KS3 Maths

Confidence • Fluency • Problem-solving • Progression

θ ONE

Series editors:

Dr Naomi Norman • Katherine Pate

ALWAYS LEARNING

PEARSON

Published by Pearson Education Limited, Edinburgh Gate, Harlow, Essex, CM20 2JE.

www.pearsonschoolsandfecolleges.co.uk

Typeset by Tech-Set Ltd, Gateshead

Cover illustration by Robert Samuel Hanson
Index by Indexing Specialists (UK) Ltd

First published 2013

16 15 14 13
10 9 8 7 6 5 4 3 2 1

British Library Cataloguing in Publication Data
A catalogue record for this book is available from the British Library

ISBN 978 1 447 96232 8

Printed in Italy by Lego S.p.A

Acknowledgements
The publisher would like to thank the following for their kind permission to reproduce their photographs:
Alamy Images: David Burton 230, PHOTOTAKE Inc. 224, Superstock 250; **Bridgeman Art Library Ltd:** Special Photographers Archive / Triangle Pattern, Vale & Betts (b.1954) / Private Collection 199; **Corbis:** STR / epa 87; **Fotolia.com:** atikinka2 61, delux 247, DURIS Guillaume 68, 94, FreshPaint 202, mskorpion 233, Myst 193, oconner 143, Victoria 1; **Getty Images:** AFP / Anja Niedringhaus 179, E+ / nullplus 91, Hulton Archive / Fin Costello 176, Yellow Dog Productions 89; **Masterfile UK Ltd:** RelaXimages 255; **Pearson Education Ltd:** Jörg Carstensen 96, Jules Selmes 30, 169; **PhotoDisc:** 73; **Photos.com:** 37, grgroup 117, 119; **Rex Features:** 145; **Science Photo Library Ltd:** Brian Bell 258, Suedhang / Cultura 63; **Shutterstock.com:** melis 127, nobeastsofierce 221; **Veer/ Corbis:** alexraths 122, Baloncici 167, Barney Boogles 3, cbrignell 153, Corbis Photography 9, Corepics 207, darrenbaker 150, Denis Dryashkin 226, Dmitry Kalinovsky 196, EpicStockMedia 148, f9photos 171, FeSeven 12, Ints Vikmanis 47, iofoto 252, Ivan Cholakov 205, John Kwan 66, majaPHOTO 101, Monkey Business Images 6, Olechowski 40, piai 228, Piccia Neri 34, PicsFive 71, Rostislav Glinsky 42, RuthBlack 32, .shock 129, stillfx 98, Tatuasha 120, tiero 45, Wavebreakmedia 15, Wavebreakmediamicrro 173, william87 103

All other images © Pearson Education

We are grateful to the following for permission to reproduce copyright material:

Graph on p14 adapted from 'Distracted Driving in the United States and Europe', Centers for Disease Control and Prevention; Mountain lion data on p27 adapted from 'Mountain Lion Research in Grand Canyon', Grand Canyon National Park; Hurricane data on p24, Unisys Weather.

Every effort has been made to trace the copyright holders and we apologise in advance for any unintentional omissions. We would be pleased to insert the appropriate acknowledgement in any subsequent edition of this publication.

CONTENTS

Unit 4 Decimals and measures 87

Unit 5 Fractions 117

Unit 6 Probability 143

Unit 7 Ratio and proportion 167

KS3 Maths

Confidence • Fluency • Problem-solving • Progression

Pedagogy at the heart – This new course is built around a unique pedagogy that's been created by leading mathematics educational researchers and Key Stage 3 teachers. The result is an innovative learning structure based around 10 key principles designed to nurture confidence and raise achievement.

Pedagogy – our 10 key principles

- Fluency
- Mathematical Reasoning
- Multiplicative Reasoning
- Problem Solving
- Progression
- Concrete-Pictorial - Abstract (CPA)
- Relevance
- Modelling
- Reflection (metacognition)
- Linking

Progression to Key Stage 4 – In line with the new National Curriculum, there is a strong focus on fluency, problem-solving and progression to help prepare your students' progress through their studies.

Stretch, challenge and support – Catering for all levels of ability, these Student Books are structured to deliver engaging and accessible content across three differentiated tiers, each offering a wealth of worked examples and questions, supported by key points, literacy and strategy hints, and clearly defined objectives.

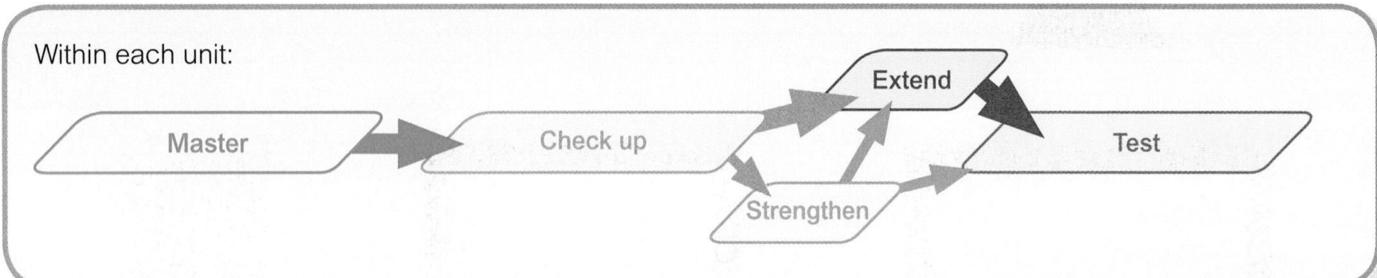

All levels of ability for Key Stage 3:

Progress with confidence!

This innovative Key Stage 3 Maths course embeds a modern pedagogical approach around our trusted suite of digital and print resources, to create confident and numerate students ready to progress further.

Help at the front-of-class – **ActiveTeach Presentation** is our tried and tested service that makes all of the Student Books available for display on a whiteboard. The books are supplemented with a range of videos and animations that present mathematical concepts along a concrete - pictorial - abstract pathway, allowing your class to progress their conceptual understanding at the right speed.

Learning beyond the classroom – Focussing on online homework, **ActiveCourse** offers students unprecedented extra practice, and a chance to reflect on their learning with the confidence-checker. Powerful reporting tools can be used to track student progression and confidence levels.

Easy to plan, teach and assess – This new **ActiveTeach Planning** provides assistance with long, medium and short term planning in outlining the Schemes of Work. Lesson plans link both front-of-class **ActiveTeach Presentation** and **ActiveCourse** and provide help with reporting, functionality and progression. Both **Planning** and **Presentation** contain the **answers** to the Student Book exercises.

Practice to progress – This new KS3 course has an extensive range of practice across a range of topics and abilities. From the **Student Books** to write-in **Progression Workbooks** through to **ActiveCourse**, there is plenty of practice available in a variety of formats whether for in the classroom or for learning at home independently.

Welcome to KS3 Maths student books!

Confidence • Fluency • Problem-solving • Progression

Starting a new course is exciting! We believe you will have fun with maths, at the same time nurturing your confidence and raising your achievement.

Here's how:

At the end of the *Master* lessons, take a *Check up* test to help you decide to *Strengthen*, or *Extend* your learning. You may be able to mark this test yourself.

Choose only the topics in *Strengthen* that you need a bit more practice with. You'll find more hints here to lead you through specific questions. Then move on to *Extend*.

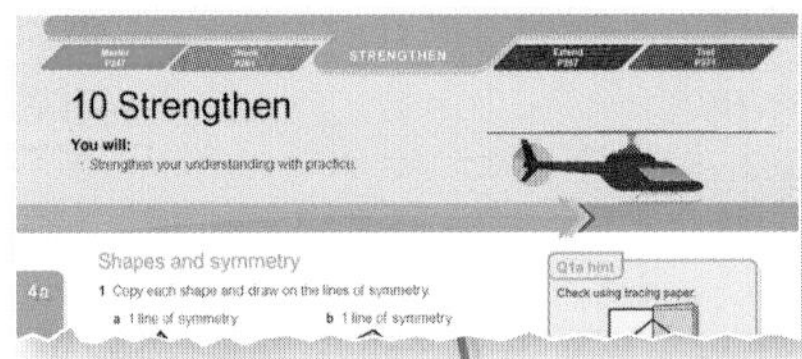

Extend helps you to apply the maths you know to some different situations. *Strengthen* and *Extend* both include *Enrichment* or *Investigations*.

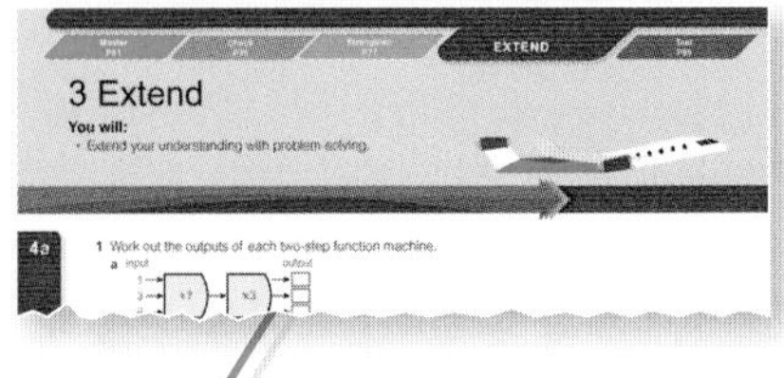

When you have finished the whole unit, a *Unit test* helps you see how much progress you are making.

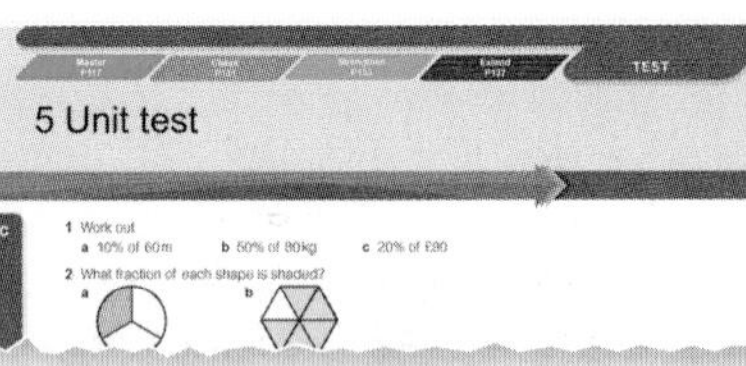

Clear *Objectives*, showing what you will cover in each lesson, are followed by a *Confidence* panel to boost your understanding and engage your interest.

Have a look at *Why Learn This?* This shows you how maths is useful in everyday life.

Improve your *Fluency* – practise answering questions using maths you already know.

The first questions are *Warm up*. Here you can show what you already know about this topic or related ones...

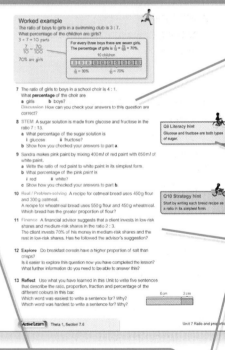

...before moving on to further questions, with *Worked examples* and *Hints* for help when you need it.

Your teacher has access to Answers in either ActiveTeach Presentation or ActiveTeach Planning.

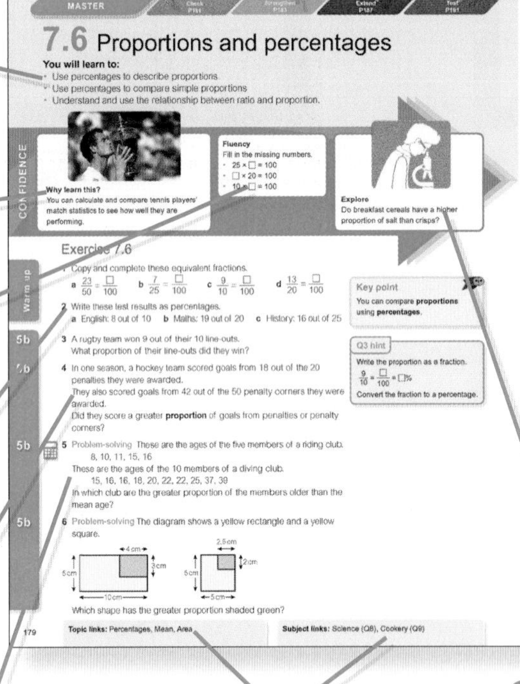

Topic links show you how the maths in a lesson is connected to other mathematical topics. Use the *Subject links* to find out where you might use the maths you have learned here in your other lessons, such as science, geography and computing .

Explore a real-life problem by discussing and having a go. By the end of the lesson you'll have gained the skills you need to start finding a solution to the question using maths.

At the end of each lesson, you get a chance to *Reflect* on how confident you feel about the topic.

STEM and Finance lessons

Context lessons expand on *Real, STEM* and *Finance* maths. Finance questions are related to money. STEM stands for Science, Technology, Engineering and Maths. You can find out how charities use maths in their fundraising, how engineers monitor water flow in rivers, and why diamonds sparkle (among other things!)

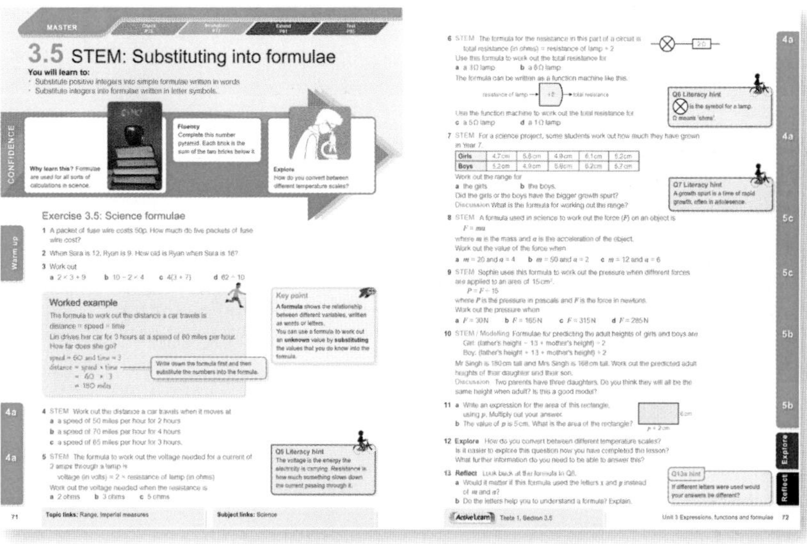
3.5 STEM: Substituting into formulae

Exercise 3.5: Science formulae

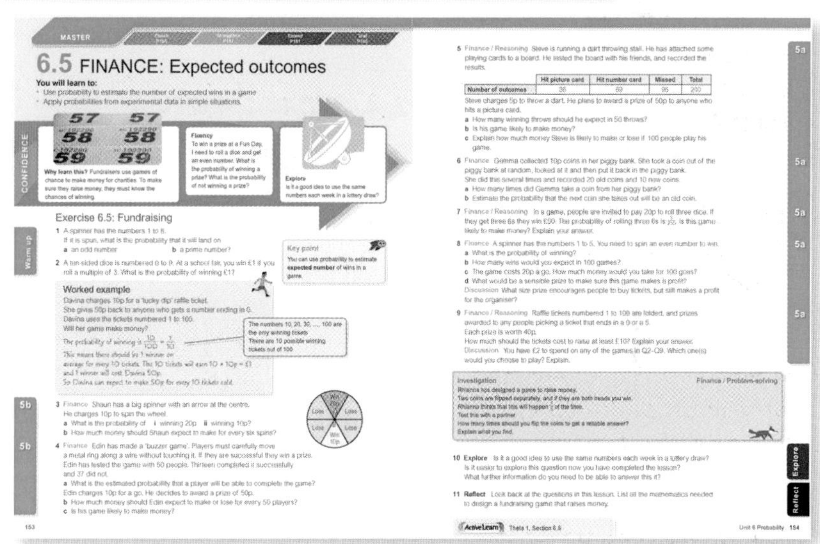
6.5 FINANCE: Expected outcomes

Exercise 6.5: Fundraising

You can improve your ability to use maths in everyday situations by tackling *Modelling, Reasoning, Problem-solving* and *Real* questions. *Discussions* prompt you to explain your reasoning or explore new ideas with a partner.

As well as hints that help you with specific questions, you'll find *Literacy hints* (to explain some unfamiliar terms) and *Strategy hints* (to help with working out).

Some questions are tagged as *Finance* or *STEM*. These questions show how the real world relies on maths. Follow these up with whole lessons that focus on how maths is used in the fields of finance, science and technology.

Further support

You can easily access extra resources that tie in to each lesson – look for the ActiveLearn icon on the lesson pages for ActiveCourse online homework links. These are clearly mapped to lessons and provide fun, interactive exercises linked to helpful worked examples and videos.

The Progression Workbooks, full of extra practice for key questions will help you reinforce your learning and track your own progress.

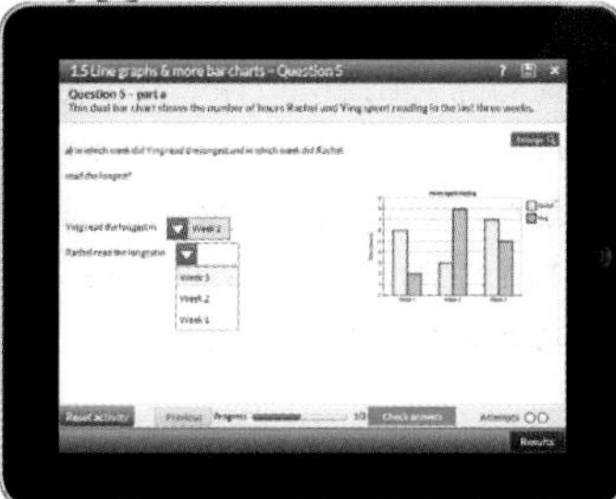

Enjoy!

1 Analysing and displaying data

MASTER

Check P18 | Strengthen P20 | Extend P24 | Test P28

1.1 Mode, median and range

You will learn to:

- Find the mode, median and range for a set of data.

CONFIDENCE

Why learn this? Broadband suppliers advertise their **median** internet speed to help customers choose the best service.

Fluency

8, 4, 5, 7, 3, 4, 5

- Which number occurs most often in this set?
- Which is the smallest of these numbers?
- Which is the largest?
- What is 12 − 4, 30 − 7?

Explore

Which country ranks middle in the world for internet speed?

Exercise 1.1

Warm up

Look at this set of data. 7, 2, 4, 2, 7, 8, 1, 1, 7

1 Which number occurs most often in this set?

2 a Write the numbers in order, from smallest to largest.
  b Which is **i** the 3rd **ii** the 6th **iii** the middle number in the ordered list?

Key point

Data is a set of information. Each piece of information is called a **value**.

4c

3 Some students spent these amounts in a café.
£2.50, £3, £1, £4, £0.50, £3, £1, £1, £2.50, £1
What is the **range** of the data?

Key point

The **range** is the difference between the smallest and largest values. The larger the range, the more spread out the values.

4b

4 Write down the **mode** for each of these sets of values.
  a TV, phone, phone, computer, iPad, TV, TV, phone, iPad, phone, iPad, computer, phone
  b 4 7 2 2 4 5 3 9 4 3
  c 0.5 0.1 0.3 0.5 0.3 0.2 0.1 0.4 0.3

Key point

The **mode** is the most common value. It is also called the **modal** value.

4b

5 Work out the range for each set of values in Q4, where possible.
Discussion Which set of data in Q4 does not have a range? Why not?

4b

6 Twenty Year 7 students recorded the number of times in a week that they visited Wikipedia for information.

10	7	4	5	6	5	9	7	6	8
7	7	5	5	6	8	8	7	10	8

Find the **modal** number of visits.

4b

7 a Write down a set of data that has two modes.
  b Write down a set of data that has no mode.

Subject links: Computing (Q14)

8 Work out the **median** for each of these sets of marks. 4b

a 5, 9, 3, 2, 7, 9, 7 **b** 11, 12, 9, 8, 15, 17, 13, 20, 12

Key point

The **median** is the middle value when the data is written in order.

Worked example

Find the median of 4, 2, 6, 7, 2, 1, 3, 6, 6, 9

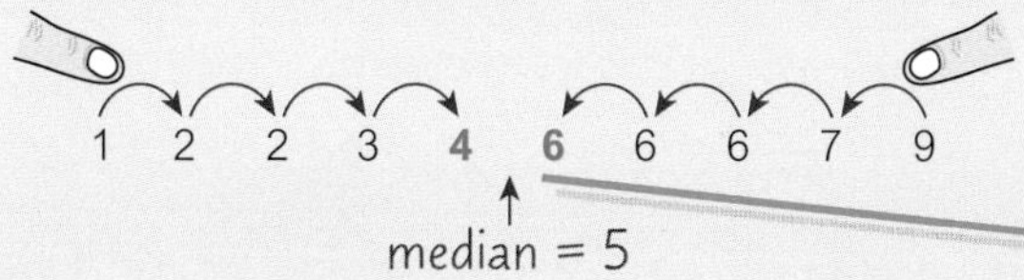

There are two middle values. The median is halfway between 4 and 6.

9 Work out the median for each of these sets of marks. 4b

a 8, 3, 2, 2, 5, 9 **b** 6, 10, 7, 15, 8, 17, 11, 9

Discussion What fraction of the values are less than the median?

10 The numbers of children in the families of some Year 7 students are 4a

4	3	2	2	1	2	3	4	3
2	1	2	1	6	2	3	3	4

Find the median.

Discussion What do you notice about the median for this set of values?

11 Reasoning Karen uses this method to find the median of a list of values: 5c

'Write the numbers in order, starting with the smallest. Count the values in the list. Add 1 to this number. Find half of the answer.
This is the position of the median in the list.'

a Does this method work for this set of numbers?

20, 5, 25, 15, 20, 40, 10, 50, 30

b Check the method works for the data in Q9.

12 Problem-solving The data below shows the numbers of hours some students spent on the internet on Sunday. One value is missing. 5c

4 0 3 4 2 1 1 ?

The median is 2.5
What could the missing value be?

Q12 Strategy hint

Try out different values.

13 Find the mode, range and median for each of these sets of data. 5c

a 9, 3, 5, 5, 7, 4, 6, 4, 8, 5, 6 **b** 30, 10, 50, 30, 30, 100, 70, 40

Investigation Problem-solving

For a set of data,

- can the mode and median be the same
- can the mode be greater than the median
- can the range be less than the mode?

Write down a simple set of data to show each answer.
The range of a set of data is 0. What can you say about the median and the mode?

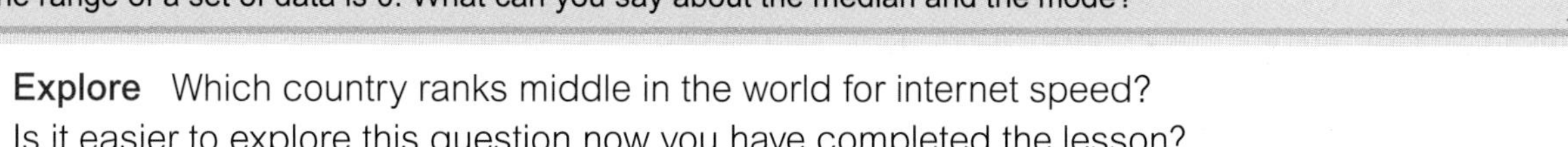

14 **Explore** Which country ranks middle in the world for internet speed? Is it easier to explore this question now you have completed the lesson? What further information do you need to be able to answer this? Explore

15 **Reflect** In this lesson, you ordered numbers to work out the median. Reflect
What other maths skills did you use to work out the median?
What maths skills did you use for other topics in this lesson?
Copy and complete this sentence until you have listed them all:
I used ____ to work out the ____.

1.2 Displaying data

You will learn to:
- Find information from tables and diagrams
- Display data using tally charts, tables, bar charts and bar-line charts.

CONFIDENCE

Why learn this? Have you ever heard someone say, 'A picture is worth a thousand words'? Diagrams are a good way to display data because they let you spot patterns or features quickly.

Fluency
- Starting at 0, count on in steps of 2
- Starting at 0, count on in steps of 5
- Work out 20 ÷ 2, 3 × 5, 15 − 7, 7 + 3 + 2 + 1

Explore
How do journalists use diagrams to show data in news stories?

Exercise 1.2

Warm up

1 Write down the number that each arrow points to on the scale.

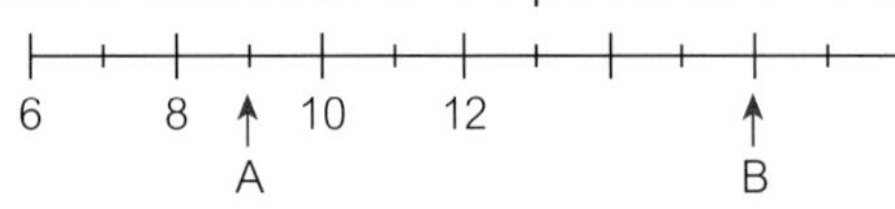

2 What does the mode tell you about a set of data?

4b

3 Real This **pictogram** shows the numbers of text messages Gary sent.

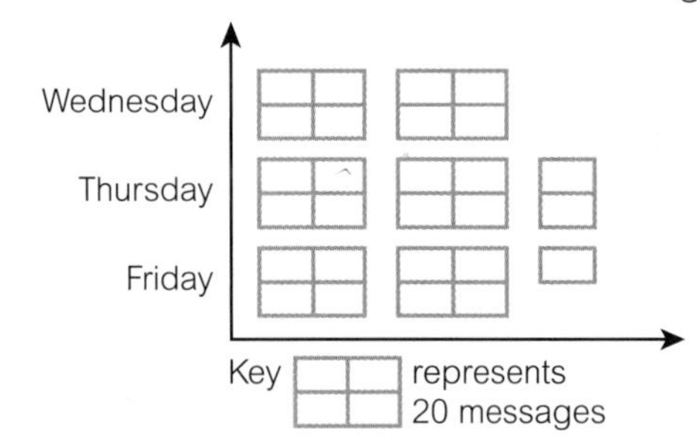

a How many messages did he send each day?

b He sent 55 messages on Saturday and 70 messages on Sunday. Draw diagrams to show this information.

c How many messages did he send altogether on these five days?

Key point
A **pictogram** uses pictures to show data. The **key** shows how many values each picture stands for.

4b

4 Real Marcia drew this **bar chart** to show her classmates' favourite cold drinks

a Which drink is the most popular?

b How many students like juice best?

c How many more students prefer fizzy drinks to juice?

d How many students are in Marcia's class?

e Discussion How can you find the mode from a bar chart?

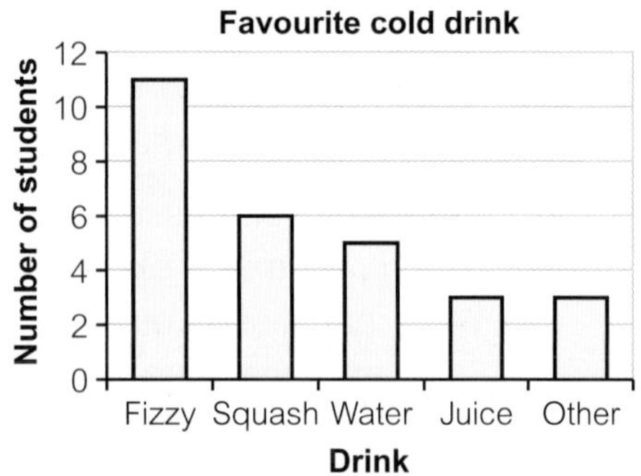

Topic links: Mode, Range

5 **Real** The table shows the types of home some Year 7 students live in.

Type of home	Number of students
detached house	3
semi-detached house	6
terraced house	8
flat	7

a How many students live in a house?

b What is the mode?

c Copy and complete the bar chart.

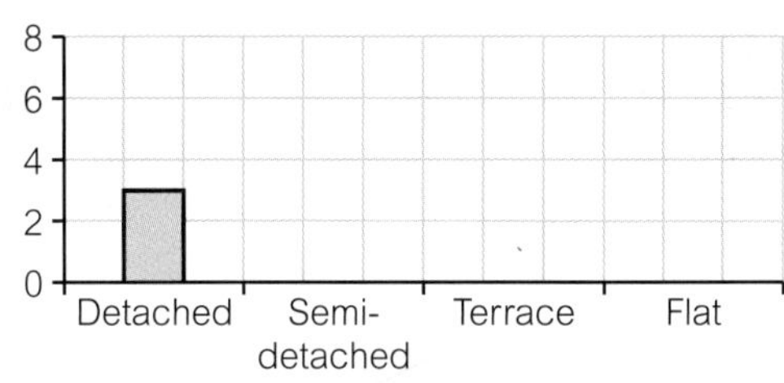

Discussion What is missing from this bar chart?

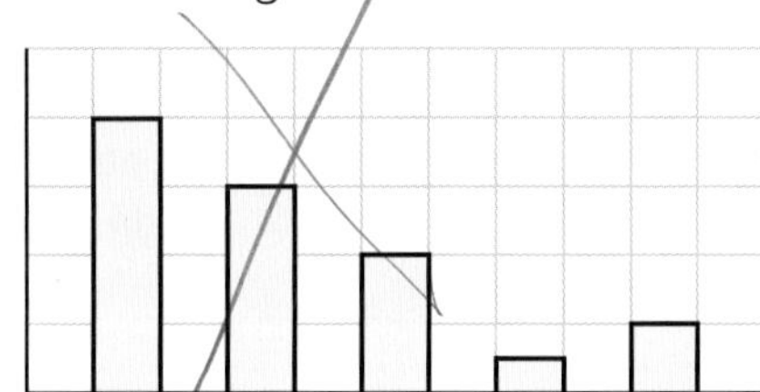

Key point

A **bar chart** uses bars of equal width to show data.
A **bar-line chart** is like a bar chart but uses lines instead of bars.

Q5c hint

Make the bars the same width. Put spaces between the bars. Label the vertical axis. Give your chart a title.

6 **Real** The **bar-line chart** shows Year 9 girls' shoe sizes.

a How many of these girls have a shoe size of 7?

b Write down the mode.

c Work out the range of the girls' shoe sizes.

Discussion In 1980, the most commonly sold shoe size was one full size smaller than today. How would the bar-line chart for Year 9 girls' shoe sizes in 1980 look different from now?

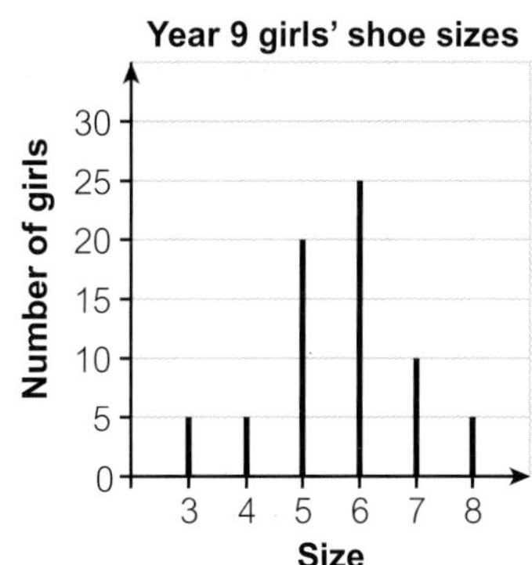

Q6c hint

What is the smallest shoe size?
What is the largest?

7 **Real** The table shows Year 9 boys' shoe sizes.

a What is the modal shoe size for these boys?

b What is the range of the shoe sizes?

c Draw a bar-line chart for the data.

d Work out the total number of boys in Year 9.

Shoe size	Number of boys
5	5
6	10
7	10
8	20
9	10
10	5

Q7c hint

Use a similar grid to Q6.

4b

8 The **tally chart** shows how some Year 7 students travel to school.

Method of travel	Tally	Frequency
walk	𝍸 𝍸 𝍸 𝍸 |	
car		16
bicycle	|||	
bus	𝍸 𝍸 𝍸	
other	||	

a How many students walk to school?

b Sixteen students travel by car. Draw the tally marks for this data.

c What is the modal method of travel?

d Write down the **frequency** of each method of travel.

> **Key point**
>
> You can record data in a **tally chart**.
> Use a tally mark | for each value.
> Group tally marks in fives like this.
>
> 
>
> The **frequency** of a value is the number of times it occurs.

4a

9 A class of Year 7 students were asked to choose their favourite social website.

Facebook (F) Instagram (I) Tumblr (Tu) YouTube (Y) Twitter (Tw)

F, Tw, F, Y, Tu, F, I, Tw, F, F, Y, I, F, Tw, Y, Tw, F,
F, Tw, Y, F, F, I, I, Tu, Y, Tw, F, Y, Tw, F

Make a tally chart for the data.

Discussion When do you need to use a tally chart?

> **Q9 hint**
>
> Look at the chart in Q8.

> **Key point**
>
> A **frequency table** shows how many of each value there are in a set of data.

4b

10 Yolanda counted the food items in 20 lunch boxes.

6, 7, 5, 6, 5, 9, 6, 4, 5, 5, 7, 6, 5, 6, 4, 7, 6, 5, 6, 4

a Copy and complete the **frequency table**.

Number of food items	4	5	6	7	8	9
Frequency						

b Draw a bar chart for the data.

> **Q10b hint**
>
> Remember that even if a data value has a frequency of 0, it should still be shown on the bar chart.

Explore

14 **Explore** How do journalists use diagrams to show data in news stories? Is it easier to explore this question now you have completed the lesson? What further information do you need to be able to answer this?

Reflect

12

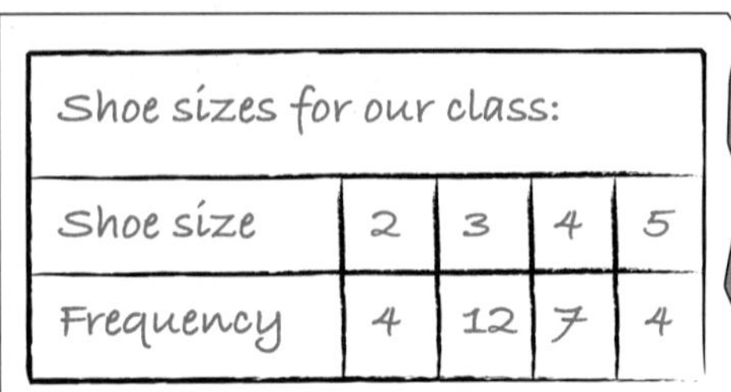

Shoe sizes for our class:

Shoe size	2	3	4	5
Frequency	4	12	7	4

Reflect Jeremy and Ashley have collected shoe size data for their class.

Jeremy says, 'The mode is 12.'

Ashley says, 'The mode is 3.'

Think carefully about what *frequency* and *mode* tell you.

Write down definitions in your own words.

Use your definitions to decide who is correct, Jeremy or Ashley.

1.3 Grouping data

You will learn to:

- Interpret simple charts for grouped data
- Find the modal class for grouped data.

CONFIDENCE

Why learn this? Managers of school canteens need to know how many of each type of snack are sold each day so that they can make sure they have enough stock to supply demand.

Fluency

- What is a tally chart?
- What values are included in the group '10–19 pencils'?
- What does the tallest bar of a bar chart show?

Explore
Do most students get enough exercise each day?

Exercise 1.3

Warm up

1 Count the tally marks.
 a 卌 卌 卌
 b 卌 |||
 c 卌 卌 卌 卌 ||

2 Find the mode of these values: 71, 76, 83, 94, 94, 71, 94, 82

5c

3 **Real** Eduardo measured the pulse rates of some classmates, in beats per minute. He crossed out each value as he made a tally mark for it in a chart.
~~81~~, ~~96~~, ~~90~~, ~~97~~, ~~78~~, 100, 88, 91, 90, 84, 96, 85, 84, 89, 80, 102, 95, 89, 109, 89
 a Complete the Tally and Frequency columns in the **grouped tally chart**.
 b What is the **modal class**?

Pulse rate	Tally	Frequency
70–79	|	
80–89	|	
90–99	|||	
100–109		

Discussion If the students exercised before Eduardo took their pulse rates, how might the tally chart be different?

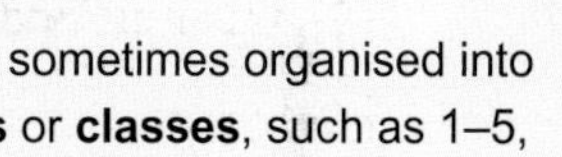

Key point
Data is sometimes organised into **groups** or **classes**, such as 1–5, 6–10, 11–15, ...
The **modal class** is the one with the highest frequency.

Q3a hint
The class 80–89 is for recording the values 80, 81, 82, 83, 84, 85, 86, 87, 88, 89

4a

4 A PE teacher asked a Year 7 class to do as many star jumps as they could in 30 seconds. The **grouped frequency table** shows the results.
 a What is the modal class?
 b How many students are in the class?
 c Darren did 37 star jumps. Which class contains this value?

Star jumps	Frequency
20–24	4
25–29	11
30–34	9
35–39	4
40–44	1

 d **Reasoning** Three more students each did 33 star jumps. Has the modal class changed? If so, how?

5 Problem-solving Sui Main asked her classmates how many coins they had on them. Here are her results.

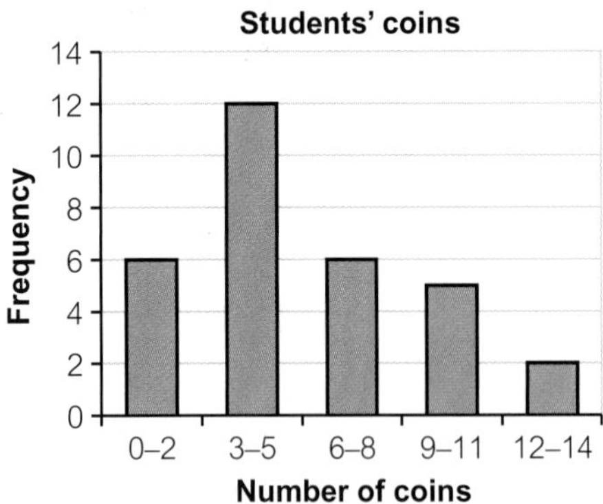

Number of coins	Frequency
0–2	6
3–5	
6–8	
9–11	
12–14	

a What is the modal class?

b Copy and complete the frequency table.

c One of Sui Main's classmates had three 5p coins and four 10p coins. What class does her number of coins belongs to?

d **Problem-solving** How many classmates had nine or more coins?

Discussion Can you tell from Sui Main's frequency table how many classmates had eight coins?

6 Pulen carried out a survey of the number of books that people in his class owned. Here are his results.

Number of books	Frequency
0–4	11
5–9	9
10–14	4
15–19	2
20–24	3
25–29	2

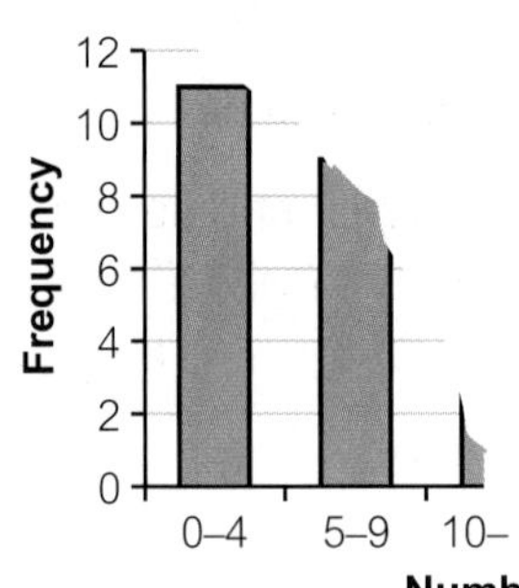

a What is the modal class?

b Copy the axes and complete the bar chart for the data.

Discussion If one student owned 99 books, would you include this value in the data?

Worked example

Abigail timed, to the nearest second, how long some students took to solve a puzzle. Draw a bar chart for the data.

Time (seconds)	Frequency
10–19	10
20–29	25
30–39	20
40–49	10
50–59	5
60–69	5

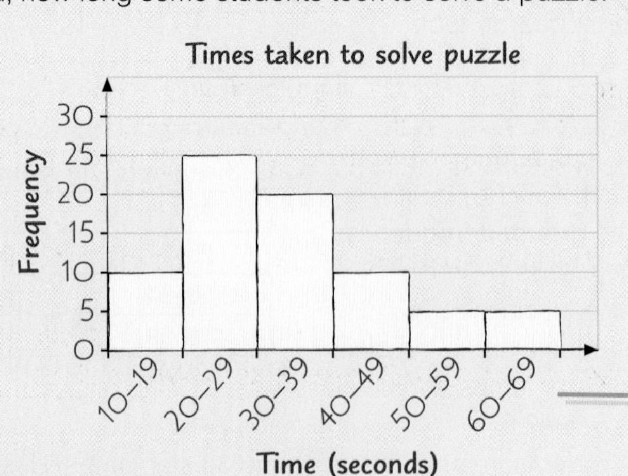

Write the class beneath each bar.

Subject links: Science (Q3), PE (Q4)

Key point

For data that comes from measuring, such as height, there are no gaps between the bars of a bar chart.

7 The frequency table shows the heights of students in a Year 7 class, measured to the nearest centimetre.

Height (cm)	Frequency
130–139	5
140–149	10
150–159	13
160–169	2

a What is the modal class?

b Draw a bar chart for the data.

Discussion Can you tell the height of the tallest student?

Q7b hint

This data is from measuring.

4a

8 Problem-solving / Reasoning The bar chart shows the volumes of liquid drunk by some Year 7 students in a day.

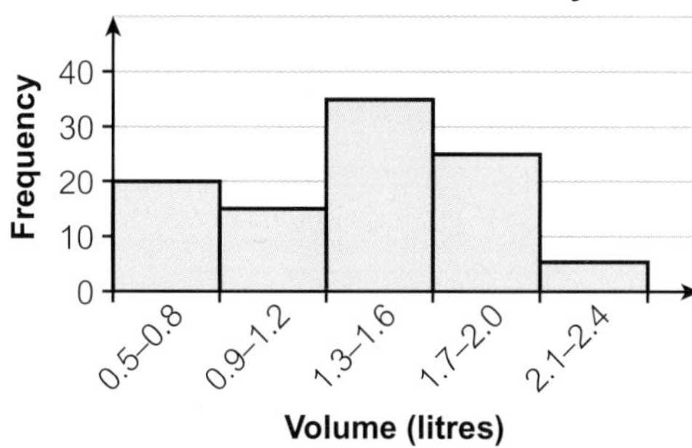

It is recommended that Year 7 students should drink about 1.2 litres a day. Are these Year 7 students drinking enough? Give a reason for your answer.

Discussion How could grouping the data differently help you to answer the question? What groups would you use?

4a

Investigation Problem-solving

1 In Q5, Sui Main could have used the classes 0–9 and 10–19. How many bars would her bar chart have had?

2 In Q6, Pulen could have used the classes 0–2, 3–5, 6–8, ... How many bars would his bar chart have had?

3 Students in a Year 7 class each sent between 0 and 45 text messages in a day. Write down the classes you would use to record the data.

Discussion What is a good rule for choosing a sensible number of classes?

9 Explore Do most students get enough exercise each day?
Is it easier to explore this question now you have completed the lesson?
What further information do you need to be able to answer this?

Explore

10 Reflect Which did you find easier: working out the modal class from a table or from a bar chart?
Think carefully about how you learn in all your subjects. Do you understand things better when there is a picture or a diagram?

Reflect

1.4 Averages and comparing data

You will learn to:
- Calculate the mean of a set of data
- Compare sets of data using their ranges and averages.

CONFIDENCE

Why learn this? Athletes use statistics to compare and improve their performance.

Fluency
Find the mode, median and range of 60, 30, 40, 20, 20, 50, 40, 20, 70, 50

Explore
Do football teams in the Premier League score more goals than teams in the lower leagues?

Exercise 1.4

Warm up

1 What is the total of 5, 3 and 7?

2 Work out 48 ÷ 8

3 Which of these pairs of numbers does 14.7 lie between?
A 10 and 17 **B** 14 and 14.5 **C** 8 and 14

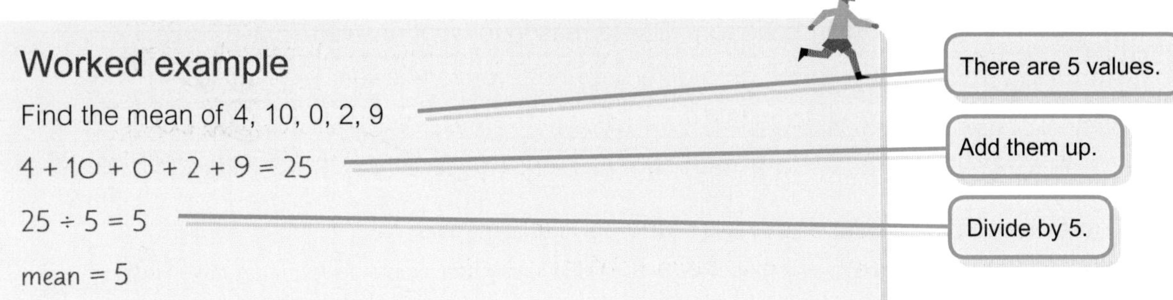

Worked example

Find the mean of 4, 10, 0, 2, 9 — There are 5 values.

4 + 10 + 0 + 2 + 9 = 25 — Add them up.

25 ÷ 5 = 5 — Divide by 5.

mean = 5

Key point
The **mean** of a set of values is the total of the set of values divided by the number of values.

5c

4 Work out the mean for each set of numbers.
a 6, 10
b 2, 0, 6, 4
c 3, 1, 1, 5, 0, 3, 2, 2, 4, 2

Discussion Can you ignore values that are 0 when working out the mean?

(modified) 6 (new Q5)

5c

5 **Real** Anna Chicherova, Olympic gold medallist, made these high jumps in the World Championships in Athletics.
189 cm, 193 cm, 197 cm, 200 cm, 203 cm
Use your calculator to work out the mean height she jumped.

Discussion How can you check that your calculated mean is correct?

Q5 hint
Remember to press the = key on your calculator after adding up the values.

Topic links: Mode, Median, Range

6 Three players scored these points in a table tennis tournament

Manjit	7, 11, 8, 13, 11, 5, 3, 12, 8, 7, 11, 9
Tony	40, 20, 60, 50, 30, 20, 60
Sebastian	8, 19, 7, 23, 9, 15

For each player, work out

a the mode **b** the median **c** the mean **d** the range.

Discussion Can the mean ever be equal to one of the values?

5c

Key point

The **average** of a set of data gives a typical value for the data.
The mode, median and mean are different ways of describing the average of a set of data.

5b

7 Problem-solving / Reasoning Here are the finishing times (in minutes) of all the runners in a cross-country race.

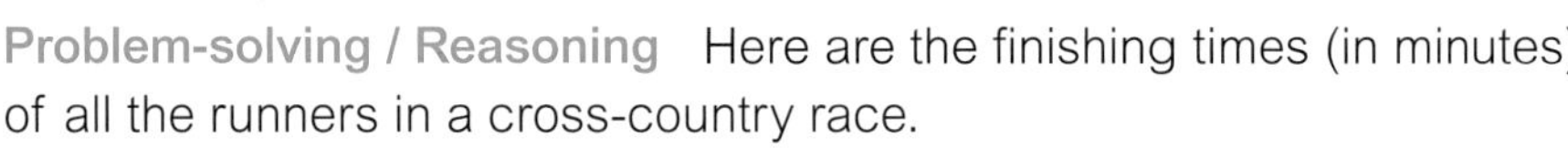

40, 36, 47, 38, 29, 35, 111

a One of the runners pulled a muscle. What was her time? How do you know?

b Which average represents the times of the runners the best?

Q7b Strategy hint

Work out the mode, median and mean.

Worked example

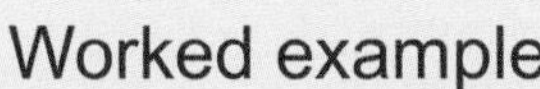

Daniel's last five long jumps were 3.7 m, 3.4 m, 4.1 m, 3.8 m, 4.1 m
Paul's last five long jumps were 3.9 m, 4.3 m, 3.2 m, 4.2 m, 3.1 m
Compare their performances.

Daniel range = 4.1 − 3.4 = 0.7 m
total = 3.7 + 3.4 + 4.1 + 3.8 + 4.1 = 19.1 m
mean = 19.1 ÷ 5 = 3.82 m

Paul range = 4.3 − 3.1 = 1.2 m
total = 3.9 + 4.3 + 3.2 + 4.2 + 3.1 = 18.7 m
mean = 18.7 ÷ 5 = 3.74 m

Paul is less consistent than Daniel because his jumps have a greater range. — Compare the ranges.

Daniel performed better on average because his jumps have a greater mean. — Compare the means.

Key point

To **compare** two sets of data, find an average (the mode, median or mean) and the range.

4a

8 Catherine and Susan carried out a survey of the sports that each of their friends enjoyed most. They each drew a bar chart of their results.

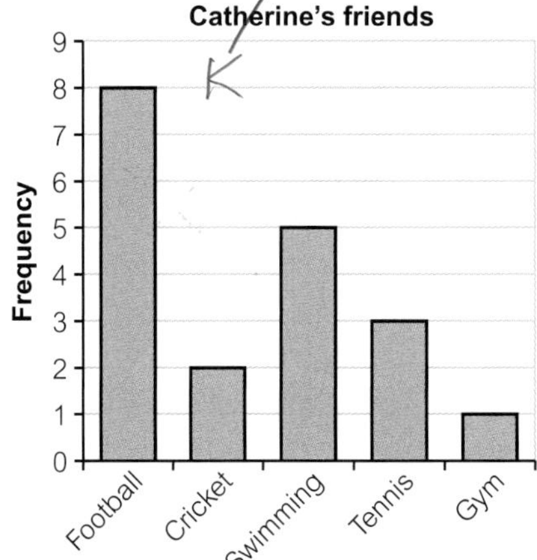

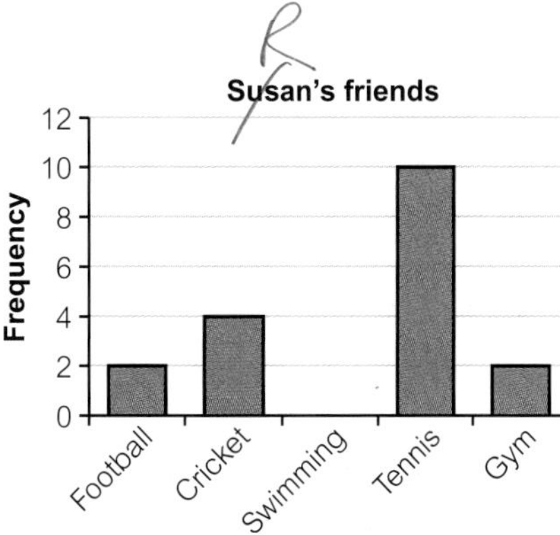

a Compare the types of sport that Catherine's and Susan's friends like least.

b Compare the types of sport that Catherine's and Susan's friends like most. Which average are you using to compare?

5c

9 **Real** The top scores in a horse riding event at the Olympics are shown in the table.

Men	76	74	81	71	75	72	76	74
Women	79	82	76	83	74	78	78	75

a Work out the range for the men and the range for the women.

b Work out the median for the men and the median for the women.

c Use the ranges and medians to write two sentences comparing the performance of the men and the women.

5b

10 A school tested the performance of some BMX bikes made from aluminium and some made from steel. The results show the times (in minutes) to complete a test course.

Steel	9.4	9.7	9.9	9.2	10.1	9.6	9.6	10.2	9.6
Aluminium	8.9	9.6	10.3	9.4	10.5	9.0	9.7	9.6	9.9

a Find the mean and range for each type of BMX bike.

b Use the means and ranges to compare the performances.

Q10b hint
Look at the Worked example.

5a

11 **Problem-solving / Reasoning** Asifa recorded the points scored by her hockey team in June. She calculated the mean score.

0 5 3 1 mean = 3

One of the scores got rubbed out accidentally.
Work out the missing score. What method did you use?
Discussion How can you use the mean of a set of values to find their total?

Investigation **Reasoning**

The table shows the heights (in centimetres) of the top ten male athletes in two sports at the 2012 Olympics.

Javelin	186	188	195	186	190	187	182	185	175	183
Shot put	180	199	204	191	186	189	193	185	196	188

Do the heights of the athletes differ between the two sports?
Explain the method you used.
Discussion What are two other sports where the contestants might differ physically? Justify your answer using information from websites.

Explore

12 **Explore** Do football teams in the Premier League score more goals than teams in the lower leagues?
What have you learned in this lesson to help you answer this question?
What other information do you need?

Reflect

13 **Reflect** You often see the word 'average' in headlines. For example, 'Average screen size of TVs grows again' or 'The changing face of the average American'.
'Average' in everyday language could be the mean, median or mode.
Write notes in your own words on the difference between the mean, median and mode.

1.5 Line graphs and more bar charts

You will learn to:

- Understand and draw line graphs
- Understand and draw dual and compound bar charts.

CONFIDENCE

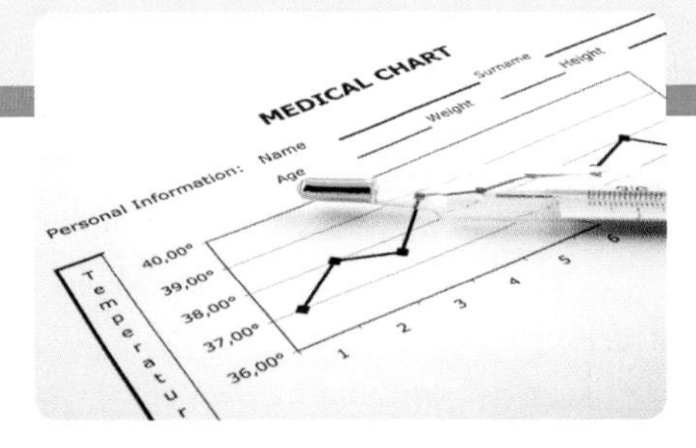

Why learn this? Nurses use line graphs to show how a patient's temperature changes.

Fluency

- What labels should every bar chart have?
- How can you find the mode from a bar chart?

Explore
Does the time of year affect the amount charities collect online?

Exercise 1.5

1 The bar chart shows the digital gadgets owned by some Year 7 students.

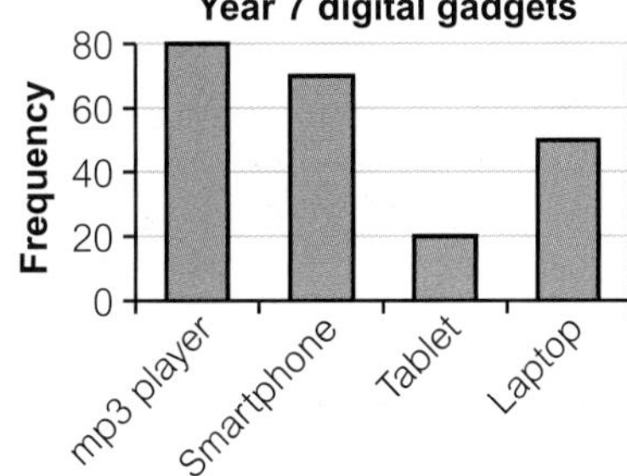

a What is the mode?

b How many digital gadgets do these students own altogether?

c These students own more smartphones than tablets. How many more?

2 Write down an abbreviation for every month of the year.

3 The **line graph** shows how Rikki's temperature changed during the morning of one day.

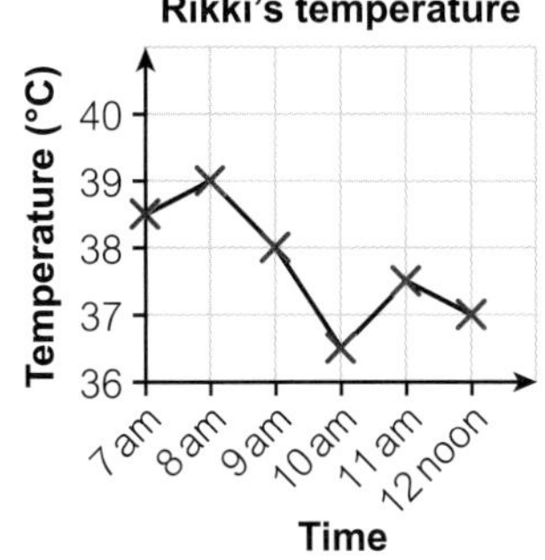

a What was Rikki's highest recorded temperature?

b When was Rikki's temperature 36.5° C?

c Normal body temperature is 37° C. How many of Rikki's readings are above this?

d Between which times was Rikki's temperature decreasing?

Key point
A **line graph** shows how quantities change over time.

Warm up

5b

5b

4 A supermarket aims to collect 100 kg of coins for charity. The line graph shows how much was donated each month.

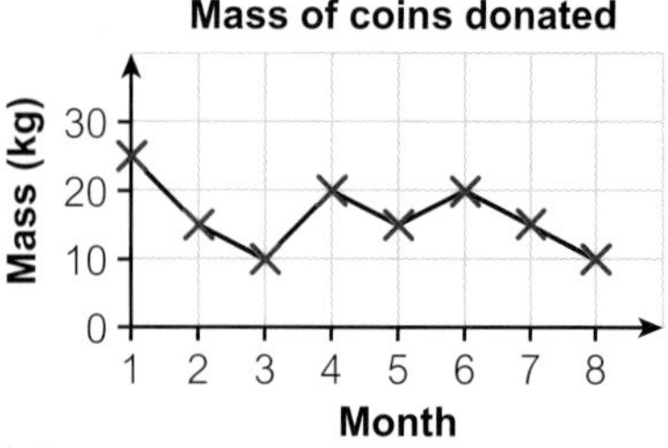

a When was the least mass of coins donated in a month?

b Which of these describes the mass of coins donated in the first three months: increasing, decreasing, or staying the same?

c In which months were more than 15 kg of coins donated?

d When did the supermarket reach its target of 100 kg?

Q4d hint

Add the masses together month by month.

5a

5 The table shows the numbers of hours that Michelle spent on Facebook each day.

Day	Fri	Sat	Sun	Mon	Tue	Wed	Thu
Time (hours)	2	5	4	0	1	2	2

a Draw a line graph for the data.

b On one day, Michelle left her smartphone at a friend's house. Which day?

c How many hours did Michelle spend on Facebook altogether?

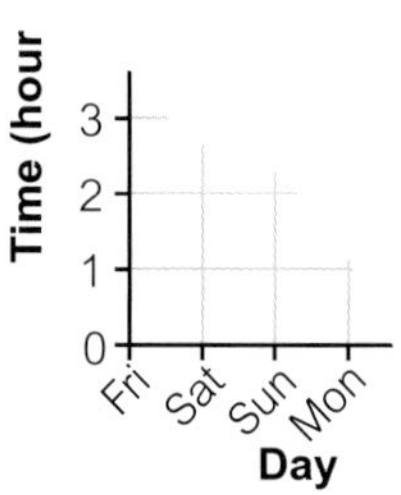

5b

6 The **dual bar chart** shows the numbers of genuine and junk emails that Aroti received each day.

Key point

A **dual bar chart** compares two sets of data.

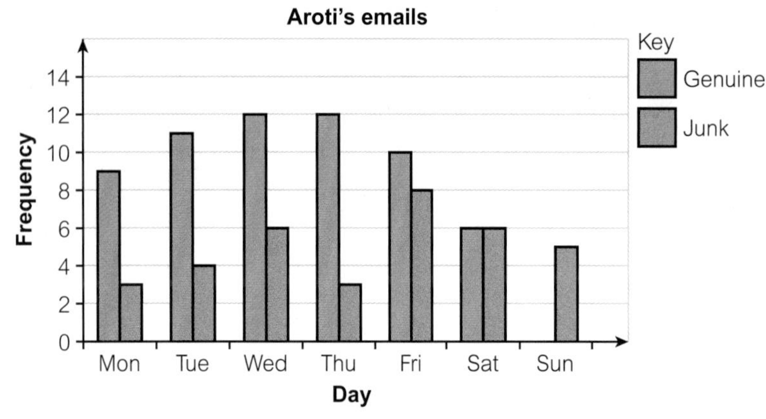

a How many junk emails did she receive on Tuesday?

b Which day did she receive equal numbers of junk and genuine emails?

c Why has Sunday only got one bar?

d Problem-solving Aroti says that about half of the emails she receives are junk. Is she correct?

5b

7 115 girls and 115 boys from Year 7 were asked what they like reading the most.

	Fiction	Graphic novels	Non-fiction	Magazines
Boys	25	35	30	25
Girls	40	25	20	30

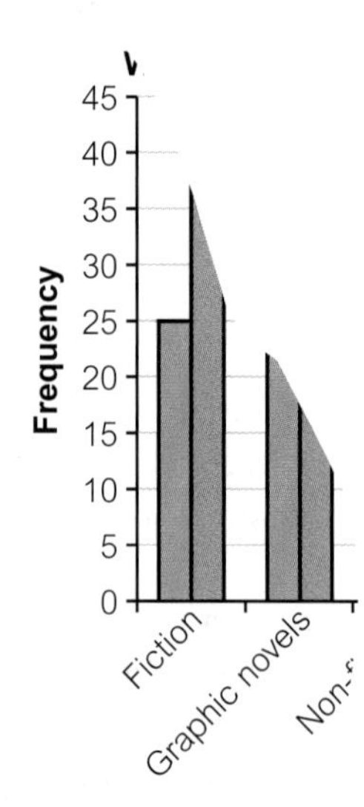

a Copy and complete the dual bar chart for the data.

b ~~Discussion~~ Do girls and boys prefer reading different things?

Topic links: Mode

Subject links: English (Investigation)

8 Real The **compound bar chart** shows some exam results for a school in 2012.

a How many students got

i a grade B in chemistry

ii a grade A or A* in biology?

b In which subjects did

i 30 students get a grade B

ii students get the most grade A passes?

c How many A* passes were there altogether in these subjects?

d Discussion Can you tell from the chart which subject is easiest?

> **Key point**
>
> A **compound bar chart** combines different sets of data in one bar.

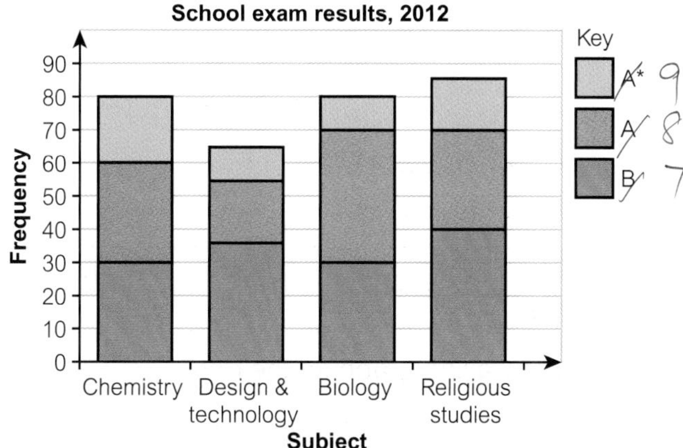

9 Here is some information about the photos Gareth uploaded.

	Facebook	Flickr	Instagram	Tumblr
Photos of Gareth	25	35	40	15
Other photos	20	35	25	50

a Copy and complete the compound bar chart for the data.

b Were there more photos of Gareth than other photos? Explain your answer.

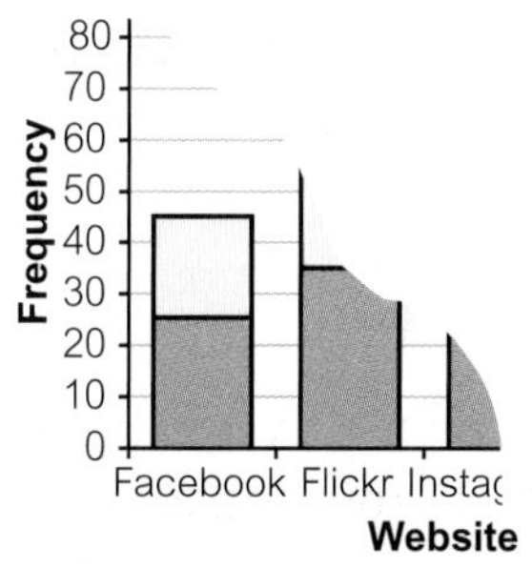

Investigation Real / Problem-solving

People in different countries were asked how often, during the last 30 days, they had talked on their mobile phones while driving. The chart shows the results.

Write a news story about the data shown in the graph. Don't forget to give it a headline.

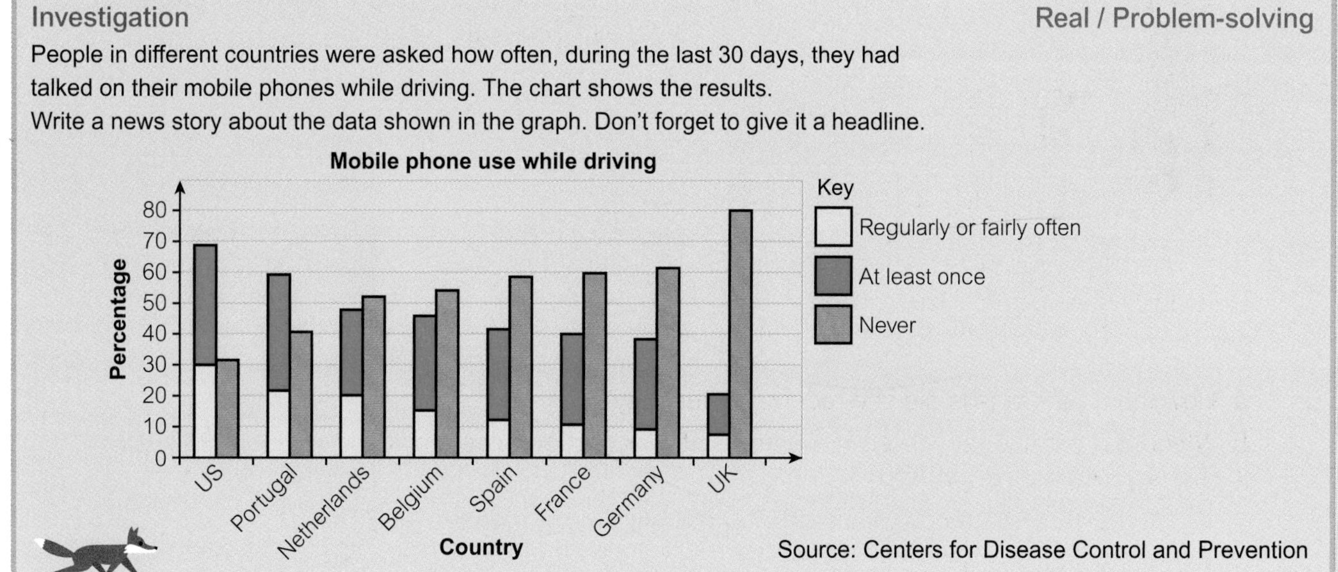

Source: Centers for Disease Control and Prevention

10 **Explore** Does the time of year affect the amount charities collect online? Is it easier to explore this question now you have completed the lesson? What further information do you need to be able to answer this?

11 **Reflect** Make a list of the questions from this lesson you found easiest to answer. What made them easier for you? Make a list of the questions from this lesson you found hardest to answer. What made them harder for you?

1.6 Using spreadsheets

You will learn to:

- Analyse and present data using spreadsheets.

CONFIDENCE

Why learn this? Computers are much faster than humans at processing data.

Fluency
Find the mode, median, mean and range for this set of data.
11, 7, 12, 12, 8, 6, 11, 12, 9, 8

Explore
What was the average score in the Eurovision Song Contest this year?

Exercise 1.6

Warm up

1 Look at this part of a spreadsheet.

	A	B
1	81	16
2	54	25

a What is the number in cell B2?

b Which cell is the number 81 in?

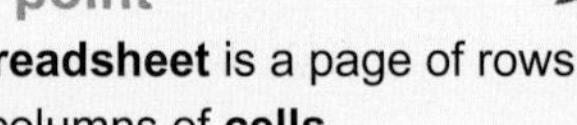

Key point
A **spreadsheet** is a page of rows and columns of **cells**.
Each cell can contain a number or text.

2 Follow these instructions to input the number 14 into cell A1.
Click on cell A1.
Type 14.
Press Enter or the Down Arrow key.
You are now ready to enter data into cell A2.

3 If you make a mistake, click the Undo button.
Try it and see what happens.

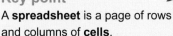

5c

4 Real The data shows the numbers of weeks the ten most popular UK singles stayed in the Top 10 in 2011.
14, 10, 12, 16, 10, 11, 11, 13, 12, 10

a Input the data into column **A** of the spreadsheet, starting at cell **A1**.

b Rearrange the numbers from smallest to largest.
  i Select the cells **A1** to **A10**.
  ii Use the sort feature to sort the data from **Smallest to Largest**.

c Find the mode.
  i Type the word **Mode** in cell **A11**.
  ii In cell **B11**, type exactly **=mode(**
  iii Select all of the numbers and press **Enter** to put the mode into cell **B11**.

d Find the median.
  i Type the word **Median** in cell **A12**.
  ii In cell **B12**, type exactly **=median(**
  iii Select the data and press **Enter** to put the median into cell **B12**.

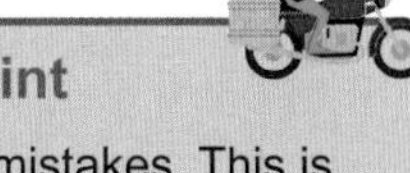

Q4 Strategy hint
Everyone makes mistakes. This is called human error. Check you have entered the data correctly.

Q4b ii hint
After sorting, check that the numbers in column A are in the order you expect.

Q4c ii hint
Typing = tells the spreadsheet to calculate something.

 Topic links: Mode, Median, Range, Bar charts

e Find the mean.

  i Type the word **Mean** in cell **A13**.

  ii In cell **B13**, type exactly **=average(**

  iii Select the data and press **Enter** to put the mean into cell **B13**.

f Find the range.

  i Type the word **Range** in cell **A14**.

  ii In cell **B14**, type exactly **=A10-A1**

  iii Press **Enter** to put the range into cell **B14**.

Discussion Experiment to find out what happens to the mode, median, mean and range if you change the value in cell **A1**. You will need to press **Enter** each time you change **A1**.

Q4e ii hint

Spreadsheets use the word 'average' instead of 'mean'.

Q4f ii hint

You don't need to type capital letters. Just type **=a10-a1**

5 Lauren kept a record of the amounts of time she spent listening to music each day on her computer. 5c

Day	Mon	Tue	Wed	Thu	Fri	Sat	Sun
Computer time (minutes)	30	20	25	20	30	45	60

a Copy the table onto a new spreadsheet, starting at cell **A1**.

b Draw a line graph for the data.

  i Select the whole table.

  ii Click the **Insert** tab on the top menu.

  iii Select the first line graph.

Discussion Right-click on the graph line and select **Format Data Series...** Experiment to see how the options change the style of the line.

Q5a hint

Click on the **Sheet 2** tab at the bottom of the screen to select a new spreadsheet.

6 Anita asked 25 girls in Year 7 which musical instrument they liked the most. 5a

Instrument	**Girls**
clarinet	3
violin	8
piano	5
saxophone	4
drum	5

a Copy the table onto a new spreadsheet, starting at cell **A1**.

b Draw a bar chart for the data.

  i Select the whole table.

  ii Click the **Insert** tab.

  iii Click Column and select the first 2D column bar chart.

  iv Give your bar chart a title and label the axes.

Discussion Make the chart box smaller. What do you notice about the vertical scale?

Q6b hint

Select the whole chart by clicking on its border. Click the **Layout** tab on the top menu. Use the **Chart Title** and **Axis Titles** buttons.

c Anita asked 25 boys in Year 7 which musical instrument they liked the most.

Instrument	**Girls**	**Boys**
clarinet	3	2
violin	8	4
piano	5	5
saxophone	4	7
drum	5	7

Add the data for the boys to the table in your spreadsheet.

d Draw a dual bar chart for the data.

e Problem-solving How do the girls and boys differ in their choice of instrument? Use the mode.

f Draw a compound bar chart for the data.

Discussion Experiment using the design and layout settings to change the appearance of your bar charts. Try drawing some horizontal bar charts too.

Q6d hint

The spreadsheet automatically draws a dual bar chart when there are two sets of data.

Q6f hint

Choose the first 2D compound bar chart from the available charts.

5b

7 Bassi made a table to show the lengths of tracks on his favourite CD.

Track length (seconds)	Frequency
50–99	3
100–149	11
150–199	6
200–249	2
250–299	3

a Copy the table onto a new spreadsheet, starting at cell **A1**.

b Draw a bar chart for the data.

c Use the **Format Data Series...** option to colour the bars yellow and give them a black border.

Q7b hint

You must close the gaps between the bars because the data values are times (in seconds), which can be measured. Right-click on a bar and select **Format Data Series...**

Investigation Modelling / STEM

This data shows the numbers of dragonflies seen in different locations one week in summer 2013.

30, 15, 90, 40, 30, 20, 40, 25, 40, 50

a Use a spreadsheet to find the mode, median, mean and range. Follow the instructions in Q4.

b Past data on dragonfly populations shows what is likely to happen the next year at a location. Use this table to predict numbers of sightings for summer 2014. Input the predicted numbers into the spreadsheet.

Sightings this year	20 or fewer	21–40	41–49	50 or more
Population next year	dies out	halves	stays the same	increases by half again

e.g. $50 + \frac{1}{2}$ of $50 = 50 + 25 = 75$

c Compare the data for summer 2013 with summer 2014.

Explore

8 **Explore** What was the average score in the Eurovision Song Contest this year? What have you learned in this lesson to help you answer this question? What other information do you need?

Reflect

9 **Reflect** You have now calculated averages and range with and without a computer. Which way did you prefer? Why? What is better or worse about each way? When might you choose to use a computer for these calculations? When would you choose to do them 'by hand'?

1 Check up

Averages and range

1 Use your calculator to find the mean for this set of lengths.

2.4 m, 3.6 m, 1.9 m, 5.2 m, 2.9 m

2 Some Year 7 students were asked how many pets they have.

0, 1, 0, 0, 2, 0, 0, 0, 3, 0, 0, 23, 3, 2, 0, 30

a Write down the mode.
b Work out the median.
c Work out the mean.
d Work out the range.

Charts and tables

3 A record was taken of the favourite big cats of some students in a Year 7 class.

tiger, lion, lion, cheetah, tiger, leopard, lion, tiger, lion, jaguar, tiger, cheetah, lion, leopard, lion

a Copy and complete the tally chart.
b What is the mode?

Big cat	Tally	Frequency
lion		
tiger		
cheetah		
leopard		
jaguar		

4 The bar-line chart shows the numbers of children in the families of some Year 7 students.

a How many families have 3 children?
b What is the mode?
c Why is there no bar for 5 children?
d How many families have fewer than 3 children?

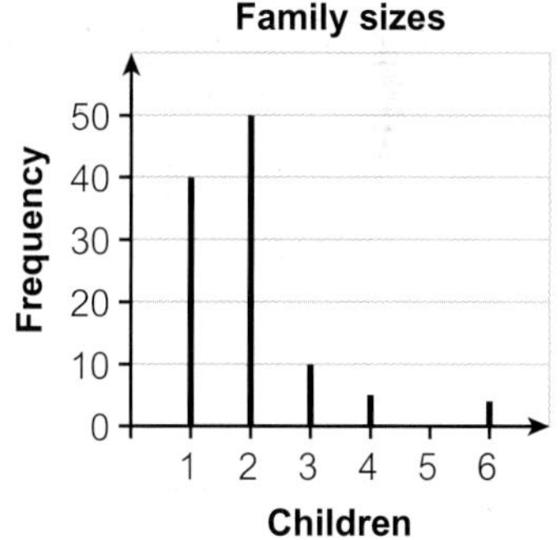

5 The line graph shows the classroom temperature every 2 hours.

a What was the temperature at 3 pm?
b When was the temperature 14° C?
c Describe what happened to the temperature between 7 am and 11 am.
d Why might the classroom temperature have dropped between 11 am and 1 pm?

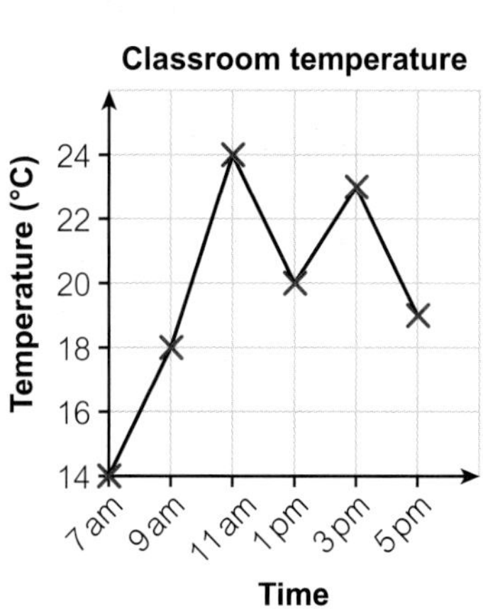

Comparing data

6 100 girls and 100 boys were asked which topics in maths they liked best.
The bar chart shows the results.

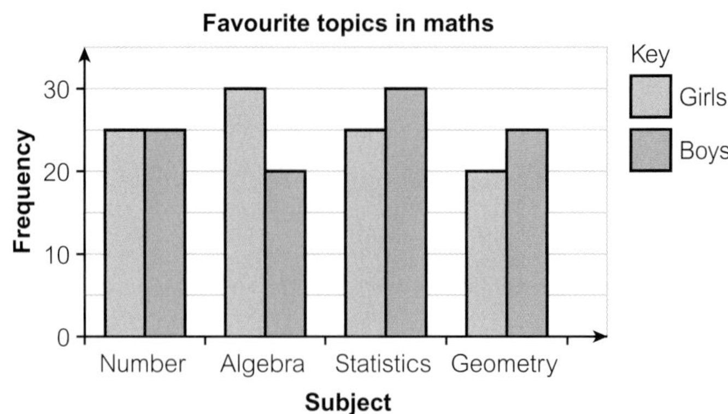

a Which was the boys' favourite topic?
b Which was the girls' favourite topic?
c Which topic did equal numbers of girls and boys like best?
d How many more boys than girls liked Statistics best?
e How many students chose Number as their favourite topic?

7 The bar chart shows the medals won by four countries at the 2012 Olympics.

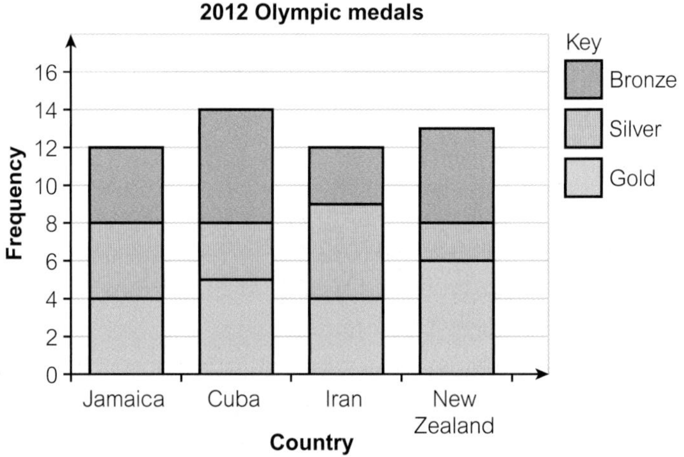

a How many gold medals did Cuba win?
b Which of these countries won the most bronze medals?
c Which of these countries won five silver medals?
d Which two of these countries won the same number of medals?

8 The table shows the distances (in kilometres) that some Year 7 students travel to school.

Oakbridge School	1.2	0.8	2.2	1.1	1.5	2.6	0.9	3.0	2.1	1.6
St John's School	3.0	0.5	6.1	1.5	1.1	5.2	9.9	2.8	8.5	1.4

a Calculate the mean travel distance for each school.
b Which school's students travel the shortest distance?
c Calculate the range for each school.
d Which school has the largest range?
e One of the schools is in a city. Which one? Give a reason for your answer.

9 **How sure are you of your answers? Were you mostly**
Just guessing **Feeling doubtful** **Confident**
What next? Use your results to decide whether to strengthen or extend your learning.

Challenge

10 a The numbers 4, 2, 7, ☐ have a mode of 2. What is the missing number?
b The numbers 4, 2, 5, ☐ have a mean of 4. What is the missing number?
c The numbers 20, 70, 10, ☐ have a range of 80. What is the missing number?
d The numbers 8, 4, 6, ☐ have a median of 5. Write down a possible value for the missing number.

1 Strengthen

You will:

- Strengthen your understanding with practice.

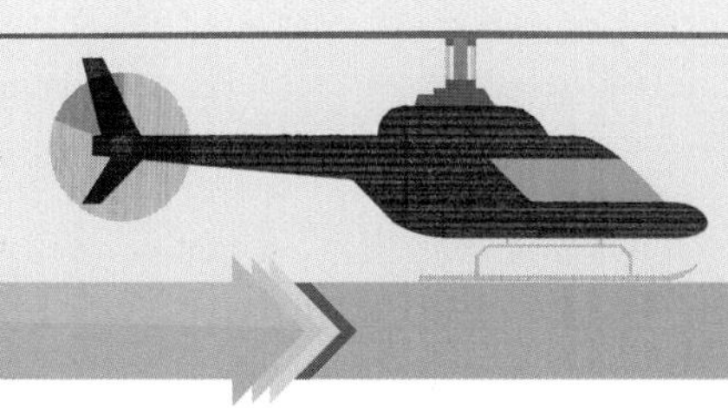

Averages and range

1 a These snacks were bought from a vending machine.

crisps, drink, crisps, chocolate, drink, crisps, chocolate, biscuits

Write down the most common item to find the mode.

b The amounts paid for the snacks are

50p, 80p, 50p, 60p, 80p, 50p, 60p, 40p

Write down the mode.

> **Q1b hint**
> Don't forget to write the units (p for pence).

4b

2 This set of data has two modes.

5, 5, 5, 6, 7, 8, 8, 8

Write down both modes.

4b

3 a Write these values in order, from smallest to largest.

9, 2, 6, 3, 5, 2, 8

9, ~~2~~, 6, ~~3~~, 5, ~~2~~, 8

smallest 2, 2, 3, ... largest

b Write down the middle value to find the median.

c Work out the median of these values.

7, 0, 6, 4, 4, 2, 7, 5, 1

> **Q3c hint**
> Write the numbers in order first.

4 Work out the median for these basketball scores for one team.

14, 30, 21, 9, 25, 18, 39, 26

> **Q4 hint**
> Write the numbers in order. Find the middle two numbers. The median is halfway between them. Use a number line to help you.

5 a Some Year 7 students did as many press-ups as they could manage.

8, 3, 15, 6, 2, 12, 6

Work out the range.

b Some pianists measured the length of their little fingers.

5.7 cm, 6.2 cm, 5.1 cm, 6.6 cm, 5.5 cm, 5.2 cm

Use a calculator to work out the range.

> **Q5a hint**
> The range is a number. Subtract the smallest value from the largest value.

6 Work out the mean of each of these sets of values.

a 8, 4, 6, 3, 4 **b** 1, 9, 2, 2, 3, 1

c 5, 3, 0, 0 **d** 0, 1, 2, 2, 3, 4

> **Q6 hint**
> Add them up. Divide by the number of values to find the mean. Make sure you count any 0 values.

7 a Use your calculator to find the mean of these lengths.

72 m, 51 m, 88 m, 10 m, 23 m, 26 m, 40 m, 13 m, 81 m, 33 m

b Check that your answer makes sense.

> **Q7a hint**
> Press the = key to get the total before you divide.

Charts and tables

4b

1 The bar-line chart shows the mass of bowling balls in a national competition.

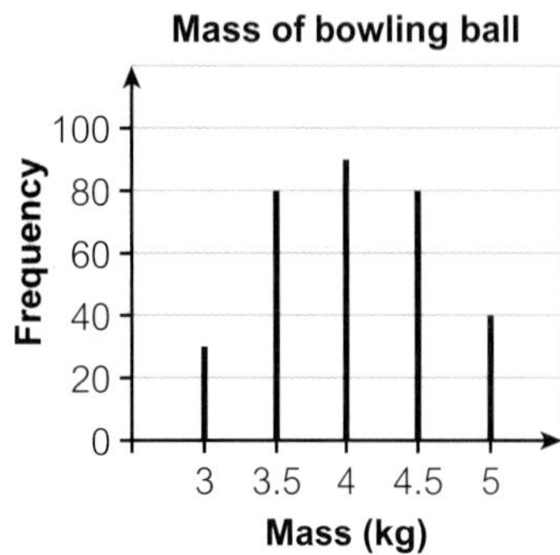

a How many bowling balls have a mass of 3 kg?

b Which mass of bowling ball did 40 players use?

c Write down the mass with the tallest bar-line to find the **modal** mass.

> **Q1a hint**
> The frequency means the number of bowling balls. The height of the bar-line for 3 kg lies halfway between 20 and 40.

> **Q1c hint**
> Make sure you write down the mass (kg) and not its frequency.

> **Q1 Literacy hint**
> The **modal** mass is the most common mass. It is another way of saying the mode.

4a

2 Scarlet won these points prizes as she played a video game.

~~50~~, ~~20~~, ~~20~~, ~~100~~, ~~50~~, ~~100~~, ~~20~~, ~~20~~, ~~20~~, ~~50~~, 200, 50, 20, 100, 100
20, 20, 200, 20, 50, 100, 50, 20, 50, 50, 200, 100, 20, 100, 20

a Copy and complete the tally chart.

Prize	Tally	Frequency
20	~~||||~~	
50	|||	
100	||	
200		

b What is the mode?

c Which prize has a frequency of 7?

d Add up the frequencies to find how many prizes Scarlet won altogether.

> **Q2a hint**
> For each value, make a tally mark. Write the tally marks in groups of five. Count the tally marks and write the totals in the Frequency column.

> **Q2d hint**
> Check your answer by counting all the prizes.

4a

3 Alex recorded the time he spent talking on his mobile phone each day for a month.

Time (minutes)	Frequency
10–19	15
20–29	9
30–39	6
40–49	0
50–59	1

Frequency: 0, 2, 4, 6, 8, 10, 12, 14, 16
Time: 10–19, 20–29

a What is the modal class?

b Copy and complete the bar chart.

> **Q3a hint**
> The class 10–19 contains all values from 10 up to and including 19. The modal class is the class with the highest frequency.

Subject links: Geography (Enrichment Q2, Q3)

5a

4 The table shows the amount of money in a charity box at the beginning of each month.

Month	Jan	Feb	Mar	Apr	May	Jun
Amount (£)	20	30	0	15	15	50

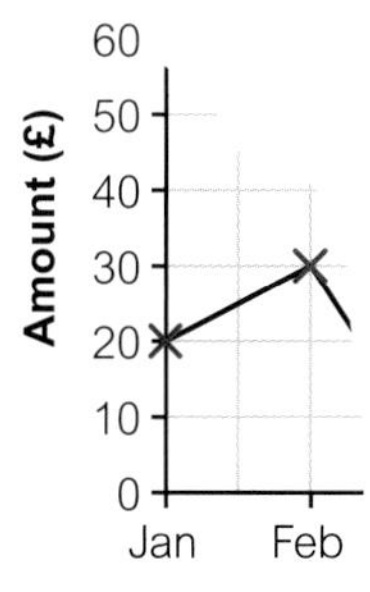

a Copy and complete the line graph for the data.

b How much was in the charity box at the beginning of February?

c When was the charity box empty?

d When was there £50 in the charity box?

Discussion What happened between March and June?

Q4a hint

Use a cross (not a dot) to plot each point. The first two crosses have been marked for you. Join the crosses with straight lines.

Comparing data

5b

1 The chart shows what the Patel and Jones families recycled one month.

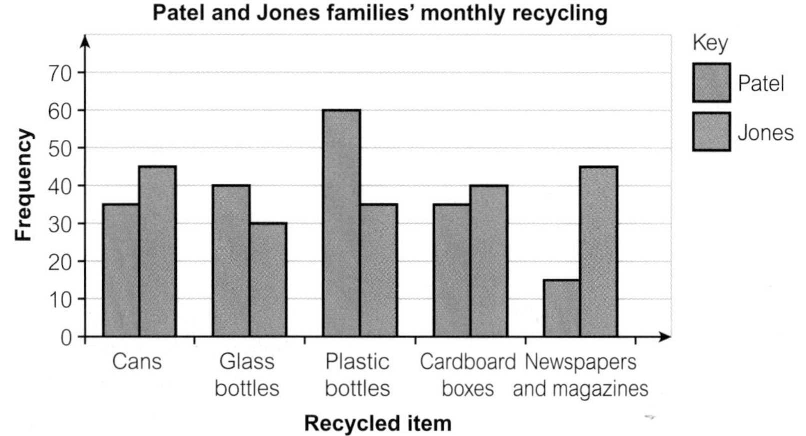

a How many cans did the Jones family recycle?

b Which item did the Patels recycle the most?

c Which family recycled more glass bottles?

d How many bottles were recycled altogether?

Q1 hint

Look at the chart carefully. Make sure you understand the key. From the top of each bar, look across to the frequency to find how many of that item were recycled.

Q1c hint

Which is the taller bar for glass bottles?

Q1d hint

Include glass bottles and plastic bottles for both families.

5c

2 Two students are neighbours. They compared their travel times (in minutes) to school by bus and by car.

Bus	15	22	19	18	21	19	20	17	21	19
Car	7	16	28	15	21	17	29	9	24	20

a i Work out the median travel time by bus.

ii Work out the median travel time by car.

iii Reasoning Use the medians to compare the travel times by bus and by car.

Travelling by car is ________ than by bus on average because the median time by bus is _______ than by car.

b i Work out the range of travel times by bus.

ii Work out the range of travel times by car.

iii Use the ranges to compare the travel times by bus and by car.

Travel times by car vary _______ than by bus because the range of car travel times is _______ than the range of bus travel times.

Q2a iii hint

Complete the sentence using the words quicker or slower, less or greater.

Q2b iii hint

Complete the sentence using the words more, less, or greater.

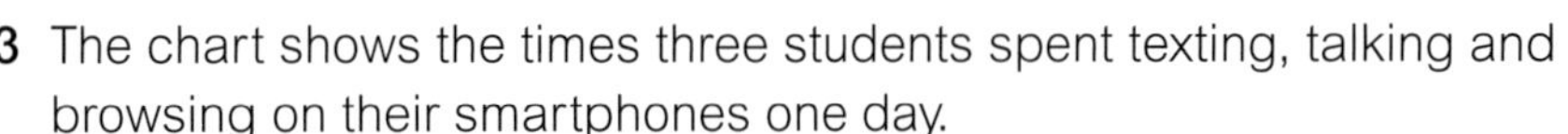

3 The chart shows the times three students spent texting, talking and browsing on their smartphones one day.

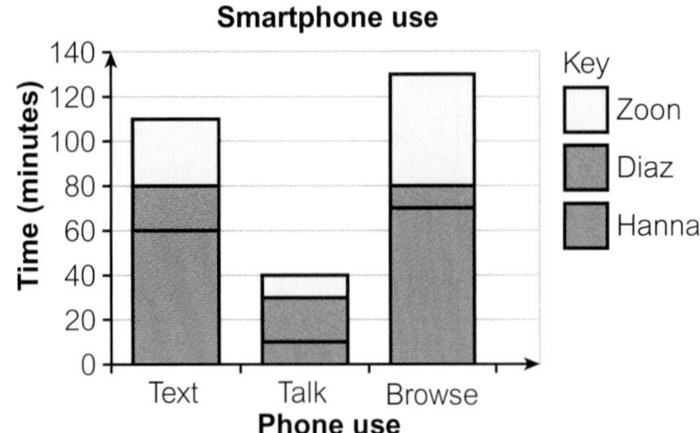

Q3 hint

Look at the chart carefully.
Make sure you understand the key and what the axes show.

Q3a hint

The yellow part of the Text bar goes from 80 minutes to 110 minutes.
Work out the difference.

a How long did Zoon spend sending text messages?

b Who spent the least time browsing?

c Copy and complete the table.

	Text	Talk	Browse
Hanna			
Diaz			
Zoon			

d How many minutes did Zoon spend texting, talking and browsing altogether?

e Which two students spent the same amount of time talking?

Enrichment

1 a i Count the letters in each word of this sentence and record the results in the tally chart shown below.

Letters	Tally	Frequency
1–2		
3–4		
5–6		
7–8		

ii What is the modal class?

iii Draw a bar chart for the data.

b i Repeat part **a** using a long sentence from a different book.

ii Compare the two sentences using the mode.

2 Real The numbers of North Atlantic hurricanes from 1995 to 2004 are
11, 9, 3, 10, 8, 8, 9, 4, 7, 9

a Write down the mode. **b** Work out the median.

c Work out the mean. **d** Work out the range.

3 Problem-solving In 2005 there were 15 hurricanes and in 2006 there were 5 hurricanes.
How does this extra data affect your answers to Q2?

Reflect

4 Reflect Write down the names of all the different charts you have learned about in this unit.
Beside each chart, write *one* thing that makes it different to the others.
Write *two* things that are the same for all charts.

1 Extend

You will:

- Extend your understanding with problem-solving.

5c

1 **a** **Real** The wind speeds (in knots) of the Atlantic hurricanes in 2005 were:

65, 130, 135, 85, 150, 100, 80, 80, 70, 150, 70, 65, 150, 100, 75

i Work out the median wind speed.

ii Work out the range of the wind speeds.

b The wind speeds (in knots) of the Atlantic hurricanes in 2010 were:

85, 115, 125, 135, 115, 105, 70, 75, 85, 65, 85

i Work out the median wind speed.

ii Work out the range of the wind speeds.

c **Reasoning** Use the medians and ranges to compare the wind speeds of hurricanes in 2005 and 2010. Write down two sentences.

5b

2 A rowing crew has eight rowers and one cox.
The cox steers the boat.

a Here are the weights of the rowers in the 2013 Oxford rowing crew.

89.8 kg, 87.1 kg, 96.2 kg, 88.9 kg, 100.2 kg, 92.5 kg, 93.9 kg, 109.8 kg

i What was their median weight?

ii Work out the range.

iii Calculate their mean weight.

b The table shows the mean, median and range of the weights of the 2013 Cambridge rowers.

Mean	Median	Range
92.0 kg	91.9 kg	19.0 kg

Compare the weights of the rowers in the two crews using

i the mean **ii** the median **iii** the range.

c The Oxford cox weighed 52.6 kg.

i Work out the median of all nine members of the Oxford crew.

ii How has the median changed?

5a

3 **Reasoning** A TV company tested two new types of remote control, A and B, on a group of viewers.
The number of wrong button presses made by each viewer was recorded during a test week.
The table shows a summary of the information.

	Mean number of wrong presses	Range
Type A	23	9
Type B	15	12

Which design would you recommend, and why?

5b

4 **Modelling** Dave wanted to estimate the average height of a Year 7 student. He measured the heights of five of his friends and calculated their mean to be 142 cm.

a Explain why Dave's friends might be different from the average for all Year 7 students.

b Explain why his mean might not be a good model for the average height of Year 7 students.

Discussion How can his model be improved?

5a

5 Gill used a spreadsheet to work out the mode, median and mean of the numbers in cells **A1** to **A8**. The values of the averages are in cells **B9**, **B10** and **B11**.
Which cell contains the

a mode   b median   c mean?

	A	B
1	20	
2	10	
3	60	
4	10	
5	40	
6	70	
7	20	
8	10	
9		20
10		10
11		30

5b

6 a The chart and table show the tools hired from Simple DIY and from Cool Tools during a week.

Cool Tools	
Tool	**Frequency**
Sander	13
Generator	9
Ladder	6
Cement mixer	7
Chainsaw	6

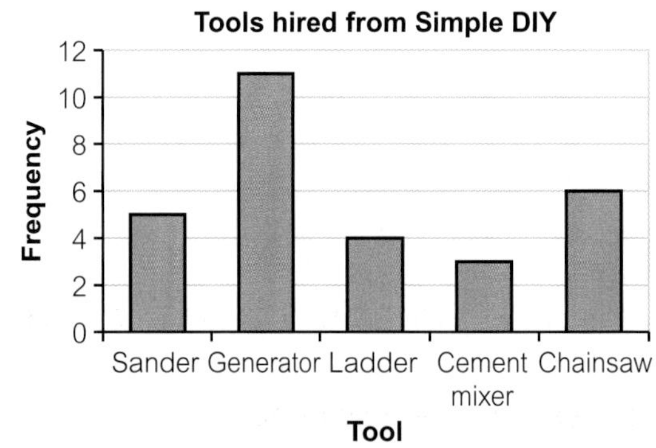

Draw a chart to compare the data for Simple DIY and Cool Tools.

b i How many tools were hired out altogether by each shop?

ii Write down the mode for each shop.

iii Write two sentences comparing the shops.

c The bar-line chart shows the number of generators hired out by Simple DIY each week during 2012.
They have 11 generators. They can borrow generators from Cool Tools if they need to.

i In how many weeks did they need to borrow generators?

ii How many generators did they need to borrow altogether in 2012?

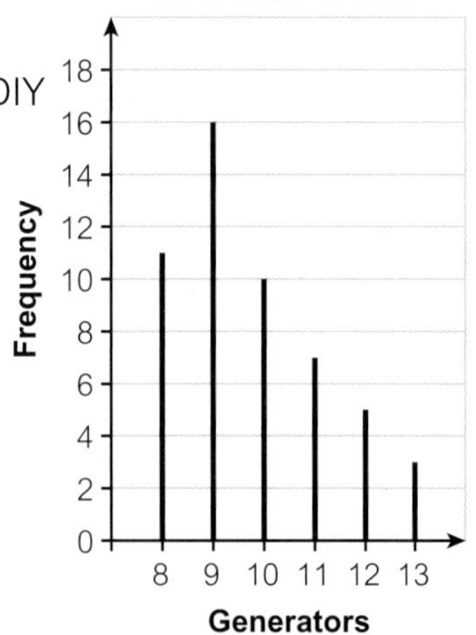

5a

7 The table shows the challenge award badges given to scouts of three troops.

	Creative	Community	Expedition	Fitness
Trascombe	4	11	7	7
Drax Valley	10	8	0	6
1st Sandon	2	5	4	12

a What was the most popular award overall?

b Draw a compound bar chart for the data. Draw one bar for each scout troop.

c Which troop got the most awards?

Subject links: Geography (Q1), Science (Q11)

8 **Problem-solving / Reasoning** Explain the method you used for each of the following questions. 5a

Q8a hint

An **integer** is a whole number.

a The mode of three integers □, □, □ is 2. Their range is 3. Find the three numbers.

b The median of the four integers 3, □, □, 7 is 5.5 Find two possible missing numbers.

c Find five integers whose mode is 1, median is 2 and mean is 3.

d The mean of three integers is 4. Work out the total of the numbers.

e The mean of the three integers 2, 3, □ is 5. Find the missing number.

f The mean of the three integers □, □, 3 is 0. Find two possible missing numbers.

9 **Real** The table shows the emergency response times for ambulances in a town during May. 5a

Time (minutes)	Frequency
3–5	12
6–8	16
9–11	10
12–14	7
15–17	3
18–20	1

a What is the modal class?

b **Reasoning** The Government's target is for ambulances to respond within 8 minutes.

i How many ambulances achieved this target?

ii How many did not?

c Draw a bar chart for the data.

d Here are the first few emergency response times for June.
4, 7, 5, 6, 10, 7, 8, 95

i What is unusual about this data? Give a possible reason for this.

ii Work out the mode, median and mean.

iii **Reasoning** Which one of these three averages best represents the data?

10 **Real** Wigan and Bradford rugby teams each played 35 games. The charts show the points they scored. 5b

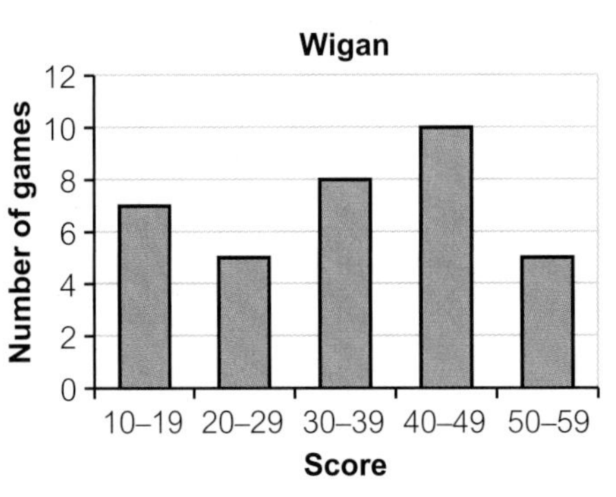

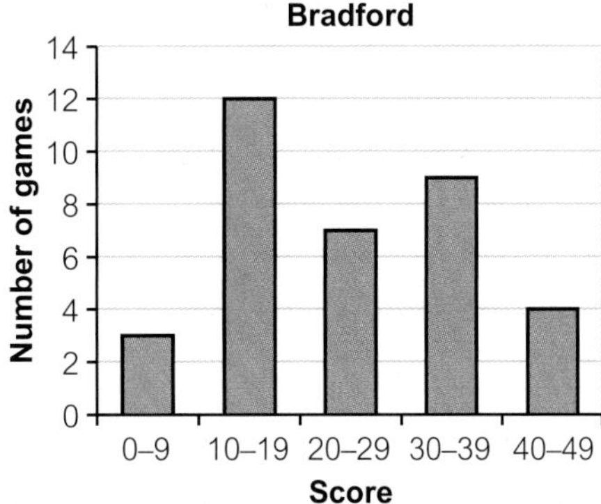

a i What is the modal class for each team?

ii Which team performed better? Give a reason for your answer.

b **Reasoning / Problem-solving** Can you tell which team had the greater range of scores? Give a reason for your answer.

11 Real / Modelling A mountain lion was tracked using an electronic tag. She travelled a distance, d miles, each day. Jamal has started a tally chart.
~~6.8~~, ~~5.7~~, ~~6.4~~, ~~3.6~~, ~~12.1~~, 9.4, 8.0, 9.2, 2.8, 3.7, 9.4, 5.6, 13.0, 6.0, 5.5, 14.2, 3.2, 4.2, 8.0, 3.8, 17.3, 8.8, 3.8, 8.7, 11.8, 8.7, 3.4, 10.1, 14.1, 19.4

Key point

The class $5 \leqslant d < 10$ includes all the values from 5 up to, but *not* including, 10.

i Copy and complete the tally chart.

ii What is the modal class?

iii On how many days did the lion travel at least 10 miles?

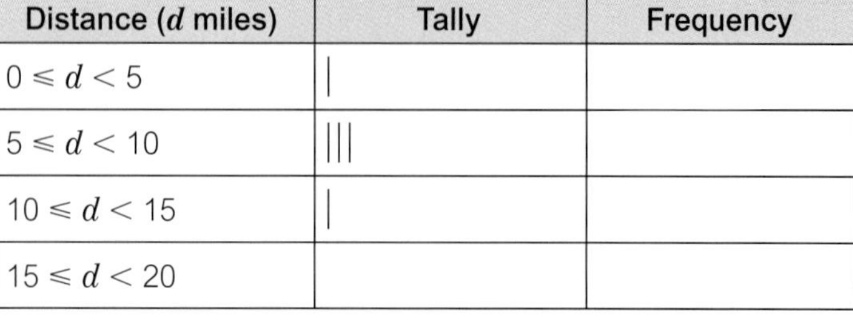

Distance (d miles)	Tally	Frequency
$0 \leqslant d < 5$	|	
$5 \leqslant d < 10$	|||	
$10 \leqslant d < 15$	|	
$15 \leqslant d < 20$		

b Jamal thinks that there should be five equal classes instead of four.

i Make a new tally chart for the data using five equal classes.

ii Write down the new modal class.

iii What would happen if you kept increasing the number of classes?

c The lion crossed the Grand Canyon during the day. The line graph shows her height above sea level, in metres, every 2 hours.

i When did the lion reach the bottom of the Grand Canyon?

ii How far above sea level is the bottom of the Grand Canyon?

iii How far did the lion ascend?

iv Compare the lion's descent and ascent.

v Estimate the height of the lion above sea level at 7.30 am.

vi Is this line graph a good model for predicting how other lions cross the Grand Canyon? Give reasons for your answer.

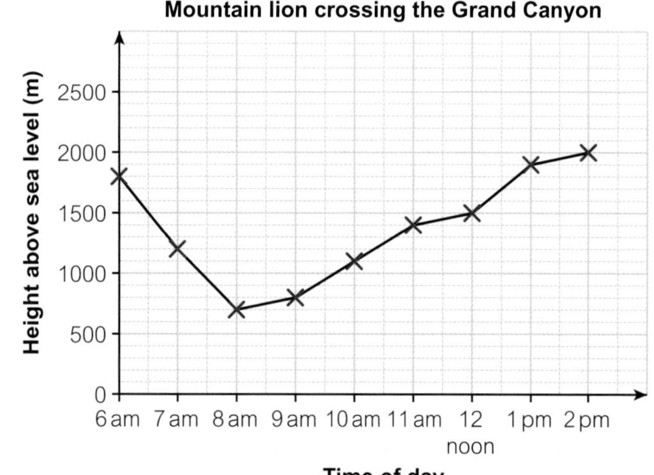

Investigation **Problem-solving**

1 **a** Work out the mean of these numbers: 2, 2, 2, 6, 8
b Add 1 to each of the numbers and work out their mean again.
c How has the mean changed?

2 Multiply each of the numbers in Q1 by 3. Work out the mean. How has it changed?

3 **a** What do you think will happen to the mean if you divide each of the numbers in Q1 by 2?
b Try it and see if your prediction is correct.

4 Investigate what happens to the means when you subtract a number from each of the numbers in Q1.

5 Investigate what happens to the mean if you multiply the numbers in Q1 by a number and then add another number to each of them.

6 **a** Write down a rule to describe what happens to the mean when you add, subtract, multiply or divide all the values.
b Test your rule using five new numbers.

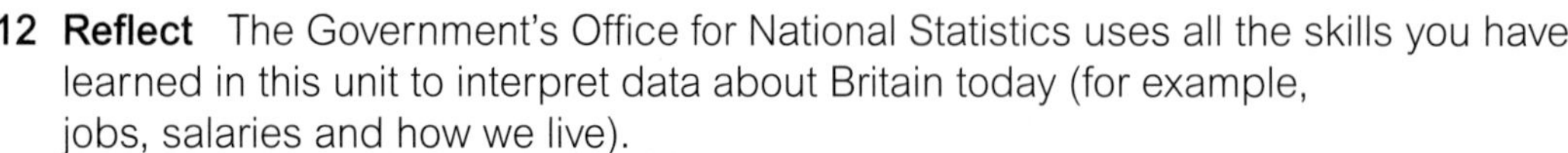

12 Reflect The Government's Office for National Statistics uses all the skills you have learned in this unit to interpret data about Britain today (for example, jobs, salaries and how we live).
What other organisations might use these skills?
What do you think they might use them for?

1 Unit test

1 a The chart shows the accidents each month on a busy road before a speed camera was fitted.

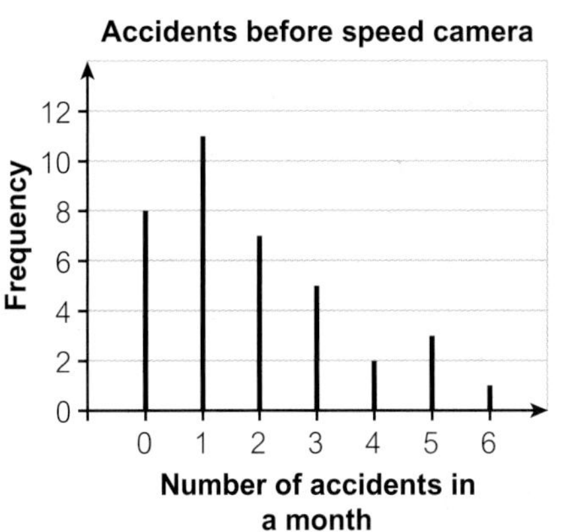

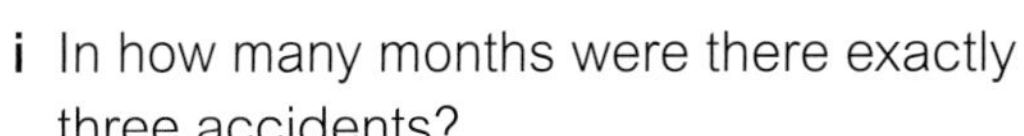

i In how many months were there exactly three accidents? 4b

ii In how many months were there more than three accidents?

iii Write down the modal number of accidents.

iv Work out the range. 4a

b The chart shows the accidents each month after a speed camera was fitted.

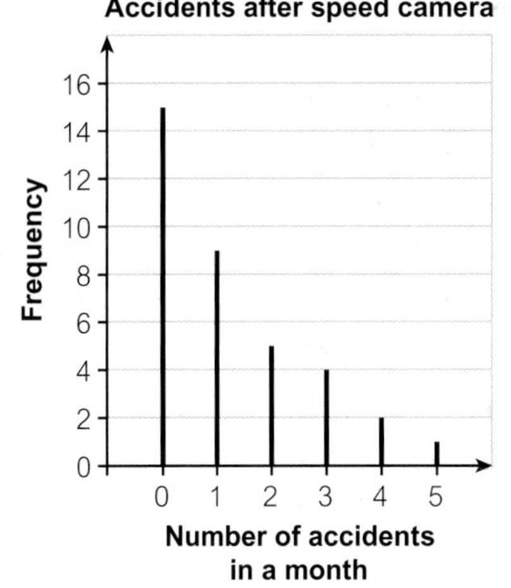

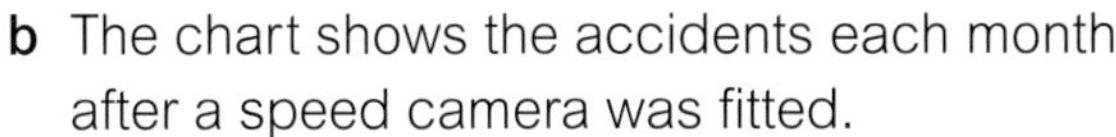

i In how many months were there no accidents? 4b

ii Write down the mode.

iii Work out the range. 4a

c Use the modes and ranges to write two sentences comparing the numbers of accidents before and after the speed camera was fitted. 4a

2 Look at this set of data.

8, 0, 5, 2, 5

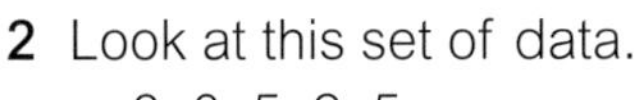

a Write down the mode. 4b

b Work out the range. 4c

c Work out the median. 4b

d Work out the mean. 5a

3 The chart shows the volume of water drunk by a rabbit each day.

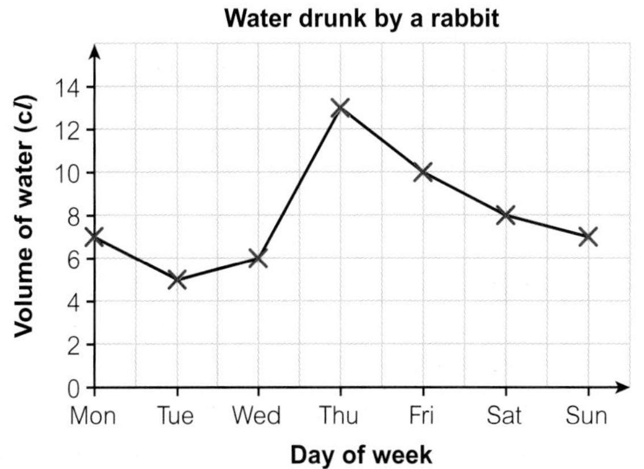

a How much water did the rabbit drink on Sunday? 4a

b When did the rabbit drink 6 c*l* of water?

c Which day do you think was the hottest? Give a reason for your answer. 5b

5a

4 Andy used electronic tagging to record the journeys of five cats. The table shows the total distances travelled (in km) over a week.

	Tizzy	Rolf	Mittens	Zoe	Patch
Daytime	1	6	3	4	3
Night	4	2	8	6	5

a Draw a compound bar chart for the data.

b Do these cats travel the furthest at night-time or during the day? Explain your answer.

5b

5 Two students each played a video game many times. The table shows some information about their scores.

	Mean	Range
Oscar	75	80
Venus	70	20

a Write two sentences comparing the performances of the students.

5a

b Which student would you like on your team? Give a reason for your answer.

6 Here are the masses of the boxes in a removal van.

32 kg, 15 kg, 51 kg, 22 kg, 30 kg, 20 kg, 44 kg, 18 kg, 27 kg, 33 kg, 38 kg, 42 kg, 33 kg, 27 kg, 19 kg, 41 kg, 30 kg, 25 kg, 36 kg, 25 kg

4a

a Work out the median.

b Copy and complete the tally chart for the data.

Mass (kg)	Tally	Frequency
15–24		

5c

c Jason says that the mean is 62 kg. Without calculating the mean, explain how you know he is wrong.

d Calculate the correct mean.

Challenge

7 You book a table for 10 people at a restaurant. The restaurant needs to know everyone's choice of meal beforehand.

a Write three choices of starter, three choices of main course, and three choices of dessert you like.

b Design a table to record everyone's choices.

Reflect

8 **Reflect** What new ideas and skills have you learned in this unit? When could these skills be useful in mathematics? Could they be useful in other school subjects?

2.1 Mental maths

You will learn to:

- Use the priority of operations, including brackets
- Use multiplication facts up to 10 × 10 and the laws of arithmetic to do mental multiplication and division
- Multiply and divide by 10, 100 and 1000.

CONFIDENCE

Why learn this? Market stallholders use mental arithmetic to work out the total cost of sales and give the correct change.

Fluency
What are the missing numbers?

- 20 + □ = 100
- 100 = □ + 35
- 100 – 82 = □
- 47 = 100 – □

Explore
How do market stallholders work out how much to charge to make a profit?

Exercise 2.1

Warm up

1 Find the sum of 25, 30 and 12.

2 Find the difference between 50 and 11.

3 Work out
a 2 × 6 b 4 × 6 c 10 × 6
d 24 ÷ 6 e 30 ÷ 6 f 42 ÷ 6

4b

4 Work out
a 3 × 2 + 5 b 3 × (2 + 5) c 10 – 5 + 2
d 3 × 0 + 8 e (12 – 8) × 7 f (9 + 3) ÷ (4 – 1)

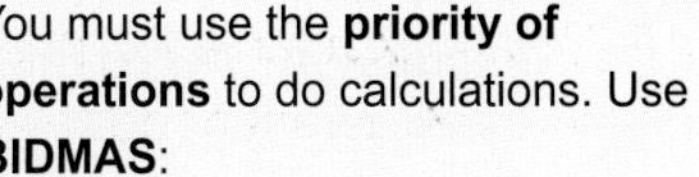

Key point

You must use the **priority of operations** to do calculations. Use **BIDMAS**:
Brackets
→ **I**ndices (powers)
→ **D**ivision and **M**ultiplication
→ **A**ddition and **S**ubtraction

4b

5 **Problem-solving** Copy these calculations. Fill in the missing operations.
a 12 * 8 * 3 * 2 = 26 b 8 * 6 * 4 * 2 = 10

4b

6 a Work out
i 2 × 3 × 4 ii 2 × 4 × 3 iii 3 × 2 × 4
iv 6 × 4 v 8 × 3

~~b What do you notice about your answers to part a?~~

Discussion Does changing the order of the multiplication change your answer? Can you split numbers to multiply them?

4a

7 Work out
a 8 × 2 × 5 b 7 × 5 × 2
c 3 × 6 × 3 d 9 × 4 × 2

Q7a hint

It is easier to do 2 × 5 first, so change the order of the multiplication.
8 × 2 × 5 = 2 × 5 × 8.

4a **8** **a** Here are two calculations using 3, 4 and 12. Write two more.

$3 \times 4 = 12$ $12 \div 4 = 3$

b $7 \times \square = 56$

i What is the missing number?

ii Write two more calculations using these numbers.

4a **9** Work out

a 50×100 **b** 10×25 **c** 1000×18

d $300 \div 100$ **e** $540 \div 10$ **f** $7200 \div 100$

Worked example

Work out

a 27×6

$27 \times 6 = 20 \times 6 + 7 \times 6$ — Split 27 into 20 + 7.

$= 10 \times 6 \times 2 + 7 \times 6$ — Split 20 into 10 × 2. It is easier to do 10 × 6 = 60 first and then 60 × 2.

$= 120 + 42 = 162$

b 4×99

$4 \times 99 = 4 \times 100 - 4 \times 1$ — For numbers ending in 9, it is easier to work with the next whole number: 99 = 100 − 1.

$= 400 - 4 = 396$

Literacy hint

This process is called **partitioning**. Partitioning splits the bigger number to make some easier multiplications.

4a **10** Work out

a 4×63 **b** 7×72 **c** 5×99 **d** 7×69

4a **11** **Real** An expedition group need a total of 22 AA batteries for all their torches. They buy four packs of two AA batteries and three packs of four AA batteries. Have they bought enough batteries?

5c **12** Work out

a $5 \times 4 + 15$ **b** $27 + 20 \div 2$ **c** $9 \div 3 + 18$

d $35 - 5 \times 15$ **e** $20 + 12 \times 4$ **f** $13 \times 3 + 4 \times 12$

Discussion Why do we need to use the priority of operations?

5c **13** **Problem-solving** $4 + 2 \times 8 - 6 \div 2$

Put sets of brackets in different places in the calculation to find as many answers as possible.

Reasoning Why does working in order help?

Discussion Would three numbers inside the brackets give you more answers?

Q13 Strategy hint

Work in order and start with (4 + 2).

Investigation — **Discussion / Reasoning**

a Use your calculator to work out

i $4 + 8 \times 2 - 7$ **ii** $2 \times 8 - 6 \div 2$ **iii** $5 \times (3 + 6)$ **iv** $(4 - 2) + 4 \times 7$ **v** $10 \times 3 \div 5 + (2 - 1)$

b Compare your answers with another person's. Are they the same?

c Does your calculator use BIDMAS? How do you know?

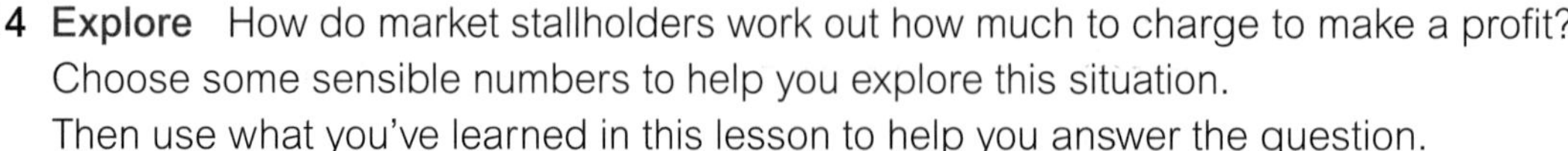

Explore **14** **Explore** How do market stallholders work out how much to charge to make a profit? Choose some sensible numbers to help you explore this situation. Then use what you've learned in this lesson to help you answer the question.

Reflect **15** **Reflect** Write the new mathematical terms and words you have learned in this lesson. Use your own words to write a definition for each of them. For each definition, make up a calculation to show what it means.

2.2 Addition and subtraction

You will learn to:
- Round whole numbers to the nearest 10, 100, 1000
- Make an estimate to check an answer
- Use a written method to add and subtract whole numbers of any size.

CONFIDENCE

Why learn this? Charity fundraisers use addition to work out how much money they have raised.

Fluency
- Find the sum of 19 and 42.
- Find the difference between 78 and 13.

Explore
How do charity fundraisers work out how much more they need to raise to reach their target?

Exercise 2.2

Warm up

1 **Round** each number to the nearest 10.
 a 92 b 538
 c 145 d 499

2 Work out
 a 314 + 143 b 267 + 124

3 Work out
 a 579 – 324 b 421 – 234

Key point
To **round** to the nearest 10, look at the digit in the units column.
To round to the nearest 100, look at the digit in the tens column.
To round to the nearest 1000, look at the digit in the hundreds column.
If the digit is less than 5, round down.
If the digit is 5 or more, round up.

4 Round each number to the nearest 100. 4c
 a 267 b 405
 c 851 d 1298

Q4a hint
The digit in the tens column is 6.
It is more than 5, so round up.

5 Round each number to the nearest 1000. 4c
 a 4320 b 5908
 c 6873 d 978

Q5a hint
The digit in the hundreds column is 3.
It is less than 5, so round down.

6 **Reasoning** Two of the calculations below are wrong. 4c
Use **estimation** to work out which two.
What mistakes have been made?

A 247 + 329 = 566

B 1375 + 2148 = 3523

C 482 + 271 = 6153

D 1482 + 6530 = 8012

Discussion When we use a written method, why do we add from right to left?

Q6 Literacy hint
In maths, **estimation** means using rounded values to do the calculation.

Q6a hint
Round the numbers to the nearest 10 and then add. Is the estimate close to the answer given?

4c **7** Website A has 326 hits on Monday.
On the same day, Website B has 118 more hits than Website A.
How many hits does Website B have?

Q7 hint

Use a bar model to help you.

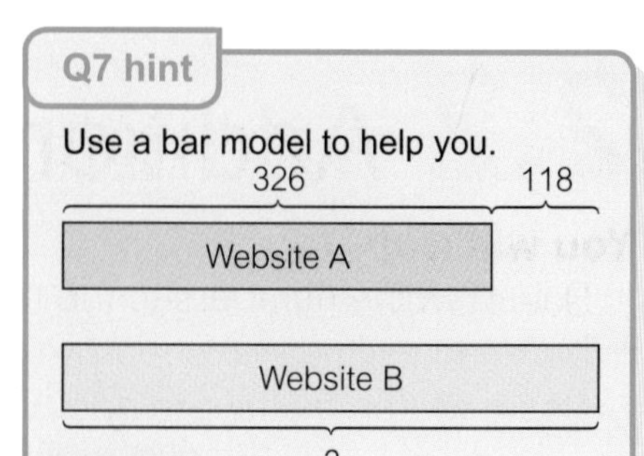

4b **8** **Problem-solving** Copy these calculations. Fill in the missing digits.

a
```
  **2
+ 13*
  396
```

b
```
  47*
+ *86
  7*1
```

c
```
  74*
- 3*6
  *23
```

d
```
  8*1
- *9*
  277
```

Discussion Compare your method with another person's.
Did you use the same approach?

Key point

Work out an estimate before you do a calculation. Use your estimate to check your answer.

5c **9** Work out these. Make an estimate first to check your answer.

- **a** 389 + 46
- **b** 1752 + 179
- **c** 247 + 2008
- **d** 1426 + 145 + 63

5c **10** **Problem-solving** A garage sells 86 more red cars than blue cars.
The garage sells 1048 blue cars.
How many red and blue cars do they sell?

Q10 hint

Use a bar model to help you.

5b **11** Work out these. Make an estimate first to check your answer.

- **a** 452 – 91
- **b** 2845 – 380
- **c** 1763 – 97
- **d** 5078 – 723 – 82

Q11d hint

Use a bar model to help you.

5078

? 723 83

5b **12** **Problem-solving / Real** Charity A raises £25 654.
Charity B raises £848 less than Charity A.
How much money do the charities raise in total?

Explore **13** **Explore** How do charity fundraisers work out how much more they need to raise to reach their target?
Choose some sensible numbers to help you explore this situation.
Then use what you've learned in this lesson to help you answer the question.

Reflect **14** **Reflect** This lesson used some bar models for problem-solving.
Would you use bar models to help you solve mathematics problems in future? Explain why, or why not.

2.3 Multiplication

You will learn to:

- Use a written method to multiply whole numbers.

Why learn this? A T-shirt seller uses multiplication to work out how much money she has made from selling T-shirts at a fixed price.

Fluency
Find the missing numbers.

- 9 × 6 = □
- □ × 8 = 64
- 4 × □ = 40
- □ × □ = 27
- 30 × 10 = □

Explore
What calculations would a T-shirt seller need to do to make sure she had enough T-shirts to sell at a festival?

Exercise 2.3

1 Work out
 a 50 × 10
 b 100 × 5
 c 30 × 20

2 Round each number to the nearest 100.
 a 218 b 658
 c 30 d 999

Key point
In the **column method** you write the numbers in the calculation in their place value columns like this:

```
  242
×   3
─────
```


Worked example

Work out 625 × 3 using the **column method**.

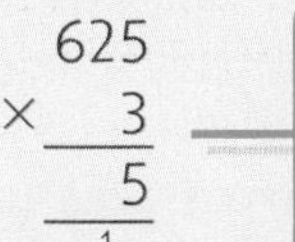

```
  625
×   3
    5
    1
```

Start in the units column. Multiply each digit in the top row by the digit in the bottom row.
5 × 3 = 15. That's 5 units and **1** ten.

```
  625
×   3
   75
    1
```

In the tens column:
2 × 3 = 6.
6 + **1** = 7.
That's 7 tens altogether.

```
  625
×   3
 1875
    1
```

In the hundreds column:
6 × 3 = 18.

Worked example

Work out 625 × 3 using the grid method.

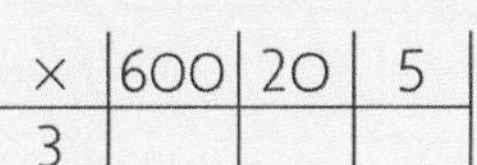

×	600	20	5
3			

Split 625 into easier numbers: 600, 20 and 5. Write them along the top of a grid.
Write 3 at the side of the grid.

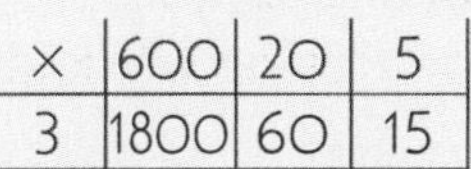

×	600	20	5
3	1800	60	15

Multiply each easier number by 3. Write the answers in the squares of the grid.

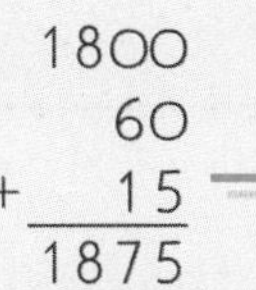

```
  1800
    60
+   15
  1875
```

Add up the numbers you worked out.

Discussion Which method is quicker?

4b **3** Work out

a 121 × 4 **b** 124 × 3 **c** 239 × 6

4b **4** **Reasoning** Three of the calculations below are wrong.
Use **approximation** to work out which three.
What mistakes have been made?

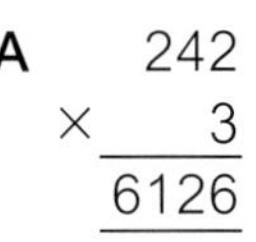

A
```
   242
×    3
  6126
```

B
```
   375
×    8
  3000
```

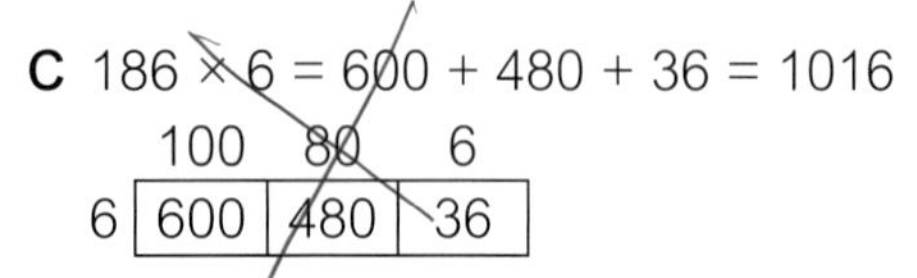

C 186 × 6 = 600 + 480 + 36 = 1016

	100	80	6
6	600	480	36

D
```
   564
×    4
  2046
```

4b **5** **Problem-solving** A bookcase has 8 shelves.

a Each shelf holds 115 books. How many books are there in total?

b There are 342 fiction books. How many books are non-fiction?

4b **6** **Reasoning** Write a one-step word problem for this bar model.
Solve your word problem.

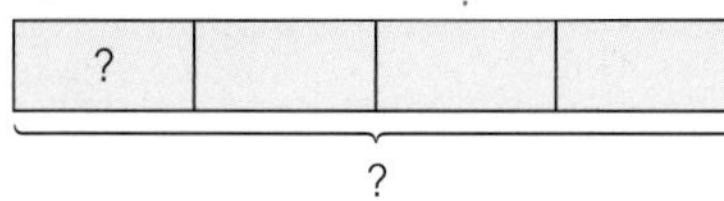
?
?

Discussion Compare your word problem with another person's.
Did you use similar mathematical words?

4b **7** **Problem-solving** A music stall has 6 rows of CDs.
There are 145 CDs in each row.
A total of 405 CDs are sold.
How many CDs are not sold?

Q4 Literacy hint
An **approximation** is a number or result that is not exact, but is close enough to the actual number for it to be useful.

Key point
You can use estimation to check the answer to a multiplication calculation. Round the numbers and then multiply.

Q4a hint
Round 242 to the nearest 100 and then multiply. Is the estimate close to the answer given?

Q5 hint
Use bar models to help you.

115 books							

? books

342 fiction	? non-fiction

Q7 Strategy hint
Try drawing bar models like those in Q5 hint.

Key point
Long multiplication is a written method to multiply by a number greater than 10.

Worked example

Work out 34 × 29

Estimate: 34 × 29 is roughly 30 × 30 = 900

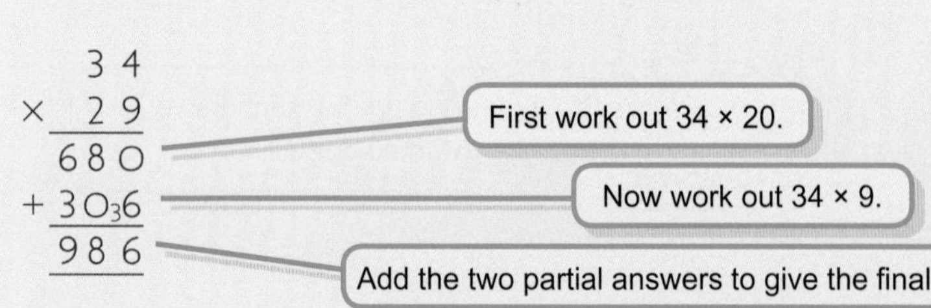

```
    3 4
×   2 9
  6 8 0
+ 3 0 6
  9 8 6
```
First work out 34 × 20.
Now work out 34 × 9.
Add the two partial answers to give the final answer.

Check: 986 is close to 900

Check the answer against the estimate.

8 Work out

a 32 × 15 b 46 × 54 c 62 × 39
d 132 × 15 e 243 × 26 f 327 × 41 **5c**

9 **Real** Malik travels by train to London 17 times a year.
Each return train ticket costs £65.
How much does he spend in total on train tickets in a year? **5c**

10 **Problem-solving** Sami has 265 followers on Twitter.
Tom has 34 times as many followers as Sami.
How many more people follow Tom than follow Sami? **5b**

11 **Real / Finance** A T-shirt seller buys 384 T-shirts at £14 each.
She sells 208 of the T-shirts at £22 each.
Has she made a profit or a loss? How much? **5b**

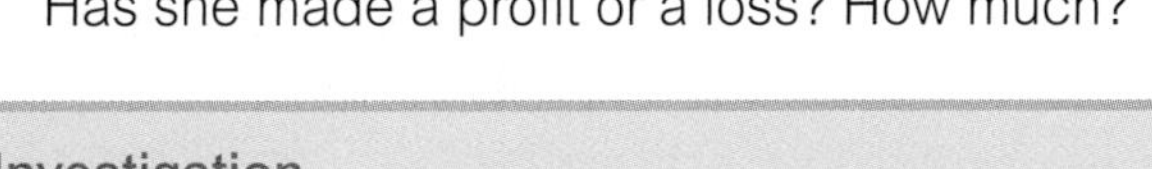

Investigation — **Problem-solving / Reasoning**

Arrange the digits 3, 5, 6, 8 as a

```
  * *
× * *
-----
-----
```

calculation.

For example:

```
  35
× 68
----
----
```

a Find the answer.

Arrange the digits in a different

```
  * *
× * *
-----
-----
```

calculation.

b How many different answers are possible?

c What is the smallest possible answer? What is the largest possible answer?

d For any four digits, will there always be the same number of answers?

12 **Explore** What calculations would a T-shirt seller need to do to make sure she had enough T-shirts to sell at a festival?
Choose some sensible numbers to help you explore this situation.
Then use what you've learned in this lesson to help you answer the question. **Explore**

13 **Reflect** Look at your working for part **a** of the investigation. Did you use a strategy to make sure you found *all* the possible answers?
If you answered 'Yes', what strategy did you use, and why?
If you answered 'No', what strategy could you have used, and why?
Could you have used a different strategy? Would this have been better? **Reflect**

2.4 Division

You will learn to:
- Use a written method to divide whole numbers
- Use inverse operations to check an answer.

CONFIDENCE

Why learn this? The entry capacity of a stadium depends on the number of spectators who can pass through all the turnstiles per hour.

Fluency
Find the missing numbers.
- 9 × 7 = □
- □ ÷ 9 = 63
- 10 × 6 = □
- □ × 20 = 120

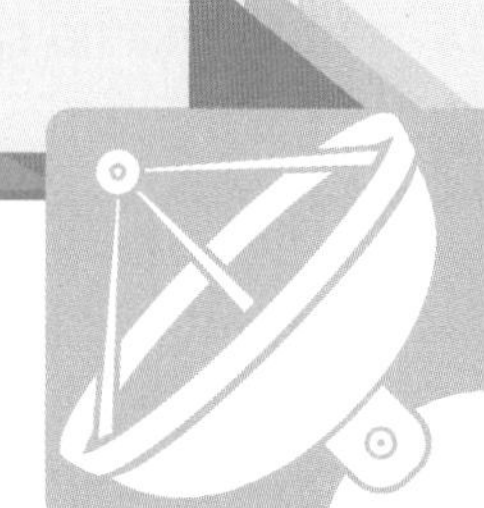

Explore
How many exits does a 40 000-seater stadium need?

Exercise 2.4

Warm up

1 a Count back in tens from 60 to 0.
  b Count back in tens from 54. What is left over?

2 a How many times does 3 go into 9?
  b How many times does 3 go into 8? What is the remainder?
  c How many times does 7 go into 20? What is the remainder?

Worked example

Work out 112 ÷ 4 using chunking.

Estimate: 112 ÷ 4 is roughly 100 ÷ 4 = 25 — Estimate the answer first.

```
4)112
 − 40  (10 × 4)
   72
 − 40  (10 × 4)
   32
 − 32  (8 × 4)
    0
```

Subtract a 'chunk' of 4. Choose an easy multiplication, like 10 × 4.

Keep subtracting 'chunks' of 4 until you can go no further. Look out for numbers in the 4 times table.

112 ÷ 4 = 10 + 10 + 8 = 28 — Add up the number of 'chunks' subtracted.

Check: 28 is close to 25 — Check the answer against the estimate.

Key point
You can use chunking or short division to divide whole numbers.

Worked example

Work out 112 ÷ 4 using short division.

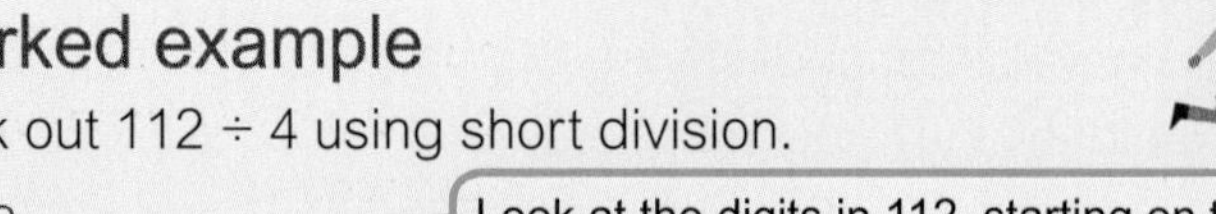

```
  2...
4)112
```

Look at the digits in 112, starting on the left.
4 doesn't go into 1, so look at 11.
4 goes into 11 twice so write a 2 in the tens column.

```
  2...
4)11³2
```

The difference between 11 and 4 × 2 is 3 so write the remainder 3 tens in the units column, to make 32.

```
  28
4)11³2
```

4 goes into 32 eight times. So write 8 in the units column.

3 Work out these divisions using **i** chunking **ii** short division.
Some of them have remainders.

a 224 ÷ 4

b 385 ÷ 5

c 128 ÷ 5

d 247 ÷ 8

Discussion Which method do you prefer – chunking or short division? Why?

Q3a hint
Estimate the answer first.

Q3c and d hint
These divisions have remainders.

4b

Worked example

Work out 448 ÷ 16

Estimate: 448 ÷ 16 is roughly 400 ÷ 20 = 20

Estimate the answer first.

```
     2 ...
16 ) 4 4 8
   - 3 2
     1 2 8
```

2 × 16 = 32. So 16 goes into 44 twice.
8 – 0 = 8, so bring down 8.

```
     2 8
16 ) 4 4 8
   - 3 2
     1 2 8
   - 1 2 8
         0
```

Try multiplying 16 by different numbers to get close to 128.
8 × 16 = 128

There is no remainder.

Key point
Long division is a written method to divide by a number greater than 10.

4 Work out these divisions.
Some of them have remainders.

a 308 ÷ 14

b 365 ÷ 15

c 684 ÷ 19

4b

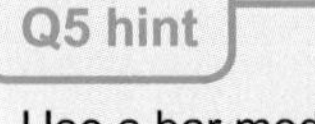

Q5 hint
Use a bar model to help you.

£336

Sioned | Ibrahim

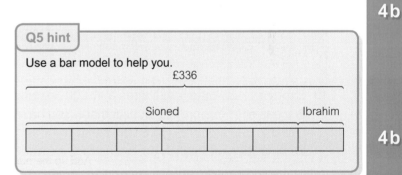

5 Sioned and Ibrahim hire a limousine at a cost of £336.
Sioned pays 6 times as much as Ibrahim.
How much does Ibrahim pay?

4b

6 Two of these calculations are wrong.
Check each multiplication by working backwards.
Which two are wrong?

A 5 × 78 = 380

B 47 × 6 = 329

C 3 × 84 = 252

4a

Key point
You can work backwards through a calculation using the **inverse** operation.
Division is the inverse of multiplication. Multiplication is the inverse of division.

Q6a Strategy hint
Which is easier to work out, 380 ÷ 78 or 380 ÷ 5?

5b

7 Work out these divisions.
   a 532 ÷ 28
   b 891 ÷ 33
   c 378 ÷ 24
   d 678 ÷ 48

Discussion Can you divide by 0?

> **Q7a hint**
> Start with, 'How many times does 28 go into 53?'

5b

8 **Real / Finance** Micah takes out a business loan of £1000.
She makes an initial repayment of £136.
She then makes 12 equal repayments.
How much is each repayment?

5b

9 **Problem-solving / Real**

Number of people at work	Number of toilets needed
76–100	5
100+	1 for every extra 25 people

A workplace has 624 employees.
How many toilets are needed?

> **Q9 hint**
> First work out the difference between 624 and 100.
> Don't forget the five toilets for the first 100 people!

Investigation — Reasoning

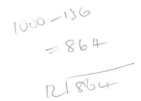

a Which of these numbers is **divisible** by 2?
18, 35, 42, 67, 74, 80, 91, 106
Write a rule to explain how you can tell when a number is divisible by 2.

b Each of these numbers is divisible by 3.
21, 36, 48, 72, 87, 108, 189, 234
Add the digits of each number together. For 21, for example, 2 + 1 = 3.
Write a rule to explain how you can tell when a number is divisible by 3.

c Which of these numbers is divisible by 2, 3 and 6?
24, 44, 54, 63, 72, 90, 102, 147
Write a rule to explain how you can tell when a number is divisible by 6.

Discussion Compare your rules with another person's. Are they the same?

> **Literacy hint**
> **'Divisible'** means 'can be divided by a number a whole number of times'.

Explore

10 **Explore** How many exits does a 40 000-seater stadium need?
Is it easier to explore this question now you have completed the lesson?
What further information do you need to be able to answer this?

Reflect

11 **Reflect** In lesson 2.3 you learned about multiplication and in this lesson you learned about division. Which was more difficult?
What made it more difficult?
Do you need more practice on any kinds of question? If so, which kinds?

2.5 FINANCE: Time and money

You will learn to:
- Round decimals to the nearest whole number
- Interpret the display on a calculator in different contexts
- Use a calculator to solve problems involving time and money.

CONFIDENCE

Why learn this? Companies spend a great deal of time and huge amounts of money on creating memorable advertising campaigns.

Fluency
- Find the total cost of three items priced at 45p, 22p and 65p.
- You pay for a 28p item with a £1 coin. How much change do you get?
- How many seconds are there in one minute?
- How many minutes are there in one hour?

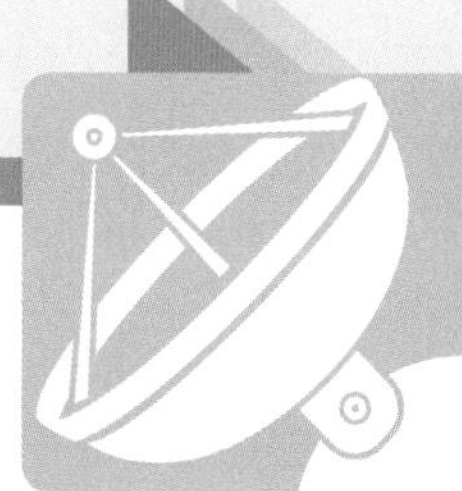

Explore
How is the price charged for adverts affected by TV viewing figures?

Exercise 2.5: Advertising

Warm up

1 a Match each decimal to the correct fraction.
   0.25   0.5   0.75
   $\frac{3}{4}$ $\frac{1}{4}$ $\frac{1}{2}$

  b Copy and complete these.
   i $\frac{1}{4}$ hour = □ minutes
   ii $\frac{1}{2}$ hour = □ minutes
   iii $\frac{3}{4}$ hour = □ minutes

2 A TV programme starts at 4.45 pm and is 40 minutes long.
What time does it finish?

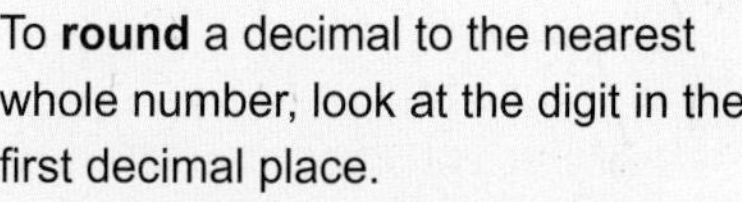

Key point
To **round** a decimal to the nearest whole number, look at the digit in the first decimal place.
If the digit is less than 5, round down.
If the digit is 5 or more, round up.

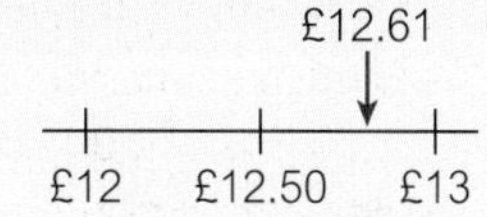

£12.61 rounds up to £13

4b

3 Round each number to the nearest whole number.
   a 4.80   b 10.29
   c 38.55   d 0.62

Q3a hint
Draw a number line or look at the digit in the first decimal place: 8.

4b

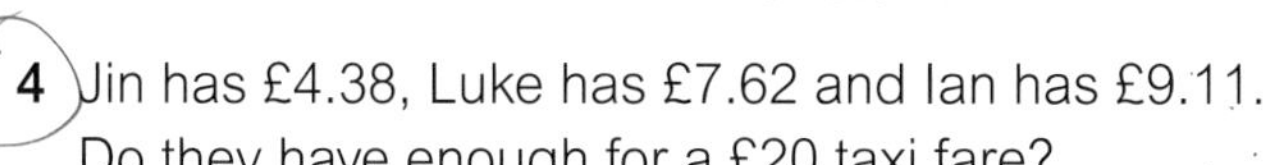

4 Jin has £4.38, Luke has £7.62 and Ian has £9.11.
Do they have enough for a £20 taxi fare?

Q4a hint
Round each amount to the nearest whole number and then add the rounded amounts.

4b

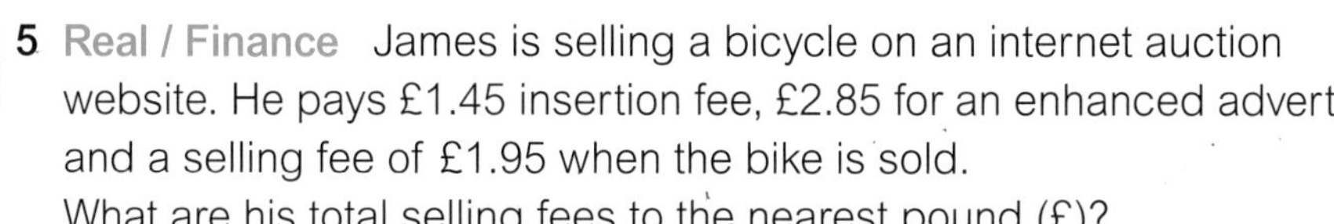

5 **Real / Finance** James is selling a bicycle on an internet auction website. He pays £1.45 insertion fee, £2.85 for an enhanced advert and a selling fee of £1.95 when the bike is sold.
What are his total selling fees to the nearest pound (£)?

4a

6 **Real / Finance** An advert in a magazine costs £2.30 per word.
Seth places an advert with 18 words.
What is the total cost?

4a

7 **Finance** A company has an advert on a billboard for 5 weeks.
The total cost is £399.50.
What is the weekly cost of the advert?

Q7 hint
Estimate the answer first so that you can check the answer given by the calculator.

5c 8 Real / Finance Shakira wants to sell her laptop on an internet website.

The prices for a week's advertising online are given in this table.

Selling price	7 days online advert
Up to £50	£3.10
£50.01– £200	£5.20
£200.01– £500	£7.50
£500.01 and above	£9.90

a How much does it cost to advertise a laptop worth £300 for 14 days?

b How much more would it cost to advertise a laptop valued at £750 for 14 days?

5c 9 Problem-solving / Reasoning A newspaper advert on a Wednesday costs £1200.

The same advert on a Saturday costs three times as much.

The same advert on a Friday costs £950 less than on a Saturday.

What is the cost of the advert on a Friday?

Q9 hint

Use this bar model to help you.

Saturday

Wednesday

£1200	£1200	£1200

Friday £950

5b 10 The calculator screens show the answers to questions on time.

A	B	C
0.75	0.5	0.25

Which screen shows an answer of

a $\frac{1}{4}$ hour b 30 minutes c 45 minutes?

5b 11 A drama is $2\frac{1}{2}$ hours long.

It has 10 advert breaks, which are evenly spaced.

How long is there between the start of each one?

2.5 ÷ 10

0.25

5a 12 Real / Finance On Channel A, a 20-second advertisement costs £388.50.

On Channel B, a 30-second advertisement costs £559.56.

Which advert is better value for money?

Discussion Can a money answer have more than two decimal places?

5a 13 Real / Problem-solving Three online clothes shops place sponsored adverts on a search engine when people search for 'checked trousers'. They pay for every click on their adverts. The more they pay for their adverts, the higher they appear on the page.

Name of shop	Cost per click	Page position	Number of clicks in a week
Fashion Heights	35p	1	23142
Legs 11	31p	2	24783
Walking Smart	28p	3	23021

a Work out how much each shop paid for their advert that week.

b Did the clothes shop that paid the most get the most clicks in a week?

Explore

14 **Explore** How is the price charged for adverts affected by TV viewing figures? Is it easier to explore this question now you have completed the lesson? What further information do you need to be able to answer this?

Reflect

15 **Reflect** Write down two new things you have learned about using a calculator for money calculations.

Which questions used this new knowledge?

When you answered these questions, did you make any mistakes? If so, check that you understand where you went wrong.

2.6 Negative numbers

You will learn to:

- Order positive and negative numbers
- Add and subtract positive and negative numbers
- Begin to multiply with negative numbers.

CONFIDENCE

Why learn this? You will experience negative g-forces when riding a roller coaster.

Fluency

- Continue the pattern:
  0 + 2 = 2
  1 + 2 = □
  2 + □ = □
  3 + □ = □
- Subtract 12 from 30.
- What is the difference between 48 and 16?

Explore
Does AYTMTB mean the same to me and you?

Exercise 2.6

Warm up

1 Look at the number line.

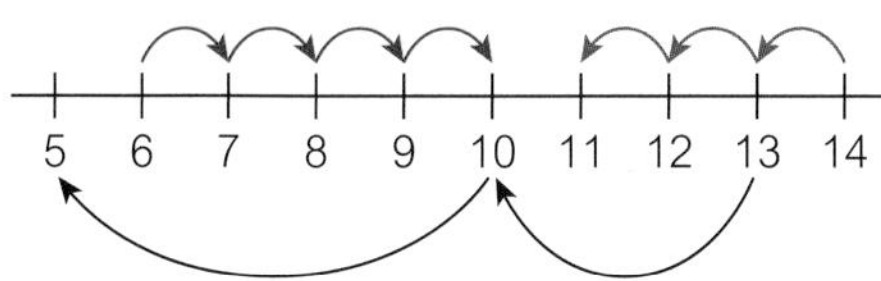

a Which colour jumps represent 6 + 4? What is the answer to 6 + 4?
b Write a calculation for the blue jumps.
c Write a calculation for the black jumps.

Q1b hint
Look carefully at the direction the arrows are going in.

2 Write this set of numbers in order. Start with the smallest.
8, 3, 0, 9, 12, 5

3 The temperature now is 14°C. It cools down by 5 degrees.
What is the new temperature?

4b

4 Write each set of temperatures in order, coldest first.
a 8 °C, 3 °C, –4 °C, –7 °C, 6 °C
b –5 °C, 2 °C, –9 °C, –1 °C, 4 °C
c 3 °C, –14 °C, –8 °C, 5 °C, –1 °C

Discussion Why are –3 and 3 closer to each other than –5 and 5?

Key point
You can show **positive** and **negative** numbers on a number line.

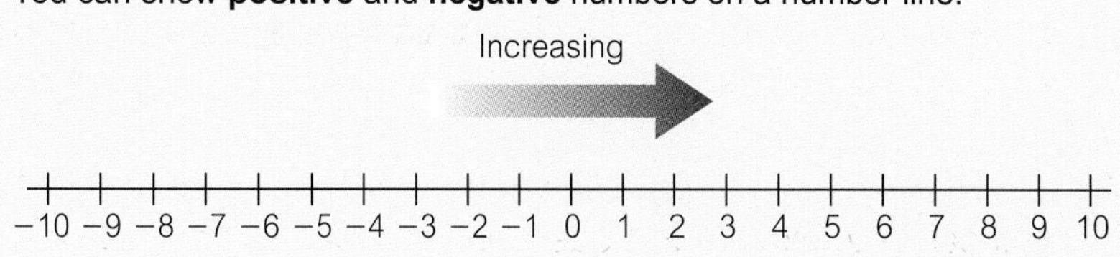

Q4a Strategy hint

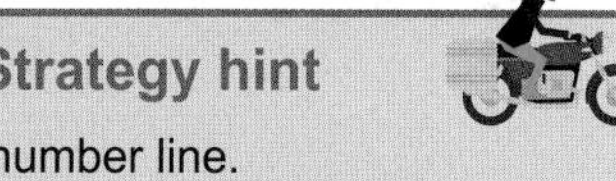

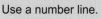

Use a number line.
Check that you have included all the temperatures in your answer.

4b **5** Copy and complete these. Write the correct sign, > or <, between each pair.

- **a** 5 °C ... −4 °C
- **b** −3 °C ... 2 °C
- **c** −7 °C ... −10 °C
- **d** −4 ... 0

4a **6** Real **a** The temperature starts at −2 °C. It gets 5 degrees colder. What is the new temperature?

b The temperature in a fridge is 5°C.
The temperature in a freezer is −20 °C.
How many degrees colder is the freezer?

4a **7** Real A scuba diver goes down 20 m below sea level. She then comes up 6 m before diving down another 8 m. How far below sea level is she now?

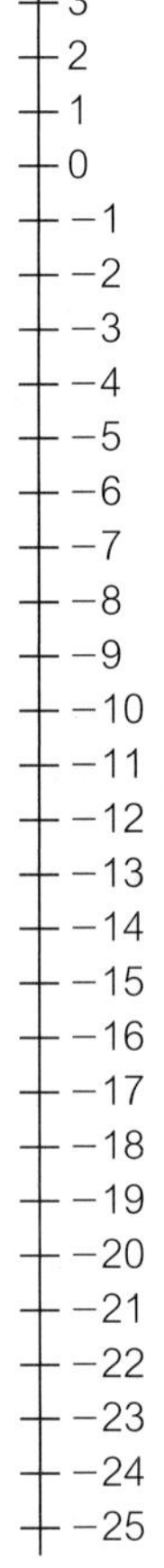

4a **8** Problem-solving / Reasoning The temperature is below 0 °C. The temperature falls by 5 degrees and then rises by 3 degrees. What could the temperature be now?
Discussion Is there more than one possible answer? Why?

5c **9** **a** Use a number line to work out

- **i** −1 + 1
- **ii** −3 + 3
- **iii** 5 − 5
- **iv** −7 + 7

b Copy and complete these.

- **i** −2 + 0 = □
- **ii** −4 + 0 = □
- **iii** −19 + 0 = □
- **iv** −24 + 0 = □

Key point

The symbol **>** means '**greater than**'. You can write '5 is greater than 2' as '5 > 2'.
The symbol **<** means '**less than**'. You can write '−6 °C is lower than −4 °C' as '−6°C< −4°C'.

Q6a hint

Use a number line. Start at −2. The temperature gets colder so count back 5.

Q6b Strategy hint

Use a number line. Mark 5 and −20 and find the difference between the two points.

Q7 Strategy hint

Use a number line to help you.

10 **a** These counters show the calculation −2 + 2.
Work out −2 + 2.

(−1) (−1)
(+1) (+1)

b These counters show the calculation −4 + 3.
Work out −4 + 3.

(−1) (−1) (−1) (−1)
(+1) (+1) (+1)

c Write the calculation shown by each set of counters.
Work out the answer to each calculation.

i 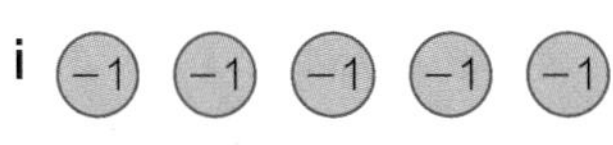
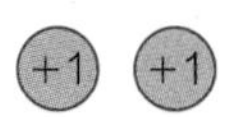

ii 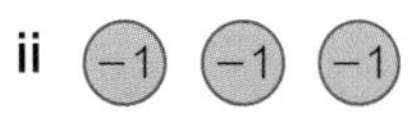
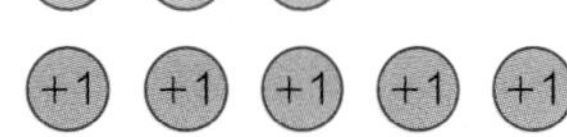

iii 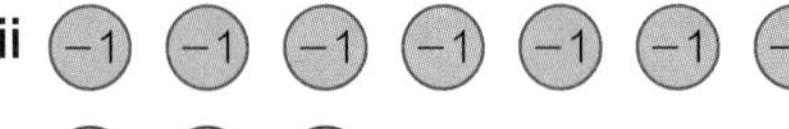

iv 

Discussion At a space shuttle launch, the ground crew announce 'T minus 9 minutes'. What does this statement mean?

11 Work out

a −4 − 2 **b** −8 − 5 **c** 1 − 4
d −5 + 12 **e** −9 + 4 **f** −10 − 2

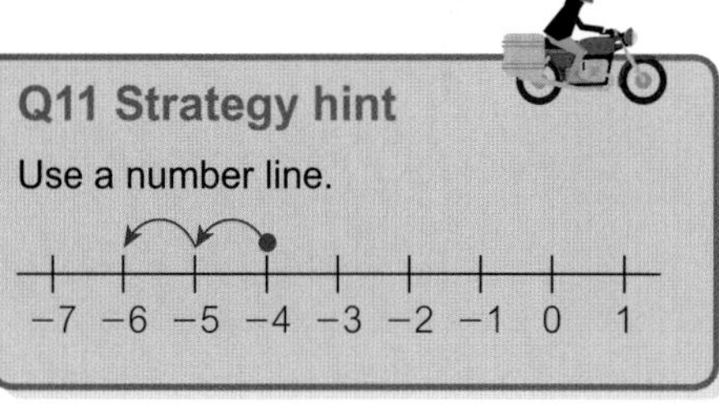

12 Five players need to work out their final scores at the end of a game. Use the table to work out the final scores for players B, C, D and E.

Player	Counters	Final score
A	(−1) (−1)	2 × −1 = −2
B	(−1) (−1) (−1) (−1)	4 × −1 =
C	(−2) (−2)	
D	(−2) (−2) (−2)	
E	(−1) (−1) (−1) (−1) (−1)	

13 **Explore** Does AYTMTB mean the same to me and you?
Look back at the maths you have learned in this lesson. How can you use it to answer this question?

14 **Reflect** Write this calculation: −1 + 2 – 3.
Without looking at this book, imagine a number line or counters and work out the answer to the calculation. Now check your answer by drawing a number line or counters.
Did imagining a number line or counters help you? If so, how?
If not, do you have a different way of imagining negative numbers?

2.7 Factors, multiples and primes

You will learn to:
- Use a calculator to explore divisibility
- Find all the factor pairs for any whole number
- Identify common factors, the highest common factor and the lowest common multiple
- Recognise prime numbers.

CONFIDENCE

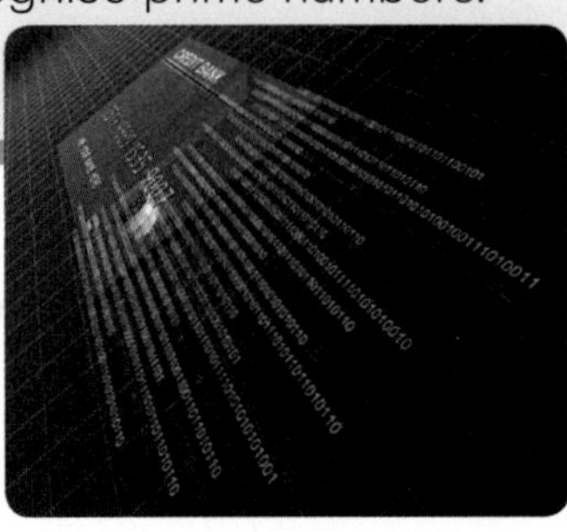

Why learn this? Prime numbers are used on the internet to code credit card information so that it remains private.

Fluency
Look at these numbers: 1, 8, 13, 29, 36, 48, 54, 72, 81.
- Which of the numbers are even?
- Which are odd?
- Which of the numbers are divisible by 2?
- Which are divisible by 3?
- Which are divisible by 6?

Explore
Two broods of cicadas emerge from their underground worlds at different time intervals. After how many years will they emerge at the same time?

Exercise 2.7

Warm up

1 Write the first five multiples of 7.

2 True or false?
   a 36 is a multiple of 9
   b 3 is a factor of 13
   c 23 is a multiple of 8
   d 6 is a factor of 18

3 Look at these numbers:
2, 3, 4, 6, 8, 9, 10, 12, 14, 15, 16, 18.

   a Which of the numbers are multiples of 2?
   b Which are multiples of 3?
   c Which are multiples of 2 and 3?
   d Copy this **Venn diagram**. Write each of the numbers in the correct section.

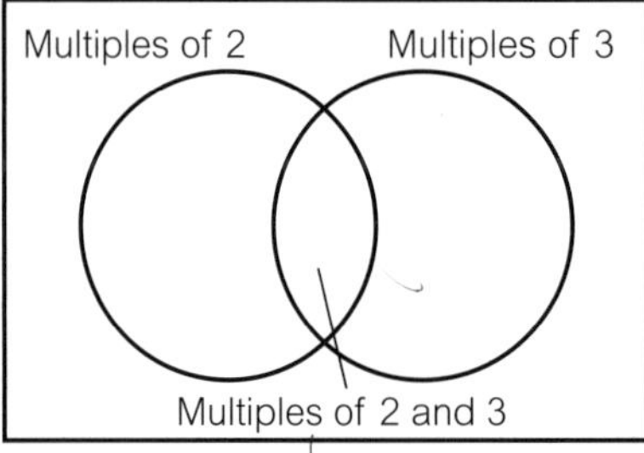

Q1 hint
A **multiple** of 7 is a number in the 7 times table.

Q2b hint
A **factor** is a whole number that divides exactly into another number.

Q3 Literacy hint
A **Venn diagram** is a way of showing sets.

4c

4 377 is exactly divisible by four different numbers. Use a calculator to find these numbers.

4b

5 a Copy and complete the Venn diagram to show the factors of 4 and 18.
   b What do the numbers in the overlapping region represent?

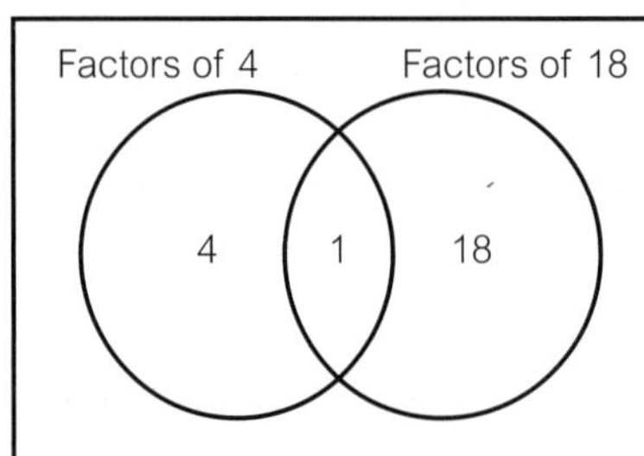

Key point
Here are the factors of 12 and 16.
12: 1, 2, 3, 4, 6, 12
16: 1, 2, 4, 8, 16
1, 2 and 4 are the **common factors** of 12 and 16.

Subject links: Science

6 a Draw a Venn diagram to show the factors of 8 and 12.
b What are the **common factors** of 8 and 12?
Discussion Have you found *all* the factors of 8? How do you know?

> **Q6a hint**
> You could write the factors in lists first.

7 Find the common factors of each of these pairs of numbers.
a 9 and 15 b 18 and 27 c 16 and 24

8 a List the factors of each of these numbers.
i 17 ii 35 iii 29
b Which of the numbers in part **a** are **prime** numbers?

> **Key point**
> A **prime** number has exactly two factors, 1 and itself.

9 a Write the prime numbers between 10 and 30.
b What do these numbers have in common?
c **Reasoning** Are all prime numbers odd? Give a reason for your answer.

10 a List the factors of 6 and the factors of 30.
b What are the common factors of 6 and 30?
c Which is the highest number in your list in part b?

> **Q10b Strategy hint**
> Use a Venn diagram or lists to help

11 Find the **highest common factor** of each of these pairs of numbers.
a 6 and 24 b 15 and 25 c 12 and 20

> **Key point**
> The **highest common factor** of two numbers is the largest number that is a factor of both numbers.

12 a Write the first six multiples of each of these numbers.
i 4 ii 6
b What is the lowest common multiple of 4 and 6?

13 Find the lowest common multiple of each of these pairs of numbers.
a 8 and 14 b 12 and 20 c 15 and 25
Discussion How many multiples do you need to write for each pair of numbers?

> **Key point**
> Here are some multiples of 2 and 3.
> 2: 2, 4, 6, 8, 10, 12, 14, …
> 3: 3, 6, 9, 12, 15, 18, …
> 6 and 12 are two of the **common multiples** of 2 and 3.
> The **lowest common multiple** of two numbers is the smallest number that is a multiple of both numbers.

14 **Problem-solving / Reasoning** Hotdog buns are sold in packs of 5. Hotdog sausages are sold in packs of 3.
a What is the smallest number of each pack you need so that no buns are left over?
b How many hotdogs could you make?
c What do you notice about your answer to part **b**?

> **Q14a Strategy hint**
> You could draw a diagram to help.

15 **Explore** Two broods of cicadas emerge from their underground worlds at different time intervals. After how many years will they emerge at the same time?
What have you learned in this lesson to help you answer this question? What further information do you need?

16 **Reflect** Write your own short definition for each of these mathematical words:
highest lowest common factor multiple
Now use your definitions to write (in your own words) the meaning of:
highest common factor lowest common multiple

4b 4b 4a 4a 5c 5c 5c 5c 5c Explore Reflect

2.8 Square and triangle numbers

You will learn to:

- Recognise square numbers and triangle numbers
- Use a calculator to find squares and square roots
- Use the priority of operations, including powers
- Use index notation for powers
- Do mental calculations with squares and square roots.

CONFIDENCE

Why learn this? Moving crowds need more space than standing crowds. One person can move freely in a 1 metre by 1 metre square. As the number of people increases, the flow rate begins to drop, which can affect crowd safety.

Fluency
What are the missing numbers?

- 3 × 3 = □
- 7 × □ = 49
- 25 ÷ 5 = □
- □ ÷ 4 = 4

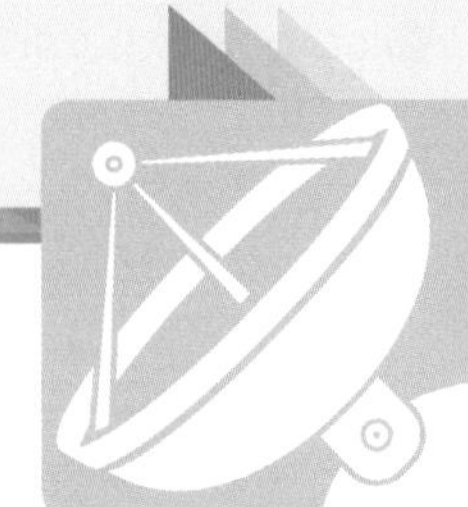

Explore
The seating in a 6000-seater stadium is to be arranged in square blocks. How many rows of seats are there in each block?

Exercise 2.8

Warm up

1 Work out 2 + 6 × 6.

2 What is 10 × 10 ÷ 20?

3 What number comes next?
a 1, 3, 5, 7, …   b 2, 6, 10, 14, …

4b

4 These patterns of dots show the first three **square numbers**.

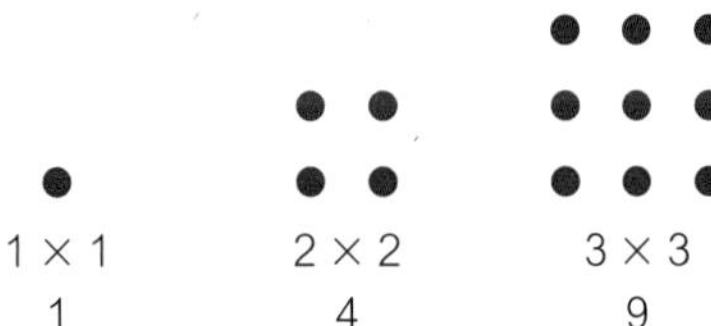

a Draw the dot pattern for the 4th square number.
b Copy and complete this calculation for the 4th square number.
4 × □ = □
c How many rows of dots are there in the 5th pattern? How many columns?
d How many dots are there in the 10th pattern?
e What is the value of the 10th square number?

Key point
Square numbers make a square pattern of dots.
To find the square of a number, you multiply it by itself.

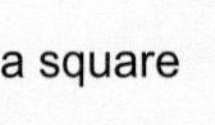

Q5 - work out squares

Q6 - Q6 (bigger no's)

4a

5 Which of the numbers in the box are square numbers?

100	8	6
15	49	
50	36	4
2	81	

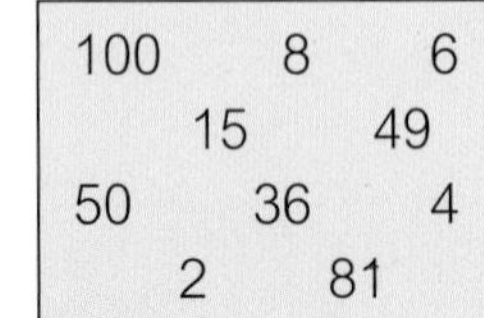

Q5 Strategy hint
Start with 1 × 1 = 1. Is this square number in the box?
Next try 2 × 2 and continue up to 10 × 10.

Topic links: Sequences, BIDMAS

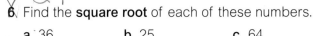

6 Find the **square root** of each of these numbers. 4a

a 36 b 25 c 64 d 100

Key point

A **square root** is a number that is multiplied by itself to produce a given number.
Finding the square root is the **inverse** of squaring.
$3 \times 3 = 9$ so $\sqrt{9} = 3$ where $\sqrt{\ }$ means square root.
You can use the $\boxed{\sqrt{\ }}$ key on your calculator to find a square root.

7 These patterns of dots show the first three triangle numbers. 4a

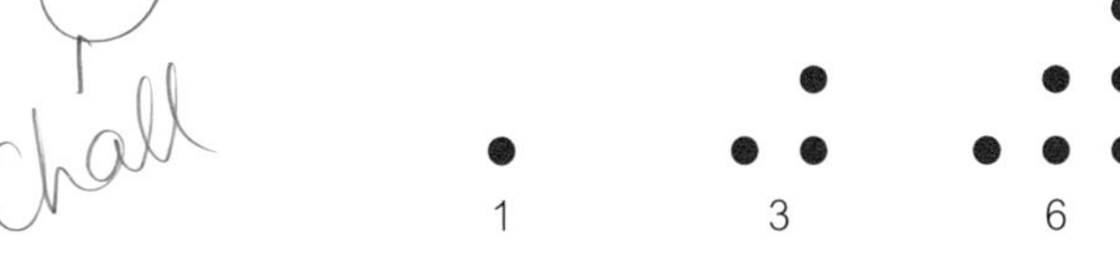

a Continue the pattern to work out the next three triangle numbers.
b Write down the first six triangle numbers.
c **Reasoning** What is being added on each time?
d Continue the pattern to work out the 7th and 8th triangle numbers.
e **Reasoning** Is 44 a triangle number? Explain your answer.

Discussion How does the way the dot pattern grows match the triangle numbers?

Q7e Strategy hint

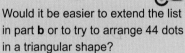

Would it be easier to extend the list in part **b** or to try to arrange 44 dots in a triangular shape?

8 Find 5c

a $\sqrt{225}$ b $\sqrt{361}$ c $\sqrt{400}$ d $\sqrt{10\,000}$

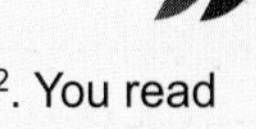

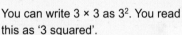

Key point

You can write 3×3 as 3^2. You read this as '3 squared'.
The '2' in 3^2 is called the power or **index**. The plural of index is **indices**.
You can use the $\boxed{x^2}$ key on your calculator to work out a square.

9 **Problem-solving** Chocolates are packed into square boxes. 5c

a Can 41 chocolates fit into a single box with no empty spaces? Explain your answer.
b Can 41 chocolates be fitted into two boxes? Explain your answer.

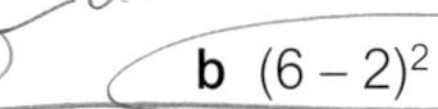

10 Work out 5b

a $2^2 \times 4 \times 5$ b $(6 - 2)^2 \times 8$ c $(6 - 2^2) \times 8$
d $(8^2 + 3) - 5$ e $15 \times (3^2 - 9)$ f $10 \times (50 - 5^2) + 4$

Q10a hint

Use BIDMAS: Work out the **I**ndices (powers) first, $2^2 = 2 \times 2 = 4$, and then the **M**ultiplication.

11 Copy and complete these. 5b

a $4 \times \square = 4^2$ b $2 \times 2 \times \square = 2^3$ c $4 \times 4 \times 4 = 4^{\square}$
d $5^3 = 5 \times \square \times \square$ e $10 \times 10 = 10^{\square}$ f $10^3 = \square$

Investigation **Discussion / Reasoning**

a Work out the square numbers from 1×1 up to and including 20×20.
b What is the pattern in the last digits of the square numbers?
c Which numbers are never the last digit of a square number?
d Test your answer to part **c** by finding three more square numbers greater than 400.

12 **Explore** The seating in a 6000-seater stadium is to be arranged in square blocks. How many rows of seats are there in each block?
Look back at the maths you have learned in this lesson. How can you use it to answer this question?

13 **Reflect** Think about the *square* of 9 and the *square root* of 9. Which is 3 and which is 81?
Make sure you know the difference between these two mathematical terms. Write down a hint in your own words to help *you* remember which is which.

Explore

Reflect

2 Check up

Written methods

1 a Round each number to the nearest 100.

i 244 **ii** 671 **iii** 105 **iv** 350

b Rupert says, '859 rounded to the nearest 1000 is 900.'
Is Rupert correct? Explain your answer.

2 Work out these. Make an estimate to check your answer.

a $\begin{array}{r} 431 \\ +\ 289 \\ \hline \\ \hline \end{array}$ **b** $\begin{array}{r} 8329 \\ -\ 6645 \\ \hline \\ \hline \end{array}$

3 Tudur wrote:
293 × 6 is about 300 × 10 = 3000
Has Tudur made a good estimate? Show working to explain your answer.

4 Work out 404 ÷ 4.
Make an estimate first to check your answer.

5 a Find the total of 756 and 1209.

b What is the difference between 2845 and 78?

c The sum of two numbers is 3264. One of the numbers is 495.
What is the other number?

6 Work out these. Make an estimate first.

a 28 × 34 **b** 419 ÷ 19

Mental work

7 Copy and complete these. Write the correct sign, < or >, between each pair.

a 3 °C ... −1 °C

b −5 °C ... 2 °C

c −4 °C ... −6 °C

8 a When a number is multiplied by 100, the answer is 2000.
What is the number?

b What must 48 be multiplied by to give 480?

c When a number is divided by 1000, the answer is 4.
What is the number?

9 a In Edinburgh the temperature was −3 °C.
In Liverpool the temperature was 5 degrees warmer.
What was the temperature in Liverpool?

b In Cardiff the temperature was 4 °C.
In Llanberis the temperature was −5 °C.
How many degrees warmer was it in Cardiff than in Llanberis?

10 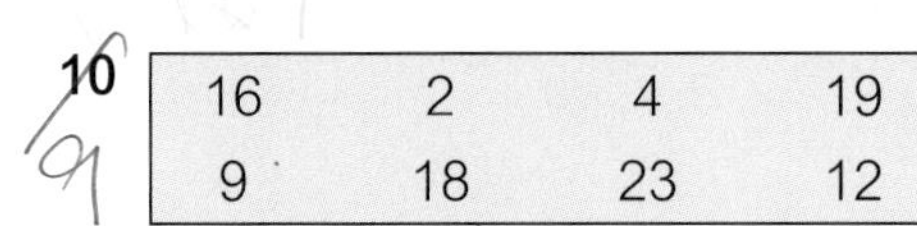

16	2	4	19
9	18	23	12

Which of the numbers in the box are

a factors of 36
b multiples of 8
c prime
d square numbers?

11 Work out

a $-2 + 5$
b $-6 + 3$
c $1 - 5$
d $-5 - 2$

12 a i Find the common factors of 12 and 14.

ii What is the highest common factor of 12 and 14?

b Find the lowest common multiple of 5 and 7.

13 Work out

a $2 + 5 \times 4$
b $6 \times (2 + 7)$
c $25 - 5 + 4$
d $6 \times 0 + 8$
e $(18 - 9) \times 4$
f $32 \div 8 \div 4$
g $4^2 + 5$
h $(2 + 3)^2 - 4$
h $64 \div (16 \div 2)$

Problem-solving

14 Phillipe spent £285 on a shopping trip.
Joe spent £189 more than Phillipe.
How much did Joe spend?

15 Lucas wants to buy three items.
The items are priced at £6.49, £10.90 and 82p.
Lucas has £20.
Use estimation to decide whether Lucas has enough to buy all three items.

16 Jordan and Stewart have a total of 632 followers on Twitter.
Jordan has three times as many followers as Stewart.
How many followers does Stewart have?

17 Andre works for a minimum wage of £3.72 per hour.
How much will he be paid for working 15 hours?

18 Abigail earns £859.20 for working 30 hours.
Ben earns £726 for working 25 hours.
Who earns more per hour? How much more per hour?

19 How sure are you of your answers? Were you mostly

Just guessing **Feeling doubtful** **Confident**

What next? Use your results to decide whether to strengthen or extend your learning.

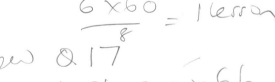

Challenge

20

2	3	5	6

Use each of the numbers in the box once and any combination of +, −, ×, ÷ and brackets to make 60.

21 When a number is subtracted from another number, the answer is −1.
What could the two numbers be?

22 When you reverse the digits of 13 you get 31.
Both 13 and 31 are prime numbers.
Find some other prime numbers which have this property.

2 Strengthen

You will:

- Strengthen your understanding with practice.

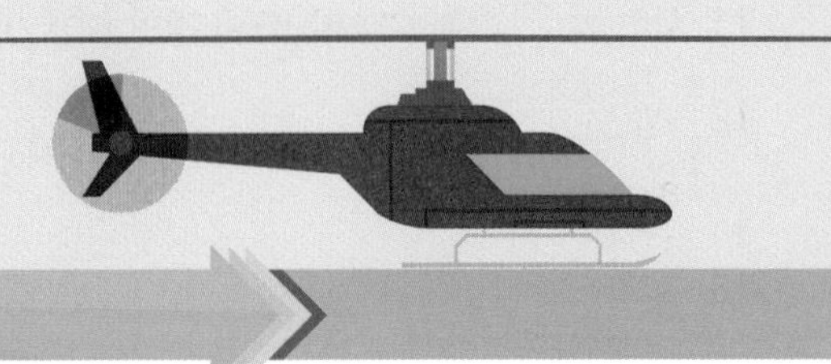

Written methods

4c **1** Round each number to the nearest 100.

a 147

b 283

c 151

Q1 Strategy hint
Mark the numbers on a number line.

4c **2** Copy and complete. Fill in the blanks.

42 = 42 units

= 4 × 10 + 2 = □ tens + □ units

= □ × 10 + 12 = □ tens + □ units

4c **3** Work out

a 224 + 148

b 237 + 125

Q3a hint
224 = 200 + 20 + 4
148 = 100 + 40 + 8

4c **4** Work out

a 392 – 256

b 764 – 429

Q4a hint
392 = 300 + 90 + 2 but 2 units is smaller than 6 units.
So use 392 = 300 + 80 + 12.

4b **5** Use approximation to work out an estimate for each of these.

a 168 × 4

b 219 × 5

c 372 × 8

Q5a hint
168 × 4 is about 200 × 4

4b **6** Use the grid method to work out

a 142 × 3

b 293 × 6

Q6a hint

	100	40	2
3	300		

142 × 3 = 300 + □ + □ = □

4b **7** Use short multiplication to work out

a 154 × 3

b 237 × 4

Q7a hint
154 = 100 + 50 + 4
What is 4 × 3?
What is 50 × 3?
What is 100 × 3?

HTU
× U
HTU

4b **8** Work out these. Make an estimate first.

a 476 × 5

b 523 × 7

c 389 × 8

4b **9** Use the bar model to work out 124 ÷ 4.

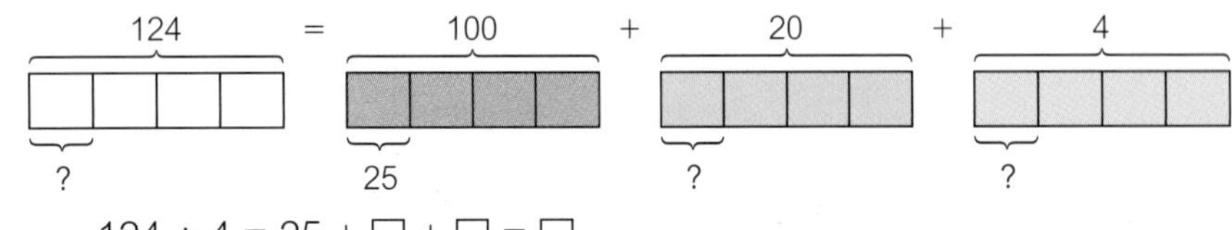

124 ÷ 4 = 25 + □ + □ = □

10 Use a bar model to work out these. Make an estimate first. 4b

a 484 ÷ 2   b 248 ÷ 4   c 336 ÷ 6

11 Use a bar model to work out 242 ÷ 6 4b

12 Work out 5b

a 24 × 15   b 37 × 21

13 Use a bar model to work out these. Make an estimate first. 4c

a 276 ÷ 12   b 279 ÷ 18   c 850 ÷ 40

Mental work

1 Write the first five multiples of 4b

a 4   b 6

2 Work out these calculations.
Use the priority of operations.

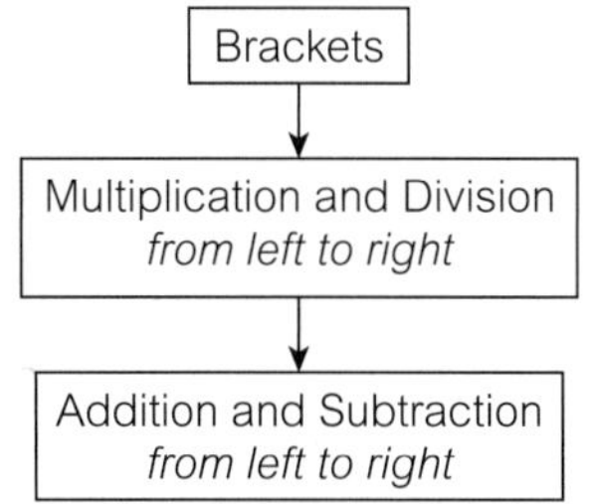

a 8 + 3 × 2   b 4 × (5 + 3)   c 3 × 6 ÷ 2

d 15 – 2 + 8   e (10 – 4) × 3   f (12 + 6) ÷ (12 – 9)

3 Write the numbers marked with crosses on the number line. 4b

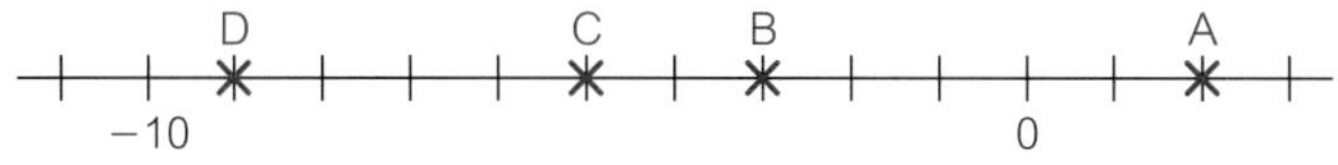

4 a Write this set of temperatures in order. Start with the coldest. 4b
3 °C, −5 °C, 0 °C, −8 °C, 2 °C, −11 °C

b Write the correct sign, < or >, between each pair.
i 4 °C ... −2 °C   ii −6 °C ... −3 °C

5 Look at Tom's answer to this question. 4b

Q: Is 4 a square number?

A: Yes, because I can make a square with 4 dots.

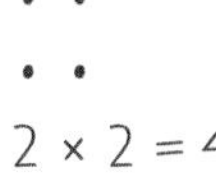

Use Tom's answer to decide whether each of these is a square number.

a 3   b 9   c 16   d 20

6 Work out 4a

a 6 × 20   b 6 × 28   c 4 × 34   d 20 × 10

Q11 hint

Choose a number you can divide by 6.

242 = 240 + 2

Q12a hint

15 = 10 + 5 = 10 + 2 + 2 + 1
What is 24 × 10? What is 24 × 2?
What is 24 × 1?

Q13a hint

276 = 240 + 36
or 276 = 120 + 120 + 36

Q13b and c hint

Parts **b** and **c** have remainders.

Q4a Strategy hint

Use a number line to help you.

Q4b i hint

Decide which number is greater.
The wider end of the symbol is by the greater number.

Q6b Strategy hint

Look for an 'easier' calculation, 28 = 20 + 8. What is 6 × 20?
What is 6 × 8?

4a

7

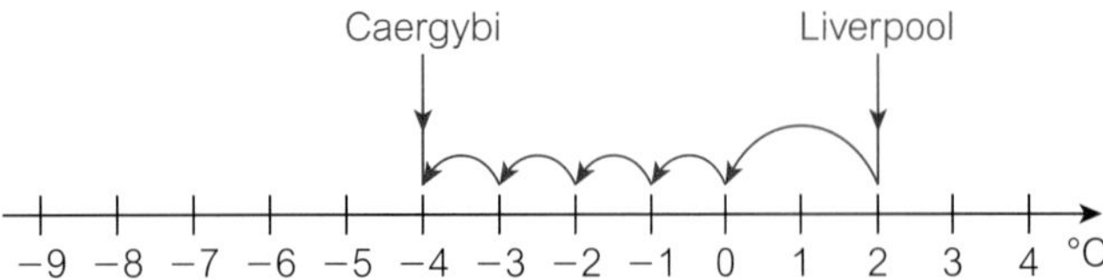

a How many degrees colder is Caergybi than Liverpool?

b The temperature in Sennybridge is −8 °C.
The temperature in Bangor is 6 degrees warmer.
What is the temperature in Bangor?

Q7b hint
Use the number line to help you.

5c

8 Work out

a −3 + 3 b −8 + 7

c 0 − 6 d −2 − 3

5c

9 a i Gwyndaf is finding the common factors of 8 and 20.
Copy and complete his working.

Factors of 8: 1, 2, ..., ...
Factors of 20: 1, 2, 4, ..., ..., ...
Common factors: 1, ..., ...

ii What is the highest common factor of 8 and 20?

b Find the highest common factor of 15 and 30.

Q9a ii hint
Circle the numbers that appear in both lists. These are the common factors.

Q9b hint
Follow the steps in part **a**.

5c

10 a Petra is finding the lowest common multiple of 5 and 8.
She lists the multiples of 5 and the multiples of 8.
Write down both of her lists. What is the lowest common multiple?

b Find the lowest common multiple of 6 and 7.

Q10a hint
Circle the numbers that appear in both lists. These are the common multiples?

Q10b hint
Follow the steps in part **a**.

5c

11 Work out:

a $3^2 + 2$ b $9 + (7 - 2)^2$

Problem-solving

4c

1 Look at the numbers in the box.

325	143	607	342	489	221	284	386

a Which two of the numbers have a sum of 626?

b Which two have a difference of 164?

Q1a hint
Use estimates to find which numbers add to around 600. Then work out accurately.

4b

2 John has £2.70, Richard has £12.84 and Lucy has £8.50.

a Round each amount to the nearest whole pound (£).

b Use your answers to part **a** to estimate how much John, Richard and Lucy have altogether.

Q2 hint
Is £2.70 closer to £2 or £3?

4b

3 Aled follows 246 people on Twitter.
Yasmin follows four times as many people.
Use the bar model to work out the number of people that Yasmin follows.

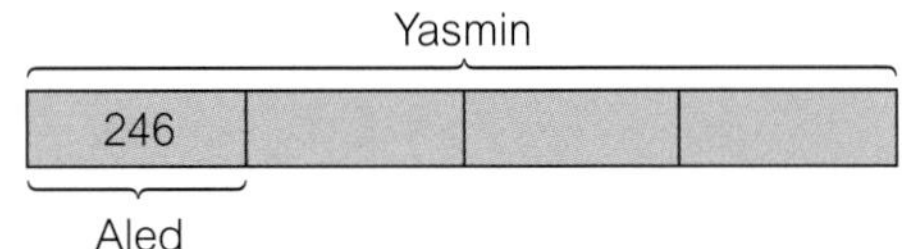

4 Reasoning Bread rolls are sold in packs of 8.
Beefburgers are sold in packs of 6.
Find the smallest number of each pack that can be bought so that no bread rolls are left over.

5c

Q4 hint

1 pack of bread rolls:
1 pack of beefburgers:

5 Real / Finance Owen takes out a business loan of £2000.
He makes 12 equal repayments of £148.
Use the bar model to work out how much he has left to repay.

£2000

148	148	148	148	148	148	148	148	148	148	148	148	?

?

5b

6 Real / Finance Motorbike insurance costs £1196.
Rena makes an initial payment of £260. She pays the remainder in 12 equal amounts.
How much is each payment?

5b

Q6 Strategy hint
Use a bar model.

Enrichment

1 Some of the numbers below have been placed into the wrong boxes.

Factors of 24	
4	14
6	16

Multiples of 7	
25	7
28	1

Square numbers	
12	9
21	4

Each box contains two incorrect numbers.
Which numbers are incorrect? Which box should they be in?

Q1 hint
These questions can help you:
Can 24 be divided by …?
Is … in the 7 times table?
Can … dots be arranged into a square?

2 **Reflect** Look back at the questions you answered in this lesson.
Some were
A calculations (for example, Mental work Q6)
B word problems (for example, Problem-solving Q2).
Sometimes you had to
C add (for example, Written methods Q3)
D subtract (for example, Written methods Q4)
E multiply (for example, Written methods Q5)
F divide (for example, Written methods Q10).

a Write down one other question number for each type of question: A, B, C, D, E and F.
b Which type of questions did you find easiest?
c Which type of questions did you find hardest? When you answered these questions, did you make some mistakes? If so, check that you understand where you went wrong.

Reflect

2 Extend

You will:

- Extend your understanding with problem-solving.

5c

1 a Work out

i $(4 + 4) \div (4 + 4)$ ii $(4 \times 4) \div (4 + 4)$

iii $(4 + 4 + 4) \div 4$ iv $4 \times (4 - 4) + 4$

v $(4 \times 4 + 4) \div 4$ vi $4 + (4 + 4) \div 4$

b **Discussion** What do you notice about your answers to part **a**?

c **Problem-solving / Reasoning** How could you use four 4s to make 7? ... to make 8?

5c

2 **Problem-solving / Reasoning** Replace each * in this addition with a digit from 1, 2, 3, 4, 5, 6, 7, 8, 9 to make the calculation correct. Use each digit only once.

Discussion Is there only one solution?

```
  * * * *
    * * *
+     * *
  -------
  6 7 5 9
```

5c

3 Work out

a $200 \div 2 \div 5$

b $\frac{200}{2 \times 5}$

c $\frac{112}{7 \times 2}$

d $\frac{108}{3 \times 6}$

5c

4 a Which of these numbers are square numbers?
123, 169, 101, 144, 230

b **Reasoning** Gwynfor says, 'There is no square number between 122 and 140.'
Is he correct?

5c

5 **Problem-solving** Adam and Bertie start a cross-country race at the same time.
Adam completes the first lap in 6 minutes.
Bertie completes the first lap in 8 minutes.
They keep running.
How many minutes after they start will they pass each other again?
How many laps will they each have done?

5c

6 **Problem-solving / Reasoning** 1 September 2010 was a Wednesday.
1 September 2011 was a Thursday.
When will 1 September next fall on a Wednesday?

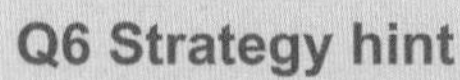

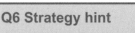

Q6 Strategy hint
Do you need to take into account that 2012 was a leap year?

5c

7 **Problem-solving / Reasoning** Jodie buys some computer games at £12 each.
Kevin buys some computer games at £15 each.
They both spend the same total amount.
They both spend less than £100.
What is the lowest amount they could each have spent?

8 Problem-solving / Reasoning Seating arrangements need to be made for 42 girls and 36 boys attending a school prom. All tables need to have the same number of girls. All tables need to have the same number of boys. All tables need to have at least one girl and one boy. 5c

a How many girls and boys could you have at one table?

b Is there more than one answer to part **a**?

c What is the maximum number of tables that can be used?

9 Two of these calculations are wrong. 5b

Use inverse operations to find out which two.

A $12 \times 28 = 363$

B $8896 \div 64 = 139$

C $7881 \div 213 = 73$

> **Q9a hint**
>
> The inverse operation would be $363 \div 12$ or $363 \div 28$

10 A laboratory experiment is carried out by 8 technicians. 5b

The experiment takes 38 hours to complete.

Each technician works on their own. They all work for the same number of hours.

How long does each technician work? Give your answer in hours and minutes.

11 Problem-solving / Real 30 000 children need an MMR vaccination. 5b

Surgery A receives 11 726 MMR vaccines.

Surgery B receives 6375 more vaccines than Surgery A.

Can all the children be vaccinated? Show working to explain your answer.

12 Problem-solving / Real A pottery production line works continuously for 24 hours. 5b

It produces 108 pieces of pottery each hour.

A total of 53 pieces are damaged.

How many good pieces of pottery are produced in total in 24 hours?

13 Problem-solving Sami has 672 followers on Twitter. 5b

Sami has 28 times as many followers as Tom.

How many fewer people follow Tom than follow Sami?

14 Work out 5b

a $(2 + 3)^2 \div (14 - 9)^2$ **b** $\frac{(2 + 3)^2}{(14 - 9)^2}$ **c** $(5^2 - 7) \div (2^2 - 1)$

d $\frac{(5^2 - 7)}{(2^2 - 1)}$ **e** $\frac{(4 + 8)^2}{(4^2 - 8)}$ **f** $(4 + 8)^2 \div (4^2 - 8)$

> **Q14a hint**
>
> Use the bracket keys on your calculator.

15 Use a mental method to work out 5a

a 28×5 **b** 15×8 **c** 5×42

d 18×16 **e** 35×12 **d** 6×34

> **Q15a Strategy hint**
>
> Think about halving and doubling. For example, $28 \times 5 = 14 \times 10$. Or, $28 \times 5 = 28 \times 10 \div 2$.

16 Work out 5a

a $3947 - 907 - 81$ **b** $731 - 39 + 256$ **c** $48 + 2609 - 146 + 397$

17 Problem-solving / Real Company A paid £48 362 in tax. 5a

Company B paid £949 more than Company A.

Company C paid £3002 less than Company B.

How much tax did the three companies pay in total?

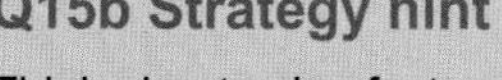

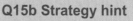

> **Q15b Strategy hint**
>
> Think about using factors. For example, $15 \times 8 = 15 \times 2 \times 4$. Or, $15 \times 8 = 15 \times 2 \times 2 \times 2$.

5a  **18 Problem-solving / Real** A supermarket sells the same brand of chocolate in three different boxes.

Box 1: £1.86 for 12 chocolates

Box 2: £2.10 for 15 chocolates

Box 3: £3.59 for 24 chocolates

a Which box is the best value for money?

b Lulu has £25. What is the largest number of chocolates that she can buy?

5a  **19 Real / Finance** Rufus is paid £150.40 for 16 hours' work.

Mamadou is paid £8.60 per hour for the first 22 hours.

He is then paid £9.90 per hour.

Who is paid more for working 32 hours? How much more?

5a **20** Work out

a $5^2 - 15$ **b** 2×4^2 **c** $(12 - 4)^2$ **d** $\sqrt{24 + 12}$

e $\sqrt{89 - 25}$ **f** $\sqrt{16} \times \sqrt{49}$ **g** $\sqrt{5^2 - 9}$

Q20d hint

Work out what is inside the square root first.

5a **21 Problem-solving / Real** A farmer has 513 eggs to pack.

She uses 12 × 12 and 15 × 15 trays.

How many trays should she use of each type, so that every tray is completely full?

5a  **22** Convert 250 hours to days and hours.

Q22 hint

1 day = 24 hours

5a  **23** Use inverse operations to check these calculations.

a $\sqrt{7} = 2.64575\ldots$

Discussion Why do you not get exactly 7?

b $23^2 = 529$

c $\sqrt{12} = 3.46410\ldots$

Q23a Strategy hint

Finding the square root is the inverse of squaring so check $(2.64575)^2$.

5a **24** Copy and complete these patterns.

a

3 + 2 = 5 (−1)

3 + 1 = 4 (−1)

3 + 0 = 3 (−1)

3 + −1 = 2

3 + −2 =

3 + −3 =

3 + −4 =

b

−3 − 2 = −5 (+1)

−3 − 1 = −4 (+1)

−3 − 0 = −3

−3 − −1 =

−3 − −2 =

−3 − −3 =

−3 − −4 =

c When you add a negative number, is the result bigger or smaller?
When you subtract a negative number, is the result bigger or smaller?

5a **25** Work out

a 2 + −4 **b** 3 + −5 **c** −2 − −6 **d** −4 − −7

Q25 hint

Use part **c** from Q24 to check your answers.

26 Which two numbers does each of these square roots lie between? Copy and complete George's working. 5a

a $\sqrt{15}$

$3^2 = 9$ and $4^2 = 16$

So the square root of 15 lies between 3 and 4

b $\sqrt{70}$

c $\sqrt{28}$

d $\sqrt{91}$

e $\sqrt{39}$

f $\sqrt{60}$

Q26a Literacy hint

'The square root of 15 lies between 3 and 4' can also be written as '$3 < \sqrt{15} < 4$'.

Q26b hint

Find square numbers either side of 70.

27 Find the lowest common multiple of each of these sets of numbers. 6c

a 4, 6 and 9 **b** 3, 4 and 5

28 Find the highest common factor of each of these sets of numbers. 6c

a 12, 18 and 36 **b** 24, 32 and 40

29 Copy and complete these patterns. 6c

a

$2 \times 2 = 4$ (−2)

$1 \times 2 = 2$ (−2)

$0 \times 2 = 0$

$-1 \times 2 =$

$-2 \times 2 =$

$-3 \times 2 =$

b

$2 \times -2 = -4$ (+2)

$1 \times -2 = -2$ (+2)

$0 \times -2 = 0$

$-1 \times -2 =$

$-2 \times -2 =$

$-3 \times -2 =$

c When you multiply a negative number by a positive number, is the answer positive or negative? When you multiply a negative number by a negative number, is the answer positive or negative?

30 Work out 6c

a -2×3 **b** -2×4 **c** -3×-3 **d** -3×-5

Q30 hint

Use part **c** from Q29 to check your answers.

31 **Problem-solving / Reasoning** The answer to a calculation was −8. 6c

a Write three different calculations that give the answer −8.

b Now write three different calculations using a different operation, +, −, ×, in each one.

32 **a** Here are two calculations using 3, −2 and −6. 6c

$-2 \times 3 = -6$ $-6 \div 3 = -2$

Write two more.

b $5 \times \square = -20$

i What is the missing number?

ii Write two more calculations using these numbers.

33 **Reflect** In these Extend lessons, do you think you did

A well **B** OK **C** not very well?

List three things that made a difference to how well you did.

They can be things that made you do better or worse.

Here are some things other students said, to give you some ideas.

'I didn't read some questions properly.'

'It helped that I can do long multiplication.'

'I chatted to John too much.'

How do you think you could have done even better in these lessons?

Reflect

2 Unit test

4c **1** **a** Round 2486 to the nearest hundred.
b Round 2486 to the nearest thousand.
c Complete this sentence:
____ rounded to the nearest hundred is 900.

4b **2** Work out 168 ÷ 8.

4b **3** **a** Show that 6 × 82 = 492.
4b **b** Work out 24 × 82. You can use part **a** to help you.

4b **4** Find the missing digits.

```
  34*
+ 2*9
  *61
```

4b **5** A weather chart shows these temperatures.
5°C, −1 °C, 3°C, −4 °C, 0 °C, −5 °C
a Copy and complete the number line to show all the temperatures.

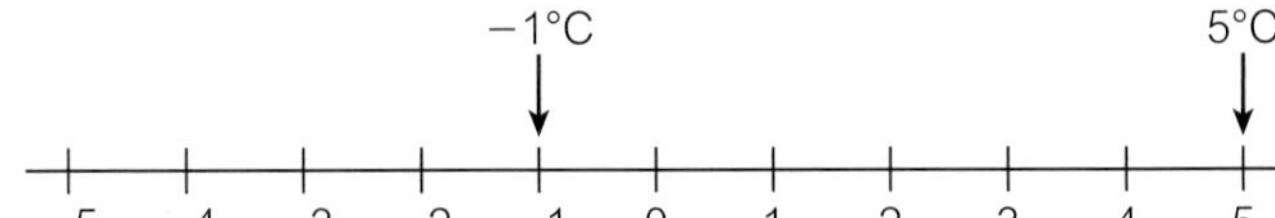

b Which is the warmest temperature?
c Is 0°C colder or warmer than −1°C?
d Write down a temperature from the list that is colder than −1°C.

4b **6** A computer costs £1420.
Nathan pays a deposit of £900.
He then pays the rest in four equal amounts.
How much is each payment?

4a **7** Karen uses a calculator to divide £9 by 2.
Look at the calculator display.

4.5

Karen says this means half of £9 is £4.05.
John says it means £4.50. Who is correct?

4a **8** **a** In Cardiff the temperature was −2°C.
In Edinburgh the temperature was 4 degrees colder.
What was the temperature in Edinburgh?
b In Dublin the temperature was 8°C.
In Llanberis the temperature was −3°C.
How many degrees warmer was it in Dublin than in Llanberis?

4a **9** Complete each calculation using one of these. × 10, × 100, ÷ 10, ÷ 100
a 8 ... = 80 **b** 200 ... = 2
c 450 ... = 45 **d** 32 ... = 320

5c **10** List all the factors of 60.

5c **11** Rhodri says, 'The factors of 56 are all even.'
Is Rhodri correct? Explain your answer.

12 There are 56 young people at a youth conference. 5c
They must be divided up into discussion groups of equal size.
What sizes of groups are possible? 5c

13 28 boxes of cookery books are delivered to a warehouse. 5c
Each box contains 42 books. How many books are delivered?

14 Work out **a** $-10 + 6$ **b** $-10 - 6$ 5c

15 George says, 'The lowest common multiple of 4 and 6 is 24.' 5c
Is George correct? Show working to explain your answer.

16 **a** Work out $\frac{100}{4 \times 5}$ 5c

b Work out $100 \div 4 \div 5$.

c What do you notice about your answers to parts **a** and **b**?

d Use what you have discovered to work out $\frac{126}{2 \times 7}$

17 Website A had 287 hits on Monday. 5b
On the same day, Website B had 34 times as many hits.
How many hits did Website B have?

18 Work out 5a

a $7^2 + 6$ **b** $72 - 5^2$ **c** $\sqrt{16 + 9}$ **d** $\sqrt{36} \times \sqrt{81}$

19 Shop 1 sells 2843 charity wristbands. 5a
Shop 2 sells 479 fewer wristbands than Shop 1.
Shop 3 sells 99 more wristbands than Shop 2.
How many wristbands do they sell altogether?

20 Steven buys 36 blank CDs. 5c
The CDs are sold in packs of four. Each pack costs £1.60.
Lucas also buys 36 blank CDs.
His CDs are sold in packs of six. Each pack costs £1.92.
Who pays more for the CDs? How much more?

21 Work out 5b

a $(63 + 35) \div (26 - 12)$ **b** $\frac{63 + 35}{26 - 12}$ **c** $(8 + 7)^2$

Challenge

22 **Reasoning** Look at these patterns of dots.

a Draw the next two shapes in the pattern.

b Complete this table to show the number of dots in each shape.

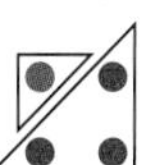

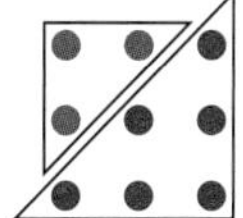

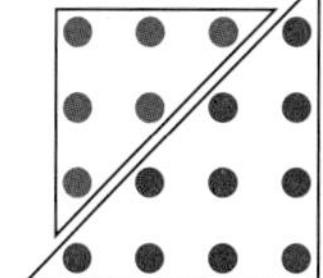

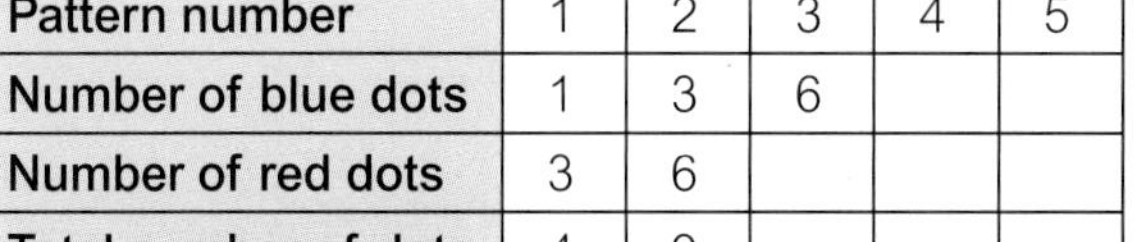

Pattern number	1	2	3	4	5
Number of blue dots	1	3	6		
Number of red dots	3	6			
Total number of dots	4	9			

c What type of numbers are represented by the blue dots?

d What type of numbers are represented by the red dots?

e What type of numbers are represented by the total numbers of dots?

23 **Reflect** Look back at the work you have done in this unit. When you answered questions, how did you decide which operation to use: addition, subtraction, multiplication or division?

Q23
Which words in problems tell you which operation to use?

Reflect

3 Expressions, functions and formulae

MASTER

Check P75 | Strengthen P77 | Extend P81 | Test P85

3.1 Functions

You will learn to:

- Find outputs of simple functions written in words and using symbols
- Describe simple functions in words.

CONFIDENCE

Why learn this? Function machines are a way of writing rules or instructions to work out all sorts of things, such as the reading age of a book.

Fluency
Write four calculations that start with the number 5 and give the answer 10.

Explore
What does this message mean?
dwwdfn dw rqfh

Exercise 3.1

Warm up

1 Work out
  a 3 add 19 b 30 divided by 5 c 9 subtract 4

2 Work out
  a 2 plus 3 then multiply by 7 b 4 divided by 2 then take away 2
  c 12 subtract 3 then add 11

3 Which operation is missing from each of these calculations: +, −, × or ÷?
  a 2 □ 3 = 6 b 5 □ 3 = 2 c 6 □ 3 = 2

Key point
A **function** is a relationship between two sets of numbers. The numbers that go into a **function machine** are called the **inputs**. The numbers that come out are called the **outputs**.

4c

4 Work out the **outputs** of each of these **function machines**.

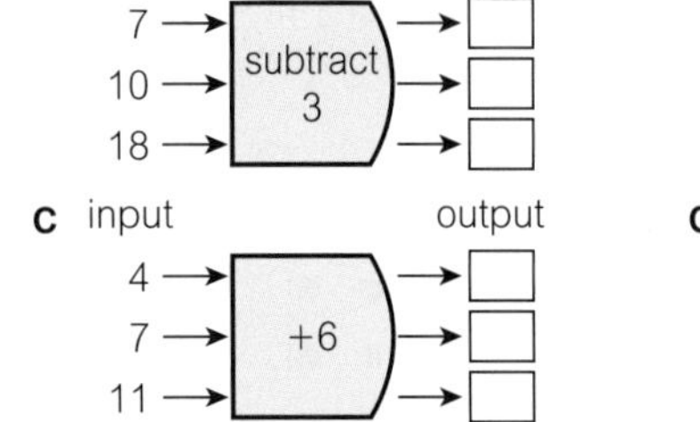

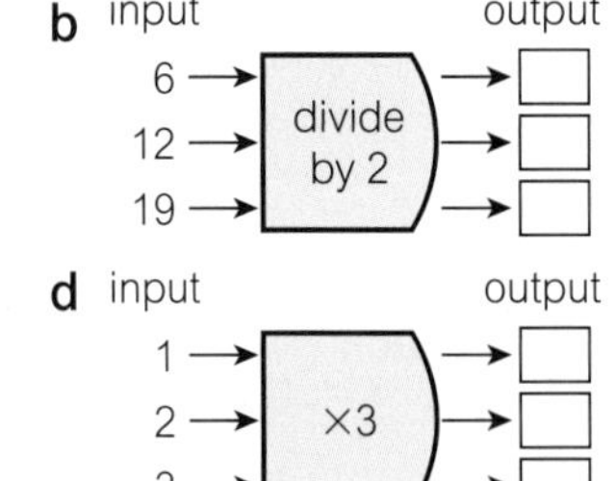

Q4a hint
The function is 'subtract 3' so you must subtract 3 from every input number to get the ourput number.
7 − 3 = 4
10 − 3 = 7
18 − 3 = □

4b

5 Write down the **function** for each machine.

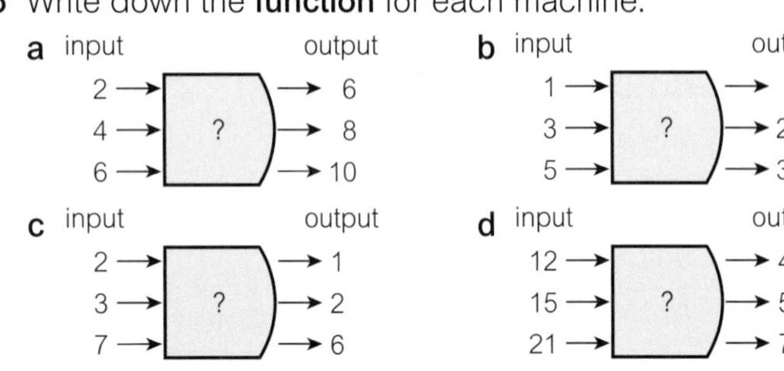

Q5a hint
Is the function '×3', or '+4' or something else?

Topic links: The four rules with whole numbers

6 Real / Problem-solving
It costs 12p for Yasmin to send one text message.
How many text messages can she send for each of these amounts of credit?
a £4.80 **b** £1.92 **c** £4.08

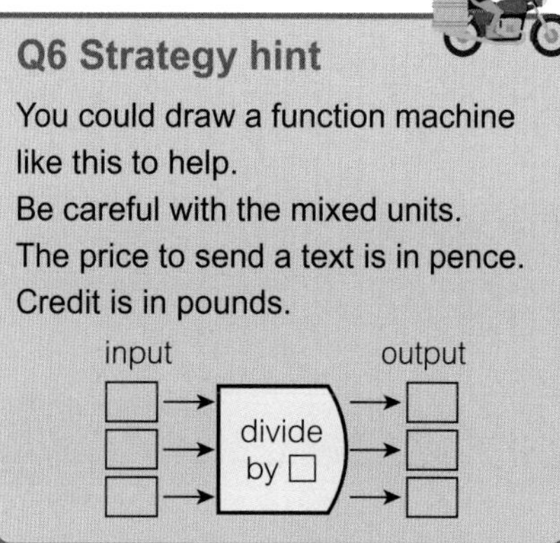

7 Work out the outputs of each of these two-step function machines.

a
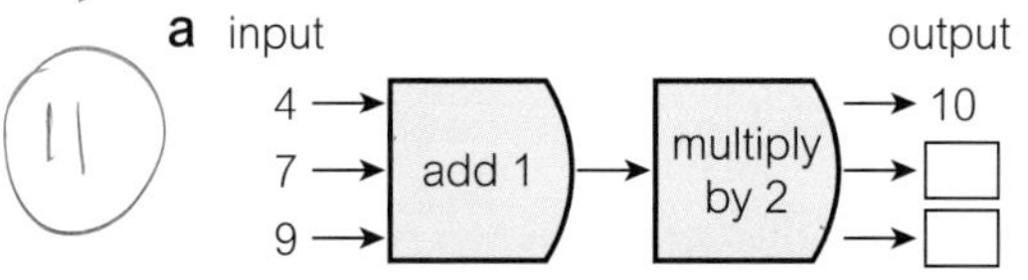

b
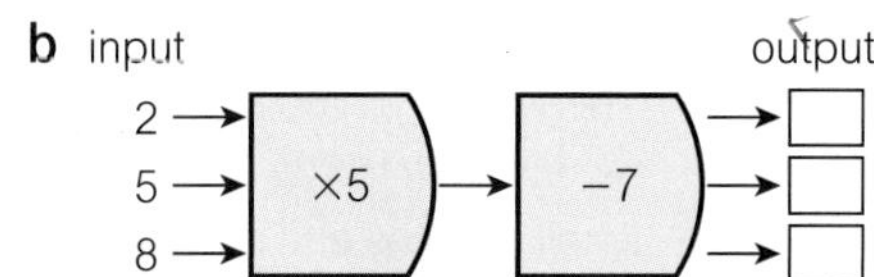

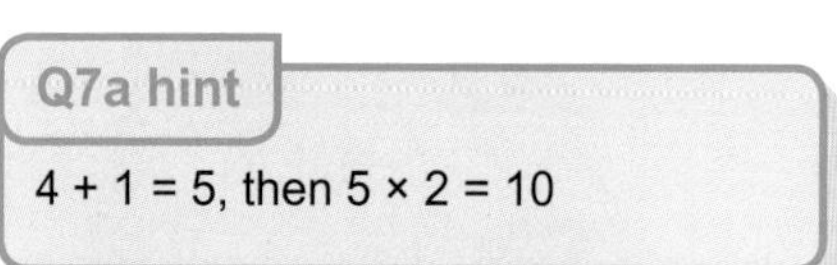

Discussion If you input a number into the function machine 'add 2, then multiply by 2', will you get the same output number as from the function machine 'multiply by 2, then add 2'?

8 Work out the outputs of this function machine.

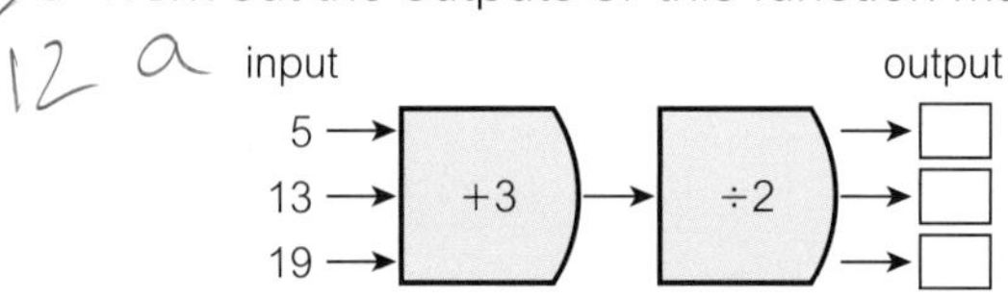

Discussion Look again at the function machine in Q8. Will the output numbers always be whole numbers, *whatever* the input numbers are?

Investigation Problem-solving

A two-step function machine takes an input of 6.
The output is 20.
Draw as many possible function machines as you can with this input and output.

Strategy hint
Make an organised list.
For example, start with '×2, then +8', followed by '×3, then +2', ... Another set could start '−1, then ×4', followed by '−2, then ×5', ...

9 **Explore** What does this message mean? dwwdfn dw rqfh
Is it easier to explore this question now you have completed the lesson?
What further information do you need to be able to answer this?

10 **Reflect** After this lesson, Orlando said, 'A function always relates an input to an output.'
Lola said, 'Each input gives only one output.'
Look back at your work on functions. Is Orlando correct? Is Lola correct?
What else can you say about functions?

3.2 Simplifying expressions 1

You will learn to:
- Simplify simple linear algebraic expressions by collecting like terms
- Use arithmetic operations with algebra.

CONFIDENCE

Why learn this? Algebra is a language that people in every country in the world can understand. It doesn't need to be translated into Japanese, Spanish or any other language.

Fluency
Match each red calculation with its blue equivalent.
2 + 2 + 2   5 + 5   3 + 3 + 3 + 3
4 × 3   3 × 2   2 × 5

Explore
This rectangle could be divided into 12 small squares and described as $12s$. How else could you describe it using small shapes all of the same kind?

s	s	s	s
s	s	s	s
s	s	s	s

Exercise 3.2

Warm up

1 Copy and complete: 4 + 4 + 4 = □ × 4 = □

2 Work out
a 3 × €6
b $15 ÷ 3

3 Work out
a 9 − (2 × 3)
b 4 × (8 − 2) + 12
c 102 + 52
d (5 + 4) × (8 − 6)

Q3 hint
Remember the priority of operations with these.

Key point
In maths, if you do not know a value, you can use a letter to represent it.

Worked example

Simplify

a $x + x + x$

$3x$

Think of a rod that is x cm long.

When you put three rods like this together, the total length is $3x$ cm.

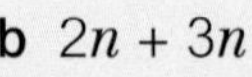

So $x + x + x = 3x$

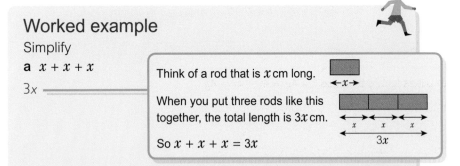

b $2n + 3n$

$5n$

Think of some blue tiles.
Each blue tile is worth n.

The question is

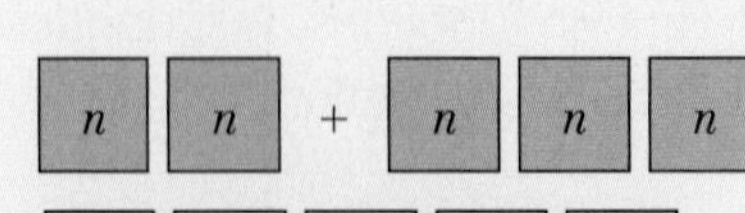

You can add together the blue tiles to give you the answer.

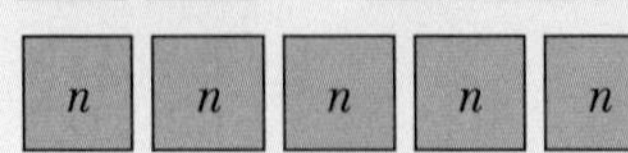

Topic links: Priority of operations, Negative numbers

Subject links: Computing (Q12)

4a

4 Josie has rods of three different lengths.
The yellow rods are x cm long.
The blue rods are y cm long.
The grey rods are z cm long.

$\leftarrow x \rightarrow$ $\leftarrow y \rightarrow$ $\leftarrow z \rightarrow$

Simplify

a $x + x + x + x$

b $y + y$

c $z + z + z$

d $2x + x$

e $3y + 2y$

f $4z - 2z$

Discussion Why is $x + x + x + x + x$ the same as $5x$?

5 Match each red calculation with its blue equivalent. 4a

$6 + 6 + 6$ $\quad z + z + z + z + z$ $\quad x + x$ $\quad y + y + y + y$

$2 \times x$ $\quad 4 \times y$ $\quad 3 \times 6$ $\quad 5 \times z$

6 Simplify 4a

a $3n + 4n$ **b** $8m + 2m$ **c** $12p - 5p$ **d** $8q - q$

e $2a + 3a + a$ **f** $6x + x - 2x$ **g** $2w - 5w$ **h** $2z + 3z - 10z$

Discussion Is $5x + 2x$ the same as $2x + 5x$? How do you know?
Is $5x - 2x$ the same as $2x - 5x$? How do you know?

Worked example

Simplify

a $4 \times y$

$4y$ — $4 \times y$ and $y \times 4$ can both be simplified to $4y$. Always write the number before the letter when multiplying.

b $y \times y$

y^2 — $y \times y$ simplifies to y^2

c $4y \times 3$

$12y$ — $4y \times 3$ simplifies to $12y$ because $3 \times 4y = 4y + 4y + 4y = 12y$

d $y \times x$

xy — $y \times x$ simplifies to xy because $y \times x = x \times y = xy$
Always write the letters in alphabetical order.

e $20p \div 10$

$2p$ — If a calculation has just multiplication and division, it doesn't matter which order you work it out.
$20 \times p \div 10 = 20 \div 10 \times p = 2 \times p$

7 Simplify 5c

a $3 \times m$ **b** $n \times 7$ **c** $p \times 5$ **d** $e \times d$

5c

8 Match the equivalent expressions.

$4a$	$a + 4$	$5b$	$3a$	$a \times b$	$a \times 3$	$b \times 3$
$4 \times a$	ab	$3 \times a$	$4 + a$	$3 \times b$	$5 \times b$	

5b

9 Simplify these expressions.

a $5 \times 2a$ b $4 \times 8b$ c $3 \times 2y$ d $16y \div 4$

e $14a \div 7$ f $0.5 \times 10c$ g $12b \div 2$ h $0.2 \times 5z$

5b

10 Problem-solving Write four multiplications or divisions that give each of these answers.

a $6a$ b $2c$ c $4t$ d $10s$

Q10a Strategy hint
Start by writing down four multiplications or divisions that give the answer 6. Then decide where to include the a.

5b

11 Copy and complete these multiplication pyramids.
Each brick is the product of the two bricks below.

a Bottom row: t, 5, 8

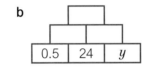

b Bottom row: 0.5, 24, y

Q11 hint
To find a product you need to multiply.

5b

12 Real Asif is in charge of the computer spreadsheets for a music festival.
One of the cells of the spreadsheet contains the formula **A10*2**.

a What might **A10*2** mean?

b The value in cell **A10** is £3.40. What is the value of **A10*2**?

c He changes the formula **A10*2** to **A10*20**. What is the value of **A10*20**?

Explore

13 **Explore** This rectangle could be divided into 12 small squares and described as $12s$. How else could you describe it using small shapes all of the same kind?

s	s	s	s
s	s	s	s
s	s	s	s

Look back at the maths you have learned in this lesson.
How can you use it to answer this question?

Reflect

14 **Reflect** In algebra, letters are used to represent values you do not know.
This lesson might be the first time you have done algebra.

Choose A, B or C to complete each statement.

In this lesson, I did …	A well	B OK	C not very well
So far, I think algebra is …	A easy	B OK	C difficult
When I think about the next lesson, I feel …	A confident	B OK	C unsure

If you answered mostly As and Bs, did your experience surprise you? Why?

If you answered mostly Cs, look back at the questions you found most tricky.
Ask a friend or your teacher to explain them to you. Then complete the statements above again.

3.3 Simplifying expressions 2

You will learn to:
- Use brackets with numbers and letters
- Simplify more complicated expressions by collecting like terms.

CONFIDENCE

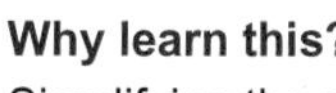

Why learn this?
Simplifying the results of a questionnaire can tell companies important information about us.

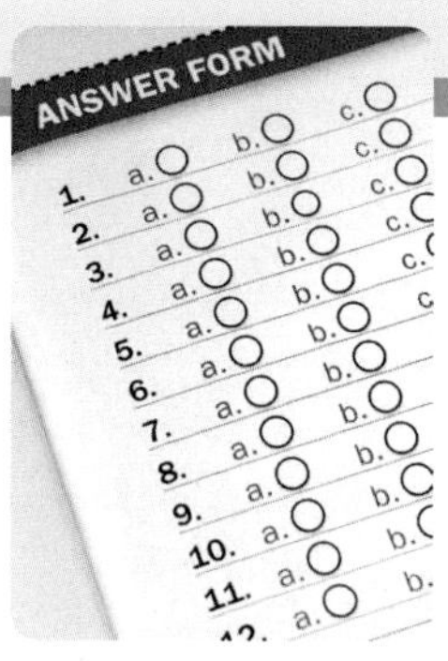

Fluency
Simplify
- $6 \times y$
- $y \times y$
- $2 \times 4y$
- $8y \div 4$

Explore
Tracey does a personality test in a magazine. There are 10 questions. Her answers are a, a, b, a, c, c, a, b, c and a. How can you describe these results as simply as possible? What do the test results tell us about Tracey?

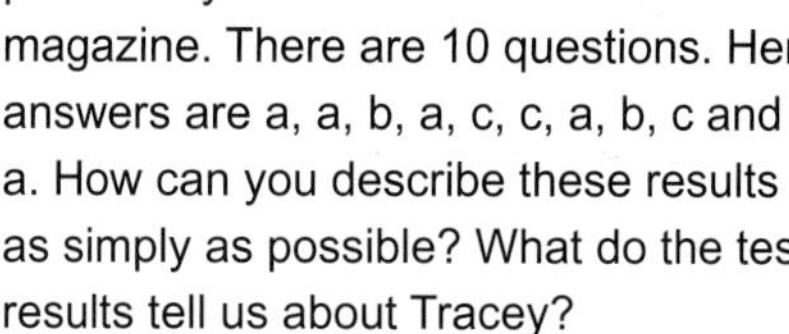

Exercise 3.3

Key point
When you multiply out a bracket, multiply every number inside the bracket by the number outside the bracket.
5 × (3 + 12) = 5 × 3 + 5 × 12
This is called the **distributive law**.

Warm up

1 Simplify
a $n + n + n + n$
b $3x + 5x$
c $4y + 2y - 5y$
d $7w + w - 10w$

2 Simplify
a $5 \times h$
b $0.5 \times 12h$
c $3 \times 4x$
d $5 \times 2y$

4a

3 Work out these. The first one has been started for you.
a $3 \times (20 + 4) = 3 \times 20 + 3 \times 4 = \square$
b $5 \times (30 + 2)$ c $2(10 + 9)$ d $2(20 - 1)$

Discussion Your answers to Q3 parts **c** and **d** should be the same. Why is this?

Q3d hint
$2 \times -1 = -2$

4a

4 Use brackets and the **distributive law** to work out these multiplications. The first one has been started for you.
a $4 \times 61 = 4 \times (60 + 1) = 4 \times 60 + 4 \times 1 = \square$
b 3×34 c 7×28 d 9×49

Q4c hint
You could use 7(20 + 8) or 7(30 − 2).

5c

5 **Simplify** these **expressions**.
a $b + b + b$
b $b + 2 + 2b + 7$
c $3b - b$
d $7b + 8b$
e $3 + 8 - 5 + b + b$
f $17b + 14 - 6b + 12 - 8 - 3b$

Key point
Like terms contain the same letter (or do not contain a letter). For example, $2x$ and $3x$ are like terms, but $2x$ and $3y$ are not like terms.
You **simplify** an **expression** by collecting like terms.

5c

6 Copy and complete these addition pyramids.
The expression in any brick is the sum of the expressions in the two bricks below.

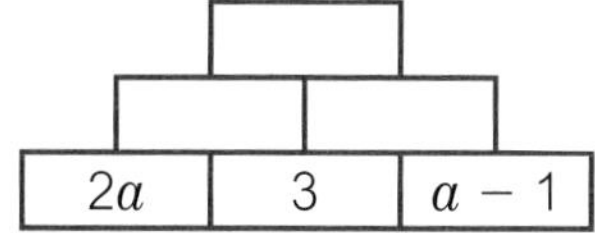

b

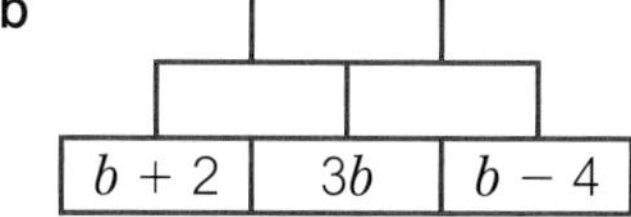

c

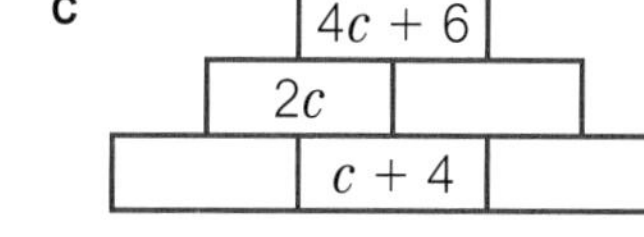
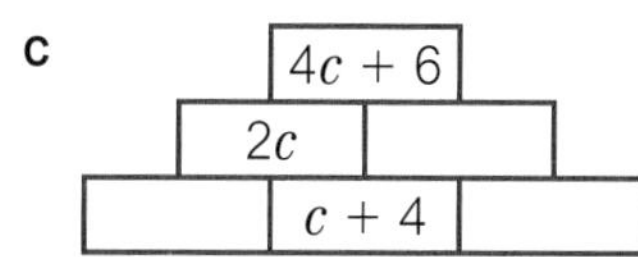

5c **7** Simplify these expressions.

- **a** $a + a + a + a - b - b$
- **b** $5a + 6 - 3 + 2b$
- **c** $2a + 5b + 6a - 7b - 8$
- **d** $17a + 9 - 5a + 4b$

5b **8** This large rectangle has been split into two smaller rectangles.

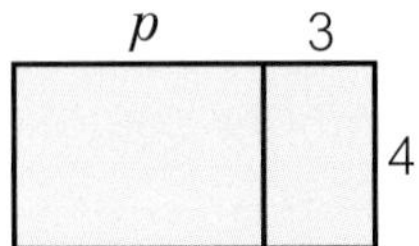

- **a** Write an expression for the width of the large rectangle.
- **b** Use your answer to part **a** to complete this sentence: area = □ × (□ + □)
- **c** Caleb wrote expressions for the areas of the two smaller rectangles. He added them together. What did he write?

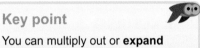

Worked example

Expand $3(x - 4)$

$$3(x - 4) = 3 \times (x - 4)$$
$$= 3 \times x - 3 \times 4$$
$$= 3x - 12$$

Multiply everything inside the brackets by 3. $3 \times x = 3x$ and $3 \times -4 = -12$.

5b **9** Multiply out the brackets.

- **a** $2(x + 7)$
- **b** $7(c - 2)$
- **c** $6(2x - 1)$
- **d** $5(3x + 4)$
- **e** $0.5(6h - 1)$

Discussion Why is $2(x + 7)$ *not* equal to $2x + 7$?

Key point

You can multiply out or **expand** expressions with brackets.

5b **10** **Problem-solving** **a** Choose a number from cloud 1 and an expression from cloud 2. Multiply them together.

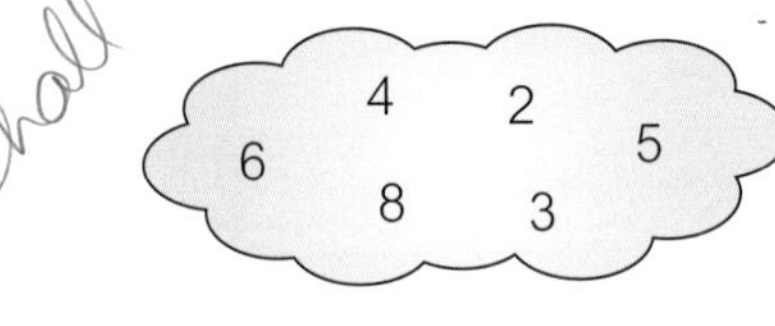

Cloud 1

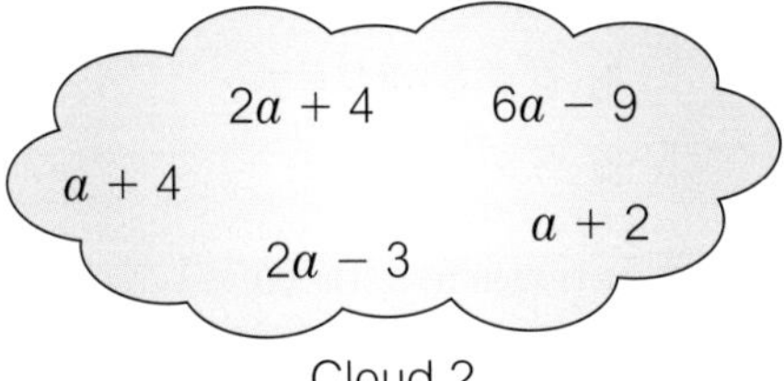

Cloud 2

- **b** Repeat this five times.
- **c** Find two calculations that give the same answer.

5b **11** Expand and simplify these. Part **a** has been done for you.

- **a** $2(x + 1) + 4x = 2x + 2 + 4x = 6x + 2$
- **b** $6(x + 4) + 5x$
- **c** $2(x + 8) + 4(x + 3)$
- **d** $5(2x + 3) + 3(x - 2)$

Explore **12** **Explore** Tracey does a personality test in a magazine. There are 10 questions. Her answers are a, a, b, a, c, c, a, b, c and a. How can you describe these results as simply as possible? What do the test results tell us about Tracey? What have you learned in this lesson to help you answer this question? What other information do you need.'

Reflect **13** **Reflect** Lilina says, 'Simplifying algebra means make the expression so that it can't be added, multiplied, divided or subtracted any more.'
Howard says, 'Simplifying algebra means getting as few terms as possible.'
Look back at your answers to all the questions in this lesson that asked you to simplify.
Do you agree with Lilina? Do you agree with Howard?
Write a definition for yourself that begins 'In algebra, 'simplify' means ...'.

Topic links: Calculating with decimals, Negative numbers

3.4 Writing expressions

You will learn to:
- Write expressions from word descriptions using addition, subtraction and multiplication
- Write expressions to represent function machines.

Why learn this? Writing expressions is like writing a foreign language. If you make mistakes, other people won't understand you!

Fluency
Start with the number 5.
Now follow one of the blue instructions. Match the outcome to the correct red answer.
Add 2 Subtract 1
Multiply by 3 Subtract from 8
15 3 7 4

Explore
How can a 'mind reader' always know your answer to this calculation?
'Think of a number, add 5, multiply the result by 2, subtract 4 and finally subtract double your original number.'

Exercise 3.4

1 Work out
a 12 add 18
b the difference between 25 and 7
c the total of 4, 6 and 12
d 14 less than 20
e 20 shared between 5
f 5 times 9
g 6 multiplied by 8
h 27 divided by 3

2 Which is the correct answer for each of these, A, B or C?

	A	B	C
a 15 decreased by 9 is	A 6	B −6	C 24
b the product of 6 and 7 is	A 1	B 13	C 42
c the sum of 8 and 4 is	A 32	B 4	C 12

3 Simplify
a $x + 2x$
b $7y - 5y$
c $2a + 3b + 4a - b$

Worked example

Alice is x years old. Ben is 5 years older and Carl is 3 years younger than Alice.
Write expressions for Ben's and Carl's ages.

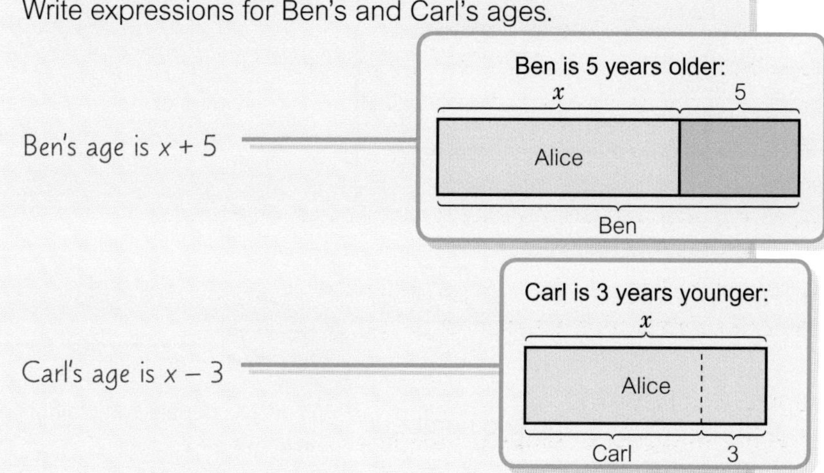

Key point

You write an algebraic expression by using letters to stand for numbers. The letter is called a **variable** because its value can change or vary.

5c

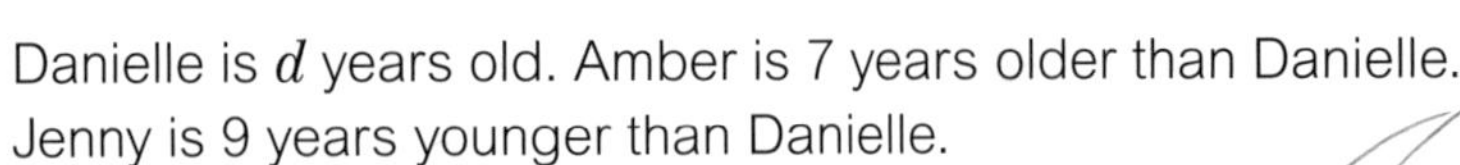

4 Danielle is d years old. Amber is 7 years older than Danielle. Jenny is 9 years younger than Danielle.
Write an expression for

a Amber's age **b** Jenny's age.

Q4 hint

Draw a bar model, like the one in the Worked example on the previous page, to help you.

5c

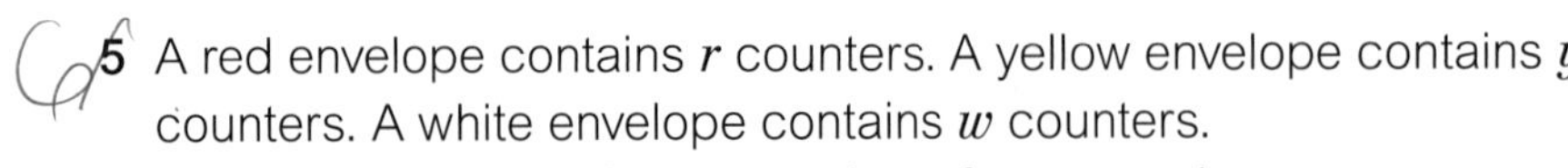

5 A red envelope contains r counters. A yellow envelope contains y counters. A white envelope contains w counters.
Write an expression for the number of counters in

a the white envelope and three more
b the red envelope and 10 more
c the yellow envelope with seven taken out
d the white envelope with eight added
e the white envelope with three taken out.

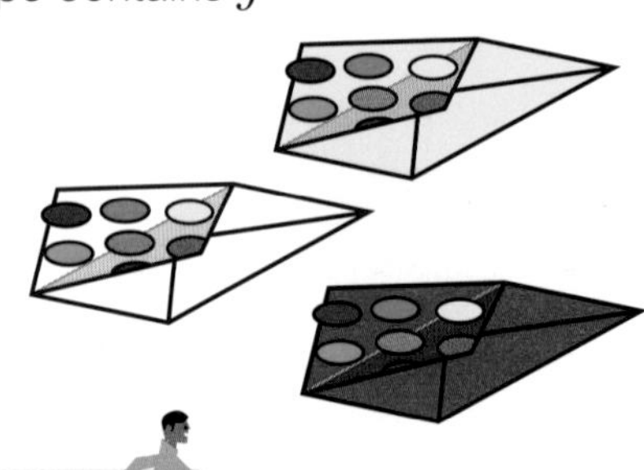

Worked example

Draw a function machine, then write an expression for y decreased by 10.

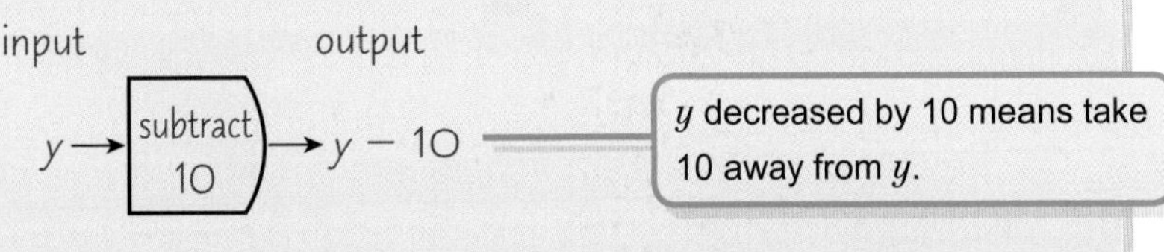

y decreased by 10 means take 10 away from y.

5c

6 Draw a function machine, then write an expression for

a 4 more than a **b** 3 less than b
c x take away 20 **d** y with 7 added on
e m with 4 removed **f** l with an extra 2.

Q6a hint

4 more than a means add 4 onto a.

5c

7 n is a mystery number. Write an expression for

a 3 more than the number **b** 21 less than the number
c the number subtracted from 50 **d** the number with 8 added.

Worked example

John thinks of two numbers, m and n. Write an expression for the sum of 3 lots of m and 5 multiplied by n.

$3 \times m = 3m$
$5 \times n = 5n$
sum $= 3m + 5n$

'3 lots of m' means $3 \times m$
'5 multiplied by n' means $5 \times n$
'Sum of' means add, so the expression is $3m + 5n$.
This cannot be simplified further as the terms are not like terms.

5b

8 Sam writes down two numbers, x and y.
Write an expression for

a double x **b** 5 times x
c the sum of the two numbers **d** the product of the two numbers
e 8 multiplied by y **f** y multiplied by 6.

Q8a hint

When you double something, you multiply it by 2.

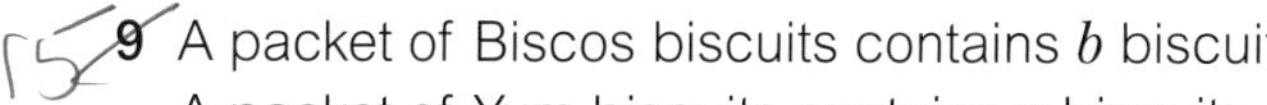

9 A packet of Biscos biscuits contains b biscuits.
A packet of Yum biscuits contains y biscuits.
A packet of Giants biscuits contains g biscuits.
Write an expression for the number of biscuits in

- **a** three packets of Giants
- **b** five packets of Biscos
- **c** seven packets of Biscos
- **d** a packet of Biscos and a packet of Giants
- **e** the total of a packet of Yum, a packet of Giants and three more biscuits.

5b

10 **Modelling** Bethany and Ajay build houses. In a two-bedroom house, they use two exterior doors and seven interior doors.

a Bethany uses this model:

1 house	$9d$
75 houses	$75 \times 9d$

i What do you think d stands for?

ii Simplify $75 \times 9d$.

b Ajay uses this model:

1 house	$2e + 7i$
75 houses	$75(2e + 7i)$

i What do you think e and i stand for?

ii Multiply out $75(2e + 7i)$.

Discussion Which is the better model? Explain why.

5b

Investigation

Problem-solving / Reasoning / Modelling

Work with a partner to solve this problem.
Greg travels by train to work each day from Monday to Friday. In a normal week, the morning journey usually takes x minutes. It usually takes 10 minutes longer to travel home from work each evening.
This is Greg's journey time information for one week in May.

	Journey time to work	Journey time home
Monday	twice as long as normal	normal
Tuesday	5 minutes longer than normal	normal
Wednesday	normal	25 minutes less than normal
Thursday	10 minutes longer than normal	twice as long as normal
Friday	day off work	day off work

Greg says, 'Even though I didn't go to work on Friday, I still spent the same amount of time travelling this week as I do in a normal week.'
Is Greg correct? Show all your working and explain your answer.

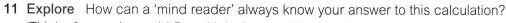

Strategy hint

Make a plan to help you solve this problem. The plan might start like this:

1. Write an expression for the normal time it takes Greg to travel home.
2. Write an expression for the total amount of time Greg spends travelling in a normal week.
3. Write an expression for the time it takes Greg to travel to work each day of the week in May.

11 **Explore** How can a 'mind reader' always know your answer to this calculation?
'Think of a number, add 5, multiply the result by 2, subtract 4 and finally subtract double your original number.'
Look back at the maths you have learned in this lesson.
How can you use it to answer this question?

12 **Reflect** This lesson suggested using bar models and function machines to help you with writing expressions. Did they help you? How?
Did you use any other methods? Explain the method(s) you used.

Reflect

3.5 STEM: Substituting into formulae

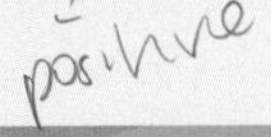

You will learn to:

- Substitute positive integers into simple formulae written in words
- Substitute integers into formulae written in letter symbols.

CONFIDENCE

Why learn this? Formulae are used for all sorts of calculations in science.

Fluency
Complete this number pyramid. Each brick is the sum of the two bricks below it.

Explore
How do you convert between different temperature scales?

Exercise 3.5: Science formulae

Warm up

1 A packet of fuse wire costs 50p. How much do five packets of fuse wire cost?

2 When Sara is 12, Ryan is 9. How old is Ryan when Sara is 16?

3 Work out
a $2 \times 3 + 9$ b $10 - 2 \times 4$ c $4(3 + 7)$ d $62 \div 10$

Worked example

The formula to work out the distance a car travels is

distance = speed × time

Lin drives her car for 3 hours at a speed of 60 miles per hour. How far does she go?

speed = 60 and time = 3
distance = speed × time
= 60 × 3
= 180 miles

Write down the formula first and then substitute the numbers into the formula.

Key point
A **formula** shows the relationship between different variables, written as words or letters.
You can use a formula to work out an **unknown** value by **substituting** the values that you do know into the formula.

4a 4 STEM Work out the distance a car travels when it moves at
a a speed of 50 miles per hour for 2 hours
b a speed of 70 miles per hour for 4 hours
c a speed of 65 miles per hour for 3 hours.

4a 5 STEM The formula to work out the voltage needed for a current of 2 amps through a lamp is

voltage (in volts) = 2 × resistance of lamp (in ohms)

Work out the voltage needed when the resistance is
a 2 ohms b 3 ohms c 5 ohms

Q5 Literacy hint
The voltage is the energy the electricity is carrying. Resistance is how much something slows down the current passing through it.

Topic links: Range, Imperial measures

Subject links: Science

6 **STEM** The formula for the resistance in this part of a circuit is 4a

total resistance (in ohms) = resistance of lamp + 2

Use this formula to work out the total resistance for

a a 3Ω lamp **b** a 6Ω lamp

The formula can be written as a function machine like this.

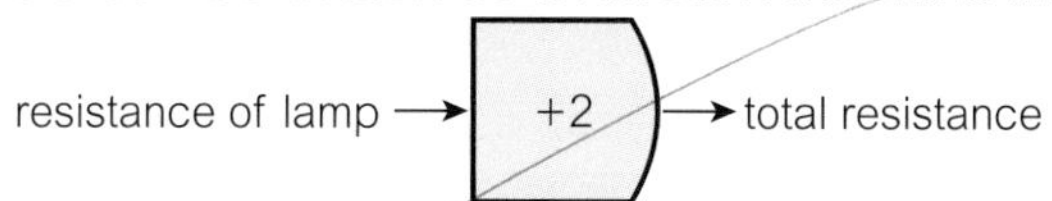

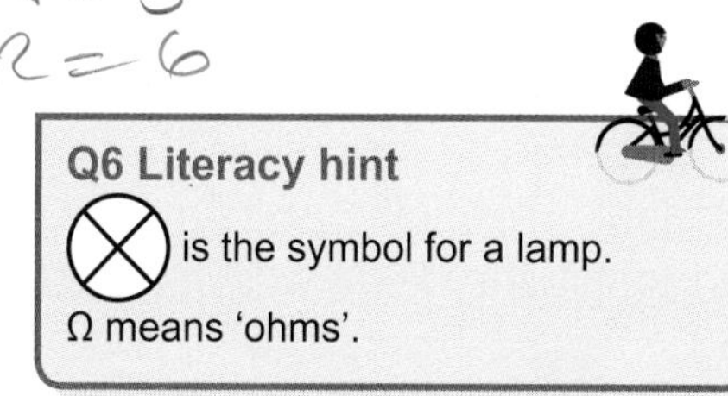

Q6 Literacy hint

⊗ is the symbol for a lamp.

Ω means 'ohms'.

Use the function machine to work out the total resistance for

c a 5Ω lamp **d** a 1Ω lamp

7 **STEM** For a science project, some students work out how much they have grown in Year 7. 4a

Girls	4.7 cm	5.6 cm	4.9 cm	6.1 cm	5.2 cm
Boys	5.2 cm	4.9 cm	5.8 cm	6.2 cm	5.7 cm

Work out the range for

a the girls **b** the boys.

Did the girls or the boys have the bigger growth spurt?

Discussion What is the formula for working out the range?

Q7 Literacy hint

A growth spurt is a time of rapid growth, often in adolesence.

8 **STEM** A formula used in science to work out the force (F) on an object is 5c

$F = ma$

where m is the mass and a is the acceleration of the object.

Work out the value of the force when

a $m = 20$ and $a = 4$ **b** $m = 50$ and $a = 2$ **c** $m = 12$ and $a = 6$

9 **STEM** Sophie uses this formula to work out the pressure when different forces are applied to an area of 15 cm². 5c

$P = F \div 15$

where P is the pressure in pascals and F is the force in newtons.

Work out the pressure when

a $F = 30$ N **b** $F = 165$ N **c** $F = 315$ N **d** $F = 285$ N

10 **STEM / Modelling** Formulae for predicting the adult heights of girls and boys are 5b

Girl: (father's height − 13 + mother's height) ÷ 2

Boy: (father's height + 13 + mother's height) ÷ 2

Mr Singh is 180 cm tall and Mrs Singh is 168 cm tall. Work out the predicted adult heights of their daughter and their son.

Discussion Two parents have three daughters. Do you think they will all be the same height when adult? Is this a good model?

11 **a** Write an expression for the area of this rectangle, using p. Multiply out your answer. 5b

b The value of p is 5 cm. What is the area of the rectangle?

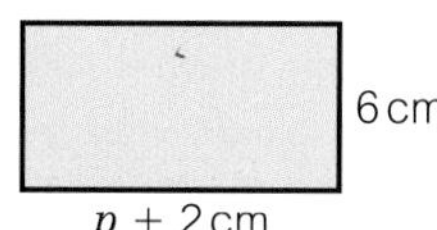

12 **Explore** How do you convert between different temperature scales? Is it easier to explore this question now you have completed the lesson? What further information do you need to be able to answer this? Explore

13 **Reflect** Look back at the formula in Q8. Reflect

a Would it matter if this formula used the letters x and y instead of m and a?

b Do the letters help you to understand a formula? Explain.

Q13a hint

If different letters were used would your answers be different?

3.6 Writing formulae

You will learn to:
- Identify variables and use letter symbols
- Write simple formulae using letter symbols
- Identify formulae and functions
- Identify the unknowns in a formula and a function.

CONFIDENCE

Why learn this? Spreadsheets can save a lot of time. Once you have entered a formula, the spreadsheet can calculate the answer whenever the data changes.

Fluency
Use the formula $T = 4n$ to work out the value of T when $n = 5$ and when $n = 12$.

Explore
How do you write formulae for calculations in a spreadsheet?

Exercise 3.6

Warm up

1 Simplify
a $x + x + x$ b $2y + 5y$ c $7z - 2z$ d $8w + w - 3w$

2 Simplify
a $2m + 3p + 8m - 2p$ b $3(x + 4)$ c $4(x - 2) + 3x$

Worked example

Aisha is making a clock face for her design project. The length of wood she needs is 10 cm more than the width of the clock face.
Write a formula that connects the length of wood, l, to the width of the clock face, w.

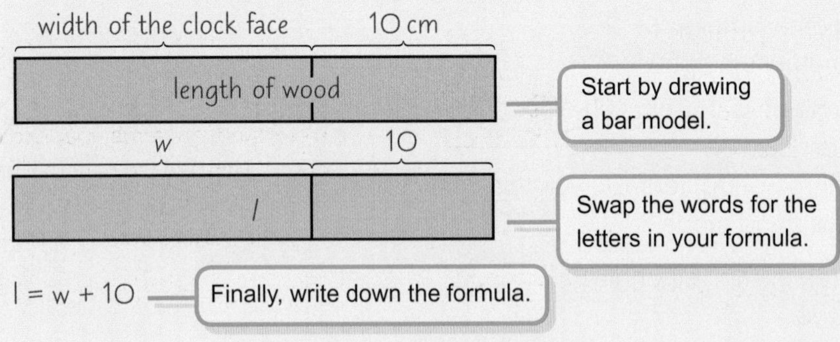
width of the clock face
10 cm
length of wood
Start by drawing a bar model.
w
10
l
Swap the words for the letters in your formula.
l = w + 10
Finally, write down the formula.

Key point
You can write a formula to work out an amount in words, and then use letters to represent the variables.

5c 3 Every day, a baker makes 12 more bread rolls than have been ordered by customers.
Write a formula that connects the number of rolls made, M, to the number of rolls ordered, R.

5c 4 All the prices on Charlie's stall have gone down £5 in a January sale.
Write a formula that connects the sale price of an item, P, to the price before the sale, x.

Topic links: The four rules with integers

5 Ali and Shiraz have decided to put together what's left of their pocket money to buy a present.
Write a formula that connects the total amount of money, M, to the amount of money Ali has, y, and the amount of money Shiraz has, z.

Worked example

Write a formula to work out the total number of players at a 5-a-side football tournament, when you know the number of teams.

1 team = 5 players, 2 teams = 2 × 5 = 10 players,
3 teams = 3 × 5 = 15 players, ...

> Start by trying different numbers to see the pattern.

number of teams × 5 = number of players

> Write the rule for the pattern in words or as a function machine.

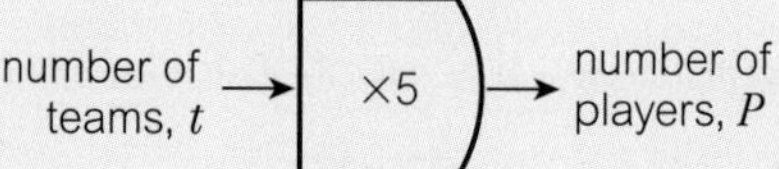

Let P = the number of players and
t = the number of teams.
$P = 5 \times t$ or $P = 5t$

> Decide on the letters you are going to use, then write your formula in its simplest form.

6 To make fruit buns you need 12 grams of fruit per bun. Write a formula that connects the amount of fruit, F, to the number of buns, b.

Q6 hint
Start by trying different numbers to see the pattern.

7 Simon is paid £8 per hour. Write a formula that connects the total he is paid, P, with the number of hours he works, h.

8 **Real** To work out the amount of food in kilograms a horse needs per day, you divide the mass of the horse in kilograms by 40.
 a Write a formula that connects the amount of food, F, to the mass of a horse, M.
 The table shows the masses of six horses at a riding stables.
 b Use your formula to work out the amount of food that each horse needs.

Name	Mass (kg)
Aurora	520
Bluegrass	500
Flanagan	480
Phantom	600
Summer	360
Tonto	460

9 **Problem-solving / Reasoning** When one cube is placed on a table, you can see five of its six faces.
When two cubes are placed side-by-side on a table, you can see eight of their faces.
How many faces can you see when there are 50 cubes placed side-by-side in a row on a table?
Discussion Tell a partner how you solved this problem.
Has your partner used a different method?

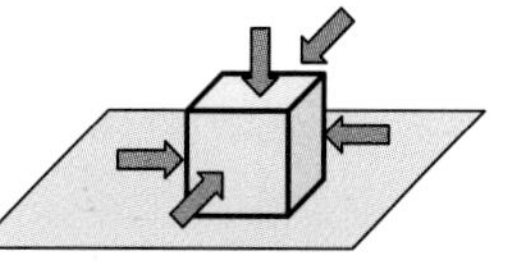

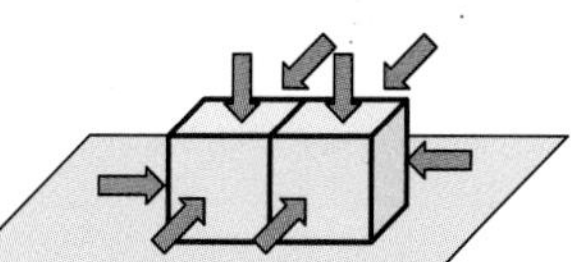

Q9 Strategy hint
Count how many faces you can see when there are three, four and five cubes. Can see the pattern? Try to write a formula connecting the number of faces and the number of cubes.

10 **Explore** How do you write formulae for calculations in a spreadsheet?
Is it easier to explore this question now you have completed the lesson?
What further information do you need to be able to answer this?

11 **Reflect** In lesson 3.5 you were given formulae to work with. In this lesson you wrote your own formulae.
 a Which did you find more difficult? b What made it more difficult?
 c Are there particular kinds of questions you need more practice on?
 If so, what kinds?

3 Check up

Functions

1 Work out the outputs of each function machine.

a

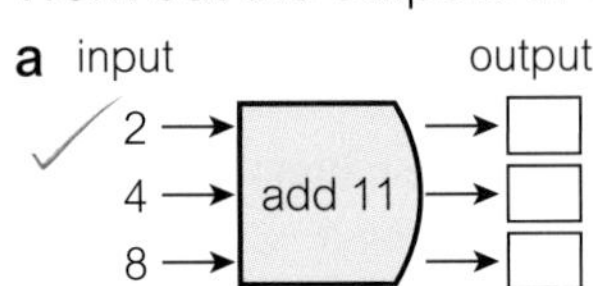

b

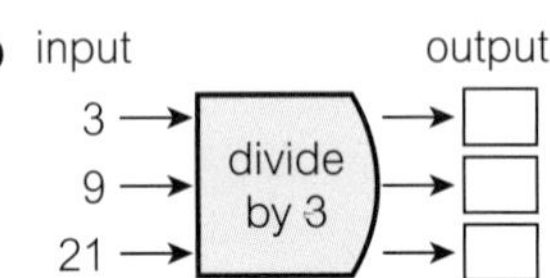

2 Write down the function for each machine.

a

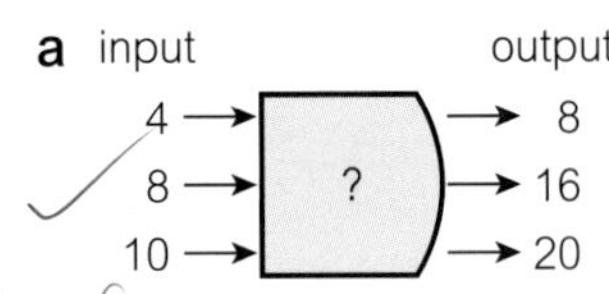

b

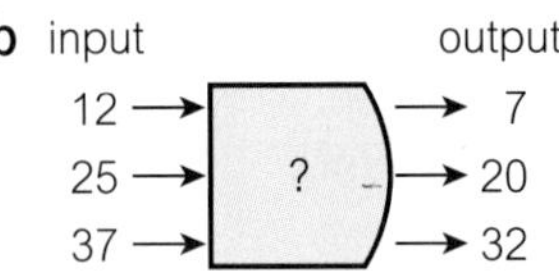

3 Work out the missing output of this function machine.

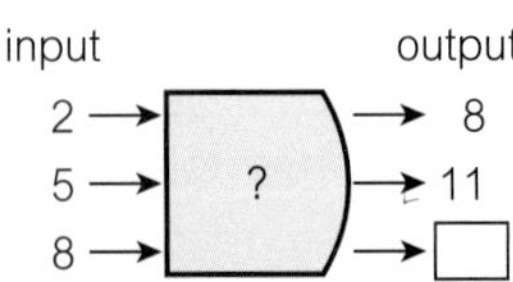

4 Work out the outputs of each two-step function machine.

a

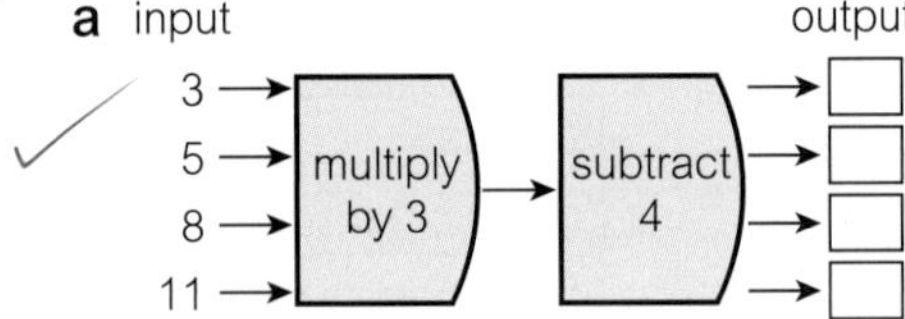

b

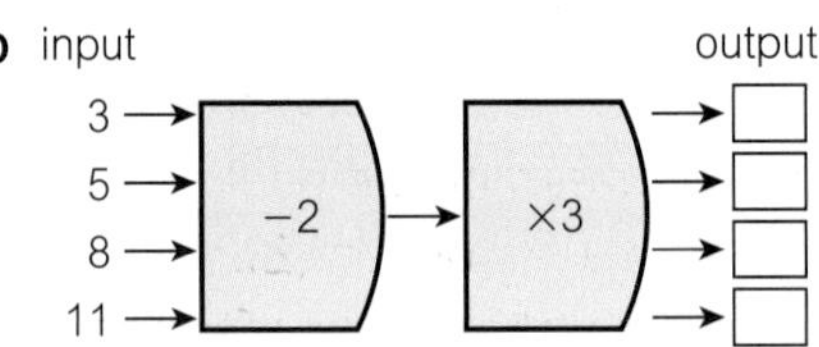

Expressions

5 Simplify

a $6k + 5k$ **b** $18h - 6h$ **c** $7b + 2b + b$ **d** $8y - y$

e $2 \times x$ **f** $z \times 9$ **g** $g \times f$ **h** $p \times q$

i $8 \times 3c$ **j** $9t \times 3$ **k** $21y \div 7$ **l** $0.5 \times 20g$

6 Gill writes down two numbers, a and b.
Write an expression for

a 4 multiplied by a

b b multiplied by 9

c the sum of the two numbers

d the product of the two numbers.

7 Work out

a $4 \times (10 + 4)$ **b** $3(40 - 2)$

8 Simplify these expressions.

a $c + 9 + 5c + 3$ **b** $14d + 11 - 4d + 2 - 6 - 2d$

9 Multiply out the brackets.

a $4(x + 4)$ **b** $6(x - 2)$ **c** $8(2x + 5)$

10 Expand and simplify $3(5x + 2) + 2(x - 1)$.

Formulae

11 The formula for working out the amount of pasta, in grams, for a meal is

amount of pasta = 125 × number of people

Work out the amount of pasta needed for

a 2 people b 10 people.

12 A formula used in science is $m = dV$.
Gethin uses the formula to work out m when $d = 20$ and $V = 5$. This is what he writes:

> $m = dV$, when $d = 20$ and $V = 5$
>
> $m = 205$

a Explain the mistake that Gethin has made.

b Use the formula to work out m when

i $d = 15$ and $V = 3$

ii $d = 25$ and $V = 6$

13 This bar model shows the difference in price (in pounds) between weekend tickets (w) and day tickets (d) for a festival.

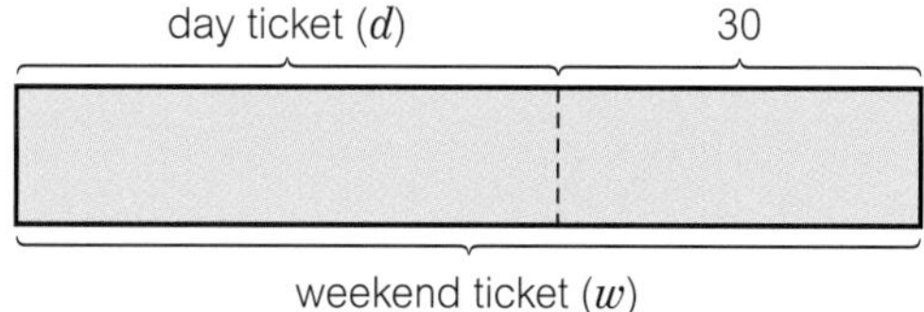

Write a formula to work out the price of a weekend ticket when you know the price of a day ticket.

14 James works out how much money he has left at the end of every month, by working out the difference between the amount he earns and the amount he spends. All amounts are in pounds (£).
Write down a formula that connects the amount of money he has left, M, to the amount of money he earns, E, and the amount of money he spends, S.

15 How sure are you of your answers? Were you mostly

Just guessing Feeling doubtful Confident

What next? Use your results to decide whether to strengthen or extend your learning.

Challenge

16 Shelby says that this function machine only gives outputs ending in 0 or 5.
Is she correct? Explain your answer.

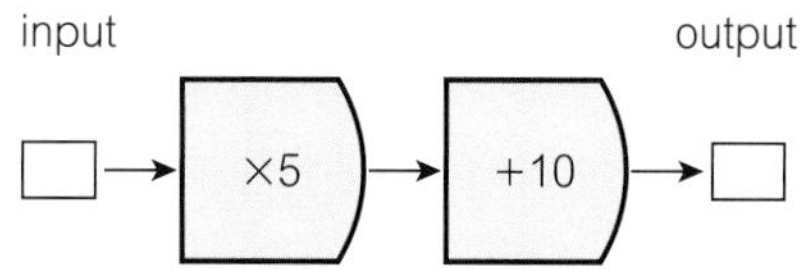

17 In this two-step function machine, the input is 6 and the output is 20.

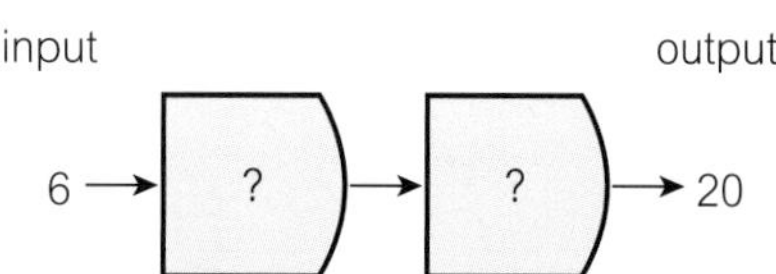

Write down three different two-step rules that this function machine could have.

18 Write four algebraic expressions that simplify to give each of these answers.

a $20x$ b $8y$

3 Strengthen

You will:
- Strengthen your understanding with practice.

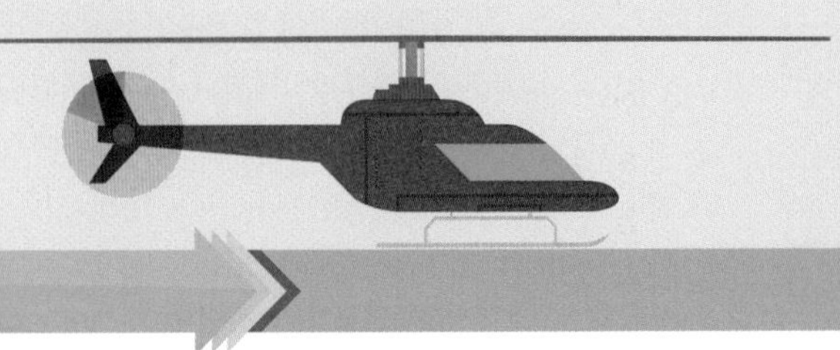

Functions

4c **1** Work out the output of each function machine.

a input 5 → add 6 → output □

b 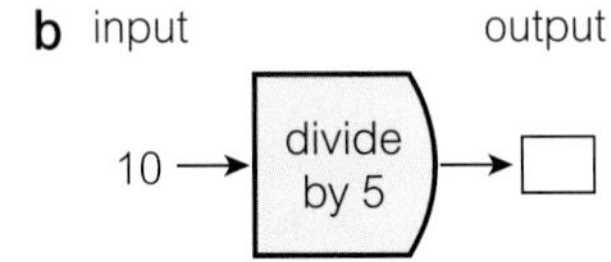

Q1a hint
Work out 5 + 6

4c **2** Work out the outputs of each function machine.

a input 6, 9, 14 → subtract 5 → output 1, □, □

b 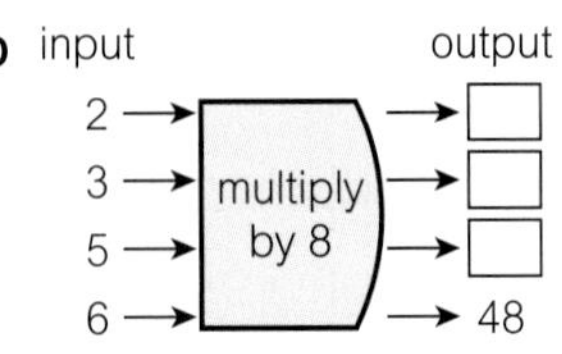

Q2a hint
input 6, 9, 14 → subtract 5 → output 1, 4, ?

4b **3** Describe the function used by each function machine.

a input 2, 5, 7 → ? → output 4, 10, 14

b 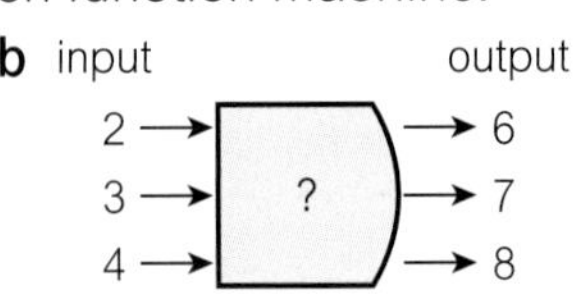

c input 2, 4, 6 → ? → output 0, 2, 4

d 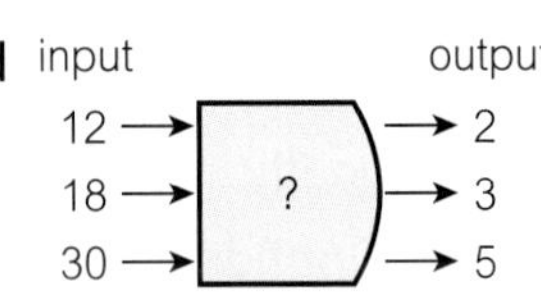

Q3a hint
To find the function ask yourself, 'What do I do to 2 to get 4?'
Does this function work to get 10 from 5, and to get 14 from 7?

4a **4** Work out the outputs of each two-step function machine.

a 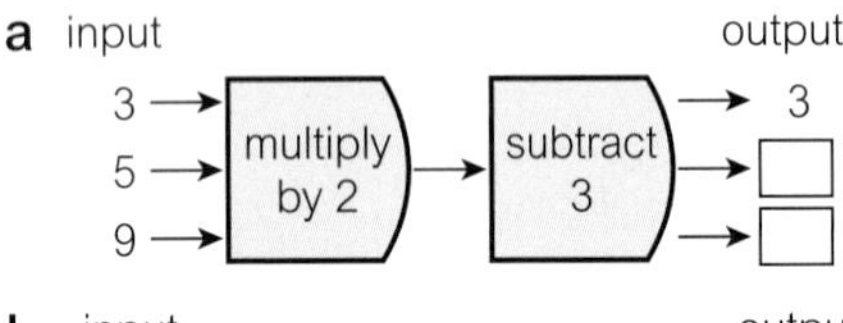

b 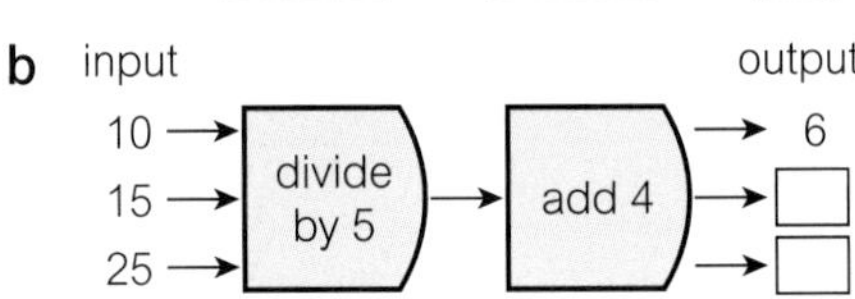

Q4a hint
3 × 2 = 6, then 6 − 3 = 3
5 × 2 = 10, then 10 − 3 = ?
Work out 9 × 2, then subtract 3
input 3, 5, 9 → multiply by 2 → 6, 10, ? → subtract 3 → output 3, ?, ?

Expressions

4a **1** Work out
a $4 \times (6 + 3)$
b $3 \times (2 + 9)$
c $8 \times (11 - 3)$
d $9 \times (5 - 2)$

Q1a hint
Think of $4 \times (6 + 3)$ as 4 lots of 6 add 4 lots of 3.

Subject links: Science – Formulae Q1

2 Fill in the gaps to show two ways of working out 5 × 76. 4a

a 5 × 76 = □ (□ + □)

b 5 × 76 = □ (□ − □)

Q2 hint

76 = 70 + □

76 = □ − □

3 Simplify 4a

a $y + y$

b $z + z + z + z$

c $b + b + b$

d $3c + 2c$

e $9a - 3a$

f $4t + 5t - 2t$

g $8r - r + 3r$

h $h + 7h - 3h - 4h$

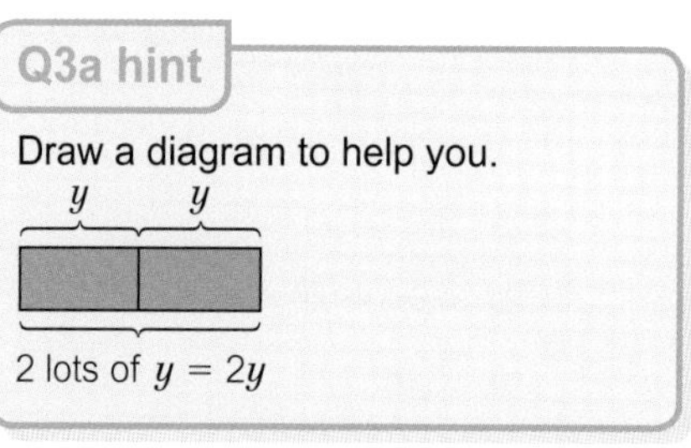

4 Simplify 5c

a $3b + y + 2b + 5y$

b $5x + 2y + 4x + 8y$

c $6r + 9s - 2r + 4s$

d $8p + 4q + 2p - q$

e $13 + 11z - 5z - 3$

Q4a hint

Start by finding the two b terms.
How many bs are there altogether?
Now do the same with the y terms.

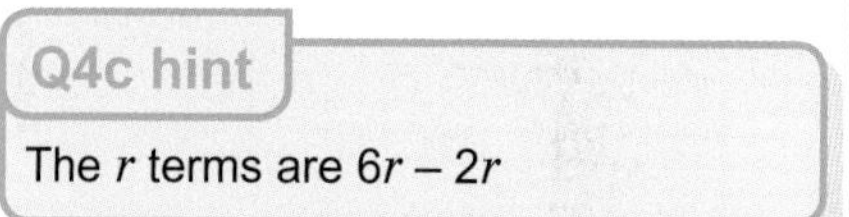

5 Simplify 5c

a $x \times 4$

b $z \times 2$

c $n \times 6$

d $p \times 4$

e $3 \times y$

f $11 \times w$

g $b \times a$

h $a \times c$

Q5a hint
Write the number before the letter.

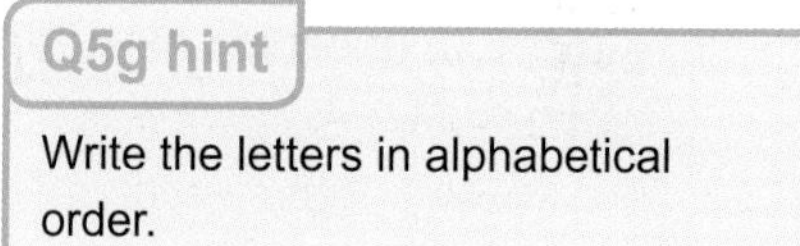

Q5g hint
Write the letters in alphabetical order.

6 Simplify 5b

a $4 \times 3x$

b $8 \times 2y$

c $6b \times 5$

d $2c \times 2.5$

e $12y \div 3$

f $16f \div 8$

g $20z \div 10$

h $4g \div 4$

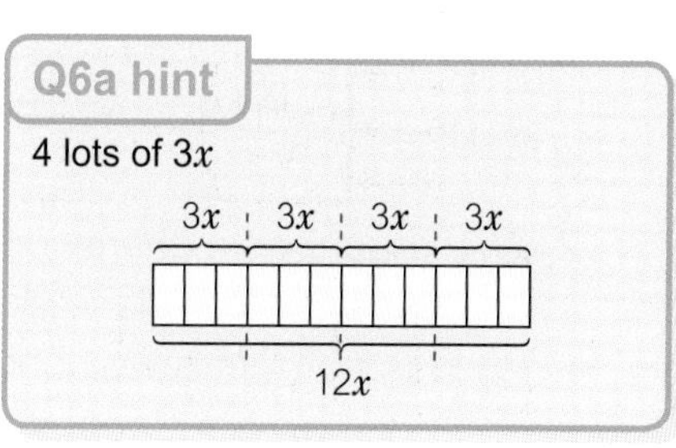

Q6a hint
4 lots of 3x
3x
3x
3x
3x
12x

7 Write an expression for 5c

a 6 more than x

b 5 less than x

c x with 4 added on

d x less than 10.

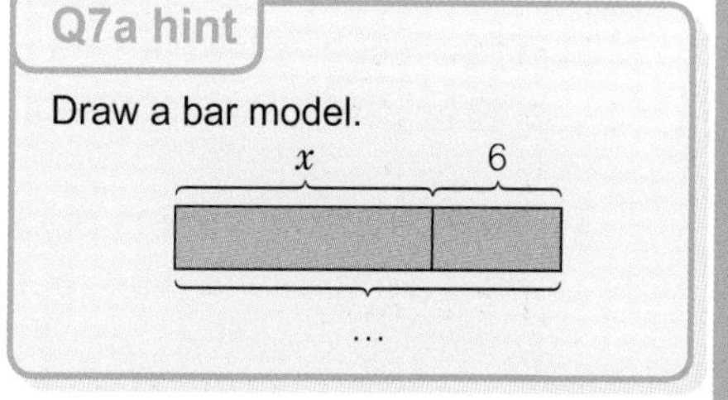

5b **8** Write an expression for

a double y

b 6 multiplied by y

c the sum of x and y

d the product of x and y.

Q8a hint

What do you multiply y by to double it?

Q8d hint

You find the product by multiplying.

5b **9** Multiply out the brackets.

a $3(x + 2)$

b $4(5 + y)$

c $2(3c + 4)$

d $4(4 + 3p)$

e $2(w - 5)$

f $4(2u - 3)$

g $3(5 - a)$

h $4(3 - 5b)$

Q9a hint

Think of $3(x + 2)$ as 3 lots of x add 3 lots of 2.

Q9e hint

Think of $2(w - 5)$ as 2 lots of w take away 2 lots of 5.
Draw a bar model to help.

5b **10** This is part of Simon's homework.

a Explain the mistake that Simon has made.

b Write down the correct answer.

Question:
Expand and simplify
$4(x + 2) + 3$

Answer:
$4(x + 2) + 3$
$= 4x + 2 + 3$
$= 4x + 5$

Formulae

5c **1** A formula used in science for a rough conversion from weight (W) to mass (M) is

$M = W \div 10$

Work out the value of M when

a $W = 60$

b $W = 500$

c $W = 85$

Q1a hint

Substitute 60 for W in the formula.
$M = W \div 10$
$= 60 \div 10$
$= \square$

5c **2** Amy organises a charity concert.
She uses this formula to work out the total amount of money (£T) she takes from ticket sales.

$T = 4C + 8A$

where C is the number of child tickets she sells and A is the number of adult tickets she sells.

Amy sells 80 child tickets and 100 adult tickets.
What is the total amount of money that she takes?

5c **3** Shem spends half his pocket money on music downloads.
Write a formula to work out the amount he spends on music downloads when you know how much pocket money he gets.

Q3 hint

Choose a letter to represent his pocket money. To work out a half, you divide by 2.

4 At a pool party, the pool manager always supplies six more cans of drink than the number of children coming to the party.
Write a formula to work out the number of cans of drink, d, when you know the number of children, c.

5 Mrs Jones has a holiday cottage that she rents to holiday makers. She charges £350 per week plus a cleaning fee of £60 per stay.
Write a formula to work out the total charge, t, when you know the number of weeks, w.

Q5 Strategy hint
£350 per week means £350 for each week.

Enrichment

1 Real / Problem-solving Eight friends pay £648 each for a holiday together.
How much do they pay in total?

Q1 hint
Split 648 into 600 + 40 + 8.
Then work out 8(600 + 40 + 8).

2 This is what Callum writes in his exercise book.

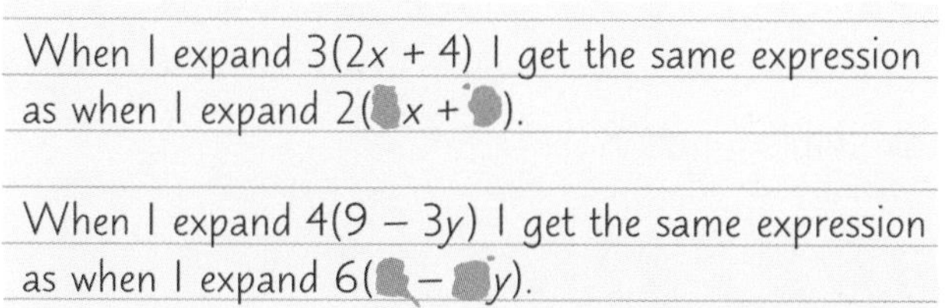

When I expand $3(2x + 4)$ I get the same expression as when I expand $2(\;x + \;)$.

When I expand $4(9 - 3y)$ I get the same expression as when I expand $6(\; - \;y)$.

Callum has spilt tea on his homework. Work out what numbers are under the tea stains.

5 **Reflect** Look back at the questions you answered in these lessons.

a Which hints were most useful? What made them more useful?

b Which hints were least useful to you? What made them less useful?

c What do your answers tell you about how you best learn maths?

3 Extend

You will:

- Extend your understanding with problem-solving.

4a **1** Work out the outputs of each two-step function machine.

a

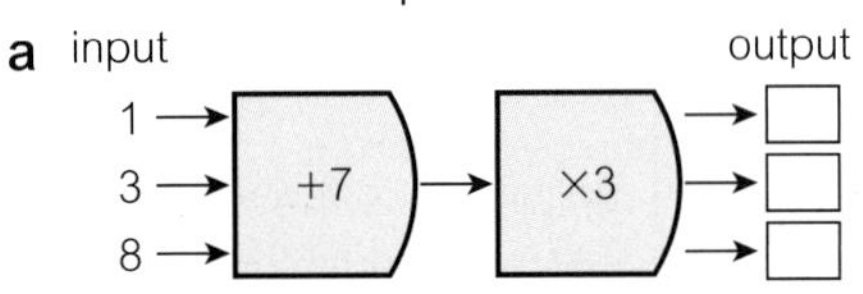

b

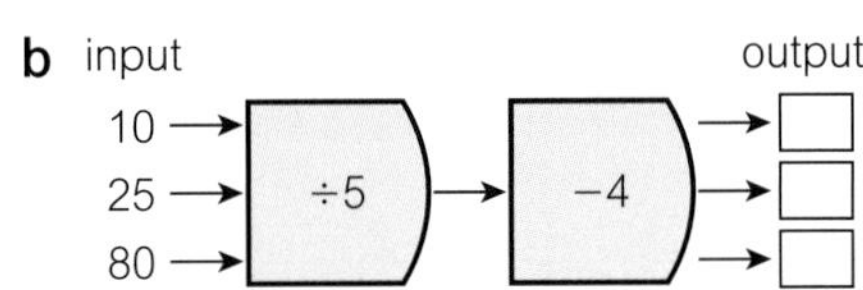

4a **2** **Problem-solving / Reasoning** Alex and Debbie look at this function machine.

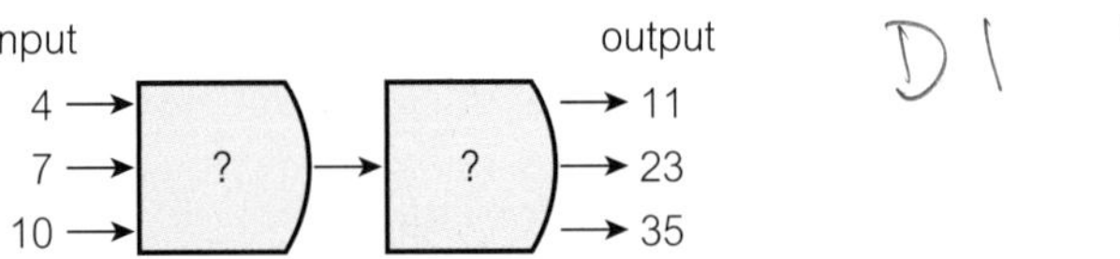

D1 U3.1 Q2

Alex says, 'I think the function is "multiply by 5, then subtract 9".'
Debbie says, 'I think the function is "multiply by 4, then subtract 5".'
Who is correct? Explain your answer.

Q2 Strategy hint
Try Alex and Debbie's functions on the input numbers.

4a **3** **Problem-solving** Sanjay has spilt tomato sauce on his homework.

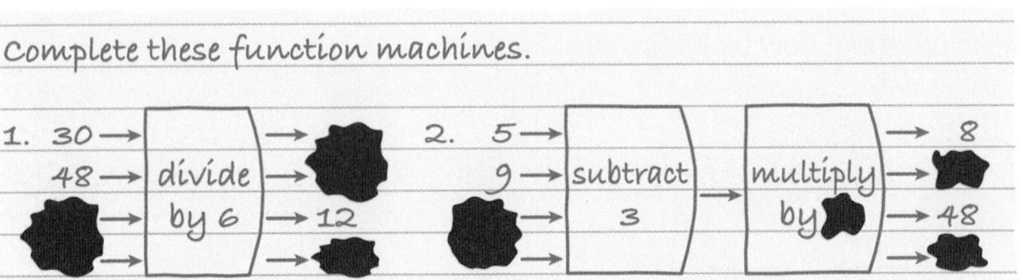

a Copy and complete the function machines. Work out the missing numbers underneath the tomato sauce.

b Is it possible to work out all the missing numbers? If not, suggest numbers that the missing numbers could be.

4a **4** Simplify

a $6a + 9a + a$ **b** $7x + x - 5x$

c $9y + 6w - 4w + 7y$ **d** $11t + 4z + 2t - 12z$

4a **5** **Problem-solving / Reasoning** In a magic square, the sums of the expressions in each row, column and diagonal are the same.
Copy and complete this magic square.
Explain the method you used.

$8n$	$5n$	
	$6n$	
		$4n$

Topic links: Mean, Mode, Square numbers

Subject links: Science (Q15, Q18, Q19), Computing (Investigation)

6 Copy and complete these addition pyramids.

The expression in any brick is the sum of the expressions in the two bricks below.

a

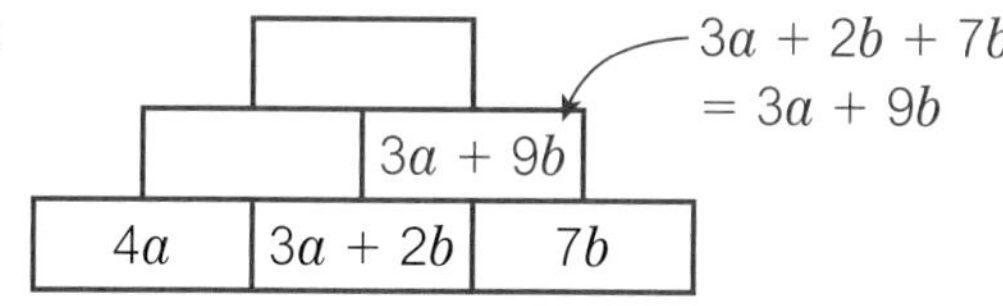

b

	$9e - 3f$	
		$4e - 2f$
$4e - 3f$		

5c

7 **Problem-solving** Sort these cards into groups that simplify to the same expression. 5b

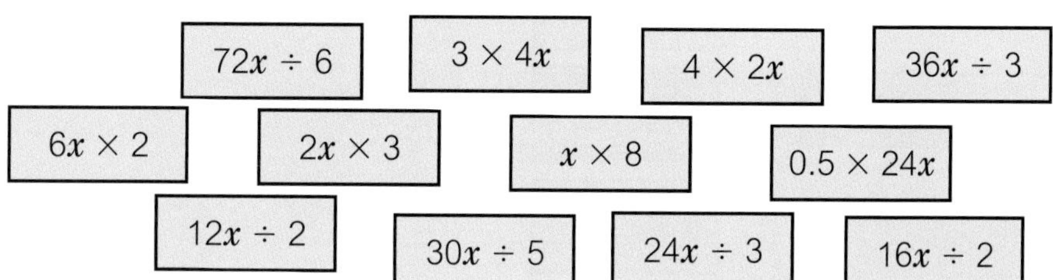

Q7 Strategy hint

Simplify the expression on each card, then sort them into groups.

8 Expand and simplify these. 5b

a $2(3x + 4) + 6(x + 2)$ b $4(x - 3) + 7(2x - 1)$

9 **Problem-solving / Reasoning** 5b

Show that $8(2x + 5) + 3(4x - 5) = 4(7x + 6) + 1$

Q9 Strategy hint

Expand and simplify each side.

10 Sam thinks of a number, n. 5a

a Write an expression for the number Sam gets when he multiplies the number by 2.

b Copy and complete this expression for the number Sam gets when he multiplies the number by 2 and then adds 5.

$\square n + \square$

11 Use m to stand for a mystery number. 5a

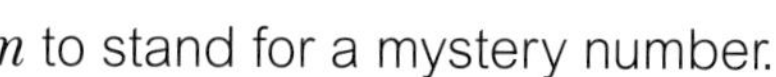

Write an expression for the number Joe gets when

a he multiplies the number by 3, then adds 10

b he divides the number by 2

c he divides the number by 5, then adds 3

d he adds 8 to the number, then multiplies by 2

e he subtracts 4 from the number, then multiplies by 6.

Q11b hint

You write $x \div 2$ as $\frac{x}{2}$

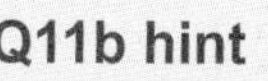

Q11d hint

When you add or subtract before you multiply, you must use brackets.

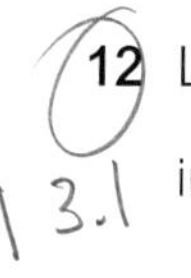

12 Look at this function machine. 5a

input → ×2 → +3 → −3 → ÷2 → output

a Try the machine for three different integers. What do you notice?

b Can you explain why this happens? You might find the words in the cloud helpful.

c **Problem-solving** What happens if you swap the last two operations, −3 and ÷2?

inverse
multiplication
undo
subtraction
division
addition

13 Eleri makes jewellery. She sells bracelets for £b each and necklaces for £n each. 5a

Write an expression for the money she makes when she sells

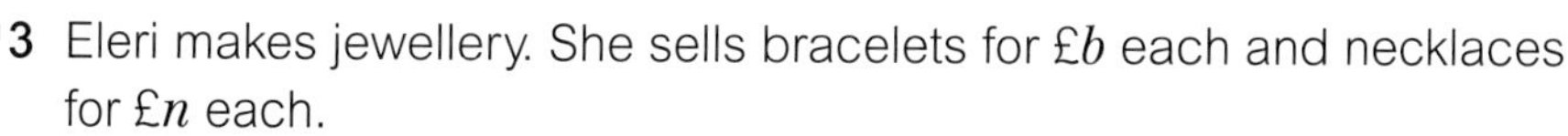

a a bracelet and a necklace

b three bracelets

c four necklaces

d three bracelets and four necklaces

e seven bracelets and five necklaces.

5a

14 a Match each description in the left-hand column to the correct expression in the right-hand column. There will be one expression left over.

DI 3.4 amended

A Multiply x by 3, then add 5	**1** $5 - 3x$
B Multiply x by 3, then subtract from 5	**2** $3(x - 5)$
C Divide x by 3, then add 5	**3** $3x + 5$
D Subtract 5 from x, then multiply by 3	**4** $3x - 5$
E Add 5 to x, then divide by 3	**5** $\frac{x}{3} + 5$
	6 $\frac{x + 5}{3}$

b Write a description for the expression that is left over.

5b

15 STEM / Modelling A personal trainer uses this formula to work out an athlete's maximum heart rate, H_{max}.

$H_{max} = 220 - A$

where A is the athlete's age in years.

Work out the maximum heart rate for athletes with these ages.

a 18 years **b** 35 years **c** 50 years

Discussion The maximum heart rate is shown by H_{max}. How might you show the minimum heart rate?

5b

16 A bicycle hire company uses this formula to work out the total cost, £C, to hire a bicycle.

DI 3.5

$C = 7d + 15$

where d is the number of days.

Work out the cost to hire a bicycle for

a 3 days **b** 5 days **c** 1 week **d** 2 weeks.

5b

17 Real To work out an approximate time (in hours) it will take to walk a distance (in kilometres), you divide the distance by 4.

a Write a formula to work out the time, t, when you know the distance, d.

Bill plans a walking holiday. The table shows the distances he plans to walk each day.

Day	Distance (km)
Monday	20
Tuesday	24
Wednesday	16
Thursday	18
Friday	26

b Use your formula to work out the time it will take Bill to do his walk each day.

5a

18 STEM A formula used in science to work out the final velocity, v, of an object is

$v = u + at$

where u is the initial velocity

a is the acceleration

t is the time.

Work out the final velocity (v) when

a $u = 10$, $a = 5$ and $t = 4$ **b** $u = 20$, $a = 8$ and $t = 6$

c $u = 8$, $a = 2$ and $t = 12$ **d** $u = 1.5$, $a = 3.5$ and $t = 10$

Q18a hint

$v = 10 + 5 \times 4$

$= 10 + 20$

$= \square$

19 **STEM** A formula used in science to work out the potential energy, P, of an object is

$$P = mgh$$

where m is the mass
g is the acceleration due to gravity
h is the height.

Work out the value of P when

a $m = 5$, $g = 10$ and $h = 3$ b $m = 8$, $g = 10$ and $h = 4$
c $m = 2$, $g = 10$ and $h = 8$ d $m = 3.5$, $g = 10$ and $h = 3$

Q19 hint
mgh means $m \times g \times h$.

5a

20 **Real / Modelling** An online shop sells packs of bath-bombs for £6 per pack plus £2.50 postage.

a Write a formula to work out the total cost of an order, T, when you know the number of packs ordered, P.
b Use your formula to work out the total cost for each of these orders.
i 2 packs ii 5 packs iii 8 packs
c Do you think that this formula is good for a large number of packs? Explain your answer.

Q20a hint
Use a two-step function machine to help you work out the formula.

5a

21 **Real** A company charges £35 per child and £40 per adult to go coasteering.

a Write an expression for the cost for C children to go coasteering.
b Write an expression for the cost for A adults to go coasteering.
c Write a formula to work out the total amount of money the company takes, T, when you know the number of children, C, and adults, A, who go coasteering.
d Use your formula to work out the value of T when
i $C = 2$ and $A = 6$ ii $C = 5$ and $A = 5$ iii $C = 10$ and $A = 4$

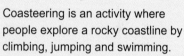

Q21 Literacy hint
Coasteering is an activity where people explore a rocky coastline by climbing, jumping and swimming.

5a

Investigation Problem-solving

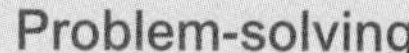

Sian enters these numbers into cells **A1** to **A10** in a spreadsheet.
1, 4, 2, 4, 3, 4, 5, 5, 8, 4

1 Work out the number that each of these formulae represents.
a **=SUM(A1:A10)**
b **=AVERAGE(A1:A10)**
c **=MODE(A1:A10)**
d **=SQRT(A2*A3*A9)**

2 Write down a different formula that you could use to give the same answer as
a **=A5+A6+A7**
b **=A4+A4+A4+A4**
c **=A3+A3+A9+A9**

25 **Reflect** What kinds of jobs involve using formulae?
What careers are you interested in? Do you think you will need to use formulae in your job? How?
What professionals are you likely to meet who might use formulae in their work?

Reflect

3 Unit test

4c **1** Work out the outputs of each function machines.

a

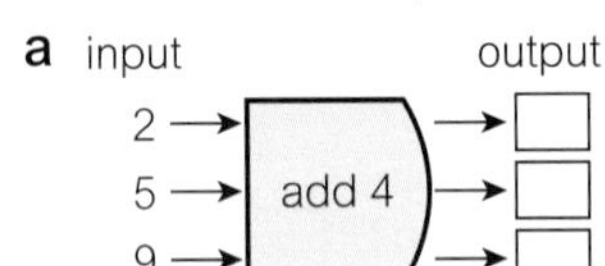

b

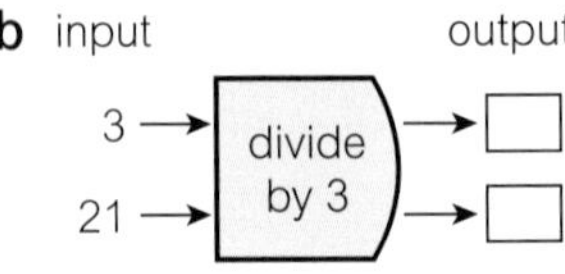

4b **2** Write the function for this machine.

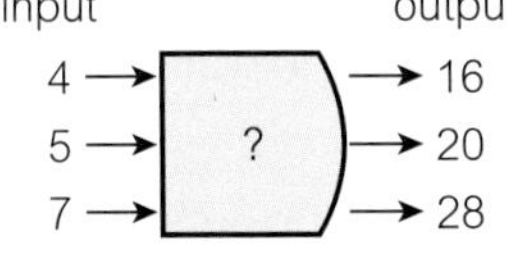

4b **3** Work out the outputs of each two-step function machine.

a

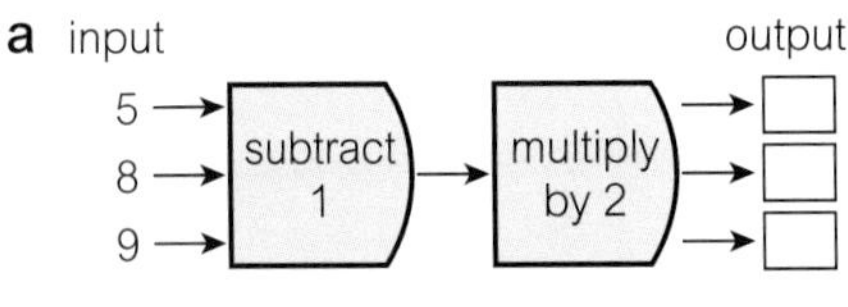

b

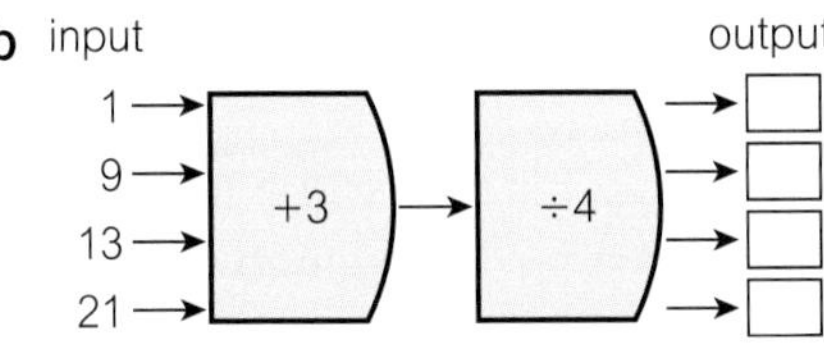

4a **4** I think of a number. I multiply it by 4 and then subtract 2. The answer is 14.
What number am I thinking of?

4a **5** Susan charges £8 per person to provide food at birthday parties.
Here are the parties that have already been booked.

16th birthday party 20 people
18th birthday party 50 people
21st birthday party 30 people

Draw a function machine to show how much she charges for each party.

4a **6** Simplify

a $x + x + x$ **b** $4m + 3m$ **c** $2q - q$ **d** $5a + 8a - a$

4a **7** Work out $4 \times (30 + 2)$.

4a **8** The cost of using broadband in a hotel is £3 per hour.
The formula to work out the total cost is

cost in pounds = 3 × number of hours

Work out the total cost of using broadband for

a 2 hours **b** 5 hours.

5c **9** Alex can think of three different ways of using function machines to change 5 into 20.
Work out the missing numbers.

a 5 → +? → 20

b

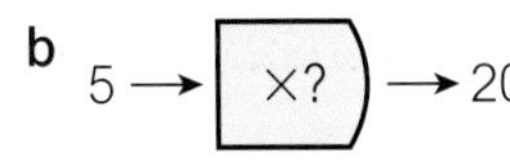

c

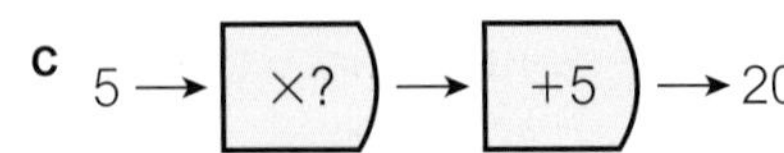

5c **10** Simplify

a $4 \times y$ **b** $z \times 8$ **c** $m \times n$ **d** $c \times b$

11 Simplify these expressions.

a $8a + 12 - 8 + 7b$ b $9a + 8b + 5a - 2b - 4$ 5c

12 Bryn is b years old. Jez is 2 years older than Bryn. Helen is 5 years younger than Bryn. 5c

Write an expression for

a Jez's age b Helen's age.

13 Every day, a butcher makes 30 more sausages than have been ordered by customers. 5c

Write a formula to work out the number of sausages made, S, when you know the number ordered, R.

14 A tutor is paid £20 per hour. 5b

Write a formula to work out the total she is paid, T, when you know the number of hours she works, h.

15 Use the formula $M = fd$ to work out the value of M when $f = 5$ and $d = 12$. 5b

16 Simplify these expressions. 5b

a $6 \times 3a$ b $4b \times 9$ c $24c \div 6$

17 Multiply out the brackets. 5b

a $4(x + 2)$ b $5(4 + 3y)$ c $2(z - 6)$

18 Write an expression for 5b

a 5 times m

b the sum of m and n

c the product of m and n.

19 Amy uses blue and yellow thread to make friendship bracelets. 5b

She uses b cm of blue thread and y cm of yellow thread.

Write a formula to work out the total length of thread, T, in centimetres.

20 I think of a number. I square it and then divide by 10. 5a

The answer is 3.6.

What number am I thinking of?

Challenge

21 Here are seven formulae cards.

$F = 2G + 4$	$B = 4G$	$D = A + 3$	
$C = E \div 10$	$E = AD$	$G = D - A$	$H = 5C + F$

a Work out the value of H when $A = 5$.

b Write down the order in which you used the formulae in part **a**.
Could you have used the formulae in a different order?

c Which formula don't you need to use to work out H?

d Write a formula that connects A to H.

Q21a Strategy hint

Sometimes it can be helpful to organise information in a table. Use a table like this one to record the value of each letter as you find it.

A	B	C	D	E	F	G	H
5							

Q21a hint

There is only one formula that you can use first.

22 **Reflect** Look back at the work you have done in this unit. Reflect

Find a question that you could not answer straight away, but that you really tried at, and then answered correctly.

How do you feel when you struggle to answer a maths question?

Write down the strategies you use to overcome your difficulty.

How do you feel when you eventually understand and get the correct answer?

4 Decimals and measures

MASTER

Check P105 | Strengthen P107 | Extend P111 | Test P115

4.1 Decimals and rounding

You will learn to:

- Measure and draw lines to the nearest millimetre
- Write decimals in order of size
- Round decimals to the nearest whole number and to one decimal place
- Round decimals to make estimates and approximations of calculations.

CONFIDENCE

Why learn this? A rounding error meant that Justin Gatlin was briefly credited with a world record of 9.76 s for the 100 m sprint in May 2006. His time of 9.766 s had been rounded down instead of up!

Fluency
Write these decimal numbers in words.

- 1.5
- 0.25
- 32.75

Explore
Which is the most crowded country in the world?

Exercise 4.1

Warm up

1 Round each number to the nearest 10.
   a 47   b 265   c 496

2 Which of the numbers in this list are square numbers?
   12, 25, 55, 36, 64, 18, 99, 81, 9, 48

4c

3 Measure the length of each line. Give your answer
   i in centimetres   ii in millimetres.
   The first one has been done for you.

   a (ruler: 0 cm 1 2 3 4 5 6 7 8 9 10)

   i 6.4 cm   ii 64 mm

   b ______   c ______

4c

4 Draw lines measuring
   a 2.6 cm   b 9.5 cm   c 42 mm

Q4 hint
Make sure you start your line at 0 on your ruler.

4b

5 Write in words the value of the 5 in each of these decimal numbers.
   The first one has been done for you.
   a 12.56 five tenths
   b 0.45
   c 24.445

Key point
Digits after the decimal point represent fractions. You can see the value of each digit in a **place value** table.

H	T	U	•	$\frac{1}{10}$	$\frac{1}{100}$	$\frac{1}{1000}$
		0	•	1		
		0	•	0	1	
		0	•	0	0	1

$0.1 = \frac{1}{10}$ (one tenth)
$0.01 = \frac{1}{100}$ (one hundredth)
$0.001 = \frac{1}{1000}$ (one thousandth)

Topic links: Square roots

Subject links: Geography (Explore)

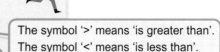

Worked example

Write > or < between each pair of numbers.
5.4 ... 5.38

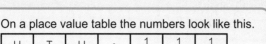

The symbol '>' means 'is greater than'.
The symbol '<' means 'is less than'.

5.4 > 5.38

On a place value table the numbers look like this.

H	T	U	•	$\frac{1}{10}$	$\frac{1}{100}$	$\frac{1}{1000}$
		5	•	4		
		5	•	3	8	

$\frac{4}{10} > \frac{3}{10}$, so 5.4 > 5.38

6 Write > or < between each pair of numbers. 4b

a 1.7 ... 1.4 **b** 3.7 ... 3.86 **c** 10.09 ... 10.9

Discussion What is the easiest way to compare 5.24 and 5.248?

Discussion Sophie says, '9.35 m is greater than 9.5 m, because 35 is greater than 5.' Is Sophie right? Explain.

Q6a hint
Use a place value table or ruler to help you.

7 Write each set of numbers in order of size, starting with the smallest. 4b

a 2.4, 1.8, 3.6, 2.7, 1.2 **b** 8.5, 8.23, 8.57, 8.11, 8.28

8 Round each number to the nearest whole number. 4b
The first one has been done for you.

a 13.72 → 14 **b** 5.3 **c** 18.05

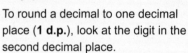

Key point
To round a decimal to the nearest whole number, look at the digit in the first **decimal place**. If the digit is less than 5, round down. If the digit is 5 or more, round up.

9 Round each number to one decimal place. 4a
The first one has been done for you.

a 15.621 → 15.6 (1 d.p.) **b** 4.78
c 23.902 **d** 0.557

Discussion How do you round 7.02 to one decimal place? ... 7.99?

Key point
To round a decimal to one decimal place (**1 d.p.**), look at the digit in the second decimal place.

10 Work out an estimate for each of these by rounding each number. 5b

a 4.7 × 5.2 **b** 8.08 × 3.95 **c** $\sqrt{10.04}$
d $\sqrt{23.8}$ × 4.05 **e** 12.55 ÷ 5.92

Discussion What is the simplest way to round to work out an estimate of 8.45 ÷ 3.06?

Q10a hint
Round 4.7 to the nearest whole number. Round 5.2 to the nearest whole number. Then multiply.

Q10c hint
Round 10.04 to 9 as you can easily work out $\sqrt{9}$.

Investigation **Reasoning**

The list shows the weights of five animals, each rounded to the nearest whole number.

dog 28 kg, cat 7 kg, hamster 138 g, guinea pig 900 g, pig 136 kg

What might the animals' exact weights be? Give two possible answers for each animal.
Explain how you worked out your answers.

11 **Explore** Which is the most crowded country in the world?
Is it easier to explore this question now you have completed the lesson?
What further information do you need to be able to answer this?

12 **Reflect** In this lesson you were rounding and estimating.
Are rounding and estimating the same thing or different? Explain.
Could rounding and estimating be useful in other subjects?

Explore

Reflect

4.2 Length, mass and capacity

You will learn to:
- Convert measurements into the same units to compare them
- Solve simple problems involving units of measurement in the context of length
- Convert between metric units of length, mass and capacity.

CONFIDENCE

Why learn this? When advertising furniture on auction websites you need to give exact measurements so that the buyer knows it will fit in their house.

Fluency
Divide 100 by each of these numbers.
- 10
- 5
- 4
- 2

Explore
How many people fit in a queue for passport control?

Exercise 4.2

Warm up

1 Work out
a 7 × 10 b 23 × 100 c 18 × 1000

2 Work out
a 80 ÷ 10 b 500 ÷ 100 c 64 000 ÷ 1000

Key point
Metric units of **length** include the **millimetre (mm)**, **centimetre (cm)**, **metre (m)** and **kilometre (km)**.
10 mm = 1 cm, 100 cm = 1 m,
1000 m = 1 km

5c 3 Copy and complete.
a 6 cm = 6 × □ = □mm b 8 m = 8 × □ = □cm
c 9 km = 9 × □ = □m d 400 cm = 400 ÷ □ = □m
e 80 mm = 80 ÷ □ = □cm f 25 000 m = 25 000 ÷ □ = □km

Discussion When you convert between units, how do you know whether to multiply or divide?

Q3a hint
The relationship between cm and mm is 1 cm = 10 mm. So for cm → mm, multiply by 10 (× 10).

5c 4 For each pair of lengths, work out which is shorter.
a 5 m or 400 cm b 300 mm or 15 cm c 6 km or 8000 m

5b 5 Copy and complete.
a 2.5 m = 2.5 × 100 = □cm b 12.5 km = 12.5 × □ = □m
c 88 mm = 88 ÷ □ = □cm d 160 cm = 160 ÷ □ = □m

Q5a hint
Use a place value table to help you. As you are *multiplying* by 100, move every digit 2 places to the *left*.

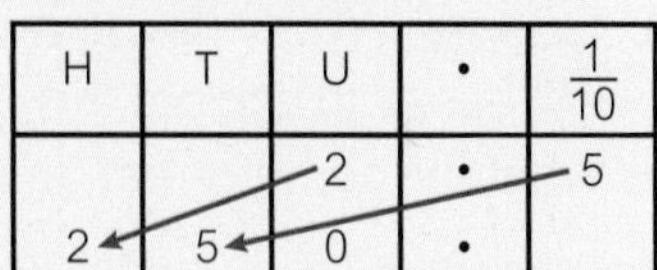

H	T	U	•	$\frac{1}{10}$
		2	•	5
2	5	0	•	

Write a 0 in the units column.

5b 6 Here are the heights (in metres) of five students.
1.54, 1.5, 1.5, 1.55, 1.53
a Write the mode. Give your answer
i in metres
ii in centimetres.
b Work out the median. Give your answer
i in metres
ii in centimetres.

Topic links: Mode, Median, Mean

Subject links: Science (Q7, Q10)

7 STEM / Modelling A boa constrictor is 45 cm long at birth. 5b
This table shows its increase in length over its first 4 years.

End of year	Increase in length
1	70 cm
2	60 cm
3	33 cm
4	13 cm

a Work out the mean increase in length over the first 4 years.
b Use your mean increase in length to estimate the length of a boa constrictor at the end of the 5th year. Give your answer in metres.
c Is the model used in part **b** a good model? Explain your answer.

Key point
Metric units of **mass** include the **gram** (g) and **kilogram** (kg).
1000 g = 1 kg
Metric units of **capacity** include the **millilitre** (ml) and **litre** (l).
1000 ml = 1 l

8 Copy and complete. 5c

a 5 kg = 5 × □ = □ g
b 7 l = 7 × □ = □ ml
c 15 000 ml = 15 000 ÷ □ = □ l
d 6000 g = 6000 ÷ □ = □ kg

Q8 hint
The relationship between kg and g is 1 kg = 1000 g.
So for kg → g, multiply by 1000 (× 1000).
The relationship between ml and l is 1000 ml = 1 l.
So for ml → l, divide by 1000 (÷ 1000).

9 Copy and complete. 5b

a 4.2 kg = 4.2 × □ = □ g
b 0.75 l = 0.75 × □ = □ ml
c 4250 ml = 4250 ÷ □ = □ l
d 875 g = 875 ÷ □ = □ kg

10 STEM A nutmeg has a mass of 10 g. 5b
A nutmeg tree produces 8000 nutmegs a year.
What is the total mass of nutmegs produced by this tree each year?
Give your answer

a in grams
b in kilograms.

11 Problem-solving The diagram shows three jugs full of water. 5b

Using only these jugs, how can you end up with

a 2500 ml in the largest jug
b 1750 ml in the largest jug?

Show your working and explain your method.

Q11a Strategy hint
Start by converting the 3 litres into millilitres, so all the units are the same.

12 Explore How many people fit in a queue for passport control?
What have you learned in this lesson to help you answer this question?
What other information do you need?

13 Reflect Look back at Q4.

- For part **a**, did you convert 5 m to cm or 400 cm to m?
- For part **b**, did you convert 300 mm to cm or 15 cm to mm?
- For part **c**, did you convert 6 km to m or 8000 m to km?

How did you decide which measure to convert for each question?
Which is easier – converting smaller measures to larger measures (like cm to m) or converting larger measures to smaller measures (like cm to mm)? Explain.

4.3 Scales and coordinates

You will learn to:
- Read scales on a range of measuring equipment
- Interpret the display of a calculator in different contexts
- Interpret metric measures displayed on a calculator
- Plot and read coordinates in all four quadrants.

CONFIDENCE

Why learn this? When selling on auction websites you have to know the mass of an item to be able to estimate the postage cost.

Fluency
Write down the coordinates of the points A and B on this coordinate grid.

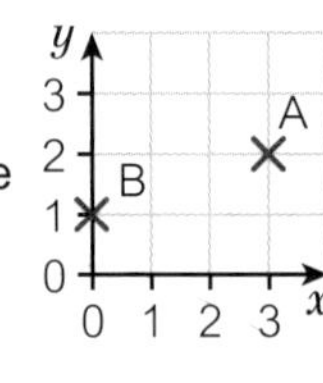

Explore
Motocross riders typically set their front tyre pressure to 12 psi and their rear tyre pressure to 13 psi. How do you think they need to change the pressures when riding on muddy or rocky ground, or when taking part in a high-speed desert competition?

Exercise 4.3

Warm up

1 Work out
- a 100 m*l* ÷ 4
- b 10 cm ÷ 10
- c 100 g ÷ 5
- d 1000 g ÷ 4

2 Which temperature is colder, −10 °C or −18 °C?

Worked example

Write the value the arrow is pointing to.

kg 0 ↑ 2

The arrow is pointing to 1.5 kg.

There are 4 divisions between 0 kg and 2 kg.
2 kg ÷ 4 divisions = 0.5 kg for each division

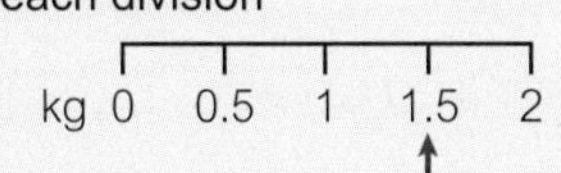

4a

3 Write the number each arrow is pointing to.

a
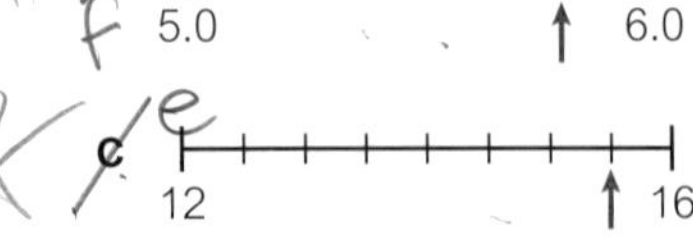

b 50 ↑ 60

c
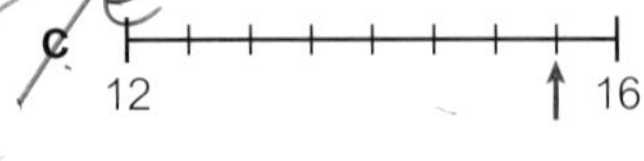

4a

4 **STEM** Write the value shown on each scale.

a
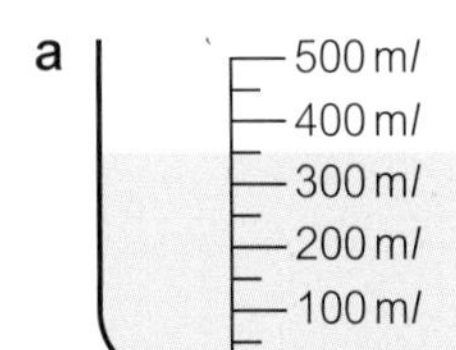

b
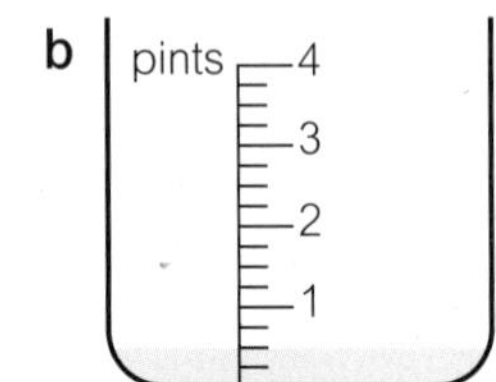

c
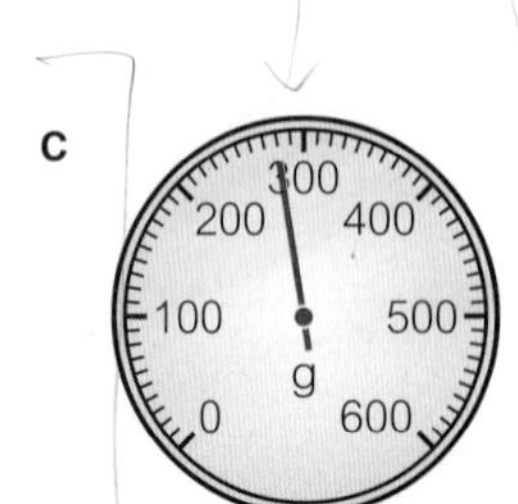

Topic links: Negative numbers, Time

Subject links: Science (Q4)

5 a Write the value shown on the speedometer. 4a
b Draw a speedometer with arrows on it to show
i 40 mph ii 58 mph iii 35 mph

6 **Real** An industrial freezer needs to be kept at a constant temperature of −22 °C. 4a
The thermometer shows the temperature inside an industrial freezer.

a Is this freezer at the correct temperature?

b What is the correct temperature of a freezer in °F?

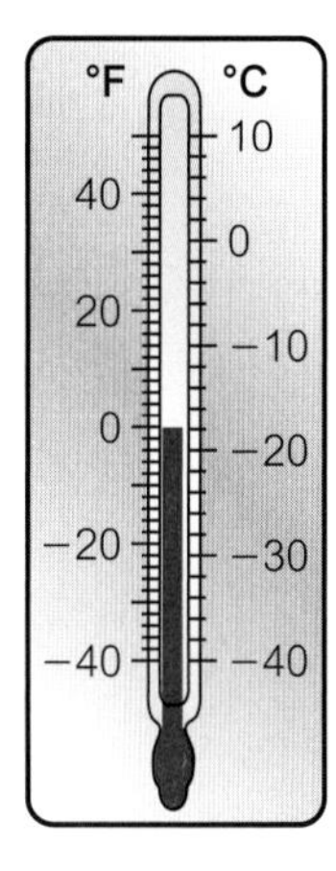

7 Use a calculator to work these out. 4a
Make sure you write the units with your answers.

a 25 × £3.16
b 6 × 19p
c 7.5 cm × 11
d 3.04 m × 8

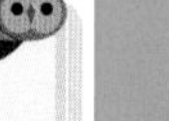

Key point

When you use a calculator to solve problems involving measures, make sure you understand the result on the calculator display. The result 9.5 can mean different things.

- If you are working with money in pounds, it means £9.50.
- If you are working with time in minutes, it means 9 minutes 30 seconds.
- If you are working with length in metres, it means 9.5 m or 9 m 50 cm.

8 **Finance** Mr Wilson's house insurance costs £342 for one year. 4a
He pays equal amounts each month.
How much does he pay each month?

9 Andy works out the answer, in metres, to a problem. 5b
The calculator display shows 12.4
Which of these statements are correct?

A The answer is 12 m 4 cm.
B The answer is 12.4 m.
C The answer is 12 m 400 cm.
D The answer is 12 m 40 cm.

Worked example

Write down the coordinates of points A, B, C and D.

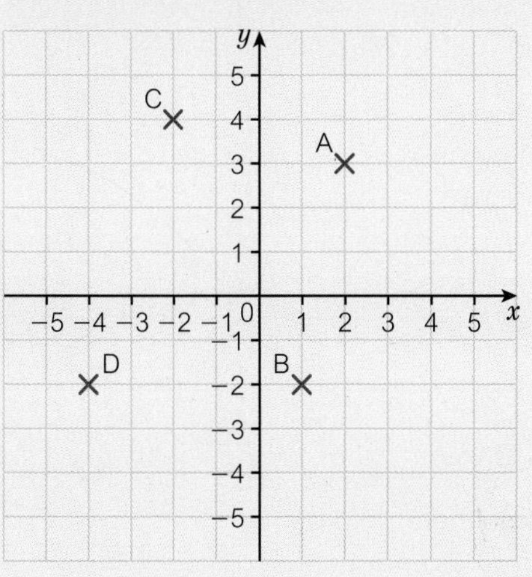

A(2, 3), B(1, −2), C(−2, 4), D(−4, −2)

Look at each point in turn. Move left or right along the x-axis to find the x-coordinate. Move up or down the y-axis to find the y-coordinate.

Key point

The x**-axis** is the horizontal axis.
The y**-axis** is the vertical axis.

5a

10 a Write the coordinates of points A, B, C and D.

Tim says that point E has coordinates (−2, 0). He is wrong.

b What are the coordinates of this point?

What mistake has Tim made?

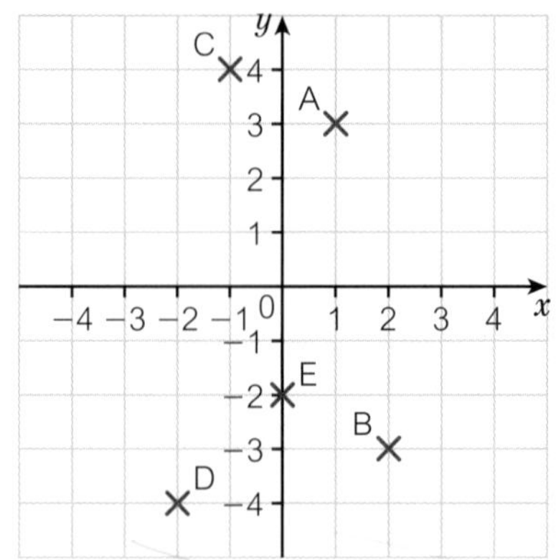

5a

11 Write the coordinates of points A, B, C, D and E.

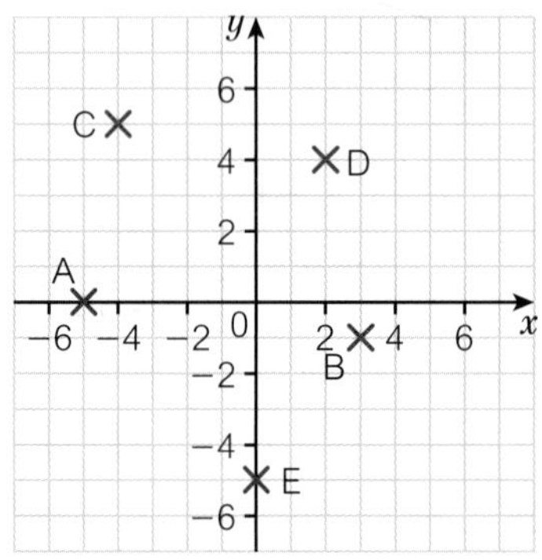

5a

12 Write the coordinates of points A, B, C, D and E.

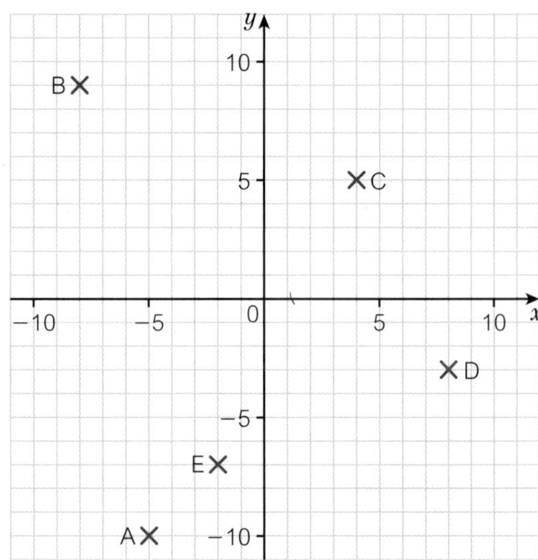

Explore

13 Explore Motocross riders typically set their front tyre pressure to 12 psi and their rear tyre pressure to 13 psi.
How do you think they need to change the pressures when riding on muddy or rocky ground, or when taking part in a high-speed desert competition?
Is it easier to explore this question now you have completed the lesson?
What further information do you need to be able to answer this?

Reflect

14 Reflect Look back at Q3, Q4, Q5 and Q6, about reading scales.
Write the steps you took to read the scales.
Make sure you include every step.
You may begin with, 'Step 1: I looked at the values on the scale either side of the arrow or marker.'
What maths operations (addition, subtraction, multiplication, or division) did you use?

4.4 Working with decimals mentally

You will learn to:

- Multiply decimals mentally
- Check a result by considering whether it is of the right order of magnitude
- Understand where to position the decimal point by considering equivalent calculations.

CONFIDENCE

Why learn this? When you go abroad on holiday, it is useful to be able to work out prices in British pounds.

Fluency
What are the missing numbers?

- 32 ÷ 10 = □
- 6 ÷ □ = 0.06
- □ ÷ 100 = 7.2

Explore
Sometimes a platform is too short for a train, and the driver cannot safely open all the carriage doors to allow passengers off. How long does a platform need to be for different size carriages?

Exercise 4.4

Warm up

1 Copy and complete these multiplications.
  a 4 × 20 = 4 × 2 × 10 = 8 × 10 =
  b 6 × 300 = 6 × 3 × 100 =

2 Copy and complete these multiplications using partitioning.
  a 3 × 23 = 3 × 20 + 3 × 3 = □ + □ = □
  b 8 × 26 = □ × □ + □ × □ = □ + □ = □

Worked example

Work out 4 × 0.2

4 × 0.2 = 4 × 2 ÷ 10 — 0.2 = 2 ÷ 10
= 8 ÷ 10 = 0.8

Key point
You can use multiplication facts to work out decimal multiplications.

4b

3 Use a mental method to work out
  a 2 × 0.2 b 0.7 × 8 c 7 × 0.05 d 0.01 × 9

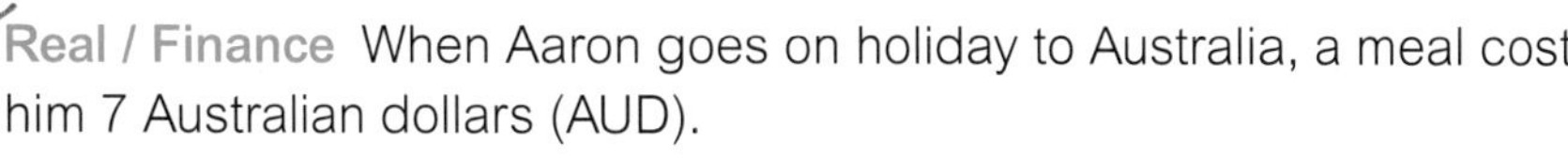

Discussion Does 0.5 × 0.8 = 0.4?

4b

4 **Real / Finance** When Aaron goes on holiday to Australia, a meal costs him 7 Australian dollars (AUD).
1 Australian dollar (AUD) is worth 0.6 British pounds (GBP).
How much does the meal cost Aaron in GBP?

Q4 hint
1 AUD = 0.6 GBP
7 AUD = 7 × 0.6 GBP

Worked example

Work out 24 × 7.5

24 × 7.5 = 12 × 2 × 7.5 — Halve of 24 is 12
= 12 × 15
= 6 × 2 × 15 — Keep doubling and halving until you reach a calculation you can do in your head.
= 6 × 30
= 180

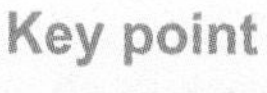

Key point
You can also use **doubling and halving** to work out decimal multiplications.

5c **5** Use doubling and halving to work out

a 8 × 3.5 **b** 6 × 7.5 **c** 4.5 × 16

Discussion To work out 3.6 × 50, which number is it better to halve?

5c **6** **Real** One ounce is approximately 28 grams.
Work out the number of grams in 2.5 ounces using doubling and halving.

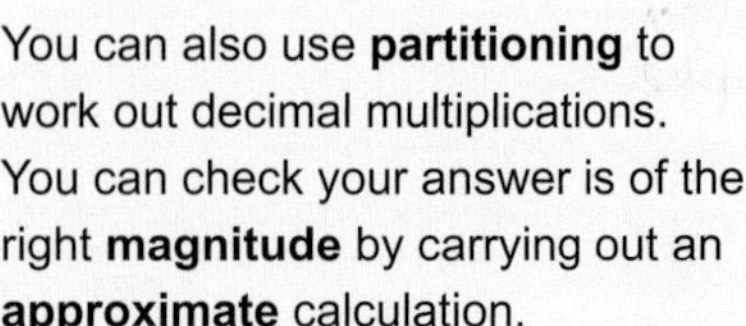

Key point

You can also use **partitioning** to work out decimal multiplications. You can check your answer is of the right **magnitude** by carrying out an **approximate** calculation.

5a **7** Copy and complete these multiplications. Check each answer.
The first one has been done for you.

a 22 × 3.4 = 20 × 3.4 + 2 × 3.4 = 68 + 6.8 = 74.8
Check: 22 ≈ 20, 3.4 ≈ 3.5, 20 × 3.5 = 70 ✓

b 38 × 1.2 = □ × 1.2 + □ × 1.2 = □ + □ = □

c 18 × 4.1 = □ × 4.1 + □ × 4.1 = □ + □ = □

Q7 Literacy hint

≈ means 'approximately equal to'.

5a **8** **Real / Finance** The exchange rate for pounds to US dollars is £1 to $1.6.
Use **partitioning** to work out how many US dollars you get for £42.
Show how you checked your answer.

5a **9** **STEM** In one tonne of ore there is 6.5 g of gold.
A dump truck carries 64 tonnes of ore.
Use partitioning to work out how much gold is in the dump truck.
Show how you checked your answer.

5a **10** 0.63 × 25 = 15.75
Use this fact to work out these. Check your answers are approximately correct.

a 6.3 × 25 **b** 0.63 × 2.5 **c** 0.063 × 0.25

Q10a hint

0.63 has changed to 6.3
6.3 = 0.63 × 10
So 6.3 × 25 = 15.75 × 10 = □

5a **11** **Problem-solving / Reasoning**

a David says, '7.4 × 0.28 is approximately 21.'
Without working out the answer, explain why David is wrong.

b Donna knows that 8.4 × 0.17 = 1.428
She says, 'It's easy to work out 0.84 × 1.7 = 1.428'
Explain how Donna can easily work this out.

Investigation **Reasoning**

Here is a number pattern.

0.3 × 1.1 = 0.33 3.3 × 1.1 = 3.63 33.3 × 1.1 = 36.63 333.3 × 1.1 = 366.63

1 Use the number pattern to write down the answer to 3333.3 × 1.1.
2 Write down the first four lines of a similar number pattern starting 0.3 × 0.11.
3 What is the answer to 3.333 × 1.1? Explain how you worked out your answer.

Explore **12** **Explore** Sometimes a platform is too short for a train, and the driver cannot safely open all the carriage doors to allow passengers off. How long does a platform need to be for different size carriages?
Is it easier to explore this question now you have completed the lesson? What further information do you need to be able to answer this?

Reflect **13** **Reflect** In this lesson you have learned three methods to help you multiply decimals mentally: multiplication facts doubling and halving partitioning
For each method, make up your own calculation to show how it works.
Work out the answer to each of your calculations. Show your working.
Explain how you chose the numbers for your calculations.

4.5 Working with decimals

You will learn to:

- Add and subtract decimals.
- Multiply and divide decimals by single-digit whole numbers.

CONFIDENCE

Why learn this? When you are given a restaurant bill, you can use division to share the cost equally between friends.

Fluency
Divide each number by 7.
- 6300
- 630
- 63

Explore
How much change from £20 would you have after buying yourself a Chinese takeaway?

Exercise 4.5

Warm up

1 Work out
a 67 + 58 b 245 + 39 c 302 − 86

2 Work out
a 48 × 6 b 8 × 234 c 65 ÷ 5 d 144 ÷ 3

Worked example

Use the column method to work out 39.82 − 8.54.
Use an estimate to check your answer.

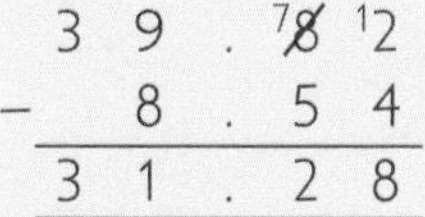

Line up the decimal points first.

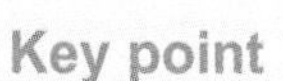

Check by rounding 39.8 to 40 and 8.5 to 9, then subtracting.

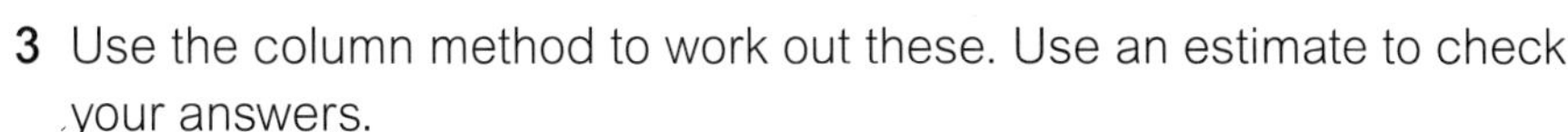

Check: 39.82 ≈ 40 and 8.54 ≈ 9, 40 − 9 = 31, 31.28 is close to 31.

Key point
You can use a **zero place holder** when adding or subtracting decimals with different numbers of decimal places. For example, write 45.9 − 23.45 as 45.90 − 23.45.

3 Use the column method to work out these. Use an estimate to check your answers. 4b
a 4.78 + 9.53 b 34.51 + 23.66 + 145.32 c 21.9 − 7.4

4 Real Craig is a plumber. He has 7.45 m of tubing. He uses 3.75 m of the tubing. How much tubing does he have left over? 4b

5 Use the column method to work out these. Use an estimate to check your answers. 5a
a 4.52 + 8.6 b 19.8 + 2.45 c 45.82 − 1.5
d 8.9 − 6.76 e 7.654 + 9.86 f 32.679 − 4.837

Discussion What is the easiest way to subtract a decimal from 1, for example 1 − 0.6 or 1 − 0.45?

5b

6 **Real** Faisal is looking for wood to make a shelter. He finds a 3 m tree branch lying on the ground.
He cuts a 1.1 m piece and a 0.76 m piece from the branch.
Each of his two saw cuts uses 0.002 m.
What length is left over?

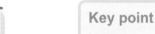

Worked example

Work out 5.6 × 4
Use an estimate to check your answer.

$$\begin{array}{r} 5\ 6 \\ \times\quad 4 \\ \hline 2\ 2\ 4 \\ \hline {}_{2}\quad \end{array}$$

56 × 4 = 224
5.6 × 4 = 22.4
Check: 5.6 ≈ 6, 6 × 4 = 24
22.4 is close to 24

Ignore the decimal point and work out 56 × 4.
56 ÷ 10 = 5.6, so work out 224 ÷ 10 to get the final answer.

Key point
You can use the column method to multiply a decimal by a whole number.

5b

7 Use column multiplication to work out these. Use an estimate to check your answers.
a 3.2 × 7 b 8 × 8.12 c 3 × 23.45

5b

8 **Real** Flexible LED party lights cost £3.75 per metre.

What is the cost of 8 m of party lights?

Worked example

Work out 73.5 ÷ 3

$$\begin{array}{r} 2\ \ 4\ .\ 5 \\ 3\overline{)7\ {}^{1}3\ .\ {}^{1}5} \end{array}$$

73.5 ÷ 3 = 24.5

First write the decimal point for the answer above the decimal point in the question. Then divide as normal, starting from the left.

Key point
You can use short or long division to divide a decimal by a whole number.

5a

9 Work out
a 94.4 ÷ 4 b 75.24 ÷ 6 c 283.76 ÷ 8

5a

10 **Problem-solving / Finance** Anna and 5 friends order a meal.

Anna orders:	Chicken Shashlik	£6.75
	Pilau Rice	£1.55
	Garlic Naan	£1.65

The total cost of the meal is £52.50.
Is Anna better off if she pays for her own food or if she pays an equal share of the bill?
Show all your working and explain your answer.

5a

11 **Real** A piece of Christmas tinsel 55.5 cm long is cut into 3 equal length pieces. How long is each piece?

Explore

12 **Explore** How much change from £20 would you have after buying yourself a Chinese takeaway?
What have you learned in this lesson to help you answer this question?
What other information do you need?

13 **Reflect** In this lesson, you added, subtracted, multiplied and divided with decimals.
Which did you find most difficult? What made it most difficult?
Do you need more practice on any kinds of question? If so, which kinds?

Topic links: Column method

4.6 Perimeter

You will learn to:
- Work out the perimeters of shapes
- Solve perimeter problems.

Why learn this?
You need to work out perimeters in all sorts of practical situations, such as working out the amount of fence you need to enclose a space.

Fluency
Work out
- 5 × 4
- 2 × 3 + 2 × 6
- 28 ÷ 4

Explore
How much ribbon is needed to decorate a wedding cake?

CONFIDENCE

Exercise 4.6

Q1 Literacy hint
A **regular polygon** is a straight-sided closed shape with all sides and all angles equal.

1 Name each of these **regular polygons**.

a 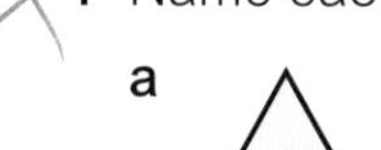
b 
c 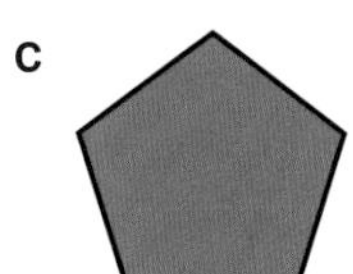
d 
e 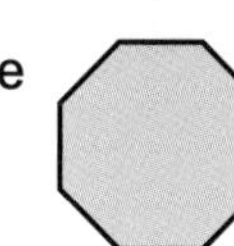

Warm up

2 Work out each side length marked with a □ in these diagrams.

a 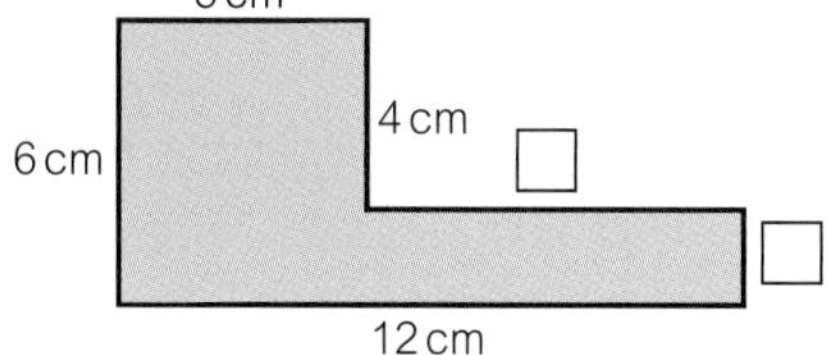

b 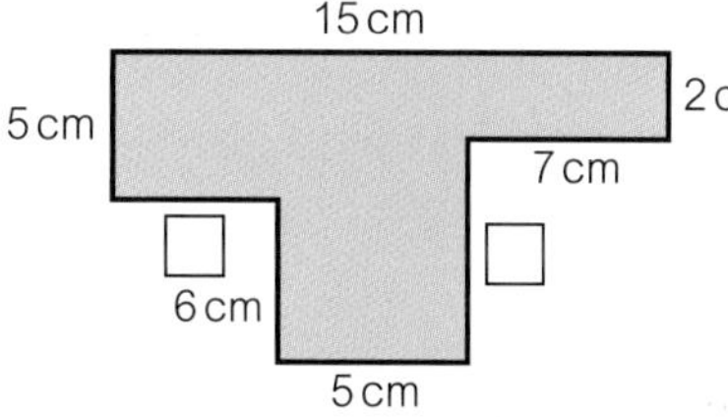

Key point
The **perimeter** is the total distance around the edge of a shape. To work out the perimeter of a shape, add up the lengths of all the sides.

4c

3 Calculate the **perimeter** of each regular polygon using the given side lengths.

a 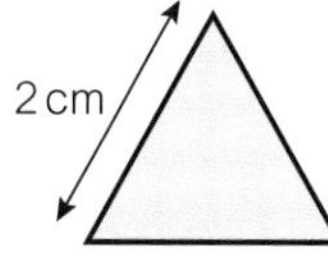

b 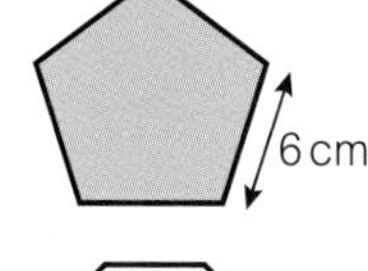

c 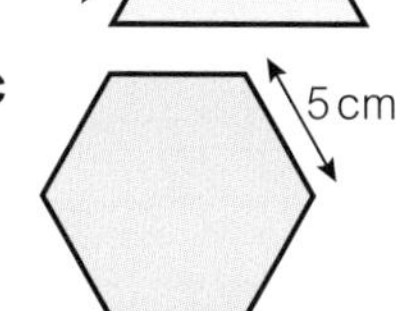

d 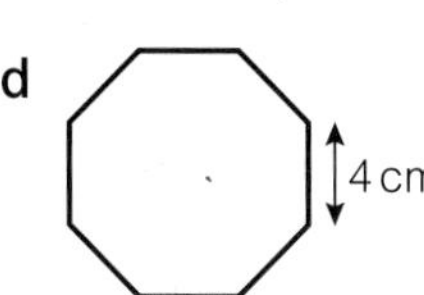

Q3a hint
perimeter = 2 + 2 + 2 = □ cm
It is quicker to multiply the side length by the number of sides.
perimeter = 3 × 2 cm = □ cm

4 This rectangle is drawn on centimetre squared paper.
What is the perimeter of the rectangle in centimetres?

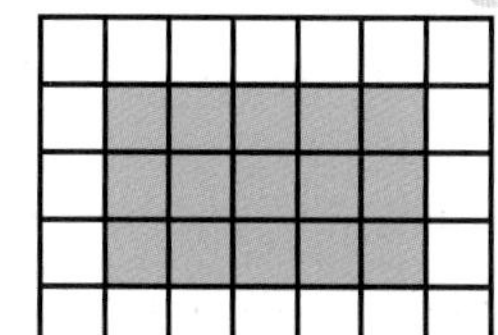

4b

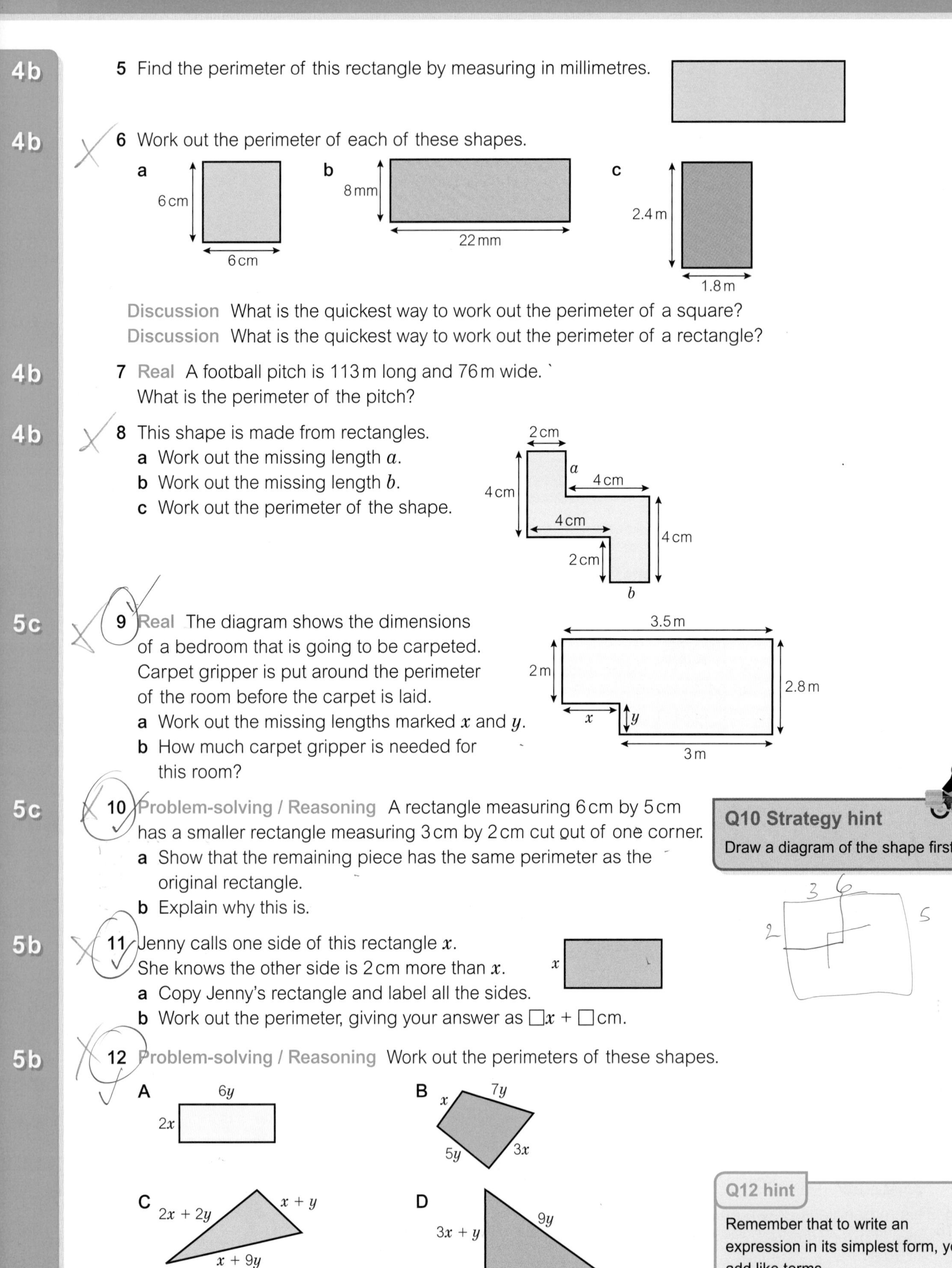

4b 5 Find the perimeter of this rectangle by measuring in millimetres.

4b 6 Work out the perimeter of each of these shapes.

a

b

c

Discussion What is the quickest way to work out the perimeter of a square?

Discussion What is the quickest way to work out the perimeter of a rectangle?

4b 7 **Real** A football pitch is 113 m long and 76 m wide.
What is the perimeter of the pitch?

4b 8 This shape is made from rectangles.

a Work out the missing length a.

b Work out the missing length b.

c Work out the perimeter of the shape.

5c 9 **Real** The diagram shows the dimensions of a bedroom that is going to be carpeted. Carpet gripper is put around the perimeter of the room before the carpet is laid.

a Work out the missing lengths marked x and y.

b How much carpet gripper is needed for this room?

5c 10 **Problem-solving / Reasoning** A rectangle measuring 6 cm by 5 cm has a smaller rectangle measuring 3 cm by 2 cm cut out of one corner.

a Show that the remaining piece has the same perimeter as the original rectangle.

b Explain why this is.

Q10 Strategy hint

Draw a diagram of the shape first.

5b 11 Jenny calls one side of this rectangle x.
She knows the other side is 2 cm more than x.

a Copy Jenny's rectangle and label all the sides.

b Work out the perimeter, giving your answer as $\square x + \square$ cm.

5b 12 **Problem-solving / Reasoning** Work out the perimeters of these shapes.

A

B

C

D

Which is the odd one out? Explain the method you used.

Q12 hint

Remember that to write an expression in its simplest form, you add like terms.

Worked example

A regular hexagon has perimeter 42 cm.
What is the side length of the hexagon?

$42 \div 6 = 7$ cm

All six sides of a regular hexagon are the same length, so divide 42 by 6 to work out the length of each side.

13 Each shape in a set of regular polygons has perimeter 24 cm.
Copy and complete the table.

Number of sides	3	4		8		24
Side length (cm)			4		2	

Q13 hint
For a regular polygon side length = perimeter ÷ number of sides

14 **a** A regular hexagon has perimeter 32.4 cm.
What is the length of each side?
b A regular octagon has perimeter 73.6 cm.
What is the length of each side?

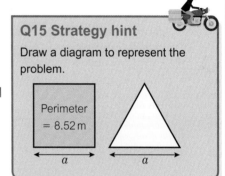

Q15 Strategy hint
Draw a diagram to represent the problem.

Perimeter = 8.52 m

a a

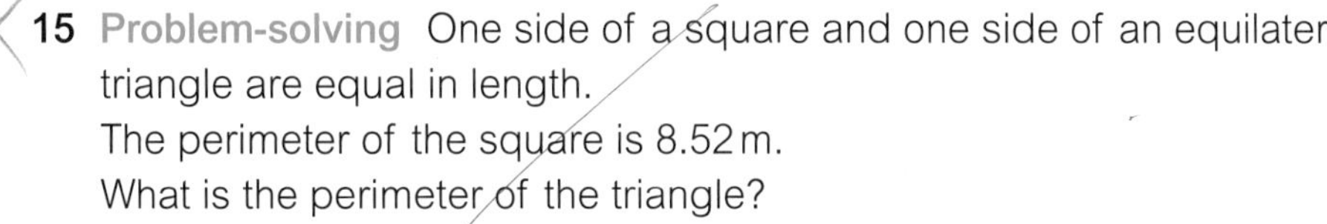

15 **Problem-solving** One side of a square and one side of an equilateral triangle are equal in length.
The perimeter of the square is 8.52 m.
What is the perimeter of the triangle?

16 **Real / Reasoning** Engineers sometimes measure the dimension of the river bed that is in contact with water.
This is called the 'wetted perimeter'. They can measure it using a heavy chain or rope.
The red lines show the chain lowered into a river.

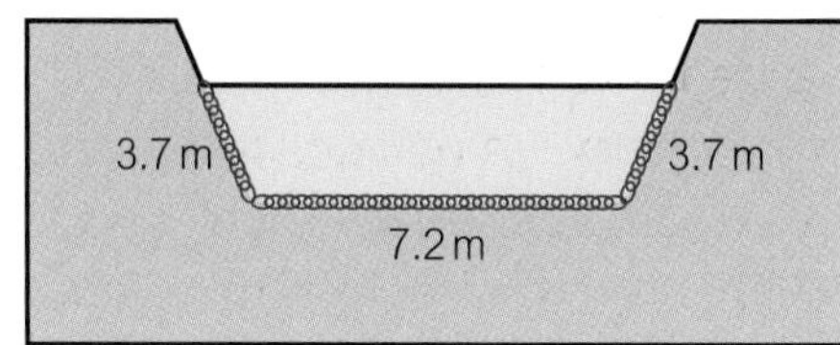

a What is the wetted perimeter at this point on this river?
b Is the wetted perimeter the same as the mathematical perimeter of a shape? Explain.

Investigation

1 On a piece of centimetre squared paper, shade in a shape made from eight squares. Here are two exaples.
Rule 1: Your shape must be made from whole numbers of squares
Rule 2: All the squares must touch side to side, not corner to corner.

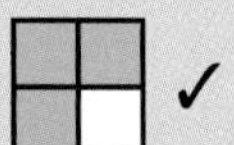 ✓ 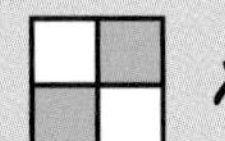 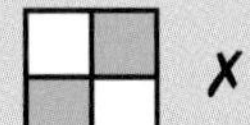 ✗

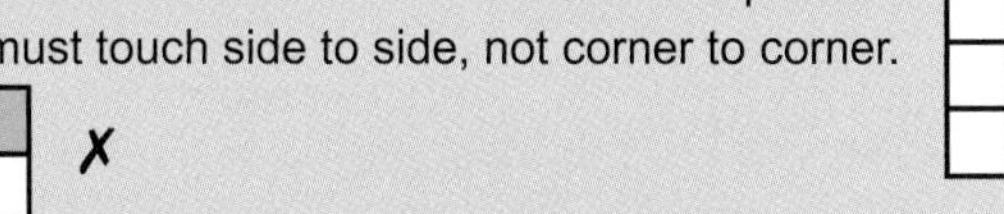
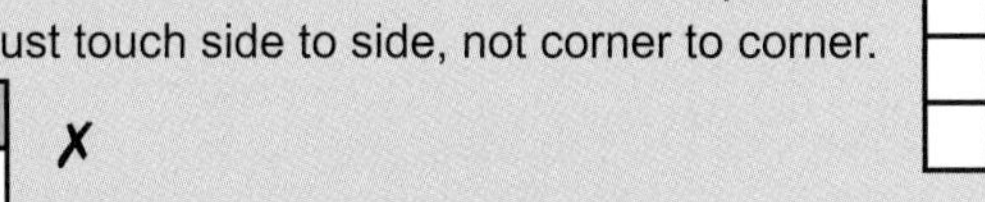

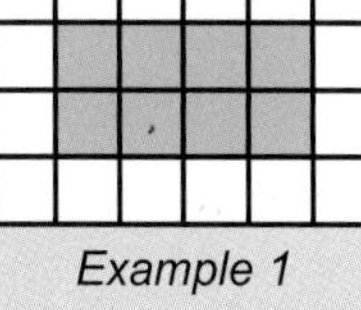
Example 1

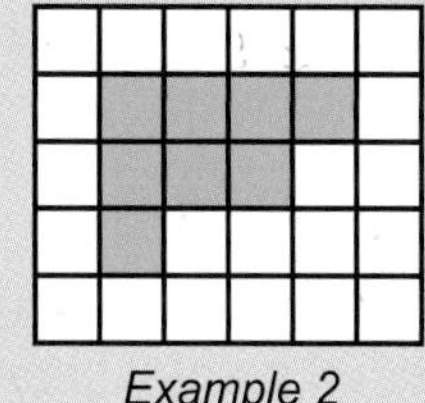
Example 2

2 Work out the perimeter of your shape in centimetres.
3 Try other shapes made from eight squares and work out the perimeter of each one.
4 Which shape has the largest perimeter and which shape has the smallest perimeter?

Discussion Compare your shapes with other people in your class.
Who has drawn the shape with the largest perimeter? ... the smallest perimeter?

17 **Explore** How much ribbon is needed to decorate a wedding cake?
What have you learned in this lesson to help you answer this question?
What other information do you need?

18 **Reflect** In this lesson, the strategy hints suggest that you draw a diagram.
Why is this a good strategy for working out the perimeter of a shape?
What other kinds of diagrams have you used to help you do maths?

4.7 Area

You will learn to:
- Find areas by counting squares
- Calculate the areas of squares and rectangles
- Calculate the areas of shapes made from rectangles
- Solve problems involving area.

CONFIDENCE

Why learn this? The grounds staff of a football stadium use area to work out the amount of turf needed for a new pitch.

Fluency
- What is 2^2 4^2 6^2
- What is the square root of each of these numbers?
  9 100 25 49 16
- Work out
  9×8 8×6 7×9

Explore
How much paint would you need to repaint the walls of your classroom?

Exercise 4.7

Warm up

1 Work out the perimeter of each shape.

a
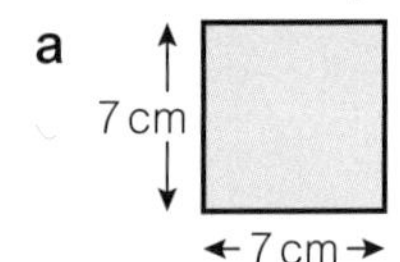

b
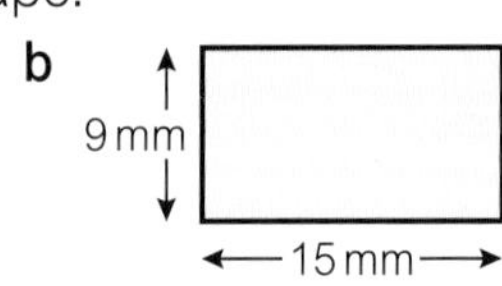

2 Simplify
a $5 \times y$ b $2x \times 4$ c $3y \times 3$ d $0.5 \times 18x$

4c

3 Find the area of each shape by counting squares. Give the units.

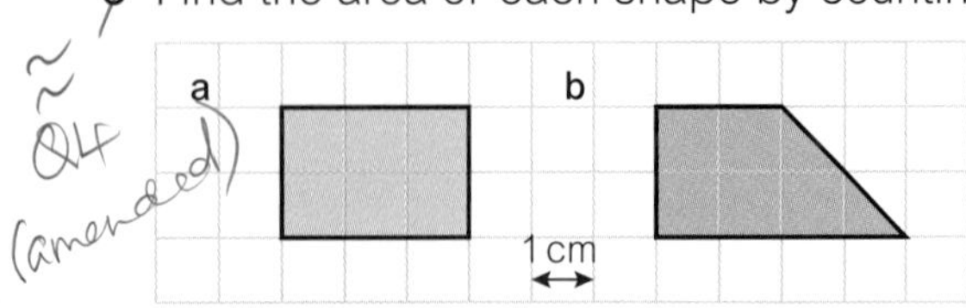

4c

4 a Draw three different rectangles on centimetre squared paper.
Label them A, B and C.
Find the area of each rectangle by counting squares.

b Write the measurements for each rectangle in a table like this one.

Rectangle	Length (cm)	Width (cm)	Area (cm^2)
A			

c What do you notice about the relationship between the length, width and area of each rectangle?

5 Which of these rectangles have area 16 cm^2?

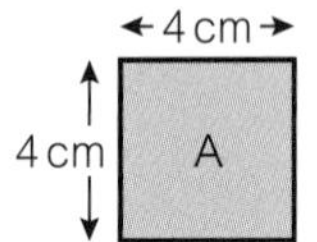

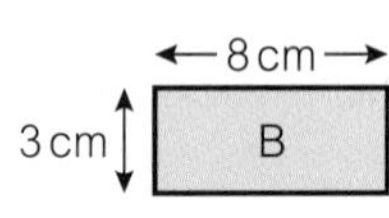

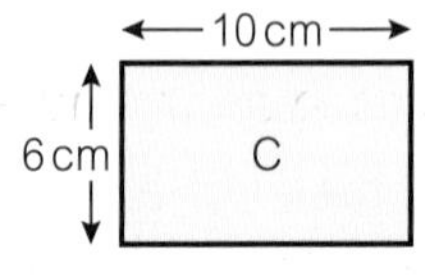

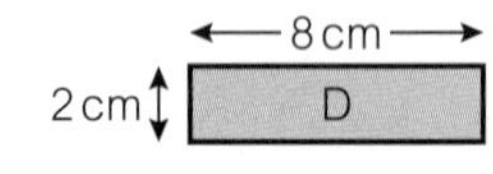

Key point
You can find the **area** of a shape drawn on squared paper by counting the squares inside it.
The **units** used for area are square units, such as mm^2, cm^2, m^2 and km^2.
A square 1 cm by 1 cm has area 1 cm^2.

Q4 Literacy hint
Read cm^2 as 'square centimetres'.

Key point
To work out the area of a rectangle or square, use
area = length × width
The length and the width must be in the same units.

Topic links: Expressions, Formulae, Square numbers, Square roots

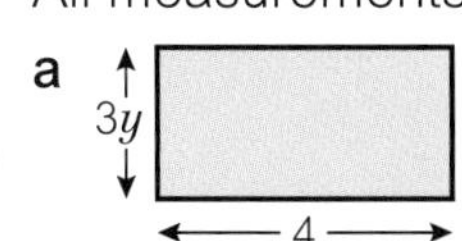

6 Work out the area of each rectangle. Write each answer in its simplest form. All measurements are in centimetres. **4a**

a $3y$ by 4 **b** $0.5w$ by 12

7 Copy and complete the workings to find the area of this shape. **5b**

area A = 5 × 3 = 15 cm²

area B = 8 × 7 = □ cm²

total area = area A + area B

= 15 + □

= □ cm²

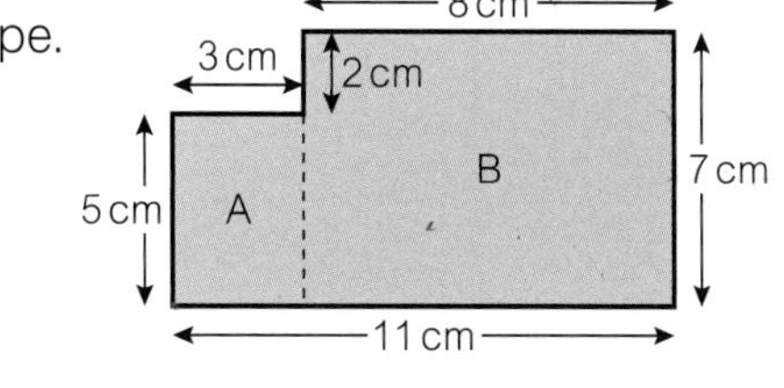

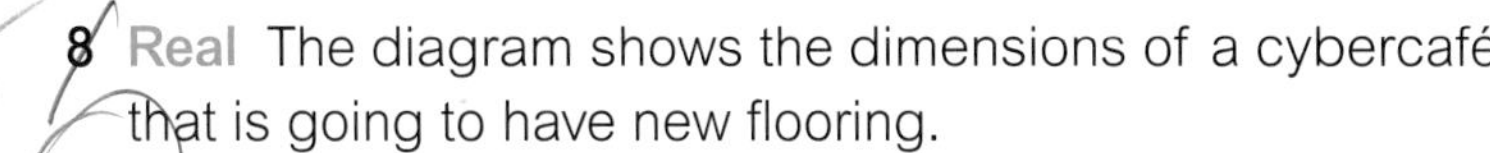

8 Real The diagram shows the dimensions of a cybercafé that is going to have new flooring. **5b**

a Work out each missing length marked with a □.

b Work out the area of flooring required.

c Discussion How many different ways are there to work out the area of the floor?

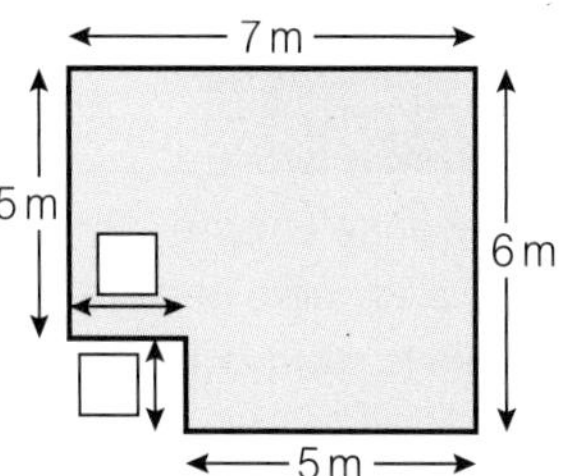

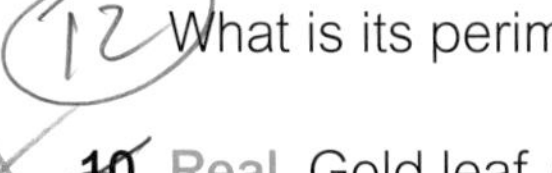

9 Problem-solving A square has area 81 cm². What is its perimeter? **5b**

Q9 Strategy hint

Start by finding the side length of the square.

10 Real Gold leaf can be bought in 8 cm square sheets. There are 25 sheets in one booklet. **5b**

a Work out the total area that can be covered using one booklet of gold leaf.

b Aiden needs to cover an area of 5000 cm² with gold leaf. How many booklets of gold leaf does Aiden need to buy?

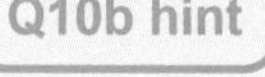

Q10b hint

He can only buy whole numbers of booklets.

Investigation

1 For each parallelogram, A, B and C

a draw the parallelogram on centimetre squared paper and cut it out

b cut along the dotted line

c arrange the pieces into a rectangle and work out the area of the rectangle.

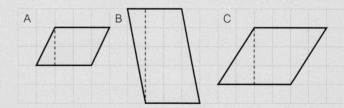

A B C

2 Copy and complete the formula for the area of a parallelogram.

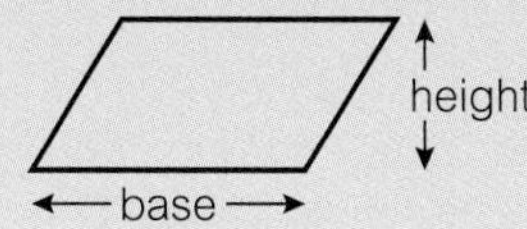

Area = ...

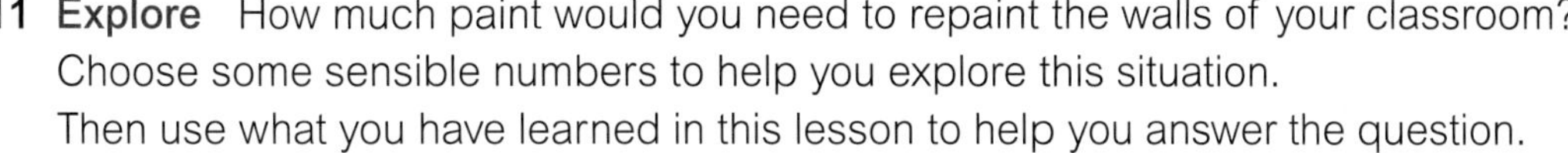

11 Explore How much paint would you need to repaint the walls of your classroom? Choose some sensible numbers to help you explore this situation. Then use what you have learned in this lesson to help you answer the question.

12 Reflect Here is a list of some jobs where you have to calculate and use area: estate agent, gardener, festival organiser.

Copy the list and write one more job where calculating and using area is important.

Write how you would use area in each job.

What career are you interested in? Do you think you will need to use area in your job? How?

Explore

Reflect

4.8 STEM: More units

You will learn to:
- Choose suitable units to estimate length and area
- Use units of measurement to solve problems
- Use metric and imperial units.

CONFIDENCE

Why learn this? Engineers need to choose appropriate units. US and UK engineers need to understand the units to be able to work together.

Fluency
What is the area of a square with side length
- 5 mm
- 8 cm
- 7 m
- 10 km

Explore
How many people can be safely carried in a lift?

Exercise 4.8: Design and construction

Warm up

1 How many
 a grams in a kilogram
 b centimetres in a metre
 c millilitres in a litre
 d millimetres in a centimetre?

2 Write < or > between each pair of measurements.
 a 0.7 m … 85 cm
 b 230 mm … 9.5 cm
 c 0.05 kg … 400 g
 d 250 ml … 1.5 l

Key point
It is important to be able to choose the most suitable **metric units** for measuring length, capacity and area. The metric units you already know are
Length: mm, cm, m, km
Capacity: ml, l
Area: mm², cm², m², km²

4b 3 Copy and complete these sentences with the most suitable metric units.
 I would use metres to measure the length of a football field.
 a I would use ________________ to measure the length of a bolt.
 b I would use ________________ to measure the capacity of a car fuel tank.

4b 4 Which unit of area would be sensible for measuring these?
 a the area of Wales
 b the area of a mobile phone screen
 c the area of the deck of a container ship

Key point
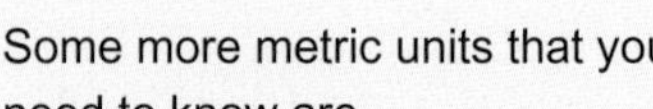
Some more metric units that you need to know are
Mass: 1 tonne (t) = 1000 kg
Area: 1 hectare (ha) = 10 000 m²
Capacity: 1 millilitre (ml) = 1 cm³

4b 5 **STEM** Civil engineers design crash barriers for roads. Each section of crash barrier is 3.5 m long.
 a What is the total length of 20 sections?
 b How many more sections are needed for 700 m?

5b 6 Copy and complete.
 a 3 t = 3 × □ = □ kg
 b 4.6 t = 4.6 × □ = □ kg
 c 5 ha = 5 × □ = □ m²
 d 2 litres = □ ml = □ cm³

Q6 hint
1 t = 1000 kg
So for t → kg, multiply by 1000.

5b 7 Copy and complete.
 a 9000 kg = 9000 ÷ □ = □ t
 b 120 000 m² = 120 000 ÷ □ = □ ha
 c 75 cm³ = □ ml
 d 3500 cm³ = □ ml = □ litres

Q7 hint
For kg → t, divide by 1000 (÷1000)

Topic links: Mean, Range, Using formulae, Area, Imperial measures

8 STEM / Modelling A construction company is building a car park.
The plot of land is a rectangle 300 m long by 150 m wide.

a Work out the area of the land **i** in m^2 **ii** in hectares.

The land costs £16 000 per hectare.

b How much does the land cost in total?

c A standard car park space is 2.4 m by 5 m.
How many spaces fit in this car park?

Discussion Is this a good model? What other space is needed in a car park?

9 STEM A hydro engineer collected data on the smallest and largest amounts of water flowing in a river from 2007 to 2011.

a Work out the mean of the smallest amount of water flowing in the river.

1 tonne of water is the same as 1000 litres.

b Convert your answer from part **a** to litres.

c Work out the range of the largest amount of water flowing in the river in litres.

	Tonnes of water every second	
Year	**Smallest**	**Largest**
2007	7	387
2008	8	893
2009	6	420
2010	5	462
2011	7	614

Q9 hint

Work out the range in tonnes, and then convert the tonnes of water to litres.

10 STEM Automotive engineers calculate the kerb weight of a car by adding the dry weight of the car to the mass of oil, water and petrol a car needs. They also add the mass of a 75 kg driver.
Here is some information about a particular model of car.
dry weight = 915 kg oil = 5 kg water = 5 kg petrol = 40 kg
Calculate the kerb weight of this car in tonnes.

11 Copy and complete.

a 3 ft = 3 × 30 = □ cm

b 150 cm = 150 ÷ 30 = □ ft

c 4 miles = 4 × 1.6 = □ km

d 160 km = 160 ÷ 1.6 = □ miles

Key point

You need know these conversions between metric and **imperial units**.
1 foot (ft) ≈ 30 cm
1 mile ≈ 1.6 km

12 STEM / Real Electric cars typically travel between 50 and 100 miles before they need charging.

a Write this range in kilometres.

b Which method did you use to convert 100 miles to kilometres?

Discussion Will you walk further if you walk 1 mile or 1 kilometre?

13 STEM / Problem-solving / Real This is a formula to estimate how far away a thunderstorm is.
Distance (in km) = time between lightning and thunder (in s) ÷ 3
After a flash of lightning, May counts 24 seconds before the thunder.
How far away is the thunderstorm in miles?

Q13 hint

11	3	10	5	6		9	2	4	5	11	7	1	8
												o	

14 **Explore** How many people can be safely carried in a lift?
Is it easier to explore this question now you have completed the lesson?
What further information do you need to be able to answer this?

15 **Reflect** Write two headings, 'metric' and ' imperial'.
Write down as many different measures as you can under each heading. Do not use this book to help you.
When you were trying to remember all the measures, what were you thinking or imagining?
Discuss your way of remembering with other students. Did anyone have another way you could try?

4 Check up

Units, Scales and coordinates

1 Which number is bigger, 23.45 or 23.8?

2 Write these numbers in order of size, starting with the smallest.
8.9, 8.47, 8.95, 8.3, 8.35

3 Copy and complete.
a 8 cm = □ mm **b** 2 kg = □ g **c** 600 cm = □ m

4 Copy and complete.
a 3.2 m = □ cm **b** 8.7 l = □ ml **c** 2400 m = □ km

5 Asif needs 0.2 pints of water for a recipe.
Has he measured the right amount? Explain.

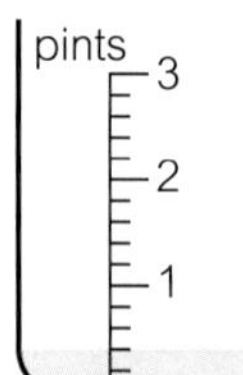

6 Josh says this is the point (−4, 2).
He is incorrect.
What are the coordinates of this point?
What mistake has Josh made?

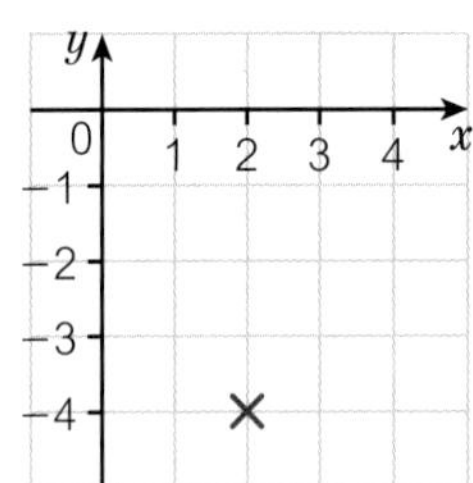

7 **a** Write the coordinates of each point marked with a square.
b Write the coordinates of each point marked with a triangle.

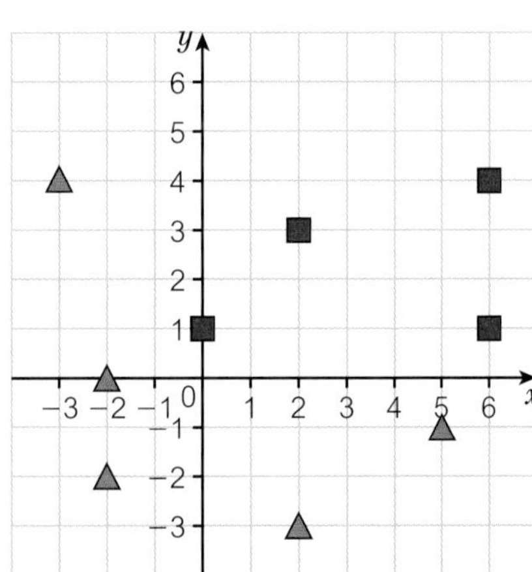

Decimals

8 Work out these. Use an estimate to check your answers.
a 12.6 + 3.9 **b** 32.8 − 17.5

9 A carpenter cuts two pieces of wood from a 3.5 m length of wood.
One piece is 1.4 m. The other piece is 0.85 m long.
a What is the total amount of wood that he cuts from the length?
b How much of the length of wood does he have left over?

10 Work out
a 3 × 0.2 **b** 0.08 × 4

11 Work out these. Use an estimate to check your answers.
a 4.6 × 8 **b** 39.6 ÷ 3

12 A potter uses 2.25 kg of clay per bowl.
How much clay does she use for 5 bowls?

13 The table shows the winning results for some of the men's track and field events in the 2012 Olympic Games. Round each result to one decimal place.

Event	Result
100 m	9.63 s
high jump	2.38 m
hammer throw	80.59 m

14 Sham says, 'If I round 13.96 to one decimal place, I get the answer 14.' Is he correct? Explain your answer.

15 0.27 × 12 = 3.24
Use this fact to work these out. Check your answers using an approximate calculation.
a 2.7 × 12 b 0.27 × 120 c 0.027 × 12

Perimeter and area

16 Calculate the perimeter of this regular hexagon.

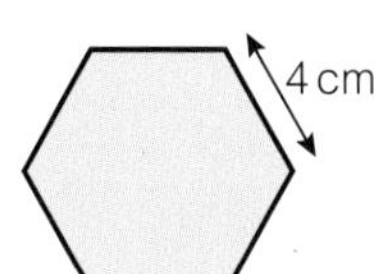

17 Work out the perimeter of each of these shapes.
Write the correct units with your answers.

a 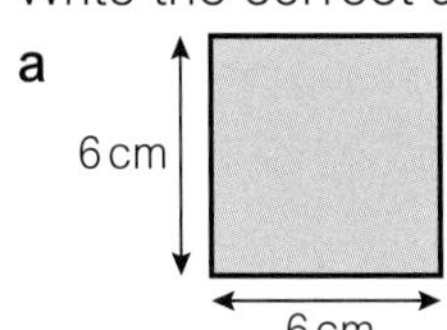

b 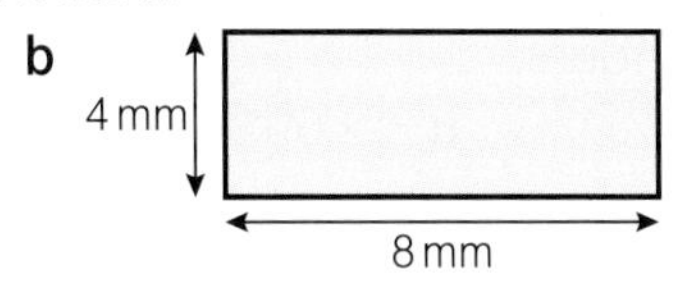

18 Work out the area of each of the shapes in Q17.
Write the correct units with your answers.

19 A square has area 9 m^2. What is its perimeter?

20 The diagram shows the dimensions of an office.
Work out the total floor area of the office.

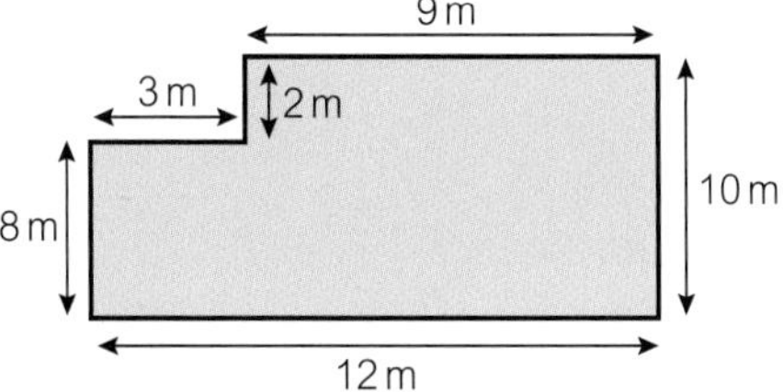

21 How sure are you of your answers? Were you mostly

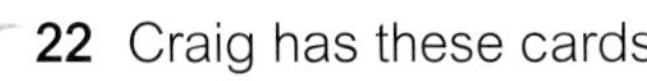

Just guessing **Feeling doubtful** **Confident**

What next? Use your results to decide whether to strengthen or extend your learning.

Challenge

22 Craig has these cards.

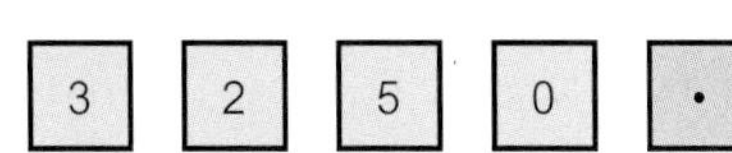

a Make five different decimal numbers.
Use all the cards in each number.
You must place the decimal point between two of the digits.
b Write your five numbers in order of size, starting with the smallest.
c What are the largest and the smallest numbers you can make using all these cards?

23 This rectangle has an area of 24 cm^2.
The length and width of the rectangle are each a whole number of centimetres.

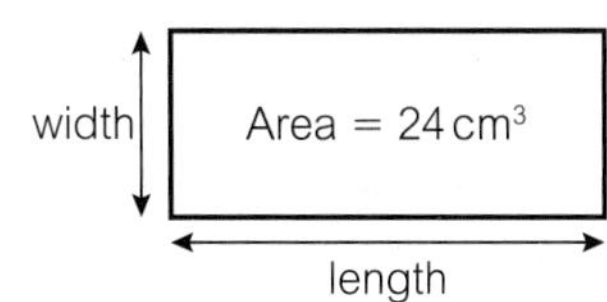

a Write three possible lengths and widths for the rectangle.
b Work out the perimeter of each rectangle you wrote in part **a**.

4 Strengthen

You will:

- Strengthen your understanding with practice.

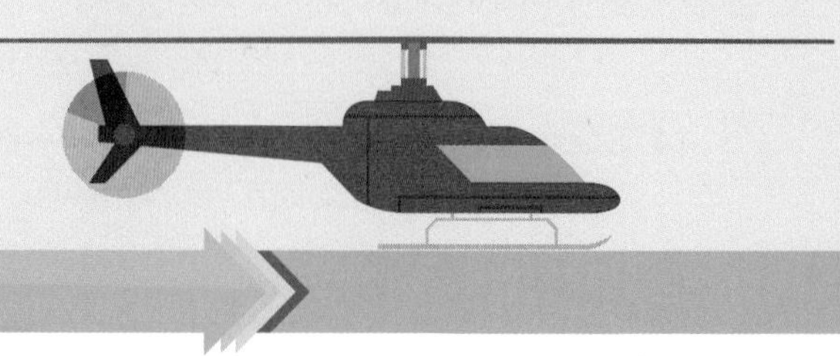

Units, scales and coordinates

4b

1 a Copy this number line. Mark on the line the numbers 4.7 and 4.3. Which is larger, 4.7 or 4.3?

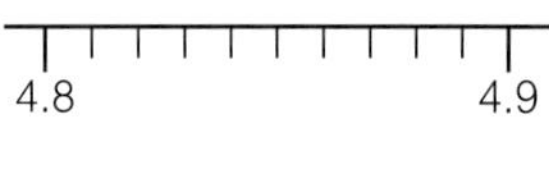

b Copy this number line. Mark on the line the numbers 4.83 and 4.9. Which is larger, 4.83 or 4.9?

Q2a hint

Use a number line to help you.

4b

2 Write > or < between each pair of numbers.

a 2.5 ... 2.3 **b** 5.75 ... 5.68 **c** 12.09 ... 12.9

3 Write each set of numbers in order of size, starting with the smallest.

a 8.6, 7.9, 8.2, 7.1

b 4.6, 4.35, 4.67, 4.33

c 8.251, 8.025, 8.421, 8.007, 8.163

Q3c hint

Use a number line to help you.

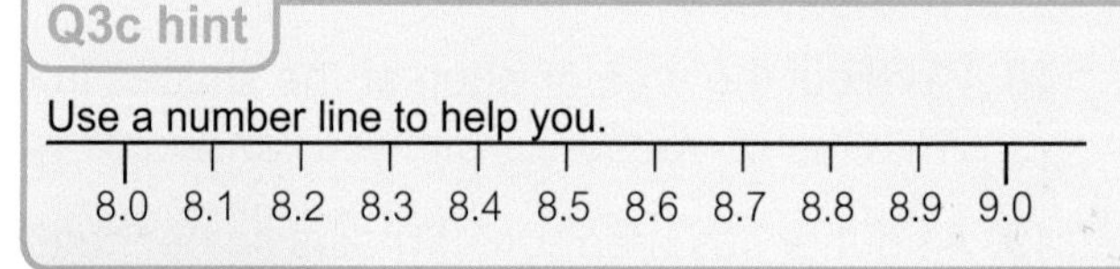

4b

4 Choose any point in the red part on this coordinate grid.

a Does it have a positive or negative x-coordinate?

b Does it have a positive or negative y-coordinate?

c Are your answers to part **a** and **b** the same for *any* point in the red part?

d Answer parts **a** to **c** above for points in

i the blue part

ii the green part

iii the yellow part.

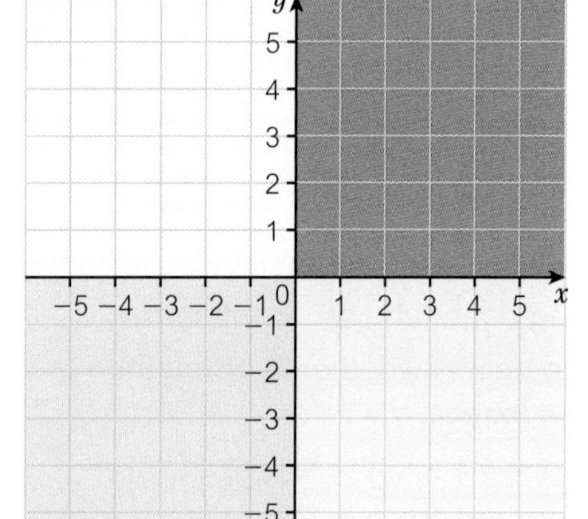

Q4 hint

The x-coordinate tells you the horizontal distance, in the direction of the x-axis.

The y-coordinate tells you the vertical distance, in the direction of the y-axis.

4a

5

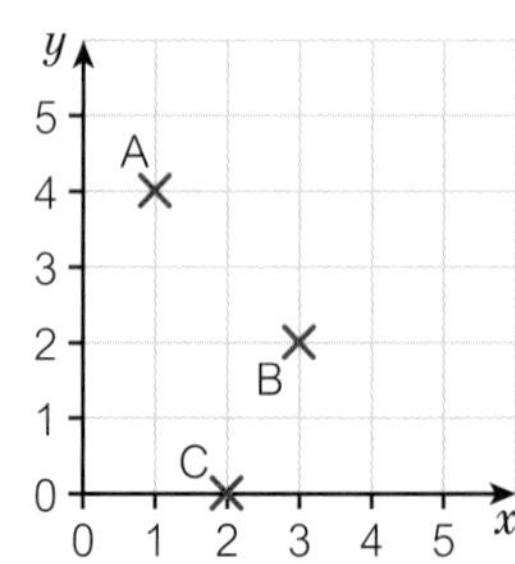

a Write the coordinates of points A, B and C.

b Copy the grid. Plot the points (5, 1), (3, 3), (0, 2) and (4, 0).

6 Copy and complete. 5c

a 1 cm = 10 mm, so 6 cm = □ mm

b 1 m = 100 cm, so 3 m = □ cm

c 10 mm = 1 cm, so 40 mm = □ cm

d 1 km = □ m, so □ km = 5000 m

e 1 kg = □ g, so □ kg = 8000 g

Q6 hint

Use number lines like this to help you.

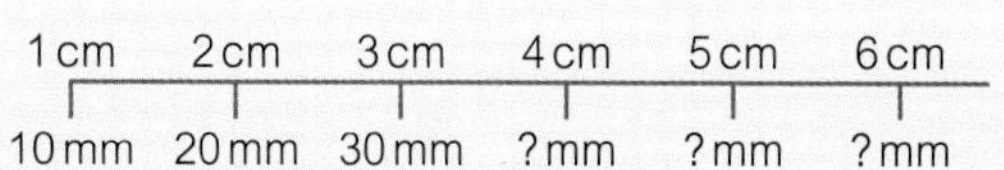

7 Copy and complete. 5b

a 4.6 m = □ cm

b 6.5 *l* = □ m*l*

c 5.25 km = □ m

d 4.8 cm = □ mm

e 0.35 kg = □ g

f 5.8 m = □ cm

Q7a hint

Use number lines like this to help you.

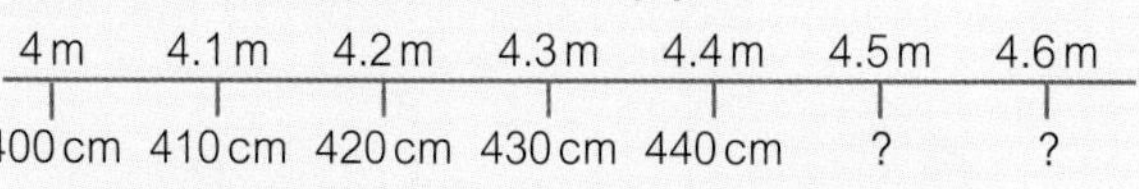

8 Copy and complete. 5b

a 240 cm = □ m

b 3250 m*l* = □ *l*

c 9200 g = □ kg

d 4280 m = □ km

e 56 mm = □ cm

f 54 cm = □ m

Q8 hint

Use number lines like this to help you.

Decimals

1 Work out these additions. Part **a** has been started for you. 4b

a 38.6 + 24.6

```
  3 8 . 6
+ 2 4 . 6
-----------
    3 . 2
-----------
  1 1
```

b 18.58 + 4.67

2 Cosmo buys a tennis racket for £28.65 and some tennis balls for £4.85. What is the total amount he spends? 4b

Q2 hint

Write one number under the other. Line up the decimal points.

3 Work out these subtractions. Part **b** has been started for you. 4b

a 45.9 − 32.7

b 8.71 − 6.38

```
  8 . 6 7 1
− 6 . 3 8
-----------
    .   3
-----------
```

4 Maya cuts 0.55 m of ribbon from a piece that is 1.8 m long. How much of the ribbon does she have left over? 4b

Q4 hint

Write one number under the other, filling empty spaces with zeros.

5 Copy and complete these number patterns. 4b

a 2 × 30 = 60 2 × 3 = 6 2 × 0.3 = 0.6 2 × 0.03 = □

b 5 × 80 = 400 5 × 8 = □ 5 × 0.8 = □ 5 × 0.08 = □

6 Use a mental method and the multiplication facts you know to work out 4b

a 4 × 0.2 b 9 × 0.4 c 0.02 × 3 d 0.08 × 4

Q6a hint

Use a number pattern.

4 × 2 = 8, 4 × 0.2 = □

7 Work out these multiplications. Use an estimate to check your answers. 5b

a 4.6 × 8 b 3.2 × 6 c 7 × 2.25 d 4 × 3.24

8 Work out these divisions. Part **a** has been started for you. 5a

a 37.2 ÷ 3

```
   1 2.□
3)3 7.¹2
```

b 31.2 ÷ 6 c 30.1 ÷ 7

Q7a hint

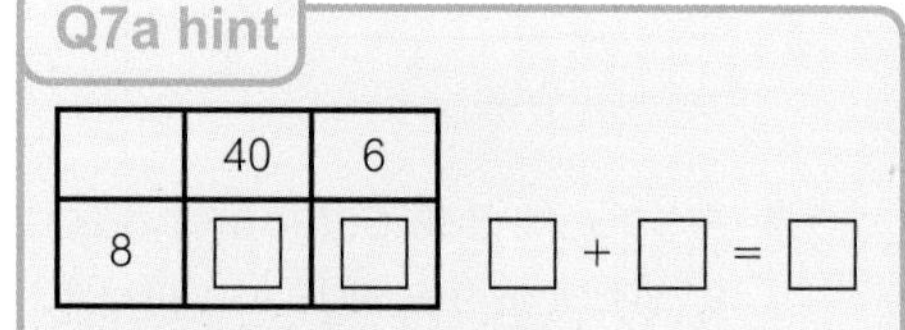

46 × 8 = □, 4.6 × 8 = □

5a **9** Which of these numbers are written to one decimal place?
4.6, 3.24, 0.559, 12.8, 5.25, 0.8, 2.44, 156.0

5a **10** Round each measurement to one decimal place.

a 4.52 m **b** 3.48 m

c 0.25 m **d** 12.98 s

Perimeter and area

4c **1** Calculate the perimeter of each of these regular polygons.

a

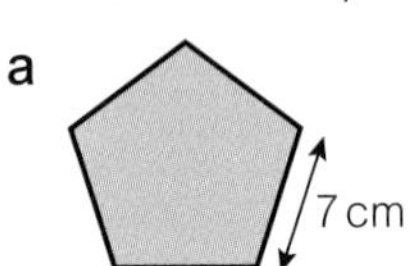

b

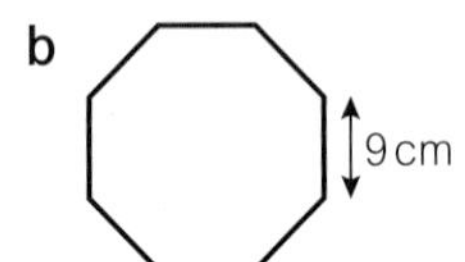

c

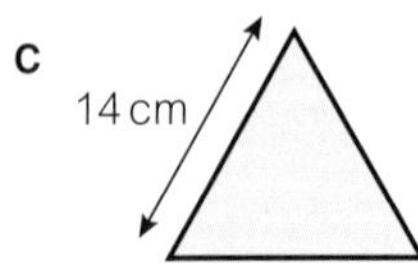

4b **2** Here is a rectangle drawn on a centimetre square grid.

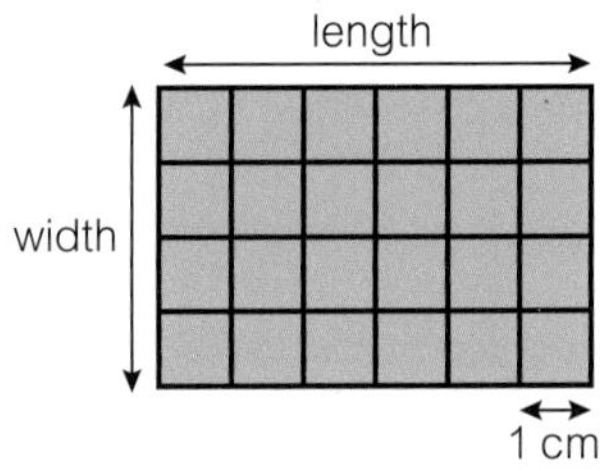

Copy and complete.

a The length of the rectangle = □ cm

b The width of the rectangle = □ cm

c The perimeter of the rectangle = □ cm

d The area of the rectangle = □ cm^2

4a **3** Copy and complete the table showing the perimeter and area of each of these shapes.

A

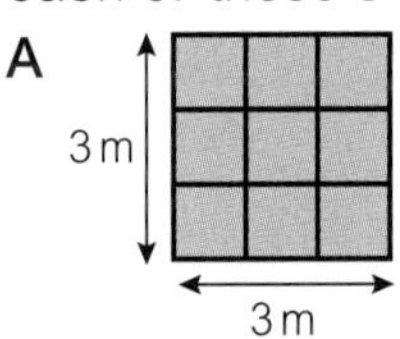

B

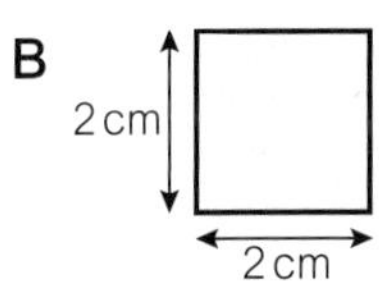

C

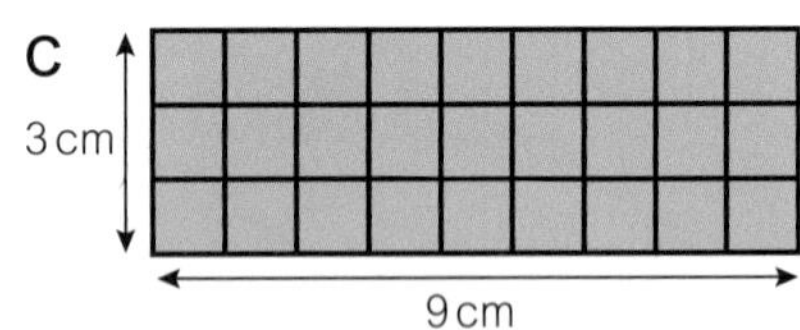

D

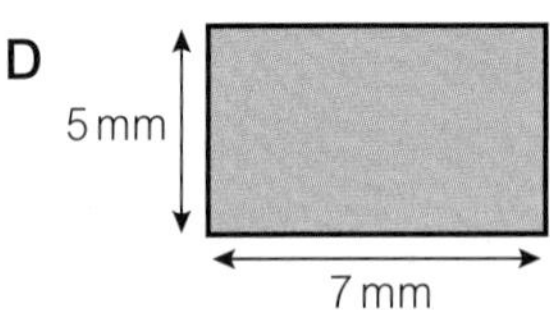

Shape	Perimeter	Units	Area	Units
A	3 + 3 + 3 + 3 = □	m	3 × 3 = □	m^2
B				
C	3 + 9 + 3 + 9 = □	cm	3 × 9 = □	cm^2
D				

4a **4** A square has perimeter 36 cm.

a What is the side length of the square?

b What is the area of the square?

Q9 hint

Which of the numbers have only one digit after the decimal point?

Q10a hint

Is 4.52 m closer to 4.5 m or 4.6 m?

Q1a hint

In a regular polygon all the sides are the same length.
Perimeter = 7 + 7 + 7 + 7 + 7 = 5 × 7 = □ cm

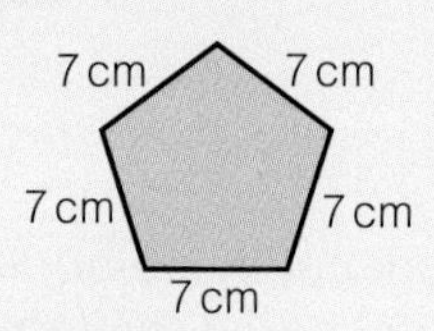

Q2a hint

Count the number of squares along the length.

Q2d hint

Work out the number of squares inside the shape.

Q3 hint

To work out the perimeter, add all the side lengths together.
To work out the area, multiply the length by the width.

Q4a hint

Each side of a square is the same length, so
? + ? + ? + ? = 36
4 × ? = 36

5 Copy and complete the workings to find the area of this shape.

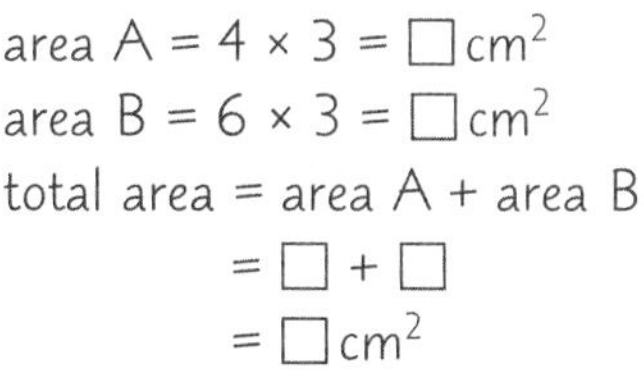

area A = 4 × 3 = □ cm^2
area B = 6 × 3 = □ cm^2
total area = area A + area B
= □ + □
= □ cm^2

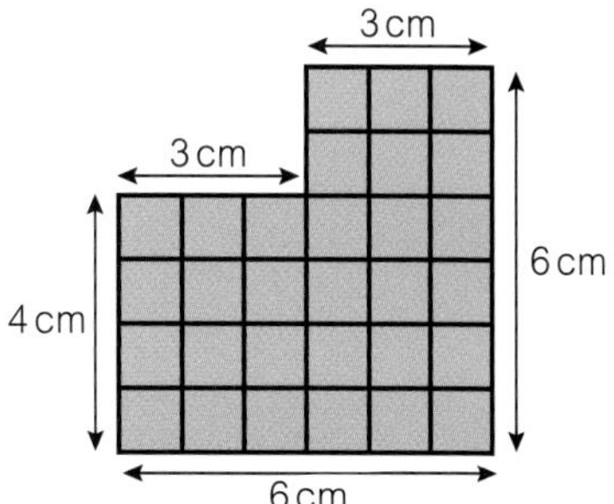

6 Work out the area of this shape.

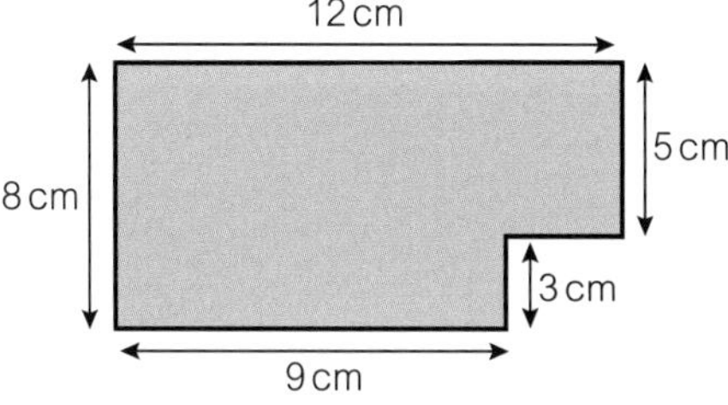

7 This square and rectangle have the same perimeter.

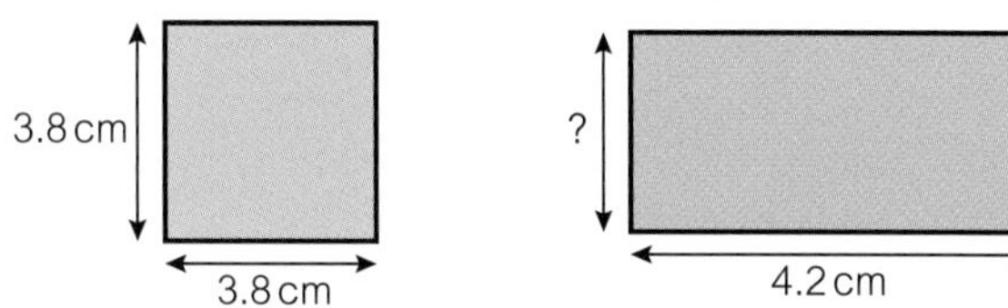

Work out the width of the rectangle.

Q5 hint

Divide the shape into two rectangles and label them A and B.

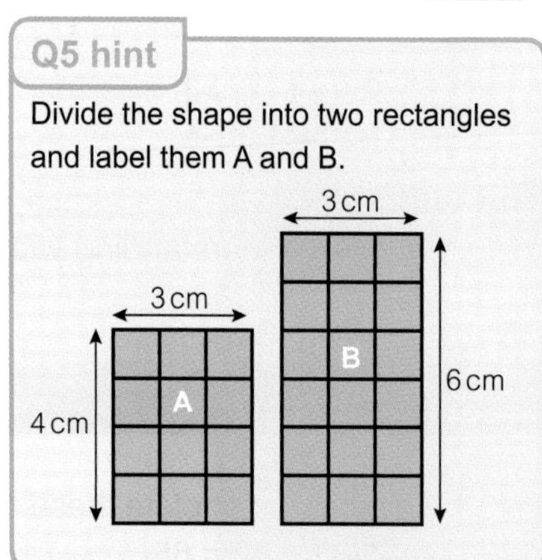

5b

Q6 hint

Divide the shape into two rectangles and label them A and B.

5b

Q7 hint

Work out the perimeter of the square. This is the perimeter of the rectangle too.
What calculation can you do to find the width of the rectangle?

5a

Enrichment

1 STEM When a hedgehog arrives at a rescue centre it is weighed and measured. Staff at the centre work out a Body Index (BI) value for the hedgehog. A hedgehog is well enough to be released when it has a BI value that is greater than 0.8 *and* its weight is greater than 0.65 kg.
The table shows the BI values and weights of some hedgehogs at a rescue centre.

Hedgehog	A	B	C	D	E	F	G	H	I
BI value	0.9	0.82	0.88	0.79	0.95	0.7	0.85	0.76	0.92
Weight (kg)	0.68	0.7	0.78	0.6	0.8	0.58	0.62	0.71	0.85

a Which hedgehogs are well enough to be released?

b Which hedgehog only needs to increase its weight to be released?

c Which hedgehog only needs to increase its BI value to be released?

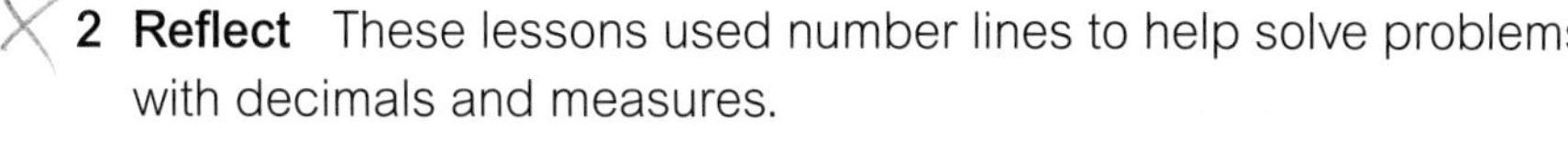

2 **Reflect** These lessons used number lines to help solve problems with decimals and measures.
Did the numbers lines help you? Explain why or why not.
Will you use number lines to help you solve mathematics problems in future? Explain why or why not.

Reflect

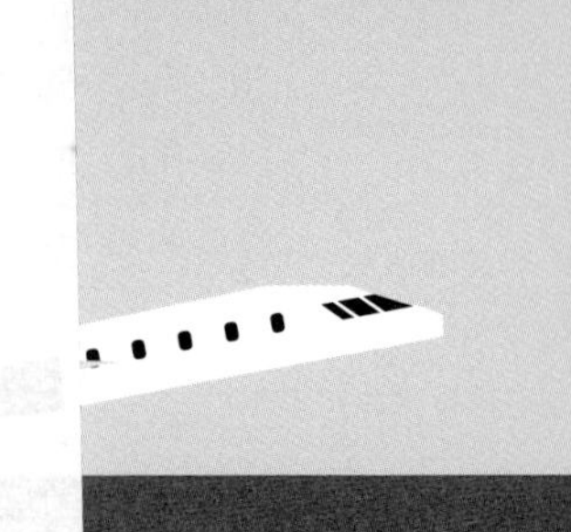

4 Exten

You will:

- Extend your unde

5a **1** Copy and con

a 2080 ÷ 32 =

208 ÷ 32 =

20.8 ÷ 32 = …

2.08 ÷ 32 = □

0.208 ÷ 32 = □

714 ÷ 0.84 = 850

714 ÷ 0.084 = □

714 ÷ 0.0084 = □

5a **2** 150 ÷ 2.5 = 60

Use this fact to work out these.

Check your answers using an approximate calculation.

a 15 ÷ 2.5 **b** 1.5 ÷ 2.5

c 1500 ÷ 2.5 **d** 150 ÷ 0.25

e 150 ÷ 0.025 **f** 150 ÷ 25

> **Q2 hint**
> Follow similar number patterns to those in Q1 to help you.

> **Q2a hint**
> Check by estimation: 15 ÷ 3 = □

4c **3** 5.4 × 37 = 199.8

Use this fact to work out these.

Check your answers using an approximate calculation.

a 0.54 × 37 **b** 0.054 × 370

c 54 × 0.37 **d** 199.8 ÷ 37

e 199.8 ÷ 3.7 **f** 19.98 ÷ 3.7

> **Q3d hint**
> Division is the inverse of multiplication.

> **Q3e hint**
> 3.7 = 37 ÷ 10, so the answer will be 10 times bigger than part **d**.

5a **4** The number 12 552 955 can be rounded in different ways.

To the nearest 10 000, it is 12 550 000.

To the nearest 100 000, it is 12 600 000.

To the nearest 1 000 000, it is 13 000 000.

Round the number 23 628 541 to the nearest

a 10 000 **b** 100 000

c 1 000 000 **d** 10 000 000

> **Q4a hint**
> 23 628 541
> 8 is greater than 5, so round the 2 up to a 3.

5a **5** **Finance** Amy buys pet insurance for her cat. The cost is £89 per year. She works out the cost per month and gets an answer of £7.41666…

Is the cost per month £7.41 or £7.42, to the nearest penny?

5a **6** **Finance** Fynn compares the costs of holiday insurance from two companies.

Company	Price
Diamond	£11.80 for 7 days
Bell	£1.72 per day

a Work out the cost of insurance per day with Diamond. Give your answer to the nearest penny.

b Which company offers the cheaper rate per day?

Topic links: Mean, Range, Formulae

7 **Real** These are the times recorded by the eight men in the 200 m kayak final at London 2012. 5a

Name	Time (s)
M Beaumont	36.688
S Craviotto Rivero	36.540
M De Jonge	36.657
M Dudas	36.830
E McKeever	36.246
M Novakovic	37.094
R Rauhe	37.553
E Salakhov	36.825

a Write each time correct to two decimal places.

b Who won the gold, silver and bronze medals?

Q7a hint

Look at the 3rd digit after the decimal point in each time to decide whether to round up or down. 36.688 rounds to 36.69.

8 **Modelling** The distances covered by some toy rockets are shown in the tables. 5a

Type A uses an air pump to release the rocket.

Type B uses a bicarbonate of soda reaction to release the rocket.

Distances covered (in metres) by Type A rockets											
6.5	4.7	12.8	0.5	8.1	4.9	7.2	10.9	5.4	2.9	4.5	8.5

Distances covered (in metres) by Type B rockets								
12.5	4.8	10.9	13.4	6.5	9.8	4.6	12.5	9.9

a Work out the mean distance covered for each type. Give your answers correct to two decimal places.

b Sam says, 'On average, the Type B rockets travel about 3 metres further than the Type A rockets.'
Is he correct? Explain your answer.

c One of the Type A rockets didn't work properly. This rocket's distance was removed from the data.

i What is the new mean for Type A rockets?

ii What effect does this new mean have on Sam's statement in part **b**?

d Based on the information you are given on the two types, do you think it is fair to say that Type B rockets go further than Type A rockets? Explain your answer.

9 Draw a grid with the x- and y-axes from −3 to +3. 5a

a Plot the coordinates (−1, −2), (2, −1), (0, 1) and (−3, 0).
Join them up with straight lines in the order they are given. Join the last point to the first one.

b Write down the name of the shape that you have drawn.

10 **Problem-solving** The diagram shows four regular polygons. 5a

The sum of the perimeters of the triangle and hexagon is equal to the sum of the perimeters of the pentagon and square.

Work out the side length of the square.

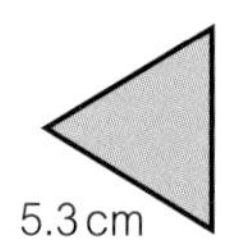

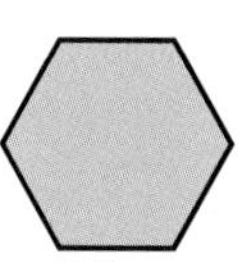

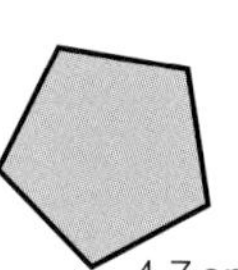

5a **11** A rectangle has length l cm and width w cm.
Jade uses this formula for the perimeter, P, of a rectangle: $P = l + l + w + w$
Nick uses this formula: $P = 2(l + w)$
Show that the two formulae are equivalent.

w cm
l cm

Q11 hint
Expand the brackets in Nick's formula. Simplify Jade's formula.

5a **12** **Real** A beach volleyball court is 16 m long and 8 m wide.
Use a formula from Q11 to work out the length of rope needed to mark out the perimeter of the court.

5a **13** **a** A regular volleyball court has a perimeter of 54 m.
The length of the court is 18 m.
What is the area of the court?

b A rugby pitch has an area of 9800 m^2. The width of the pitch is 70 m.
What is its perimeter?

Q13a hint
Draw a diagram to help you.

5a **14** The Great Pyramid of Giza has a square base.
The perimeter of the base is 921.6 m.
What is the area of the base?
Give your answer to the nearest square metre.

5a **15** A square board game has an area of 2500 cm^2.
What is the perimeter of the board?

5a **16** Give an example to show why each of these statements is wrong.

a The perimeter of a rectangle cannot be an odd number.

b When the length and the width of a rectangle are doubled, the area is also doubled.

c Ignoring the units, the area and the perimeter of a square are always different.

Q16a hint
What if one side is a decimal?

5a **17** For this shape, work out

a the perimeter

b the area.

4 cm
7 cm
5 cm
3 cm
□ □
4 cm
14 cm

Q17 hint
First work out the missing lengths marked with a □.
Add all the lengths to find the perimeter.
Split the shape into three rectangles to work out the area.

5a **18** Work out the area of each of these rectangles.
Write your answers in the units given.
Give your answers to parts **c** and **d** correct to two decimal places.

a 0.6 m, 20 cm, area = □cm^2

b 3 cm 2 mm, 7 mm, area = □mm^2

c 3 m 54 cm, 2.6 m, area = □m^2

d 2.75 m, 85 cm, area = □m^2

Q18 hint
Before you work out the area, convert the lengths to the correct uits.

5a **19** **Finance / Modelling** A 2 km long stretch of road needs to be resurfaced. The width of the road is 8.3 m.

a Model this stretch of road as a rectangle. Work out the area of road that needs to be resurfaced in m^2.

Resurfacing this road costs £30 per square metre.

b What is the total cost to resurface this road?

20 Real / Problem-solving The table shows the heights and lengths of some roller coasters in theme parks around the world.

5a

Roller coaster	Country	Height (feet)	Length (feet)
Kingda Ka	USA	456	3118
Leviathan	Canada	306	5486
Millennium Force	USA	310	6595
Steel Dragon 2000	Japan	318	8133
The Ultimate	UK	107	7442
Tower of Terror II	Australia	377	1235

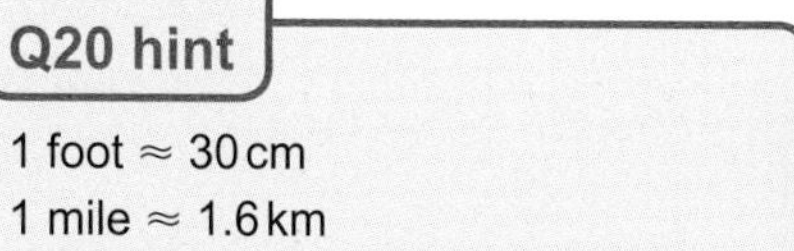

a Work out the height and length of Kingda Ka in metres.

b Which roller coasters are more than 2 km in length?
Give the names of these roller coasters and their length in km, correct to two decimal places.

c What is the range in heights of the six roller coasters, in metres?

d Millennium Force travels at a speed of 150 kilometres per hour.
Steel Dragon 2000 travels at a speed of 95 miles per hour.
Which travels faster? Explain your answer.

21 Real / Problem-solving Chico orders a mat for a giant chessboard set. It is a square of side length 9 feet.

5a

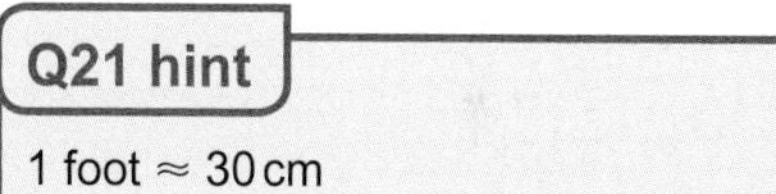

a What is the perimeter of the mat in metres?

b What is the area of the mat in square metres?

There are 64 squares on a chessboard. Half are black and half are white.

c What area of the mat is black?
Give your answer in square metres correct to two decimal places.

d What is the area of one of the squares on the mat?
Give your answer in square metres correct to two decimal places.

Investigation

1 Draw these rectangles on centimetre squared paper and work out their areas.
a 3 cm by 2 cm **b** 30 mm by 20 mm **c** 5 cm by 4 cm **d** 50 mm by 40 mm

2 Draw a 1 cm by 1 cm square.
Copy and complete.
area of 1 cm by 1 cm square = □ cm^2
area of 10 mm by 10 mm square = □ mm^2
1 cm^2 = □ mm^2

3 Use the fact you found in Q2 to copy and complete these conversions.
a 5 cm^2 = □ mm^2 **b** 9 cm^2 = □ mm^2 **c** 4.2 cm^2 = □ mm^2
d 300 mm^2 = □ cm^2 **e** 800 mm^2 = □ cm^2 **f** 360 mm^2 = □ cm^2

4 **a** Use the same method as above to work out the connection between m^2 and cm^2, and between km^2 and m^2.
b Convert some areas in m^2 to cm^2, and some areas in cm^2 to m^2.
c Convert some areas in km^2 to m^2, and some areas in m^2 to km^2.

22 Reflect Write a definition of a decimal, in your own words. Be as accurate as you can.
Remember to explain decimal notation in your definition.
Check your definition against some of the decimal numbers in this unit.
Does your definition fully describe them?

Literacy hint
Mathematical notation means the symbols used in maths. For example, the notation = means 'equals', the notation < means 'less than'.

Reflect

4 Unit test

4c **1** Calculate the perimeter of this square.

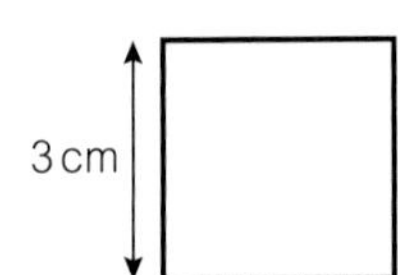

4b **2** Write > or < between each pair of numbers.

a 12.39 ... 12.55 **b** 8.6 ... 8.07 **c** 29.8 ... 29.37

4b **3** Write these numbers in order of size, starting with the smallest.

3.8, 3.85, 3.35, 3.09, 3.3

4b **4** Work out

a 2×0.4 **b** 8×0.3 **c** 0.09×4

4b **5** A recipe for ice cream uses 0.2 litres of cream per person.
How much cream is needed to make ice cream for 8 people?

4b **6** Write the correct units from the box for each of the statements.

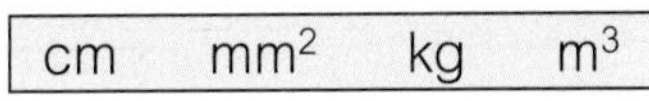

a area of a square = 16□ **b** perimeter of a rectangle = 18□

4a **7** For each shape work out **i** the perimeter **ii** the area.

a

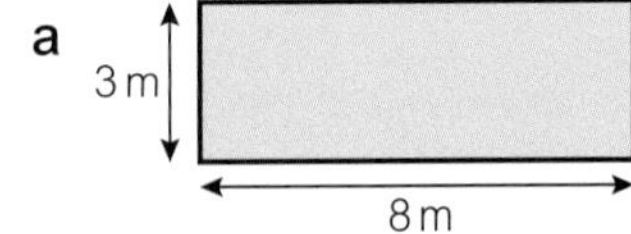

b

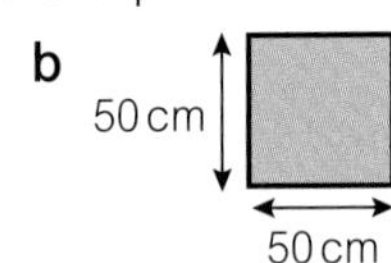

Write the correct units with your answers.

4a **8** Round 55.25 to one decimal place.

4a **9** Olga says, 'If I round 27.02 to one decimal place, I get the answer 27.'
Is she correct? Explain your answer.

5c **10** Copy and complete.

a 800 cm = □m **b** 2 *l* = □m*l* **c** 9000 g = □kg

5b **11** Copy and complete.

a 550 cm = □m **b** 400 g = □kg **c** 4.5 km = □m

5b **12** Dave has a mass of 95.45 kg. Caz has a mass of 62.8 kg.

a What is their total mass?

Dave is 1.8 m tall and Caz is 1.55 m tall.

b What is the difference in their heights?

5b **13** Work out these multiplications.
Use an estimate to check your answers. Show your working.

a 8.7×4 **b** 5×4.23

5b **14** A baker uses 4.32 kg of dough per tray of rolls.
How much dough does he use for 4 trays of rolls?

5b **15** A square has perimeter 20 cm. What is the area of the square?

16 For this shape, work out 5a

a the perimeter

b the area.

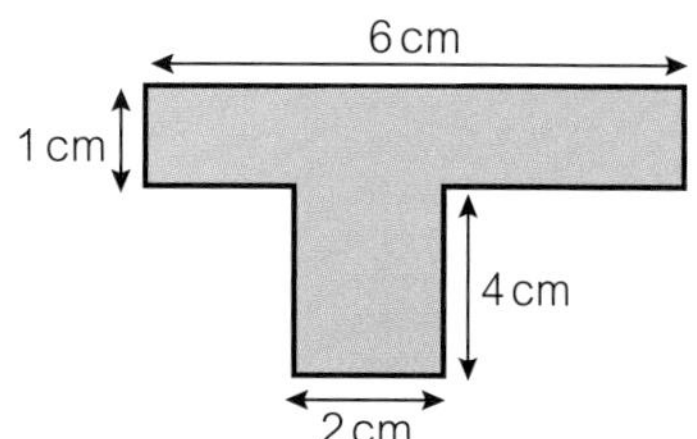

17 Work out these divisions. 5a

a 39.6 ÷ 4 b 84.15 ÷ 3

18 Sammi orders 4 pairs of 3D glasses for his TV. The total cost of the glasses is £139.80. 5a
How much does each pair of 3D glasses cost?

19 $18 \times 4.7 = 84.6$ 5a
Use this fact to work out these. Check your answers using an approximate calculation.

a 18×0.47 b 180×4.7 c 0.18×4.7

20 This square and rectangle have the same perimeter. 5a

a What is the area of the square

i in square millimetres ii in square metres?

b Work out the length of the side of the rectangle marked □.

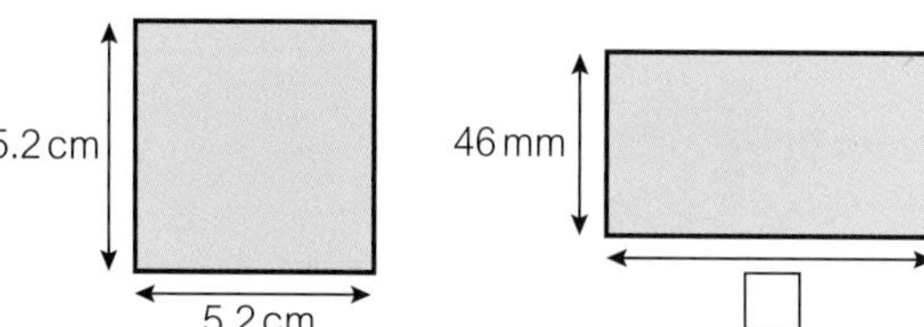

21 Draw a grid with the x- and y-axes from −5 to +5. 5a

a Plot the points A (1, 3), B (0, −2) and C (2, −2). Join them with straight lines. What sort of triangle is this?

b Plot the point D at (−5, −1). Join the points A, B, C and D with straight lines. What shape is this?

22 Round the number 34 514 978 to the nearest 5a

a 10 000 b 1 000 000

Challenge

23 Work out the missing digits in each of these.

a

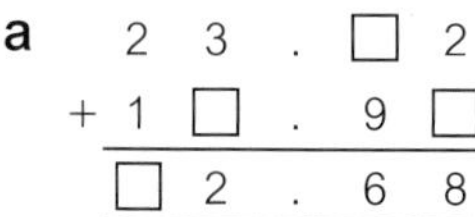

b

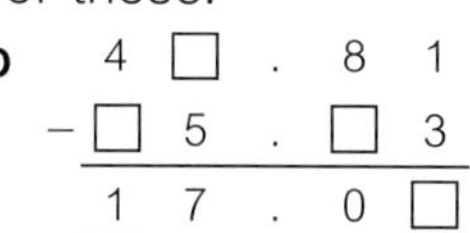

24 A rectangle has perimeter 22 cm and area 24 cm^2.
Work out the side lengths of the rectangle.

25 **Reflect** Put these topics in order, from easiest to hardest. Reflect
(You could just write the letters.)

A Writing decimals in order

B Converting measures

C Rounding decimals

D Multiplying and dividing decimals

E Adding and subtracting decimals

F Perimeter

G Area

Think about the two topics you said were hardest.
What made them hard?
Write at least one hint to help you for each topic.

5 Fractions

MASTER

Check P131 | Strengthen P133 | Extend P137 | Test P141

5.1 Comparing fractions

You will learn to:

- Use fraction notation to describe parts of a shape
- Compare simple fractions
- Use a diagram to compare two or more simple fractions.

CONFIDENCE

Why learn this? You can compare fractions to find the best deal in the sales.

Fluency
Write these numbers in order of size, smallest to largest.
18, 7, 15, 5, 9, 13

Explore
Can you make one whole by adding together unit fractions and without using any fraction more than once (i.e. $\frac{1}{2} + \frac{1}{2}$ is not allowed).

Exercise 5.1

Warm up

1 Which of these shapes are $\frac{1}{2}$ shaded?

A 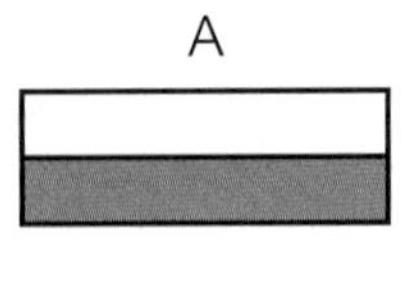 B 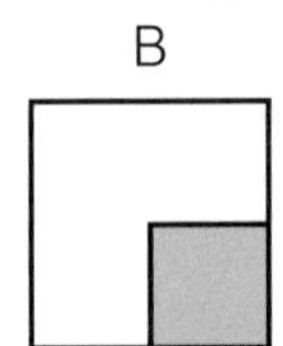 C 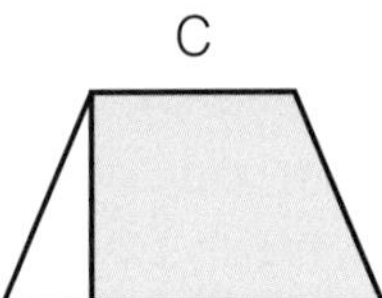 D 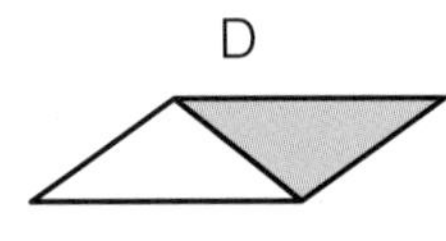

2 For each pair of diagrams, are the shaded **fractions** equivalent?

a 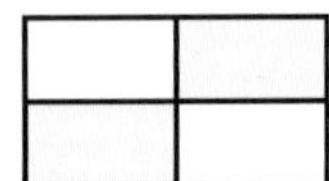

b 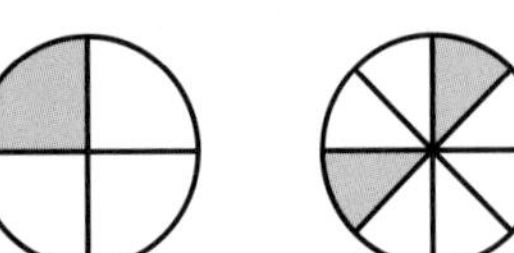

c  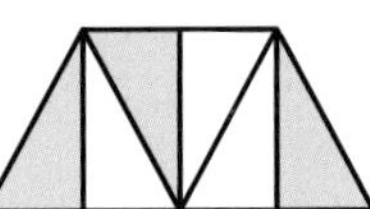 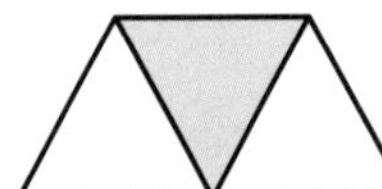

Key point
A **fraction** is part of a whole. The top number of a fraction is the **numerator**. The bottom number is the **denominator**.

4b

3 What fraction of each shape is shaded?

a 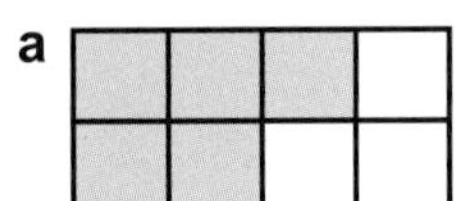 **b** 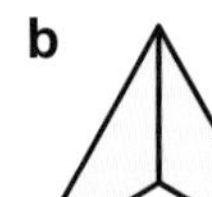 **c** 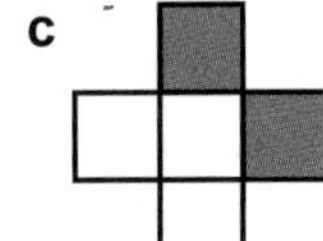 **d** 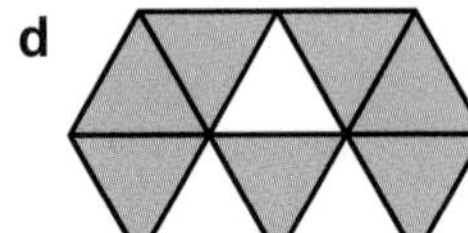

Q3 hint
First count the total number of parts. This will be the bottom number of the fraction.
Then count the number of parts that are shaded. This will be the top number of the fraction.

4 What fraction of each shape is
i shaded
ii unshaded?

a b c d

4b

Discussion Look again at your answers to Q4. How can you use the two numerators in each part to check your answers are correct?

5 Make four copies of this rectangle on squared paper.

4b

Using a new rectangle for each part, shade

a $\frac{1}{6}$ b $\frac{1}{2}$ c $\frac{1}{3}$ d $\frac{1}{12}$

Q5d hint
Draw in extra lines to divide the rectangle into 12 equal parts.

Investigation **Problem-solving / Reasoning**

Work with a partner to answer these questions.

1 a $\frac{1}{3}$ of this shape is shaded.
How many other ways can you find to shade $\frac{1}{3}$ of the shape?
b Do you think there are more ways or fewer ways to shade $\frac{1}{2}$ of the shape?
c Test your answer.

2 Make a copy of this shape and shade in $\frac{1}{2}$.
How many other ways can you find to shade $\frac{1}{2}$ of the shape?

6 **Problem-solving** What fraction of this shape is unshaded?

4b

Q6 Strategy hint
Copy the diagram and add some extra lines of your own.

7 Write the correct sign, > or <, between each of these pairs of fractions.

4b

a $\frac{3}{4} \dots \frac{1}{4}$ b $\frac{4}{5} \dots \frac{2}{5}$ c $\frac{3}{8} \dots \frac{5}{8}$ d $\frac{4}{9} \dots \frac{7}{9}$

Discussion When the denominators are the same, how can you decide which fraction is larger without drawing a diagram?

Q7a hint
Draw two bars the same length. Shade $\frac{3}{4}$ of one and $\frac{1}{4}$ of the other.

Worked example

Write the correct sign, > or <, between these fractions: $\frac{1}{2} \dots \frac{1}{3}$.

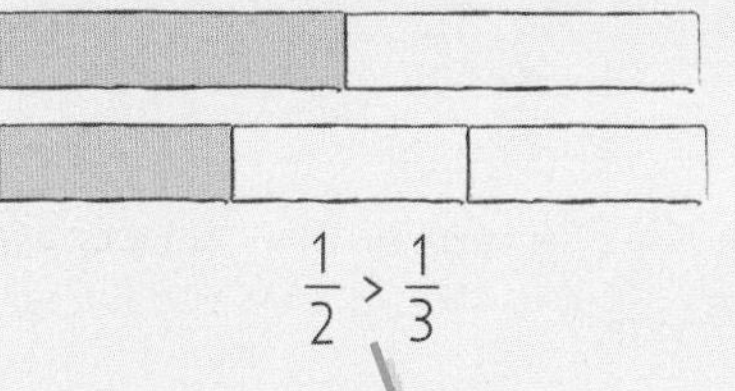

Draw two bars the same length.

Shade $\frac{1}{2}$ of the first bar.

Shade $\frac{1}{3}$ of the second bar.

$\frac{1}{2} > \frac{1}{3}$

$\frac{1}{2}$ is greater than $\frac{1}{3}$, so write the 'greater than' symbol, >, between them.

Key point
A **unit fraction** has numerator 1.
For example, $\frac{1}{2}$, $\frac{1}{3}$ and $\frac{1}{4}$ are unit fractions.

4b **8** Write the correct sign, > or <, between each of these pairs of fractions.

a $\frac{1}{2} \cdots \frac{1}{4}$ **b** $\frac{1}{5} \cdots \frac{1}{3}$ **c** $\frac{1}{8} \cdots \frac{1}{6}$ **d** $\frac{1}{7} \cdots \frac{1}{10}$

Discussion When you are given two unit fractions, how can you decide which is larger without drawing a diagram?

Q8 hint
The wider end of the > and < signs points to the larger fraction.

4b **9** **Real** Two shops sell the same pair of flip-flops at the same original price. Both shops have a sale.

Which pair of flip-flops is cheaper? Explain your answer.

4b **10** Use the fraction wall to work out which fraction is larger in each pair.

a $\frac{2}{3}$ or $\frac{3}{4}$ **b** $\frac{3}{7}$ or $\frac{2}{5}$ **c** $\frac{1}{4}$ or $\frac{2}{7}$ **d** $\frac{4}{5}$ or $\frac{7}{8}$

$\frac{1}{8}$
$\frac{1}{7}$
$\frac{1}{6}$
$\frac{1}{5}$
$\frac{1}{4}$
$\frac{1}{3}$
$\frac{1}{2}$

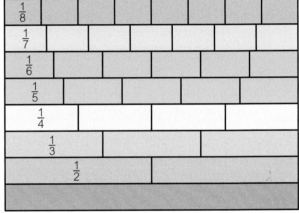

4b **11** Write these fractions in order of size, starting with the smallest.

$\frac{5}{7}, \frac{3}{5}, \frac{2}{3}$

4b **12** **Problem-solving** Use the grid to decide which is larger, $\frac{3}{4}$ or $\frac{7}{12}$.

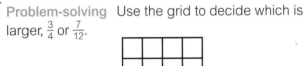

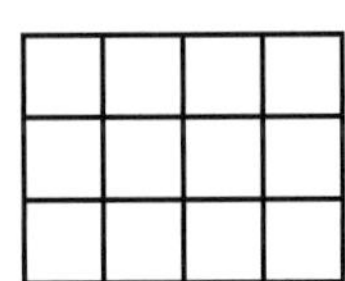

Q12 Strategy hint
Start by making two copies of the grid.

Explore

13 **Explore** Can you make one whole by adding together unit fractions and without using any fraction more than once (i.e. $\frac{1}{2}+\frac{1}{2}$ is not allowed).
Look back at the maths you have learned in this lesson.
How can you use it to answer this question?

Reflect

14 **Reflect** This may be the first time you have studied fractions since primary school.
Choose A, B or C to complete each statement.

In this lesson, I did …	A well	B OK	C not very well
So far, I think fractions are …	A easy	B OK	C difficult
When I think about the next lesson, I feel …	A confident	B OK	C unsure

If you answered mostly As and Bs, did your experience surprise you? Why?
If you answered mostly Cs, look back at the questions you found most tricky. Ask a friend or your teacher to explain them to you. Then complete the statements above again.

5.2 Simplifying fractions

You will learn to:
- Change an improper fraction to a mixed number
- Identify equivalent fractions
- Simplify fractions by cancelling common factors.

CONFIDENCE

Why learn this? Writing fractions in different ways helps you to compare amounts, for example when adapting recipes.

Fluency
Copy and complete these.
- 4 × □ = 12
- 8 ÷ □ = 2
- □ × 3 = 15

Explore
On average, humans spend $\frac{1}{3}$ of each day asleep. How does this compare with the fraction of the day that other animals sleep?

Exercise 5.2

1 a How many thirds in 2 wholes?

b How many halves in 3 wholes?

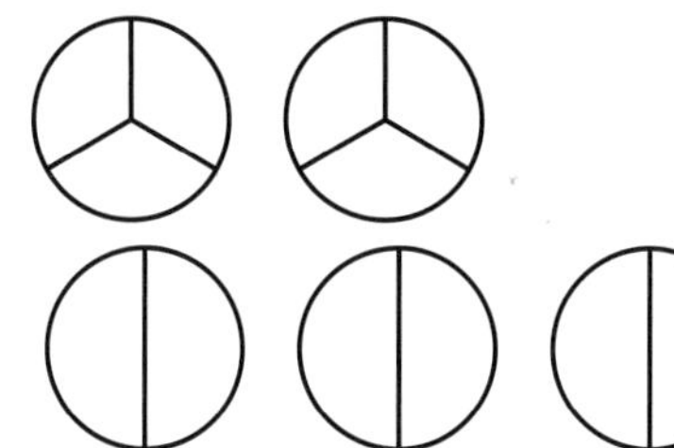

2 Work out the highest common factor (HCF) of
a 6 and 8 b 5 and 15 c 12 and 20

3 Convert these **improper fractions** to **mixed numbers**.
a $\frac{5}{3}$ b $\frac{12}{5}$ c $\frac{11}{6}$ d $\frac{7}{4}$ e $\frac{9}{5}$ f $\frac{21}{8}$

4 Reasoning Sam changes $\frac{10}{3}$ to $1\frac{7}{3}$. Liz changes $\frac{10}{3}$ to $2\frac{4}{3}$.
Jeff changes $\frac{10}{3}$ to $3\frac{1}{3}$.
Whose answer is best?

5 Real A chef calculates that he needs $\frac{17}{4}$ litres of vegetable stock.
How much is this as a mixed number?

Key point
An **improper fraction** has a numerator that is bigger than its denominator, for example $\frac{4}{3}$.
A **mixed number** has a whole number part and a fraction part, for example $1\frac{1}{3}$.

Warm up

Q3a hint
Think of $\frac{5}{3}$ as 5 thirds.

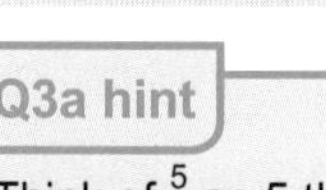

You can see that 5 thirds is the same as 1 whole with 2 thirds left over.

4a 4a 4a

Worked example

Complete the equivalent fraction $\frac{2}{3} = \frac{8}{\square}$

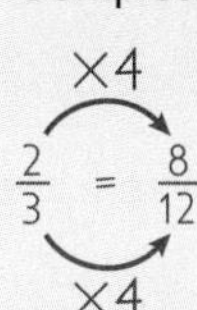

$\frac{2}{3} \overset{\times 4}{=} \frac{8}{12}$

2 has been multiplied by 4 to give 8.
Multiply 3 by 4 to give 12.
You can see from the diagram that $\frac{2}{3}$ and $\frac{8}{12}$ have the same value.

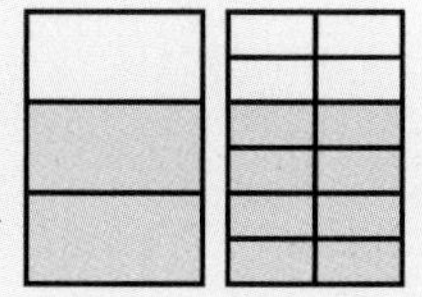

Key point
Equivalent fractions are fractions that have the same value.
For example,

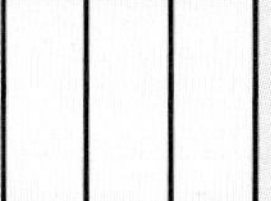
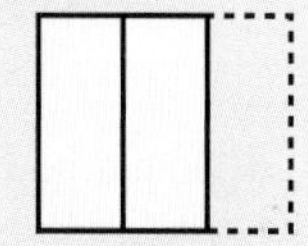

$\frac{1}{2}$ is the same as $\frac{2}{4}$

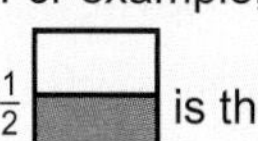
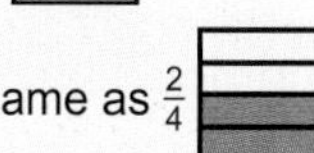

You can find equivalent fractions by multiplying or dividing the numerator and denominator by the same number.

4a

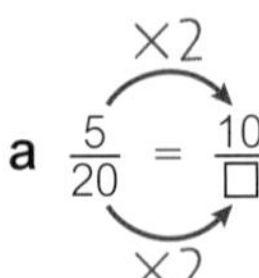

6 Copy and complete these equivalent fractions.

a $\frac{5}{20} = \frac{10}{\square}$ (×2, ×2) b $\frac{1}{5} = \frac{\square}{25}$ (×5, ×5) c $\frac{5}{7} = \frac{15}{\square}$ d $\frac{2}{5} = \frac{\square}{40}$

e $\frac{8}{10} = \frac{4}{\square}$ (÷2, ÷2) f $\frac{4}{12} = \frac{\square}{3}$ (÷4, ÷4) g $\frac{30}{36} = \frac{\square}{6}$ h $\frac{12}{21} = \frac{4}{\square}$

Key point

You can **simplify** fractions by **cancelling** common factors. A fraction is in its **simplest form** when it cannot be cancelled any further. You cancel a fraction to its simplest form by dividing the numerator and denominator by their highest common factor (HCF).

5b

7 Write each fraction in its **simplest form**.

a $\frac{12}{14}$ b $\frac{15}{20}$ c $\frac{20}{30}$ d $\frac{16}{24}$ e $\frac{18}{36}$ f $\frac{14}{21}$

Q7a hint

The HCF of 12 and 14 is 2, so divide the top and bottom of the fraction by 2.

5b

8 **Reasoning** This is how Gary and Lowri cancelled the fraction $\frac{16}{20}$ to its simplest form.

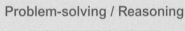

Gary

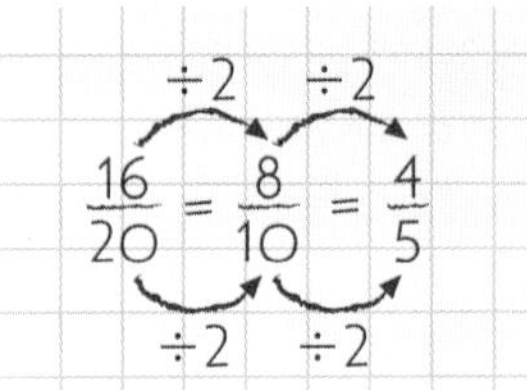

Lowri

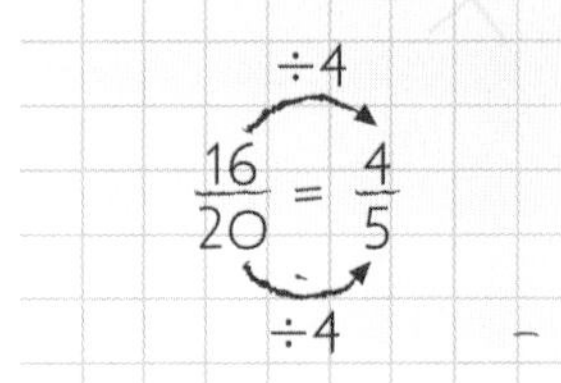

They have cancelled differently but arrived at the same answer. Explain why.

Discussion Does it matter how many steps it takes to cancel a fraction to its simplest form?

Investigation

Problem-solving / Reasoning

Work with a partner to answer this question.

a Copy and complete these fractions. They are all equivalent to $\frac{1}{2}$.

$\frac{1}{2}, \frac{2}{4}, \frac{\square}{6}, \frac{\square}{8}, \frac{5}{\square}$

b Write each of the fractions in part **a** as a coordinate pair.
(1, 2), (2, 4), …

c Make a copy of the grid shown.
Plot all the coordinate pairs on the grid. The first two have been done for you.

d Join together all the points you have plotted. Do they all lie on one straight line?

Discussion Why do you think the points all lie on a straight line?

Explore

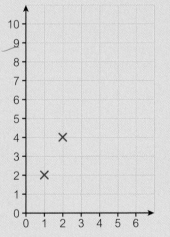

9 **Explore** On average, humans spend $\frac{1}{3}$ of each day asleep. How does this compare with the fraction of the day that other animals sleep?
What have you learned in this lesson to help you answer this question?
What other information do you need?

Reflect

15 **Reflect** After this lesson, Lucy said, 'Fractions are not really like whole numbers.'
Kala said, 'Yes! Fractions can be written in many different ways.'
Look back at your work on fractions.
a What do you think Lucy means?
b What do you think Kala means?

5.3 Working with fractions

You will learn to:
- Add and subtract simple fractions
- Calculate simple fractions of quantities.

CONFIDENCE

Why learn this? A vet needs to be able to calculate a fraction of a dose of medicine depending on the size of the animal to be treated.

Fluency
What fraction of each shape is shaded?

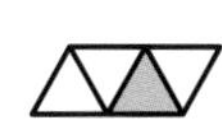 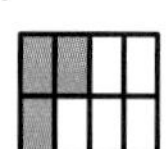 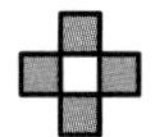

Explore
How would a vet decide how much flea control treatment is needed for a small dog or a large dog?

Exercise 5.3

Warm up

1 Work out
   a $30 \div 6$
   b $14 \div 7$
   c $45 \div 5$
   d $18 \div 2$

2 Work out
   a $\frac{1}{2}$ of £12
   b $\frac{1}{3}$ of 15 kg
   c $\frac{1}{4}$ of 20 m
   d $\frac{1}{5}$ of 30 kg

Worked example

Work out $\frac{1}{3} + \frac{1}{3}$

$$\frac{1}{3} + \frac{1}{3} = \frac{2}{3}$$

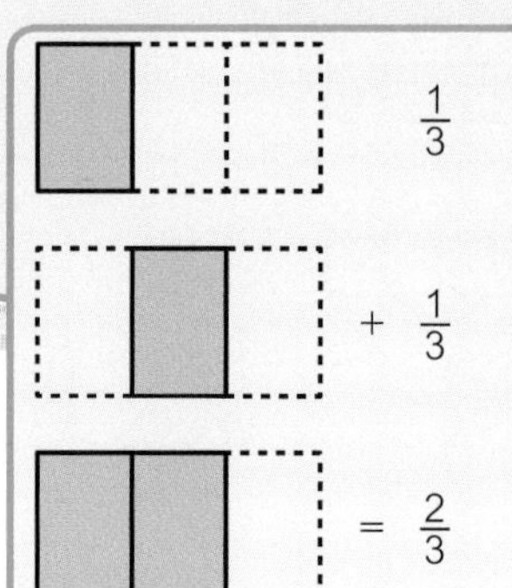

Key point

When you add or subtract fractions with the same denominator, add or subtract the numerators then write the result over the same denominator.

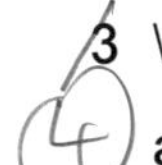

3 Work out
   a $\frac{1}{5} + \frac{1}{5}$
   b $\frac{3}{7} + \frac{2}{7}$
   c $\frac{2}{9} + \frac{5}{9}$
   d $\frac{1}{11} + \frac{6}{11}$

   e $\frac{4}{5} - \frac{3}{5}$
   f $\frac{4}{7} - \frac{2}{7}$

   g $\frac{3}{5} - \frac{2}{5}$
   h $\frac{8}{9} - \frac{1}{9}$

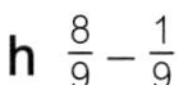

Q3e hint

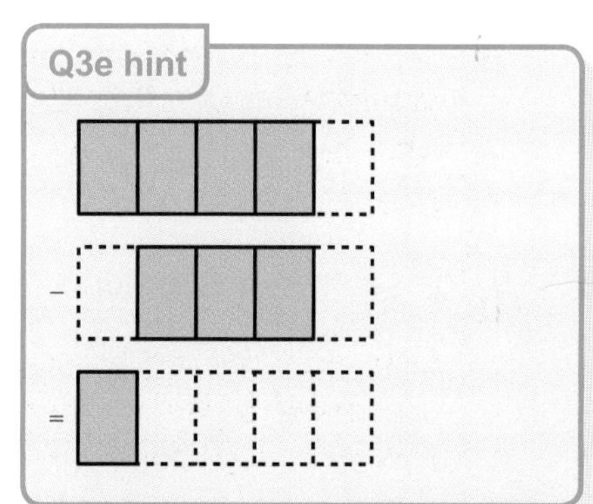

5c

5c

4 Work out

a $\frac{5}{6}+\frac{1}{6}$ b $\frac{3}{5}+\frac{2}{5}$

c $\frac{4}{9}+\frac{5}{9}$ d $1-\frac{4}{5}$

e $1-\frac{5}{7}$ f $1-\frac{2}{9}$

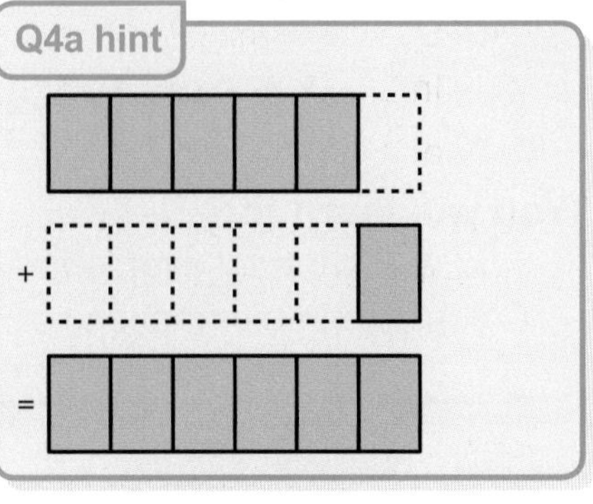

5c

5 Work out these. Give each answer in its simplest form.
The first one has been started for you.

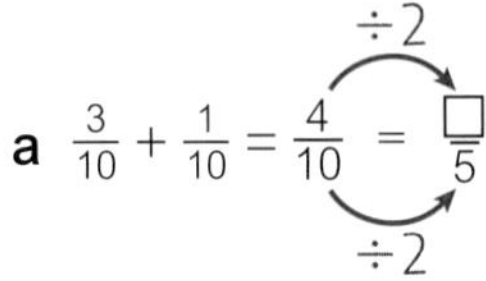

a $\frac{3}{10}+\frac{1}{10}=\frac{4}{10}=\frac{\square}{5}$ (÷2 numerator and denominator)

b $\frac{1}{4}+\frac{1}{4}$ c $\frac{1}{8}+\frac{5}{8}$

d $\frac{2}{9}+\frac{4}{9}$ e $\frac{3}{4}-\frac{1}{4}$

f $\frac{3}{8}-\frac{1}{8}$ g $\frac{9}{10}-\frac{3}{10}$

h $\frac{11}{12}-\frac{7}{12}$

5c

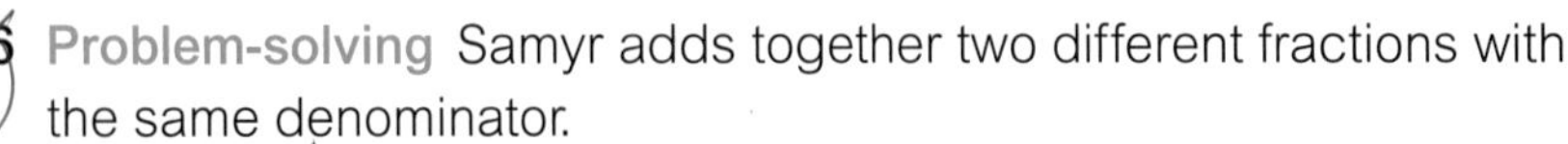

6 **Problem-solving** Samyr adds together two different fractions with the same denominator.
He gets the answer $\frac{1}{4}$. Write down two fractions that Samyr might have added.

Discussion Did you get the same fractions as other people in your class?

Q6 Strategy hint

You could begin by finding some fractions that are equivalent to $\frac{1}{4}$.

$\frac{1}{4}=\frac{\square}{\square}$

5b

7 Work out

a $\frac{1}{7}$ of £14 b $\frac{1}{9}$ of 36 cm

c $\frac{1}{8}$ of 24 t d $\frac{1}{10}$ of 250 ml

Worked example

Work out $\frac{2}{3}$ of 12 m.

$\frac{1}{3}$ of 12 m = 12 ÷ 3 = 4 m

$\frac{2}{3}$ of 12 m = 2 × 4 = 8 m

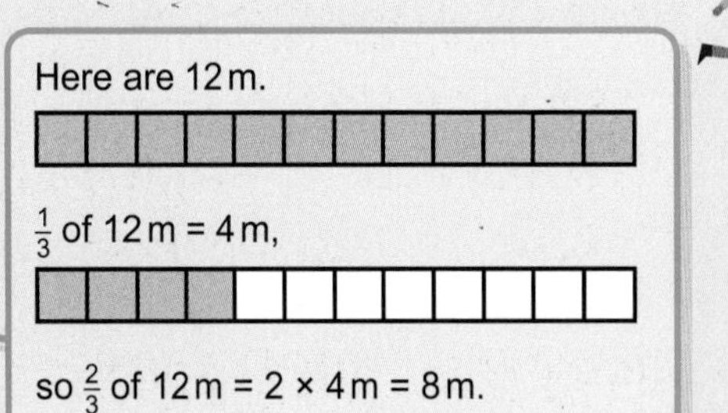

Key point

When you work out a fraction of a quantity, you divide the quantity by the denominator, and then multiply by the numerator.

5b

8 Work out

a $\frac{2}{3}$ of \$27 b $\frac{3}{4}$ of 20 m

c $\frac{5}{8}$ of 16 km d $\frac{4}{5}$ of 30 kg

5b

9 **Reasoning** a Joe works out $\frac{2}{5}$ of £15 by doing 15 ÷ 5 = 3, 3 + 3 = 6.
Ben does 15 ÷ 5 = 3, 3 × 2 = 6.
Why do they both end up with the same answer?

Discussion Which is the better method and why?

b Here is a calculation: 16 ÷ 4 × 3. Write a question that uses this calculation.

Topic links: Using formulae, Conversions

Subject links: Science (Q10, Q13)

10 STEM Red gold is an alloy made from $\frac{3}{4}$ gold and $\frac{1}{4}$ copper. 5b
In 24 g of red gold, how many grams are there of
a gold **b** copper?

> **Q10 Literacy hint**
> An alloy is a mixture of metals.

11 Real The diagram shows the petrol gauge of a car. 5b
The petrol tank holds 56 litres when full.
How much petrol is in the tank?

12 Real The formula to convert a distance in kilometres to a distance in miles is 5b

distance in miles = $\frac{5}{8}$ of distance in kilometres

Tanya sees this sign on holiday in France.
How far, in miles, is she from Disneyland Paris?

Disneyland 60 km

13 Modelling Hannah carries out a science experiment. 5b
The table shows her results for the values of A and B.

A	14	41	66	240
B	21	60	110	380

Hannah says, 'The value of A is always $\frac{2}{3}$ of B.' Is this a good mathematical model?

14 Real / Finance When Sally works on a Sunday she is paid her normal wage plus half again. Sally is normally paid £9 per hour. 5a
How much is she paid per hour on Sundays?

Investigation **Problem-solving**

Work in pairs to solve this problem.
Here is a set of fractions dominoes.

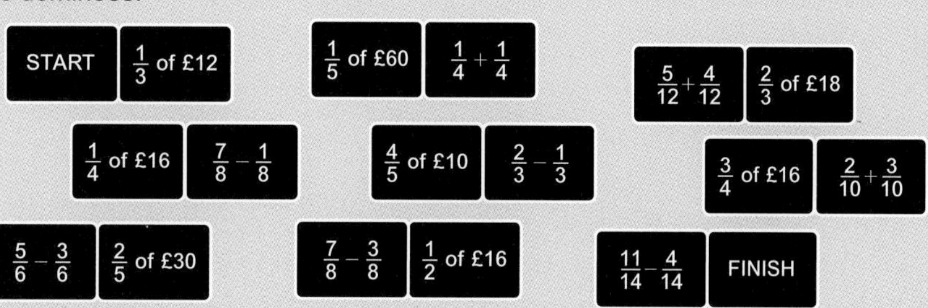

Work out a way to link the dominoes together. A domino can only link with another domino that gives the same answer.
The first two dominoes are

Discussion Is there more than one way to link the dominoes?

14 Explore How would a vet decide how much flea control treatment is needed for a small dog or a large dog? Explore
Is it easier to explore this question now you have completed the lesson?
What further information do you need to be able to answer this?

15 Reflect Reflect
a Write down an easy fraction.
b Write down a difficult fraction
c What makes one fraction easier or harder than the other.

5.4 Fractions and decimals

You will learn to:

- Work with equivalent fractions and decimals
- Write one number as a fraction of another.

CONFIDENCE

Why learn this? Understanding equivalent fractions and decimals can help you choose the best deal in a supermarket.

Fluency

- What is the highest common factor of 6 and 10, 12 and 100?
- Work out 100 ÷ 2, 100 ÷ 5, 100 ÷ 4

Explore

Did the UK meet the EU target for recycling batteries in 2012?

Exercise 5.4

Warm up

1 What is the value of the digit 7 in each of these numbers?

a 274.25 **b** 14.75 **c** 112.97

2 Write each fraction in its simplest form.

a $\frac{2}{10}$ **b** $\frac{18}{100}$ **c** $\frac{45}{100}$

Key point

You can write fractions as decimals. Three important examples are $\frac{1}{4} = 0.25$, $\frac{1}{2} = 0.5$, $\frac{3}{4} = 0.75$.

You can convert a decimal to a fraction by looking at the place value.

Worked example

Write 0.32 as a fraction in its simplest form.

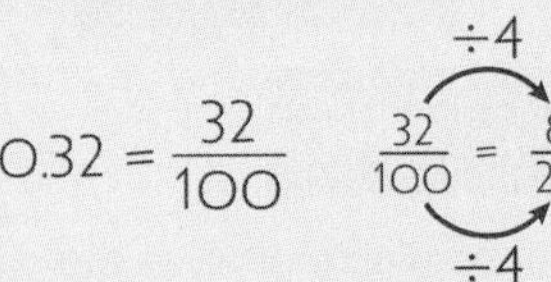

Look at 0.32 in a place value table.

...	H	T	U	•	$\frac{1}{10}$	$\frac{1}{100}$	...
			0	•	3	2	

0.32 is the same as $\frac{32}{100}$

3 Write each decimal as a fraction in its simplest form.

a 0.9 **b** 0.6

c 0.5 **d** 0.36

e 0.25 **f** 0.62

g 0.75 **h** 0.81

4 In the 2013 Wimbledon final, 0.64 of Andy Murray's first serves were in.
He won 0.72 of his first serve points.

Write each decimal as a fraction in its simplest form.

a 0.64 **b** 0.72

Topic links: Highest common factor

5 Write each fraction as a decimal. 4b

a $\frac{1}{5} = \frac{\square}{10} =$ b $\frac{3}{20} = \frac{\square}{100} =$ c $\frac{12}{25}$ d $\frac{17}{50}$

Key point

You can convert a fraction to a decimal by writing an equivalent fraction with a denominator of 10, 100, 1000, ... and then using place value.

6 In a rugby match, the British Lions won 12 out of the 20 line-outs. 4b

Write $\frac{12}{20}$ as a decimal.

Discussion Is there more than one way to change $\frac{12}{20}$ to a decimal?

7 **Problem-solving** In the same rugby match, the British Lions missed 18 out of the 40 missed tackles. 4b

Write $\frac{18}{40}$ as a decimal.

Q7 Strategy hint

Work out how to change 40 into 100.

8 A shop sells 30 pairs of flip-flops in one day. Five of the pairs are pink. 5b

What fraction of the flip-flops sold are pink?

Q8 hint

Write the fraction $\frac{\text{pink flip-flops}}{\text{total flip-flops}}$

Write the fraction in its simplest form.

9 There are 17 members in a Scout group. 5b

Seven of the members go caving.

What fraction of the group go caving?

10 **Real** There were 70 000 spectators at a football match. 5b

42 000 of them supported Manchester United.

What fraction of the spectators supported Manchester United?

Write the fraction in its simplest form.

11 **Problem-solving / Real** In the 2012 Tour de France there were 9 flat stages, 4 medium mountain stages, 5 mountain stages and 2 individual time-trial stages. 5b

a What fraction of the stages were not medium mountain stages?

b Write your answer to part **a** as a decimal.

Q11a Strategy hint

Start by working out the total number of stages.

Investigation **Problem-solving / Reasoning**

Work with a partner to answer these questions.

1 Use a calculator to work out $\frac{1}{9}$, $\frac{2}{9}$, and $\frac{3}{9}$ as decimals.

For $\frac{1}{9}$ work out 1 ÷ 9, for $\frac{2}{9}$ work out 2 ÷ 9, ...

2 Describe the pattern you see. What do you think $\frac{7}{9}$ is, as a decimal?

3 Check your prediction with a calculator.

Discussion What happens to the pattern when you reach $\frac{9}{9}$, $\frac{10}{9}$ and beyond?

12 **Explore** Did the UK meet the EU target for recycling batteries in 2012? Explore

What have you learned in this lesson to help you answer this question?

What other information do you need?

13 **Reflect** After this lesson, Faiz says, 'Decimals are just another way to write fractions.' Reflect

Do you agree with Faiz? Explain.

5.5 Understanding percentages

You will learn to:
- Understand percentage as 'the number of parts per 100'
- Convert a percentage to a number of hundredths or tenths
- Work with equivalent percentages, fractions and decimals.

CONFIDENCE

Why learn this? You can compare the performances of sports teams by looking at the fraction or percentage of games they each win.

Fluency
Find pairs of equivalent fractions in this list.
$\frac{8}{100}$, $\frac{3}{20}$, $\frac{2}{10}$, $\frac{2}{25}$, $\frac{15}{100}$, $\frac{1}{5}$

Explore
An ebook tells you what percentage of the book you have read. How will it change when you read one page of short and long books?

Exercise 5.5

Warm up

1 Work out
a $320 \div 100$ b 0.52×100 c $25 \div 100$ d 6.9×100

2 Write each of these fractions in its simplest form.
a $\frac{4}{10}$ b $\frac{50}{100}$ c $\frac{8}{100}$ d $\frac{25}{100}$

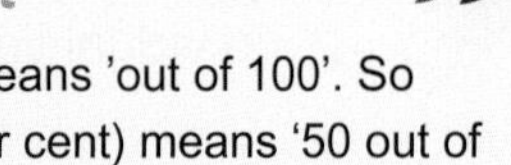

Key point
Per cent means 'out of 100'. So 50% (50 per cent) means '50 out of 100', which is $\frac{50}{100}$

4c

3 What **percentage** of each block is
i shaded ii unshaded?

a
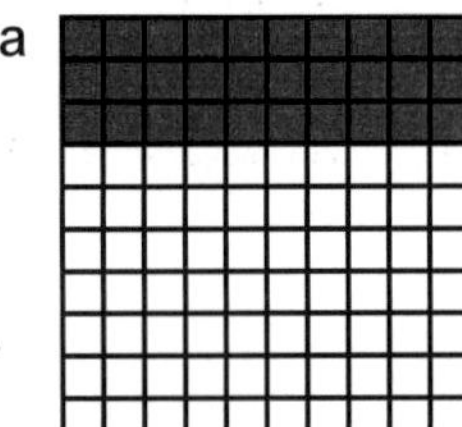
b
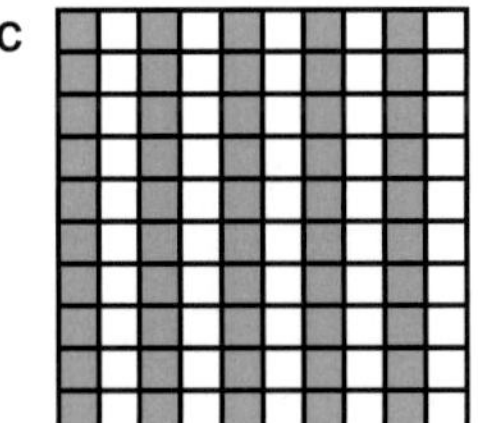
c

d Show how you checked each pair of answers.

Q3a hint
30 out of 100 ($\frac{30}{100}$) squares are shaded.

Q3 hint
Check your answers are correct by adding the percentage shaded and the percentage unshaded. They should total 100%.

4c

4 **Reasoning** The manager of Model Fashions has designed a new shop layout.

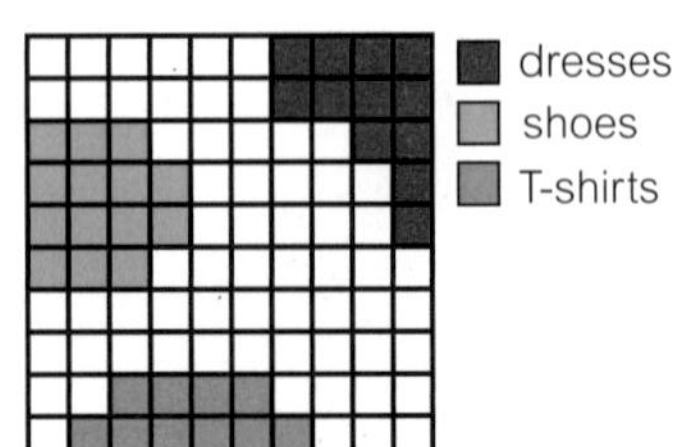

a What percentage of the layout is for
i shoes ii dresses iii T-shirts?

b The manager says, '74% of the shop is empty floor space'. Without counting the squares, how can you tell that the manager is wrong?

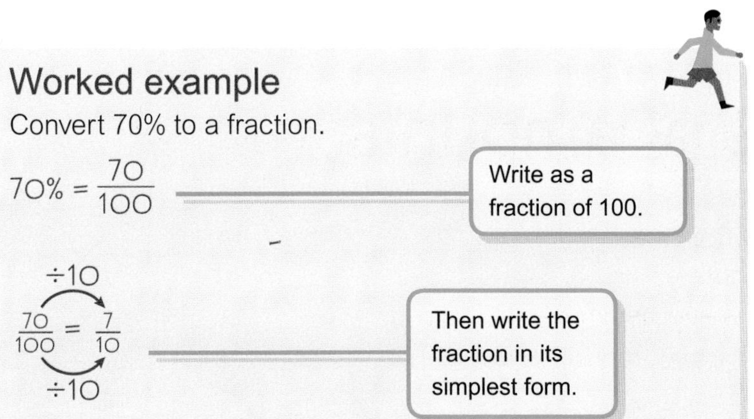

Worked example

Convert 70% to a fraction.

$70\% = \frac{70}{100}$ — Write as a fraction of 100.

$\frac{70}{100} = \frac{7}{10}$ (÷10 top and bottom) — Then write the fraction in its simplest form.

Key point

You can write any **percentage** as a fraction with denominator 100.

5 Convert these percentages to fractions. Write each fraction in its simplest form. The first and third parts have been started for you. 4b

a $27\% = \frac{\square}{100}$ b 99%

c $10\% = \frac{\square}{100} = \frac{\square}{10}$ d 30%

6 A clothes shop makes a different percentage profit on each brand of clothing. Write each percentage profit as a fraction. 4b

a 37% b 79% c 61% d 119%

7 A shoe shop gives different percentage discounts on shoes in the sale. Write each percentage discount as a fraction in its simplest form. 4b

a 20% b 60% c 40% d 90%

Discussion Is it possible to give a 150% discount?

Key point

To convert a percentage to a decimal, you divide by 100. For example, 45% = 45 ÷ 100 = 0.45.
To convert a decimal to a percentage, you multiply by 100. For example, 0.08 = 0.08 × 100 = 8%.

8 Convert these percentages to decimals. The first one has been started for you. 4b

a 35% = 35 ÷ 100 = □ b 40% c 110%

9 Convert these decimals to percentages. The first one has been started for you. 4b

a 0.45 = 0.45 × 100 = □ % b 0.7 c 0.03

Investigation — Problem-solving / Reasoning

1 Make three copies of this rectangle on squared paper.
2 Shade in 65% of the first rectangle. How many squares is this?
3 Shade in 0.3 of the second rectangle. How many squares is this?
4 Ask a partner to shade, on the third copy, a percentage or decimal that you choose. If it is not possible with a whole number of squares, explain why.
5 Explain how you can work out how to choose a percentage or decimal that is a whole number of squares.

10 Explore A ebook tells you what percentage of the book you have read. How will it change when you read one page of short and long books? Choose some sensible numbers to help you explore this situation. Then use what you have learned in this lesson to help you answer the question. Explore

11 Reflect After this lesson, Alex says, 'Percentages are just another way to write fractions.' Do you agree with Alex? Explain. Reflect

5.6 Percentages of amounts

You will learn to:

- Use different strategies to calculate with percentages
- Express one number as a percentage of another.

CONFIDENCE

Why learn this? In tennis, the percentage of first serves in tells the fans how well a player is serving.

Fluency
Work out
- 80 ÷ 10
- 9 ÷ 10
- 25 ÷ 10
- 170 ÷ 10

Explore
What percentage of people are left-handed?

Exercise 5.6

Warm up

1 Work out
a $\frac{1}{2}$ of £18 b $\frac{1}{3}$ of 21 km c $\frac{1}{4}$ of 12 cm

2 Change each fraction to a percentage.
a $\frac{4}{100}$ b $\frac{7}{10}$ c $\frac{11}{50}$

Key point

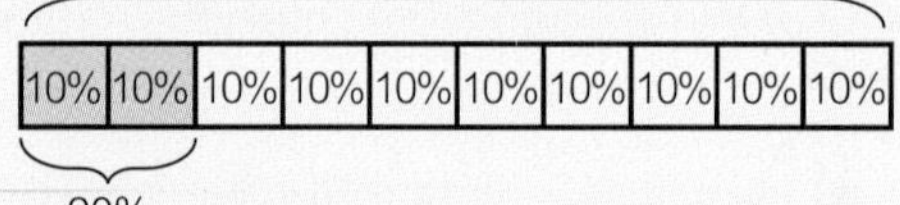

$10\% = \frac{10}{100} = \frac{1}{10}$
To find 10% of an amount, you divide by 10. You can then use 10% to find other percentages.

4c

3 Work out
a 10% of 80 kg b 10% of 150 ml
c 10% of 1500 m d 10% of £45
e 20% of £50 f 80% of 20 t
g 40% of 350 g h 30% of 25 km

Q3d hint
Remember to write money correctly.
£36 ÷ 10 = £3.60, not £3.6

Q3e hint
First find 10%.

4c

4 **Real / Finance** Five hundred tickets went on sale for a charity concert. Ninety per cent were sold.
a How many tickets were sold?
The tickets cost £12 each.
b What was the total amount of money taken in ticket sales?
Discussion How did you work out 90% of 500?

4c

5 Work out
a 50% of £40 b 25% of 300 kg c 75% of 20 mm
Discussion In the UK and in the USA, about 10% of the population have blood group B. Is this the same number of people in each country?

Q5 hint
50% is the same as $\frac{1}{2}$
25% is the same as $\frac{1}{4}$
75% is the same as $\frac{3}{4}$

4a

6 **Finance / Real** Charities can claim an extra 25% of the value of a donation back from the Government. This is called Gift Aid.
Work out how much Gift Aid a charity can claim on a donation of £273.50. Give your answer to the nearest penny.

Topic links: Measures, Bar charts

Worked example

Work out 26% of 60 m.

10% → 60 m ÷ 10 = 6 m
20% → 2 × 6 m = 12 m
5% → 6 m ÷ 2 = 3 m
1% → 6 m ÷ 10 = 0.6 m
26% → 12 m + 3 m + 0.6 m = 15.6 m

Break down the 26% into 20% + 5% + 1%.
Start by finding 10% of 60 m, then use this to find 20%, 5% and 1%.
Write down the individual parts as you find them.

Finally add the parts together to give 26%.

Key point

When you are working out more complicated percentages of amounts, you can make notes or use **jottings** to help you.

7 Work out these percentages. Use **jottings** to help. 5b

a 15% of £40
b 35% of 90 kg
c 21% of 50 m
d 85% of 120 km

Discussion How did you work out the answer to part **d**?

8 Rewrite these statements, giving the numbers as percentages. 5a

a 20 out of 25 students like drawing.
b 43 out of 50 people play a sport.
c 7 out of 10 people have a passport.

Q8a hint

Write 20 out of 25 as a fraction, then change it to an equivalent fraction with a denominator of 100.
The numerator is the percentage.

Key point

You can use a **multiplier** to work out a percentage, by using the decimal equivalent of the percentage.

100% = 0.1

0.1	0.1	0.1	0.1	0.1	0.1	0.1	0.1	0.1	0.1

20% = 0.2

10% = $\frac{10}{100} = \frac{1}{10}$ = 0.1
To find 10% you multiply by 0.1, to find 20% you multiply by 0.2, ...

9 Use a **multiplier** to work out 5a

a 20% of £8
b 30% of 35 kg
c 40% of 32 litres
d 60% of 7 t

Q9a hint

2 × 8 = 16, so 0.2 × 8 = ...

10 Real The organisers of a dog agility competition decide to give 20% of the profit they make to charity. 5a
They make £854.87 profit. How much do they give to charity?
Round your answer to a suitable amount.

11 **Explore** What percentage of people are left-handed?
What have you learned in this lesson to help you answer this question? What other information do you need?

12 **Reflect** In this lesson you found 20% of a quantity in two different ways.
Strategy 1: finding 10%, then multiplying by 2.
Strategy 2: using the multiplier 0.2.

a Look back at the questions where you used these different strategies.
b Which strategy did you like better? Explain.
c Which strategy would you use if an item was 20% off in a shop? Explain.
d Write down any advantages or disadvantages of each of these strategies.

Explore

Reflect

5 Check up

Fractions

1 What fraction of each shape is shaded?

a

b

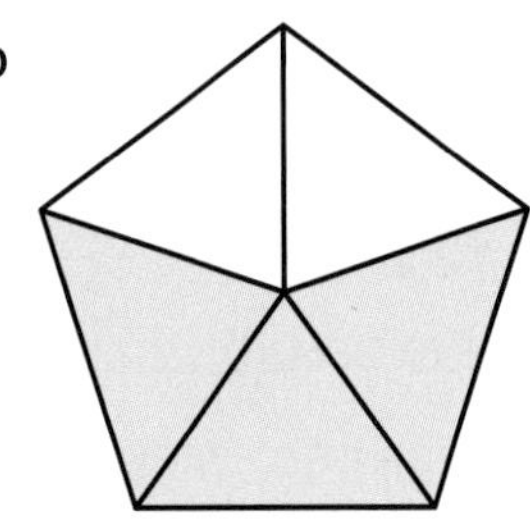

2 Rob says, '$\frac{5}{7}$ of this shape is shaded'. Is he correct? Explain your answer.

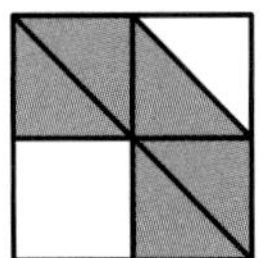

3 **a** Choose one fraction from the cloud to complete this statement: '$\frac{1}{4}$ is larger than $\square$'.

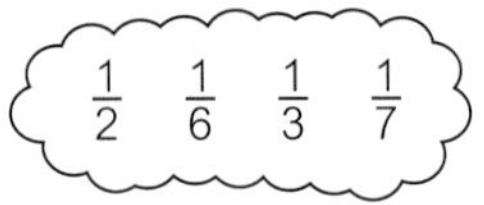

b Choose two fractions from the box to complete this statement:

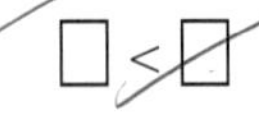

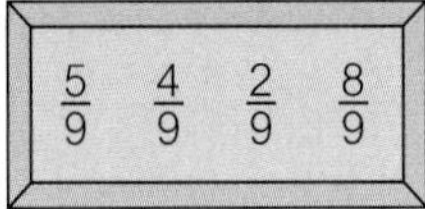

4 Gill says, '$\frac{1}{15}$ is greater than $\frac{1}{14}$ because 15 is greater than 14.' Is she correct? Explain your answer.

5 Copy and complete these equivalent fractions.

a $\frac{3}{7} = \frac{12}{\square}$ **b** $\frac{30}{40} = \frac{\square}{8}$

6 Convert these improper fractions to mixed numbers.

a $\frac{5}{4}$ **b** $\frac{23}{6}$

7 Work out

a $\frac{2}{5} + \frac{1}{5}$ **b** $\frac{8}{9} - \frac{3}{9}$

8 Work out these calculations. Give each answer in its simplest form.

a $\frac{1}{12} + \frac{5}{12}$ **b** $\frac{13}{20} - \frac{7}{20}$

9 Anil cancels the fraction $\frac{12}{18}$ to its simplest form.
This is what he writes.
Is Anil correct? Explain your answer.

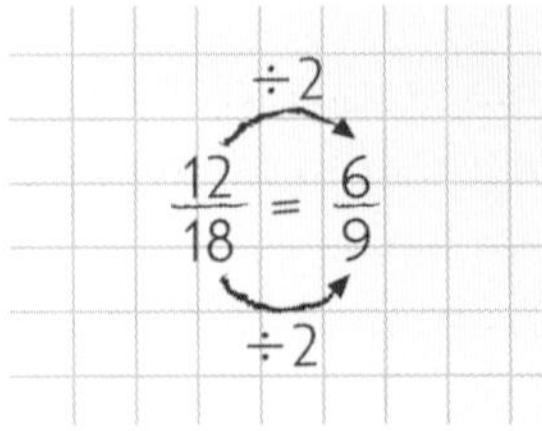

10 Work out

a $\frac{1}{6}$ of £18 **b** $\frac{3}{4}$ of 12 km **c** $\frac{5}{7}$ of 21 kg **d** $\frac{4}{9}$ of 54 mm

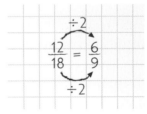

Fractions, decimals and percentages

11 Write each decimal as a fraction in its simplest form.

a 0.13 b 0.7 c 0.2 d 0.42

12 Write each fraction as a decimal.

a $\frac{9}{10}$ b $\frac{49}{100}$ c $\frac{7}{20}$ d $\frac{2}{5}$

13 Write each percentage as a fraction in its simplest form.

a 23% b 60% c 8% d 75%

14 Write each fraction as a percentage.

a $\frac{42}{100}$ b $\frac{3}{10}$ c $\frac{41}{50}$ d $\frac{11}{25}$

15 Copy and complete this table.

Fraction	Decimal	Percentage
$\frac{1}{2}$		
		70%
	0.25	
		6%

16 There are 12 dogs in a dog training class. Five of them are spaniels. What fraction of the dogs are spaniels?

17 There are 8 men and 6 women members in a diving club. What fraction of the members are women?

Percentages

18 Work out

a 10% of £40 b 50% of 18 cm c 30% of 60 km d 25% of 200 kg

19 Seven out of 10 people own a pet. Write this number as a percentage.

20 Work out 16% of £30. Use jottings to help.

21 Choose a decimal number from the circle to complete each of these statements.

a To find 10% of an amount, you multiply by …

b To find 20% of an amount, you multiply by …

c To find 70% of an amount, you multiply by …

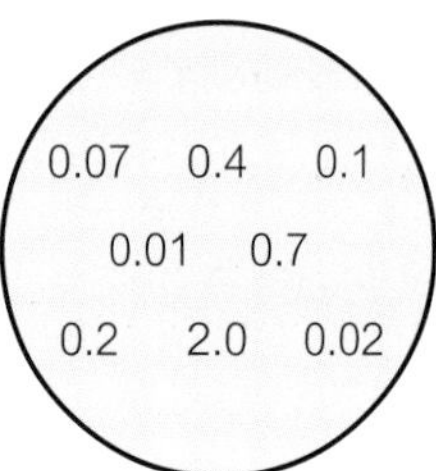

22 How sure are you of your answers? Were you mostly

Just guessing Feeling doubtful Confident

What next? Use your results to decide whether to strengthen or extend your learning.

Challenge

23 Make two copies of this rectangle.
Show two different ways to shade in $\frac{3}{8}$ of the rectangle.

24 Write down three different pairs of fractions that add together to give $\frac{1}{2}$.

25 $\frac{3}{8}$ of £16 = £6
Write down three different 'fraction of an amount' questions that have the answer £6.

5 Strengthen

You will:

- Strengthen your understanding with practice.

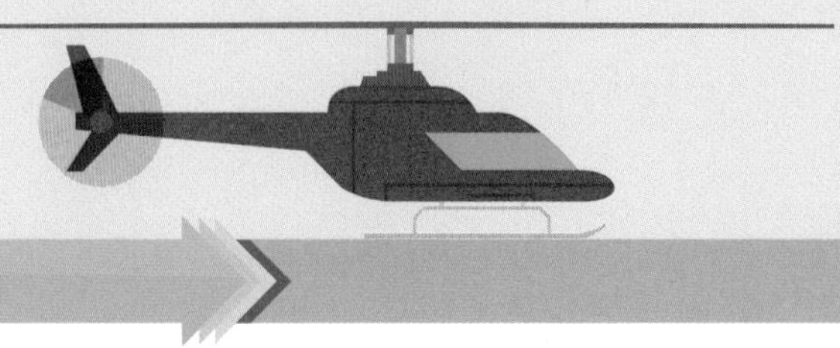

Fractions

4b **1** Copy each shape and shade the fraction shown.

a $\frac{3}{5}$ **b** $\frac{7}{10}$

c $\frac{5}{8}$

> **Q1a hint**
>
> To shade $\frac{3}{5}$, you must shade 3 out of the 5 equal parts.

4b **2** Copy and complete to find the fraction of each shape that is shaded.

a $\frac{\text{number of parts shaded}}{\text{total number of equal parts}} = \frac{\square}{\square}$

b 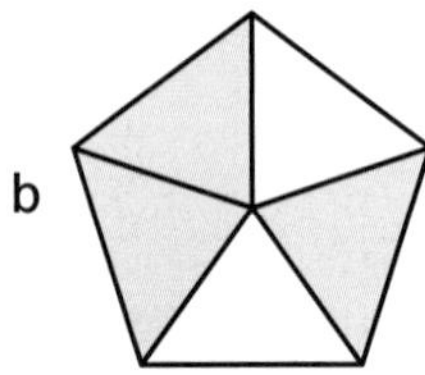 $\frac{\text{number of parts shaded}}{\text{total number of equal parts}} = \frac{\square}{\square}$

c 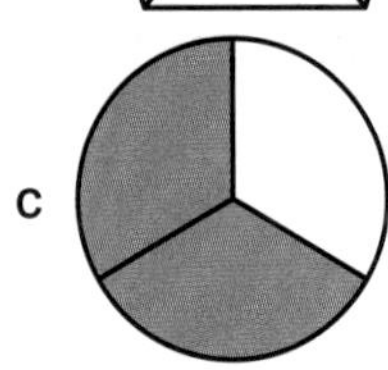 $\frac{\text{number of parts shaded}}{\text{total number of equal parts}} = \frac{\square}{\square}$

> **Q2a hint**
>
> 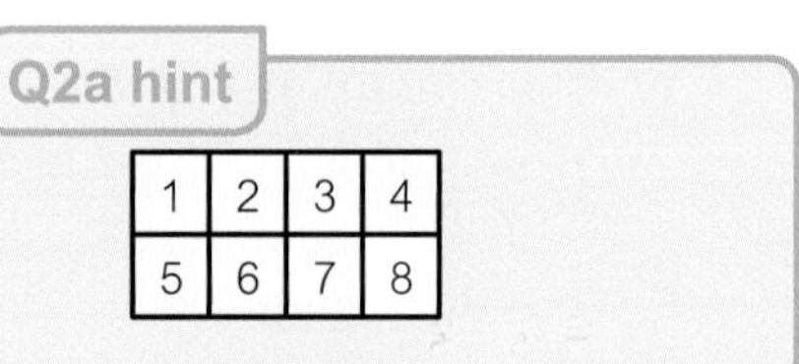
>

4b **3** Which fraction is larger in each pair?

a $\frac{3}{5}$ or $\frac{1}{5}$

b $\frac{1}{4}$ or $\frac{3}{4}$

> **Q3a hint**
>
> Divide a bar into 5 equal parts. The larger the number of shaded parts, the bigger the fraction.
>
> 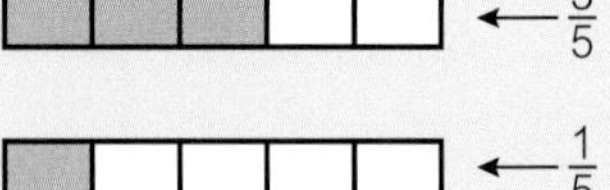
>

4b **4** Which fraction is larger in each pair?

a $\frac{1}{2}$ or $\frac{1}{5}$

b $\frac{1}{3}$ or $\frac{1}{4}$

> **Q4a hint**
>
> Divide a bar into 2 equal parts and 5 equal parts.
>
> 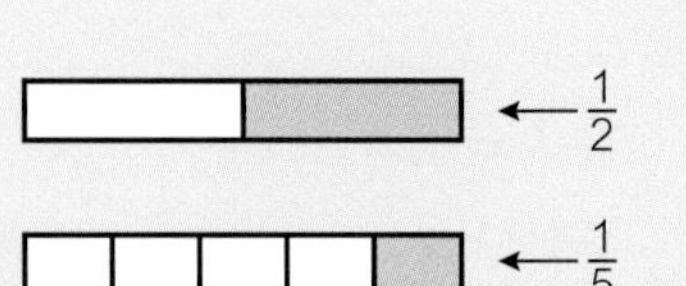
>

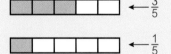

4b **5** Write each set of fractions in order of size, starting with the smallest.

a $\frac{7}{9}, \frac{3}{9}, \frac{5}{9}$

b $\frac{1}{7}, \frac{1}{2}, \frac{1}{11}$

> **Q5 hint**
>
> **a** The denominators are the same, so compare the numerators.
> **b** These fractions all have the numerator 1, so they are unit fractions.

Topic links: Common factors

4a

6 How many

  a sixths in a whole

  b quarters in a whole

  c tenths in a whole?

4a

7 Convert each improper fraction to a mixed number.

  a $\frac{9}{4}$

  b $\frac{16}{5}$

  c $\frac{13}{6}$

  d $\frac{11}{2}$

Q7a hint

Draw nine quarters. Count how many wholes and how many quarters left over.

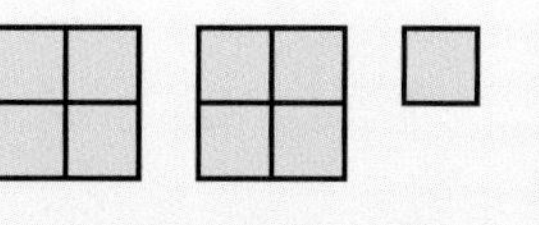

Q7b hint

Read the fraction aloud: 'sixteen fifths'. How many fifths in a whole?

5c

8 Work out

  a $\frac{1}{5} + \frac{2}{5}$

  b $\frac{4}{8} + \frac{1}{8}$

  c $\frac{3}{9} + \frac{2}{9}$

  d $\frac{4}{10} + \frac{3}{10}$

  e $\frac{4}{5} - \frac{1}{5}$

  f $\frac{3}{7} - \frac{1}{7}$

  g $\frac{7}{9} - \frac{2}{9}$

Q8a hint

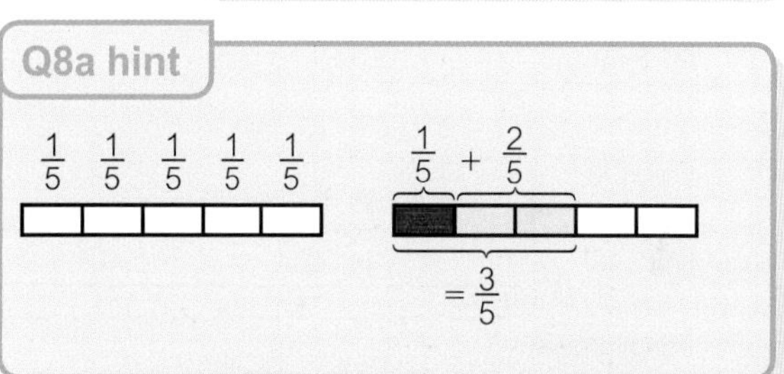

Q8e hint

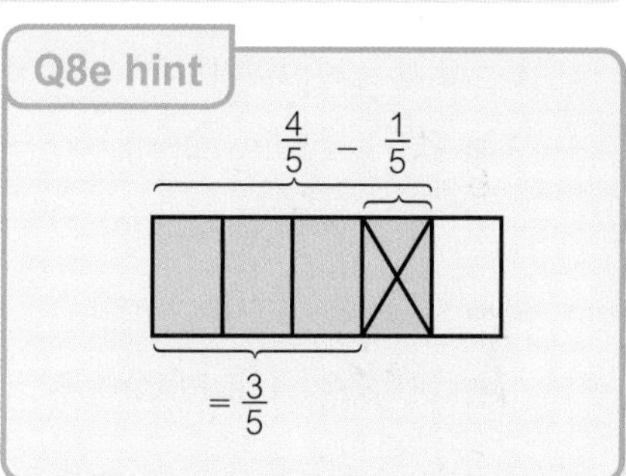

5b

9 Write each fraction in its simplest form. The first two have been started for you.

  a 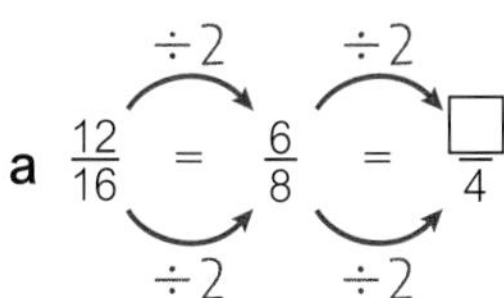

  b 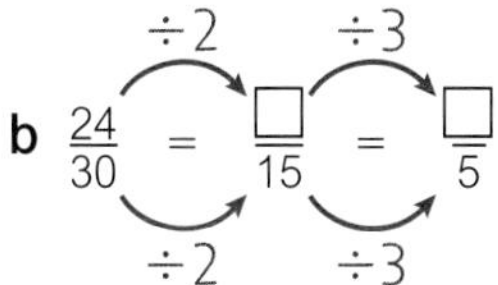

  c $\frac{18}{20}$

  d $\frac{9}{15}$

  e $\frac{16}{24}$

  f $\frac{40}{48}$

  g $\frac{30}{45}$

Q9a hint

The easiest way to simplify is to divide by the smallest number you can. Here, 2 is the smallest number that divides into 12 and 16.
When you have divided, check to see if you can divide again.

Q9d hint

Can you start by dividing by 2?
What can you divide by?

5b

10 Work out

a $\frac{1}{4}$ of £8

b $\frac{1}{3}$ of 12 km

c $\frac{1}{5}$ of 30 kg

d $\frac{1}{6}$ of 24 cm

Q10a hint

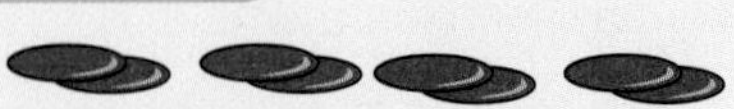

Use counters to represent £1 coins. Arrange 8 counters into 4 equal piles. How many counters are in each pile?

Q10b hint

Use counters to represent kilometres. Arrange 12 counters into 3 equal piles.

Fractions, decimals and percentages

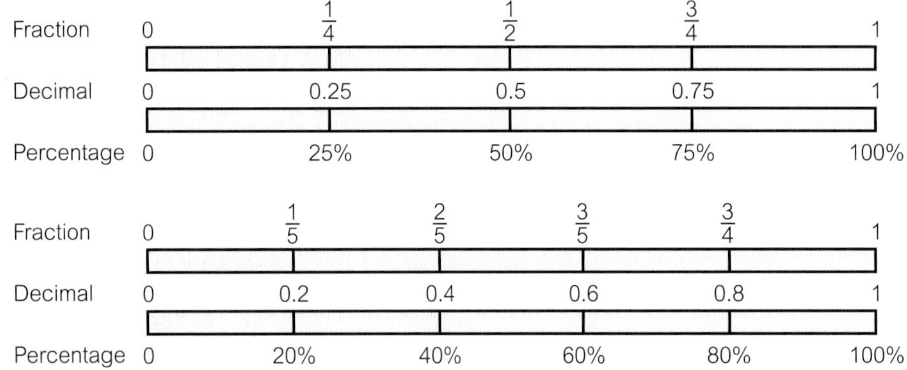

4b

1 Copy and complete. Use the diagrams above to help.

a 0.5 = □ (fraction)

b $\frac{1}{4}$ = □ (decimal)

c 75% = □ (fraction)

d 0.25 = □ (percentage)

e 20% = □ (decimal)

f 0.6 = □ (percentage)

g 80% = □ (fraction)

h $\frac{4}{5}$ = □ (decimal)

4b

2 Copy and complete this diagram.

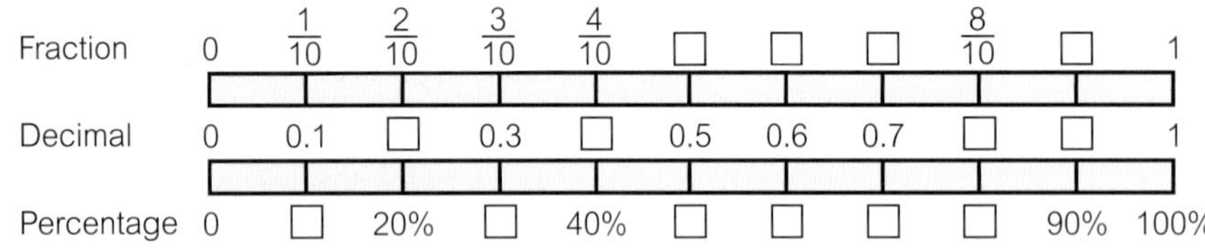

Q2 hint

Use the diagrams from Q1 to help.

4b

3 Copy and complete the calculations.

a $27\% = \frac{\square}{100}$

b $66\% = \frac{\square}{100} = \frac{\square}{50}$

c $44\% = \frac{\square}{100} = \frac{\square}{50} = \frac{\square}{25}$

d $\frac{35}{100} = \square\%$

e $\frac{3}{10} = \frac{\square}{100} = \square\%$

f $\frac{9}{20} = \frac{\square}{100} = \square\%$

Q3a hint

27% means 27 out of 100.

5b

4 a There are nine cats in a rescue centre. Seven of them are black. What fraction of the cats are black?

b There are 12 dogs in the rescue centre. Five of them are male. What fraction of the dogs are male?

Q4a hint

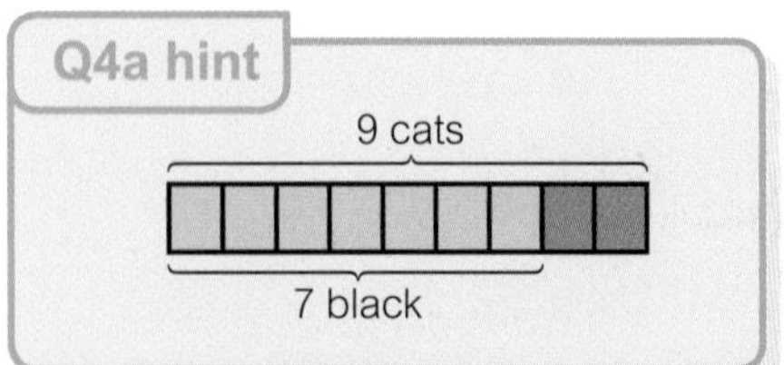

Percentages

4c

1 Work out
i 10% ii 50% iii 25% iv 75% of each of these amounts.

a £20
b 30 kg
c 50 ml
d 80 m
e £120

Q1a hint

Use counters to represent £1 coins.

Q1b hint

Find 10% or $\frac{1}{10}$ first, by dividing 30 by 10.

4a

2 Work out

a 20% of £12
b 30% of 45 kg
c 40% of 24 litres
d 70% of 9 t

Q2a hint

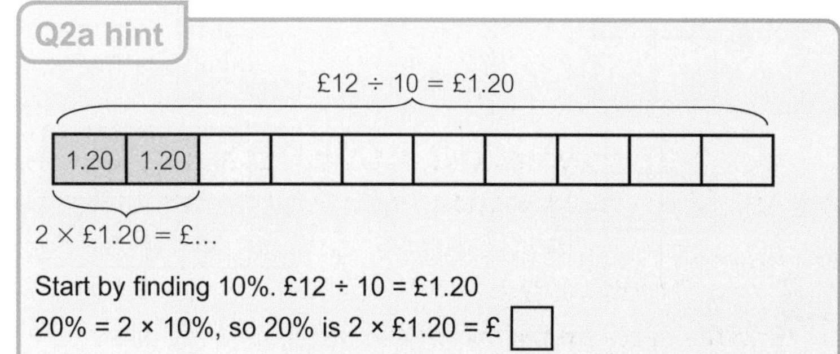

Start by finding 10%. £12 ÷ 10 = £1.20
20% = 2 × 10%, so 20% is 2 × £1.20 = £ ☐

5a

3 Rewrite these statements, giving the numbers as percentages.

a 40 out of 50 students like chocolate cake.
b 7 out of 25 people go to the gym.
c 12 out of 20 people have a pet.
d 8 out of 10 children like fruit.
e 2 out of 5 students play sport regularly.

Q3b hint

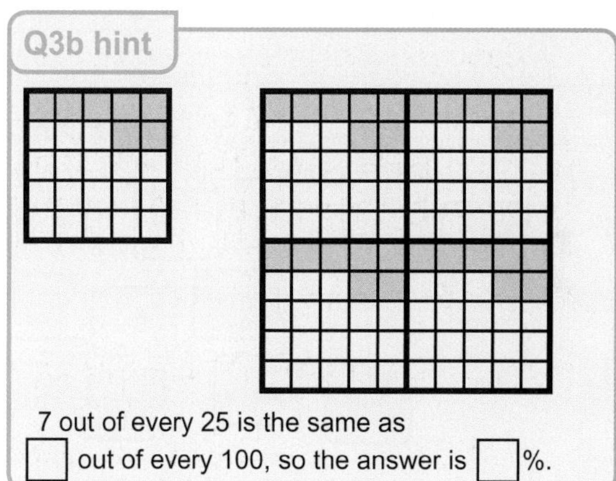

7 out of every 25 is the same as ☐ out of every 100, so the answer is ☐%.

Enrichment

1 Problem-solving / Reasoning Shelly thinks that the same fraction of each of these shapes is shaded.

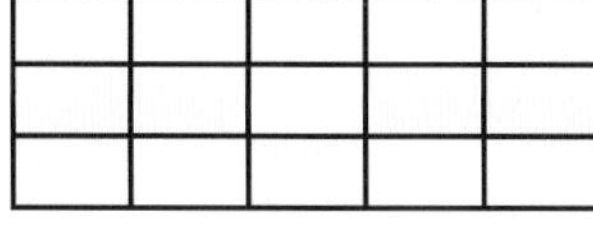

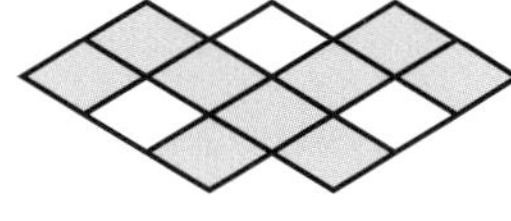

Is Shelly correct? Explain your answer.

2 **Reflect** Caspar says 'In the lesson I am doing lots of division.'

Look back at your work in this lesson. Where did you use division? How did you use it?

Reflect

5 Extend

You will:

- Extend your understanding with problem-solving.

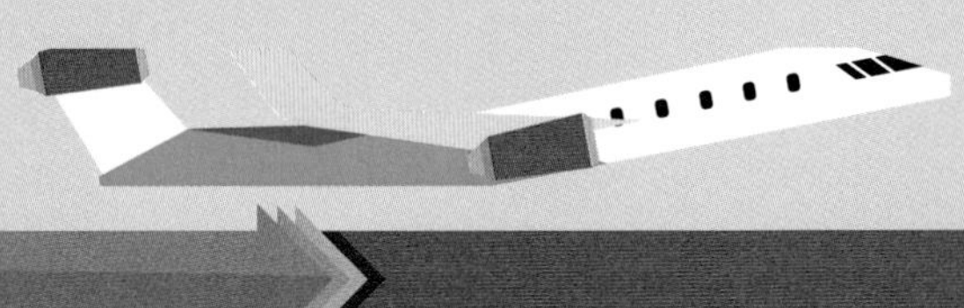

4b

1 Write down how much of each shape is shaded

i as a fraction **ii** as a percentage.

a 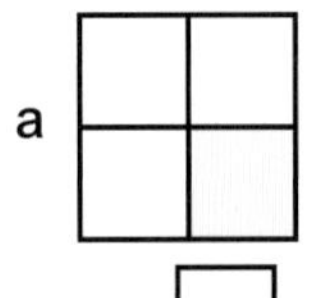 **b** 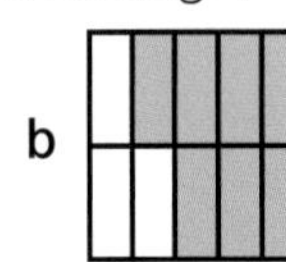

c 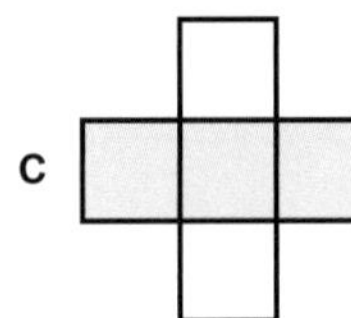 **d** 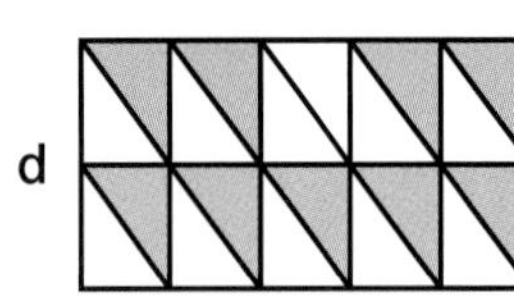

Q1 hint

To convert a fraction to a percentage, first write it as a fraction with denominator 100.

4b

2 Write each set of fractions in order, smallest first.

a $\frac{1}{4}, \frac{1}{5}, \frac{1}{2}, \frac{1}{8}$ **b** $\frac{1}{7}, \frac{1}{3}, \frac{1}{9}, \frac{1}{6}$

c $\frac{4}{6}, \frac{1}{6}, \frac{5}{6}, \frac{2}{6}$ **d** $\frac{8}{10}, \frac{3}{10}, \frac{5}{10}, \frac{9}{10}$

4b

3 **Problem-solving** Sort these cards into groups of equivalent values. Which card does not belong in any of the groups?

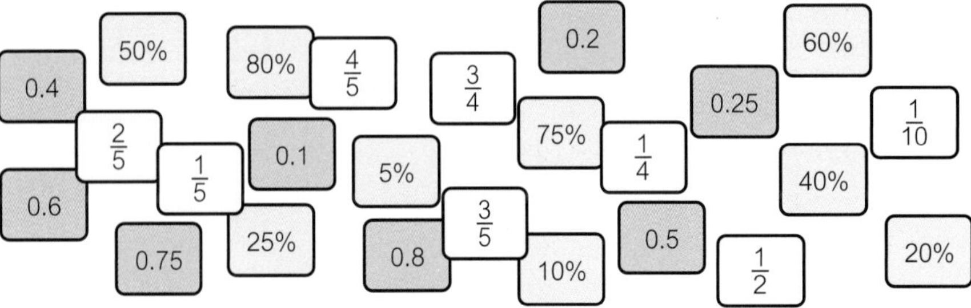

4a

4 a What fraction of this shape is shaded?

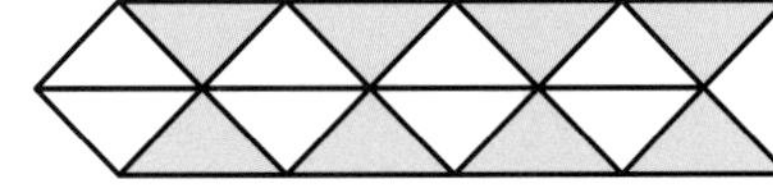

b **Problem-solving / Reasoning** How many *more* triangles must be shaded so that $\frac{3}{4}$ of the shape is shaded? Explain how you worked out the answer.

5b

5 Work out these additions. Give each answer as a mixed number in its simplest form.

The first one has been done for you.

a $\frac{3}{4} + \frac{3}{4} = \frac{6}{4} = 1\frac{2}{4} = 1\frac{1}{2}$ **b** $\frac{5}{6} + \frac{5}{6}$

c $\frac{7}{8} + \frac{5}{8}$ **d** $\frac{11}{12} + \frac{7}{12}$

e $\frac{7}{9} + \frac{8}{9} + \frac{5}{9}$ **f** $\frac{9}{10} + \frac{7}{10} + \frac{6}{10}$

Topic links: Bar charts, Perimeter and area

Subject links: Science (Q6, Q18)

6 **STEM / Reasoning** A blood test shows that 11 ml out of 20 ml is plasma. The rest of the blood is a mix of red blood cells, white blood cells and platelets. 5b

a Write the amount of plasma in the blood

i as a fraction **ii** as a percentage.

b What percentage of the blood is red blood cells, white blood cells and platelets combined?
Explain how you worked out your answer.

Q6a i hint
Write 11 out of 20 as a fraction.

Q6a ii hint
Convert your fraction in part **i** to an equivalent fraction with denominator 100.

7 **Finance** Ruth invests £2000. At the end of one year she receives £60 interest. 5b

Write the interest she receives

a as a fraction **b** as a percentage

of the amount she invests.

Q7a hint
Remember to write your fraction in its simplest form.

8 **STEM** **a** The tower of a wind turbine weighs 35 tonnes. 5b
The total weight of the wind turbine is 50 tonnes.
Write the weight of the tower

i as a fraction **ii** as a percentage

of the total weight of the wind turbine.

b The tower of a wind turbine costs £37 500.
The total cost of the wind turbine is £250 000.
Write the cost of the tower

i as a fraction **ii** as a percentage

of the total cost of the wind turbine.

Q8a i hint
Remember to write your fraction in its simplest form.

9 **Finance** A chocolate company asks people to invest £2000 in the company. Instead of being paid interest in money, they are given four boxes of chocolates each year. The chocolates normally cost £17.50 per box. 5b

a What is the value of the chocolates each year as a fraction of the investment?

b If the people had invested money in the bank, they would have got approximately 2% interest each year.
Do you think investing in the chocolate company is a good idea?
Give a reason for your answer.

10 **a** Copy and complete these equivalent fractions. 5a

i $\frac{5}{6} = \frac{\square}{12}$ **ii** $\frac{2}{3} = \frac{\square}{12}$ **iii** $\frac{3}{4} = \frac{\square}{12}$

b Write the fractions $\frac{5}{6}$, $\frac{2}{3}$, and $\frac{3}{4}$ in order, starting with the largest.

Q10b hint
Use your answer to part **a** to help.

11 Write these fractions in order, largest first. 5a
$\frac{3}{5}$, $\frac{7}{10}$, $\frac{13}{20}$

Q11 hint
Start by writing the fractions as equivalent fractions with the same denominator.

5a

12 Rewrite these statements, giving the numbers as percentages.

a 23 out of 40 students have a bicycle.

b 27 out of 80 people went abroad this year.

c 237 out of 250 people watch football on TV.

d 72 out of 125 students have a mobile phone.

Q12a hint

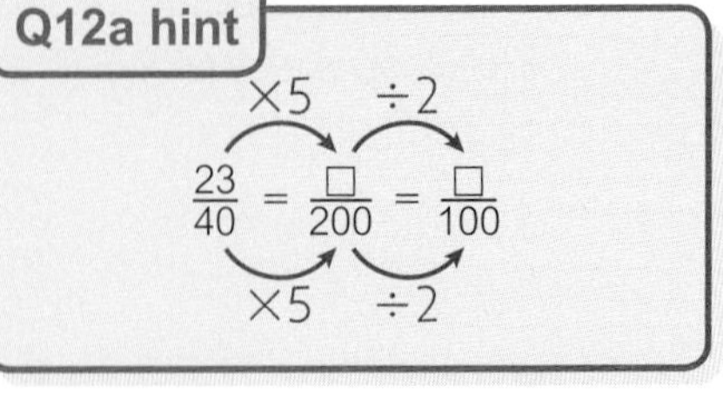

5a

13 Work out

a $\frac{5}{6} \times 24$

b $\frac{3}{8} \times 72$

Q13a hint

Use the same method as you would to work out $\frac{5}{6}$ of £24.

5a

14 Which of these calculations gives an answer that is different from the other two?

A	B	C
$\frac{4}{9} \times 36$	$\frac{2}{5} \times 45$	$\frac{2}{3} \times 24$

5a

15 Copy and complete.

a $\frac{4}{5}$ of 21 kg $= \frac{84}{5} = 16\frac{\square}{5}$ kg

b $\frac{2}{3}$ of 19 m $= \frac{38}{3} = \square\frac{\square}{3}$ m

c $\frac{3}{7}$ of 15 km $= \frac{\square}{7} = \square\frac{\square}{7}$ km

d $\frac{5}{9}$ of 40 mg $= \frac{\square}{\square} = \square\frac{\square}{\square}$ mg

Q15a hint

21 will not divide exactly by 5, so work out 4 × 21 first. Write this answer with denominator 5 as an improper fraction. Then change it to a mixed number.

5a

16 **Problem-solving** The bar chart shows the numbers of T-shirts sold in a zoo shop on one day.

Two-fifths of the T-shirts sold were child sizes.

The rest were adult sizes.

How many adult size T-shirts were sold on that day?

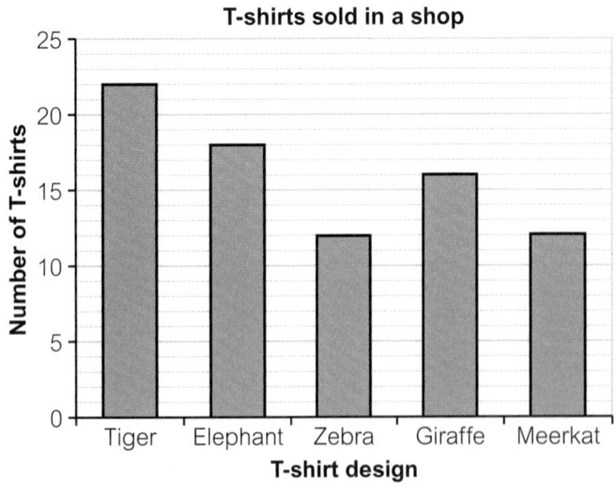

5a

17 **Problem-solving** A square field has a perimeter of 1.2 km.

Two-thirds of the field is to be grazed by sheep, the rest by cattle.

What area of the field is to be grazed by cattle?

Give your answer in square metres.

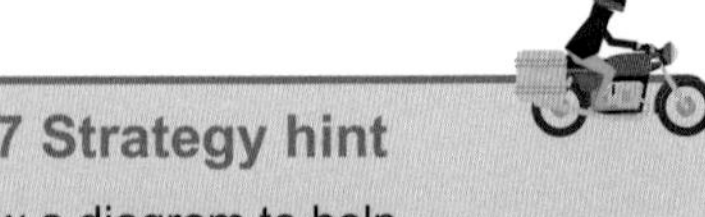

Q17 Strategy hint

Draw a diagram to help.

18 **STEM** Put these temperatures in order, lowest first.
77° F, 59° F, 10° C, 20° C

Q18 hint

To convert a temperature from Fahrenheit to Celsius:
- Subtract 32 from the temperature in Fahrenheit.
- Find $\frac{5}{9}$ of that value.

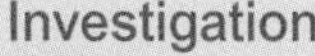

Investigation **Modelling / Reasoning**

Bamboo is the fastest growing plant on the planet. There are over 1200 different species, which grow at different rates. Bamboo grows to its full height in a growing season of 3 to 4 months.

One species of bamboo grows at a rate of 60 cm per week for 12 weeks.

1 Copy this table and complete the first and second rows.

Week	1	2	3	4	5	6	7	8	9	10	11	12
Height of bamboo at start of week (cm)	0	60	120									
Height of bamboo at end of week (cm)	60	120	180									
Fraction increase	–	1	$\frac{1}{2}$									
Percentage increase	–	100%	50%									

2 How tall will the bamboo be at the end of 12 weeks?

3 Complete the third and fourth rows of the table.
For example

Week 2 fraction increase $= \frac{\text{increase in height}}{\text{height at start of week}} = \frac{60}{60} = 1$, percentage increase = 100%

Week 3 fraction increase $= \frac{\text{increase in height}}{\text{height at start of week}} = \frac{60}{120} = \frac{1}{2}$, percentage increase = 50%

Use a calculator to work out the equivalent percentages you don't know by multiplying the fraction by 100. If necessary, round your answers to one decimal place. For example, $\frac{1}{3}$ as a percentage is 1 ÷ 3 × 100 = 33.3% (to one decimal place).

4 What do you notice about the pattern in the fraction increases?

5 What do you notice about the pattern in the percentage increases?

6 Would the pattern of fraction and percentage increases be the same for a bamboo that grows at a rate of 40 cm per week? Explain your answer.

7 Would the pattern of fraction and percentage increases be a good mathematical model to use for any bamboo? Explain your answer.

19 **Reflect** Look back at the questions you have answered in these lessons.
Which question(s) did you find easiest? What made them easy?
Which question(s) did you find most difficult? What made them difficult?
Are there particular kinds of questions you need more practice with?
If so, which kinds?

5 Unit test

4c

1 Work out

a 10% of 60 m **b** 50% of 80 kg **c** 20% of £90

2 What fraction of each shape is shaded?

a

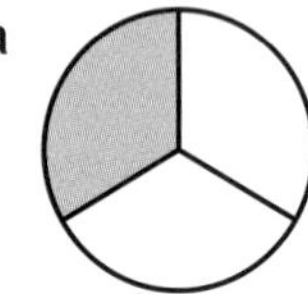

b

4b

3 Sharon has started to shade this rectangle.
How many *more* triangles must she shade so that $\frac{7}{12}$ of the rectangle is shaded?

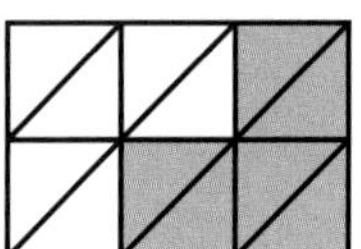

4b

4 **a** Which is larger, $\frac{1}{8}$ or $\frac{1}{9}$?

b Write these fractions in order of size starting with the smallest.
$\frac{5}{7}, \frac{2}{7}, \frac{4}{7}$

4b

5 Copy and complete these percentage and fraction conversions.

a $47\% = \frac{\square}{100}$ **b** $3\% = \frac{\square}{100}$ **c** $70\% = \frac{\square}{100} = \frac{\square}{10}$

d $\frac{38}{100} = \square\%$ **e** $\frac{9}{100} = \square\%$ **f** $\frac{3}{10} = \square\%$

4b

6 Copy and complete these decimal and percentage conversions.

a $0.75 = \square\%$ **b** $0.4 = \square\%$ **c** $0.05 = \square\%$

d $\square = 50\%$ **e** $\square = 4\%$ **f** $\square = 25\%$

4b

7 **a** Write $\frac{1}{10}$ as a decimal.

b Use your answer to part **a** to write $\frac{2}{10}$ and $\frac{3}{10}$ as decimals.

4b

8 Write the fraction $\frac{9}{20}$ as a percentage and as a decimal.
Show all your working.

4a

9 Convert these improper fractions to mixed numbers.

a $\frac{6}{5}$ **b** $\frac{19}{4}$

4a

10 Copy and complete these equivalent fractions.

a $\frac{7}{9} = \frac{21}{\square}$ **b** $\frac{24}{32} = \frac{\square}{16}$

4a

11 Which is the correct answer for each of these: A, B, C or D?

a 20% of £32 **A** £16 **B** £6.40 **C** £1.60 **D** £0.64

b 40% of 8 kg **A** 32 kg **B** 5 kg **C** 3.2 kg **D** 0.5 kg

5c

12 Work out

a $\frac{1}{7} + \frac{3}{7}$ **b** $\frac{4}{5} - \frac{3}{5}$

5c

13 Use the diagram to work out which is larger, $\frac{3}{5}$ or $\frac{4}{7}$.

14 Write the fraction $\frac{24}{32}$ in its simplest form. 5b

15 Work out 5b

a $\frac{1}{3}$ of 21 cm b $\frac{3}{5}$ of 60 km

16 Nine out of 10 people have a mobile phone. 5b
Write this number as a percentage.

17 Some students were asked the name of their favourite author. The pictogram shows the results. 5b

What percentage of the students said Michael Morpurgo was their favourite author?

Malorie Blackman	
Roald Dahl	
Michael Morpurgo	
J K Rowling	
Jacqueline Wilson	

Key:  represents 2 students

18 Write whether each of these statements is true (T) or false (F). 5a
Give a reason for each of your answers.

a To find 30% of an amount, you multiply by 0.3

b To find 1% of an amount, you multiply by 0.1

Challenge

19 Copy this code box.

I																										?
8	21		15		7	12	9	6	27	12	36		15		5	18	15	5		7	15	4	4	12	13	

Work out the answer to each of the calculations below. Then use your answers to fill in the letters in the code box and find the secret message. The first one has been done for you.

$\frac{2}{3}$ of 12 = 8, so 8 = **I**

I	$\frac{2}{3}$ of 12	**D**	$\frac{1}{4}$ of 20	**S**	$\frac{3}{5}$ of 35
Y	10% of 60	**G**	30% of 90	**N**	90% of 40
P	$\frac{1}{7}$ of 49	**O**	$\frac{4}{9}$ of 27	**A**	$\frac{5}{6}$ of 18
L	25% of 36	**T**	50% of 26	**E**	75% of 24
R	1% of 400				

20 Write your own message and questions for encoding it.

21 **Reflect** Use what you have learned in this unit to work out if any of these three statements are true: Reflect

A 9% is the same as $\frac{1}{9}$

B 9% and $\frac{1}{9}$ are both the same as 0.9

C 0.9 is the same as 'remainder 9'

Explain your answers.

6 Probability

6.1 The language of probability

You will learn to:

- Use the language of probability
- Use a probability scale with words
- Understand the probability scale from 0 to 1.

CONFIDENCE

Why learn this? Weather forecasters use the language of probability to describe the weather we can expect.

Fluency
What do these words mean?
possible, impossible, certain, predict, likely, unlikely

Explore
What does it mean when weather forecasters give a percentage chance of rain? When would you decide to take an umbrella?

Exercise 6.1

Warm up

1 Match each number with its equivalent percentage.

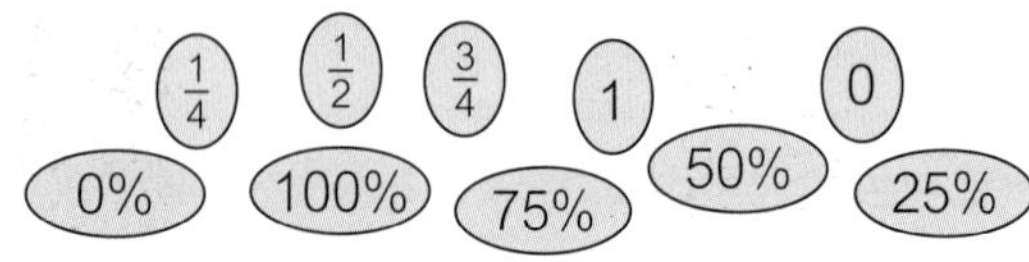

2 Write each number as a percentage.
a 0.5 b 0.75 c 0.25 d 0.1

> **Key point**
> **Probability** is the **chance** that something will happen.
> **Even chance** means that something is as likely to happen as it is not.

4a

3 How would you describe the **probability** of each **event**.
Choose from: impossible, unlikely, even chance, likely, certain.
a getting a 5 when you roll an ordinary dice
b scoring between 0% and 100% on a maths test
c picking a card with a number from an ordinary pack of playing cards
d a domino landing on its end when you drop it on the floor.

> **Q3 Literacy hint**
> The word **event** is used in probability to mean something that might happen, for example, a coin landing on heads, and so on…

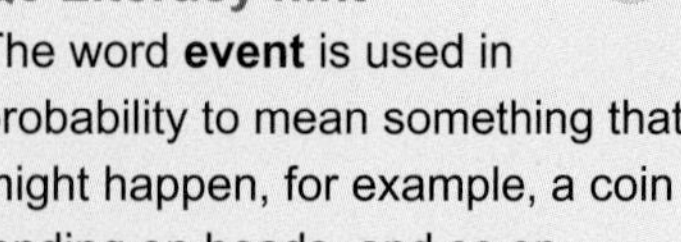

4a

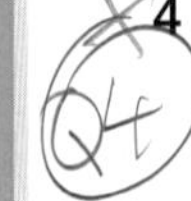

4 Copy the **probability scale** below. Mark each event from Q3 on your scale.

impossible | very unlikely | unlikely | even chance | likely | very likely | certain

> **Key point**
> Probabilities range from impossible to certain. You can show a probability on a **probability scale**.

4a

5 Problem-solving Write down an event which is
a impossible b unlikely c even chance
d likely e certain.

Topic links: Percentages, Fractions, Decimals

Subject links: PSHE (Q7)

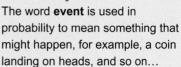

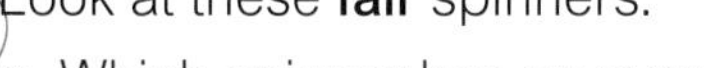

6 Look at these **fair** spinners.

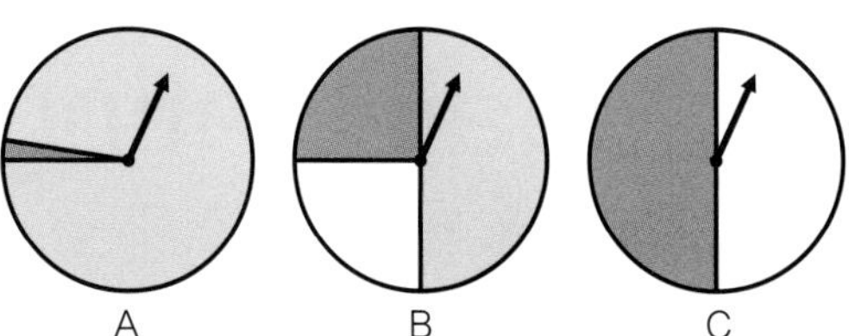

a Which spinner has an even chance of stopping on red?
b Which spinner is unlikely to stop on white?
c Which spinner is very likely to stop on blue?
d Which is more likely – Spinner A stopping on red or Spinner B stopping on white? Explain your answer.
e Problem-solving Draw a spinner where red is unlikely and where blue and white are equally likely.

Q6 Literacy hint
Fair means that the pointer on the spinner is equally likely to stop at any position.

4a

7 a Copy the probability scale shown below and mark these probabilities on it. Use their capital letters.

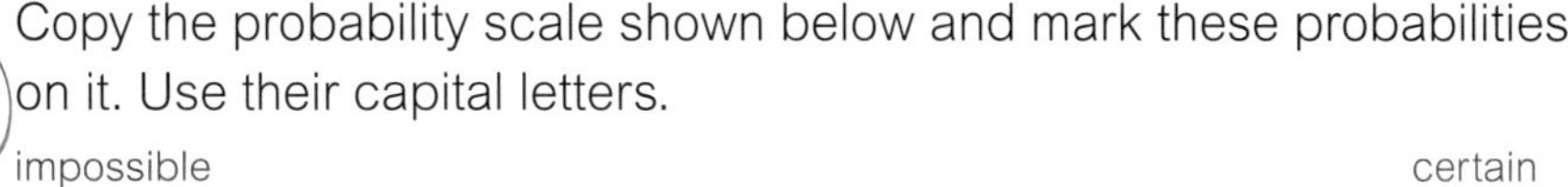
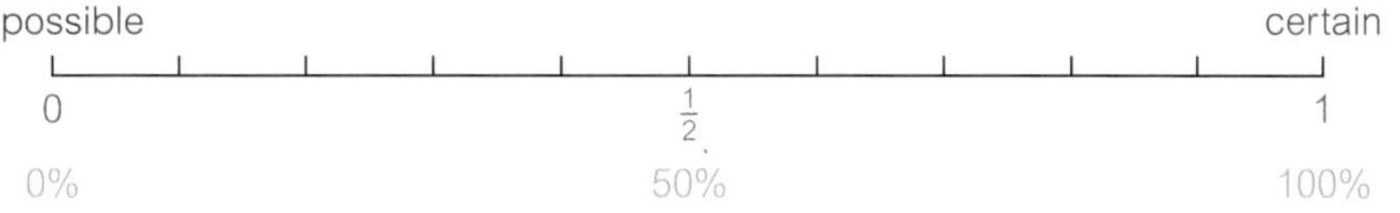

A The probability that someone will grow taller than their father is 50%.
B The probability of someone born in 2012 living to 100 is about 33%.
C The probability of having twins is 1%.
D The probability of an identical twin having twins is still 1%.
E The probability of a non-identical twin having twins is 6%.

b Who is more likely to have twins – someone who is an identical twin or someone who is a non-identical twin? Explain.

Key point
All probabilities have a value between 0 and 1.
You can use fractions, decimals and percentages to describe probabilities.

5c

Discussion What are the advantages of using numbers to describe probabilities?

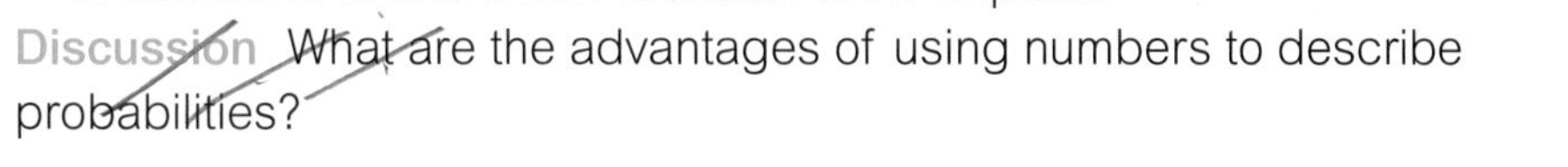

8 Finance / Discussion The probability of a business failing in the first 5 years is 56%.
Does this mean that people should not start new businesses? Explain your answer.

5c

9 Problem-solving / Reasoning An expert predicted that there was a 40% chance that Ferrari would win the next Grand Prix.
If Ferrari win, what could the expert say to justify her prediction?

5c

Investigation Reasoning / Discussion

Insurance companies estimate the probability of a person having a car accident in the next year.
The higher the probability, the more they charge for insuring the person.

1 a Which people are most likely to have a car accident?
b Which people are less likely?
c Write each description on a probability scale.
2 Do your classmates agree?
3 Repeat the investigation, looking at the probability of a different event.

10 Explore What does it mean when weather forecasters give a percentage chance of rain? When would you decide to take an umbrella?
Choose some sensible numbers to help you explore this situation. Use what you've learned in this lesson to help you answer the question.

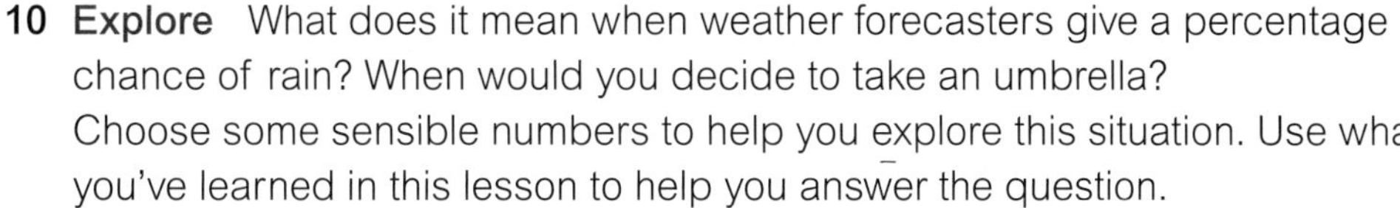

Explore

11 Reflect This lesson used a probability scale labelled in different ways.
a Did the scale help you to understand probability, or not? Explain.
b List at least two other areas of maths where you have used a scale.
c Do these scales help you understand the maths?

Reflect

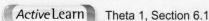

6.2 Calculating probability

You will learn to:
- Identify outcomes and equally likely outcomes
- Calculate probabilities
- Use a probability scale from 0 to 1.

CONFIDENCE

Why learn this? Games designers often try to make sure the probability of winning is low, but not zero. An example is the game show 'Who wants to be a millionaire?'

Fluency
- Write these numbers in order, from smallest to largest: $\frac{7}{10}, \frac{3}{10}, \frac{9}{10}, \frac{1}{10}$
- Write these numbers in order, from smallest to largest: $\frac{5}{6}, \frac{1}{6}, \frac{3}{6}, \frac{4}{6}$

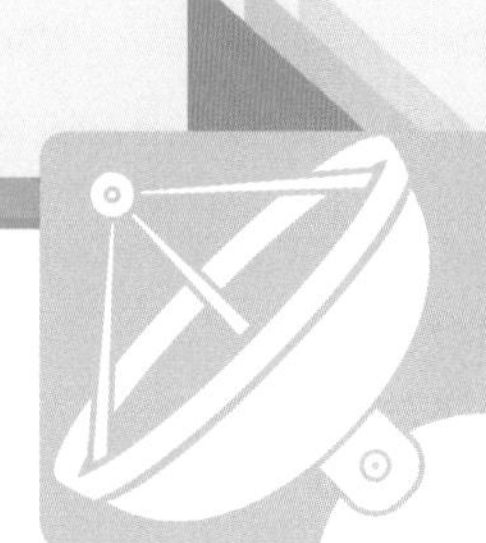

Explore
Why do you get so many vowel tiles in the game of Scrabble®?

Exercise 6.2

Warm up

1 There are five ice creams. One of them is strawberry. Write this as a fraction.

2 Three out of six plums are rotten. Write this as a percentage.

3 Here is a fair spinner.

a Use words to describe the probability that the spinner will land on
   i red   ii blue.

b Which colour is the spinner more likely to land on – red or white?

c Copy the probability scale shown below.

impossible — unlikely — even chance — likely — certain

Mark the probability of each colour on your scale.

Key point
An **outcome** is an end result. For example, one outcome of flipping a coin is heads.

5b

4 Each of these fair dice is rolled once. For each dice

a write all the possible **outcomes**

b write the total number of possible outcomes.

c **Reasoning** With which dice is the outcome 1 most likely?

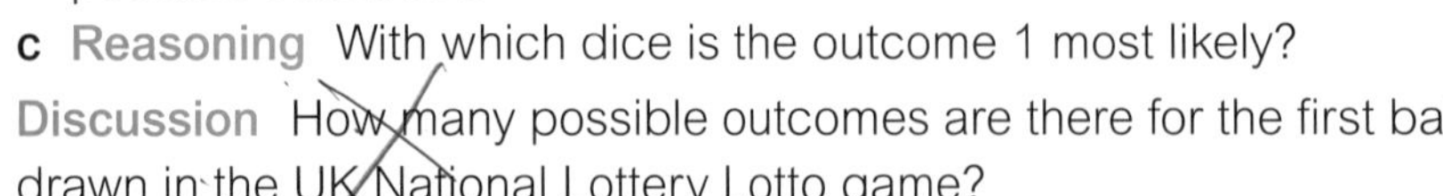

Discussion How many possible outcomes are there for the first ball drawn in the UK National Lottery Lotto game?

Q4a hint
Each dice could land on any of its faces.

Q4b hint
Count the possible outcomes you listed in part **a**.

5b

5 This spinner is spun once.

a It lands on an even number. What are the **successful outcomes**?

b It lands on a multiple of 3. What are the successful outcomes?

c It lands on a prime number. What are the successful outcomes?

Q5a Literacy hint
Successful outcomes are the outcomes you want.

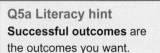

Topic links: Multiples and factors, Prime numbers, Square numbers, Fractions, Percentages

Worked example

Find the probability that this spinner will land on blue.

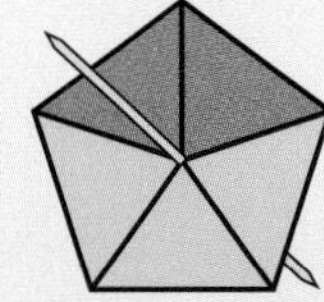

Probability that spinner lands on blue = $\frac{3}{5}$

There are three successful outcomes: blue, blue, blue.
The total number of possible outcomes is 5.

Key point

Probability of an event happening = $\frac{\text{number of successful outcomes}}{\text{total number of possible outcomes}}$

6 Dewi spins this fair spinner once. What is the probability (as a fraction) that it lands on

a pink **b** green **c** blue **d** white?

5b

Q6a hint

The successful outcome is pink. What is the number of successful outcomes? What is the total number of possible outcomes for this spinner?

7 The numbers on the faces of a 10-sided dice are

5 100 20 10 1 1000 15 50 20 1

Leah rolls the dice once.

5b

a What is the probability (as a fraction) it will land on

i the number 1 **ii** a 2-digit number

iii a number greater than 1 **iv** a multiple of 10?

b Write your answers to part **a** as decimal probabilities.

c Write your answers to part **a** as percentage probabilities.

8 Work out these probabilities, giving your answers as fractions.

5b

a An ordinary six-sided dice lands on an odd number.

b The first ball drawn in a game of Bingo is over 60. (There are 100 balls, numbered from 1 to 100.)

c New Year's Day falls on a Tuesday.

d You pick a picture card at **random** from an ordinary shuffled pack of 52 playing cards. (The picture cards are the Jack, Queen and King of each suit.)

Discussion What is the probability of a baby being born at the weekend? Explain your answer.

Q8d Literacy hint

Picking an item at **random** means that each item has exactly the same chance of being picked.

9 Reasoning Ollie says, 'The probability of a football team winning is $\frac{1}{3}$ because winning is only one out of the three possible outcomes – win, lose, draw.' Explain why Ollie is wrong.

5b

10 Problem-solving / Real

5b

a A single-wheel lock (with numbers 0–9) can be opened by the number 2. What is the probability that a stranger can open the lock in one attempt?

b A different lock has two wheels of numbers.

i How many possible combinations are there?

ii What is the probability that a stranger can open this lock at the first attempt?

c If the lock has three wheels, what is the probability that a stranger can open it at the first attempt?

5b

11 Jarvis rolls a 12-sided dice numbered from 1 to 12.

a Work out the probability that Jarvis rolls

A an even number

B a number greater than 0

C a multiple of 5

D a number less than 10

E a prime number

F a square number.

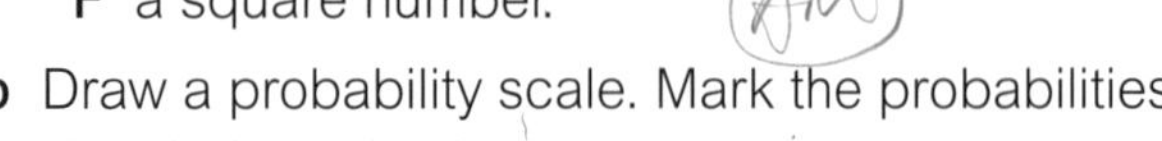

b Draw a probability scale. Mark the probabilities from part **a** on it. Use their capital letters.

> **Q12a hint**
> You do not need to simplify the fractions.

> **Q12b hint**
> Number the scale in twelfths: $\frac{0}{12}, \frac{1}{12}, \ldots, \frac{12}{12}$

5a

12 A bag contains 2 chocolates, 3 toffees and 5 chews.
Lin takes a sweet from the bag without looking.
What is the decimal probability that the sweet is

a a chew

b a toffee

c a chocolate?

> **Investigation** — **Problem-solving / Reasoning**
>
> **Pick a counter**
>
> Kayla puts red, green, yellow and black counters in a bag.
> She picks a counter at random.
> The probabilities of getting each of the colours are:
>
> green $\frac{1}{4}$ red $\frac{1}{2}$ yellow $\frac{1}{5}$ black $\frac{1}{20}$
>
> What is the smallest number of counters that there could be in the bag?
> How many counters of each of the colour are in the bag?

Explore

13 Explore Why do you get so many vowel tiles in the game of Scrabble®?
What have you learned in this lesson to help you answer this question?
What other information do you need?

Reflect

14 Reflect Andy and Kofi are playing a game with a fair six-sided dice.
Andy needs a 6 to win. He rolls a 2!
Andy says, 'It's not fair. It's harder to roll a 6 than a 2.'
Use what you have learned in this lesson to decide if Andy is correct.
Explain.

6.3 More probability calculations

You will learn to:

- Calculate more complex probabilities
- Calculate the probability of an event *not* happening.

CONFIDENCE

Why learn this? If you know the probability that it will be windy tomorrow, you can decide whether to go kite surfing or not.

Fluency

Work out

- $1 - \frac{1}{4}$
- $1 - 0.6$
- $100\% - 12\%$
- $1 - \frac{2}{5}$
- $1 - 0.9$
- $1 - \frac{3}{10}$

Explore

In a tombola you win a prize for numbers ending in 0 or 5. What's the chance of winning?

Exercise 6.3

Warm up

1 Roopa spins this fair spinner once.

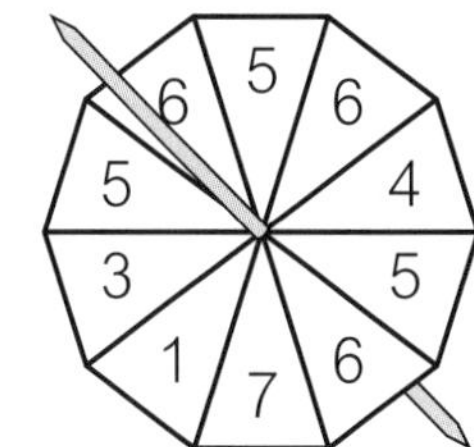

a What is the probability of it landing on 5?

b What is the probability of it landing on an odd number? Write your answer as a decimal.

c What is the probability of it landing on an even number? Write your answer as a percentage.

2 At a disco, there are 3 red, 2 green and 1 yellow laser lights. A computer turns one on at random. What is the probability it is 5b

a green or red

b red or yellow

c yellow

d red or green or yellow?

Q2a hint

There are 3 + 2 + 1 laser lights altogether. There are 3 + 2 laser lights that are either red or green.

3 Claire takes a card from the top of a shuffled pack of 52 playing cards. 5b

What is the probability that it is

a the 3 of clubs or the 2 of diamonds

b a 3 or a 2

c a club, a diamond or a heart

d a Jack or an odd number?

Discussion What is the probability that Claire takes a club or a picture card?

4 Olivia's mp3 player has 100 music tracks and is set to play on random. 5b

There are 20 rock tracks, 40 pop songs, 10 classical tracks and 30 folk songs.

a Work out the percentage probability that the next track played is

i rock or pop

ii classical or folk

iii rock, pop or classical.

Olivia adds 20 more classical tracks to her mp3 player.

b Work out the percentage probability that the next track played is classical.

c Work out the decimal probability that the next track played is folk.

Investigation

Problem-solving / Reasoning

a What is the probability of flipping heads with a coin?
b What is the probability of *not* flipping heads with a coin?
c Add the two probabilities together.
d What is the probability of rolling a 3 with an ordinary dice?
e What is the probability of *not* rolling a 3 with an ordinary dice?
f Add the two probabilities together.
g Write a general rule for adding together the probability of an event happening and the probability of it *not* happening.

Worked example

The probability that a segment of a mandarin contains a pip is approximately $\frac{3}{10}$.
What is the probability that a segment does *not* contain a pip?

Probability that a segment does not contain a pip is $\frac{7}{10}$.

$1 - \frac{3}{10} = \frac{10}{10} - \frac{3}{10} = \frac{7}{10}$

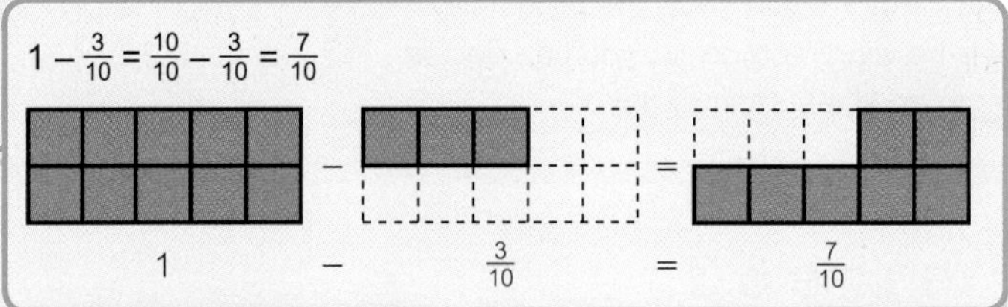

Key point
To find the probability of something *not* happening, subtract the probability of it happening from 1.

5a **5** **Real** Gordon is a goalkeeper. The probability that he saves a penalty is 0.3.
What is the probability that Gordon will *not* be able to save a penalty?
Discussion Can the probability of something happening be 0? Can the probability of something happening be the same as the probability of it *not* happening?

5a **6** **Real / STEM**
A baby has a 5% chance of being born on its due date.
What is the probability that a baby is *not* born on its due date?

Key point
Percentage probability of something *not* happening = 100% − percentage probability of it happening

5a **7** **Problem-solving** The probability that Haroon does *not* hit the bullseye of a dartboard is 0.8.
What is the probability that he hits the bulls eye with the next dart?

Explore **8** **Explore** In a tombola you win a prize for numbers ending in 0 or 5.
What's the chance of winning?
Is it easier to explore this question now you have completed the lesson? What further information do you need?

Reflect **9** **Reflect** In this lesson, you found probabilities using an ordinary dice, a 10-sided spinner and a coin.
Would you find it easier to use a fraction, a decimal or a percentage to write the probability for
a rolling 1 on the dice
b landing on 1 on the spinner
c flipping the coin and getting a head?
Explain your answers.

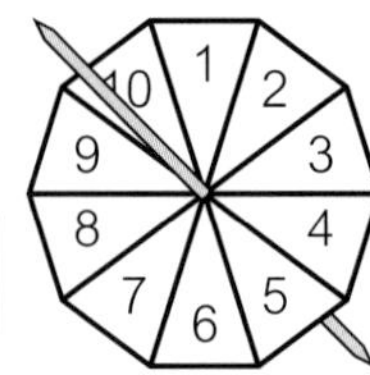

6.4 Experimental probability

You will learn to:
- Record data from a simple experiment
- Estimate probability based on experimental data
- Make conclusions based on the results of an experiment.

CONFIDENCE

Why learn this? Scientists repeat experiments to make sure of the results.

Fluency
- Out of a bag of 20 balloons, three exploded as they were being blown up. What fraction exploded? What fraction did not explode?
- 95 seeds out of a packet of 100 seeds produced a flower. What percentage produced a flower? What percentage did not produce a flower?

Explore
Will it snow on Christmas Day in the UK?

Exercise 6.4

Warm up

1 a The tally chart shows the colours of flowers that grew from a mixed packet of seeds. Copy and complete the table.

Colour	Tally	Frequency
Red	卌 卌 ||	
Blue		7
White	卌 |	

b What is the total frequency?

c What fraction of the flowers are red?

2 How would you describe each of these probabilities. Choose from: impossible, unlikely, even chance, likely, certain.

a 0.4 b $\frac{19}{20}$ c 0.5

d $\frac{1}{50}$ e 60% f 0

Key point

You can estimate the probability of an event using the results of an **experiment**. This is called finding the **experimental probability**.

Experimental probability $= \frac{\text{frequency of event}}{\text{total frequency}}$

Worked example

Andrew dropped a drawing pin lots of times.
It could fall point up or down.
He recorded the results in a frequency table.

a Work out the total frequency.

b Work out the experimental probability that the pin will fall point up.

c Work out the experimental probability that the pin will fall point down.

Position	Frequency	Experimental probability
Point up	83	$\frac{83}{100}$
Point down	17	$\frac{17}{100}$
Total frequency	100	

The total number of times Andrew dropped the drawing pin = 83 + 17 = 100

Experimental probability

$= \frac{\text{number of times pin pointed up}}{\text{total number of drops}}$

$= \frac{83}{100}$

= 83% or 0.83

Notice that the probabilities add up to 1 because $\frac{83}{100} + \frac{17}{100} = \frac{100}{100} = 1$

5b

3 Real / STEM A hospital tried out a new kind of knee surgery on some patients. After two years, patients were asked how they felt. The results are shown in the frequency table.

Outcome	Frequency	Experimental probability
symptom free	60	
some improvement	15	
no improvement	5	
Total frequency		

a Copy the table. Work out the total frequency.

b Calculate the **experimental probabilities**.

c The hospital claims that patients undergoing the new surgery are very likely to improve. Comment on this claim.

5b

4 Real A skateboard manufacturer gave 100 customers a set of newly-designed wheels to try out. The table shows how long the wheels performed well for.

Time (months)	Frequency	Experimental probability
5	7	
6	14	
7	35	
8	25	
9	15	
10	3	
11	1	

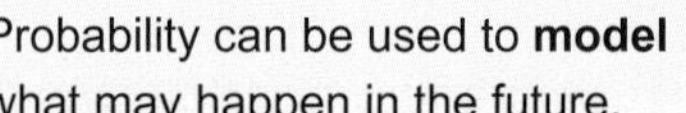

Key point

Probability can be used to **model** what may happen in the future.

a Copy the table. Work out the experimental probabilities for the different times the wheels performed well. Write your answers as percentages.

b Estimate the percentage probability that the wheels will perform well for longer than 8 months.

c Reasoning Why do you think the wheels performed well for different amounts of time?

Discussion When you repeat an experiment, will you get the same results?

5b

5 Real A manufacturer tested a new kind of mobile phone battery. They claim that there is a 95% experimental probability that the battery will last 30 hours with average use.

a Can you tell from the probability how many batteries they tested?

b What would make you confident that their claim was correct?

Key point

The more times an experiment is repeated, the more reliable the estimated probability.

5b

6 Real Hal counted the passengers in the first 100 cars passing his school. He found that 38 of the cars had no passengers. Estimate the probability that the next car will have

a no passengers

b some passengers.

5b

7 Real / Modelling Records show that more than 10 cm of rain fell in Orkney during 415 of the last 1000 months.

a Estimate the probability that there will be more than 10 cm of rain next month.

b Is this a good model for predicting the rainfall in the month of July? Give a reason for your answer.

Topic links: Frequency tables, Median

Subject links: Science (Q3 and Q9)

8 **Problem-solving** An optician's records show that 17 of the last 50 customers bought tinted lenses, and 23 of them bought two pairs of glasses. 5b

a Estimate the probability that the next customer orders

i tinted lenses   ii two pairs of glasses.

b The optician's assistant worked out 17 + 23 = 40 and estimated that the probability of a customer ordering tinted lenses or two pairs of glasses is $\frac{40}{50}$.
Explain why he might be wrong.

9 **Real / STEM** An amateur astronomer recorded the number of shooting stars she saw each night between midnight and 1 am. 5b

Shooting stars	0	1–2	3–5	6–10	11–20	more than 20
Frequency	3	12	20	22	15	8

a For how many nights did she record the number of shooting stars?

b Estimate the probability that she will see at least three shooting stars during the next night.

10 **Reasoning** The median number of customers visiting Lydia's café each day is 36. 5b
What is the probability that more than 36 customers will visit the café tomorrow?

Discussion For which of these events can you work out the exact probability?

A The next train is late.

B Picking a particular coloured counter from a bag.

C A piece of toast falling on the floor butter-side down.

D Next year's price of your favourite magazine.

Investigation **Real / Discussion**

Work in a group of five.

1 Each person draws a straight line between 1 cm and 30 cm long, secretly noting its length.
2 Take turns to show your line to the group.
3 Each person estimates the length of the line.
4 Record each estimate of the length.
5 Check if the estimate is within 10% of the true length. (Work out 10% of the true length. Add and subtract this to the true length to give the range of estimates within 10% of the true value.)
6 Repeat until each person's line has been estimated.
7 Record all of the results in the same tally chart. Use the rows 'good estimate and 'poor estimate'.
8 Work out the experimental probability of a person making a good estimate.

11 **Explore** Will it snow on Christmas Day in the UK? Explore
What have you learned in this lesson to help you answer this question?
What other information do you need?

12 **Reflect** In the Investigation in this lesson, you collected your own data and worked out the experimental probability. Other questions gave you data. Reflect
Which was easier? Explain.

6.5 FINANCE: Expected outcomes

You will learn to:

- Use probability to estimate the number of expected wins in a game
- Apply probabilities from experimental data in simple situations.

CONFIDENCE

Why learn this? Fundraisers use games of chance to make money for charities. To make sure they raise money, they must know the chances of winning.

Fluency
To win a prize at a Fun Day, I need to roll a dice and get an even number. What is the probability of winning a prize? What is the probability of not winning a prize?

Explore
Is it a good idea to use the same numbers each week in a lottery draw?

Exercise 6.5: Fundraising

Warm up

1 A spinner has the numbers 1 to 8.
If it is spun, what is the probability that it will land on
a an odd number **b** a prime number?

2 A ten-sided dice is numbered 0 to 9. At a school fair, you win £1 if you roll a multiple of 3. What is the probability of winning £1?

Key point
You can use probability to estimate **expected number** of wins in a game.

Worked example

Davina charges 10p for a 'lucky dip' raffle ticket.
She gives 50p back to anyone who gets a number ending in 0.
Davina uses the tickets numbered 1 to 100.
Will her game make money?

The probability of winning is $\frac{10}{100} = \frac{1}{10}$.

The numbers 10, 20, 30, …, 100 are the only winning tickets
There are 10 possible winning tickets out of 100.

This means there should be 1 winner on average for every 10 tickets. The 10 tickets will earn $10 \times 10\text{p} = £1$ and 1 winner will cost Davina 50p.
So Davina can expect to make 50p for every 10 tickets sold.

5b 3 **Finance** Shaun has a big spinner with an arrow at the centre.
He charges 10p to spin the wheel.
a What is the probability of **i** winning 20p **ii** winning 10p?
b How much money should Shaun expect to make for every six spins?

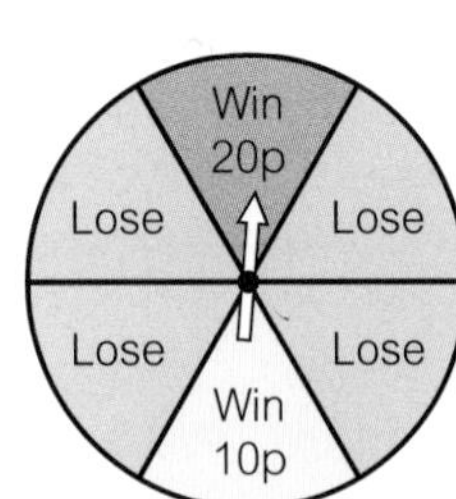

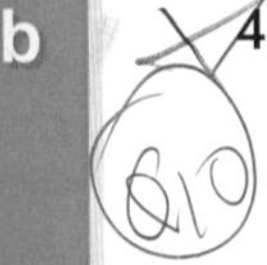

5b 4 **Finance** Edin has made a 'buzzer game'. Players must carefully move a metal ring along a wire without touching it. If they are successful they win a prize.
Edin has tested the game with 50 people. Thirteen completed it successfully and 37 did not.
a What is the estimated probability that a player will be able to complete the game?
Edin charges 10p for a go. He decides to award a prize of 50p.
b How much money should Edin expect to make or lose for every 50 players?
c Is his game likely to make money?

5 Finance / Reasoning Steve is running a dart throwing stall. He has attached some playing cards to a board. He tested the board with his friends, and recorded the results. 5a

	Hit picture card	Hit number card	Missed	Total
Number of outcomes	36	69	95	200

Steve charges 5p to throw a dart. He plans to award a prize of 50p to anyone who hits a picture card.

a How many winning throws should he expect in 50 throws?
b Is his game likely to make money?
c Explain how much money Steve is likely to make or lose if 100 people play his game.

6 Finance Gemma collected 10p coins in her piggy bank. She took a coin out of the piggy bank at random, looked at it and then put it back in the piggy bank. 5a
She did this several times and recorded 20 old coins and 10 new coins.

a How many times did Gemma take a coin from her piggy bank?
b Estimate the probability that the next coin she takes out will be an old coin.

7 Finance / Reasoning In a game, people are invited to pay 20p to roll three dice. If they get three 6s they win £50. The probability of rolling three 6s is $\frac{1}{216}$. Is this game likely to make money? Explain your answer. 5a

8 Finance A spinner has the numbers 1 to 5. You need to spin an even number to win. 5a

a What is the probability of winning?
b How many wins would you expect in 100 games?
c The game costs 20p a go. How much money would you take for 100 goes?
d What would be a sensible prize to make sure this game makes a profit?

Discussion What size prize encourages people to buy tickets, but still makes a profit for the organiser?

9 Finance / Reasoning Raffle tickets numbered 1 to 100 are folded, and prizes awarded to any people picking a ticket that ends in a 0 or a 5. 5a
Each prize is worth 40p.
How much should the tickets cost to raise at least £10? Explain your answer.

Discussion You have £2 to spend on any of the games in Q2–Q9. Which one(s) would you choose to play? Explain.

Investigation Finance / Problem-solving

Rhianna has designed a game to raise money.
Two coins are flipped separately, and if they are both heads you win.
Rhianna thinks that this will happen $\frac{1}{3}$ of the time.
Test this with a partner.
How many times should you flip the coins to get a reliable answer?
Explain what you find.

10 **Explore** Is it a good idea to use the same numbers each week in a lottery draw?
Is it easier to explore this question now you have completed the lesson?
What further information do you need to be able to answer this it? Explore

11 **Reflect** Look back at the questions in this lesson. List all the mathematics needed to design a fundraising game that raises money. Reflect

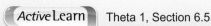

6 Check up

The language of probability

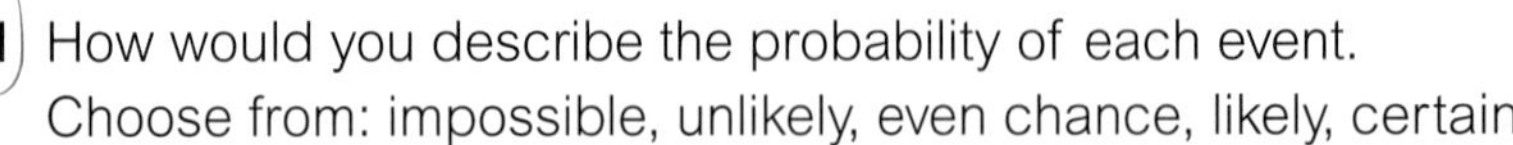

1 How would you describe the probability of each event.
Choose from: impossible, unlikely, even chance, likely, certain.
A You roll a number greater than 1 with an ordinary dice.
B A stamp falls on the floor sticky side up.
C One of your classmates was born on 30 February.
D A student chosen at random in assembly has a name beginning with Q.
E This maths lesson will end before 6 pm.

2 Mark each event in Q1 on a copy of this probability scale. Use their capital letters.

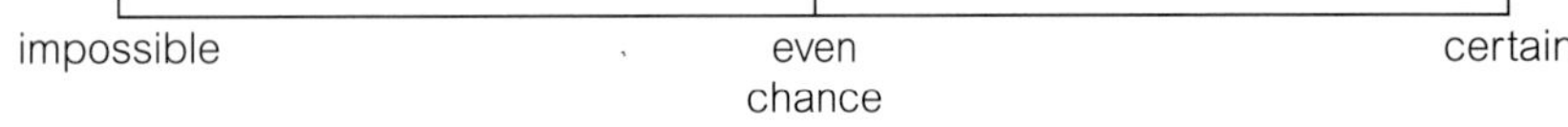

3 Describe each probability using words.
A 0.8 **B** 0 **C** 0.25 **D** 1 **E** 0.5

4 If divers come up too fast, they can become ill. About 12% of them have damaged nerves.
Use words to describe the probability of a diver having damaged nerves.

Calculating probability

5 Look at these fair spinners.
a List all the possible outcomes for Spinner A.
b What is the total number of possible outcomes for Spinner A?
c **i** How many ways can Spinner A land on white?
ii What is the probability that Spinner A lands on white?
iii What is the probability that Spinner A lands on red or white?

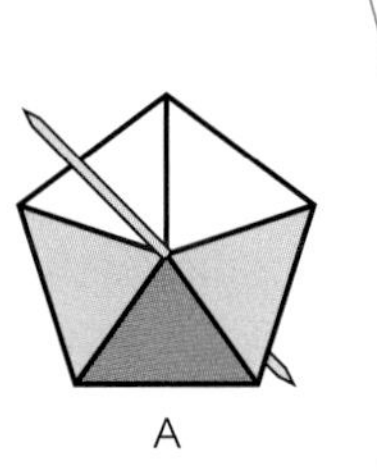
A

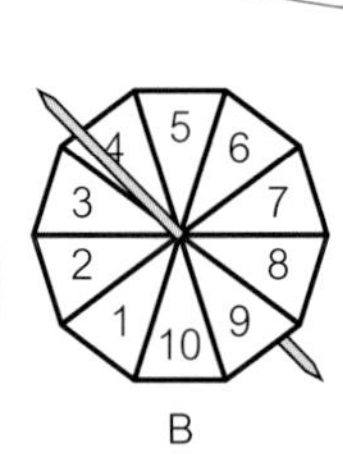

B

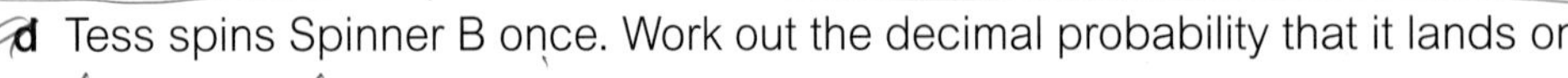

d Tess spins Spinner B once. Work out the decimal probability that it lands on
i 4 **ii** an odd number **iii** a number less than 7.

6 These letter cards are shuffled. Jim chooses one of the cards at random.

a Work out the percentage probability that he picks
i the letter S **ii** a vowel
iii not the letter P **iv** a green letter or the letter I.
b Which is more likely – a green letter or a blue letter? Explain your answer.

7 Frances removes all of the diamonds from an ordinary pack of 52 playing cards.
She shuffles the pack and looks at the top card. What is the probability that it is
a the 5 of hearts **b** a club **c** a club or a spade
d a picture card **e** a 3 or a club?

8 Look at this fair spinner.
Javier says, 'One of the three possible outcomes is blue, so the probability of the spinner landing on blue is $\frac{1}{3}$.' Explain why he is wrong.

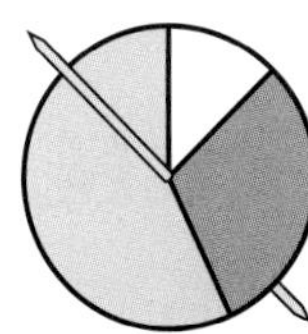

9 The probability that a new smartphone will develop a fault in the first 12 months is 0.1
What is the probability that it does *not* develop a fault?

10 Elephant calves have a survival rate of 98%.
- **a** If an elephant is born, is it likely to survive?
- **b** What is the probability of the elephant calf *not* surviving?

Experimental probability

11 Riikka recorded how long her new laptop battery lasted each day.

Time (hours)	Frequency	Experimental probability
7	5	
8	9	
9	16	
10	7	
11	3	
Total frequency		

- **a** Copy and complete the table.
- **b** Riikka said that the battery is unlikely to last more than 8 hours in a day.
  - **i** Estimate the probability that her battery will last more than 8 hours tomorrow.
  - **ii** Based on the data, is Riikka correct?
- **c** Are the experimental probabilities a good model for predicting how long Riikka's battery will last
  - **i** the day after the experiment finished
  - **ii** 6 months later?

  Explain your answers.

12 The chart shows how a plantation's bananas were used.
- **a** How many bananas were grown altogether?
- **b** Estimate the probability that a banana
  - **i** will go to the supermarket
  - **ii** will be dried or processed.

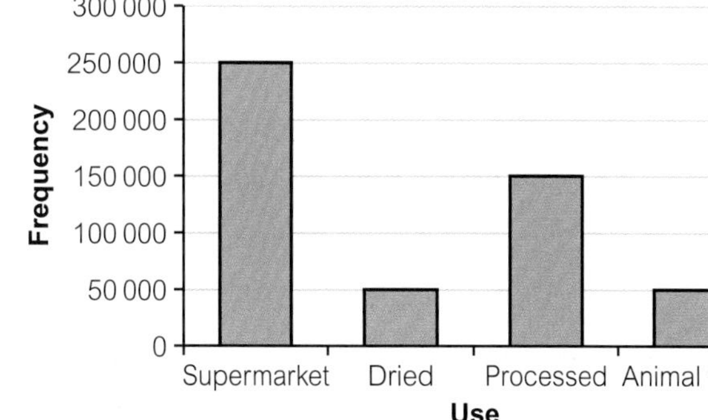

13 A quality control inspection of 200 watches found that 20 were faulty.
Estimate the probability that a watch will be faulty.

14 How sure are you of your answers? Were you mostly

Just guessing **Feeling doubtful** **Confident**

What next? Use your results to decide whether to strengthen or extend your learning.

Challenge

15 Think about your favourite sport. Describe an event that is
a impossible **b** likely **c** very unlikely **d** certain.

16 Design a spinner using the colours blue, yellow, black and white.
The probability of the spinner landing on blue must be 25%, on yellow 0.1, on black $\frac{1}{2}$.

6 Strengthen

You will:

- Strengthen your understanding with practice.

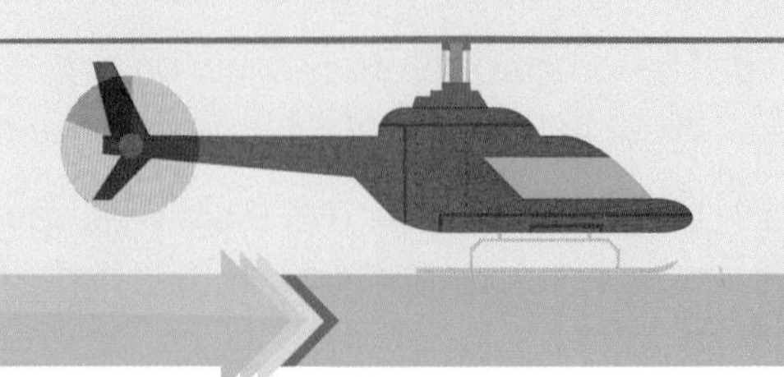

The language of probability

4a **1** Match each event to a probability.

An event

1 cannot happen **2** often happens **3** rarely happens

4 happens as many times as it does not happen

5 must happen.

Its probability is

A unlikely **B** even chance **C** certain

D likely **E** impossible.

4a **2** Here is a fair spinner.

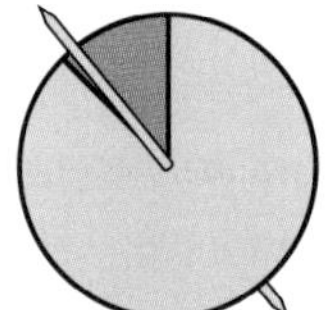

a Which colour is the spinner likely to land on?

b Which colour is the spinner unlikely to land on?

> **Q2a hint**
> Is there a reason for the spinner to land on one colour more often?

4a **3** Jen spins this spinner once. Which of these statements is true?

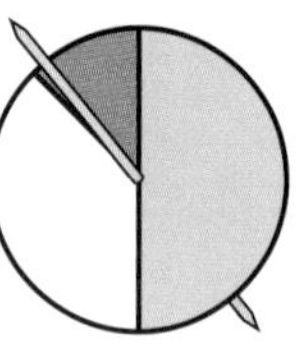

A The spinner is likely to land on blue.

B The spinner is unlikely to land on blue.

C The spinner has an even chance of landing on blue.

4a **4** Misha rolls an ordinary dice, numbered 1 to 6. Draw a probability scale and mark on it the letter of each event.

The dice lands on

A the number 5 **B** an odd number **C** the number 9

D a number greater than 2 **E** a number less than 7.

> **Q4 hint**
> Decide if each event is impossible, unlikely, even chance, likely or certain.

5c **5** **a** Copy this percentage probability scale.

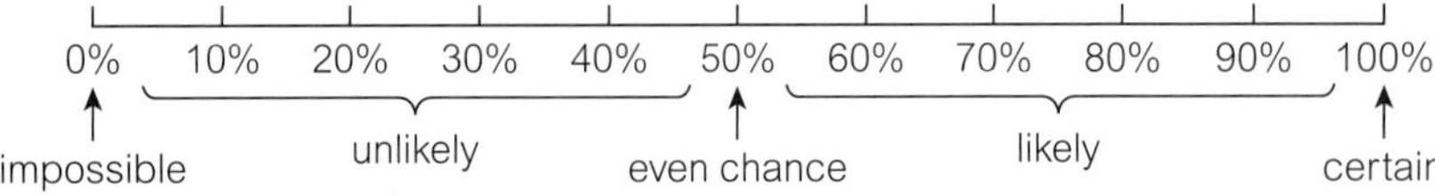

Mark on it the letter of each of these events.

A There is a 50% chance that the first student through the school gate tomorrow will be female.

B A teacher says there is a 10% probability that the school will be closed due to snow next week.

C There is a 100% probability that the school will close later today.

D If you cheat in a maths exam, the probability of being caught is 90%.

b Describe each of the events in part **a** using probability words.

Topic links: Fractions, decimals and percentages

Subject links: Science (Calculating probability Q3, Q4; Experimental probability Q3)

Calculating probability

1 This four-sided dice has a shape drawn on each side.

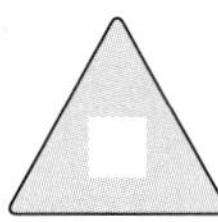 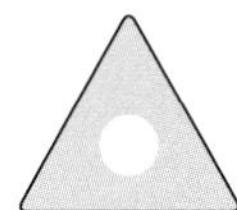 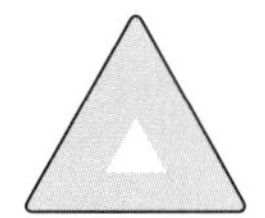 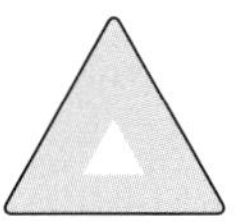 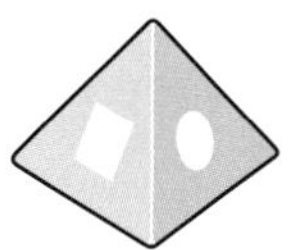

a How many possible outcomes are there?

b The dice is rolled once. How many successful outcomes are there for each event?

A The dice lands on a triangle.

B The dice lands on a circle.

C The dice lands on a shape with straight sides.

c Write the probability of each event in part **b**.

2 Alessandra put these counters in a bag and then took one out without looking.

     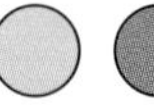     

a How many possible outcomes are there?

b What is the probability (as a fraction) that the counter is

i blue

ii red

iii pink

iv blue or pink

v not pink?

c How would you describe each of the probabilities in part **b**.
Choose from: impossible, unlikely, even chance, likely or certain.
Use the probability scale below to help you.

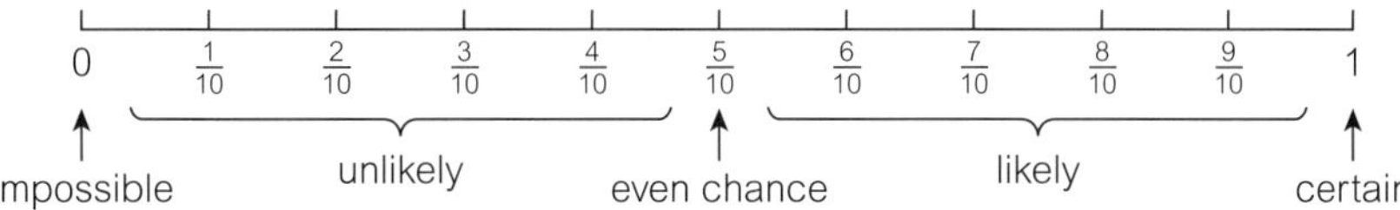

d Write each of the probabilities as a decimal.

e Write each of the probabilities as a percentage.

f Alessandra wrote each letter of her name on a counter and picked one at random.

      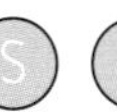      

What is the probability the counter is

i the letter A

ii blue and the letter A

iii blue or the letter A?

Q1 hint

Event A can happen in two ways because there are two triangles. There are two successful outcomes for event A.

Q1c hint

The probability of an event happening $= \frac{\text{number of successful outcomes}}{\text{total number of possible outcomes}}$

For event A, there are 2 successful outcomes and 4 possible outcomes.
Probability of event happening $= \frac{2}{4}$
You can leave the answer as $\frac{2}{4}$ or simplify the fraction to $\frac{1}{2}$.

Q2a hint

How many different ways can Alessandra take a counter out of the bag? Some counters have the same colour but they are still different from one another.

Q2b i hint

There are 5 successful outcomes and 10 possible outcomes.

Q2d hint

$\frac{1}{10} = 0.1$, $\frac{2}{10} = 0.2$, $\frac{3}{10} = 0.3$, $\frac{4}{10} = 0.4$, $\frac{5}{10} = 0.5$, …

Q2e hint

0.1 = 10%, 0.2 = 20%, 0.3 = 30%, 0.4 = 40%, 0.5 = 50%, …

Q2f iii hint

You must not count the same counter twice. Cover up the blue counters. Cover up those with the letter A. Count the letters you have covered up.

5a **3** Due to weather conditions, the probability that there will be a NASA rocket launch tomorrow is $\frac{1}{10}$.
Work out the probability that there will *not* be a launch.

5a **4** Astronomers predict that there is a 45% chance of a solar storm tomorrow.
What is the probability that there will *not* be a solar storm tomorrow?

Q3 hint

Probability of *not* a launch
= 1 − probability of a launch

1 whole = 10 tenths = $\frac{10}{10}$

$\frac{1}{10}$	$\frac{1}{10}$	$\frac{1}{10}$	$\frac{1}{10}$	$\frac{1}{10}$	$\frac{1}{10}$	$\frac{1}{10}$	$\frac{1}{10}$	$\frac{1}{10}$	$\frac{1}{10}$

not a rocket launch — rocket launch

Experimental probability

4b **1** Sanchez's teacher secretly put 10 cubes in a bag. Some were blue, some yellow and some black.
Sanchez took one out and recorded its colour in the tally chart below.
Then he put the cube back into the bag. He repeated this 20 times.

Colour	Tally	Frequency	Experimental probability
Blue	卌 卌 |||	13	$\frac{13}{20}$
Yellow	卌		
Black	||		
	Total frequency		

a Complete the Frequency column.

b Calculate the total frequency.

c Calculate the experimental probability of picking each colour.

d Which counter is more likely to be picked from the bag – black or yellow?

Q1b hint

The total frequency is the total number of times Sanchez took a cube from the bag.

Q1c hint

Write each frequency as a fraction with denominator 20.

5b **2** The tally chart shows the visits to some Post Office cashier desks on a Saturday morning.

Cashier desk	Tally	Frequency	Estimated probability
1	卌 卌 ||||	14	$\frac{14}{100}$ = 14%
2	卌 卌 卌 |		
3	卌 卌 卌 卌 卌		
4	卌 卌 卌 卌 卌 卌		
5	卌 卌 卌		
	Total frequency		

a **i** Copy the table and complete the Frequency column.
ii Which cashier desk was visited by the most customers?

b Work out the estimated probability that the next customer will visit cashier desk 3.
Write your answer as a percentage.

c **Reasoning** The Post Office manager says that the probability of a customer visiting cashier desk 1 next Monday is 14%.
Explain why this might not be true.

Q2c hint

Think of a reason why things might be different in the Post Office on Monday compared with on Saturday.

3 Real / STEM The bar chart shows the wildlife spotted on a Scottish boat trip in July.

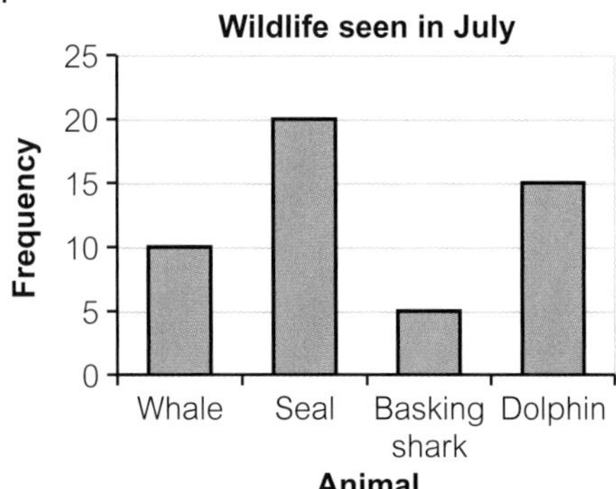

a How many animals were spotted altogether?

b Estimate the probability that the next animal spotted will be a basking shark.

c Reasoning Is your answer a good estimate for spotting a basking shark on a boat trip in January? Give a reason for your answer.

Q3a hint

Add up the frequencies of the bars.

Q3b hint

Probability = $\frac{\text{number of basking shark}}{\text{total number of animals}}$

Q3c hint

Think about the temperature of the water at different times of year.

Enrichment

1 Problem-solving **a** Write six numbers to label a blank six-sided dice so that the probability of rolling an even number is unlikely.

b Write ten numbers to label a blank ten-sided dice so that there is an even chance of rolling a number greater than 3.

2 Some two-letter words begin with a vowel: in, an, of, …
Others do not: be, to, we, …

a Close your eyes, turn to a random page in this book and point to a random place on the page.
Start reading and record the first two-letter word you come to.
Repeat this 20 times.

b **i** Work out the experimental probability of a two-letter word in this book beginning with a vowel.

ii Describe this probability using words.

Discussion If you repeated the experiment with 20 more two-letter words, would the results be the same? Explain your answer.

c Make up a different experiment. For example, record 20 three-letter words.

Q2 Literacy hint

The vowels are: a, e, i, o, u.

3 **Reflect** Copy and complete this sentence with three different endings.
In this unit I learned to ____.

4 **Reflect** Choose, copy and complete at least four of these sentences.
I showed I am good at ____ .
I found ____ hard.
I got better at ______ by ____ .
I was surprised by ____ .
I was happy that ____ .
I still need help with ____ .

Reflect

6 Extend

You will:

- Extend your understanding with problem-solving.

5b **1** The one-armed bandit machine has a paper strip stuck to its wheel. You pull the handle once and the strip shows your winnings. An unhappy face means you lose.

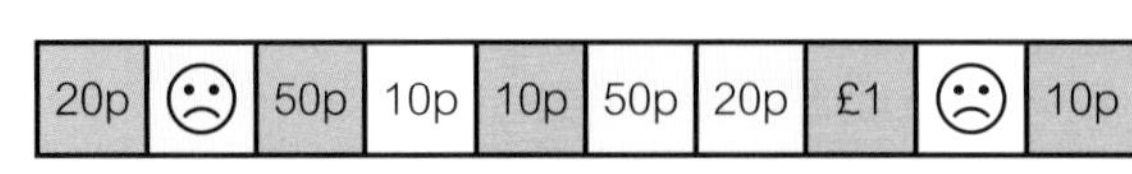

a Use words to describe the probability that the wheel lands on
  - **i** a yellow square
  - **ii** a yellow or a blue square
  - **iii** a black square.

b Write as a fraction the probability that the wheel lands on
  - **i** a blue square
  - **ii** a 10p prize
  - **iii** a blue square or a 10p prize.

c Work out the decimal probability of winning
  - **i** 50p
  - **ii** less than 20p
  - **iii** a multiple of 20p.

d Work out the percentage probability that the wheel lands on
  - **i** a 10p prize on a blue square
  - **ii** a prize of £1 or less
  - **iii** a prize of at least 20p.

e Work out the probability that the wheel does *not* land on
  - **i** an unhappy face
  - **ii** a blue square
  - **iii** a blue square or a 10p prize.

5b **2** **Problem-solving** Toni rolls an ordinary six-sided dice once.
Describe a possible event with each of these probabilities.

a impossible **b** 50% **c** unlikely
d $\frac{5}{6}$ **e** 1 **f** $\frac{1}{3}$

5a **3** There is a 40% chance that a fatal car accident on New Year's Day in the USA involves alcohol.
What is the probability that alcohol is *not* involved?

5a **4** The probability that Dana will *not* get a seat on the 8.10 am train to work is 0.28
Work out the probability that she will get a seat.

5a **5** **Real** About 200 000 people are chosen to sit on a **jury** each year in the UK. They are chosen from a population of 48 million adults.

a What is the probability that a particular adult will be chosen next year? Write your answer as a fraction in its simplest form.

b Describe this probability using words.

c What is the probability that a particular adult will *not* be chosen for a jury? Write your answer as a fraction.

> **Q5 Literacy hint**
> A **jury** is a group of 12 randomly chosen members of the public who decide the outcome of a court case.

Topic links: Fractions, decimals and percentages, Time

Subject links: Science (Q11)

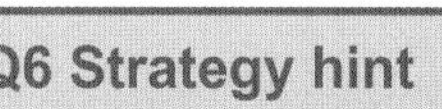

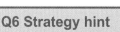

5a

6 **Problem-solving** A fair 8-sided spinner is going to be marked with letters. Jake has marked some events on a probability scale.

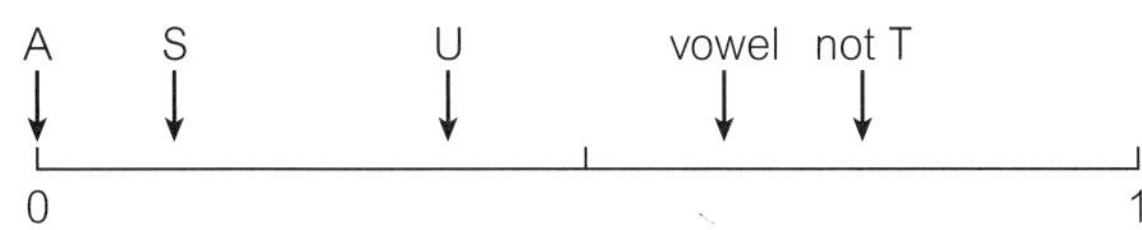

Design a possible spinner for these probabilities.

Q6 Strategy hint

Sketch the spinner. Use a pencil to fill in the easiest letters first. The probability scale might not show all of the possible letters on the spinner.

Worked example

If you flip a coin 10 times, how many heads do you expect?

The total frequency is 10.

Expected number of heads = $\frac{1}{2} \times 10 = \frac{1}{2}$ of 10 = 5

The probability of heads is $\frac{1}{2}$, so you expect heads to happen half the time.

Discussion If you flip a coin 10 times, do you expect to get exactly 5 heads and 5 tails?

Key point

If you know the probability of an event happening, you can work out the number of times you expect it to happen. This is called the **expected frequency**.

Expected frequency of an event = probability of event × total frequency

7 **a** How many tails do you expect if a coin is flipped 50 times? 5a

b How many 2s do you expect if an ordinary dice is rolled 30 times?

c How many even numbers do you expect if a 10-sided dice is rolled 80 times?

d You take a card from a shuffled pack of 52 playing cards and put it back. How many hearts do you expect if you do this 20 times?

e How many times do you expect the one-armed bandit in Q1 to land on a blue square in 40 goes?

8 In cricket, a googly is a way of bowling the ball. 5a

The probability that Nate bowls a googly is 0.15.

How many googlies would you expect Nate to bowl in 40 deliveries?

9 Find an object that has at least two different ways of landing when it is dropped. 5a

a Sketch the possible outcomes of dropping the object. Give each a short description.

b Drop the object on the table 20 times and record the results in a tally chart.

c **i** Work out the experimental probability of the object falling each way up.

ii Write your answer as a percentage.

d **i** Repeat the experiment by dropping the object 25 times.

ii Work out the experimental probabilities.

iii Compare your experimental probabilities with those from the experiment in part **b**.

e **i** Combine your results into a single frequency table.

ii Calculate the experimental probabilities for the combined data.

iii If you dropped the object 180 times, how many times would you expect it to land each way up?

Discussion If you repeat an experiment, will you get the same experimental probabilities?

Q9c ii hint

Change the probability to an equivalent fraction with denominator 100 then work out the percentage.

Q9d iii hint

Compare the percentage probabilities.

10 In 2011, the probability of a driver making an insurance claim was 0.13
In 2012, there were 33 million insured drivers in the UK.
Estimate the number of drivers making an insurance claim in 2012.

11 **Reasoning / STEM** The probability that a computer microchip is faulty is 0.22 when the production process is working properly.
A company employee found that six microchips were faulty out of a batch of 20.
Is the production process working properly? Explain your answer.

12 Rojas recorded the numbers of people entering a lift on the ground floor of a department store on Saturday morning.

People	Frequency
0	2
1	5
2	5
3	8
4	7
5	6
6	3
7	2
8	2

a Next time the lift arrives at the ground floor. Estimate the probability that
  i 3 people enter
  ii 3 or 4 people enter
  iii no-one enter
  iv more than 6 people enter
  v some people enter.

b The lift left the ground floor 50 times the following Saturday morning. Estimate the number of times 3 people entered the lift.

c **Modelling** Are your estimated probabilities a good model for lift activity on Monday? Explain your answer.

d **Modelling** Are your estimated probabilities a good model for people entering the lift on the top floor? Explain your answer.

13 **Problem-solving** At Christmas, the store lift continuously plays these five songs, one after the other, without any gaps between them. Their durations are shown in minutes.
Jingle Bells (150 sec), Silent Night (140 sec), White Christmas (180 sec), We Three Kings (120 sec), Away in a Manger (160 sec)
Work out the probability that White Christmas will be playing when Izzy enters the lift. Write your answer as a decimal.

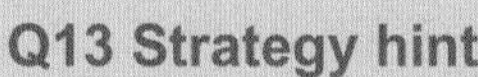

Q13 Strategy hint
Work out the total duration of the songs.

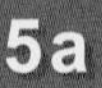

14 When Jamie's computer is switched on, it randomly chooses one of two background images – the sky or the beach. Jamie switched on his computer on Wednesday and on Thursday.

a Write the possible outcomes for the background images.

b Work out the probability that the background image will be the beach on both days.

Q14a hint
Make sure you list them all.

Wednesday	**Thursday**
sky	sky
sky	beach
…	…

15 Fatima flipped a coin and dropped a playing card on the table.

a Write all of the possible outcomes.

b What is the probability that Fatima flipped heads and the card fell face down?

Q15a hint
She could have flipped heads and the card could have fallen face down. Write this outcome as: Heads, Face Down. What are the other possible combinations?

16 **a** Write the possible outcomes for flipping two coins at the same time.

b What is the probability of flipping a head and a tail?

c Estimate the number of times you would expect to get a head and a tail with 100 flips.

17 Morine recorded the darts thrown by two of her favourite players.

	Tom Sharp	Sneaky Joe
Single	39	8
Double	30	5
Treble	25	7
25 ring	5	3
Bull	1	2

6.5

a Draw a suitable graph for the data.

b Estimate the probability of each player hitting a treble.

c Which player is more likely to hit a treble? Explain your answer.

d **Modelling** Whose estimated probability is a more reliable model for their future dart throws? Explain why.

e If Sneaky Joe threw 200 darts tomorrow, estimate the number of trebles he would hit.

Q17b hint

Write the probabilities as percentages.

5a

18 a A tennis ball is made by covering a rubber ball with two identical yellow patches. One patch is marked with an X.

i What is the probability that the ball will land on the marked patch after being hit?

ii Estimate the number of times it will land on the marked patch after 30 hits.

6.5

b A rugby ball is made by stitching four identical patches together. One patch is marked with an X.

i What is the probability that the ball will land on the marked patch after being kicked?

ii Estimate the number of times it will land on the marked patch after 60 kicks.

c About 360 million square kilometres of the Earth's surface is sea. The other 150 million square kilometres is land. If a globe of the Earth rolls across the floor, what is the probability of it stopping on land?

5a

Investigation **Problem-solving**

In a game, four animal cards are placed in a bag. Two animal cards are randomly picked out together. If the numbers of legs on the animals add to more than 6, then you win. If less than 6, then you lose. (Ignore any times when the legs add up to 6.)

Choose animals for the cards so that

- there is an even chance of winning
- there is a greater chance of winning than losing.

19 **Reflect** Probability is used in many jobs, for example

- sport
- medicine
- insurance
- forensic science
- weather forecasting.

For each one, write down one way it uses probability.

What career are you interested in? Do you think you will need to use probability in your job? How?

Reflect

6 Unit test

4a **1 a** Use impossible, unlikely, even chance, likely or certain to describe the probability of each of these events.

- **A** You choose the King of hearts from a shuffled pack of 52 playing cards.
- **B** You get 110% in your next maths exam.
- **C** A letter is delivered to your home next week.
- **D** You run a mile in 3 minutes.
- **E** You get an odd number when you roll an ordinary dice.

b Copy the probability scale. Mark each event from part **a** on it. Use their capital letters.

impossible — unlikely — even chance — likely — certain

5c **2** Describe each of these probabilities using words.

a $\frac{3}{4}$ **b** 0.2 **c** 50% **d** 0 **e** 100%

5b **3** Duane spins this fair spinner.

a List all of the possible outcomes.

b Write the probability that the spinner lands on

- **A** the number 4
- **B** the number 3
- **C** an even number
- **D** the number 6
- **E** a number less than 10.

c Copy the probability scale. Mark each event from part **b** on it. Use their capital letters.

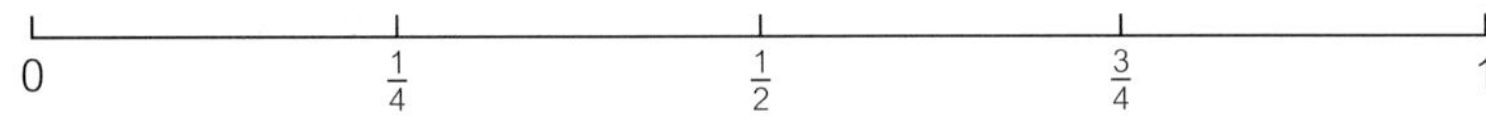

5b **4** Emily wrote these words on her fridge using magnetic letters.

a One of the letters falls off the door when it is closed. What is the decimal probability that it is

- **A** the letter o
- **B** n, o or d
- **C** a red letter
- **D** a black vowel
- **E** a blue letter or a vowel?

b Copy the probability scale. Mark each event from part **a** on it. Use their capital letters.

0 — 0.5 — 1

5b **5** A fair 10-sided dice numbered 0, 1, 2, 3, 4, 5, 6, 7, 8, 9 is rolled once. Work out the percentage probability that it lands on

a the number 3 **b** not the number 3

c a square number **d** a prime number.

5a **6** The probability of a stolen car being found is 0.3
What is the probability of a stolen car *not* being found?

5a **7** A government website says the chance of catching flu this year is 20%.
What is the probability that a person will *not* catch flu?

8 As part of an experiment, Luke cut off part of a rubber ball. 5a
He predicted that the ball would be unlikely to land on the curved surface when dropped.
Here are Luke's results.

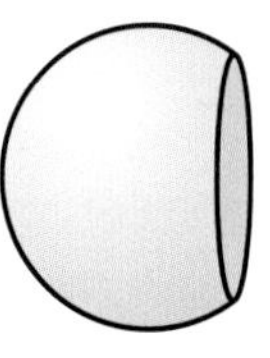

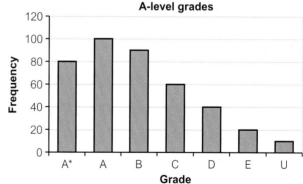

Outcome	Tally	Frequency	Experimental probability
curved surface	𝍸 |||		
flat surface	𝍸 𝍸 ||		
	Total frequency		

a How many times did Luke drop the ball?

b Work out the experimental probabilities.

c Is Luke's prediction correct? Explain your answer.

d How can Luke improve his estimates of the experimental probabilities?

9 In an honesty experiment, 100 purses were left on the pavement. 5a
The table shows what happened.

Action taken	Frequency	Experimental probability
handed in at the nearest shop	25	
handed in at the police station	20	
stolen	15	
Total frequency		

a Copy and complete the table.

b Another purse is left on the pavement. Estimate the probability that it will be handed in.

10 In a video racing game, an obstacle randomly appears on the race track five times every 40 laps. 5a
Work out the probability that an obstacle appears on the track during a particular lap.

11 The bar chart shows the A-level mathematics grades achieved by some students one year. 5a

a How many students got a grade of B or C?

b How many students took A-level mathematics?

c Estimate the probability that a student will get a grade of B or C next year.

A-level grades

Frequency: 0, 20, 40, 60, 80, 100, 120

Grade: A*, A, B, C, D, E, U

Challenge

12 Draw a four-sided and a six-sided fair spinner.
Put the numbers 1, 2 or 3 on the sections of each spinner.
You can use each number as often as you like.
Make up three probability questions about each spinner.
Work out the answers to your questions.

13 **Reflect** Think carefully about the work you have done in this unit.

a Write down, in your own words, a short definition for

i probability ii probability scale

iii possible outcomes iv successful outcomes.

b The word 'event' is used a lot in probability. How is it used differently in probability to everyday life?

Reflect

7 Ratio and proportion

7.1 Direct proportion

You will learn to:

- Use direct proportion in simple contexts
- Solve simple problems involving direct proportion
- Use the unitary method to solve simple word problems involving direct proportion.

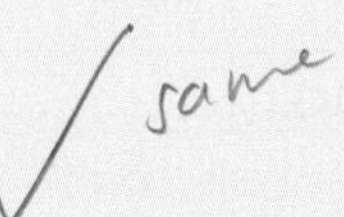

CONFIDENCE

Why learn this? When adapting a recipe for any number of people you must keep the ingredients in the same proportion.

Fluency
Divide 30 by each of these numbers.
2, 3, 4, 5

Explore
How much rice would you need to make a paella for your class?

Exercise 7.1

Warm up

1 Work out
  a 250 g ÷ 5 b £1.20 ÷ 6 c 35 kg ÷ 7 d 40 mm ÷ 8

2 Work out
  a 40 ÷ 5 × 3 b 20 ÷ 4 × 6 c 16 ÷ 8 × 5 d 50 ÷ 10 × 12

5c

3 **Real** A ticket to a theme park costs £21. Work out the cost of
  a 3 tickets b 4 tickets c 9 tickets.

Worked example

A recipe for four people uses 120 g of cheese.
How much cheese is needed for

a 8 people

4 × 2 = 8 people
120 g × 2 = 240 g

4 people need 120 g
8 people would need twice as much.
120 g × 2 = 120 g + 120 g
= 240 g

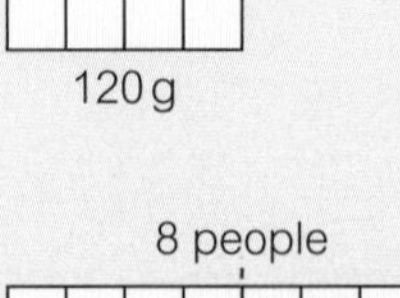

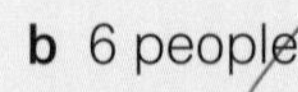

b 6 people?

4 people + 2 people = 6 people
2 people = half of 4 people
Half of 120 g = 60 g
120 g + 60 g = 180 g

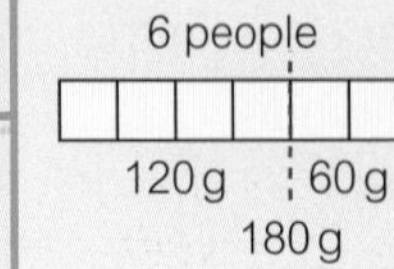
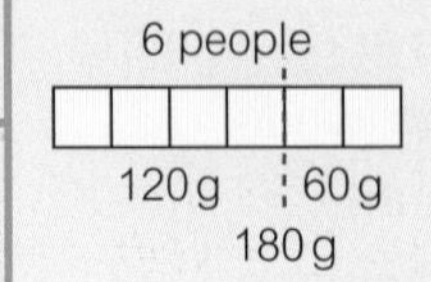

 Topic links: Measures

Subject links: Cookery (Q4), Science (Q5)

4 **Real** A recipe for six people uses four eggs. How many eggs are needed for
a 12 people
b 3 people
c 9 people
d 15 people?

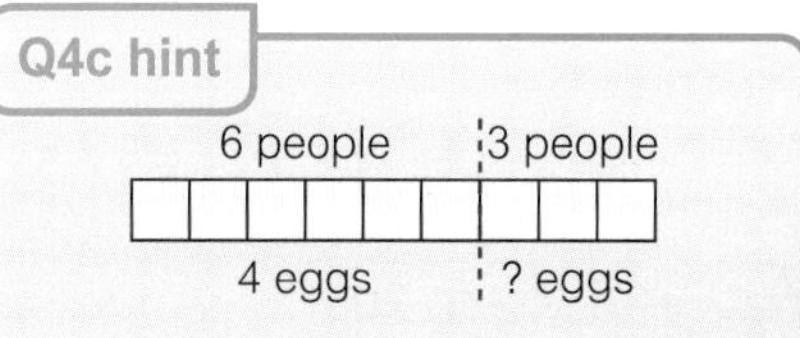

5b

Discussion Four tickets to a music concert cost £140. Discuss the different ways you can work out the cost of 14 tickets. Which method is best? Why?

Key point

In the **unitary method** you find the value of one item before finding the value of more.

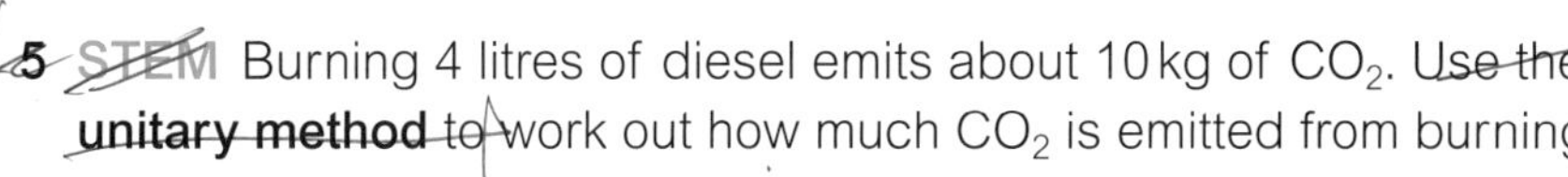

5 **STEM** Burning 4 litres of diesel emits about 10 kg of CO_2. Use the **unitary method** to work out how much CO_2 is emitted from burning

a 1 litre of diesel b 5 litres of diesel c 7 litres of diesel.

5a

6 It takes a music examiner 1 hour to test three students. How long will it take the examiner to test eight students?

Q6 Strategy hint

Change the hour into minutes first.

5a

7 **Problem-solving / Real** A scout leader orders a mug for each of the 31 scouts in his group. The total value of the order is £93. Four more scouts join the group, so he orders an extra four mugs. What is the total value of the order now?

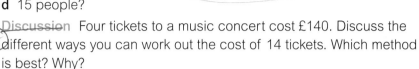

5a

Key point

When two quantities are in **direct proportion**, as one increases or decreases, the other increases or decreases at the same rate.
Two quantities in direct proportion have a straight-line graph through zero.

Investigation **STEM / Finance**

People buy and sell gold to make money.
The graph shows the price of gold on one particular day.

1 Explain what the points A, B and C on the graph tell you.
2 What is the cost of 0 g?
3 What is the cost of
 a 1 g b 2 g c 3 g d 4 g?
4 Complete this sentence: For every 1 g increase in weight of gold, the cost increases by £_________.
5 How much gold can you buy for £425?
6 How can you use the graph to work out the cost of 28 g of gold?
7 Think of two questions to ask about the graph.
 Make sure you work out the answers yourself first.

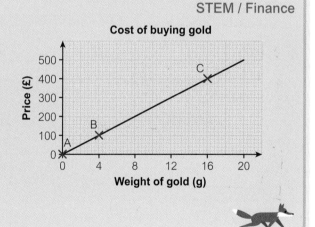

Cost of buying gold

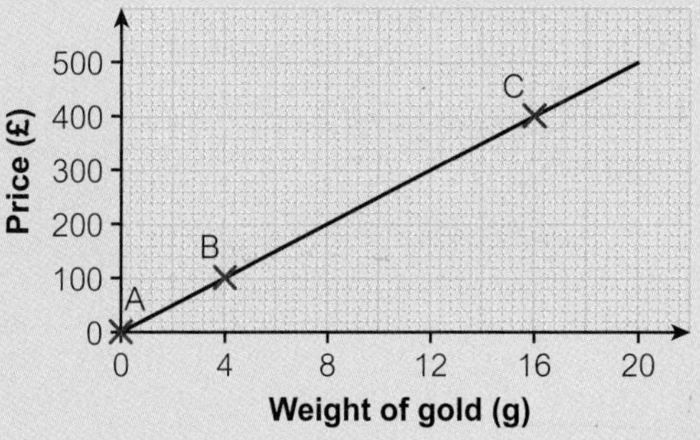

(Graph: Price (£) 0–500 against Weight of gold (g) 0–20; points A at (0, 0), B at (4, 100), C at (16, 400).)

8 **Explore** How much rice would you need to make a paella for your class? Look back at the maths you have learned in this lesson. How can you use it to answer this question?

Explore

9 **Reflect** Alan tells his mum he spotted two examples of **direct proportionality** at the petrol station:

A Mum's car: 30 litres of fuel costs £42
 Next car: 10 litres of fuel costs £14

B In our queue six people are served in 10 minutes.
 In the other queue, four people are served in 6 minutes.

His mum is impressed!
Should his mum be impressed? Explain.

Reflect

7.2 Writing ratios

You will learn to:

- Use ratio notation
- Reduce a ratio to its simplest form
- Reduce a three-part ratio to its simplest form by cancelling.

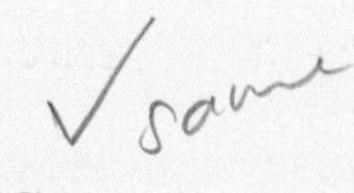

CONFIDENCE

Why learn this? For concrete to be strong you need to use the correct ratio of cement, sand and aggregate.

Fluency
Find the HCF of these pairs of numbers: 12 and 16, 20 and 35, 18 and 36.

Explore
Were there enough toilets at the Glastonbury festival?

Exercise 7.2

Warm up

1 Work out
a $24 \div 6$ b $30 \div 5$ c $49 \div 7$ d $56 \div 8$

2 Work out the mean of each set of numbers.
a 8, 4, 9 b 10, 5, 15, 2, 8

Key point
A **ratio** is a way of comparing two or more quantities.

5c

3 Write the **ratio** of blue beads to yellow beads for each necklace.
a b c d

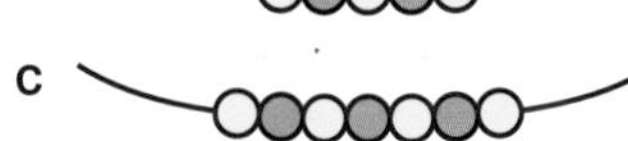

Q3a hint
There are two blue beads and three yellow beads in the necklace. Write the ratio 'blue : yellow' using the numbers.

5c

4 Draw beads to show the ratios
a blue to yellow 5 : 1 b blue to yellow 1 : 5.

Discussion Is the ratio 3 : 2 the same as 2 : 3?

5c

5 Problem-solving These are the points scored in different matches by a netball club's 'A' team and 'B' team.

'A' team	8	12	15	18	16	10	17	22	21	16	21
'B' team	10	17	9	6	18	10	14	18	15	11	15

a Write the teams' mean scores as a ratio A : B.
b What does this tell you about the teams' performances?

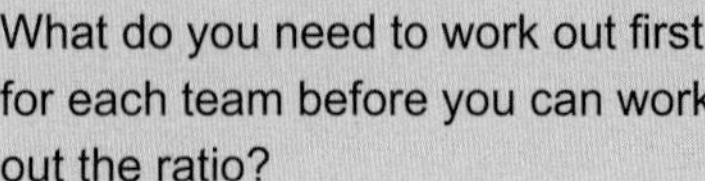

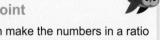

Q5a Strategy hint
What do you need to work out first for each team before you can work out the ratio?

5b

6 Write the ratio of blue beads to yellow beads for each necklace. Simplify each ratio if possible. The first one has been started for you.
a blue : yellow = 4 : 2 = 2 : □

b c

Key point
You can make the numbers in a ratio as small as possible by **simplifying**. You simplify a ratio by dividing the numbers in the ratio by the **highest common factor**.

Topic links: Highest common factor, Mean, Bar graphs

7 Write each ratio in its simplest form. 5b

a 2 : 20 b 25 : 5 c 4 : 24 d 6 : 30

e 8 : 24 f 6 : 10 g 30 : 25 h 24 : 10

i 16 : 6 j 40 : 15

Q7a hint

$$2:20 \xrightarrow{\div 2} 1:\square$$

Q7b hint

$$25:5 \xrightarrow{\div 5} \square:\square$$

8 **Real** At a nursery there are five members of staff and 20 two-year-old children. 5b

The recommended ratio of staff to children is 1 : 4.

Has the nursery got the correct ratio?

9 **STEM** Digital television screens usually have a width : height ratio of 16 : 9. 5b

This screen has width 80 cm and height 45 cm.

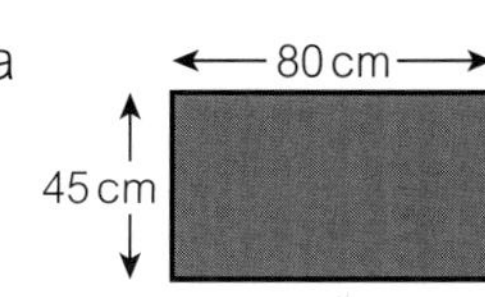

Does the screen have a ratio of 16 : 9?

Show how you worked out your answer.

10 **Problem-solving / Reasoning** The bar graphs show the number of recorded delivery and special delivery letters a company sends during one week. 5b

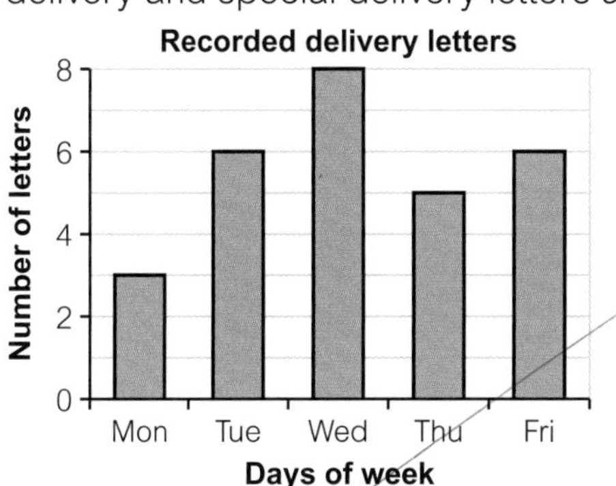

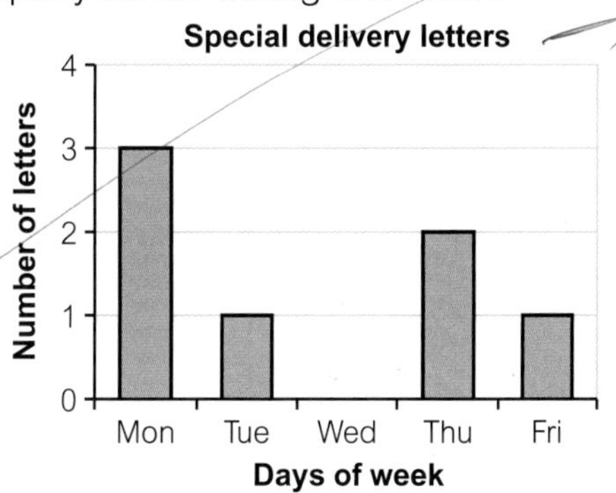

a What is the ratio of recorded delivery to special delivery letters? Write your answer in its simplest form.

b The secretary of the company says that they send three times as many recorded delivery letters as special delivery letters. Is the secretary correct? Explain your answer.

Q10 hint

What do you need to work out first, before you can work out the ratio?

11 Write each ratio in its simplest form. 5a

a 8 : 24 : 12 b 20 : 12 : 16 c 24 : 30 : 18

d 14 : 21 : 42 e 25 : 15 : 35 f 8 : 32 : 56

Q11a hint

The highest common factor of 8, 24 and 12 is 4, so divide all three numbers by 4.

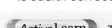

$$8:24:12 \xrightarrow{\div 4} \square:\square:\square$$

12 **STEM** A pink gold bracelet is made from 30 g of gold, 8 g of copper and 2 g of silver. 5a

Write the ratio of gold : copper : silver in its simplest form.

13 **Explore** Were there enough toilets at the Glastonbury festival? Explore

Is it easier to explore this question now you have completed the lesson?

What further information do you need to be able to answer this?

14 **Reflect** After this lesson Miguel and Judith discussed what they noticed about ratios.

Miguel said, 'A ratio tells you how much of one thing there is compared to another.'

Judith said, 'The things must always be the same kind. So, they must all be numbers of objects, or all numbers of people, or all lengths.'

Look back at the questions you answered about ratios. Is Miguel correct?

Is Judith correct? What other quantities or amounts could you write in a ratio?

7.3 Using ratios

You will learn to:
- Divide a quantity into two parts in a ratio given in words
- Divide a quantity into two parts in a given ratio
- Solve word problems involving ratio.

CONFIDENCE

Why learn this? When you know the ratio of the precious metals in jewellery you can work out the value of the jewellery.

Fluency
Here is a bag containing red, white and blue balls.
Write the ratio of red : white : blue balls in the bag.

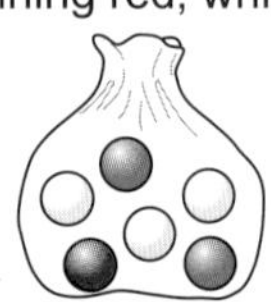

Explore
How many staff are needed to take your year group on a school trip?

Exercise 7.1

Warm up

1 In an ICT suite there are 36 computers and 3 printers.
Write the ratio of computers to printers in its simplest form.

2 Work out

a 28 ÷ 4   b 36 ÷ 6   c 60 ÷ 5   d 44 ÷ 11

4a 3 In a necklace there is one blue bead for every four yellow beads.
There are 15 beads altogether.
a How many blue beads are there?
b How many yellow beads are there?
c How can you check that your answers to parts **a** and **b** are correct?

Q3 hint
There are five beads (one blue, four yellow) in each section. For 15 beads you need 15 ÷ 5 = 3 sections.

5c 4 A game requires at least 16 counters in total. There must be one white counter for every two black counters. How many of each colour counter must be included in the game box?

Discussion Two people buy a lottery ticket between them and they win £1000. One paid 40p and the other 60p for the ticket. Is it fair that they get £500 each?

5b 5 Share these amounts between Alice and Ben in the ratios given.
Show how you check your answers.

a £21 in the ratio 2 : 1   b £45 in the ratio 2 : 3
c £96 in the ratio 7 : 5   d £28 in the ratio 4 : 3
e £72 in the ratio 3 : 5   f £60 in the ratio 11 : 4

Q5a hint

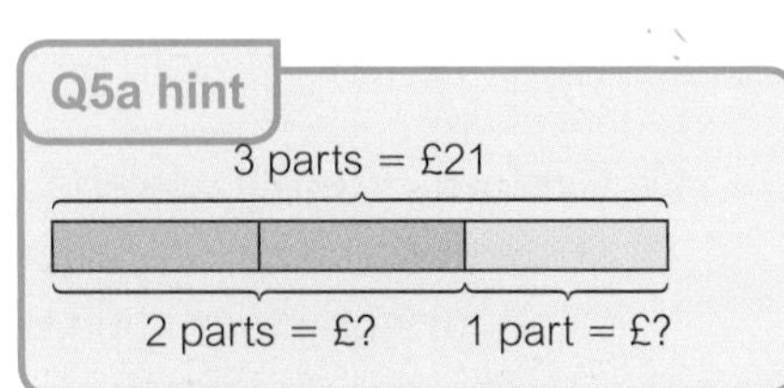

5b 6 **STEM / Real** Red gold is made from copper and gold in the ratio 1 : 3.
A red gold necklace weighs 24 g.
a How much copper is in the necklace?
b How much gold is in the necklace?
1 g of copper costs 0.5p, 1 g of gold costs £27.60.
c Work out the value of the metal in the necklace.

Discussion Why might the necklace cost more than your answer to part **c**?

Subject links: Science (Q6)

7 **Real** In the UK the ratio of men to women over 80 is approximately 4 : 7. 5b
In a village there are 110 people over 80.

a How many would you expect to be men?

b **Discussion** Why can't you be sure this is the exact number of men?

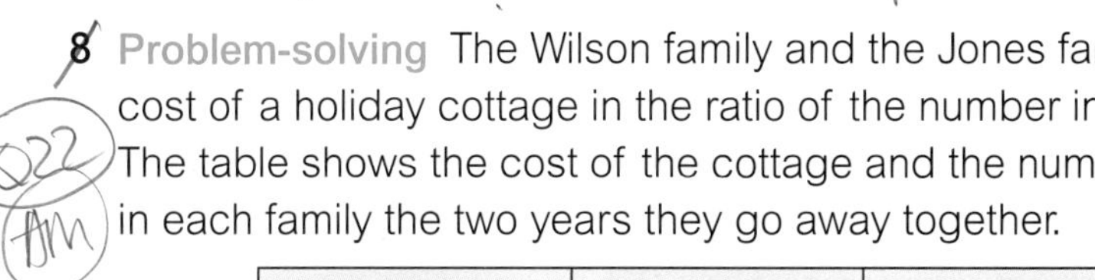

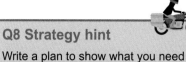

8 **Problem-solving** The Wilson family and the Jones family share the cost of a holiday cottage in the ratio of the number in each family. The table shows the cost of the cottage and the number of people in each family the two years they go away together. 5a

> **Q8 Strategy hint**
> Write a plan to show what you need to work out at each step.

	Number in Wilson family	Number in Jones family	Cost of holiday cottage
2010	2	3	£450
2013	4	5	£630

a How much more do the Jones family pay in 2013 than in 2010?

b Which family has the biggest increase in price from 2010 to 2013?

Worked example

The ratio of chilli to garlic in a recipe is 1 : 3.
George uses 4 teaspoons of chilli.
How many teaspoons of garlic does he use?

$3 \times 4 = 12$

George uses 12 teaspoons of garlic.

> Multiply each part by the same number to get an equivalent ratio.
>
> 1 : 3
> ×4 ×4
> 4 : 12

9 **Real** Hummingbirds eat nectar made from sugar and water in the ratio 1 : 4. How much water is needed for 3 teaspoons of sugar? 5a

10 **Real** A recipe for Thai chicken uses Thai sauce and fresh ginger in the ratio 2 : 1. Anna uses 4 tablespoons of Thai sauce. How much ginger does she use? 5a

5a

11 **Finance / Problem-solving** Harry invests some money in low-risk and high-risk investments in the ratio 7 : 3. 5a
He invests £1800 into the high-risk investments.
How much money does he invest altogether?
Discussion Is there more than one way to work out the answer to this question?

12 **Explore** How many staff are needed to take your year group on a school trip? Explore
Is it easier to explore this question now you have completed the lesson?
What further information do you need to be able to answer this?

13 **Reflect** Look back at the questions you answered in this lesson. Reflect
For type A questions, you were given the ratio and total and asked you to find the parts (Q5).
For type B questions you were given the ratio and one part, and asked you to find the other part (Q10).
Find two other questions for types A and B.
What maths operations (addition, subtraction, multiplication, or division) did you use to solve each type of question?

7.4 Scale and measures

You will learn to:
- Use ratios and measures.

CONFIDENCE

Why learn this?
Converting between units is useful when cutting out fabric to make clothes.

Fluency
Fill in the missing numbers.
- 1 cm = □ mm
- 1 kg = □ g
- □ cm = 1 m

Explore
What is the ratio of your height to some of the world's tallest buildings?

Exercise 7.4

Warm up

1 Work out the missing values.
   a 100 × □ = 700   b 10 × □ = 80
   c 1000 × □ = 3200   d 100 × □ = 950

2 Work out
   a 1000 ml ÷ 5   b 1000 g ÷ 10   c 100 cm ÷ 4

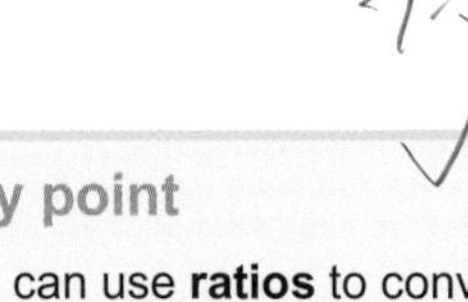

Key point
You can use **ratios** to convert between **metric units**.

5b 3 Copy and complete.
Every 1 cm is the same as _____ mm. The **ratio** cm : mm is 1 : 10.

5b 4 Write these conversions as ratios.
   a mm : cm   b cm : m   c km : m
   d kg : g   e ml : l f m : cm

5b 5 Complete these conversions.
   a 9 m = □ cm   b 2 cm = □ mm   c 7 l = □ ml
   d 5000 m = □ km   e 200 cm = □ m   f 30 mm = □ cm
   g 12 000 ml = □ l h 10 cm = □ mm   i 100 m = □ km

Q5a hint
m : cm
1 : 100
×9 ×9
9 : □

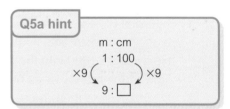

5b 6 Complete these conversions.
   a 3.6 m = □ cm   b 2.8 kg = □ g   c 3.1 cm = □ mm
   d 8.9 kg = □ g   e 3900 m = □ km   f 630 cm = □ m
   g 84 mm = □ cm   h 8600 ml = □ l i 70 m = □ cm

Q5d hint

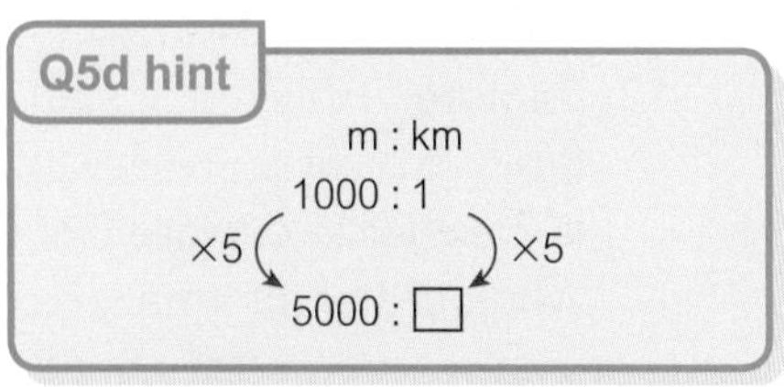

5b 7 Six adults share 1.5 litres of lemonade equally between them.
Their children have a 330 ml can each.
Who gets the most?

5b 8 A carpenter has a piece of wood 1.2 m long.
He cuts the wood into two pieces in the ratio 2 : 3.
Work out the length of the shorter piece of wood.
Give your answer in centimetres.

Q8 hint

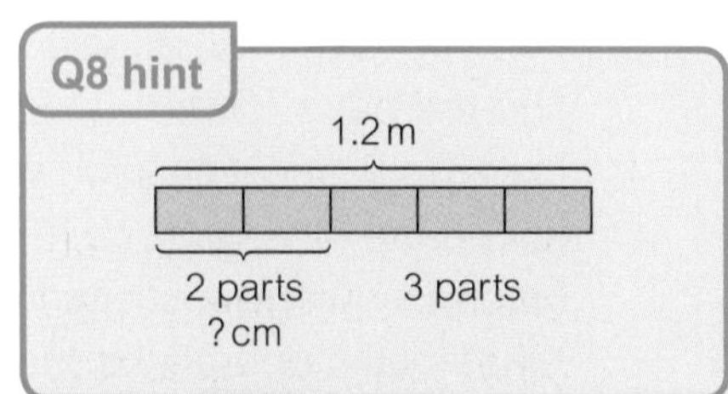

Topic links: Measures, Using formulae

Subject links: Science (Q12, Q14, Q15), PE (Q9)

9 Real / Problem-solving One length of a swimming pool is 25 m. Alison swims 60 lengths of the pool. How many more lengths must Alison swim to complete 1 mile?

Q9 hint
1 mile is 1.6 km.

Q9 Strategy hint
Start by working out how far she has already swum.

10 Real / Problem-solving A nurse uses this formula to work out the amount of medicine a patient needs each hour.

$$A = B \times M \times 60$$

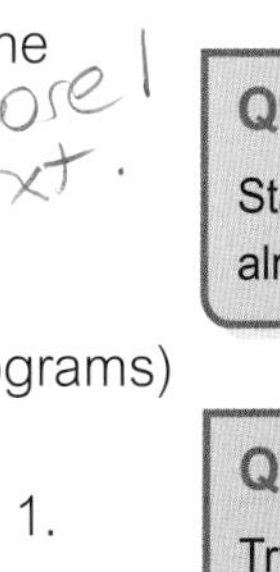

where A is the amount of medicine per hour (in micrograms)
B is the amount of medicine per kg body mass (in micrograms)
M is the mass of the patient (in kg)

The ratio for converting from micrograms to milligrams is 1000 : 1.
Work out the value of A when B = 18 and M = 62.
Give your answer in milligrams.

Q10 Strategy hint
Try some easier numbers in the formula first such as B = 20 and M = 60.

Worked example

What value is the arrow pointing to?
Give your answer in grams.

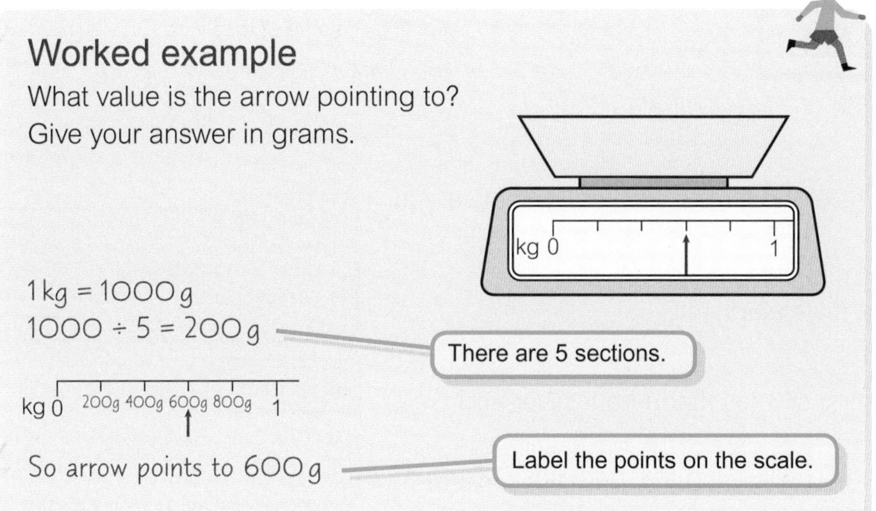

1 kg = 1000 g
1000 ÷ 5 = 200 g — There are 5 sections.

kg 0 200g 400g 600g 800g 1

So arrow points to 600 g — Label the points on the scale.

11 What value is the arrow pointing to?

a Give your answer in centimetres.

b Give your answer in grams.

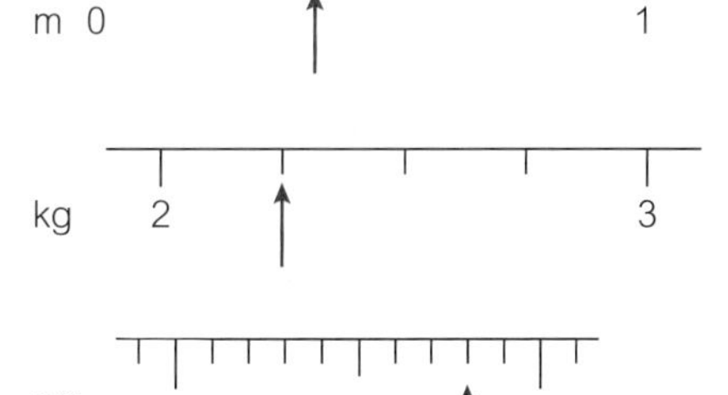

c Give your answer in millimetres.

d Give your answer in millilitres.

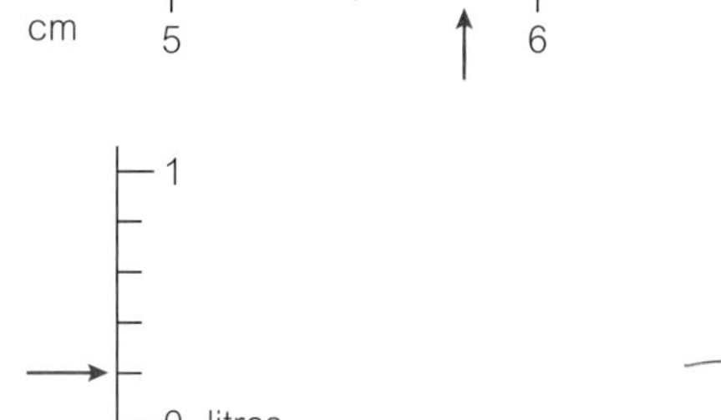

12 Problem-solving In a science experiment Heidi mixes together equal quantities of sand, sugar and cornstarch.
She has the correct amount of sand and sugar, and 25 g of cornstarch, on the scales shown.
How much more cornstarch does she need to add?

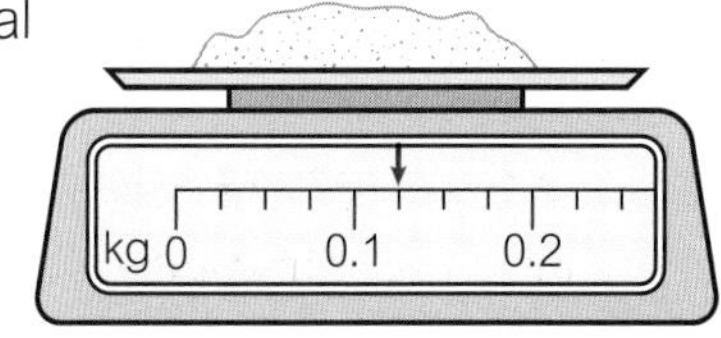

Worked example

The height of a man and a tree are in the ratio 1 : 6.
The man's height is 180 cm. What is the height of the tree in metres?

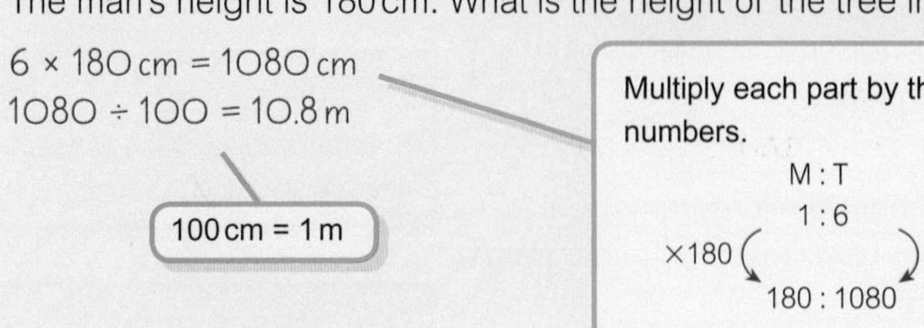

6 × 180 cm = 1080 cm
1080 ÷ 100 = 10.8 m
100 cm = 1 m
Multiply each part by the same numbers.
M : T
1 : 6
×180
×180
180 : 1080

5a

13 This advert is projected onto the side of a building. The side lengths of the image shown and of the projection are in the ratio 1 : 300.

How tall is the advert on the side of the building?
Give your answer in metres.

5a

14 STEM The greatest mass of male and female Asian elephants are in the ratio 9 : 7.
The greatest mass of a female elephant is 4200 kg.
What is the greatest mass of a male elephant?
Give your answer in tonnes.

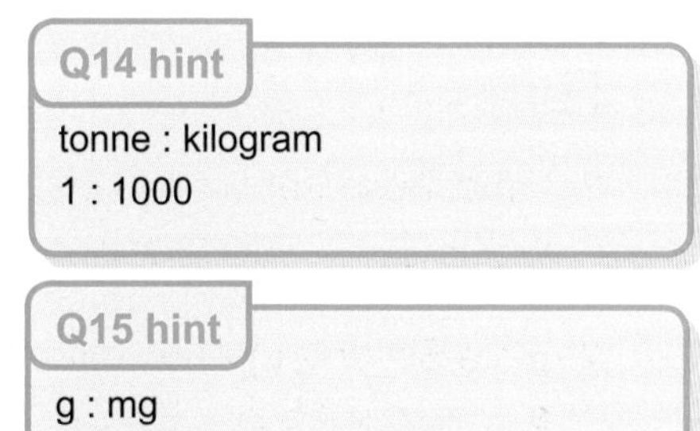

5a

15 STEM / Problem-solving Sterling silver is made from silver and copper in the ratio 37 : 3.
What is the total mass of a sterling silver ring that contains 600 mg of copper? Give your answer in grams.

Investigation

Here are some scales.

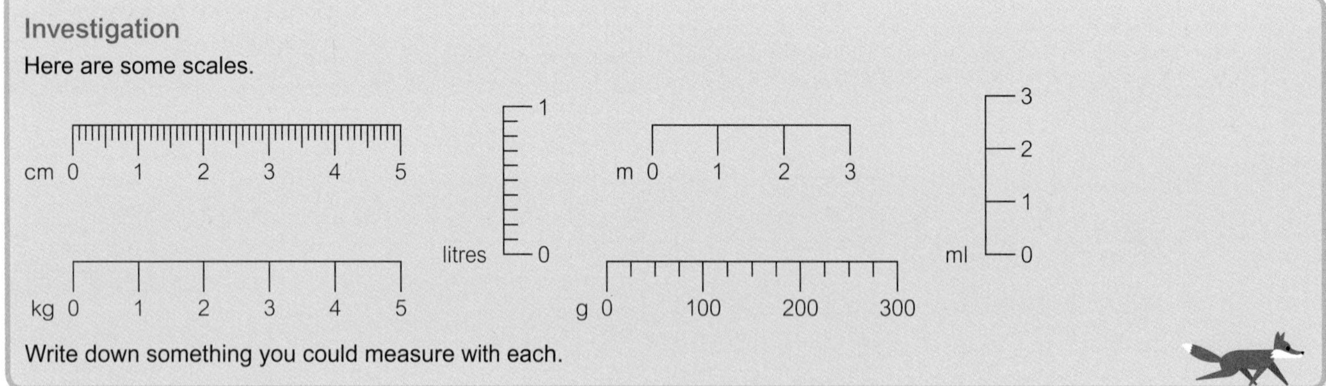

Write down something you could measure with each.

Explore

16 **Explore** What is the ratio of your height to some of the world's tallest buildings?
What have you learned in this lesson to help you answer this question?
What other information do you need?

Reflect

17 **Reflect** Where does 8 go on this scale?
Copy this scale exactly. Mark 8 on your scale as accurately as possible.

Write down step-by-step instructions for how you did it.

7.5 Proportions and fractions

You will learn to:

- Use fractions to describe and compare proportions
- Understand and use the relationship between ratio and proportion.

CONFIDENCE

Why learn this? You can compare the fractions of people who go to different music festivals to see which festival is the most popular with students.

Fluency
Write these fractions as pairs of equivalent fractions.
$\frac{4}{5}, \frac{2}{3}, \frac{12}{15}, \frac{20}{24}, \frac{8}{12}, \frac{5}{6}$

Explore
How has the proportion of people going to university in the UK changed since 1970?

Exercise 7.5

Warm up

1 Write these fractions in order of size starting with the smallest.
 a $\frac{3}{8}, \frac{7}{8}, \frac{1}{8}$ b $\frac{1}{2}, \frac{1}{5}, \frac{1}{3}$ c $\frac{11}{15}, \frac{4}{15}, \frac{7}{15}$

2 Write Simon's age as a fraction of Debbie's age when
 a Simon is 15 and Debbie is 20 b Simon is 20 and Debbie is 25
 c Simon is 45 and Debbie is 50.

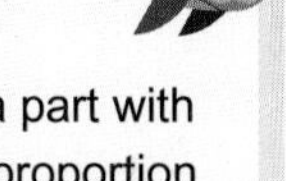

Key point
A **proportion** compares a part with a whole. You can write a proportion as a fraction, a decimal or a percentage.

Worked example

In a biscuit tin, there are 10 chocolate and 4 shortbread biscuits.
What **proportion** are
a chocolate **b** shortbread?

$10 + 4 = 14$ — Work out the total number of biscuits.

a $\frac{\text{chocolate biscuits}}{\text{total biscuits}} = \frac{10}{14} = \frac{5}{7}$ — Write each amount as a fraction of the total. Simplify.

b $\frac{\text{shortbread biscuits}}{\text{total biscuits}} = \frac{4}{14} = \frac{2}{7}$ — Check your answer: $\frac{5}{7} + \frac{2}{7} = 1$.

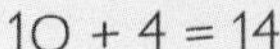

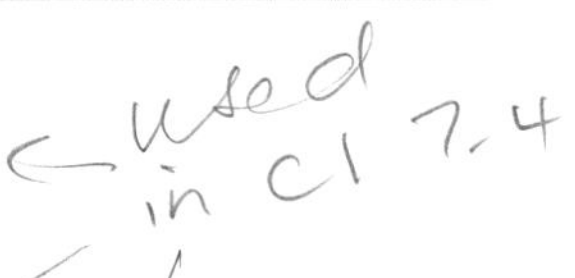

3 A zoo has five adult tigers and three tiger cubs.
What **proportion** of the zoo's tigers are cubs? 5b

4 In class 7G, 14 students are 11 years old and 16 students are 12 years old.
Write down the proportion of each age. 5b

5 **Discussion** In class 7G there are 12 boys and 18 girls. Is the proportion of boys $\frac{12}{18}$?

5 In a shoe shop, six of the 42 pairs of shoes sold were size 5.
In a different shoe shop 12 out of the 60 shoes sold were size 5.
Which shop sold the greater proportion of size 5 shoes? 5b

Q5 hint
Cancel each fraction to its simplest form, then compare the fractions.
$\frac{6}{42} = \frac{\square}{\square}, \frac{12}{60} = \frac{\square}{\square}$

5b **6** There are 32 children in class 7H. Twenty of them are boys.
There are 24 children in class 7T. Nine of them are boys.
Which class has the greater proportion of boys?

5b **7** The table shows the number of toffee-fudge ice creams and the total number of ice creams sold one weekend.

Day	Number of toffee-fudge ice creams sold	Total number of ice creams sold
Saturday	25	150
Sunday	15	120

Which day had the greater proportion of sales of toffee-fudge ice cream?

5b **8** **Real** The table shows the number of seats for season-ticket holders and the total number of seats at two football stadiums.

Stadium	Seats for season-ticket holders	Total number of seats
Manchester City FC	36 000	48 000
Reading FC	18 000	24 000

Which stadium has the greatest proportion of seats for season-ticket holders?

5b **9** **Problem-solving / Finance** The graph shows the income from souvenirs, photos and refreshments at a children's farm one weekend.

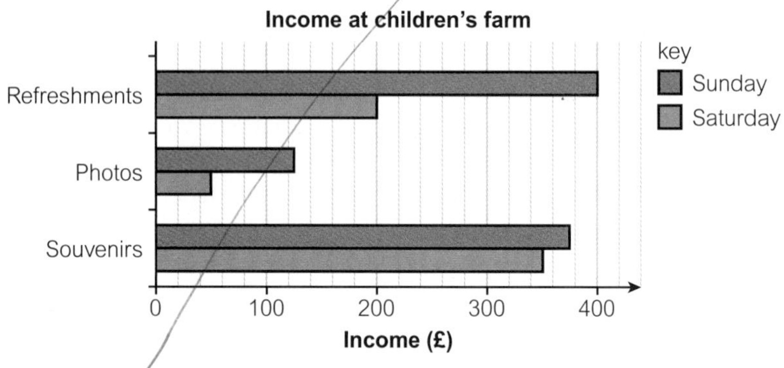

a Which day had the greater income from souvenirs?

b Which day had the greater proportion of income from souvenirs?

Q9 Strategy hint

What do you need to work out before you can work out the fraction of the income that came from souvenirs?

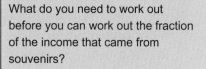

5a **10** In a stir fry, Adam makes a sauce using soy sauce and chilli sauce in the ratio 3 : 1.
What fraction of the sauce is

a soy sauce

b chilli sauce?

Discussion How can you check your answers to this question are correct?

Q10a hint

soy	soy	soy	chilli

Three out of every four parts are soy.
The fraction of soy is $\frac{\square}{4}$

5a **11** **Real** Brass is made from copper and zinc in the ratio 7 : 3.

a What fraction of brass is

i copper ii zinc?

b Show how to check your answers to part **a**.

Topic links: Bar charts

Subject links: Cookery (Q10), Science (Q11)

12 Helen makes orange paint by mixing red and yellow paint in the ratio 5 : 8.

a What fraction of the orange paint is

i red paint ii yellow paint?

b Show how to check your answers to part **a**.

c Helen needs 26 litres of paint. How many litres of each colour does she need?

5a

13 **Problem-solving** A music website sells singles and albums in the ratio 9 : 5.
A different website sells singles and albums in the ratio 5 : 2.
Which website sells the greater proportion of albums?

Q13 Strategy hint
Use equivalent fractions to compare.

5a

14 **Problem-solving** A school trip to a theme park has four full coaches of staff and students. One coach seats 52 people. Altogether there are 16 staff.
Write the answer to these questions in their simplest form.

a What fraction of the people on the trip are staff?

b What is the ratio of staff to students?

Q14 Strategy hint
How can you work backwards from a fraction to a ratio?

5a

15 **Problem-solving / Reasoning** Tim makes orange squash by mixing 50 ml of squash with 450 ml of water.
Peter makes orange squash by mixing 30 ml of squash with 210 ml of water.
Who has made the stronger squash? Explain your answer.

5a

Investigation **Modelling**

In about 1490 Leonardo da Vinci made a drawing to show the proportions of the human body.

- The length of a person's ear is one-third of the length of their face.
- A person's armspan is equal to their height.
- The distance from the top of the head to the bottom of the chin is $\frac{1}{8}$ of a person's height.
- The distance from the elbow to the tip of the hand is $\frac{1}{5}$ of a person's height.
- The length of a person's foot is $\frac{1}{7}$ of a person's height.
- The length of a person's hand is $\frac{1}{10}$ of a person's height.

1 Write these statements as ratios.

2 Are any of these statements true for you?

16 **Explore** How has the proportion of people going to university in the UK changed since 1970?
Is it easier to explore this question now you have completed the lesson?
What further information do you need to be able to answer this?

Explore

17 **Reflect** Look back at the questions you answered in this lesson.
For type A questions, you wrote proportions as fractions (Q3)
For type B questions, you wrote proportions as fractions and then cancelled (Q5)
For type C questions, you wrote ratios as fractions (Q10).
Find one other question for types A, B and C.
When you answered these different types of questions, did you make any mistakes? If so, check that you understand where you went wrong.

Reflect

7.6 Proportions and percentages

You will learn to:
- Use percentages to describe proportions
- Use percentages to compare simple proportions
- Understand and use the relationship between ratio and proportion.

CONFIDENCE

Why learn this?
You can calculate and compare tennis players' match statistics to see how well they are performing.

Fluency
Fill in the missing numbers.
- 25 × □ = 100
- □ × 20 = 100
- 10 × □ = 100

Explore
Do breakfast cereals have a higher proportion of salt than crisps?

Exercise 7.6

Warm up

1 Copy and complete these equivalent fractions.
a $\frac{23}{50} = \frac{\square}{100}$ b $\frac{7}{25} = \frac{\square}{100}$ c $\frac{9}{10} = \frac{\square}{100}$ d $\frac{13}{20} = \frac{\square}{100}$

Key point
You can compare **proportions** using **percentages**.

2 Write these test results as percentages.
a English: 8 out of 10 b Maths: 19 out of 20 c History: 16 out of 25

5b 3 A rugby team won 9 out of their 10 line-outs.
What proportion of their line-outs did they win?

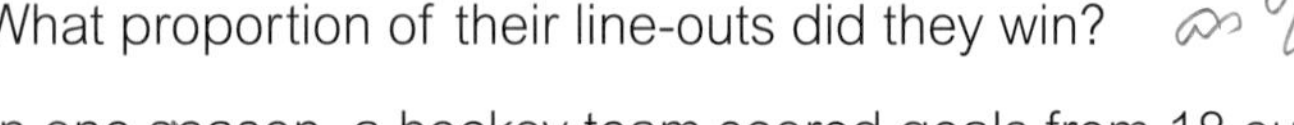

Q3 hint
Write the proportion as a fraction.
$\frac{9}{10} = \frac{\square}{100} = \square\%$
Convert the fraction to a percentage.

5b 4 In one season, a hockey team scored goals from 18 out of the 20 penalties they were awarded.
They also scored goals from 42 out of the 50 penalty corners they were awarded.
Did they score a greater **proportion** of goals from penalties or penalty corners?

5b 5 **Problem-solving** These are the ages of the five members of a riding club.
8, 10, 11, 15, 16
These are the ages of the 10 members of a diving club.
15, 16, 16, 18, 20, 22, 22, 25, 37, 39

In which club are the greater proportion of the members older than the mean age?

5b 6 **Problem-solving** The diagram shows a yellow rectangle and a yellow square.

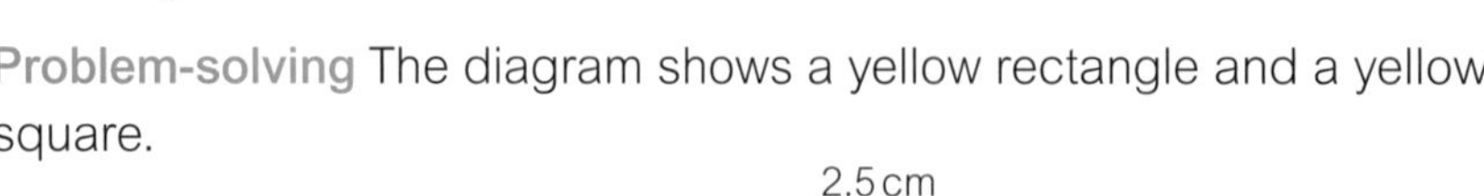

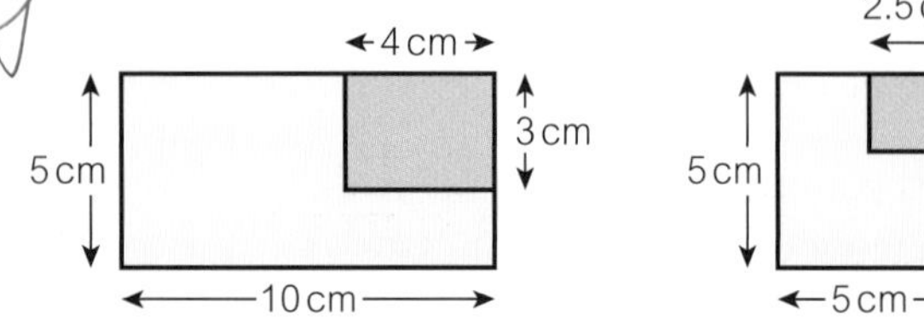

Which shape has the greater proportion shaded green?

Topic links: Percentages, Mean, Area

Subject links: Science (Q8), Cookery (Q9)

Worked example

The ratio of boys to girls in a swimming club is 3 : 7.
What percentage of the children are girls?

3 + 7 = 10 parts

$\frac{7}{10} = \frac{70}{100}$

70% are girls

For every three boys there are seven girls.
The percentage of girls is $\frac{7}{10} = \frac{70}{100} = 70\%$.

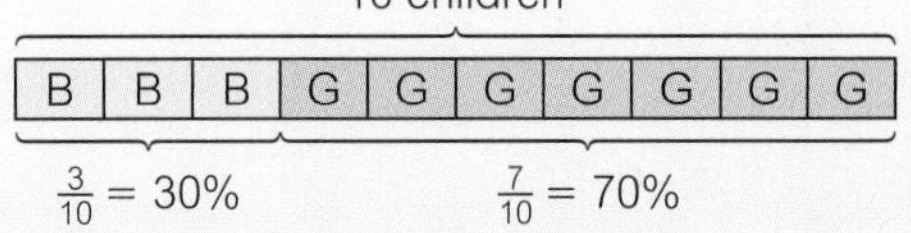

7 The ratio of girls to boys in a school choir is 4 : 1.
What **percentage** of the choir are
a girls b boys?
Discussion How can you check your answers to this question are correct?

8 STEM A sugar solution is made from glucose and fructose in the ratio 7 : 13.
a What percentage of the sugar solution is
i glucose ii fructose?
b Show how you checked your answers to part **a**.

Q8 Literacy hint
Glucose and fructose are both types of sugar.

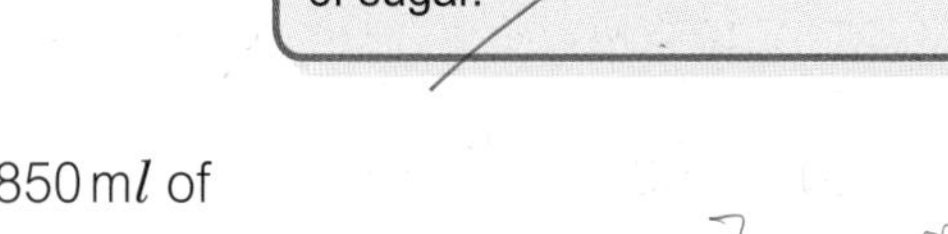

9 Sandra makes pink paint by mixing 400 ml of red paint with 850 ml of white paint.
a Write the ratio of red paint to white paint in its simplest form.
b What percentage of the pink paint is
i red ii white?
c Show how you checked your answers to part **b**.

10 Real / Problem-solving A recipe for oatmeal bread uses 450 g flour and 300 g oatmeal.
A recipe for wheatmeal bread uses 550 g flour and 450 g wheatmeal.
Which bread has the greater proportion of flour?

Q10 Strategy hint
Start by writing each bread recipe as a ratio in its simplest form.

11 Finance A financial advisor suggests that a client invests in low-risk shares and medium-risk shares in the ratio 2 : 3.
The client invests 70% of his money in medium-risk shares and the rest in low-risk shares. Has he followed the advisor's suggestion?

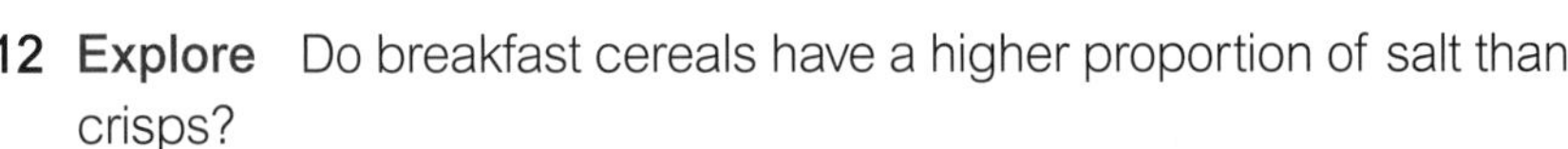

12 **Explore** Do breakfast cereals have a higher proportion of salt than crisps?
Is it easier to explore this question now you have completed the lesson?
What further information do you need to be able to answer this?

13 **Reflect** Use what you have learned in this Unit to write five sentences that describe the ratio, proportion, fraction and percentage of the different colours in this bar.
Which word was easiest to write a sentence for? Why?
Which word was hardest to write a sentence for? Why?

6 cm 2 cm

7 Check up

Direct proportion

1 A ticket to the cinema costs £6. Work out the cost of
a 3 tickets b 7 tickets c 11 tickets.

2 A recipe for four people uses 200 g flour. How much flour is needed for
a 8 people b 2 people c 6 people?

3 It takes Mary half an hour to clean four dog kennels at a rescue centre.
She works from 8 am to 11 30 am.
Has Mary got enough time to clean all 30 kennels?
Show your working.

4 Three packets of cashew nuts cost £6. Work out the cost of
a 1 packet b 2 packets c 5 packets.

5 It costs eight people £320 to go horse riding. How much will it cost five people?

Ratio

6 Katy keeps chickens. For every one white egg she gets five brown eggs.
There are 30 eggs altogether.
a How many white eggs are there? b How many brown eggs are there?

7 a Share £45 in the ratio 2 : 3.
b Show how you checked your answer is correct.

8 This is Sara's solution to a problem.
a Explain the mistake that Sara has made.
b Work out the correct solution to the problem.

Question
Amy and Kieran share 30 sweets in the ratio 1 : 2.
How many sweets does Kieran get?

Answer
Kieran gets 30 ÷ 2 = 15 sweets

9 Write each of these ratios in its simplest form.
a 2 : 12 b 28 : 4
c 10 : 15 d 16 : 12

10 Joe uses coriander and turmeric in a curry in the ratio 3 : 1.
How much coriander does he use with 2 teaspoons of turmeric?

11 The ratio of boys to girls in a volleyball club is 4 : 3.
Twelve club members are boys.
a How many members are girls?
b What is the total number of members in the club?

12 The lengths of two roller coasters are in the ratio 3 : 20.
The length of the shorter roller coaster is 360 m.
What is the length of the longer roller coaster? Give your answer in kilometres.

Comparing proportions

13 There are four boys in a dance group of five students.

a What fraction of the dance group are boys?

There are nine boys in a dance group of 10 students.

b What fraction of this dance group are boys?

c Which dance group has the greater proportion of boys? Explain how you worked out your answer.

14 In their first season, a football team scored no goals in 7 out of the 20 matches they played.

a Write 7 out of 20 as a percentage.

In their second season, they scored no goals in 9 out of the 25 matches they played.

b Write 9 out of 25 as a percentage.

c In which season did they score no goals in a greater proportion of their matches?

15 Problem-solving These are the ages of the members of two badminton clubs.

Dragons	12 14 15 15 17 17 19 20 22 22
Swifts	11 11 13 14 14 15 15 16 16 16 17 19 19 20 21 21 22 24 25 25

Which badminton club has the greater proportion of members over the age of 18?

16 When Gill makes bread, she uses white flour and wholemeal four in the ratio 3 : 1.
What fraction of the flour is

a white flour b wholemeal flour?

c Gill needs 300 g of flour. How much of each type of flour does she use?

17 The ratio of girls to boys in a school orchestra is 2 : 3.

a What percentage of the orchestra are

i girls ii boys?

b Show how you checked your answers to part **a**.

18 Sam makes light blue paint by mixing 250 ml of blue paint with 750 ml of white paint.
Tony makes light blue paint by mixing 400 ml of blue paint with 1600 ml of white paint.
Who has made the lighter blue paint? Explain your answer.

19 How sure are you of your answers? Were you mostly

Just guessing Feeling doubtful Confident

What next? Use your results to decide whether to strengthen or extend your learning.

Challenge

20 Copy this rectangle on to squared paper.

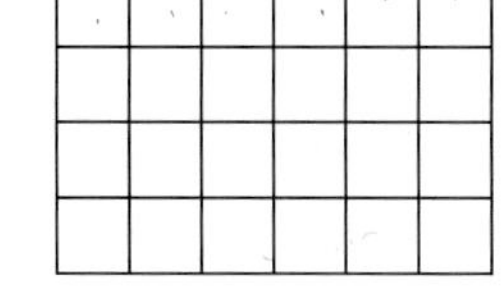

a Show three different ways that you can divide the rectangle into two parts so that the areas of the two parts are in the ratio 3 : 1.

b Show three different ways that you can divide the rectangle into two parts so that the areas of the two parts are in the ratio 1 : 2.

21 The ratio of boys to girls in a swimming club is 4 : 5.
Write three different numbers of boys and girls that could be in the swimming club.
In each case give the total number of children in the swimming club.

7 Strengthen

You will:

- Strengthen your understanding with practice.

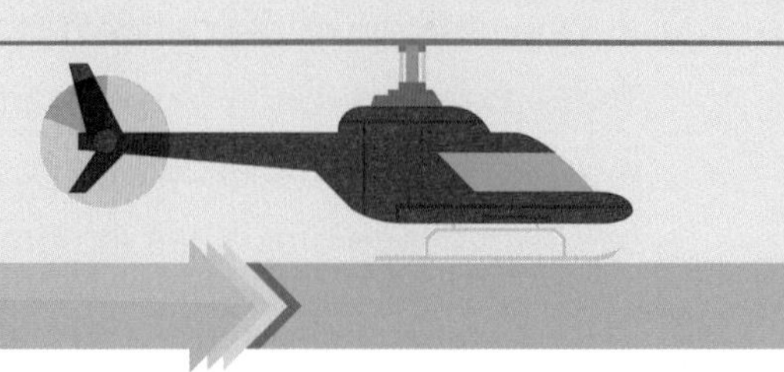

Direct proportion

5c **1** A raffle ticket at a charity event costs £4. Work out the cost of

a 2 tickets
b 3 tickets
c 5 tickets.

Q1a hint
2 × £4 = □ | £4 | £4

5b **2** It costs £42 for six children to go sledging in a snowdome. How much does it cost for

a 12 children
b 3 children
c 9 children?

Q2 hint
6 children: £42; 3 children: £?
12 children: £42, £42

5a **3** Three boxes of cat food cost £6. Work out the cost of

a 1 box
b 2 boxes
c 5 boxes.

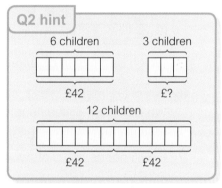

Q3a hint
3 boxes: £6; 1 box: £2 £2 £2
£6 ÷ 3 = £2

5a **4** Real There are 100 calories in 5 teaspoons of sugar. How many calories are there in 8 teaspoons of sugar?

Ratio

4a **1** Ian plants tomato seeds. For every four seeds that do grow, there is one that does not. Ian plants 15 seeds altogether.

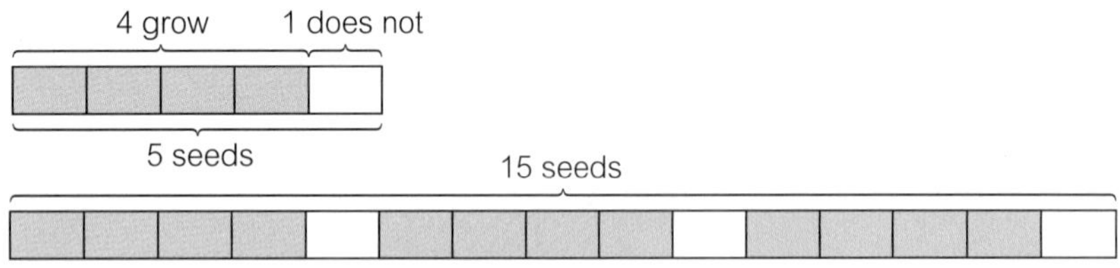

a How many of the seeds grow?
b How many of the seeds don't grow?
c Show how you checked your answers to parts **a** and **b**.

Q1c hint
Add together your answers to parts **a** and **b**. The total should be the number of seeds planted.

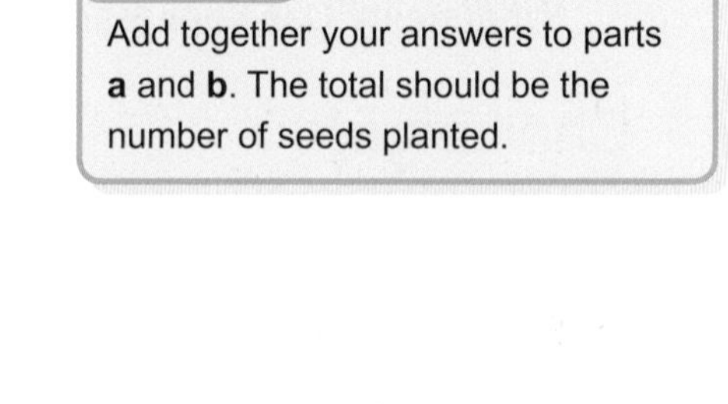

4a **2** Real A hairdresser makes hair colouring by mixing 1 part dye with 2 parts peroxide solution. He wants 60 ml of hair colouring.

a How much dye does he use?
b How much peroxide solution does he use?
c Show how you checked your answers to parts **a** and **b**.

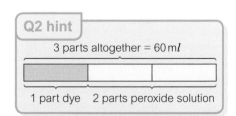

Q2 hint
3 parts altogether = 60 ml
1 part dye | 2 parts peroxide solution

Topic links: Fractions, Percentages

Subject links: Science (Ratio Q10, Ratio Q13), Cookery (Ratio Q8, Comparing proportions Q6)

3 a Copy and colour these circles to show the ratios 5c

i 5 : 7 **ii** 1 : 5 **iii** 3 : 9 **iv** 1 : 3.

b What do you notice about your answers to parts **iii** and **iv**?

4 Write 2 : 6 in its simplest form. 5b

Q4 hint

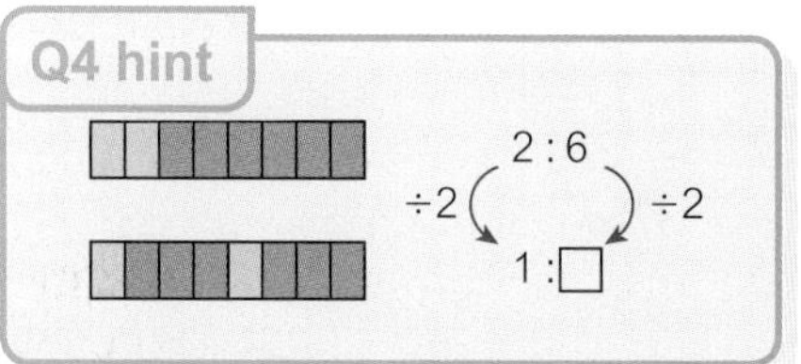

5 Write each ratio in its simplest form. 5b

a 2 : 4

b 6 : 3

c 3 : 12

d 30 : 5

e 6 : 8

f 6 : 27

g 16 : 24

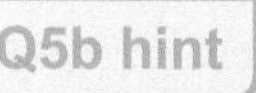

Q5b hint

You cannot divide by 2.
Try dividing by 3.

6 This is how Ian cancels the ratio 36 : 54 to its simplest form. 5b
Has Ian got the correct simplest form?
Explain your answer.

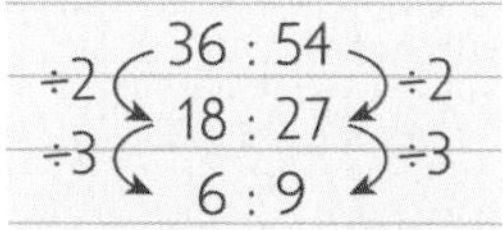

7 Real A campsite has pitches for 20 static caravans and 35 touring caravans. 5b
Write the ratio of static caravans to touring caravans in its simplest form.

Q7 hint

20 : 35 = □ : □
Try dividing by 2, by 3, by 4, … until you find one that works for both numbers.

8 Real Jan uses basil and oregano in a bolognese sauce in the ratio 1 : 2. 5a
She uses 2 teaspoons of basil. How much oregano does she use?

9 The ratio of boys to girls in a gym club is 2 : 3. 5a
There are six boys in the club.

a How many girls are in the club?

b What is the total number of children in the club?

Q9a hint

B G

6

B : G
2 : 3
×□ ×□
6 : □

10 STEM The ratio of steel to plastic in a washing machine is 10 : 7. 5a
The steel in one washing machine weighs 40 kg.
How much does the plastic in the washing machine weigh?

11 Share these amounts between Andy and Bern in the ratios given. 5b

a £12 in the ratio 1 : 3

b £15 in the ratio 1 : 2

c £20 in the ratio 4 : 1

Q11a hint

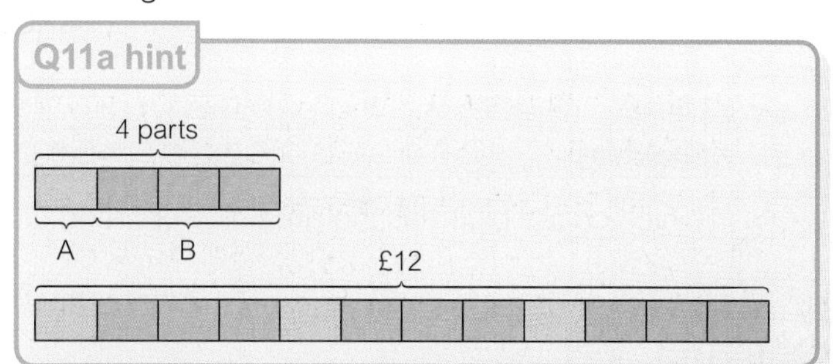

5b 12 Share these amounts between Carole and Dave in the ratios given.

a £21 in the ratio 5 : 2

b £28 in the ratio 3 : 4

c £45 in the ratio 2 : 7

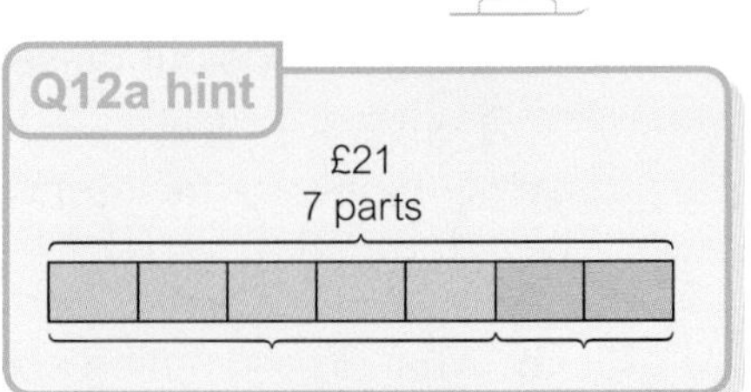

5b 13 STEM Electrum is made from gold and silver in the ratio 2 : 3. How much gold is in 100 g of electrum?

Comparing proportions

5c 1 There are 7 chocolate muffins in a pack of 10 muffins. What proportion of the pack are chocolate muffins?

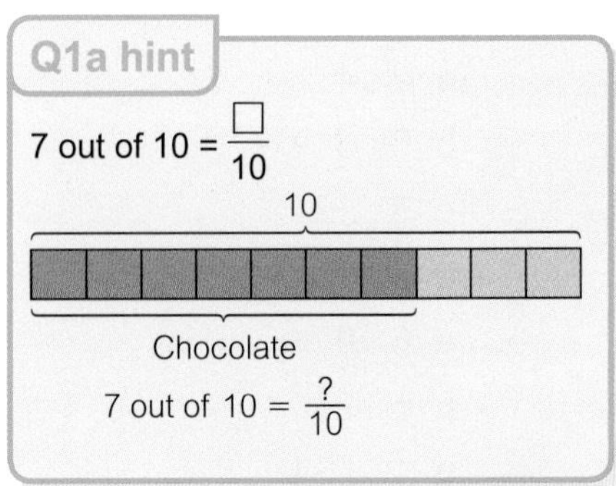

Q1a hint
7 out of 10 = □/10
10
Chocolate
7 out of 10 = ?/10

5b 2 There are three boys in a group of eight students.

a What fraction of the group are boys?

There are two boys in a group of five students.

b What fraction of this group are boys?

c Which group has the greater proportion of boys?

Q2c Strategy hint

Compare the fractions

5b 3 There are three red and seven blue marbles in box A.

a What fraction of the marbles are red?

There are two red and three blue marbles in box B.

b What fraction of the marbles are red?

c Which box has the greater proportion of red marbles?

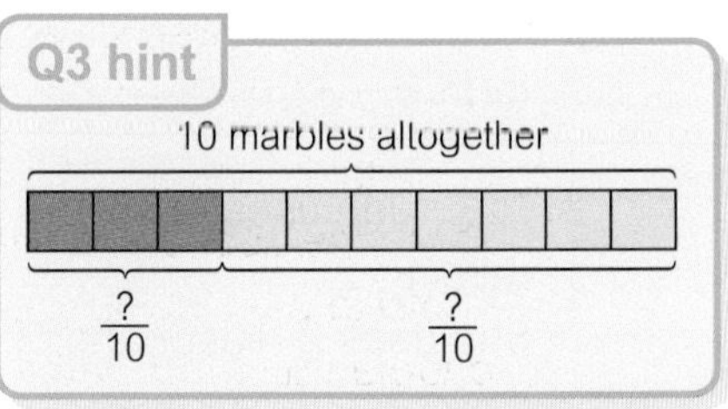

5b 4 Ellie has five songs on a playlist. Three of them are R&B.

a Write 3 out of 5 as a percentage.

Dai has 25 songs on a playlist. Fourteen of them are R&B.

b Whose playlist has the greater proportion of R&B songs?

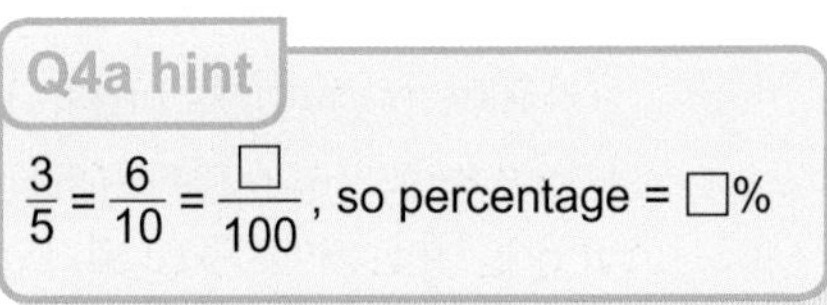

5b 5 Problem-solving The table shows the gender of the members of two canoe clubs.
G stands for girls, B stands for boys.

Seals	G B B G B B G G G G
Dolphins	B B B G G B G G G B G B G G B B G G G B

Which canoe club has the greater proportion of girls?

Q5 Strategy hint

For each club

1 count the number of girls and the total number of children

2 write the number of girls as a fraction of the total number of children

3 change the fraction to a percentage

4 compare the percentages.

6 Real When Sally bakes a teabread, she makes a topping out of syrup and water in the ratio 2 : 1.

What fraction of the topping is

a syrup b water?

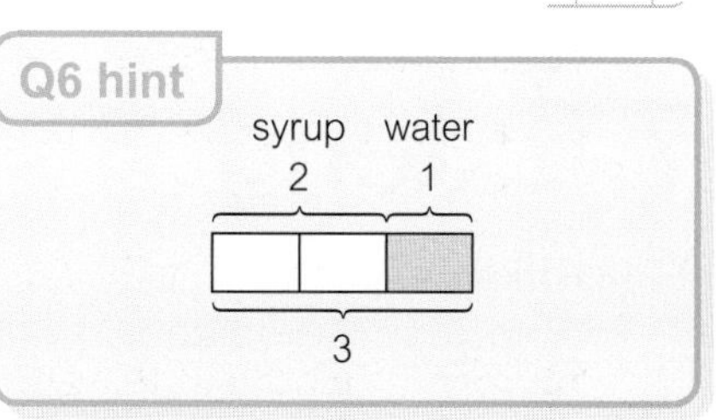

7 Abbie makes light green paint by mixing 20 ml of green paint with 80 ml of white paint.
Emma makes light green paint by mixing 15 ml of green paint with 35 ml of white paint.
Who has made the darker green paint? Explain your answer.

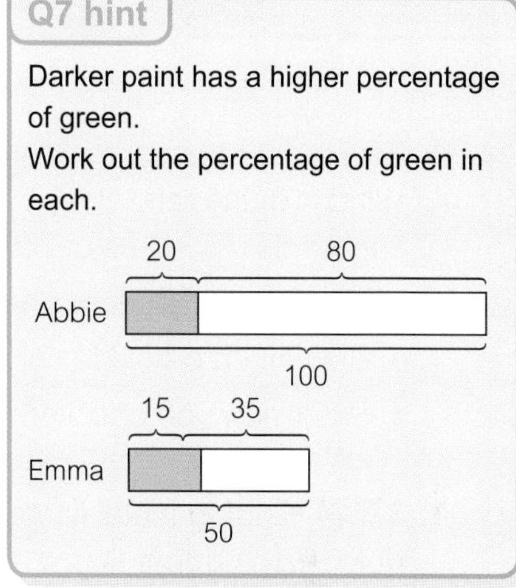

Q7 hint
Darker paint has a higher percentage of green.
Work out the percentage of green in each.
20
80
Abbie
100
15
35
Emma
50

Enrichment

1 Real / Problem-solving Twenty-one friends go to the cinema. They order taxis to take them from the cinema to a restaurant. One taxi carries four passengers.

a What is the smallest number of taxis they need to order?

b Write down three ways that the 21 people can fit in the taxis. No more than four people are allowed in one taxi.

c Each taxi charges £15 for the journey, and the people in each taxi share the cost equally between them. Which of the three ways you found in part **b** would be the fairest way to travel, so that all the people pay roughly the same?

2 In a surfing lesson $\frac{2}{3}$ of the group are boys and the rest are girls.

Harry says, 'The ratio of boys to girls is 2 : 3.'

Lily says, 'The ratio of boys to girls is 2 : 1.'

Who is correct? Explain your answer.

3 **Reflect** These lessons used bar modelling to help you solve ratio and proportion problems. Did the bar models help you or not? Explain.

7 Extend

You will learn to:

- Extend your understanding with problem-solving.

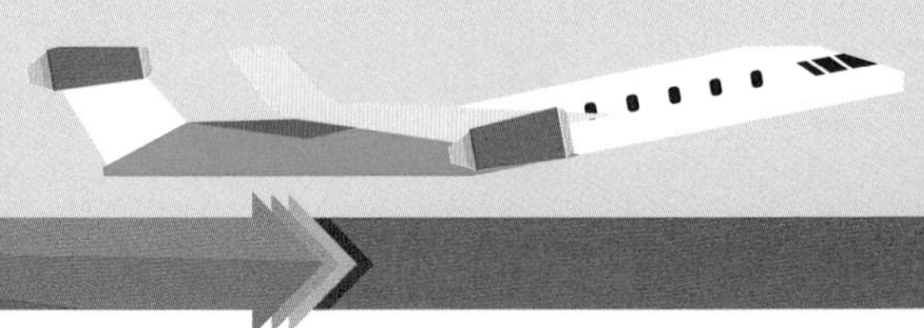

5b

1 **Real** A hairdresser makes hair colouring by mixing dye with peroxide solution in the ratio 1 : 2.
She wants 0.45 litres of hair colouring.

a How much dye does she use?

b How much peroxide solution does she use?

c Show how you checked your answers to parts **a** and **b**.

Q1 hint

Start by changing 0.45 litres into millilitres.

5b

2 **STEM** Gilding metal is made from zinc and copper in the ratio 1 : 19.
How much copper is in 1.2 kg of gilding metal?
Show how you checked your answer.

Q2 Literacy hint
Gilding metal is used to make products such as bullets, badges and jewellery.

5b

3 **STEM** A recycling plant takes the glass out of plasma TVs. Half the weight of a plasma TV is glass and iron in the ratio 3 : 2.
What is the weight of the glass in a plasma TV that weighs 30 kg?
Show how you checked your answer.

5b

4 **STEM** A wind turbine has three components: the tower, the rotor and the nacelle.

The bar chart shows the mass of the components of two turbines, the S200 and the S300.

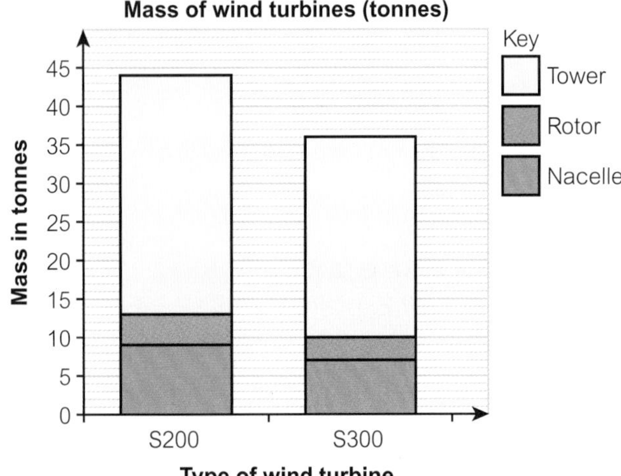

In the most efficient wind turbines, the rotor accounts for a higher proportion of the turbine's mass.
Which wind turbine is likely to be the more efficient?

Q4 Literacy hint
The nacelle is the part of the wind turbine that contains all the generating components such as the generator and gearbox.

used in core / ext

Topic links: Bar charts, Pictograms, Measures

Subject links: Science (Q2, Q3, Q4, Q9, Q14, Q16), Cookery (Q5, Q10, Q13)

5 **Real** The table shows the number of teaspoons of different spices used in two different curry recipes. 5b

Spice mix	Chicken curry	Egg curry
Turmeric	1	2
Chilli	2	1
Coriander	6	3
Cumin	5	1
Garam masala	4	1

Which curry has the greater proportion of chilli in the spice mix?

6 The table shows the Saturday and Sunday golf scores of the players at a golf club. 5b

Saturday	67	68	68	69	70	72	72	73	73	73	74	74	75	78		
Sunday	66	67	69	70	70	70	71	71	72	72	72	72	75	75	76	76

a Work out the percentage of players that scored less than 71 on Saturday.

b Work out the percentage of players that scored less than 71 on Sunday.

c On which day did the greater proportion of players score less than 71?

Q6a hint

$\frac{5}{14}$ scored less than 71.
Change $\frac{5}{14}$ to a percentage using your calculator like this:
5 ÷ 14 × 100 = □% (1 d.p.)

7 The pictogram shows the number of boys and girls having boardrider lessons at a leisure centre, over a bank holiday weekend. 5b

In Core 1 ext.

Key: represents 2 boys represents 2 girls

Saturday

Sunday

Monday

Which day had the greater proportion of girls?

Q7 hint

Work out the fraction of the children each day that were girls. Convert each fraction to a percentage using your calculator.

8 **Real** The table shows the number of visitors to the top three zoos in the UK in 2011 and 2012. 5a

Zoo	2011	2012
Chester	1 425 319	1 405 233
London	1 090 741	974 433
Whipsnade	502 785	476 226

a David says, 'In 2012, more than half of the visitors to the top three zoos went to Chester.'
Was this correct? If not, suggest what David meant to say.

b Jem said 'In 2011, a third of the visitors to the top three zoos went to Whipsnade.'
Was this correct? If not, suggest what Jem meant to say.

9 **STEM** 60 g of green gold contains 45 g of gold, 12 g of silver, and the rest is copper. 5b

In Core 1 ext

a Write the ratio of gold : silver : copper in its simplest form.

b A green gold ring weighs 8 g.
What is the weight of the gold in the ring?

5b

10 **Real** The diagram shows the amount of each ingredient in 800 ml of salad dressing.

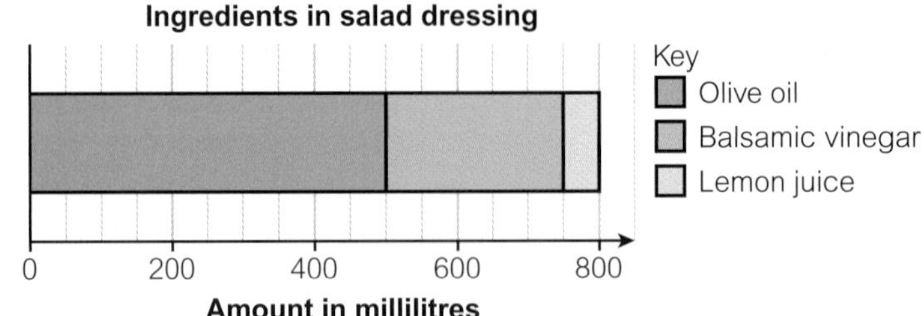

a Write the ratio of olive oil : balsamic vinegar : lemon juice in its simplest form.

b Work out the amount of balsamic vinegar needed for 2.4 litres of salad dressing.

5a

11 In a class of students $\frac{2}{5}$ have brown hair and $\frac{3}{5}$ have black hair. Write the ratio of students with brown hair to black hair.

Q11 hint

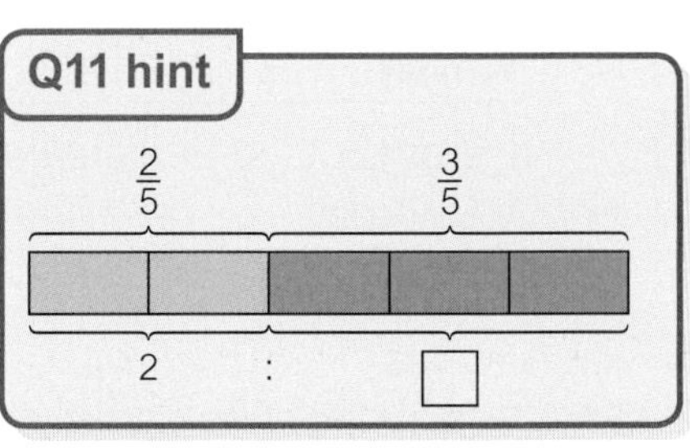

5a

12 In a class of students $\frac{5}{6}$ are right handed and $\frac{1}{6}$ are left handed. Write the ratio of right-handed students to left-handed students.

5a

13 **Real** In a gluten-free loaf $\frac{3}{8}$ of the flour is gram flour, $\frac{1}{8}$ is rye flour and $\frac{4}{8}$ is rice flour.
Work out the ratio of gram flour to rye flour to rice flour.

5a

14 **STEM / Problem-solving** A saline solution is $\frac{1}{20}$ salt. The rest is water.
Write down the ratio of salt to water in the saline solution.

Q15 hint

blue : yellow : white
20 : 25 : 55
□ : □ : □

5a

15 Alun mixes his own paint. 20% of the paint is blue, 25% is yellow and 55% is white.
Write these proportions as a ratio in its simplest form.

5a

16 **STEM / Problem-solving** A recycling plant separates materials from fridges. In a fridge, 50% of its mass is iron, 10% is other metals and the rest is plastic.

a Write the ratio of the mass of iron to other metals to plastic in its simplest form.

b What fraction of the mass of the fridge is plastic?

Q16b hint

Write your answer in its simplest form.

5a

17 Four cans of beans weigh the same as six boxes of chocolates.

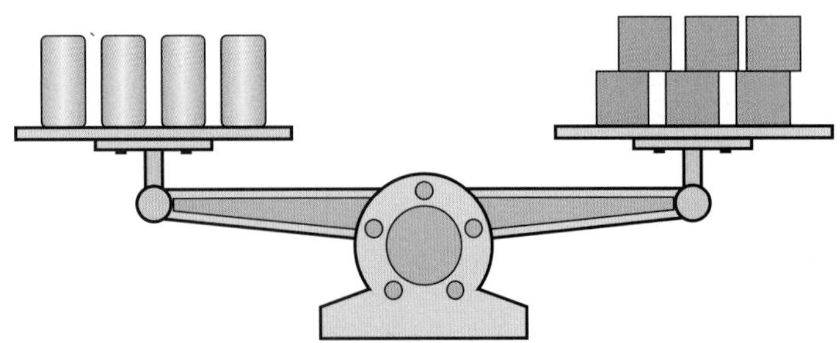

Copy and complete the sentences.

a Eight cans of beans weigh the same as □ boxes of chocolates.

b Six cans of beans weigh the same as □ boxes of chocolates.

c □ cans of beans weigh the same as 30 boxes of chocolates.

d □ cans of beans weigh the same as 15 boxes of chocolates.

Q17 hint

Start by writing the ratio 4 : 6 in its simplest form. Then multiply both sides of the ratio by different numbers to work out the missing values.

18 Here are some equivalent metric and imperial measures. 5a

1 mile ≈ 1.6 km 1 ft ≈ 30 cm 1 lb ≈ 450 g

1 pint ≈ $\frac{1}{2}$ litre 1 gallon ≈ 4.5 litres

Convert these amounts into the units shown.

a 4 lb ≈ ☐ g **b** 6 ft ≈ ☐ cm

c 3 miles ≈ ☐ km **d** 6 pints ≈ ☐ litres

e 4 gallons ≈ ☐ litres

Q18 hint

The symbol '≈' means 'is approximately equal to'.

Q18a hint

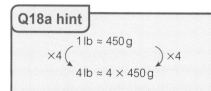

1 lb ≈ 450 g

×4 ×4

4 lb ≈ 4 × 450 g

19 **Real** In the Olympic games the marathon is 26.22 miles. 5a

How far is this in kilometres?

20 The ratio of small to medium to large dogs at a dog agility competition is 2 : 1 : 7. 6c

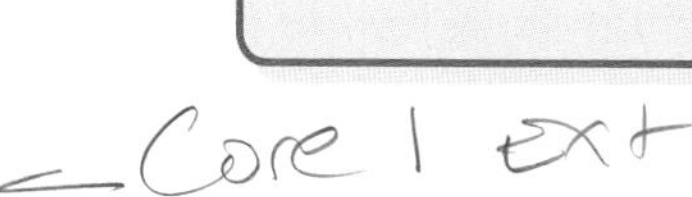

Altogether there are 300 dogs at the competition.

a How many

i small **ii** medium **iii** large dogs are there?

b Show how you checked your answers to part **a**.

21 **Finance** Pete invests £6000 into Premium Bonds, Income Bonds and Growth Bonds in the ratio 1 : 5 : 2. 6c

a How much does he invest in

i Premium Bonds

ii Income Bonds

iii Growth Bonds?

b Show how you checked your answers to part **a**.

Q20 hint

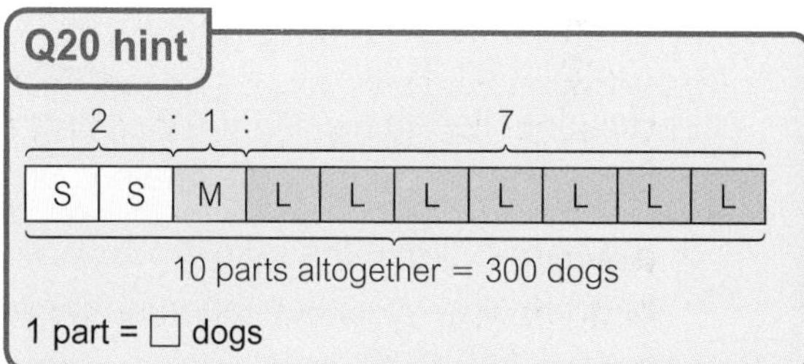

1 part = ☐ dogs

Investigation **Modelling / Reasoning**

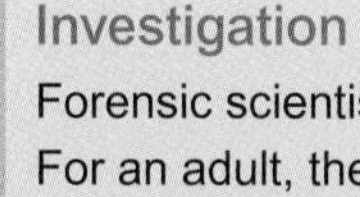

Forensic scientists use the length of a footprint to predict the height of a criminal.

For an adult, the usual ratio of length of foot to height is 3 : 20.

1 Predict the height of the criminals who have left these footprints.
Give your answer in metres.

A

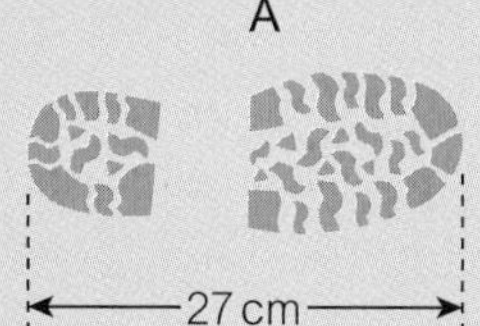

27 cm

B

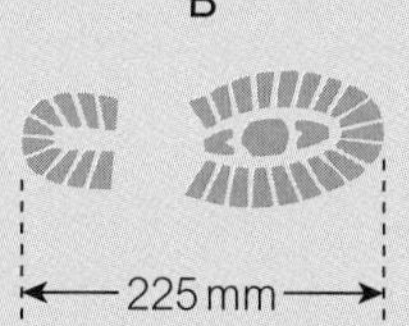

225 mm

C

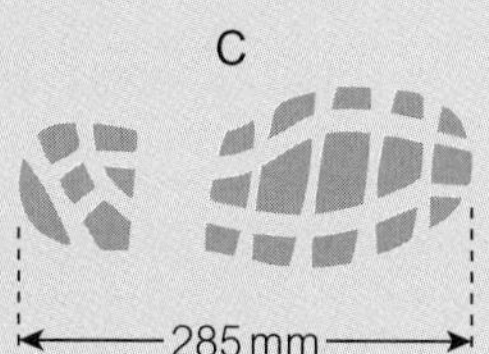

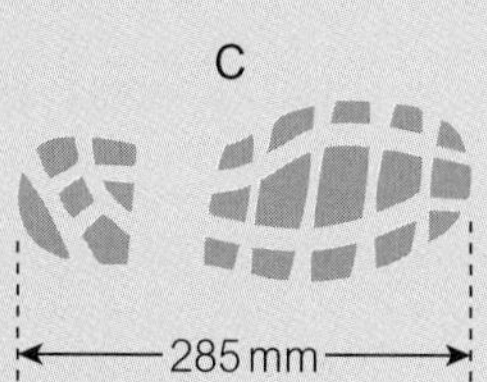

285 mm

2 Measure your foot length and see if this ratio works for you.

3 Is this a good model to use for animals?
Do you think this would work for paw prints or hoof prints?
Explain your answer.

22 **Reflect** In these lessons you were asked questions about ratios and proportions.

Are ratio and proportion the same thing or different? Explain.

In which other subjects might understanding ratio and proportion be useful to you?

Q22 hint

Look at this bar:

Find the ratio of grey to pink. Find the proportion of the bar that is grey.

When do you compare one part to another part?

When do you compare a part with the whole?

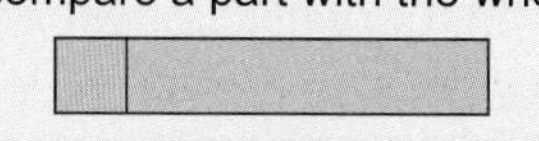

Reflect

7 Unit test

4a

1 Abbie makes a necklace out of beads.
For every red bead, she uses three green beads. She uses 24 beads altogether.
a How many red beads does she use?
b How many green beads does she use?

5c

2 A T-shirt costs £3.
Work out the cost of
a 3 T-shirts **b** 5 T-shirts **c** 11 T-shirts.

5b

3 There are 4 teaspoons of sugar in 200 m*l* of cola.
How many teaspoons of sugar are there in these amounts of cola?
a 400 m*l* **b** 100 m*l* **c** 1 litre?

5b

4 It takes a kitchen assistant 4 minutes to make six slices of toast.
The kitchen assistant has 20 minutes to make 35 slices of toast.
Has the kitchen assistant got enough time to complete the order?
Show your working and explain your answer.

5b

5 a Share 27 kg in the ratio 4 : 5.
b Show how you checked your answer is correct.

5b

6 Write each ratio in its simplest form.
a 3 : 15 **b** 30 : 5 **c** 15 : 25 **d** 80 : 60

5b

7 There are 4 blue lights in a row of 10 disco lights.
a What fraction of the disco lights are blue?
There are 7 blue lights in a row of 20 disco lights.
b What fraction of this row of disco lights are blue?
c Which row of disco lights has the greater proportion of blue lights?
Explain how you worked out your answer.

5b

8 The first time Abu played darts he missed the dartboard in 3 out of 10 throws.
a Write 3 out of 10 as a percentage.
The second time Abu played darts he missed the dartboard once in 5 throws.
b Write 1 out of 5 as a percentage.
c Did Abu miss the dartboard on a greater proportion of throws the first or the second time?

5b

9 Problem-solving These are the times, in minutes, for members of two clubs to swim 100 lengths.

Dolphins	62 74 75 75 87 87 89 90 102 116
Sharks	51 71 73 74 74 75 75 76 76 78 78 79 89 90 91 91 92 94 95 95

Which swimming club has the greater proportion of members with times under 80 minutes?

5a

10 Three memory sticks cost £12.
Work out the cost of
a 1 memory stick **b** 2 memory sticks **c** 8 memory sticks.

11 It cost £420 for six tickets to watch a Swansea City football match.
How much did it cost for five tickets? **5a**

12 Greg uses petrol and oil in his chainsaw in the ratio of 50 : 1.
How much oil does he use with 1500 m*l* of petrol? **5a**

13 The ratio of girl to boy members in a club is 2 : 3. **5a**
There are eight girl members.
a How many boy members are there?
b What is the total number of children in the club?

14 When Gavin makes a fruit cake, he uses cherries and sultanas in the ratio 1 : 4. **5a**
a What fraction of the fruit is
i cherries
ii sultanas?
b Gavin uses 250 g of fruit. How much of each type of fruit does he use?

15 The ratio of home to away supporters at a basketball match is 7 : 3. **5a**
a What percentage of the supporters are
i home supporters **ii** away supporters?
b Show how you checked your answers to part **a**.

16 Rob makes a rice pudding using 800 m*l* of milk and 200 m*l* of cream. **5a**
a Write the ratio of milk to cream in its simplest form.
b What percentage of the milk and cream mix is
i milk **ii** cream?

17 Debbie makes lemon squash by mixing 100 m*l* of squash with 900 m*l* water. **5a**
Sian makes lemon squash by mixing 40 m*l* of squash with 460 m*l* water.
Who has made the stronger squash? Explain your answer.

Challenge

18 Here are seven cards with ratios written on them.

1 : 2	1 : 3	1 : 4	2 : 3	3 : 5	3 : 7	4 : 5

Follow these steps.
1 Start with £1000.
2 Choose a card and share £1000 in the ratio written on it.
Circle the larger amount.
3 Choose a different card and share the circled amount in this ratio.
Circle the smaller amount.
4 Choose a different card and share the circled amount in this ratio. Circle the larger amount.
5 Continue these steps until you can go no further.

> **RULES**
> Use each card once only.
> Only use a card if it shares the amount exactly into whole numbers of pounds.

> **EXAMPLE**
> £1000 shared in the ratio 3 : 5 is £375 : (£625)
> £625 shared in the ratio 2 : 3 is (£250) : £375
> £250 shared in the ratio 3 : 7 is £75 : (£175)
> £175 shared in the ratio 1 : 4 is (£35) : £140
> £35 cannot be shared by any of the other ratios so STOP.

a What is the smallest final amount you can find?
b Is there a strategy you can use to try and find the smallest amount?
Explain your answer.

19 **Reflect** List five new skills and ideas you have learned in this unit. **Reflect**
What mathematics operations did you use most (addition, subtraction, multiplication and division)?
Which lesson in this unit did you like best? Why?

8 Lines and angles

MASTER

Check P209 | Strengthen P211 | Extend P215 | Test P219

8.1 Lines, angles and triangles

You will learn to:
- Describe and label lines, angles and triangles
- Identify angle, side and symmetry properties of triangles.

CONFIDENCE

Why learn this? Lines and angles drawn on graphs help investors tell whether share prices are going up or down.

Fluency
How many degrees are there in a full turn? ... half a turn? ... a quarter of a turn ... three quarters of a turn?

Explore
What shape and measurements would you need to create a template for a bag that fits in the frame of a bicycle?

Exercise 8.1

Warm up

1 Copy these shapes. Draw in the line of symmetry.

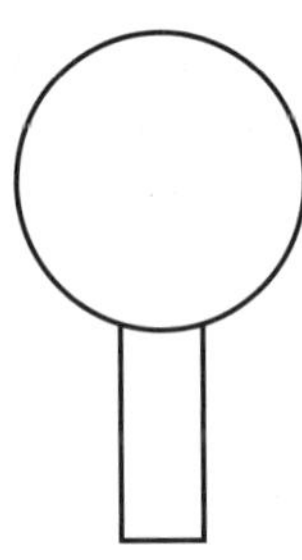 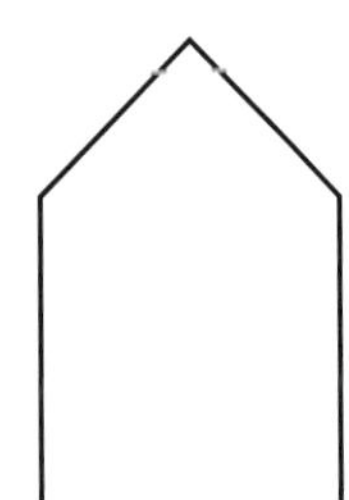 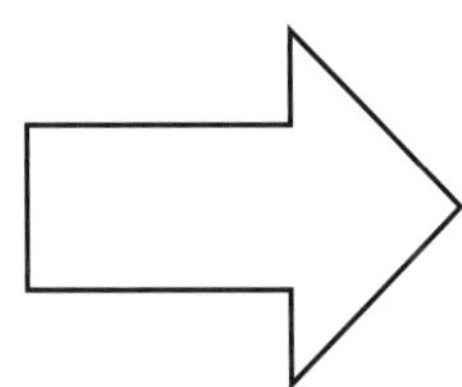

2 Name each triangle. Choose from scalene, isosceles, equilateral or right-angled.

a 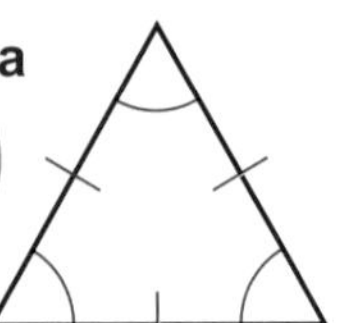 b 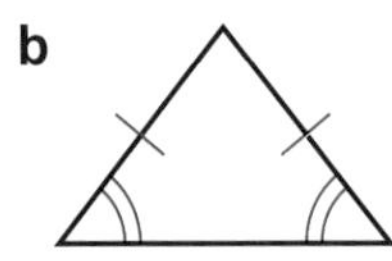 c d 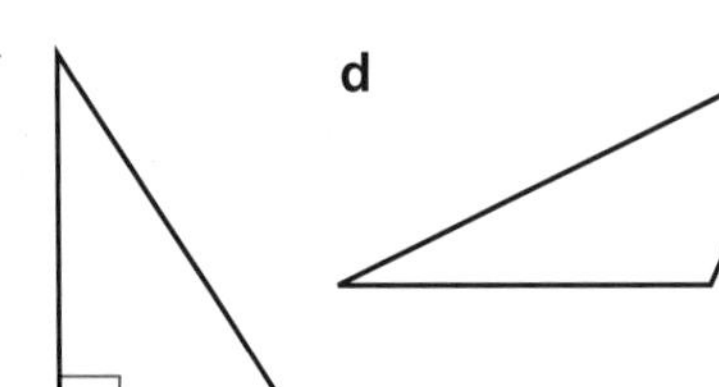

Q2 hint
The dashes show sides of equal length.
and show equal angles.

4c

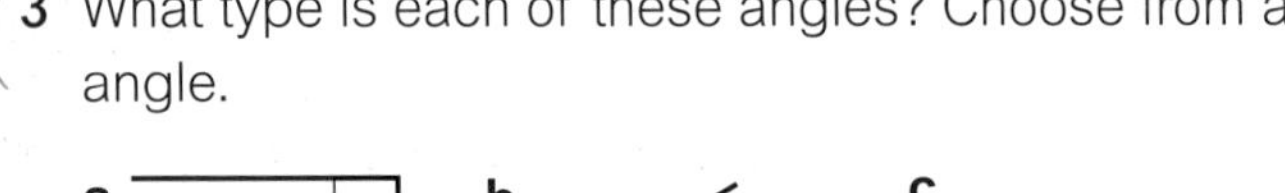

3 What type is each of these angles? Choose from acute, obtuse or right angle.

a 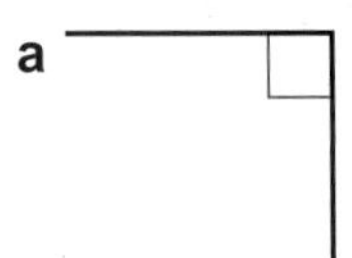 b 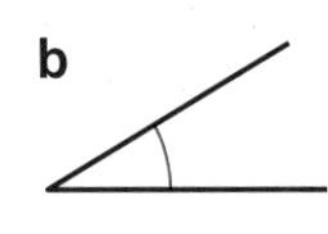 c  d 

Subject links: Science (Q5, Q9), Design and technology (Q5, Q9)

4 For each angle, write the angle name and the type. Choose from acute, obtuse or **reflex**.

a

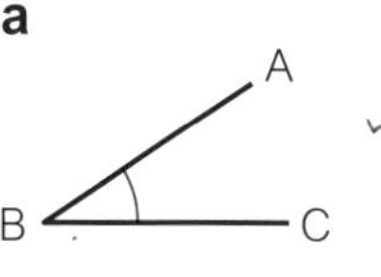

b

D E F

c

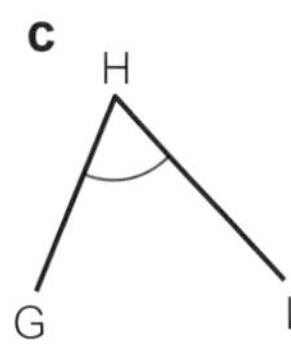

d

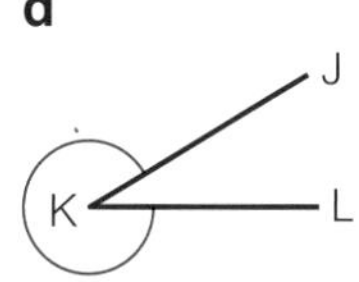

Discussion If you add two acute angles, do you get an obtuse angle?

5 **STEM** This is a Howe truss. It was used in wooden railway bridges.

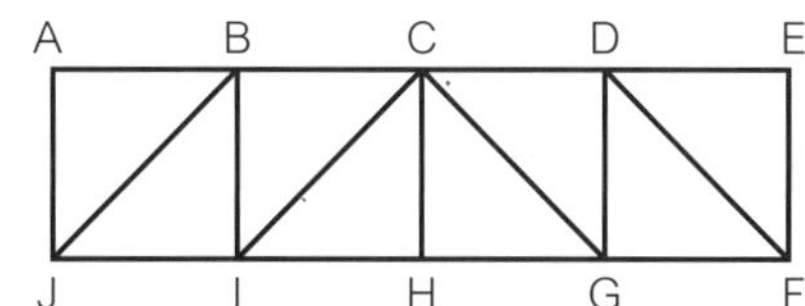

a Write a line that is

i **parallel** to CD

ii **perpendicular** to DG.

b Are CI and CG parallel? Explain your answer.

c What type of angle is ∠GCD?

d What type of angle is $E\hat{F}D$?

e Write a 90° angle.

6 Sketch a triangle XYZ with three acute angles.

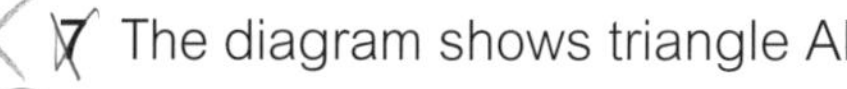

7 The diagram shows triangle ABC.

Write down

a a letter at one **vertex** of the triangle

b the equal sides

c the type of triangle

d the equal angles.

A
C B

Discussion Can an equilateral triangle be made using right-angled triangles?

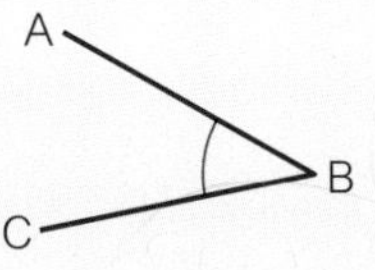

Key point

This angle is called angle ABC or $A\hat{B}C$ or ∠ABC,
or angle CBA or $C\hat{B}A$ or ∠CBA.

Key point

A **reflex** angle is more than 180°, but less than 360°.

Key point

Perpendicular lines are at right angles (90°) to each other.
Parallel lines are always the same distance apart and never meet.

Key point

You can describe a triangle using the letters at its **vertices** (the plural of **vertex**). The vertices are the corners.
This is triangle DEF.

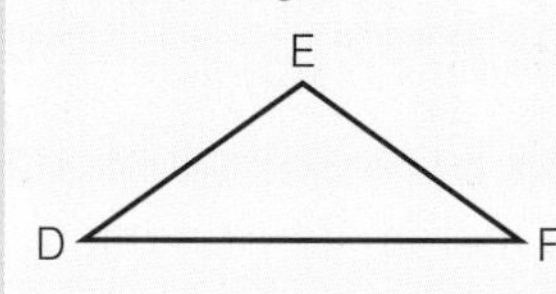

4b

4b

4a

4a

Investigation **Reasoning**

Use a 3 × 3 square on square dotted paper.
Draw as many *different* triangles as you can, by joining three dots.

Here is one example. 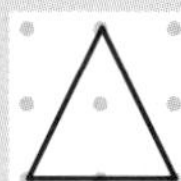

1 How many different triangles can you draw?

2 Label the triangles: scalene, isosceles, equilateral, right-angled.

3 Which triangles are **symmetrical**? How many lines of symmetry do they have?

Literacy hint

If a shape is **symmetrical** it has a line or lines of symmetry.

4a **8** How many lines of symmetry does this triangle have?

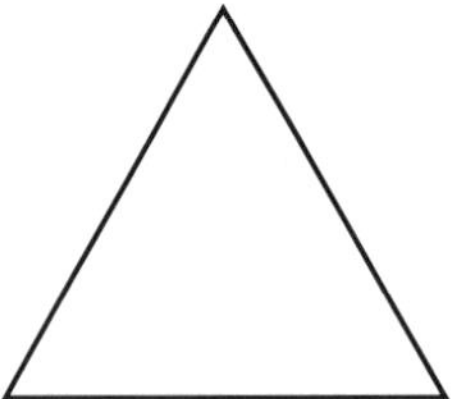

5c **9** **STEM** This is a common truss. It is used to support roofs.

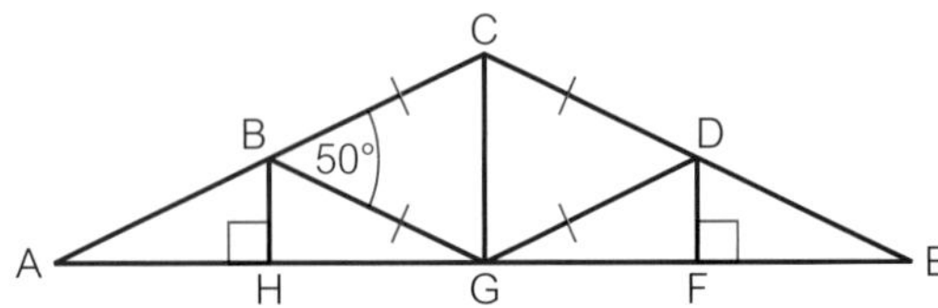

a What type of triangle is BGC?

b How many right-angled triangles are there?

c Write down two lengths which are equal.

d Write down two angles which are equal.

e Which angle is labelled 50°?

f How many lines of symmetry does triangle ACE have?

g **Reasoning** Is ∠CDG 50°? Explain your answer.

Discussion Can a right-angled triangle be isosceles?

> **Q9d hint**
> Use a protractor to check.

Explore

10 **Explore** What shape and measurements would you need to create a template for a bag that fits in the frame of a bicycle?
Is it easier to explore this question now you have completed the lesson?
What further information do you need to be able to answer this?

Reflect

11 **Reflect** 'Notation' means symbols. Mathematics uses a lot of notation.
For example:

= means 'is equal to' ° means 'degrees' ∟ means 'a right angle'

Look back at this lesson on angles, lines and triangles. Write a list of all the maths notation used.
Why do you think mathematicians use notation?
Could you have answered the questions in this lesson without understanding the maths notation?
What other kind of notation was used in this lesson?
What other subjects use notation?

> **Q11 hint**
> Look at the symbols at the ends of all the sentences!

8.2 Estimating, measuring and drawing angles

You will learn to:
- Use a protractor to measure and draw angles
- Estimate the size of angles
- Solve problems involving angles.

CONFIDENCE

Why learn this? Solar panels must be set at a specific angle to capture the most energy from the Sun.

Fluency
Which of these angles are acute? ... obtuse? ... reflex?
- 137°
- 42°
- 12°
- 271°
- 92°
- 350°

Explore
At what angle from the horizontal should a solar panel be set to collect the most energy?

Exercise 8.2

Warm up

1 Measure the length of line XY. Give your answer in millimetres.

X ———————————————— Y

2 What angle is shown here? 4b

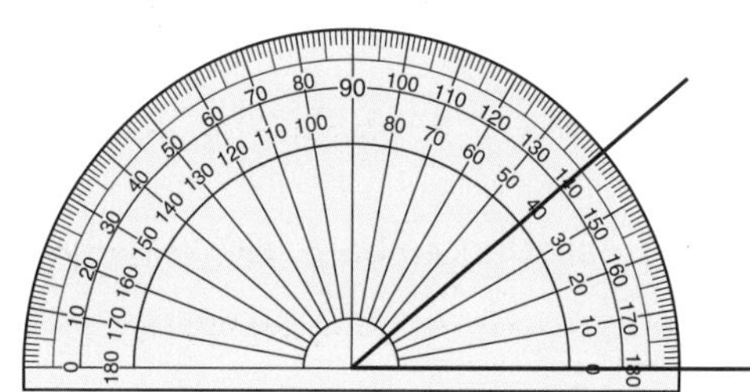

Q2 hint
Read up from 0 on the inner scale.

3 Look at these angles. 4b

Q3 hint
Place the cross of the **protractor** on the point of the angle.
Line up the zero line with one line of the angle.
Read up from 0 on the inner scale.

a What type of angles are they?
b Measure each angle.
Give your answers to the nearest degree. Check they are sensible.

4a

4 Measure each angle to the nearest degree.

a

b

4a

5 Isabel needs to measure these angles to the nearest degree.

a **b**

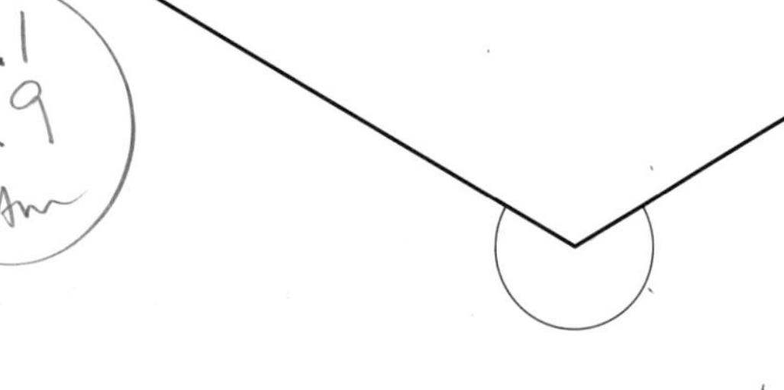

Copy and complete Isabel's work.

a smaller angle = 120°, so marked angle = 360° − 120° = □

b smaller angle = □, so marked angle = □

Discussion Why do you subtract the smaller angle from 360°?

4a

6 Look at these triangles.

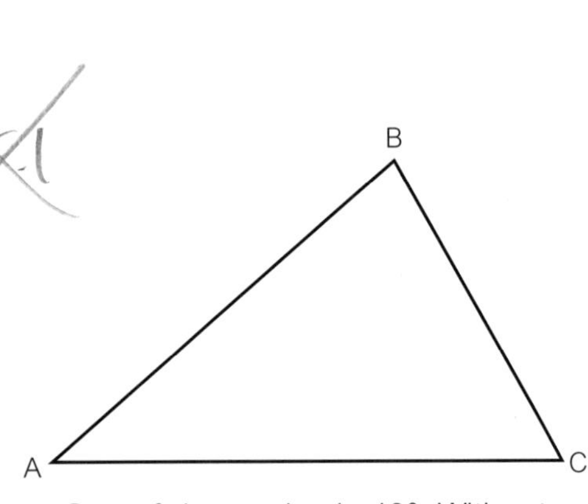

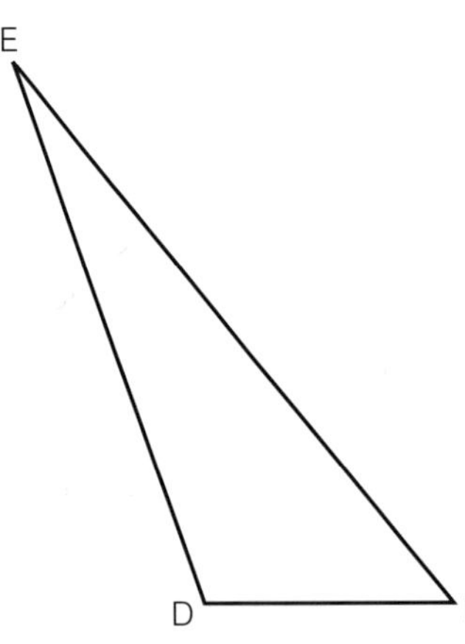

a One of the angles is 40°. Without using a protractor, decide which one.

b Estimate the size of ∠FDE.

c Estimate the size of ∠BCA.

d Which angle looks less than 40°?

e Use a protractor to check your answers to parts **a** to **d**.

Q6b hint

First decide whether the angle is less than or more than 90°.

Topic links: Reading scales, Metric conversions, Probability

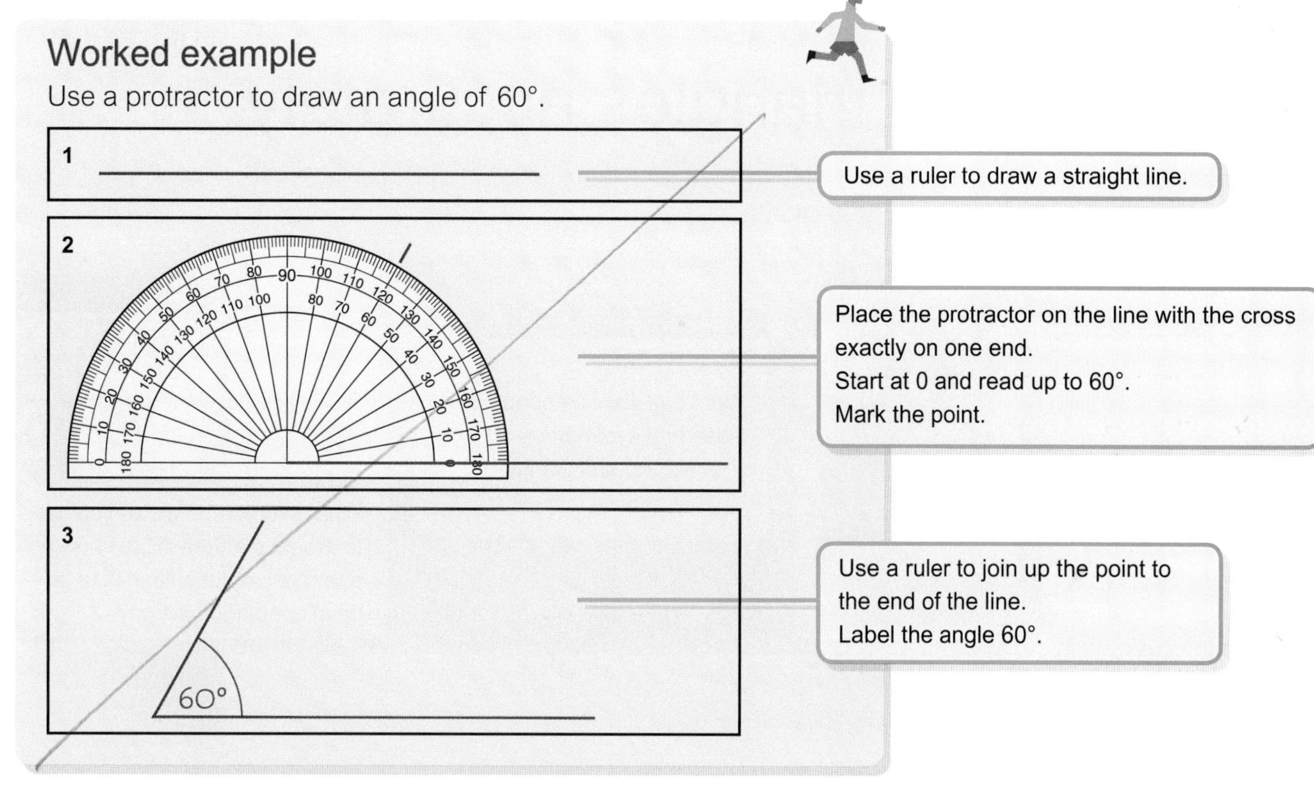

Worked example
Use a protractor to draw an angle of 60°.
1
Use a ruler to draw a straight line.
2
Place the protractor on the line with the cross exactly on one end.
Start at 0 and read up to 60°.
Mark the point.
3
Use a ruler to join up the point to the end of the line.
Label the angle 60°.
60°

7 Use a protractor to draw these angles.

a 80° **b** 75° **c** 37° **d** 100°
e 145° **f** 220° **g** 315°

Q7f hint

If you have a semicircular protractor, work out 360° − 220° = 140°, then draw an angle of 140°.
The reflex angle is 220°.

8 Problem-solving This spinner has four sectors. Each sector wins a prize.

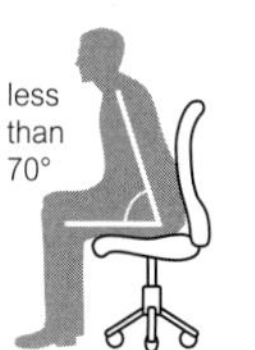

a Which prize do you have the best chance of winning?

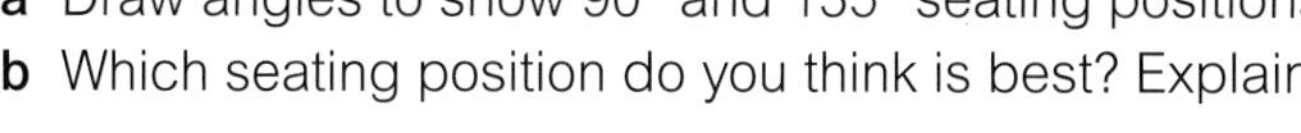

b Which prize do you have the least chance of winning?

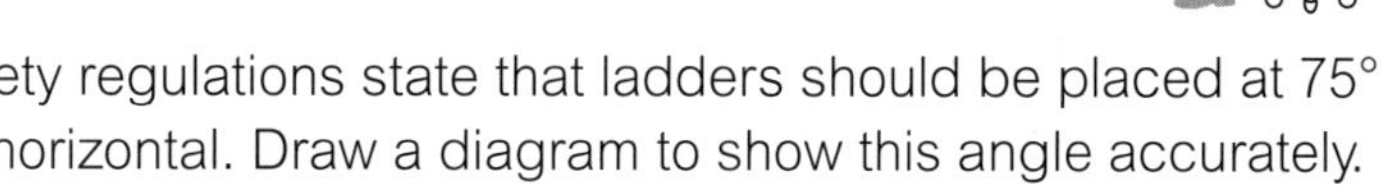

Q8 hint

Use a protractor to measure the angles.

9 Real / STEM A study looked at the best position for sitting at a desk. One seating position is shown.

less than 70°

a Draw angles to show 90° and 135° seating positions.
b Which seating position do you think is best? Explain.

10 Real Safety regulations state that ladders should be placed at 75° from the horizontal. Draw a diagram to show this angle accurately.

11 **Explore** At what angle from the horizontal should a solar panel be set to collect the most energy?
Look back at the maths you have learned in this lesson.
How can you use it to answer this question?

12 **Reflect** Look back at Q6.
First you estimated the size of angles, and then you measured them accurately.
Why is estimating first a good strategy?
Write other maths topics where you have used this strategy.
Why is it a good strategy for other maths topics?
Can you use this strategy in other subjects too? Explain.

5c 5c 5c 5c Explore Reflect

8.3 Drawing triangles accurately

You will learn to:

- Use a ruler and protractor to draw triangles accurately
- Solve problems involving angles and triangles.

CONFIDENCE

Why learn this? Many artists find inspiration in maths and construct triangles in their works of art.

Fluency
What can you say about the sides and symmetries of
- an equilateral triangle
- an isosceles triangle?

Explore
What information would you need to produce a drawing to show how a triangular plot of land is to be developed and built on?

Exercise 8.3

Warm up

1 Draw each of these lines accurately.
  a 7 cm b 6.2 cm c 50 mm

2 Use a ruler and protractor to draw an acute angle and an obtuse angle.

3 Use a protractor to draw these angles.
  a 25° b 120°

4 On a scale drawing 1 cm represents 1 m.
  Use a ruler to draw a line to represent 6 m.

Worked example

Use a ruler and protractor to draw this triangle accurately.

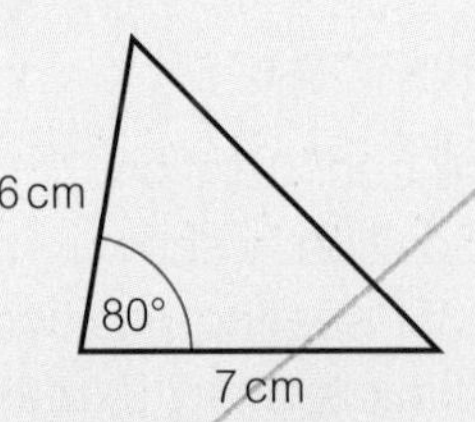

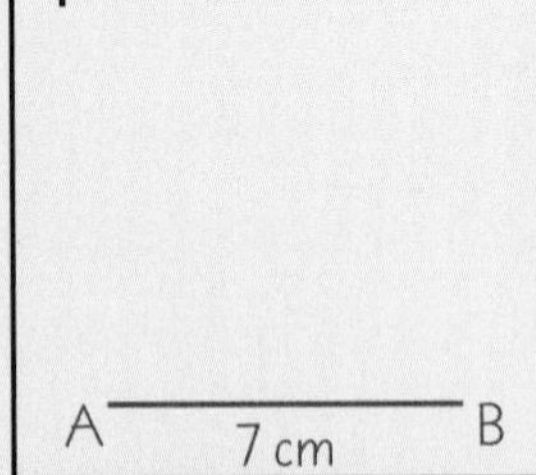

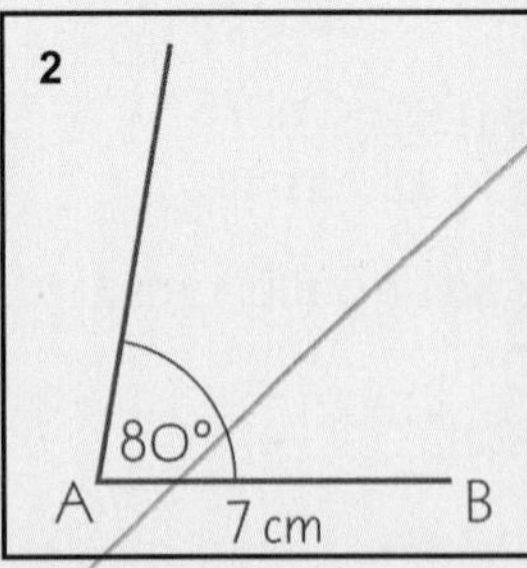

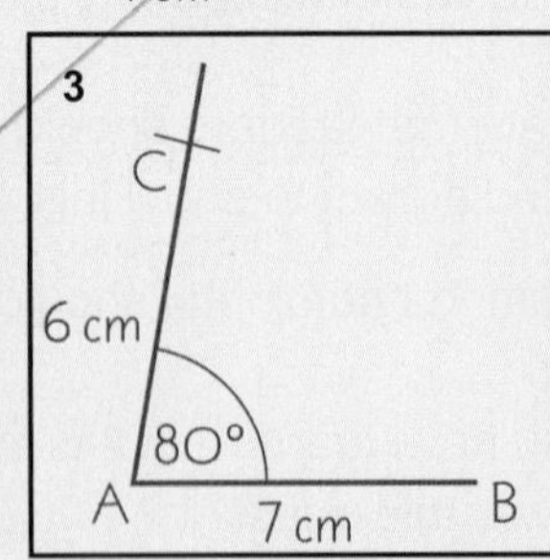

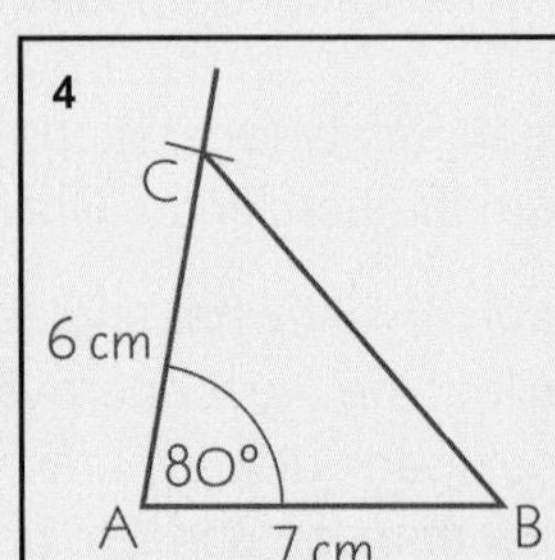

1 Use a ruler to draw the line AB with length 7 cm.
2 Use a protractor to draw an angle of 80° at A. Draw a long line through the 80° mark.
3 Use a ruler to draw the line AC with length 6 cm.
4 Draw in the third side of the triangle.

Topic links: Reading scales, Metric conversions

Subject links: Music (Q10), Physics (Q10)

5 Use a ruler and protractor to draw these triangles accurately.

a

8 cm, 7 cm, 50°

b

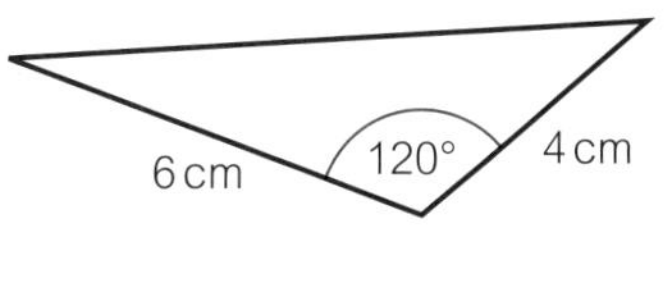

Q5 hint

First draw a side with a length you know.

6 a Make an accurate drawing of this triangle.

b Measure the length of AB, to the nearest millimetre.

c Measure the sizes of angles CAB and CBA.

d **Reasoning** What type of triangle is ABC?

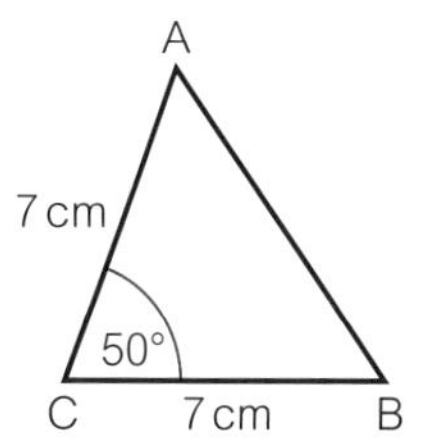

Q6 hint

You must use a ruler and protractor to make an accurate drawing.

Worked example

Make an accurate drawing of this triangle.

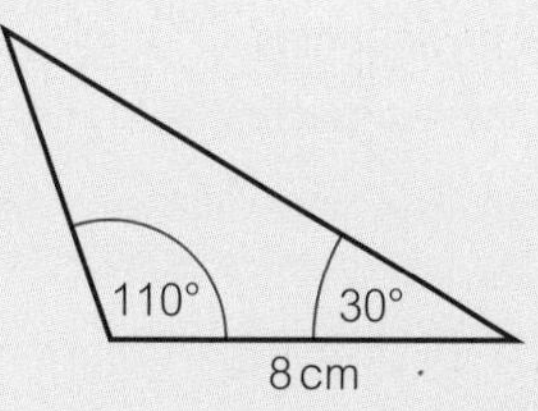

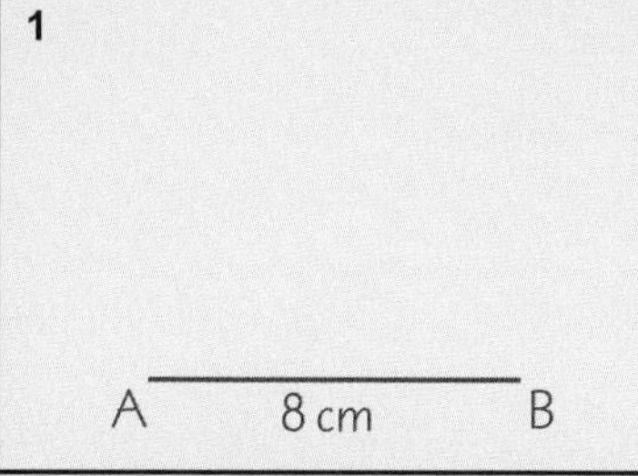

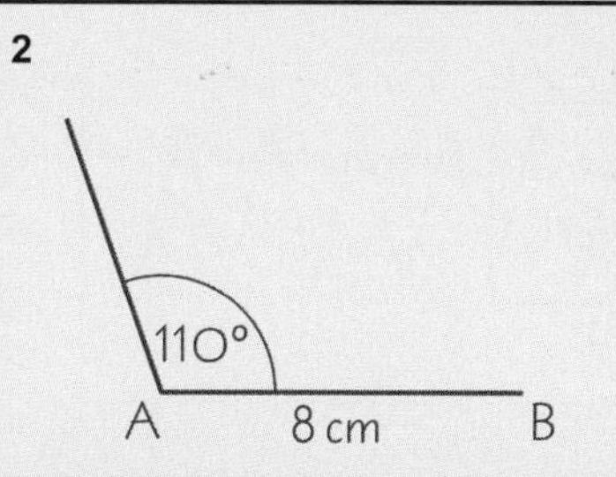

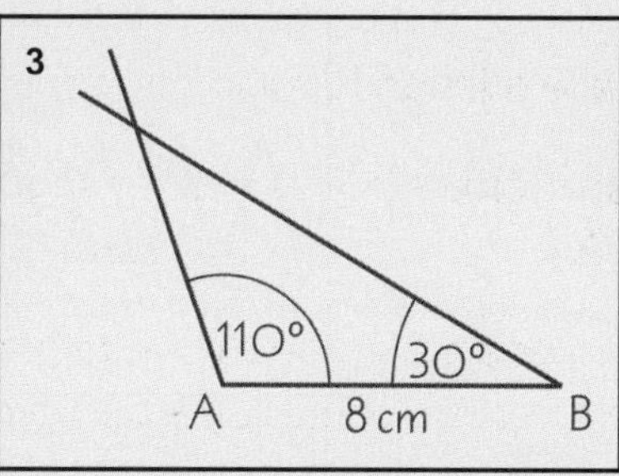

1 Use a ruler to draw the line AB with length 8 cm.

2 Use a protractor to draw an angle of 110° at A. Draw a long line through the 110° mark.

3 Use a protractor to draw an angle of 30° at B. Draw a line through the 30° mark until it crosses the 110° line.

7 Use a ruler and protractor to draw these triangles accurately.

a

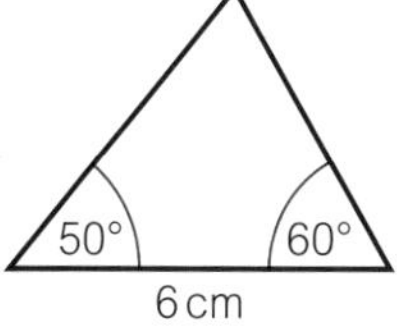

b

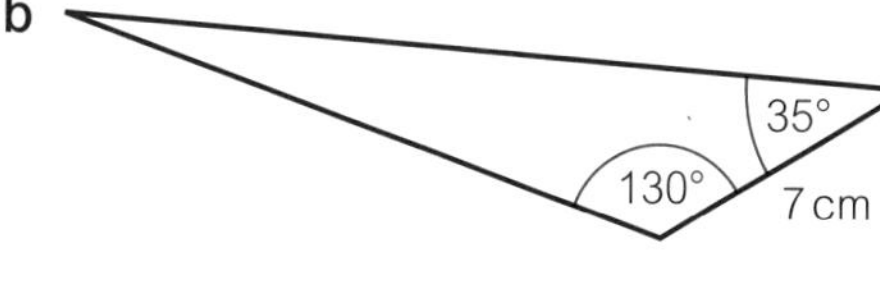

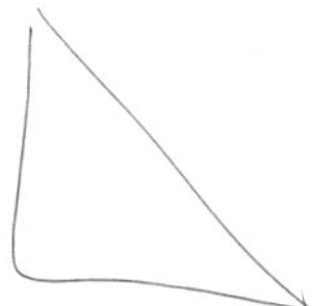

8 a Make an accurate drawing of this triangle.

b Measure the lengths of AC and AB.

c Measure the size of ∠CAB.

d **Reasoning** What type of triangle is ABC?

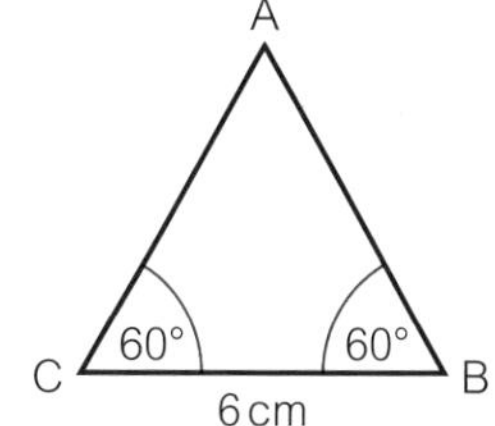

5b 5a 5a 5a

5a

9 Problem-solving / STEM This is a common roof truss.

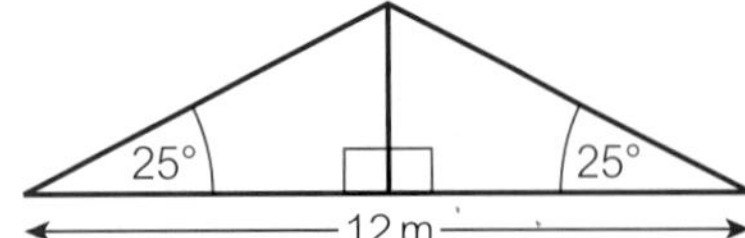

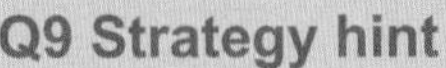

Q9 Strategy hint
Measure the central height of the truss. Work to the nearest metre.

a Make an accurate drawing of the truss. Use 1 cm to represent 1 m in real life.

b Ray needs a truss with a height of 4 m. Is this truss big enough? Explain your answer.

Investigation — Reasoning

1 Use a ruler and protractor to accurately draw an equilateral triangle with side length 8 cm.
2 Mark the **midpoint** of each side at 4 cm.
3 Use a ruler to join up the three midpoints.
4 Measure the side lengths of all the triangles.
5 Measure the angles of all the triangles.
6 What can you say about these triangles?

Literacy hint
The **midpoint** is half way between two points.

5a

10 Real / STEM The diagram shows the sound waveform created when a guitar string is plucked.

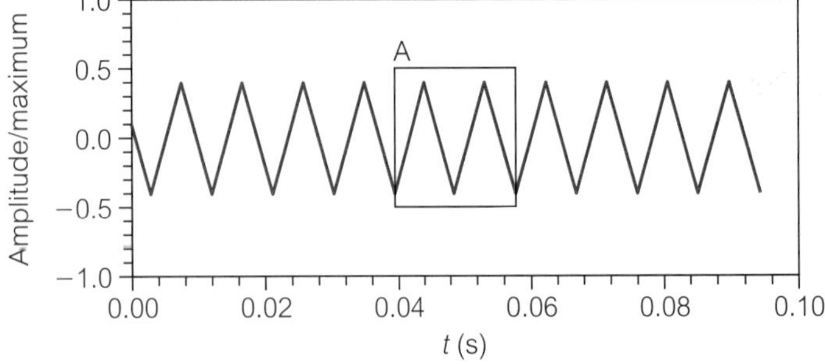

The waveform is close to a triangle wave. Here is a sketch of one of the enlarged triangles.

a Make an accurate drawing of the triangle.

b Use it to make an accurate drawing of section A of the waveform.

Explore

11 Explore What information would you need to produce a drawing to show how a triangular plot of land is to be developed and built on?
What have you learned in this lesson to help you answer this question?
What other information do you need?

Reflect

12 Reflect In this lesson you used two tools to help you draw triangles accurately – a ruler and a protractor.
Which did you find more difficult to use? Why?
Write down a hint or hints, in your own words, to help you use this tool in future.

8.4 STEM: Calculating angles

You will learn to:
- Use the rule for angles on a straight line, angles around a point and vertically opposite angles
- Solve problems involving angles.

CONFIDENCE

Why learn this? Diamonds are cut to reflect the light in different directions, which makes them sparkle.

Fluency
- How many degrees are there in a right angle?
- Work out

a 180 − 60 b 180 − 90
c 180 − 125 d 360 − 120
e 360 − 90 f 360 − 205

Explore
How does a periscope use angles of light so you can see round corners?

Exercise 8.4: Light

Warm up

1 Find the missing numbers.

a 40 + □ = 180 b 180 = 65 + □

c 280 + □ = 360 d 360 = 175 + □

2 a What is 360 ÷ 3?

b Divide 360 into nine equal parts.

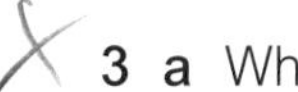

3 a What is 60 × 6?

b What must 180 be multiplied by to give a total of 360?

4b

4

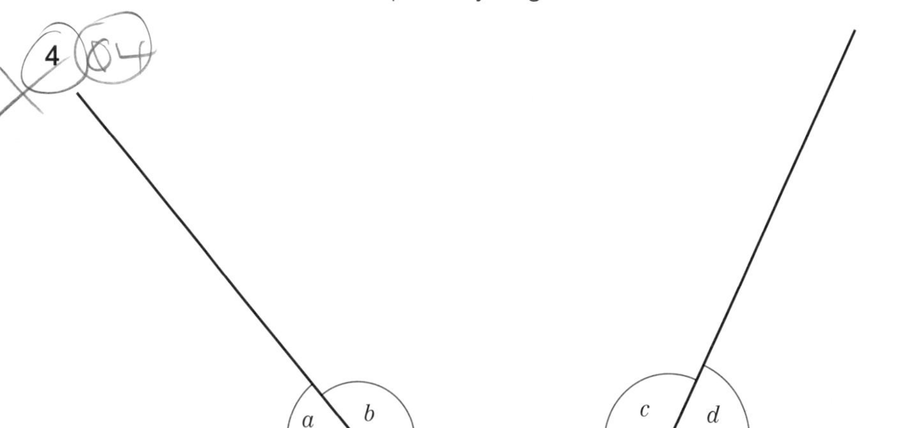

a Measure the angles marked with letters.

b Work out $a + b$ and $c + d$.

c What do you notice about your answers to part **b**?

Key point
Angles are sometimes labelled with lower case letters inside the angle.
The angles on a straight line add up to 180°.
$a + b = 180°$

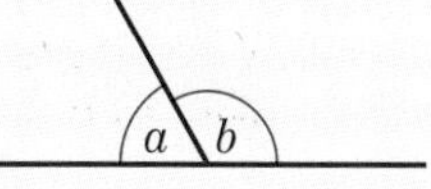

4b

5 Calculate the size of each unknown angle.

a
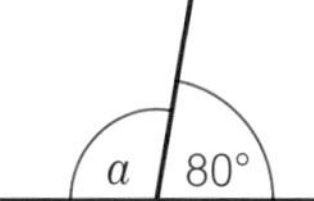

b
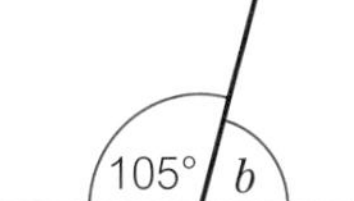

c
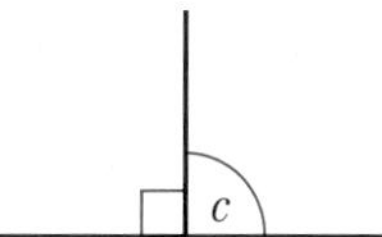

Q5a Strategy hint
You can think of the calculation in two ways.
$180° - 80° = a$ or $a + 80° = 180°$

4a **6** STEM When light is reflected, the **angle of incidence** (i) equals the **angle of reflection** (r).

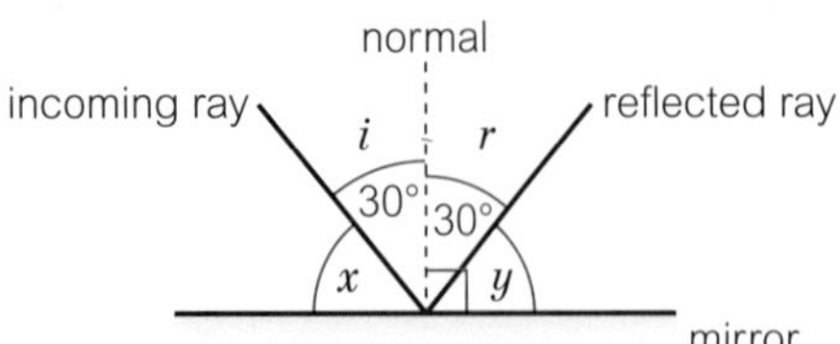

Work out

a angle x **b** angle y.

Q6 Literacy hint

In science, you calculate angles of light to the *normal*. The normal is an imaginary line at 90° to a surface. The **angle of incidence** is between the incoming ray and the normal. The **angle of reflection** is between the normal and the reflected ray.

4a **7** Problem-solving / Reasoning Angle A is five times the size of angle B. What are the sizes of angle A and angle B?

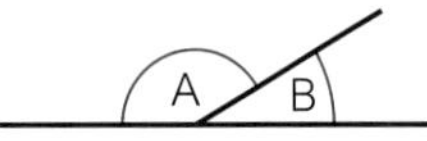

Q7 Strategy hint

Use the ratio A : B.
5 : 1

4a **8** **a** Measure the angles marked with letters.

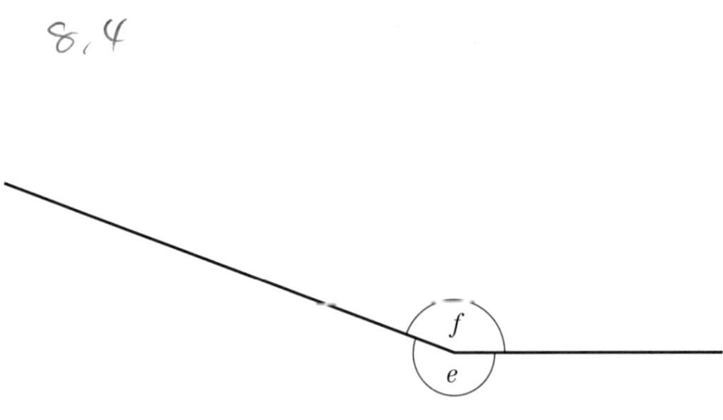

b Work out $e + f$ and $g + h$.

c What do you notice about your answers to part **b**?

Discussion How do the sums of angles on a straight line and round a point relate to the half turn and full turn?

Key point

The angles around a point add up to 360°.

$a + b = 360°$

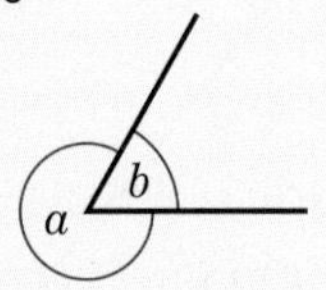

4a **9** Calculate the size of each unknown angle.

a

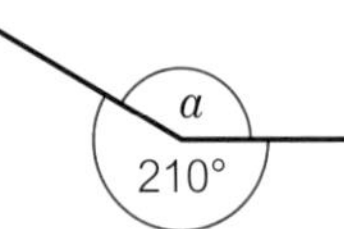

b

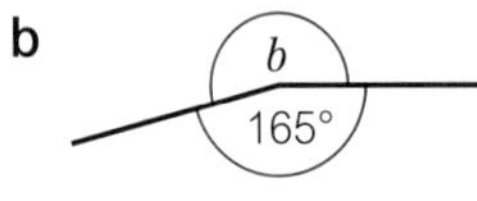

c

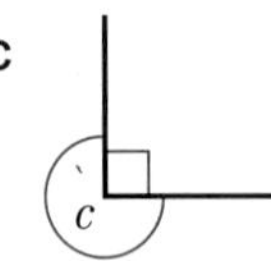

Q9 Strategy hint

You can think of the calculation in two ways.

$360° - 210° = a$ or $a + 210° = 360°$

5c **10** STEM Light refracts when it goes from one material to another. Work out the missing angles in these refraction diagrams.

a

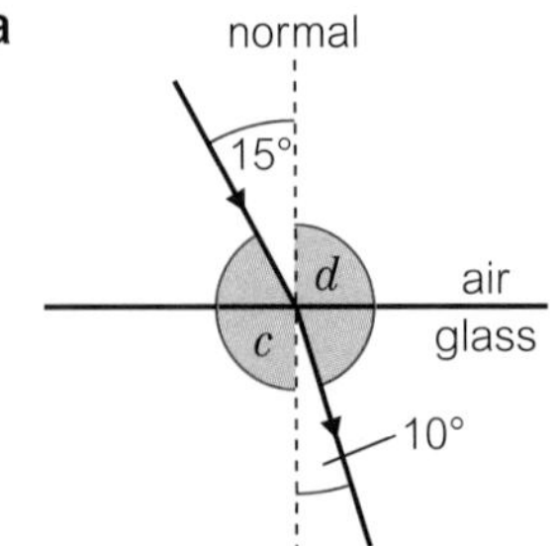

b

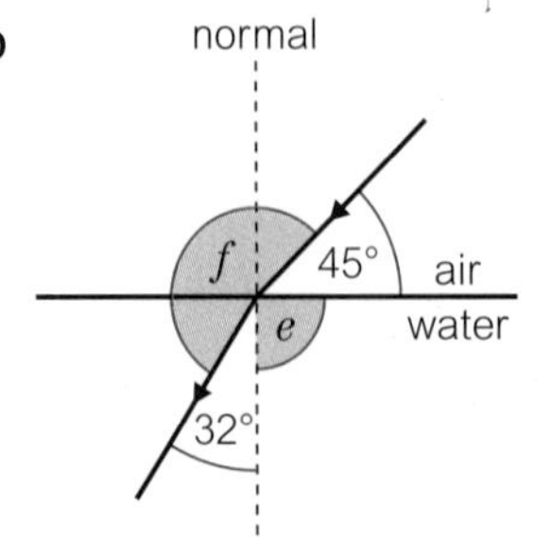

Q10 Literacy hint

When light refracts, the ray of light changes direction.

Subject links: Science

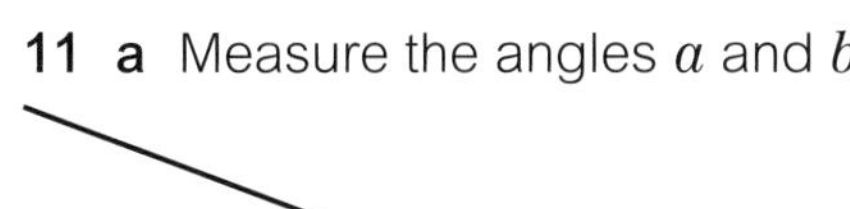

11 a Measure the angles a and b.

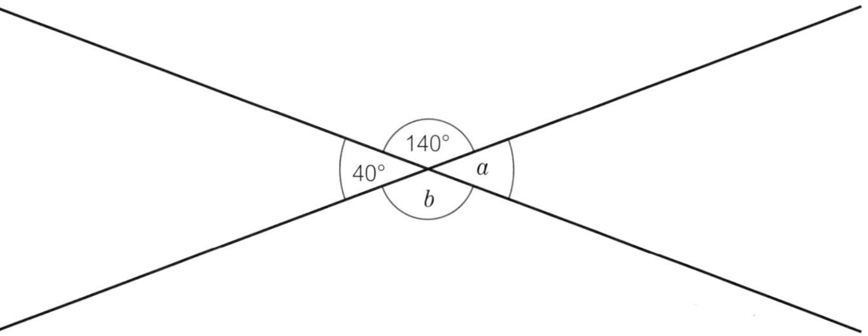

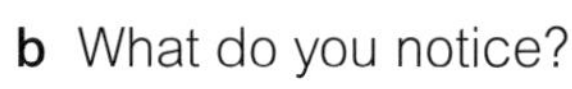

b What do you notice?

Discussion Can you work out the size of angles a and b without measuring?

Key point

Vertically opposite angles are equal.
The green angles are equal.
The blue angles are equal.

12 Work out the sizes of the unknown angles.

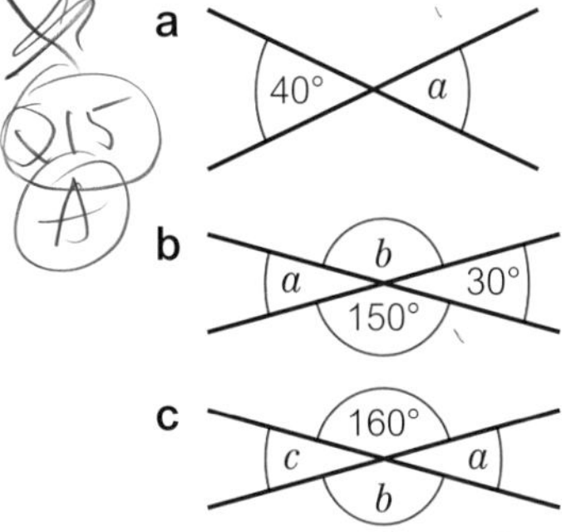

c

160°
c a
b

Q12c hint

The angles a and 160° make a straight line.

13 STEM Light is refracted when it passes through a glass lens.
Work out the angles m and n.

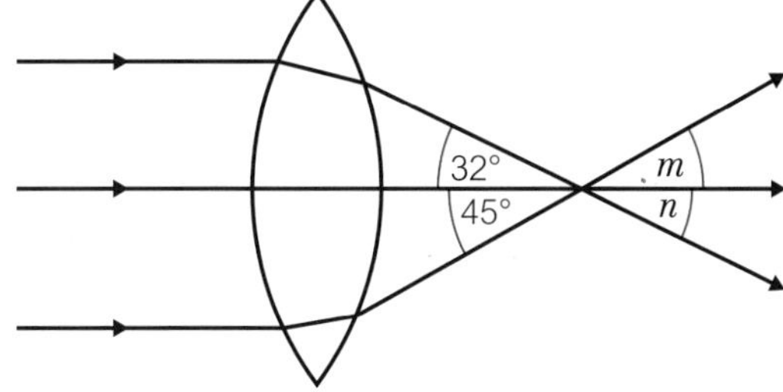

14 Explore How does a periscope use angles of light so you can see round corners?
Look back at the maths you have learned in this lesson.
How can you use it to answer this question?

15 Reflect Some questions in this lesson were about angles only.
Some questions were about angles and light.
Look back at questions of both types. When you answered them:

- What did you do the same for both types?
- What did you do differently for each type?
- Which type of question do you prefer? Why?
- Which type of question was easier? Why?

8.5 Angles in a triangle

You will learn to:
- Use the rule for the sum of angles in a triangle
- Calculate interior and exterior angles
- Solve angle problems involving triangles.

CONFIDENCE

Why learn this? Aircraft engineers work out the angles of the triangular surfaces of a stealth attack aeroplane.

Fluency
Work out
- 90 + 60
- 90 − 25
- 35 + 70
- 180 − 105
- 180 − 75 − 10

Explore
At what angle does a snooker ball bounce off the second cushion at a corner?

Exercise 8.5

Warm up

1 Work out the unknown angles.

a 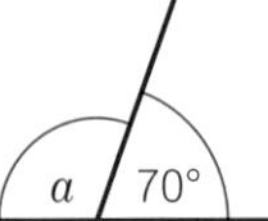

b 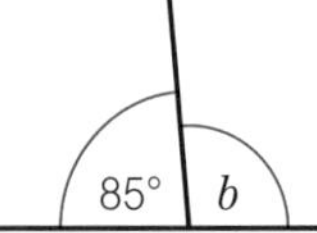

c 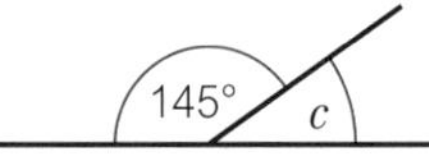

2 Which triangle am I?
 a I have one angle of 90°.
 b All my sides are equal.
 c All my sides are different lengths.

5c

3 a Draw a rectangle.
 Draw one straight line to divide the rectangle into two right-angled triangles.
 b Draw another rectangle.
 Draw two straight lines to divide the rectangle into four isosceles triangles.

Q3b hint
An isosceles triangle has two equal angles.

5c

4 For each diagram, write down the size of
 i the **interior** angle ii the **exterior** angle.

a 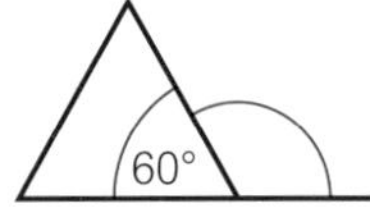

b 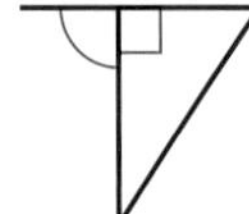

c 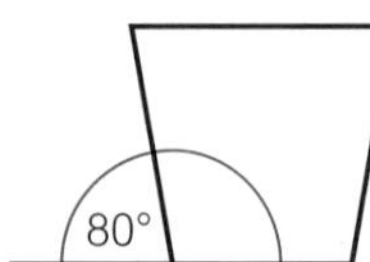

Key point

An **interior** angle is inside a shape.
An **exterior** angle is outside the shape on a straight line with the interior angle.

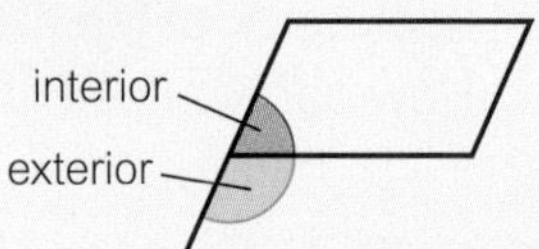

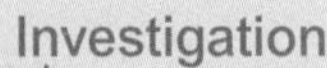

Investigation
1 Draw a triangle with angles a, b and c.
2 Cut out the triangle and tear off each of the corners.
3 Arrange the three parts in a straight line so that angles a, b and c meet.
4 Reasoning What does this tell you about the angles in a triangle?
 Does this work for all triangles?

Topic links: Symmetry

Subject links: Science (Q10)

5 Calculate the size of each unknown angle. 5b

a

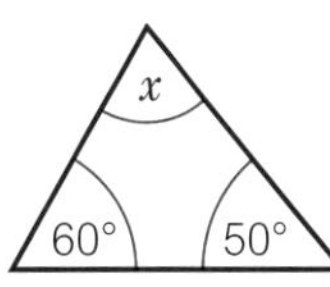

b

45°, 75°, x

c

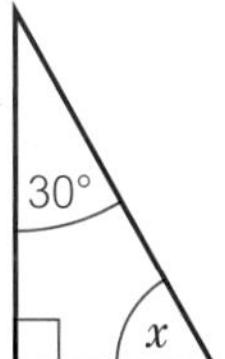

Discussion Is there a quick way of working out the missing angle in a right-angled triangle?

> **Key point**
>
> The angles in a triangle add up to 180°.
>
> $a + b + c = 180°$
>
> 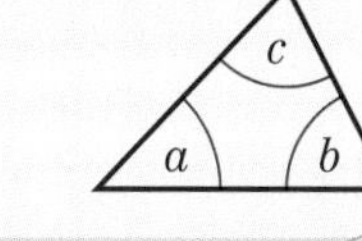
>

6 **Reasoning** Work out the size of each angle in an equilateral triangle. 5b

7 **Problem-solving** One of the angles of an isosceles triangle is 50°. 5b
What are the other two angles?
Reasoning Is there more than one possible answer?

8 Work out the missing angles. 5b

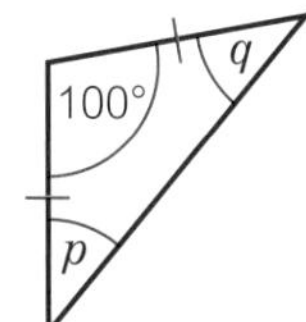

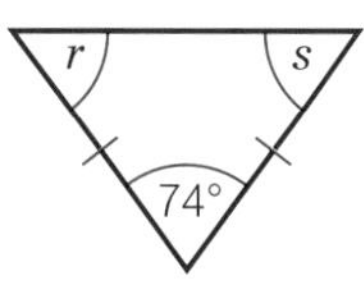

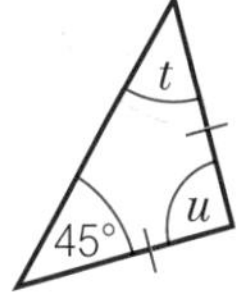

9 Calculate the size of each unknown angle. 5b

a

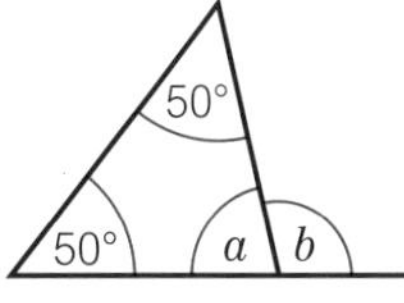

b

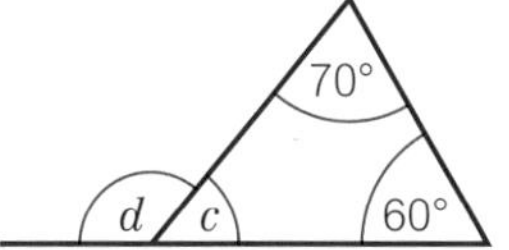

c

f, 40°, e, 120°

Discussion Is an equilateral triangle isosceles?

> **Q9a hint**
>
> $a + 50 + 50 = 180°$
> $a + b = ?$

> **Q9c hint**
>
> Work out e first.

10 **Problem-solving / STEM** This is a scissor truss. It is used to build a cathedral or vaulted ceiling. 5b

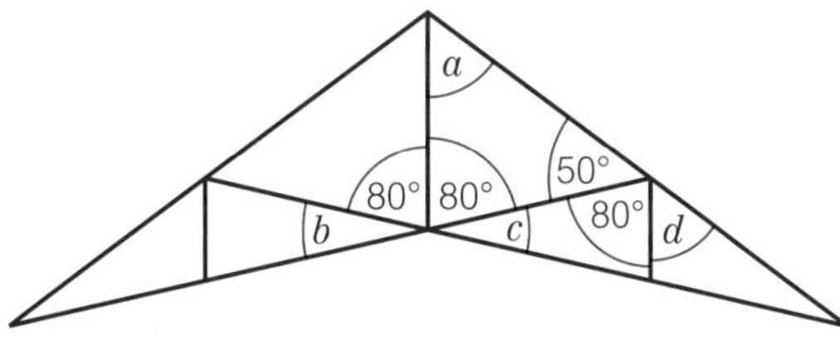

Work out the size of each unknown angle.

> **Q10 hint**
>
> Which two angles are vertically opposite?

11 **Explore** At what angle does a snooker ball bounce off the second cushion at a corner?
Choose some sensible numbers to help you explore this situation.
Then use what you have learned in this lesson to help you answer the question.

Explore

12 **Reflect** In this lesson you did a lot of subtracting from 180°.
What strategy did you use to mentally subtract from 180°?
Would your strategy still work to subtract 46°? If not, what strategy would you use?
Would your strategy still work to subtract a number from 360°?
If not, what strategy would you use?

> **Q12 hint**
>
> Describe what you did when you mentally subtracted from 180°. For example, did you subtract tens first? Or did you use a different method?

Reflect

8.6 Quadrilaterals

You will learn to:

- Identify and name types of quadrilaterals
- Use the rule for the sum of angles in a quadrilateral
- Solve angle problems involving quadrilaterals.

CONFIDENCE

Why learn this? The shapes and angles in a bicycle frame affect the strength of the bicycle.

Fluency
How many sides does a quadrilateral have?
Work out

- 60 + 90 + 120
- 85 + 145 + 105
- 360 − 150 − 90 − 20
- 360 − 110 − 85 − 85

Explore
Can you make a patchwork quilt using any type of quadrilateral?

Exercise 8.6

Warm up

1 How many lines of symmetry does each of these shapes have?

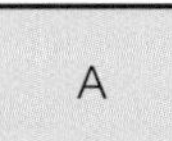

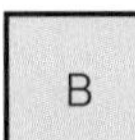

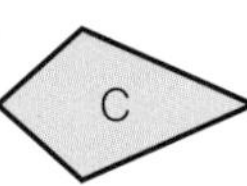

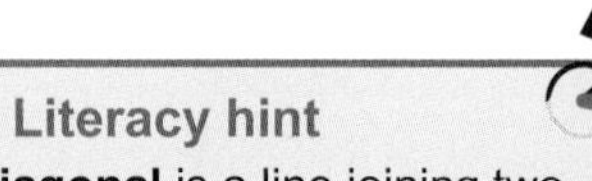

Q2 Literacy hint
A **diagonal** is a line joining two opposite vertices.

2 Imagine a rectangle with both **diagonals** drawn. Remove one of the triangles. What type of triangle is it?

5c **3** Name each of these quadrilaterals. Choose from square, rectangle, rhombus, parallelogram, trapezium, kite or arrowhead.

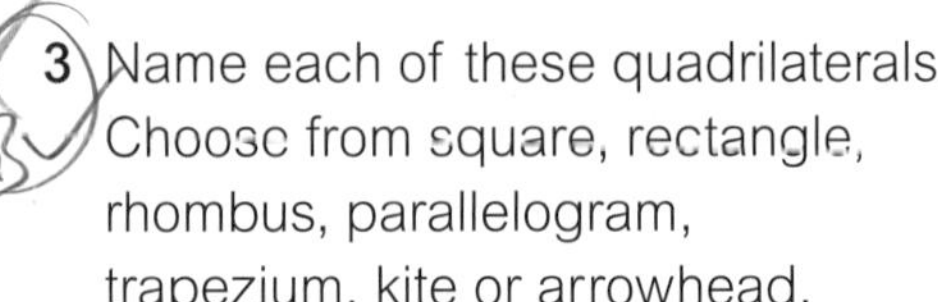

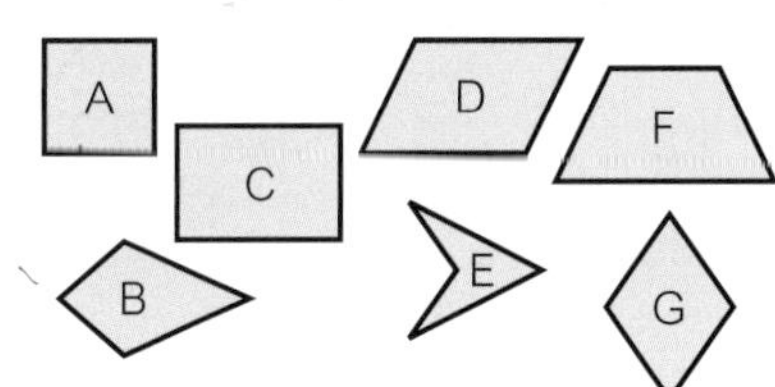

5c **4** Which quadrilateral am I?

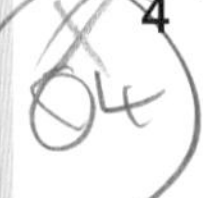

- **a** I have four right angles. All my sides are equal.
- **b** I have four equal angles and two pairs of equal sides.
- **c** I have one pair of parallel sides.
- **d** I have no right angles. My opposite sides are equal and parallel.

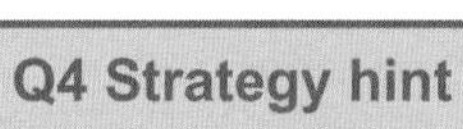

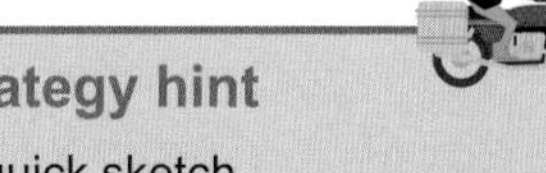

Q4 Strategy hint
Draw a quick sketch.

5b **5** Here is a rectangle cut in two.

- **a** Name the two new shapes that are made.
- **b** Write down the properties of each shape.

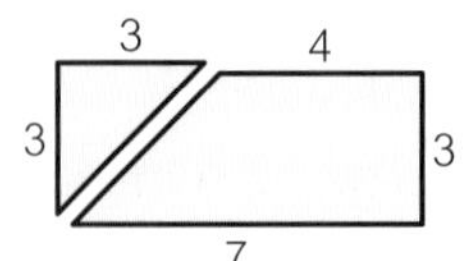

Q5b Literacy hint
The properties of a shape are facts about its angles, symmetry and sides.

5a **6** **Reasoning** Show how two identical isosceles triangles can be joined together to make

a a rhombus **b** a square.

5a **7** **Reasoning** In this diagram the diagonal divides the quadrilateral into two triangles.

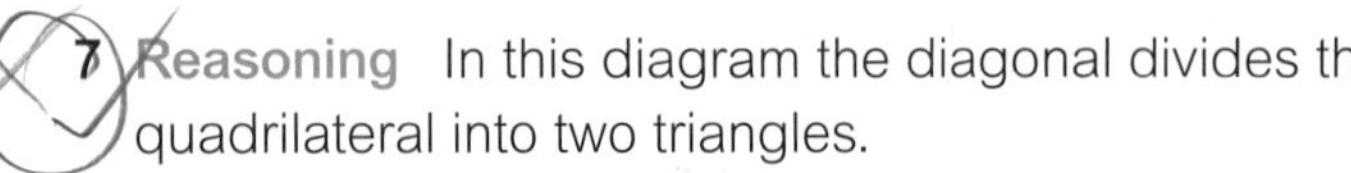

- **a** What do the three red angles add up to?
- **b** What do the three blue angles add up to?
- **c** What do all the angles in the quadrilateral add up to?
- **d** Will this work for *any* quadrilateral?

Q7d hint
Sketch some and see.

Worked example

Work out the size of angle x.

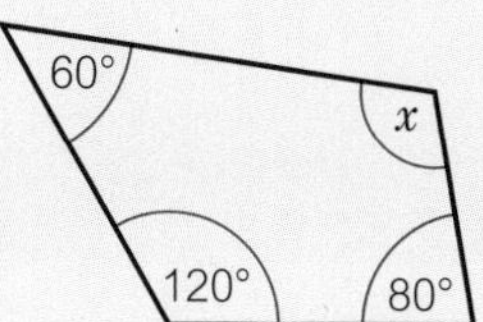

$x = 360° - 120° - 80° - 60°$

$x = 100°$

Key point

The angles in a quadrilateral add up to 360°.

$a + b + c + d = 360°$

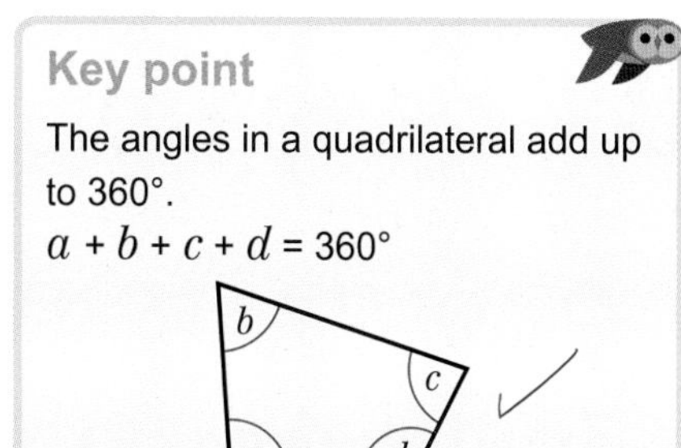

8 Calculate the size of each unknown angle.

a

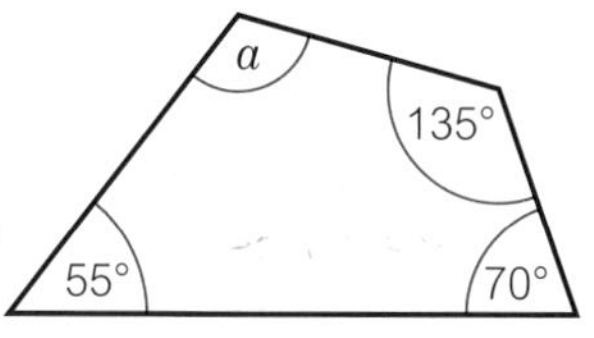

b

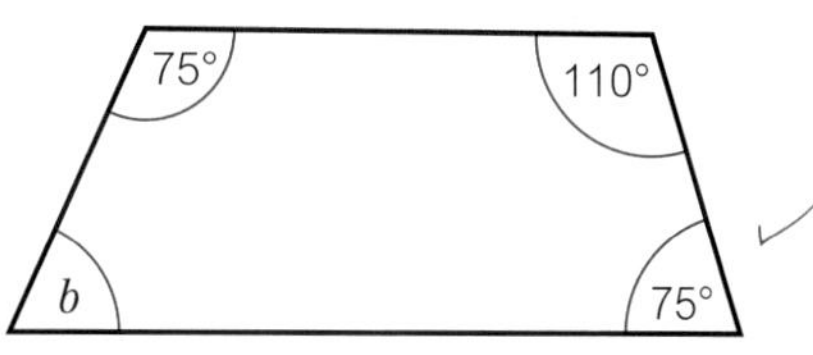

c

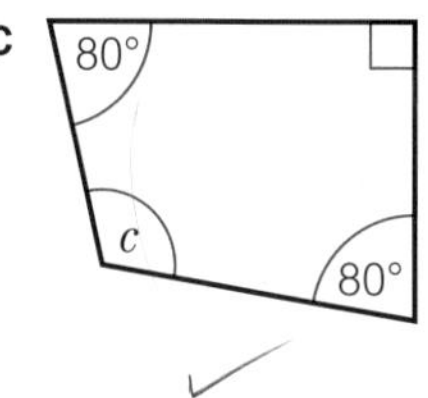

d

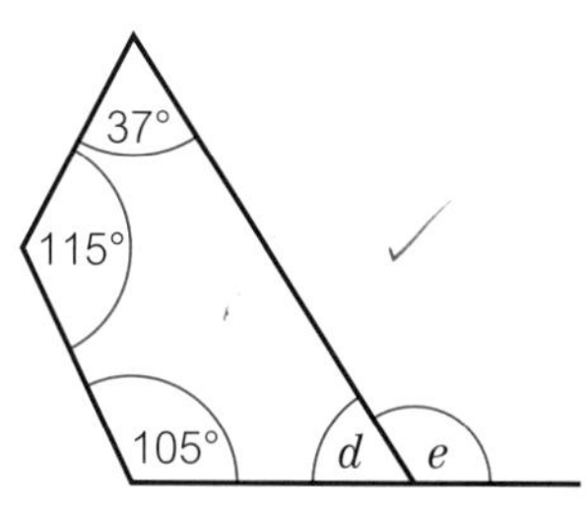

9 Problem-solving The diagram shows a bicycle frame. Work out the missing angle.

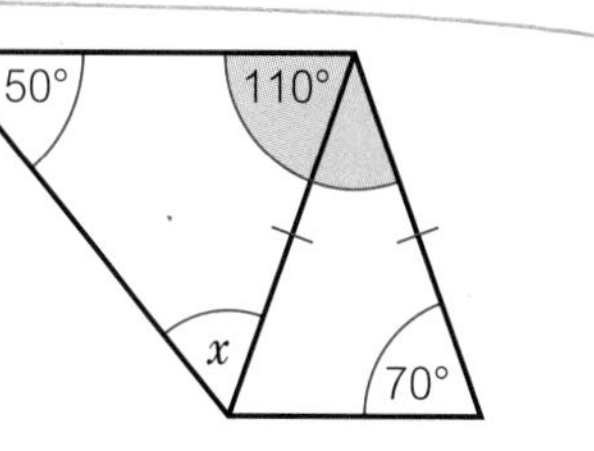

Investigation

Reasoning

Take two squares of any size and overlap them to make another shape. For example

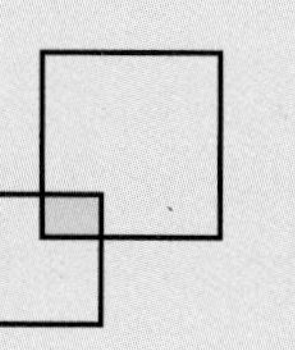

Which of these shapes can be made?

rectangle, rhombus, isosceles triangle, kite, trapezium

Discussion Why can't some of the shapes be made?

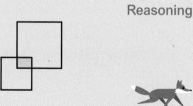

10 Explore Can you make a patchwork quilt using any type of quadrilateral? Choose some sensible shapes to help you explore this situation. Then use what you have learned in this lesson to help you answer the question.

11 Reflect Look back at all the lessons you have completed in this unit so far. Write down at least two new or important mathematics words you have learned. Make sure you spell them correctly. Beside each word write a definition in your own words. You can draw diagrams to help. Write down at least two new or important mathematics facts you have learned. Make up a question (with an answer) that uses each fact.

ActiveLearn Theta 1, Section 8.6

8 Check up

Measuring angles

1 **a** What type of angle is each of these?
b Measure each angle. Write your answers to the nearest degree.

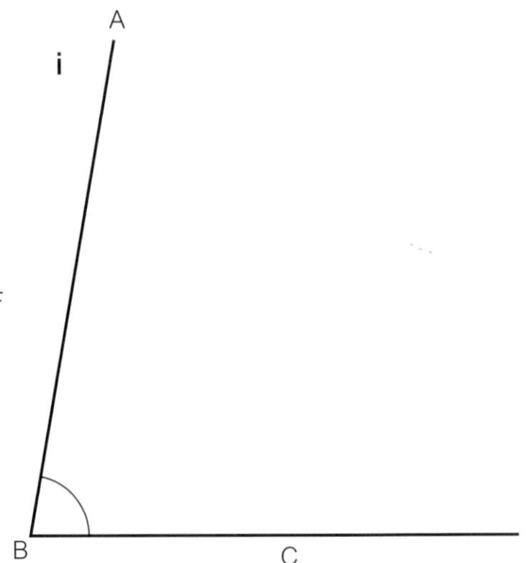

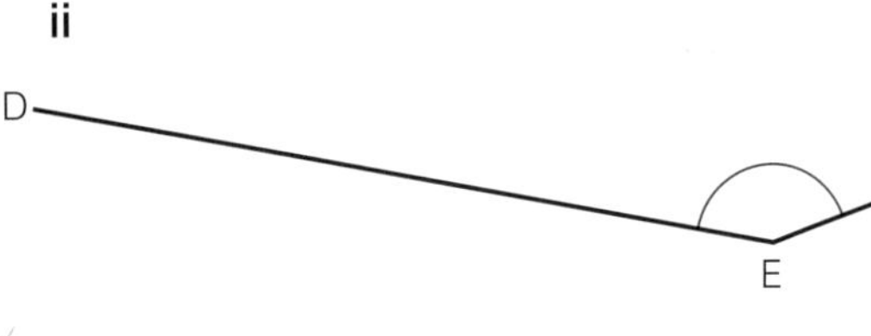

2 The diagram shows an angle.
Kevin measures the angle. He says,
'The angle is 120°.'
Is he correct? Explain your answer.

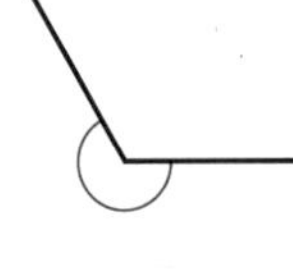

3 Use a protractor to draw an angle of 115°.

4 **a** Make an accurate drawing of this triangle.
b Measure angle ACB.
c What type of triangle have you drawn?

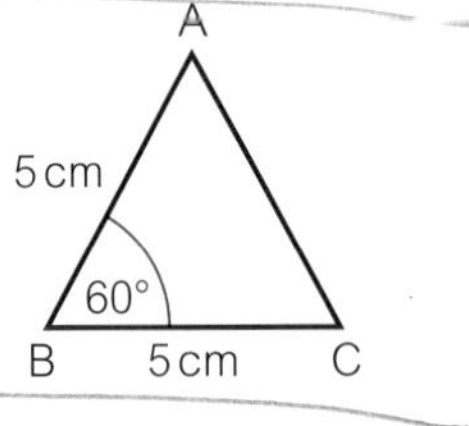

Calculating angles

5 Work out the size of each unknown angle.

a

a 70°

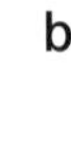

b

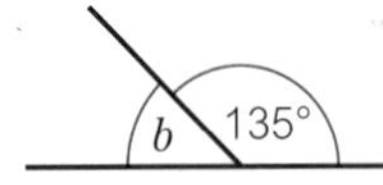

6 Work out the size of angle a. Show your working.

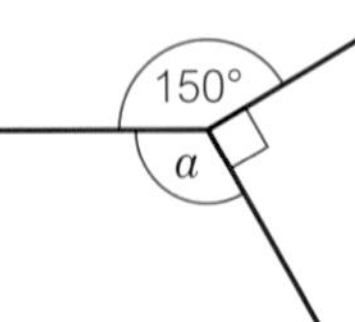

7 Calculate the size of each unknown angle.

a

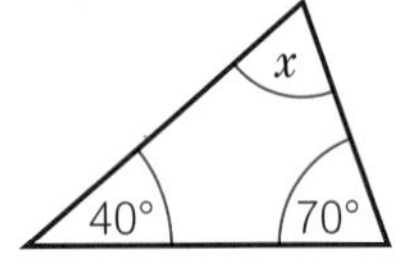

b

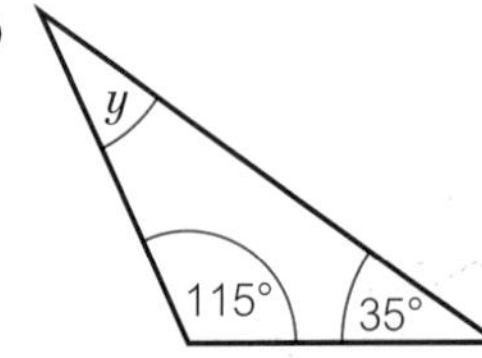

8 Calculate the size of each unknown angle. Show your working.

a

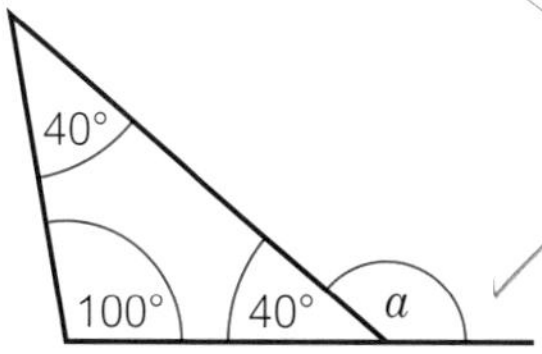

b

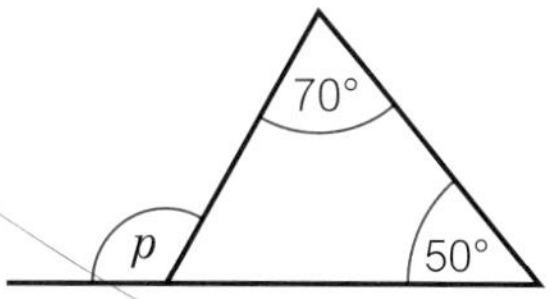

9 The diagram shows two straight lines crossing.

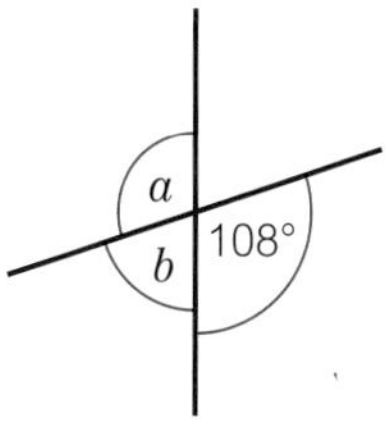

a Joe says, 'Angle a is 72°.'
Is he correct? Explain your answer.

b What is the size of angle b?

10 The diagram shows a quadrilateral.
Calculate the size of the unknown angle.
Show your working.

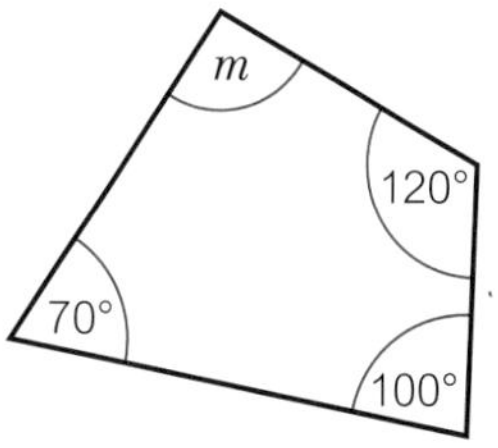

Solving geometric problems

11 Write down the name of each of these quadrilaterals.

a

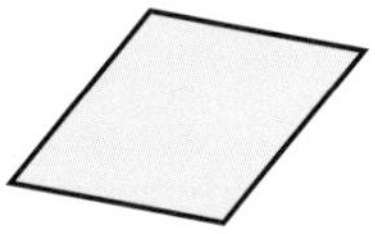

b

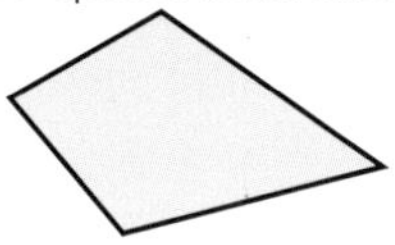

12 The diagram shows a triangle.
Rhiannon says, 'Angle a is 48°.
Is she correct? Explain your answer.

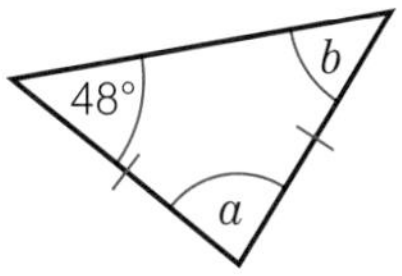

13 Work out the size of each unknown angle.

a

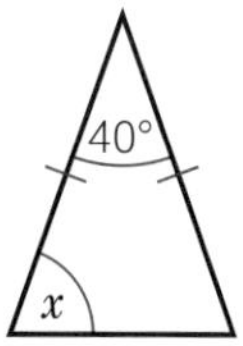

b

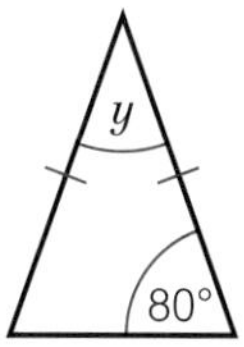

14 How sure are you of your answers? Were you mostly

Just guessing **Feeling doubtful** **Confident**

What next? Use your results to decide whether to strengthen or extend your learning.

Challenge

15 Reasoning Use a 4 × 4 square on square dotted paper.
Draw as many different quadrilaterals as you can.
Here is one example.

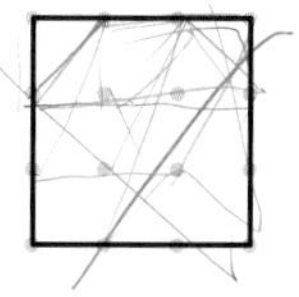

a Name the quadrilaterals you have drawn.

b Which of your quadrilaterals are symmetrical?
How many lines of symmetry does each of them have?

8 Strengthen

You will:

- Strengthen your understanding with practice.

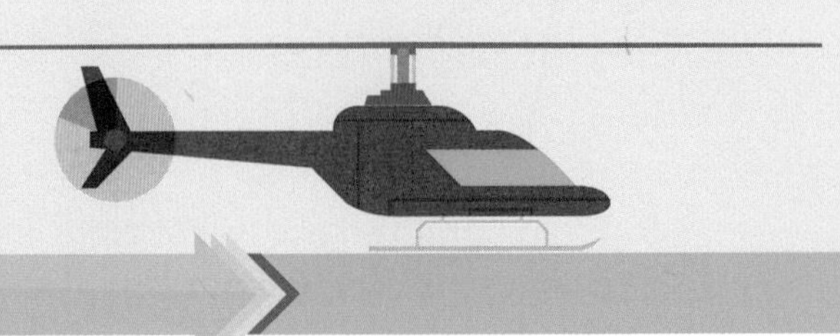

Measuring angles

4c **1** Read off the size of each angle from the protractor.

a

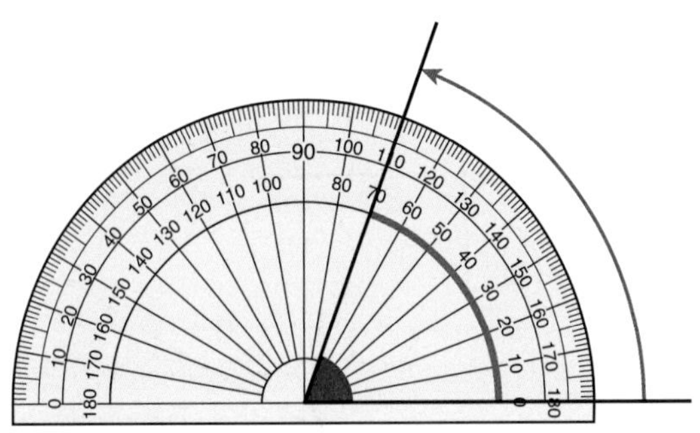

b

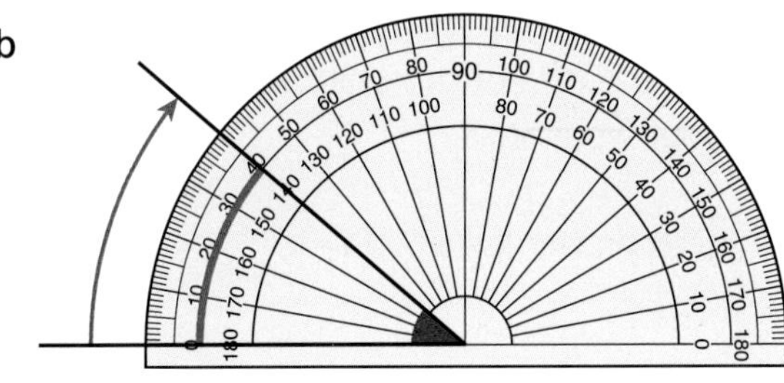

4b **2** Mehdi uses a protractor to measure angle ABC.
He says, 'Angle ABC is 40°.'
Without using a protractor, can you say whether or not he is correct?
Give a reason for your answer.

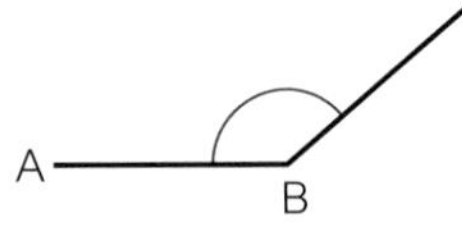

Q2 hint
What type of angle is angle ABC?

4b **3** Use a protractor to measure these angles.

a

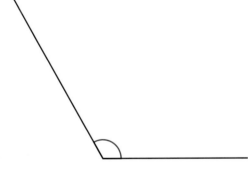

b

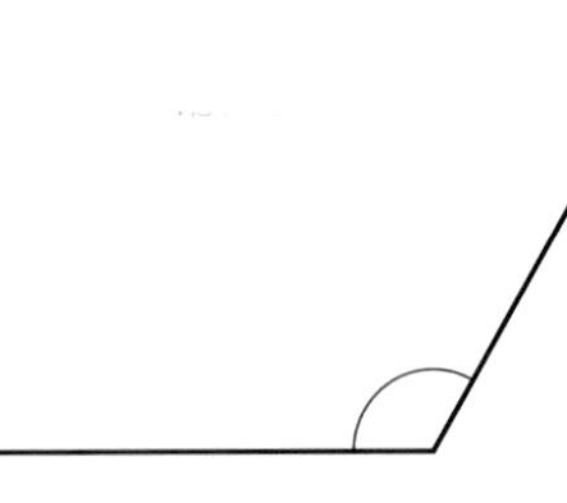

Q3 hint
Place the cross of the protractor on the point of the angle.
Line up the zero line with one line of the angle.

5b **4** **a** Use a ruler to draw a line of length 6 cm. Label it AB.

b Use a protractor to draw an angle of 130° at point A.

c Draw in the other lines needed to complete this triangle accurately.

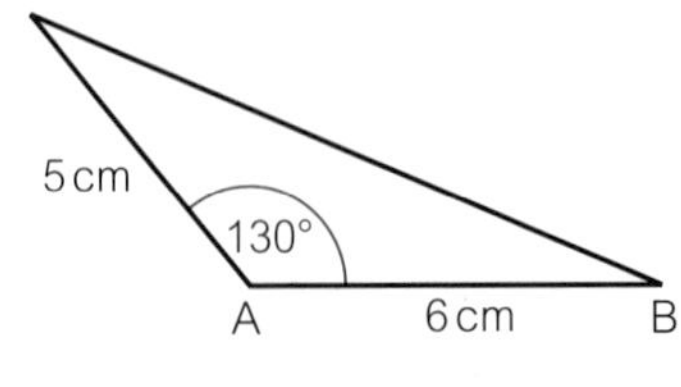

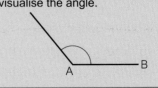

Q4b Strategy hint
A quick sketch can help you visualise the angle.

A B

Subject links: Science (Enrichment Q1)

Topic links: Fractions

Calculating angles

4c

1 a How many degrees are there in half a turn?

b How many degrees are there in a quarter turn?

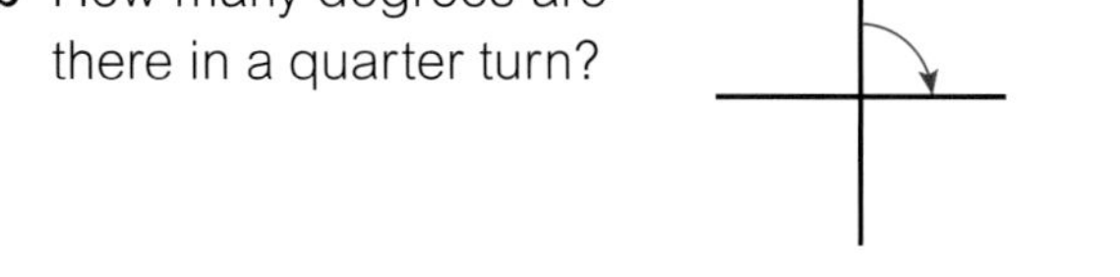

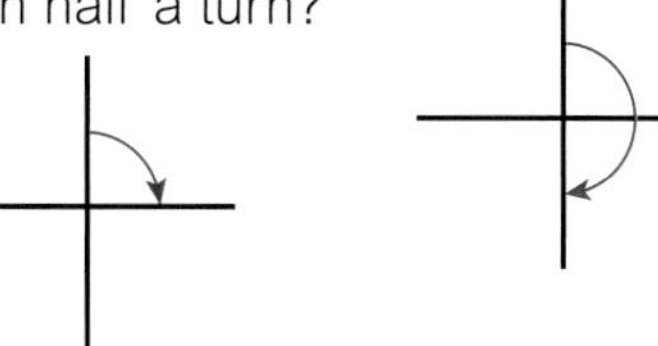

> **Q1 hint**
>
> Full turn = 360°
>
> $\frac{1}{2}$ of 360° = □ $\frac{1}{4}$ of 360° = □

4b

2 Work out the size of each angle marked with a letter.

a

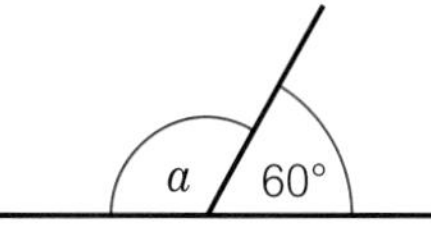

b

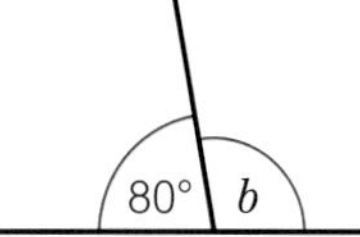

> **Q2a hint**
>
> 180° − 60° = a

4a

3 Calculate the size of each unknown angle.

a

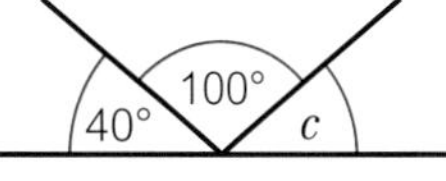

b

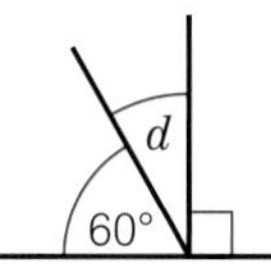

> **Q3b hint**
>
> = 90°

4a

4 a What do the angles around a point add up to?

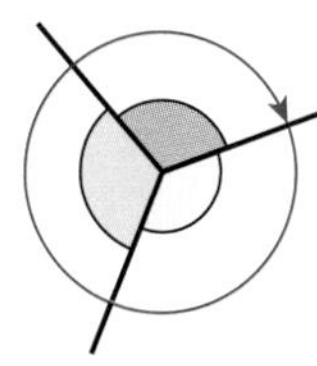

b Work out the size of angle x.

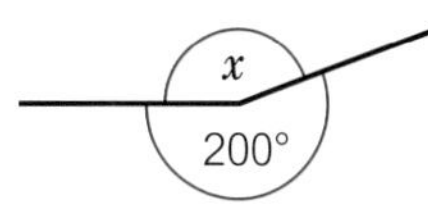

> **Q4b hint**
>
> 360° − 200° = x

5c

5 Work out the size of each angle marked with a letter.

a

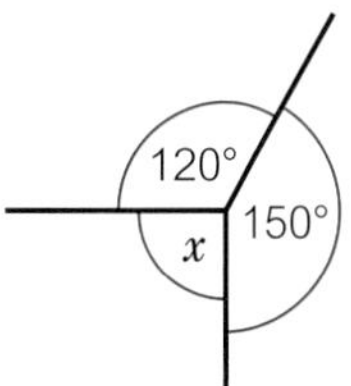

b

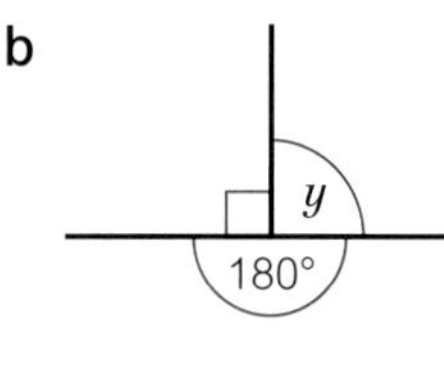

5c

6 Calculate the size of each unknown angle.

a

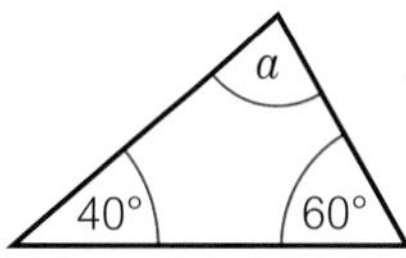

b

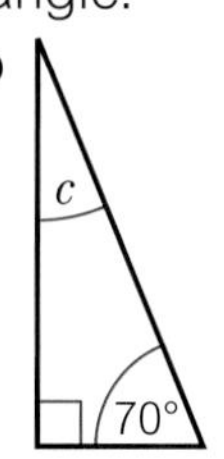

> **Q6 hint**
>
> What do the angles in a triangle add up to?

5b

7 The diagram shows two straight lines crossing.
Catrin says, 'Angle a is also 60°.'
Explain why Catrin is correct. Choose from

A Angles on a straight line add up to 180°.

B Vertically opposite angles are equal.

C The angles look the same size.

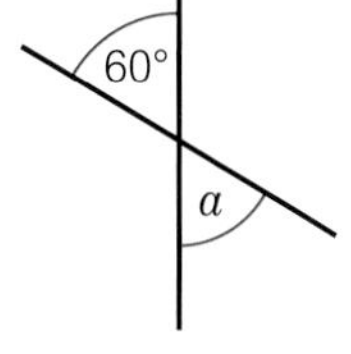

> **Q7 Literacy hint**
>
> **Vertically opposite** means the angles are opposite and meet at their vertices.

5b

8 a Complete the working to find the sizes of angles a and b.

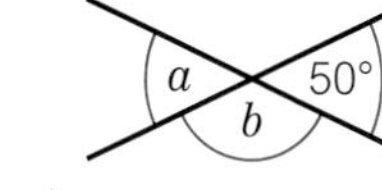

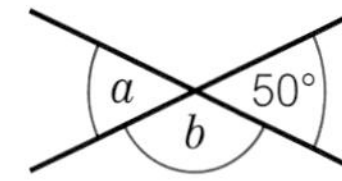

angle a = □ Vertically opposite angles are __________.

angle b = 180° − □ ° = □ ° Angles on a _______ add up to □°.

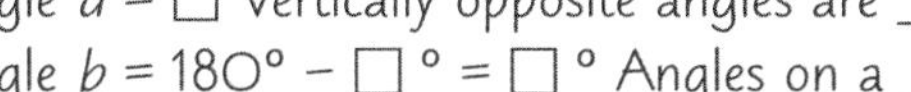

b Work out the size of each unknown angle. Write down the reasons.

i ii

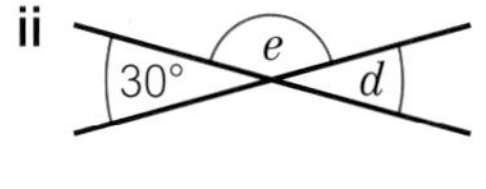

5a

9 Reasoning Draw a **quadrilateral** with angles A, B, C and D. Cut out the quadrilateral and tear off each of the corners.
Arrange the torn-off corners so that angles A, B, C and D meet around a common point.
What does this tell you about the angles in a quadrilateral?

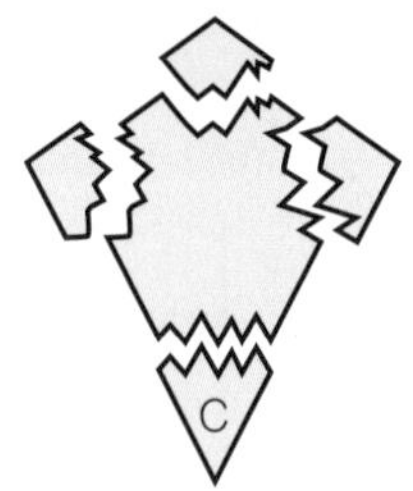

Q9 Literacy hint
A **quadrilateral** is a shape with four straight sides.

5a

10 Work out the size of each unknown angle.

a

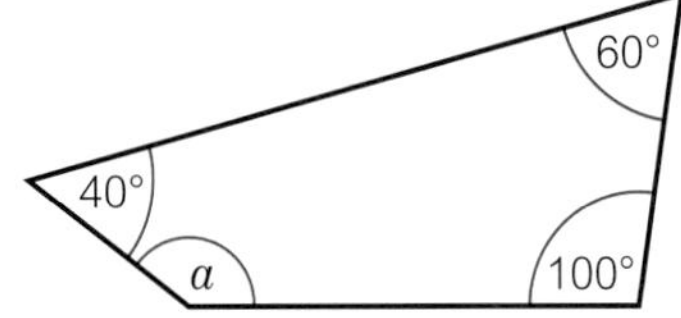

b

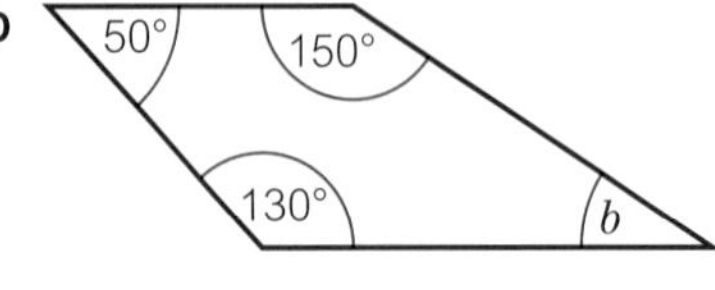

Q10a hint

$360° - 100° - 60° - 40° = a$

Solving geometric problems

4a

1 Match up each description with the correct diagram. Name each of the shapes.

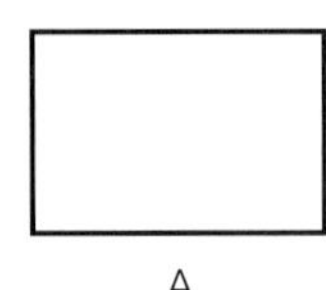

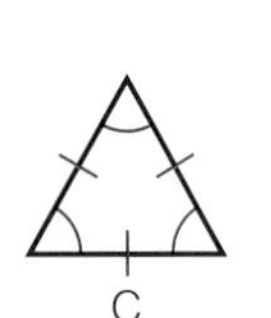
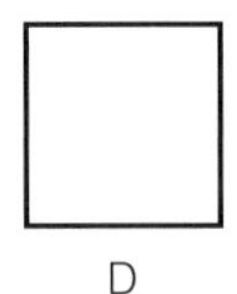

A B C D

a I have four equal sides and four angles of 90°.

b I have three equal sides and three equal angles.

c I have two pairs of equal sides and four right angles.

d I have three sides. Two of my sides and two of my angles are equal.

Q1 hint

Dashes show equal sides.

and are equal angles.

4a

2 Reasoning

a Diagram A shows one side of a square.

i Copy the diagram on squared paper and draw three more lines to complete the square.

ii Draw on the lines of symmetry.

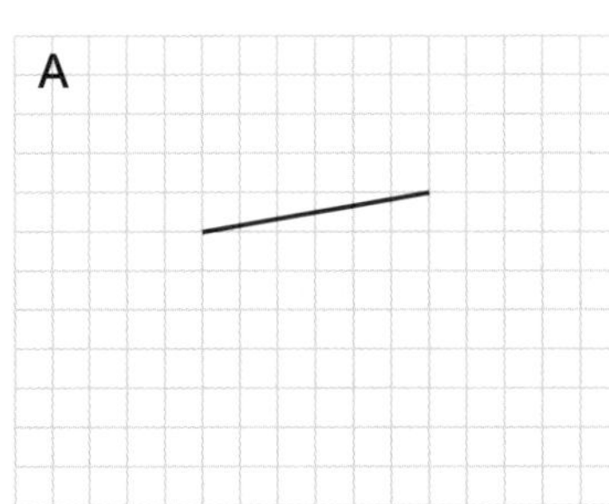

Q2a hint

Use a protractor to draw the angles.

b Diagram B shows one side of a quadrilateral. The opposite sides of this quadrilateral are equal.

i Copy the diagram on squared paper and draw three more lines to show what the quadrilateral could be.

ii Copy the diagram again and draw three more lines to show a different quadrilateral that it could be.

iii What are the names of the shapes that you have drawn?

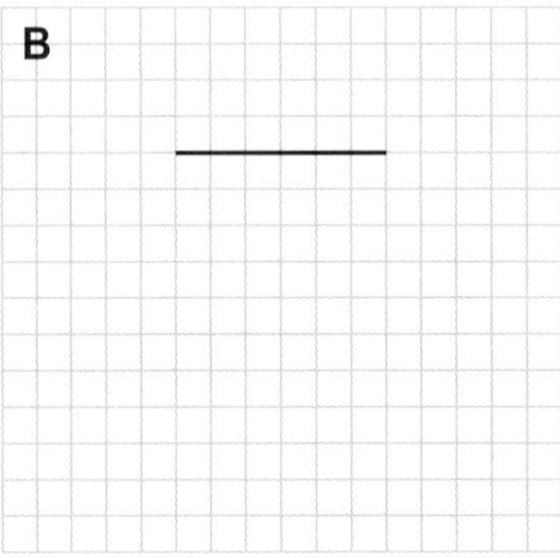

3 Problem-solving This cake was cut into equal slices. Two of the slices are left. How many slices have been eaten? 5c

Q3 Strategy hint
Draw a sketch to show how many 60° slices there are in 360°.

4 a Show how two of these scalene triangles can be joined together to make a parallelogram. 5b

b Show how two right-angled triangles can be joined together to make a parallelogram.

5 a The diagram shows a triangle ABC. 5a

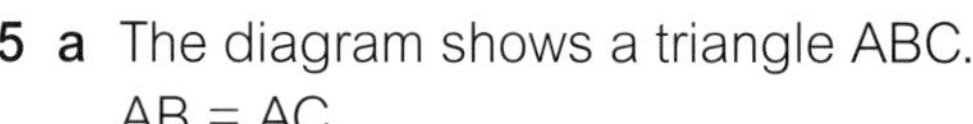

AB = AC

i How are the equal sides shown on the diagram?

ii What is the name of this type of triangle?

iii What is the size of angle a?

Q5 hint
AB = AC means that the length of AB is the same as the length of AC.

b The diagram shows a triangle DEF.

i What is the size of angle e? Give a reason for your answer.

ii Work out the size of angle f.

Q5b hint
What type of triangle is DEF?

6 Work out the size of angle x. 5a

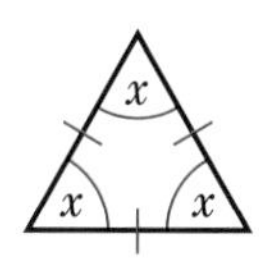

Enrichment

1 STEM In a science experiment a mass hangs on a wire. 5c

a Work out the size of the unknown angle x.

b What would change if the mass was greater?

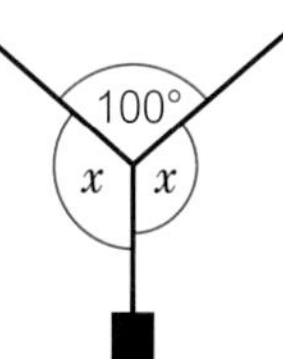

2 Problem-solving The pie chart shows the results of a survey on types of television programmes. 5a
The angle of the sector for reality programmes is the same size as the angle for music programmes.
Find the size of this angle.

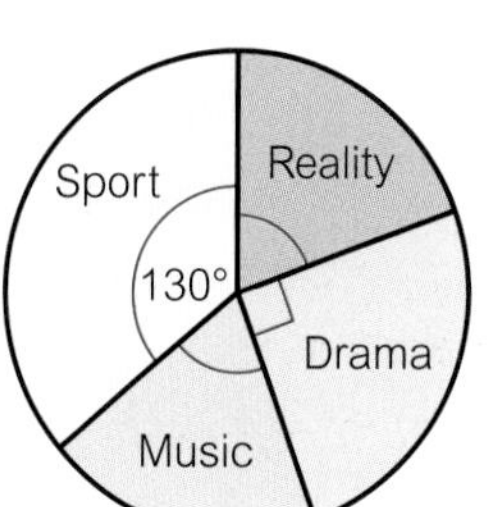

3 Problem-solving / Reasoning The diagram shows a tilted platform. 5a

a Work out the size of angle x.

b Work out the size of angle y.

c As the platform is tilted further, the 70° angle decreases to 65°. What happens to angle y?

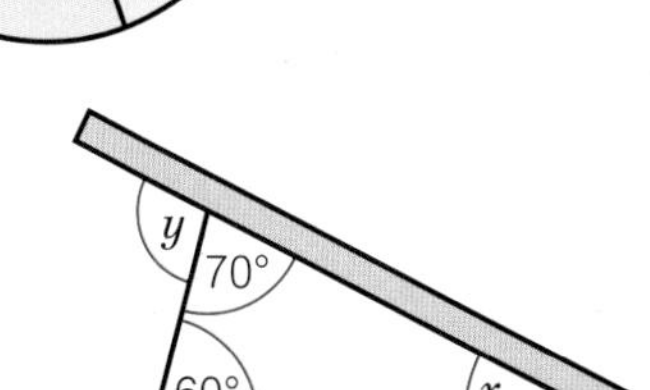

4 **Reflect** Write down one thing you find easy and one thing you find difficult when

- drawing angles accurately
- calculating angles
- solving geometric problems.

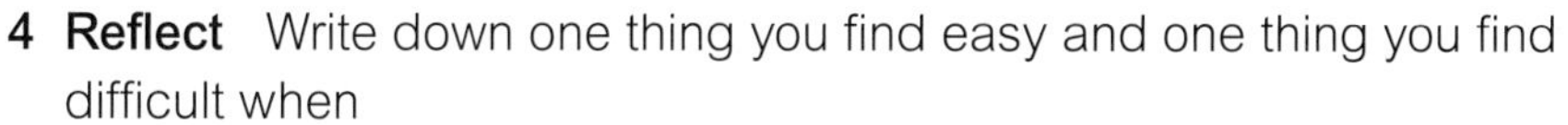

For each thing you find difficult, write a hint in your own words.

Q4 hint
Look back at the questions in these strengthen lessons to help you.

8 Extend

You will:

- Extend your understanding with problem-solving.

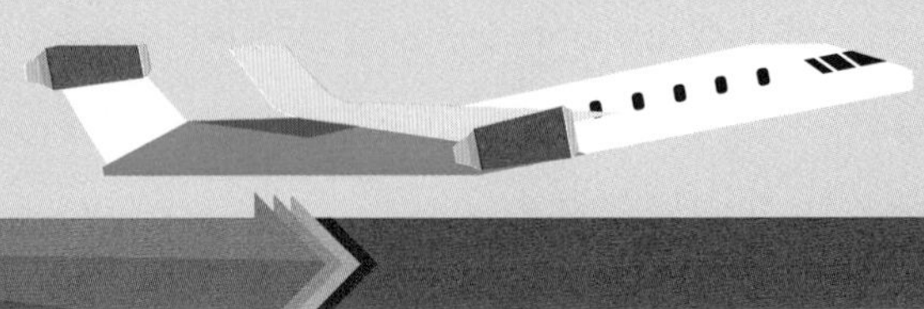

5c **1 Problem-solving / STEM** The mirror in a periscope is set at an angle x.
Work out the size of angle x.

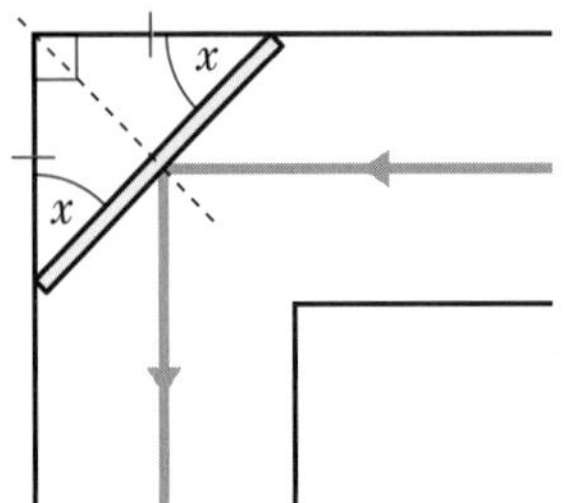

> **Q1 hint**
> The two angles labelled x are equal.

5c **2 Problem-solving** The pie chart shows the results of a survey on hobbies.
Calculate the size of the angle for social media.

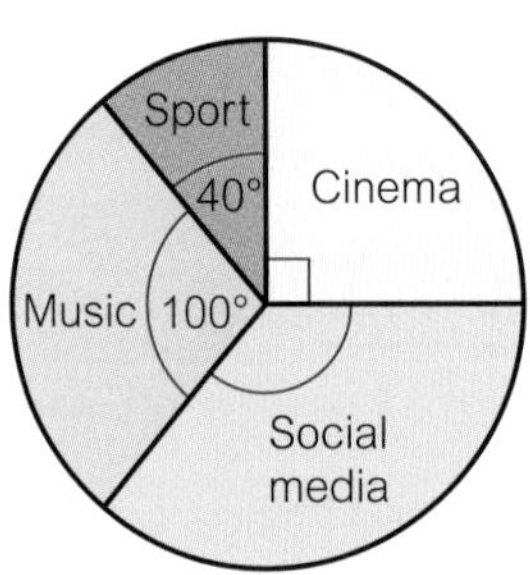

5b **3** Accurately draw triangle ABC with AB = 8 cm, BC = 6 cm and angle ABC = 80°.

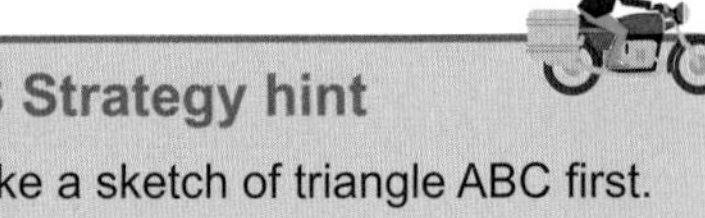

> **Q3 Strategy hint**
> Make a sketch of triangle ABC first.

5b **4 Problem-solving** A regular hexagon is divided into six identical triangles like this.

a What is the size of one angle at the centre?

b Reasoning What type of triangles are these? Explain your answer.

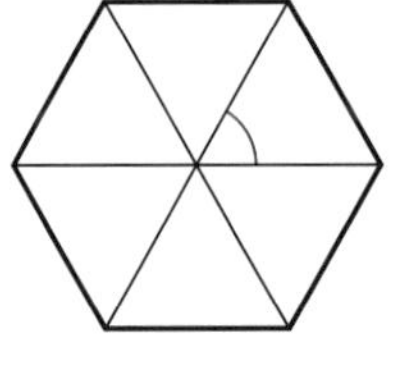

> **Q4b Literacy hint**
> In a regular polygon all sides and all angles are equal.

5b **5 Problem-solving** A regular **polygon** is divided into identical triangles.
One angle at the centre is 30°.
How many sides does the polygon have?

> **Q5 Literacy hint**
> **Polygons** are 2D shapes with straight sides.

5b **6** Calculate the size of angle a.
Show all your working.

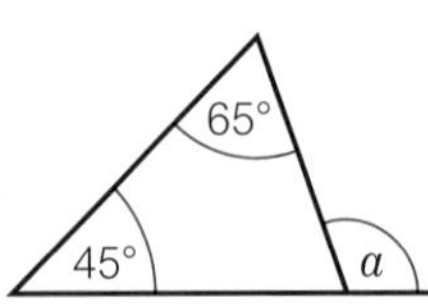

5b **7** Work out the size of each unknown angle.

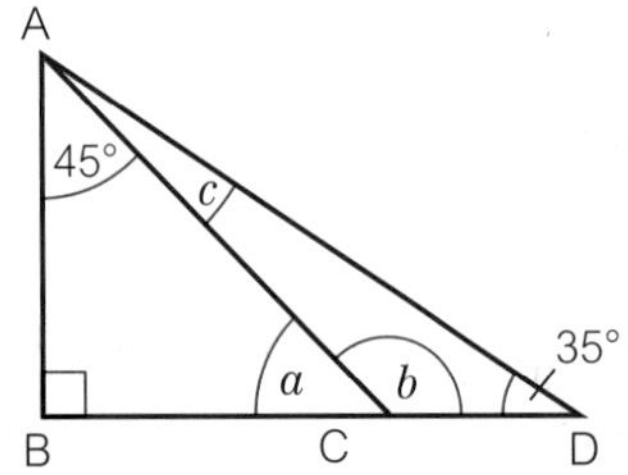

> **Q7 Strategy hint**
> Sketch the diagram. Write on the angles as you work them out.

Subject links: Science (Q1, Q20)

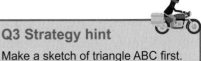

8 Work out the size of angle x in each diagram.

a

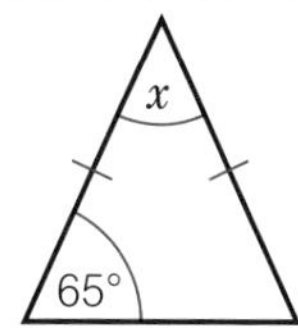

b

120°
x

c

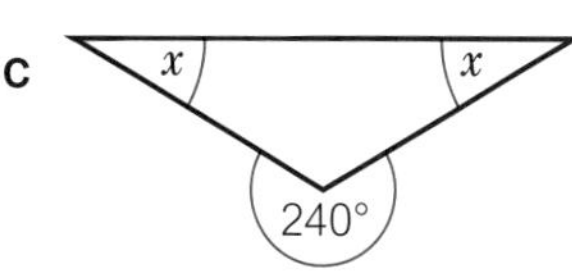

d

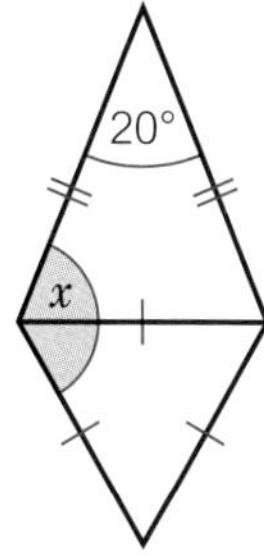

e

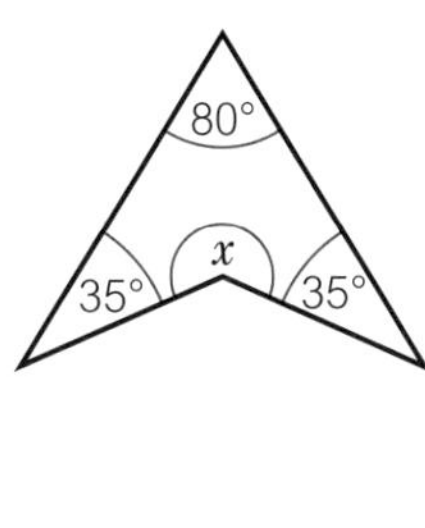

Discussion Why can a triangle never have a reflex angle but a quadrilateral can?

5a

9 **Problem-solving** In triangle ABC, AB = AC and angle CAB = 40°.
Line DC **bisects** angle ACB.
Work out the sizes of angles x, y and z.

Discussion A square is a special type of rhombus. Why?
What similar statements can you make about the other quadrilaterals?

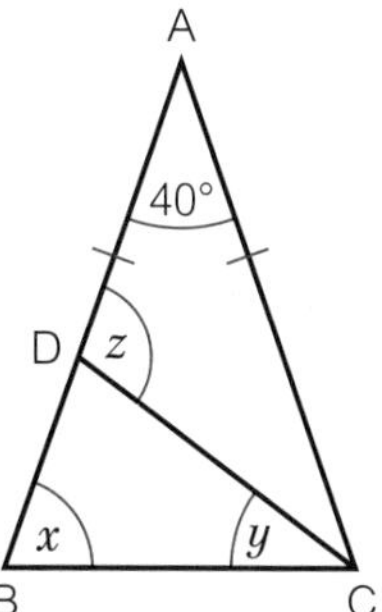

Q9 Literacy hint
Bisects means 'cuts in half'.

5a

Investigation Reasoning / Problem-solving

Make a large copy of this table.

1 Write each of these quadrilaterals in the correct position in the table:
rectangle, rhombus, kite, parallelogram, arrowhead, trapezium

		Number of pairs of parallel sides		
		0	1	2
Number of pairs of equal sides	0			
	1			
	2			

2 One of the shapes can fit in more than one box. Which shape?

3 Draw a quadrilateral to fit in each empty box. Use markings to show which sides are parallel and which are equal.

Hint
Think carefully about the definitions of each shape.

5a

10 Work out the sum of the three exterior angles shown on this diagram.

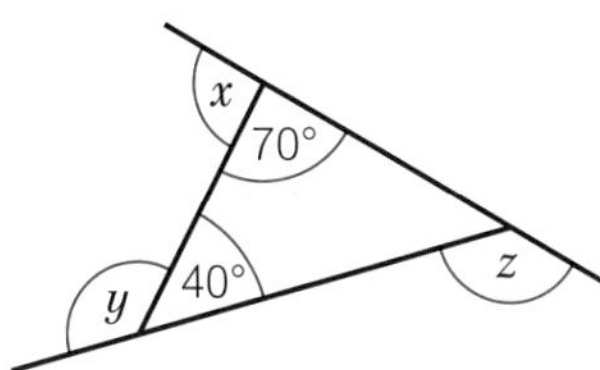

5a

11 a Accurately draw a triangle XYZ with YZ = 6 cm, angle XYZ = 50° and angle XZY = 60°.
b What is the size of angle ZXY?
c Extend the line XZ. Measure the size of the external angle at Z.
d Add together angles XYZ and ZXY. What do you notice?

Q11 Literacy hint
'Extend the line' means continue it outside the triangle.

5a **12** Look at this diagram.

a Measure angles ABC and ACB.

b Add together angles ABC and ACB.

c Measure the external angle at A. What do you notice?

Discussion How can you use what you have found in Q11 and Q12 to help you solve problems involving external angles of triangles?

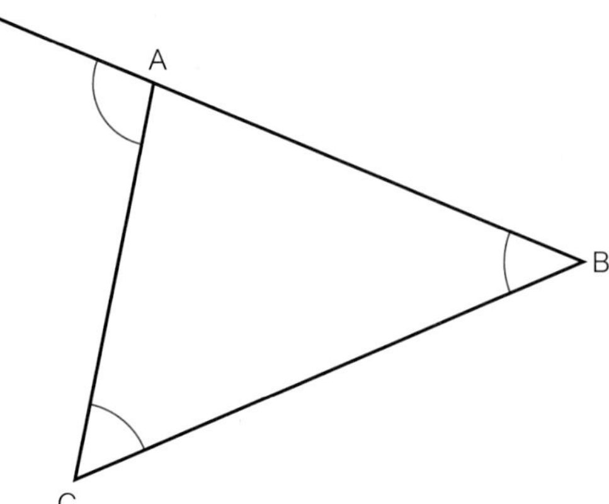

5a **13** Work out the size of each unknown exterior angle.

a

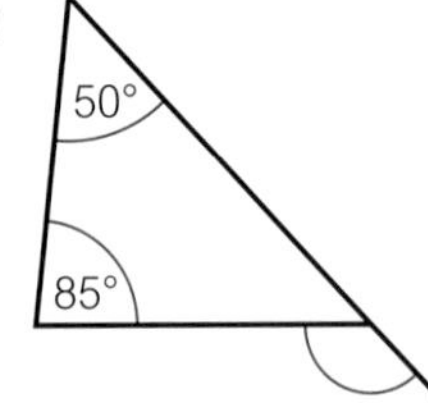

b

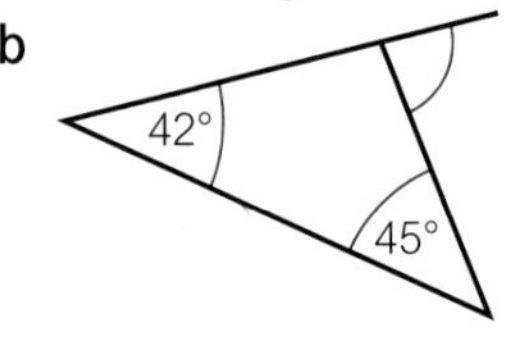

Q13a hint

Use what you discovered in Q11 and Q12.

5a **14** Accurately draw a triangle ABC with ∠ABC = ∠ACB.

Discussion Is it possible to accurately draw a triangle with two obtuse angles?

5a **15** Is it possible to draw this triangle accurately?

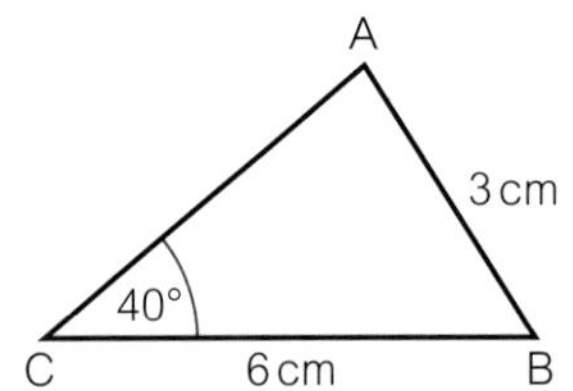

5a **16** The diagram shows a rhombus.

a Measure angles ABC, BCD and BAD.

b What do you notice about the opposite angles of a rhombus?

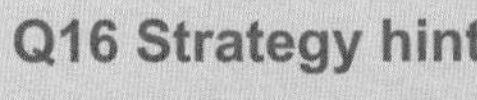

Q16 Strategy hint

Draw diagrams to help with your explanations.

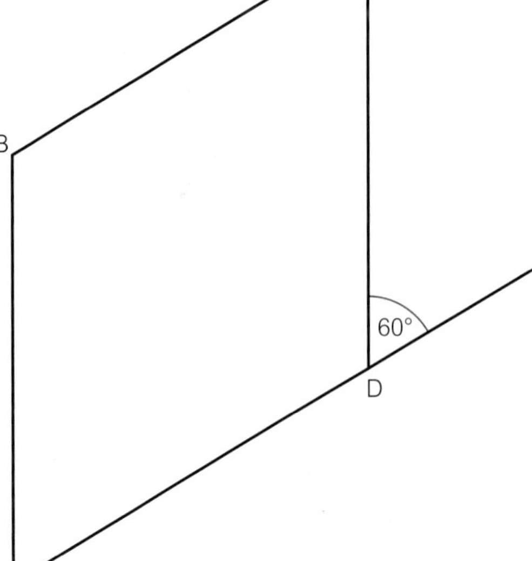

5a **17** **Reasoning** Andre says, 'A rhombus is a parallelogram, but a parallelogram is not a rhombus.'

Is he correct? Explain your answer.

18 Problem-solving This pattern is made up of three identical red rhombus tiles and three identical blue rhombus tiles.

a Work out the size of angle x.

b What is the size of angle y? Show your working.

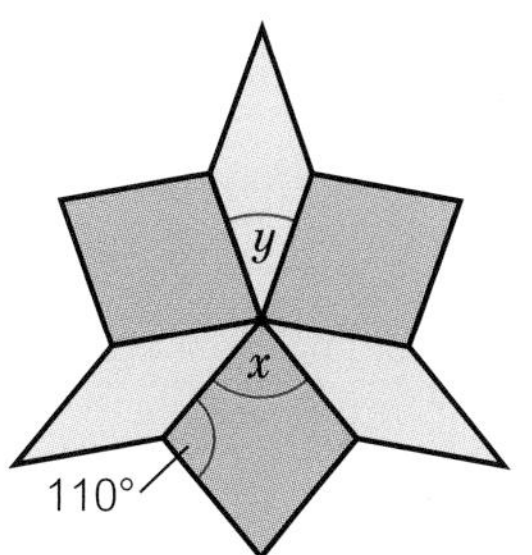

5a

19 Real The diagram shows the correct 1 in 4 rule for using a ladder safely.

Q19 hint

The '1 in 4 rule' means 1 unit out for every 4 units up.

6c

Russell has set up a ladder like this.

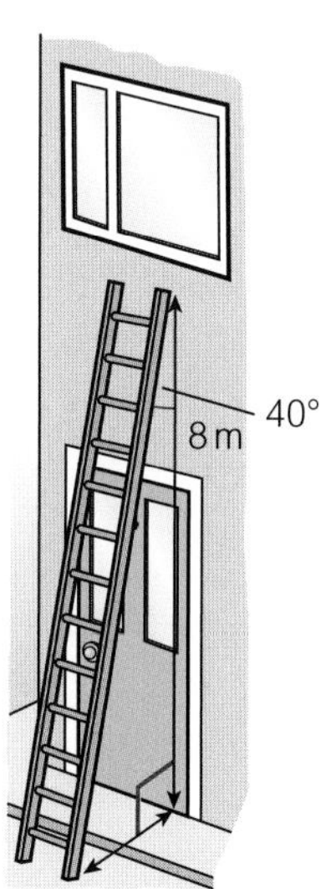

a Make a scale drawing to show his ladder.

b Has he set up the ladder correctly?

Q19b hint

Measure the distance away from the wall.
Has Russell used the 1 in 4 rule?

20 Problem-solving / STEM An ash tree is 20 m tall. It casts a 12 m shadow on the ground.

a Accurately draw a triangle to represent this.

b What angle does the light from the Sun make with the ground?

Discussion Are the angles of a triangle on a scale drawing the same size as the angles in the actual triangle?

6c

21 Reflect In these extend lessons you have answered questions about angles and: a pie chart a periscope a ladder
Where else do you think it is useful to have an understanding of angles in maths, in science and in real life?

Q21 hint

Use a vertical line to represent the tree.

Reflect

8 Unit test

4b **1** The diagram shows two angles.
Work out the size of angle m.

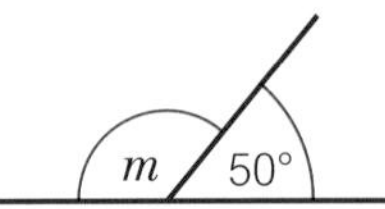

4a **2** One of these angles measures 140°.

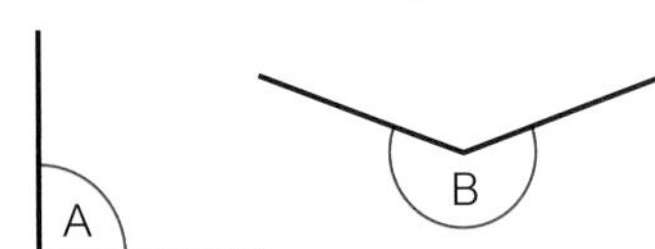

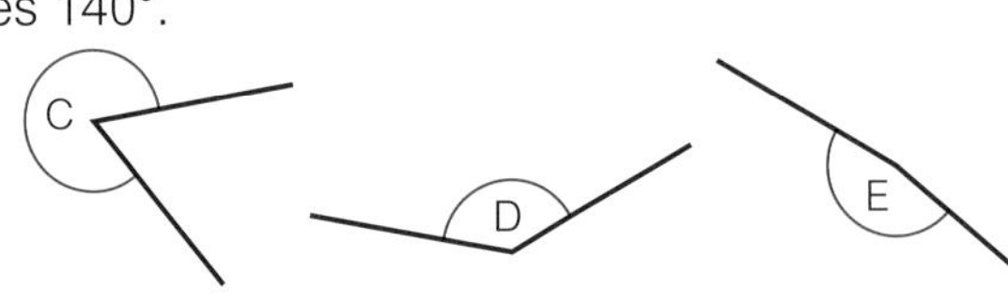

Without using a protractor, decide which one.

4a **3** Make an accurate drawing of this angle.

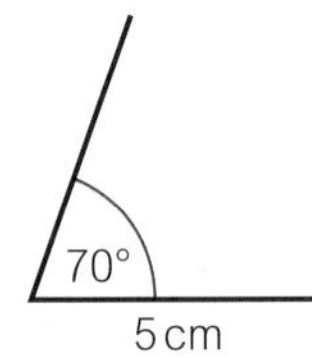

5c **4** Alan measured the angles in a triangle.
He said, 'The angles are 40°, 50° and 100°.'
Is he correct? Explain.

5c **5** Calculate the size of angle x in each diagram. Show your working.

a

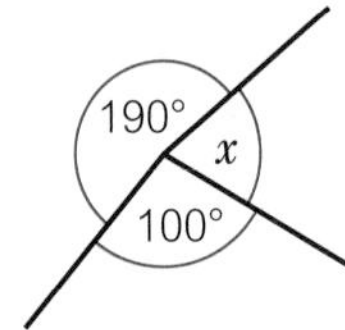

b

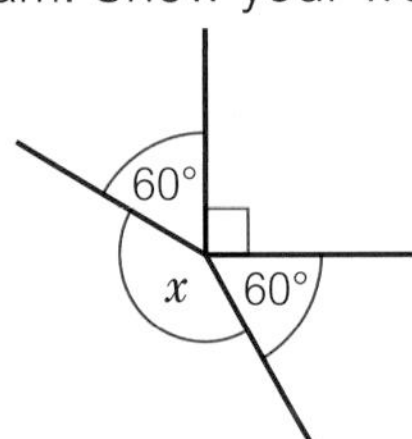

5c **6** A pizza is cut into equal slices like this.
How many slices are there?

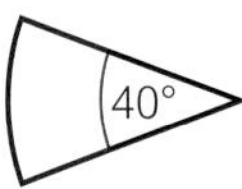

5b **7** **a** Triangle ABC has three equal sides.
What are the sizes of the angles in this triangle?
b The right-angled triangle DEF has two equal sides.
What are the sizes of the angles in this triangle?

5b **8** Work out the sizes of angles x and y.

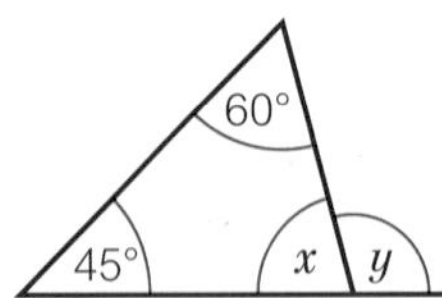

5b **9** Make an accurate drawing of this triangle.

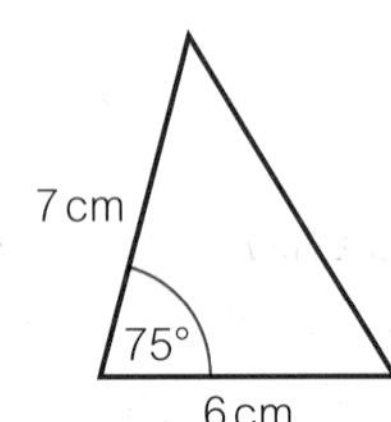

10 Here is a list of some types of quadrilaterals. 5b
kite, parallelogram, rectangle, rhombus, square
a Write down the names of the quadrilaterals which have two pairs of parallel sides.
b Write down the names of the quadrilaterals which must have two pairs of equal sides.

11 The diagram shows triangle ABC. 5b
Work out the sizes of angles a, b and c.

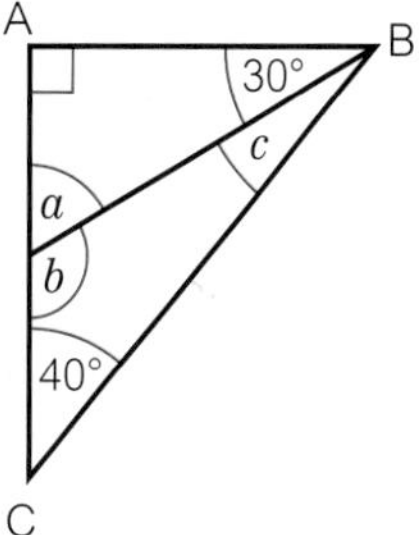

12 The diagram shows triangle ABC. 5a
AB = AC
a Work out the size of angle ACB.
b Work out the size of angle DBA.

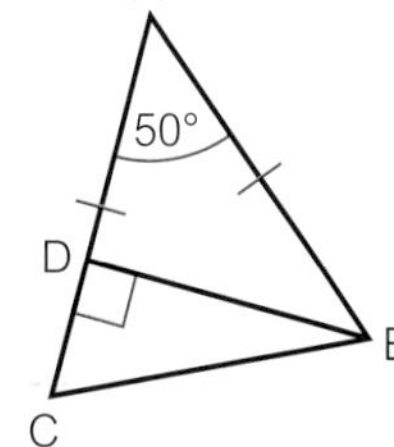

13 ABCD is a quadrilateral. 5a
Work out the size of angle c.

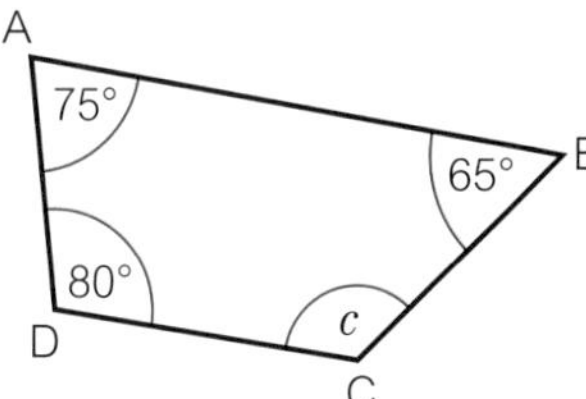

14 A general rule for a wheelchair ramp is that for every 1 cm of rise, a 12 cm length of ramp is required. 5a
a Draw an accurate triangle to represent this.
b What is the angle between the bottom of the ramp and the ground?

Challenge

15 Start with these two shapes.
a What new shapes can you make by joining them together?
b What are the properties of each new shape?

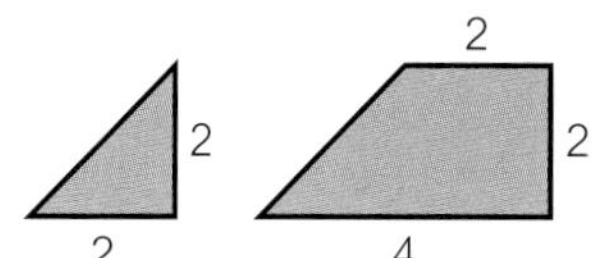

18 **Reflect** Look back at the questions you answered in this test.
Find a question that you could not answer straight away, or that you really had to think about. While you worked on this question how did you feel?
- What were you thinking about? Were you calm? Were you panicky?
- Did you keep trying until you had an answer? Did you give up before reaching an answer, and move on to the next question?
- Did you think you would get the answer correct or incorrect?

Write down any strategies you could use to stay calm and positive when answering tricky maths questions in tests. Compare your strategies with other people's.

Reflect

9 Sequences and graphs

MASTER | Check P235 | Strengthen P237 | Extend P241 | Test P245

9.1 Sequences

You will learn to:
- Recognise, describe and continue number sequences
- Generate terms of a sequence using a term-to-term rule
- Find missing terms in a sequence.

CONFIDENCE

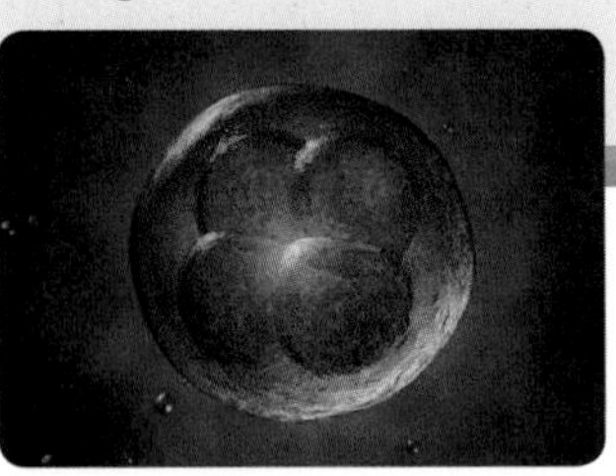

Why learn this? When an embryo is developing, the numbers of cells it contains form a sequence. Understanding this sequence can help doctors select healthy embryos for IVF treatment.

Fluency
- Find the difference between −10 and −7
- Work out 0.4 + 1.2

Explore
Will there be a FIFA World Cup in 2054?

Exercise 9.1

NEW Q5

Warm up

1 Count up in threes starting at 14. Stop when you get to 26.

2 Starting at 24, keep halving until you get a mixed number.

3 Count up in fives starting at 8. What do you notice?

Worked example

a Write down the next three terms in this sequence.
4, 7, 10, …

4, 7, 10, 13, 16, 19 — Work out how to get from one term to the next. Continue the pattern for the next three terms.

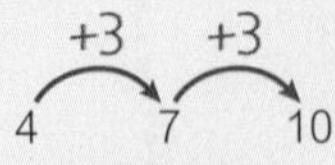

b Write down the first term and the term-to-term rule.

First term is 4.
Term-to-term rule is 'add 3'. — Write down the first term and the rule to get from one term to the next.

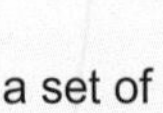

Key point
A number **sequence** is a set of numbers that follow a rule. Each number in a sequence is called a **term**.

Key point
The **term-to-term rule** tells you how to get from one term to the next in a sequence. It can use adding, subtracting, multiplying and dividing.

4b

Q6 4 Write down the next three **terms** of each **sequence**.

a a 6, 11, 16, 21, … ✓ b 23, 27, 31, 35, … new c, d

b c 60, 52, 44, … ✓ c d 3, 3.2, 3.4, … new d

Topic links: Decimals, Negative numbers, Fractions

Subject links: Science (Q10)

5 Write down the first term, the **term-to-term** rule and the next three terms of each sequence. 4b

a 2, 5, 8, 11, ___ , ___ , ___

b 52, 48, 44, ___ , ___ , ___

c 1, 2, 4, 8, ___ , ___ , ___

d 160, 80, 40, ___ , ___ , ___

Discussion If you count on in tens, will the sequence be finite or infinite?
What if you count on in hundreds? Does it make a difference where you start?

> **Q5 hint**
> What do you need to do to get from one term to the next? Do you add, subtract, multiply or divide?

> **Key point**
> Sequences where the numbers **increase** are **ascending** sequences.
> Sequences where the numbers **decrease** are **descending** sequences.
> A sequence that carries on for ever is **infinite**.
> A sequence with a fixed number of terms or a 'last term' is **finite**.

6 A sequence has first term 2. The term-to-term rule is 'add 5'. 4b
The last term is 42.

a Write down all the terms in the sequence.

b Is the sequence **ascending** or **decending**? Is it **finite** or **infinite**?

7 A sequence has first term 1. The term-to-term rule is 'add 2'. 4b

a Write down the first 10 terms in the sequence.

b Is the sequence ascending or descending? Is it finite or infinite?

c What is the name for the terms in this sequence?

Discussion If you write down the sequence of all odd numbers and the sequence of all even numbers, will you have written all the numbers that exist?

> **Key point**
> When you know the first term and the term-to-term rule, you can work out all the terms in the sequence.

8 Use the first term and the term-to-term rule to generate each sequence. 4a

a First term 0, term-to-term rule '+ 0.2'. Stop at 2.

b First term 10, term-to-term rule '− 0.4'. Stop at 6.

c First term 7, term-to-term rule '+ 0.6'. Stop at 13.

d Write down a first term and a term-to-term rule for another increasing sequence that includes the term 7.6

9 **Modelling** Rasheed reads on a website that his height should increase by 8 cm a year. 4a
His height is 131 cm when he is 10 years old.

a Write down his predicted heights for the next six years.

b What about the five years after that?

c Is this a good mathematical model? Explain your answer.

10 **Problem-solving / STEM** The number of cells in a bacteria sample doubles every 20 minutes. 5c
There is one bacteria cell in a dish.

a How many cells will there be after 40 minutes?

b How many minutes until there are 16 cells?

> **Q10c Strategy hint**
> You could draw a table like this to help.

Minutes	0	20	40	...
Cells	1			

5b

11 a Write down the next four terms of each sequence.

i 1.2, 1.4, 1.6, …
ii $1\frac{1}{2}$, 2, $2\frac{1}{2}$, 3, …
iii −9, −7, −5, …
iv 57.1, 57.8, 58.5, …
v $\frac{1}{2}$, $\frac{1}{4}$, $\frac{1}{8}$, $\frac{1}{16}$, …
vi 2, 0, −2, …

b Which of the sequences in part **a** are decreasing?

12 Work out the missing terms in each sequence.

a ___, ___, ___, 18, 21, 24
b ___, ___, ___, 55, 58, 61
c 23, ___, 15, ___, 7
d −5, ___, −15, ___, −25
e 3.8, 4.0, 4.2, ___, ___, ___, ___, 5.2
f 7.9, 8.3, ___, 9.1, ___, 9.9, ___, ___
g 0.45, ___, ___, 0.6, 0.65, ___, 0.75, ___

Q12a hint
From 18 to 21 the term-to-term rule is 'add 3'. □ + 3 = 18

Q12c hint
Find the difference between two of the terms, then halve it to find the term-to-term rule.

5b

13 Finance You are offered two options for investing your money.

Option A
Month 1: deposit £3000
Month 2: balance is £3010
Month 3: balance is £3020
Month 4: balance is £3030
and so on.

Option B
Month 1: deposit £1
Month 2: balance is £3
Month 3: balance is £9
Month 4: balance is £27
and so on.

Which option is better? Explain your answer.

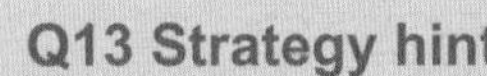

Q13 Strategy hint
Write each option as a sequence until Month 10.

Investigation **Problem-solving**

A sequence begins 1, 4, …

1 What could the next term be?
2 What is the term-to-term rule?
3 Find another term-to-term rule. What is the next term for this rule?
4 Write as many term-to-term rules as you can for sequences that start 1, 4, …
5 Answer Q1–4 for the sequence that begins $\frac{1}{2}$, $\frac{1}{4}$, …

Discussion Will $\frac{1}{27}$ be a term in any of your sequences? Why, or why not?

Explore

14 Explore Will there be a FIFA World Cup in 2054?
Is it easier to explore this question now you have completed the lesson?
What further information do you need to be able to answer this?

Reflect

15 Reflect Think carefully about your work on sequences. How would you define a sequence in your own words? Write down your definition. Compare your definition with someone else's in your class.

9.2 Pattern sequences

You will learn to:

- Find patterns and rules in sequences.
- Describe how a pattern sequence grows.
- Write and use number sequences to model real-life problems.

CONFIDENCE

Why learn this? A sequence of diagrams can help in making predictions about the spread of a virus.

Fluency

- What is the 10th multiple of 3?
- What is the term-to-term rule for the sequence 4, 6, 8, 10, …?

Explore
How long will it take for a rumour to spread?

Exercise 9.2

Warm up

1 What is the term-to-term rule of each sequence.
  a 12, 18, 24, 30, … b 23, 33, 43, 53, …

2 Write down the next four terms of this sequence: 5, 9, 13, 17, …

3 A **sequence** has first term 4 and term-to-term rule '– 2'.
Write down the first four terms of the sequence.

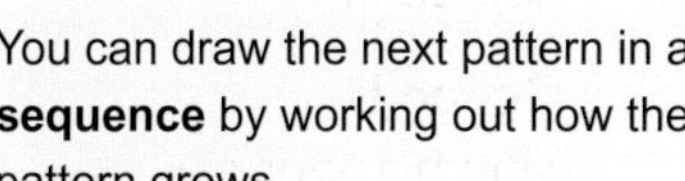

Key point
You can draw the next pattern in a **sequence** by working out how the pattern grows.
You can describe how a sequence grows by explaining how to get from one pattern to the next.

4a

4 Look at this sequence of patterns made from counters.

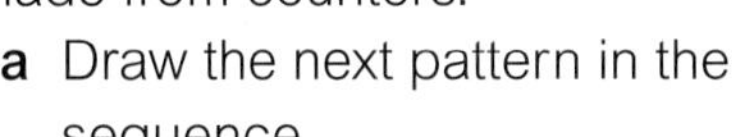

a Draw the next pattern in the sequence.

b Copy and complete this table for the sequence.

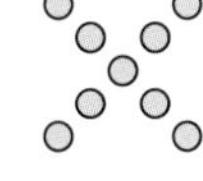

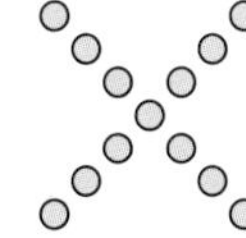

Pattern 1 Pattern 2 Pattern 3

Pattern number	1	2	3	4	5
Number of counters					

c Describe how the sequence grows.

Q4a hint
Look at how the number of counters in each 'arm' of the pattern increases.

Q4c hint
Explain how to make the next pattern in the sequence.

4a

5 Look at this sequence of patterns made from squares.

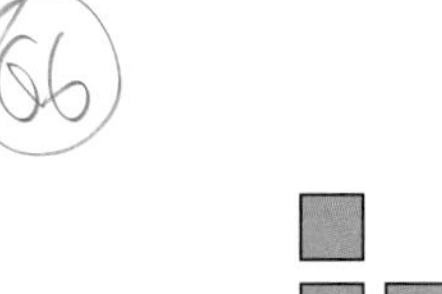

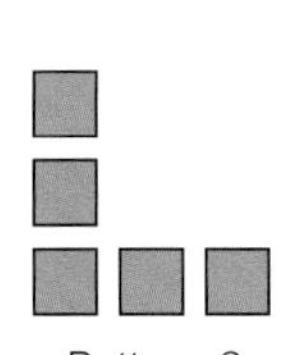

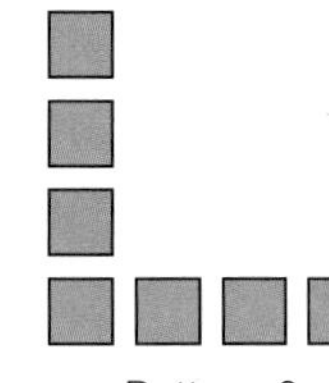

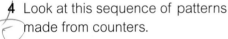

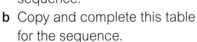

Pattern 1 Pattern 2 Pattern 3

a Draw the next pattern in the sequence.

b Copy and complete this table for the sequence.

Pattern number	1	2	3	4	5
Number of squares					

c Describe how the sequence grows.

4a **6** Jack is collecting trading cards.
He starts with a gift pack of 15 cards.
He plans to buy 10 cards every week until he has 75.

a Copy and complete the table to show the number of cards he will have each week.

Week number	1	2	3	4	5
Number of cards	15	25			

b In which week will he reach his target?

Q7b hint
Continue the table up to 75 cards.
Read the week number.

5c **7** This is a sequence of growing rectangles.

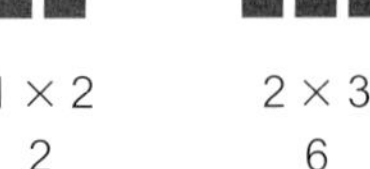

1 × 2	2 × 3	3 × ____	____ × ____	____ × ____
2	6	____	____	____

a Complete the multiplications for the rectangles.

b Describe in your own words how this sequence grows.

c The 2nd rectangle is 2 × 3. What will the 8th rectangle be?

5c **8** Finance Abi and Ben are both saving up for a computer game that costs £40.
Abi starts with £20 and saves £4 per week.
Ben starts with £10 and saves £8 per week.
Who will be first to have enough money for the game?
Discussion How many ways are there to solve this?

Investigation — Modelling / STEM / Problem-solving

A potato in the middle of a tray has gone rotten! It is making all the potatoes around it rotten too.
Each potato immediately next to a rotten potato goes rotten in a day.
This diagram shows the number of rotten potatoes (including the original one) after one day.

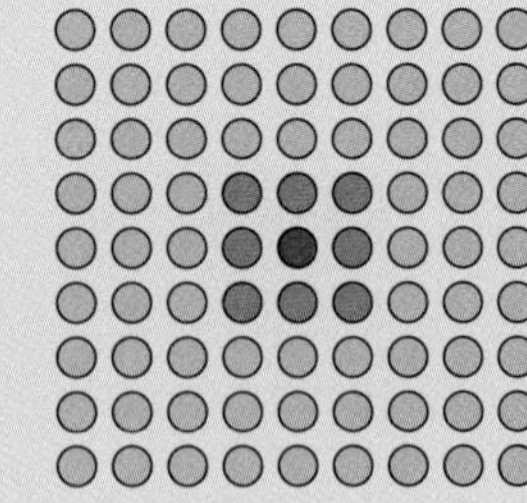

1 Copy the diagram on to squared paper. Continue the pattern.
The sequence showing the number of new rotten potatoes each day begins 1, 8, …
2 How does it continue?
Discussion Would this model be a realistic way to predict the spread of a virus in humans?

Explore **9** **Explore** How long will it take for a rumour to spread?
What have you learned in this lesson to help you answer this question?
What other information do you need?

Reflect **10** **Reflect** Look back over this lesson. Sequences are shown in three different ways:
A Diagrams **B** Tables **C** Lists of numbers
Which of these ways helped you most to understand sequences and answer the questions?
Give one other area of mathematics where you have found this way useful.

9.3 Coordinates

You will learn to:
- Generate and plot coordinates from a rule
- Solve problems and spot patterns in coordinates
- Find the midpoint of a line segment.

CONFIDENCE

Why learn this? The army has used coordinates for hundreds of years to pinpoint locations.

Fluency
- Work out half of 12, 8, 17.
- Sketch a parallelogram.
- Worlk out –3 + 5

Explore
How could you tell a computer program exactly where to display graphics?

Exercise 9.3

Warm up

1 Work out the difference between −3 and 6.

2 Add 4 and 10, then halve the answer.

5c

3 a Write down the coordinates of points A, B and C.
b A, B and C are three vertices of a rectangle.
Write down the coordinates of the fourth vertex, D.

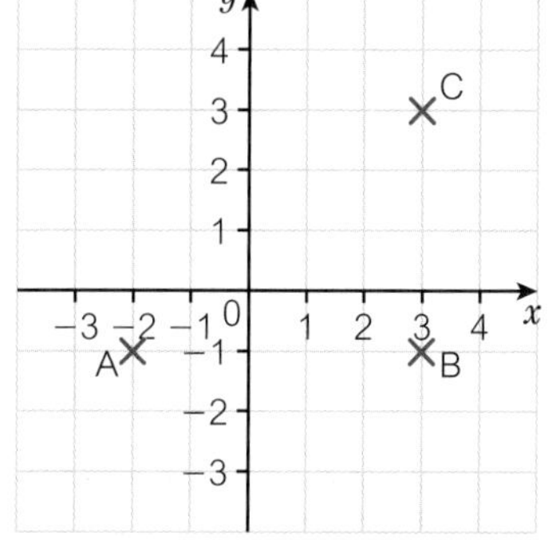

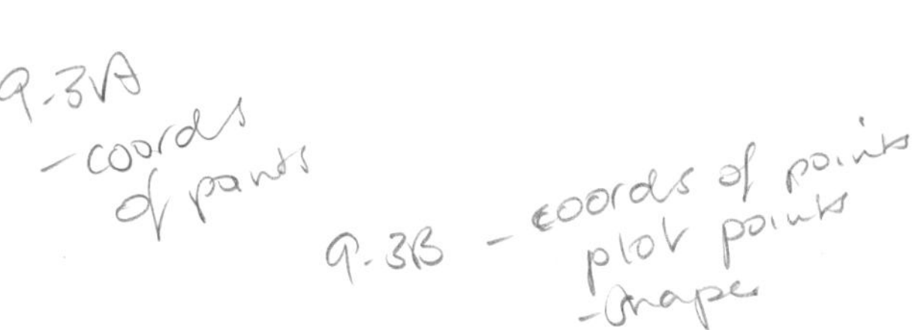

5c

4 a Copy and complete the table of values for this function machine.

x → multiply by 8 → y

x	1	2	3	4	5
y					

b The y-values make a sequence. What is the term-to-term rule of the sequence of y-values?

Q4 hint
Put each x-**coordinate** through the function machine to get the y-**coordinate**.

5b

5 This function machine generates coordinates.
When you input an x-coordinate, it outputs the y-coordinate.

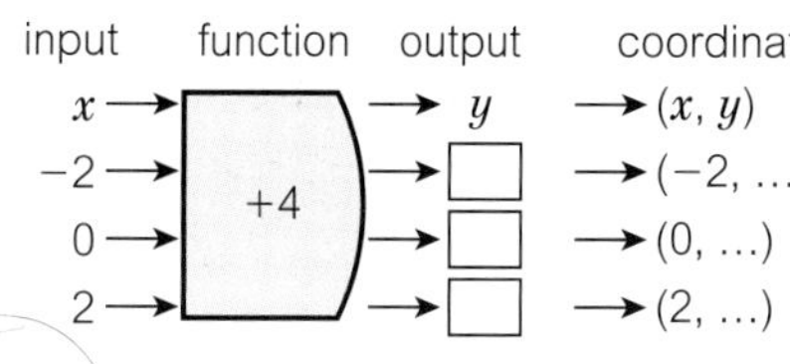

a Work out the missing y-coordinates.
b Draw a grid with x- and y-axes from −2 to 6. Plot the coordinates from part **a** on the grid and join them with a straight line.
c Write down the coordinates of another point that lies on the straight line.

Discussion Try other input values between −5 and +5. Are the coordinates on your line?

d Write down the rule for the function machine using algebra. Label your graph with this rule.

Q5d hint
Your rule should start $y = \ldots$

5b

6 Copy and complete the table to work out the **midpoint** of each of these **line segments**.

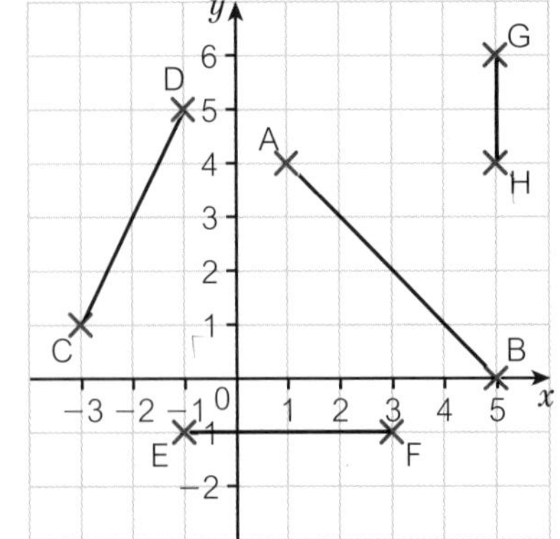

Key point

The **midpoint** of a line segment is the point exactly in the middle.

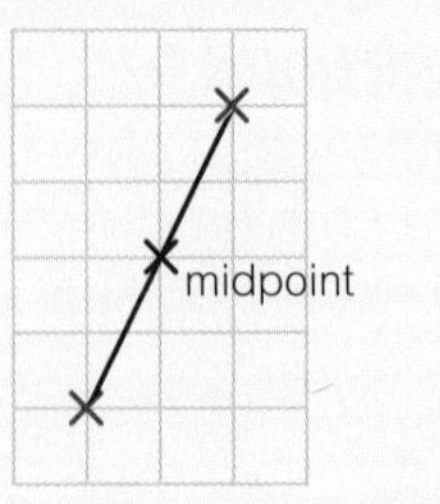

Line segment	Beginning point	Endpoint	Midpoint
AB	(1, 4)	(5, 0)	
CD	(−3, 1)		

Q6 Literacy hint

These are **line segments** and not just lines because they have a definite beginning and end.

Discussion Look at your table. How can you find the midpoint of a line segment by just looking at the beginning and end coordinates?

Worked example

Work out the midpoint of this line segment.

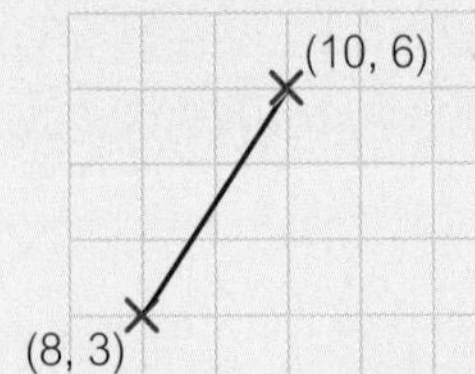

$(8 + 10) \div 2 = 9$ — Add the two x-coordinates together and divide by 2.

$(3 + 6) \div 2 = 4.5$ — Add the two y-coordinates together and divide by 2.

midpoint = (9, 4.5) — These are the x- and y-coordinates of the midpoint.

5a

7 Work out the midpoint of each of these line segments.

a

b

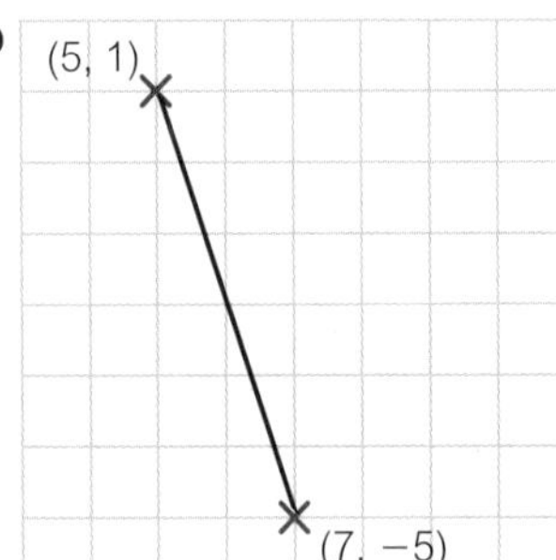

c

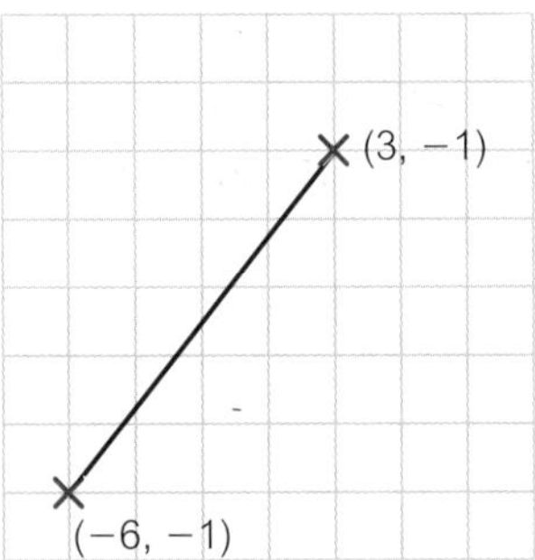

Explore

8 Explore How could you tell a computer program exactly where to display graphics?
What have you learned in this lesson to help you answer this question?
What other information do you need?

Reflect

9 Reflect Patty, Sally and Dave are talking about this line.
Patty says 'One end is at the point (2, −2).'
Sally says 'The midpoint is at (−3, 0).'
Dave says 'The other end is at the point (2, 2).'

a Who is right and who is wrong?

b Write a hint on reading coordinates, in your own words, to help the students who are wrong.
Check your hint. Will it stop them making their mistakes?

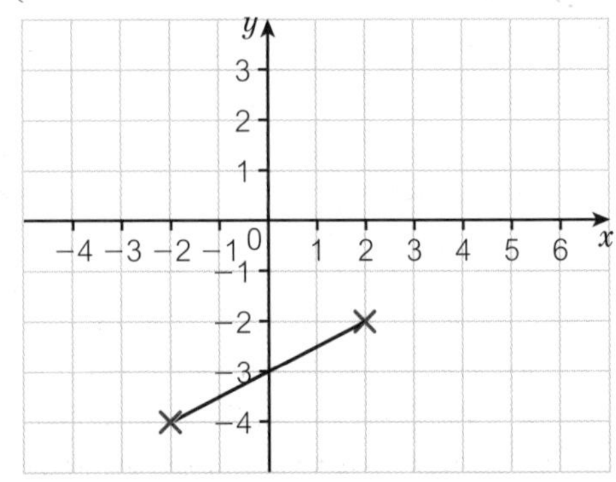

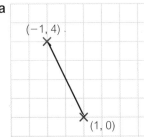

9.4 Extending sequences

You will learn to:

- Describe and continue special sequences
- Use the term-to-term rule to work out more terms in a sequence
- Recognise an arithmetic sequence.

CONFIDENCE

Why learn this?
Many things around us follow a pattern. Knowing how a pattern continues can help us know what to expect.

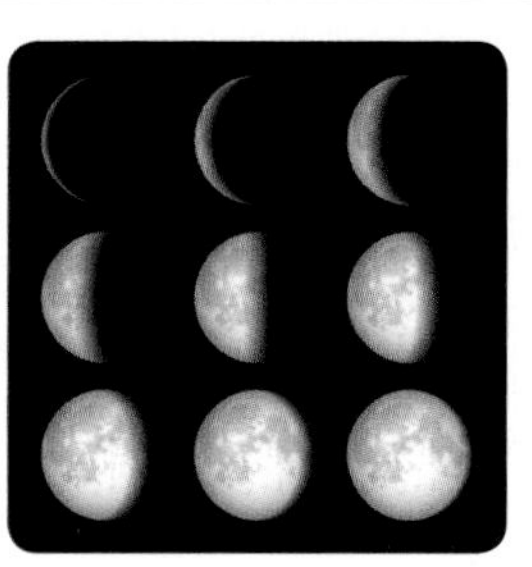

Fluency
What are the term-to-term rules for these sequences?

- 2, 6, 10, 14, 18, …
- 3, 6, 12, 24, 48, …
- 15, 12, 9, 6, 3, …

Explore
In a group of friends, everyone hugs each other once. How many hugs is this?

Exercise 9.4

Warm up

1 Work out the outputs for each function machine.

a
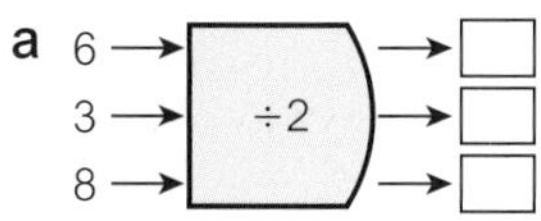

b
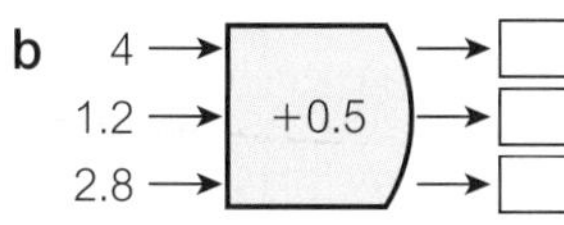

2 Work out

a $2 \times 3 + 4$ b $15 \div 3 + 1$ c $(10 + 6) \div 4$

4b

3 Look at these patterns made from counters.

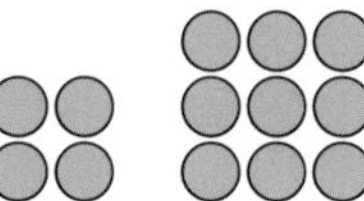

a Draw the next pattern in the sequence.
b The first three terms of the sequence are 1, 4, 9.
Write down the next three terms.
c What is the special name for the numbers in this sequence?
d **Reasoning** Is this an **arithmetic sequence**? Explain your answer.

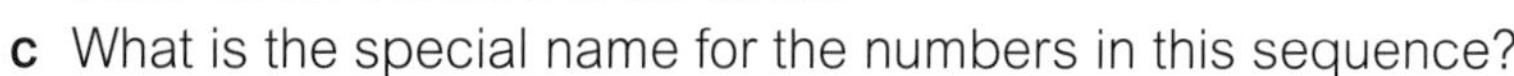

Key point
An **arithmetic sequence** goes up or down in equal steps. For example, the sequence 14, 11, 8, 5, 2, … goes down in steps of 3.

4a

4 Look at this sequence: 2, 5, 10, 17, 26, …
a What is the term-to-term rule?
b Write down the next three terms in the sequence.
c **Reasoning** Is this an arithmetic sequence? Explain your answer.

Q4a hint
Look at the differences between terms.

4a

5 Write the first five terms of each sequence.
a first term 5, term-to-term rule 'multiply by 2, then add 1'
b first term 7, term-to-term rule 'multiply by 2, then subtract 3'
c first term 127, term-to-term rule 'subtract 1, then divide by 2'
d first term 2, term-to-term rule 'multiply by 3, then subtract 4'
e first term 32, term-to-term rule 'divide by 2, then add 4'

Q5a hint
Be careful when the rule has two steps. Use the correct priority of operations.
$5 \times 2 + 1 = 10 + 1 = 11$

Q5c hint
Use a function machine like this

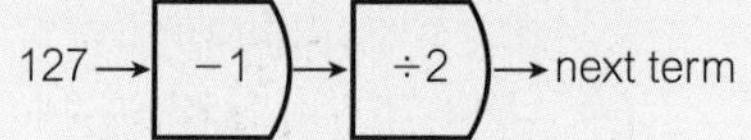

or brackets like this
$(127 - 1) \div 2 =$ next term

4a

6 Use first term 2. Choose three term-to-term rules with two steps, for example 'multiply by 2, then add 3'.
a Write down the first five terms of each sequence.
b Which sequence increases or decreases fastest?

Worked example

This pattern sequence is made from counters.

a Complete this table for the sequence.

Pattern number	1	2	3	4	5
Number of counters	1	4	7	10	13

+3 +3 +3 +3

Use the term-to-term rule to fill in the numbers of counters for the 4th and 5th patterns.

b Work out the number of counters in the 10th pattern.

1st pattern: 1
2nd pattern: 1 + 3 = 4
3rd pattern: 1 + 3 + 3 = 7
4th pattern: 1 + 3 + 3 + 3 = 10
10th pattern: 1 + 9 × 3 = 1 + 27 = 28

The number of times you add 3 is one less than the pattern number.
2nd pattern: 1 + 1 × 3
3rd pattern: 1 + 2 × 3
4th pattern: 1 + 3 × 3

5b

7 This pattern sequence is made from beams.

a Copy and complete this table for the sequence.

Pattern number	1	2	3	4	5
Number of beams					

b Work out the number of beams in the 10th pattern.

5b

8 **Real / Problem solving** Polly is told to exercise her leg after an injury. She exercises for an hour each day for the first week, then decreases the daily time by 12 minutes each week.

a In which week does Polly first exercise her leg for less than half an hour each day?

b In which week doesn't she need to exercise her leg any more?

c Do the daily exercise times each week form an arithmetic sequence? Explain your answer.

Discussion How did you solve part **a** and part **b**?

Q8a hint

Convert hours to minutes.

5b

9 Which of these sequences are arithmetic? For each arithmetic sequence, write down the first term and the common difference.

a 3, 5, 6, 8, 9, 11, …
b 0.5, 1.5, 2.5, 3.5, 4.5, …
c 1, 2, 3, 1, 2, 3, 1, …
d 1, 2, 4, 8, 16, ...
e 25, 20, 15, 10, 5, …
f 98, 89, 80, 71, 62, …

Key point

You can describe an arithmetic sequence using the first term and the **common difference** (the difference between terms). For the sequence 14, 11, 8, 5, 2, … , the first term is 14 and the common difference is −3.

Explore

10 **Explore** In a group of friends, everyone hugs each other once. How many hugs is this? Choose some small numbers to help you explore this question. Then use what you have learned in this lesson to help you answer the question.

Reflect

11 **Reflect** Mickey says this riddle about a sequence.

'My first term is 2. My fourth term is 14. I am arithmetic. What is in between?'

a Write down every step you take to work out Mickey's sequence. You might begin 'I write down all the numbers I know, leaving gaps for any missing numbers: 2 ___ , ___ , 14.'

b Look at the steps you have written down. Underline any of them (or parts of them) that you think might help you when problem-solving in mathematics in the future.

9.5 Straight-line graphs

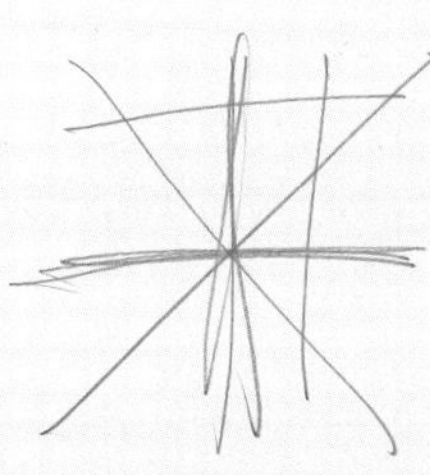

You will learn to:
- Recognise, name and plot graphs parallel to the axes
- Recognise, name and plot the graphs of $y = x$ and $y = -x$
- Plot straight-line graphs using a table of values
- Draw graphs to represent relationships.

CONFIDENCE

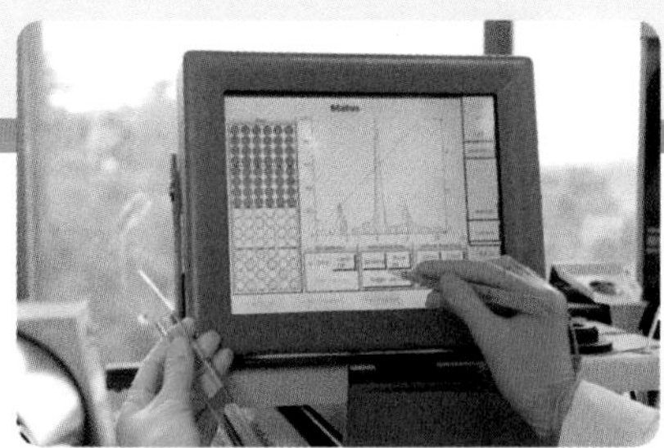

Why learn this?
Using a graph to plot results from a science experiment will help to show a relationship.

Fluency
- Work out 3 × 2 + 1.
- In (4, 1), which is the x-coordinate and which is the y-coordinate?
- $n = 4$. What is the value of $3n$?

Explore
How could you tell a computer program how a character should travel across the screen?

Exercise 9.5

Warm up

1 $y = 5x$. Work out the value of y when x is equal to
a 6 b 1 c 4

2 Work out the value of $3p + 4$ when p is equal to
a 1 b 2 c 6

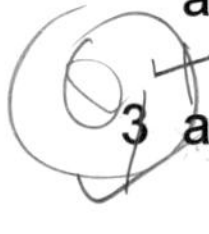

5b

3 a Aisha's rule for generating coordinates is 'whatever the x-coordinate is, the y-coordinate is always 4.'
Which of these coordinate pairs satisfy Aisha's rule?
(5, 5), (4, 4), (1, 4), (4, 3), (−1, 4), (5, −4), (0, 4), (4, 5)

b Copy this grid and plot your points from part **a**. Join the points with a straight line. What do you notice?

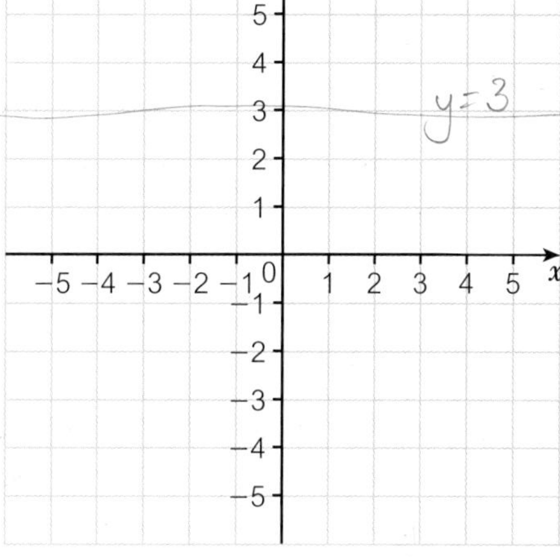

c Duane's rule for generating coordinates is 'whatever the x-coordinate is, the y-coordinate is always 2.'
Duane generates these coordinates: (5, 2), (4, 2), (0, 2), (3, 2).
Where do you think these points will be on the grid?

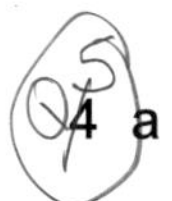

5b

4 a Write down the coordinates of all the points on line A.
b What do you notice about the coordinates?
c Copy and complete these sentences.
i The equation for line A is $y = \ldots$
ii The equation for line B is $x = \ldots$
iii The equation for line C is $y = \ldots$

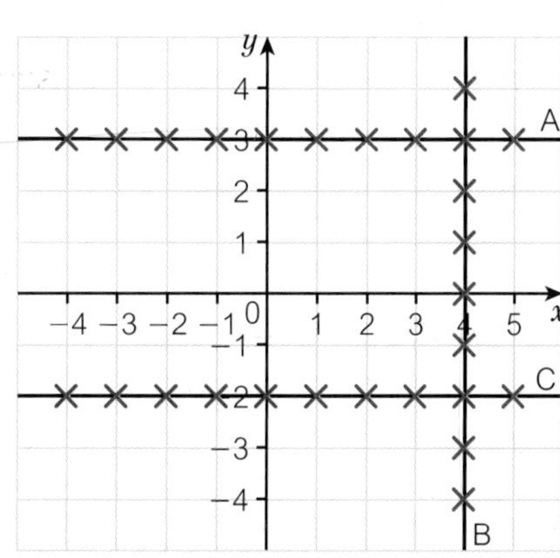

5a **5** Write down the equations of the lines labelled A, B, C and D.

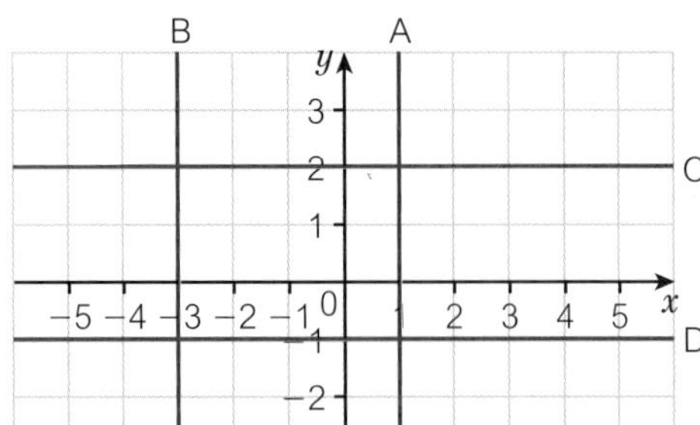

Key point

The equation $y = 2$ means the y-coordinate is always 2, whatever the x-coordinate is. The line is **parallel** to the x-axis.
The equation $x = 3$ means the x-coordinate is always 3, whatever the y-coordinate is. The line is parallel to the y-axis.

5a **6** Draw a grid with x- and y-axes from −5 to +5.
Draw and label these graphs.

a $y = 5$ **b** $x = 2$ **c** $y = 3$

Discussion Are these lines or line segments?

Key point

When you draw a graph, it should go to the edge of the grid.

Q6 Literacy hint

Labelling a graph means writing the equation of the graph next to the line.

Worked example

a Complete this table of values for the equation $y = 2x + 4$.

x	1	2	3	4	5
y	6	8	10	12	14

To find each missing y-coordinate multiply the x-value by 2 and then add 4.

b Write down five coordinate pairs from the table.
(1, 6), (2, 8), (3, 10), (4, 12), (5, 14)

When $x = 1$, $y = 6$, giving (1, 6).

5a **7** **a** Copy and complete this table of values for the equation $y = 3x$.

x	1	2	3	4	5
y					

b Copy and complete these coordinate pairs from the table of values.
(1, __), (2, __), (3, __), (4, __), (5, __)

c Draw a coordinate grid with x-axis from 0 to 6 and y-axis from 0 to 20. Plot the coordinates.
Draw a straight line that goes through all the points and to the edges of the grid. Label the graph with its equation.

d What is the value of y when $x = 6$?

Q7d hint

Draw a line from 6 on the x-axis up to your graph, then across to the y-axis.

5a **8** **a** Copy and complete this table of values for the equation $y = 3x + 4$.

x	1	2	3	4	5
y					

b Write down the coordinate pairs from the table of values.

c Draw the graph of $y = 3x + 4$.

d What is the value of y when $x = \frac{1}{2}$?

Discussion Look at the graphs you drew for Q7 and Q8. What do you notice?

Q8a hint

Use this two-step function machine to help you.

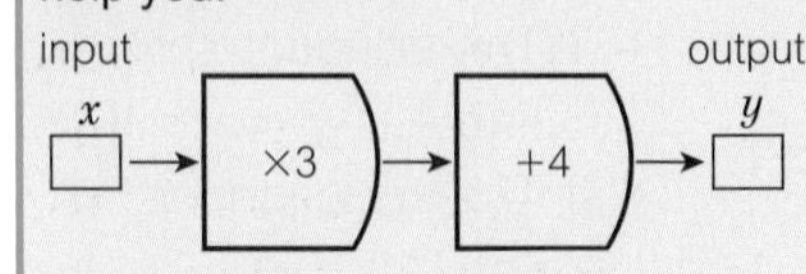

Topic links: Substitution, Parallel lines

Subject links: Science (Investigation), Computing (Q1)

9 **a** Complete this table of values for the function $y = x$.

x	−3	−2	−1	0	1	2	3
y	−3		−1			2	

b Copy the grid from Q3 and plot the coordinates from the table. Join them with a straight line.

10 This is the graph of $y = -x$.

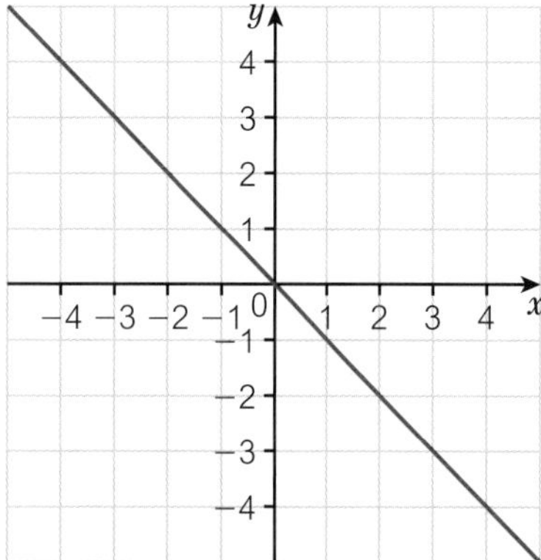

a Write down three pairs of coordinates that lie on the line $y = -x$.

b Write down three pairs of coordinates that you know will *not* lie on the line $y = -x$.

Discussion What is the same and what is different about the graphs of $y = x$ and $y = -x$?

Investigation **STEM / Real**

This spring is 10 cm long.
Jermaine puts different masses on the end and measures the spring.
He records his results in this table.

Mass (g)	100	150	200	250
Length of spring (cm)	12	13	14	

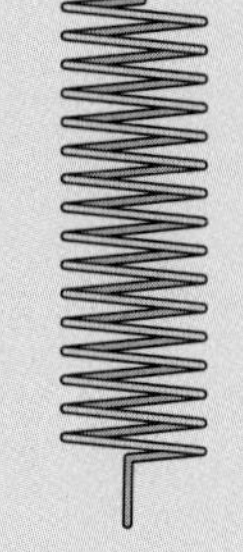

1 How long will the spring be when he adds the 250 g mass?

2 Copy and complete this sentence.
Each time Jermaine adds another __g, the spring extends by __cm.

3 Krysta does the same experiment with a different spring. Here are her results.

Mass (g)	0	50	100	150	200	250	300
Length of spring (cm)	4	8	12	16	18	19	19.5

4 How long was Krysta's spring to begin with?

5 Copy the grid and use it to plot Krysta's results.

6 Write down the coordinates of the point where the line starts to curve.

Discussion What do you think has happened to the spring?

11 **Explore** How could you tell a computer program how a character should travel across the screen?
What have you learned in this lesson to help you answer this question?
What other information do you need?

12 **Reflect** Here are three things you have done in this lesson.

A Completed a table of coordinate pairs.
B Drawn a straight-line graph.
C Read coordinates from a straight-line graph.

Which of these things did you find easiest? What made it easy?
Which of these things did you find most difficult? What made it difficult?
Do you think you need more practice on any of these things? If so, which one(s)?

9.6 Position-to-term rules

You will learn to:
- Generate terms of a sequence using the position-to-term rule
- Use linear expressions to describe the nth term of simple sequences.

CONFIDENCE

Why learn this? Scientists and economists sometimes want to see what will happen if trends continue for a year, for 2 years and beyond.

Fluency
- What is the 7th term of this sequence? 3, 5, 7, 9, 11, 13, …
- I am thinking of a number, n.
  What is
  a 3 times my number
  b 3 more than my number
  c 2 less than my number?

Explore How much does a monthly subscription to a film rental site cost in total?

Exercise 9.6

Warm up

1 Write down the missing rule for each function machine.

a 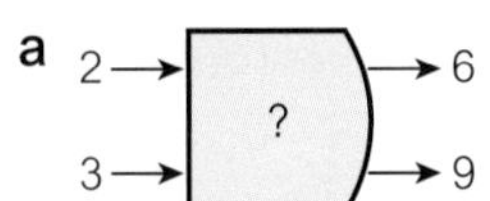

b 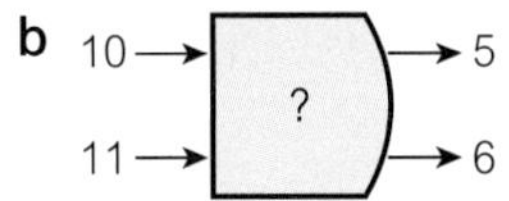

c 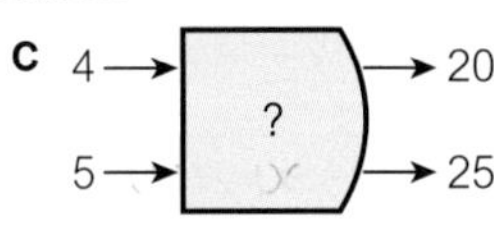

2 Match each expression on a green card to its simplified form.

$5 \times n$ 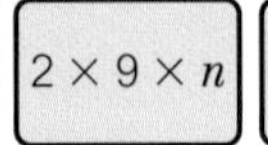 $2 \times 9 \times n$ 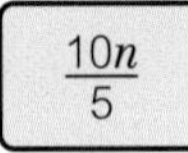 $\frac{10n}{5}$ $2n$  $18n$ 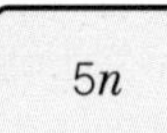 $5n$

5a

3 Look at these shapes made from squares.

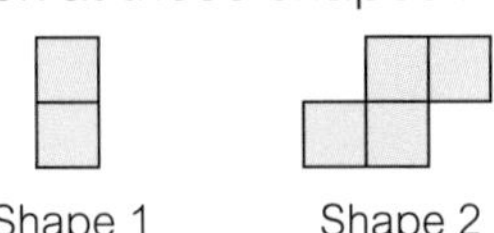

Shape 1 Shape 2

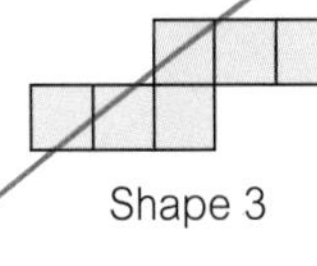

Shape 3

Shape 4

a Draw the next shape.
b Copy and complete the table.

Shape number (position)	1	2	3	4	
Number of squares (term)					

c Write down the term-to-term rule.
d How many squares are in the 6th shape?
e Copy and complete this formula to describe the **position-to-term** rule.
number of squares = shape number × ______
f Use the position-to-term rule to find the 10th term in the sequence.

5a

4 a Write the first six terms of the sequence for each of these position-to-term rules.
i position number + 6
ii 2 × position number
iii (2 × position number) + 1
iv (3 × position number) − 2

b Write down the term-to-term rule for each of the sequences in part **a**.

Discussion What is the relationship between the term-to-term rule and the position-to-term rule?

Key point
Each term in a sequence has a position.
The 1st term is in position 1, the 2nd term is in position 2, the 3rd term is in position 3, and so on.
The **position-to-term** rule tells you how to work out a term in a sequence when you know its position.

Q4a hint
The 1st term of the sequence is at position 1.
So the 1st term is 1 + 6 = 7
The 2nd term of the sequence is at position 2.
So the 2nd term is 2 + 6 = 8.

Topic links: Square numbers, Triangle numbers

5 Look at this sequence.

6, 8, 10, 12, 14, …

Signe said, 'The position-to-term rule of this sequence is "position number + 2".' Explain why Signe is wrong.

Worked example

Work out the nth term of this sequence.

6, 12, 18, 24, 30, …

Position:	1	2	3	4	5	…	n
	×6	×6	×6	×6	×6		×6
Term:	6	12	18	24	30	…	$6 \times n$

Work out what you do to the position number to get the term.

$6n$ — $6 \times n = 6n$.

Key point

You use algebra to write the position-to-term rule.
It is called the ***n*th term** because it tells you how to work out the term at position n (any position).

6 For each sequence below,

i write down the term-to-term rule

ii describe the position-to-term rule in words

iii write down the ***n*th term** using algebra.

a

Position	1	2	3	4	5
Term	7	14	21	28	35

b

Position	1	2	3	4	5
Term	4	5	6	7	8

7 Find the nth term of each of these sequences.

a 2, 4, 6, 8, 10, … b 10, 20, 30, 40, 50, …

8 Write down the term-to-term rule for each of the sequences in Q7.

Discussion What do you notice about the term-to-term rule and the nth term?

9 **STEM / Modelling** Elena is training for a marathon. She runs for 12 minutes on her first day, then 12 minutes more each time she goes for a run.

a Continue this sequence to the 6th term.
12, 24, ...

b What is the nth term for this sequence?

c How many hours will Elena run for on the 10th day?

d Do you think Elena will be able to stick to the model for 50 days? Explain your answer.

Q9c hint

Convert the number of minutes to hours.

10 **Explore** How much does a monthly subscription to a film rental site cost in total? Is it easier to explore this question now you have completed the lesson? What further information do you need to be able to answer this?

15 **Reflect** Think about the term-to-term rule and the position-to-term rule for the 5 times table.
Which rule is '× 5' and which is '+ 5'?
Make sure you know the difference between the term-to-term rule and the position-to-term rule. Write down a hint, in your own words, to help you remember which is which.

9 Check up

Sequences

1 What are the next three terms in each sequence?

a 10, 20, 30, … **b** 1, 3, 5, … **c** 4, 7, 10, …

2 This rule generates a sequence: Start at 0. Add 2 each time.

a Write down the first five terms.

b What is this sequence called?

3 Use the first term and the term-to-term rule to generate the first five terms of each sequence.

a first term 9, term-to-term rule '− 4'

b first term 0, term-to-term rule '+ 8'

c first term 2, term-to-term rule '× 3'

d first term 48, term-to-term rule '÷ 2'

4 a Draw the next shape in this pattern sequence.

b Describe how the sequence grows.

c Write down the number of dots in the first three patterns of this sequence.

d Write down the next four terms of the number sequence.

Pattern 1 Pattern 2 Pattern 3

5 Write down the next four terms of each sequence.

a 6, 13, 20, 27, …

b −8, −10, −12, −14, …

c $\frac{1}{3}, \frac{1}{5}, \frac{1}{7}, \frac{1}{9}, \ldots$

d Which of these sequences are arithmetic? Explain your answer.

6 Work out the missing terms in each sequence.

a 6, ___ , 0, −3, ___ **b** 1.5, ___ , 0.5, ___ , ___

c ___ , 4, ___, −10, −17 **d** ___ , −3.2, −2.3, ___ , −0.5, ___

The nth term

7 This function machine finds terms of a sequence from their position.

a Write down the missing rule for the function machine.

b Use the position-to-term rule to work out the 20th term of the sequence.

c Write down the nth term of the sequence.

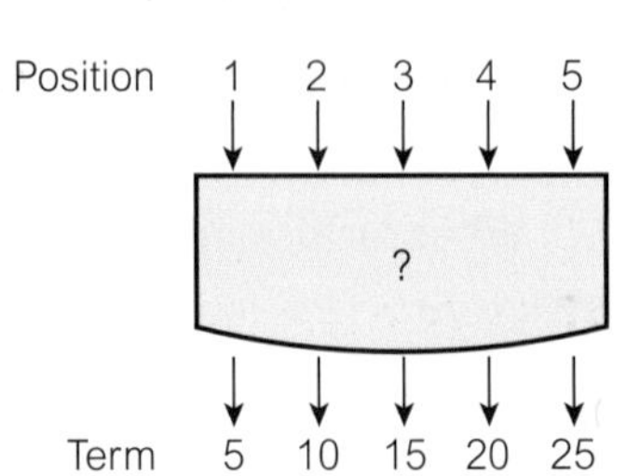

8 a Find the position-to-term rule for this sequence.

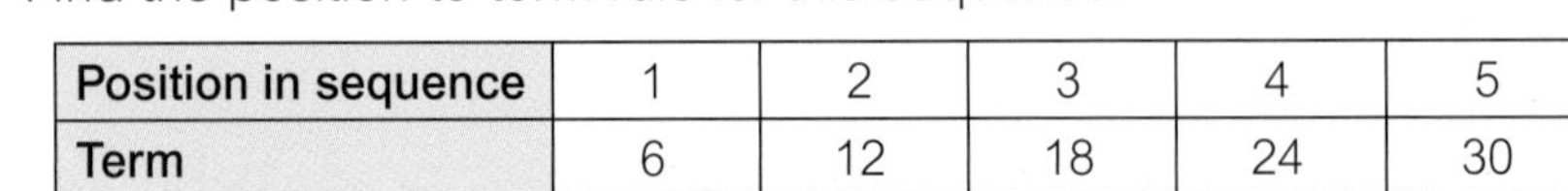

Position in sequence	1	2	3	4	5
Term	6	12	18	24	30

b Use your rule to find the 10th term and the 50th term.

c What is the nth term of this sequence?

9 Find the nth term of this sequence: 3, 4, 5, 6, …

10 A sequence begins 3, 6, 9, 12, …
Nawaz says, 'The nth term of this sequence is $n + 3$.'

a What mistake has he made?

b Find the nth term of the sequence.

Graphs

11 Draw a grid with x- and y-axes from −6 to +6.

a Plot the points (2, 1), (4, 3) and (5, 4).

b Plot the points (0, −1) and (−2, −3).

c What do you notice about all these points?

12 Write down the equation of each line marked with a letter.

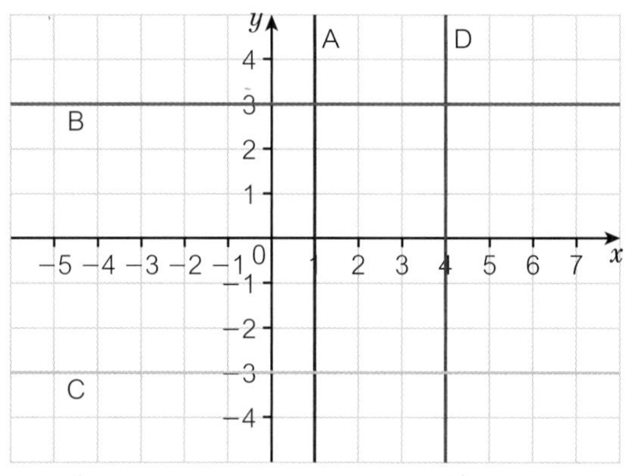

13 Draw a grid with x- and y-axes from −5 to +5. Draw and label the graphs of

a $y = 2$ b $x = 4$ c $y = -1$ d $x = -2$

14 a Copy and complete this table of values for the equation $y = 4x + 2$.

x	1	2	3	4	5
y	6				

b Use the values in the table to draw the graph of $y = 4x + 2$.

c Use your graph to find the value of y when $x = \frac{1}{2}$.

15 Draw a grid with x- and y-axes from −6 to +6. Draw and label the graphs of $y = x$ and $y = -x$.

16 How sure are you of your answers? Were you mostly

☹ Just guessing 😐 Feeling doubtful ☺ Confident

What next? Use your results to decide whether to strengthen or extend your learning.

Challenge

17 Write down three different arithmetic sequences with term-to-term rule '− 8'.

18 a Draw these lines on a grid: $x = 5$, $x = 1$, $y = -2$, $y = 2$

b Copy and complete this sentence.
The lines are four sides of a ________ .

c Write down equations of four lines that are the sides of a rectangle.

d Write down equations of three lines that are the sides of a triangle.

9 Strengthen

You will:
- Strengthen your understanding with practice.

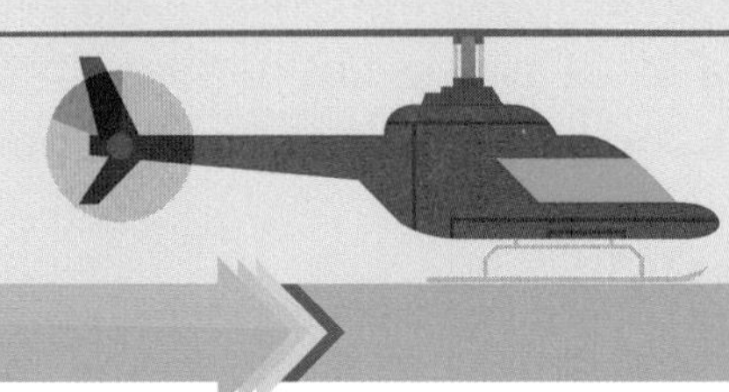

Sequences

4b

1 Write down the first five terms of each sequence.

a first term 3, term-to-term rule 'add 2'

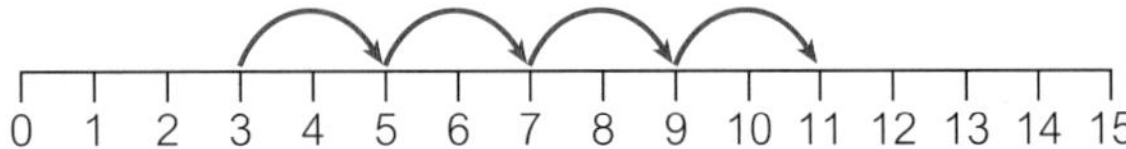

b first term 15, term-to-term rule 'subtract 6'

c first term 3, term-to-term rule 'multiply by 10'

d first term 36, term-to-term rule 'halve'

Q1a hint
Start at 3 on the number line.
Count on 2 to get the next term each time.

Q1c hint
Multiply the first term by 10 to get the second term.

4b

2 Here is a sequence of patterns made from yellow hexagons.

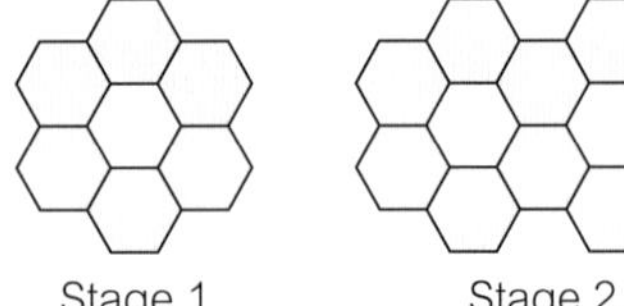

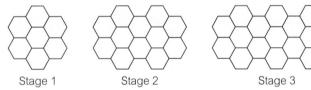

Stage 1 Stage 2 Stage 3

a Write down the terms of the number sequence.
This is an arithmetic sequence.

b How many yellow hexagons are added between Stage 1 and Stage 2?

c How many yellow hexagons are added between Stage 2 and Stage 3?

d How many hexagons will be in Stage 4?

e **Reasoning** What method did you use to work this out? What different method could you have used?

f The number sequence begins 6, 10, 14, ...
Write down the next five terms.

Q2a hint
Count and write down the number of hexagons in each pattern.

Q2c hint
This should be the same as your answer to part **b** because it is an arithmetic sequence.

4a

3 Write down the first five terms of each sequence.

a first term 4, term-to-term rule 'multiply by 2, then add 3'

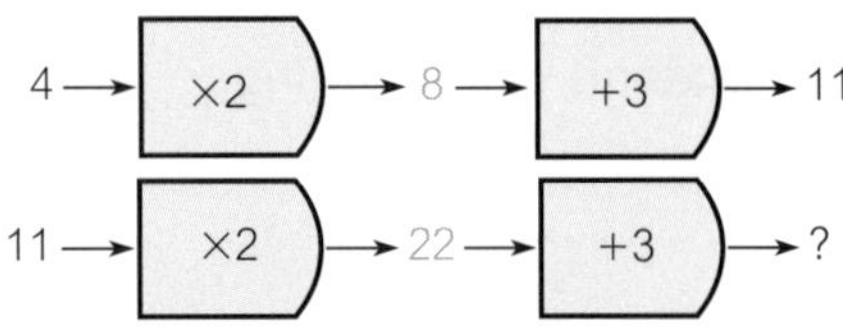

b first term 0, term-to-term rule 'multiply by 2, then add 5'

c first term 5, term-to-term rule 'subtract 1, then multiply by 2'

d first term 4, term-to-term rule 'multiply by 10, then add 1'

Q3a hint
When you input each term into the term-to-term rule, the output is the next term.

5c

4 Write down the next three terms and the term-to-term rule for each sequence.

a 45, 50, 55, ... b 12, 20, 28, ... c 100, 96, 92, ...

d −15, −7, 1, ... e −20, −13, −6, ...

Q4a hint
What do you have to add or subtract to get from one term to the next?.

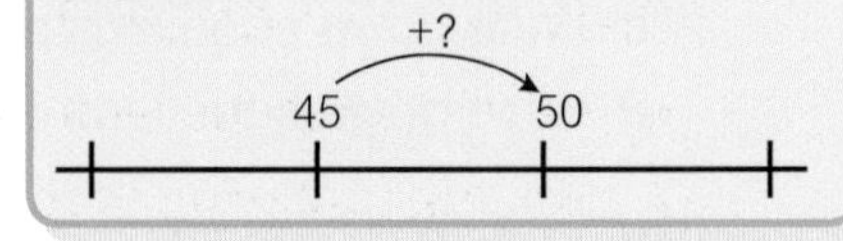

5 Work out the missing terms in each sequence. 5c

a ___ , 13, ___ , 19, 22

b 30, ___ , ___ , 42, 46

c ___ , 4, ___ , −10, ___

d ___ , −1, ___ , 0, ___

Q5a hint

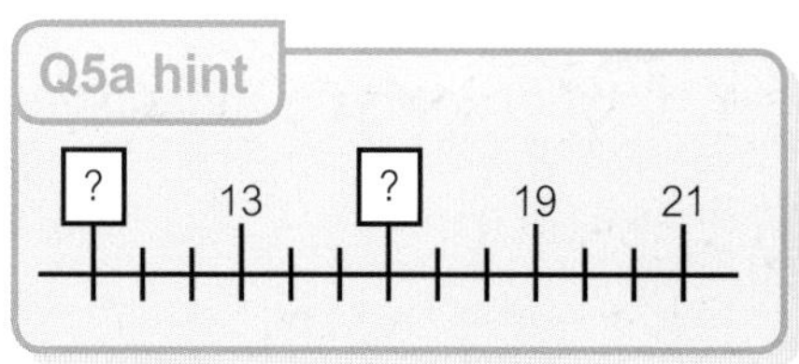

The *n*th term

1 Find the position-to-term rule for each sequence. 5c

a

Position in sequence	1	2	3	4	5
Term	5	6	7	8	9

b

Position in sequence	1	2	3	4	5
Term	11	12	13	14	15

c

Position in sequence	1	2	3	4	5
Term	5	10	15	20	25

d

Position in sequence	1	2	3	4	5
Term	7	14	21	28	35

Q1a hint

You could draw a function machine with input 'position' and output 'term'. What is the rule for this function machine?

input (position)

1 2 3 4 5

?

5 6 7 8 9

output (term)

2 Use the position-to-term rule to write the 10th term and the 50th term for each sequence in Q1. 5a

Q2a hint

The positions are 10 and 50. Input them into the **position-to-term rule**.

3 Write down the nth term for each sequence in Q1. 5a
Show that you have checked your answers. The first one has been done to help you in the hint for Q3a.

Q3a hint

The position-to-term rule is '+ 4'.
So the ***n*th term** is $n + 4$
Check your answer.
nth term is $n + 4$
1st term is 1 + 4 = 5 ✓
2nd term is 2 + 4 = 6 ✓
3rd term Is 3 + 4 = 7 ✓

4 Look at this sequence. 5a

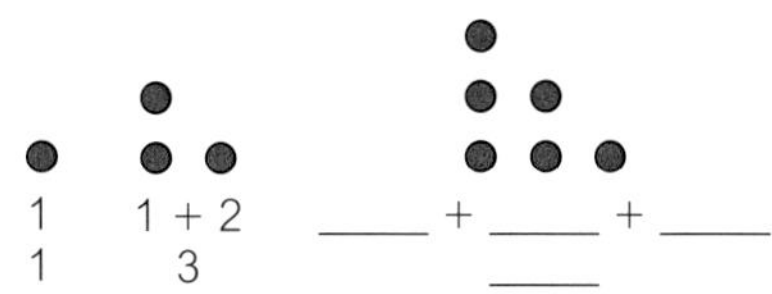

a Copy and complete the sequence, filling in the numbers for the 3rd term.

b Draw the next two terms, including the numbers.

c What is the name of this number sequence?

Uzma says, 'The 4th term is found by adding a row of four dots on the bottom.'

d Is Uzma using the term-to-term rule or the position-to-term rule?

Craig says, 'The 4th term is found by adding all the numbers up to 4.'

e Is Craig using the term-to-term rule or the position-to-term rule?

f Use the position-to-term rule to find the 10th term of the sequence.

Q4c hint

Look at the shapes that the sequence makes.

Graphs

5c **1** Write down the coordinates of each point marked with a letter.

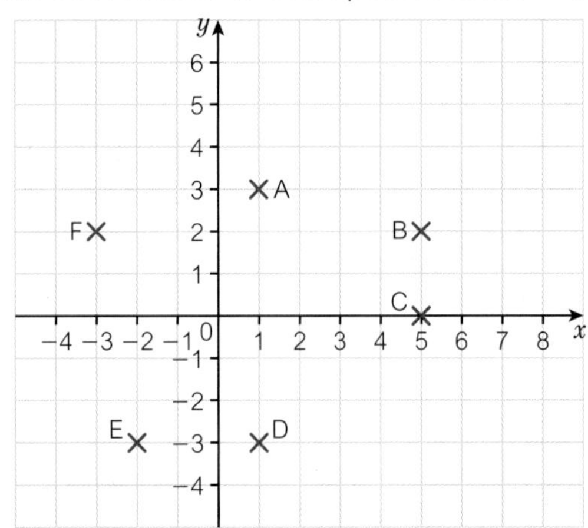

> **Q1 hint**
>
> How to read coordinates:
> The first coordinate is where the line down reaches the x-axis (4, □).
> The second coordinate is where the line across reaches the y-axis (□, 2).
>
> 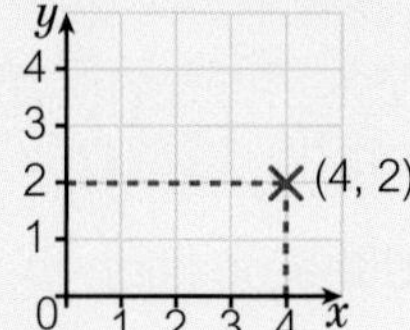
>
> The coordinates of the point shown are (4, 2).

5a **2** Copy the grid from Q1.
Plot the points (3, 2), (1, 5), (6, 3), (−1, −4), (−2, 2) and (4, −3).

5a **3** **a** Draw a grid with x- and y-axes from −5 to +5. Plot four points with y-coordinates of 2.

b Join all your points with a straight line. Where does the line cross the y-axis?

c The equation of the line is $y = 2$. Which of these points will also lie on the line?

(0, 2), (4, −2), (5, 2), (−2, −2), (−1, 2), (2, 2)

d Write a sentence about the y-coordinates of the points that do *not* lie on the line.

> **Q3c hint**
>
> Find each point. Does it lie on the line $y = 2$?

5a **4** Draw a grid with the x- and y-axes from −5 to +5. Draw the lines

a $x = 4$ **b** $x = 1$ **c** $x = -3$

> **Q4a hint**
>
> Plot some points whose x-coordinate is 4, then draw a line through them.

5a **5** Reasoning **a** Sophie tried to plot the line $x = 3$.
What mistake did she make?

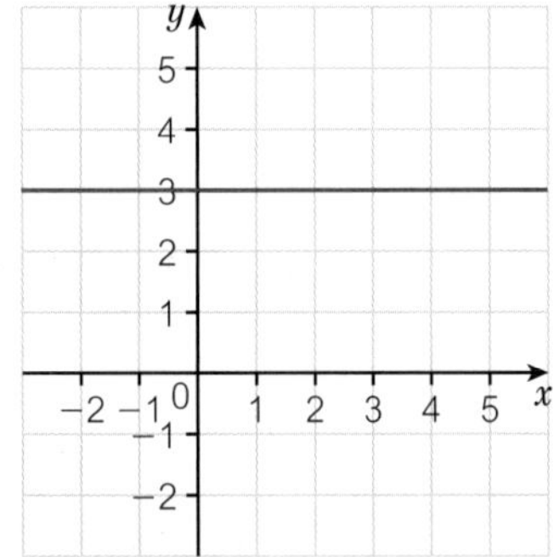

b Write Sophie a hint, explaining how to plot the graph of a line like $x = 3$.

> **Q5b hint**
>
> You could use these words to help.
> x-coordinate straight axis

5a **6** This question is about the function $y = 4x$.

a Copy and complete this table with the value of y for each value of x.

x	0	1	2	3	4
y	0	4			

b Write down the five pairs of coordinates generated by the table.

c Draw a grid with the x- and y-axes from 0 to 16.
Plot the coordinates on the grid.

d Join the points with a straight line and label the line $y = 4x$.

> **Q6a hint**
>
> $y = 4x$, so multiply each value of x by 4 to get the value of y.

7 This question is about the function $y = 3x + 1$.

a Copy and complete this table with the value of y for each value of x.

x	1	2	3	4	5
y	4				

b Draw a grid with x-axis from 0 to 5 and y-axis from 0 to 20.
Plot the points from your table of values.

c Draw a straight line through the points and label the line $y = 3x + 1$.

d What is the point where the graph crosses the y-axis?

Q7a hint

Input the x-coordinatese to work out the y-coordinates.

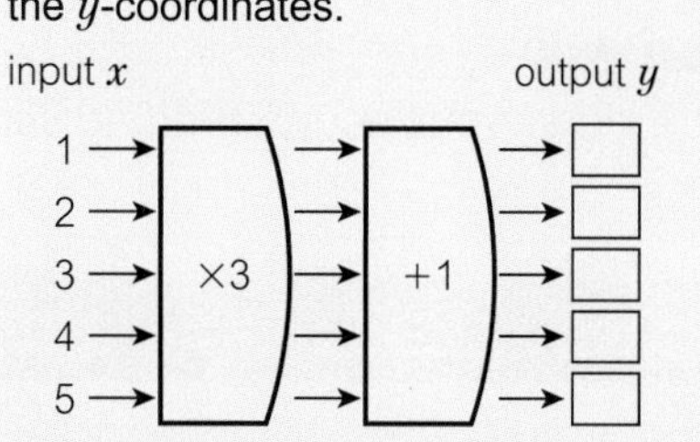

Q7d hint

Move your finger along the graph until it reaches the y-axis.

Enrichment

1 Look at this sequence of dominoes.

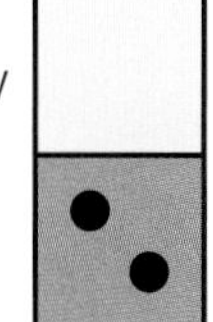
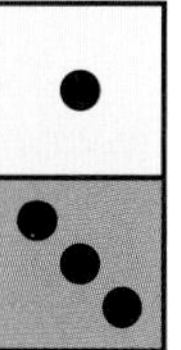
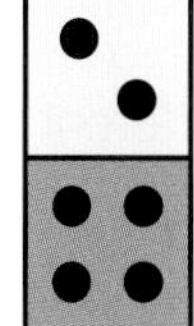

a How many dots will be in the yellow section of the next domino?

b What is the term-to-term rule for the sequence of dots in the pink sections?

c Draw the next domino in the sequence.

d You can use the dominos to generate coordinates: (yellow, pink).
The first domino gives the coordinates (0, 2).
Write down the next three pairs of coordinates?

e Plot the four pairs of coordinates on a grid.

f Complete this function machine.

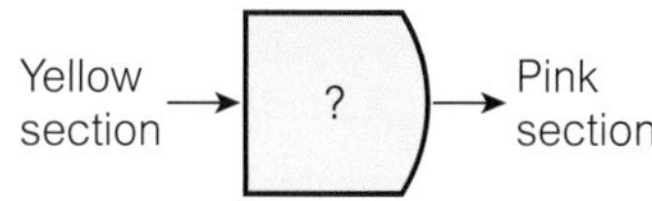

Q1b hint

Are dots added, subtracted, multiplied or divided each time?

Q1e hint

Think about what size grid you need to draw. Look at the smallest and largest x-coordinates and the smallest and largest y-coordinates.

2 Real / Reasoning / Modelling Each branch on a particular tree grows two new branches each week.

The sequence generated by the number of branches begins 1, 3, 7, ...

a Write down the next two terms of the sequence.

b Describe what is happening to the term-to-term rule each week.

c Do you think real trees grow like this? Explain.

d Each branch on a different type of tree grows three new branches each week. What sequence is generated by the number of branches?

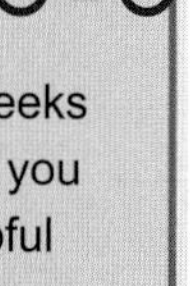

Q2a Strategy hint

You could draw the tree at Week 4 and at Week 5.

Q2d Strategy hint

You could draw the first few weeks of this tree's growth and see if you spot a pattern. It might be helpful to use a different colour for the new branches each week.

3 **Reflect** Lars says 'The words "term" and "coordinates" are used a lot in these lessons. These must be important words for understanding sequences and graphs.'
Write definitions, in your own words, for 'term' and 'coordinates'.

Reflect

9 Extend

You will:

- Extend your understanding with problem-solving.

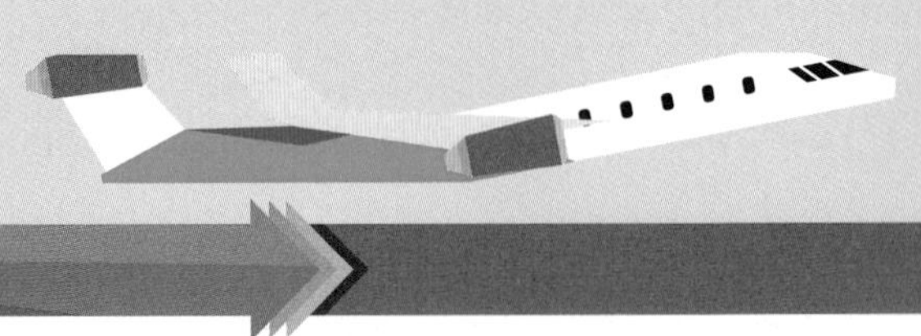

4a **1** For each of these sequences, write down the first term and the term-to-term rule.

a 16, 160, 1600, 16 000, … **b** 0.25, 0.5, 1, 2, … **c** 1, 1, 2, 3, 5, 8, …

5c **2** **Problem-solving** Write two different ways to continue each of these number sequences.
Write down the term-to-term rule you used and the next three numbers.

a 1, 3, … **b** 1, 5, … **c** 3, 5, … **d** 0, 4, …

5c **3** This is a sequence of integers: 88, 44, 22, …
Is the sequence infinite? Explain your answer.

Q3 Literacy hint
An **integer** is a whole number.

5c **4** **Finance** Carol invests £250.

a After a year, her investment doubles, but she has to pay £40 tax. How much does she have at the end of the first year?

b The next year, the same thing happens again. How much does she have at the end of the second year?

Q4 Literacy hint
People hope to make money by investing in savings accounts or company shares. However, when they make over a certain amount, they have to pay the Government some tax.

5b **5** Write a sequence containing these numbers, with at least one term in between them. Describe the term-to-term rule that you use.

a 1 and 12 **b** 3 and 15 **c** 6 and 20

d 1 and 100 **e** 4 and 10

5b **6** Decide whether each of these sets of numbers is finite or infinite.

a multiples of 5 **b** birthday dates

c even numbers **d** temperatures on one day

e integers less than 100

Reasoning Are there more even numbers than multiples of 5?

5a **7** Look at this pattern made from squares.

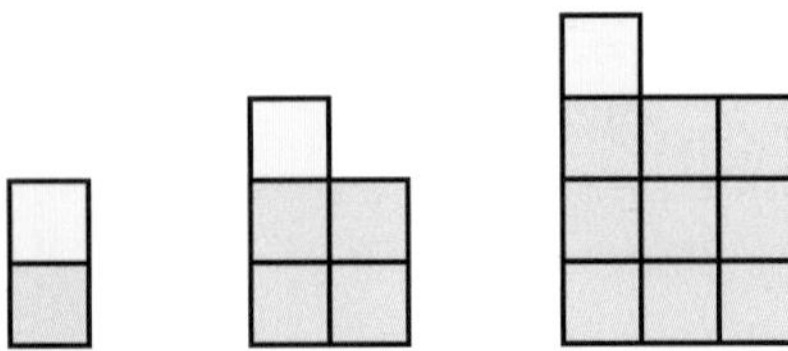

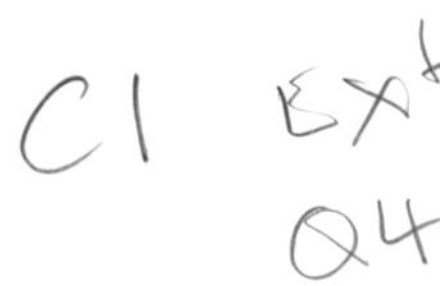

a How many blue squares will there be in the 4th pattern?

b What is the special name for the number sequence generated by the blue squares?

c How many yellow squares will there be in the 4th pattern?

d How many yellow squares will there be in the 100th pattern?

e Think about the sequences of numbers generated by the pattern of blue squares and the pattern of yellow squares. Is either of them an arithmetic sequence? Explain your answer.

f What calculation will you do to work out the total number of squares in the 6th pattern?

g Write down the sequence generated by the total numbers of squares in the first four patterns.

Q7e hint

Look back at Lesson 9.4 for the definition of an arithmetic sequence.

8 Susannah has plotted some coordinates from a function. 5a

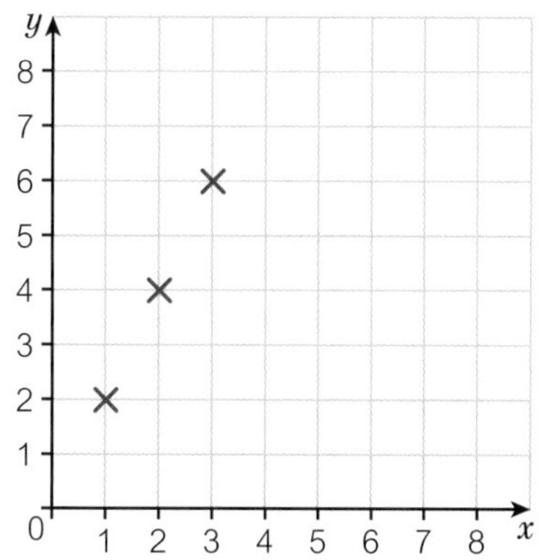

She used this function machine to generate the coordinates.

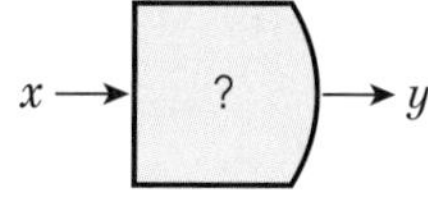

a What is the rule for the function machine?

b Write down the equation of the line through Susannah's points.

c Copy the grid and plot the graph of Susannah's function.

d Plot the graph of $y = x$ on the grid.

e Write down one difference and one similarity between the two graphs.

Q8a Strategy hint

Write down the coordinates of the points to help you.

Q8b hint

Write $y = \ldots$

Check that your equation works for two points on the line.

9 This question is about the function $y = 3x + 1$. 6c

a Copy and complete the table with the value of y for each value of x.

x	−2	−1	0	1	2	3
y	−5					

b Use the table of values to draw the graph of $y = 3x + 1$.
Draw a grid with x-axis from −2 to 3 and y-axis from −5 to 12.

c What is the point where the graph crosses the y-axis?

10 Repeat each step of Q9 using the function $y = 3x + 3$. 6c
Plot the graph on the same axes.

Discussion What is the same and what is different about the two graphs in Q9 and Q10?

11 **STEM** Jan is designing a building using a computer. She wants to place a stairwell at the midpoint of a wall. The wall goes from (5, 4) to (33, 6). What are the coordinates of the stairwell? 5a

Q11 hint

Look back to Lesson 9.3 for the definition of the midpoint.

5a **12** Write the nth term for a sequence where the terms are

a the multiples of 3 **b** the multiples of 6 **c** the even numbers.

5a **13** **a** The nth term for a sequence is $2n + 3$.
Finish the spreadsheet to find the first six terms of the sequence.

	A	B	C	D	E	F	G	H
1	Position	1	2	3	4	5	6	
2	Term	=B1*2+3	=C1*2+3					

b Use a spreadsheet to generate the first six terms in each sequence.

i $2n + 2$ **ii** $2n - 5$ **iii** $2n + 10$

c What do you notice about the term-to-term rule for the sequences in part **b**?

5a **14** Use a spreadsheet to answer this question.

Step 1: Type a number into cell **A1**.

Step 2: In cell **A2**, type the formula **=(A1+4)/2**. Press **Enter**.

Step 3: Click and drag cell **A2** down using its bottom-right hand corner, so the formula repeats itself.

a Describe in words what the formula does.

b What do you notice about the numbers in the sequence?

c What happens if you change the number in cell **A1**?

d Repeat this process with a similar formula, replacing **+4** with a different number. What happens?

e **Reasoning** Use the spreadsheet to plot a graph of the sequence generated in Q14d. Write a sentence about the shape of the graph.

Q14e Strategy hint

Look at the shape of the graph. When do the y-coordinates stop changing?

5a **15** Write the nth term for a sequence where the terms

a include 24 and 33 **b** are not whole numbers.

5a **16** Look at this sequence of dominoes.

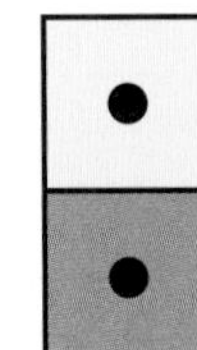 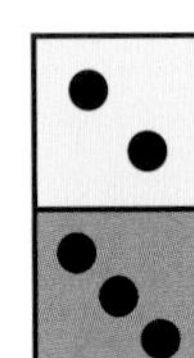 

a How many dots will be in the yellow section of the next domino?

b What is the term-to-term rule for the sequence of dots in the pink sections?

c Draw the next domino in the sequence.

d In words, write a rule to explain how to work out the number of dots in the pink section when you know the number of dots in the yellow section.

e Complete this function machine.

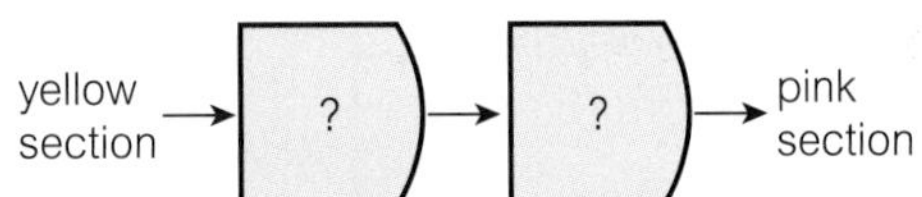

f Use the function machine to write down an algebraic function using y and p.

g You can use these dominos to generate coordinates: (yellow, pink). The first domino will have coordinates (1, 1). What will the next three pairs of coordinates be?

h Plot the four pairs of coordinates on a grid.

17 Find the nth term of each of these sequences. 5a

a 9, 18, 27, …

b 7, 14, 21, …

c 100, 200, 300, …

Key point

The nth term is sometimes called the **general term**.

18 Find the first five terms and the 100th term of each sequence. 5a

a **general term** $n - 4$

b general term $n^2 + 1$

c general term $2n - 6$

d general term $200 - n^2$

19 **Problem-solving / Reasoning** Look at these sequences. 6c

A 2, 5, 8, 11, 14, 17, 20, … B 1, 2, 4, 8, 16, 32, …

C 4, 5, 6, 7, 8, 9, 10, … D 3, 12, 27, 48, 75, …

a Which ones are arithmetic sequences?

b Plot a graph for each sequence using a computer.

c What do you notice about the graphs of the arithmetic sequences?

d Here is another sequence.

1, 5, 1, 5, 1, 5, …

Sketch what you think its graph will look like.

Now plot the sequence using a computer. Were you correct?

Q19b hint

In a spreadsheet, type each sequence into a separate column, highlight the column, and click the line graph icon.

Q19d Literacy hint

Sketching a graph means drawing it without rulers or numbers on the axes. It helps you see the shape of a graph quickly.

Investigation Real / Problem-solving / STEM

Strontium-90 is a radioactive isotope found in spent nuclear fuel. It has a half-life of 29 years. This means that after 29 years, half of the atoms will have decayed, forming a new element. After another 29 years, half of the remaining atoms will have decayed. Strontium-90 can be very harmful to animals and humans. If a field is exposed to 128 grams of strontium-90, how many years would you wait before planting in the field again?

Strategy hint

Use this table to help keep track of the amount of strontium-90. How else could you display this information?

Time (years)	0	29	58	87	116	145	174
Amount of strontium-90 left (g)	128	64					

Hint

Think about how the strontium is distributed over the field and about how many grams of strontium-90 are considered to be safe. 1 gram? 2 grams? None?

Discussion Will nuclear waste ever stop being radioactive?

20 **Reflect** Sandra says 'Sequences and straight-line graphs are all about following patterns.'
Look back at the work you have done in this unit. Write three sentences that describe how what you have learned is all about 'following patterns'.

Reflect

9 Unit test

4c **1** Write down the next term in each of these sequences.

a 0, 50, 100, 150, … **b** 17, 15, 13, 11, … **c** 1, 10, 100, 1000, …

4b **2** Write down the term-to-term rule and the next three terms for each of these sequences.

a 100, 90, 80, 70, … **b** 40, 52, 64, 76, …

c 8, 9.5, 11, 12.5, … **d** $\frac{1}{2}, \frac{1}{4}, \frac{1}{8}, \frac{1}{16}, \ldots$

4b **3** Write down the missing numbers in these sequences.

a ___ , 7, ___, 17, 22, ___ **b** ___, 3, 6, 12, 24, ___

4a **4** Sushma makes a bracelet from beads.

It grows like this.

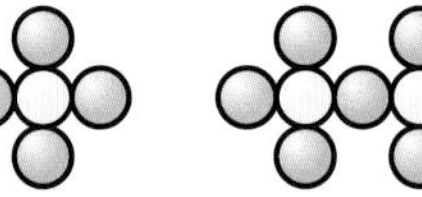

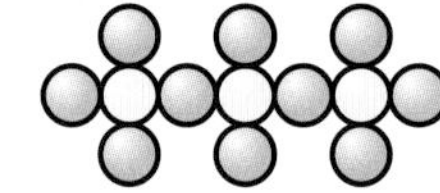

a Copy and complete this table.

Number of flowers	1	2	3	4	5
Number of beads	5	9			

b Describe the term-to-term rule of the sequence.

5c **5** Write down the coordinates of points A, B, C and D.

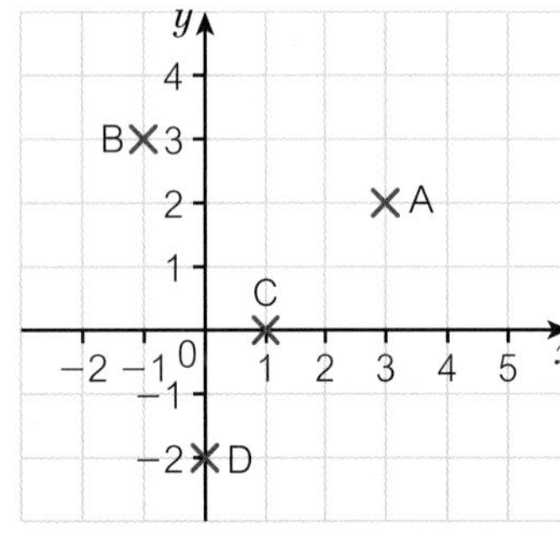

5a **6** Jemima generates this table of coordinates from an experiment.

x	1	2	3	4	5
y	3	3	3	3	3

a Copy this grid and plot the coordinate pairs.

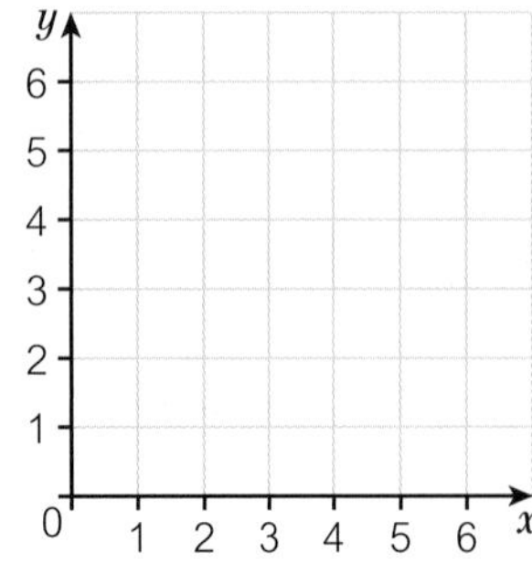

b Draw a line through the points. What is the equation of the line?

c Copy and complete this sentence.

When $x = 50$, the y-coordinate is ___.

7 a Copy and complete this table of values for the graph of $y = 2x + 1$. 5a

x	1	2	3	4	5
y	3	5			

b What is the y-coordinate when the x-coordinate is 10?

8 a Complete this table of values for the graph of $y = 3x - 3$. 5a

x	1	2	3	4
y				

b Draw a grid with x- and y-axes from 0 to 10 and plot the graph of $y = 3x - 3$.

9 a Find the position-to-term rule for this sequence. 5a

Position in sequence	1	2	3	4	5
Term	0.5	1	1.5	2	2.5

b Use your rule to find the 10th term and the 50th term.

c What is the nth term of this sequence?

10 Write the first five terms of the sequence whose nth term is 5a

a $3n + 4$ b $6 - n$ c $n^2 + 6$ d $100 - n^2$

11 Look at your sequences from Q10. Which of them are arithmetic sequences? 5a

12 Look at this sequence: 4, 8, 12, 16, … 5a

a Write down the next three terms of the sequence.

b Write a formula for the nth term of the sequence.

13 a Copy the table of values from Q8. Complete it for i $y = x$ ii $y = 3x$ 6c

b Copy the grid from Q6. Plot the graph of i $y = x$ ii $y = 3x$.

c Write down the coordinates of the point where the two lines meet.

Challenge

14 Investigate the number of squares in each of these shapes.
Use the steps below to begin.

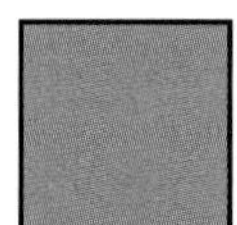 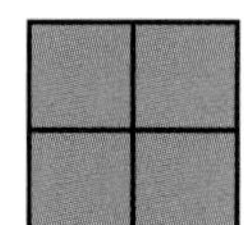 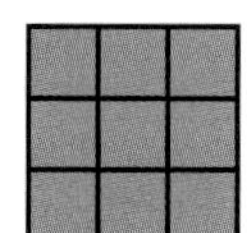 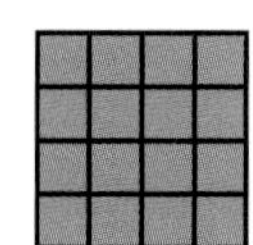

a Write a sequence for the *total* number of squares you can see at each stage.

b Use your sequence to predict the *total* number of squares in the 5th shape.

c Can you find a way of working out the *total* number of squares in the 6th pattern using your answer to part **b**?

d Can you find any other number patterns in these shapes?

Q14a hint
Don't forget to count squares made of smaller squares.

Q14b hint
Draw the 5th shape to test your answer.

Q14c Strategy hint
Use a systematic method for counting the total number of squares.

15 **Reflect** Write a heading 'Five important things about sequences and graphs'.
Now look back at the work you have done in this unit and list the five most important things you think you have learned.
For example, you might include:

- words (with their definitions)
- methods for working things out
- mistakes you made (with tips on how to avoid them in future).

Reflect

10 Transformations

MASTER

Check P261 | Strengthen P263 | Extend P267 | Test P271

10.1 Congruency and enlargements

You will learn to:
- Identify congruent shapes
- Use the language of enlargement
- Enlarge shapes using given scale factors
- Work out the scale factor given an object and its image.

CONFIDENCE

Why learn this? Logo designers must think about what a logo will look like when enlarged from their small computer screen on to big advertisements.

Fluency
Work out
- 6 × 3
- 5 × 2
- 8 × 4
- 7 × 5

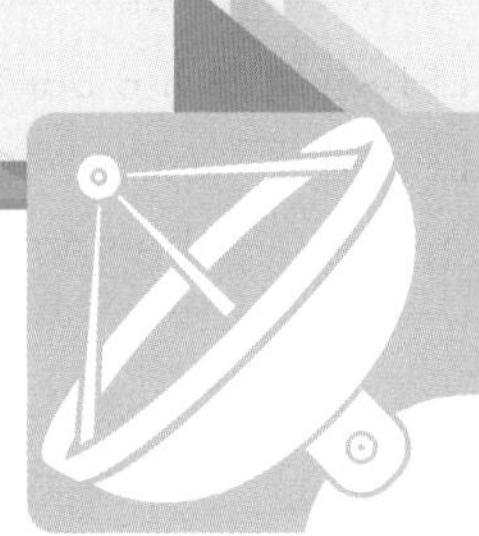

Explore
Does Andy Warhol use congruency in any of his art works?

Exercise 10.1

Warm up

1 Which one of these shapes is not the same as the other two?

a A  B  C

b A 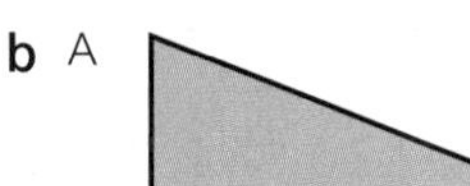 B 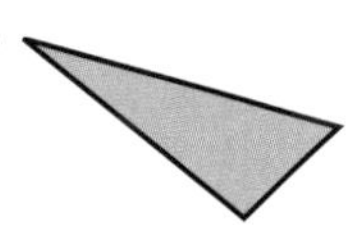 C 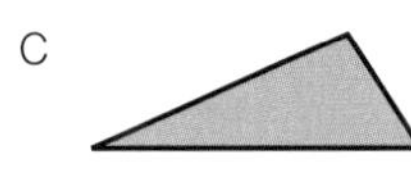

2 Copy and complete

a 2 × □ = 8   b □ × 3 = 12   c 18 ÷ 6 = □   d 15 ÷ □ = 5

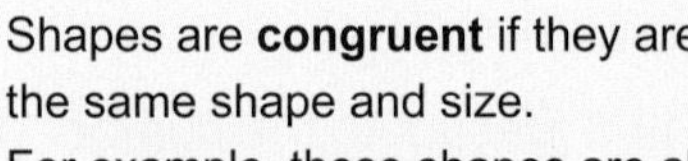

Key point
Shapes are **congruent** if they are the same shape and size.
For example, these shapes are all congruent.

5c

3 Copy each shape. Shade in the **congruent** parts of each shape in the same colour.
The first one is done for you.

a 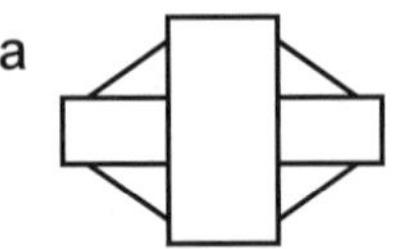 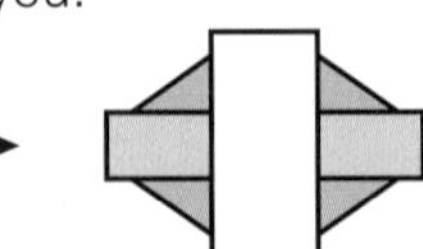

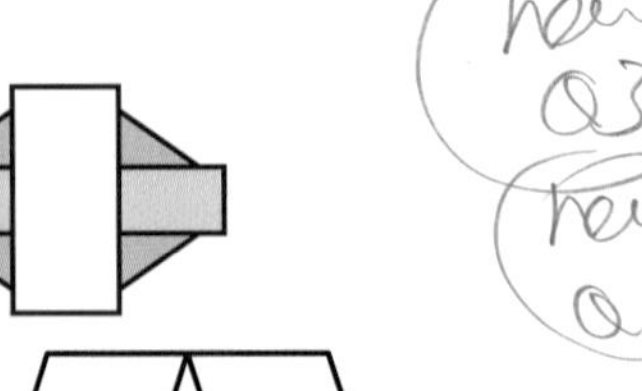

b  c 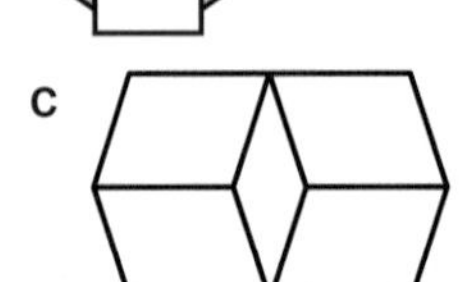

Q3a hint
The blue triangles are the same shape and size.
The green rectangles are the same shape and size.

Discussion What congruent shapes are there in the flags of Great Britain?

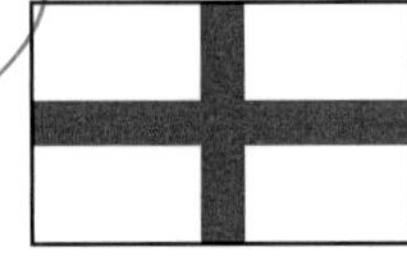 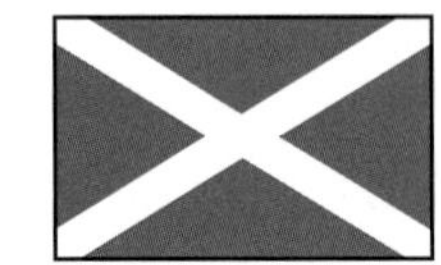  

Topic links: Ratio, Perimeter, Measures, Multiplying whole numbers

4 Copy each shape. Then split them into the number of congruent shapes shown. The first one is done for you.

a four congruent triangles

b two congruent triangles

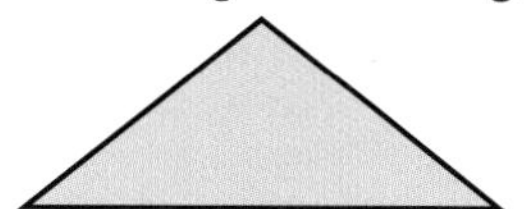

c two congruent triangles and two congruent rectangles

Key point

In congruent shapes, **corresponding sides** and **corresponding angles** are equal.

5c

5 These two triangles are congruent.
Copy and complete these sentences.

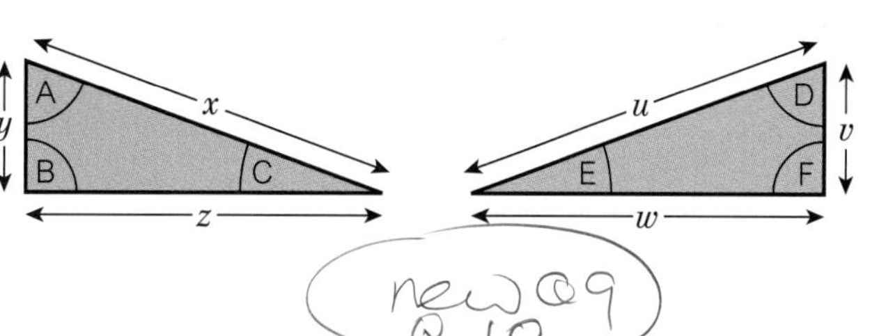

a Length x is the same as length □.

b Length □ is the same as length v.

c Angle A is the same size as angle □.

d Angle □ is the same size as angle E.

5c

Investigation **Problem-solving**

A pentomino is a shape made from five congruent squares that touch side-to-side.
The diagram shows four congruent pentominoes.
Design your own pentominoes.
How many *different* pentominoes can you draw?
How many congruent pentominoes are there for each design?

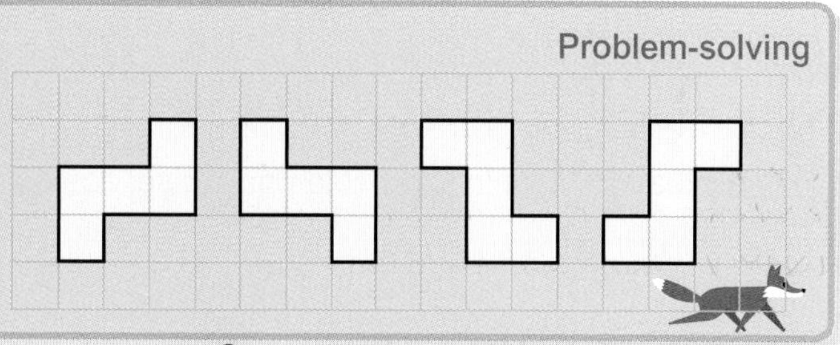

Worked example

Enlarge this shape by scale factor 2.

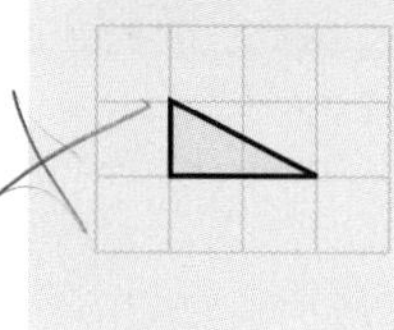

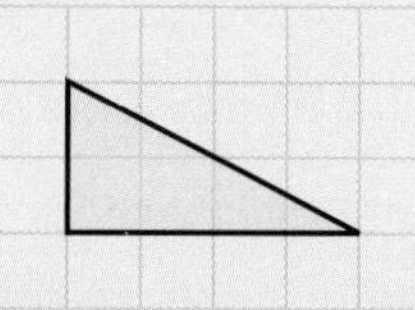

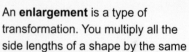

Multiply each side by 2.
Draw the height and base of the new triangle first, then join to make the third side.

Key point

An **enlargement** is a type of transformation. You multiply all the side lengths of a shape by the same number.
The number that the side lengths are multiplied by is called the **scale factor**.

6 Copy each shape on to squared paper. Now **enlarge** each shape by
i scale factor 3 ii scale factor 5.

a

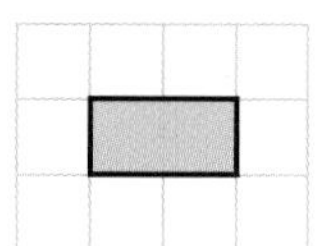

b

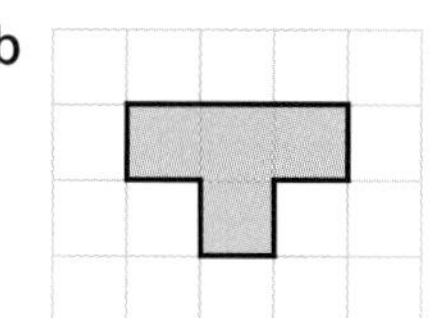

c

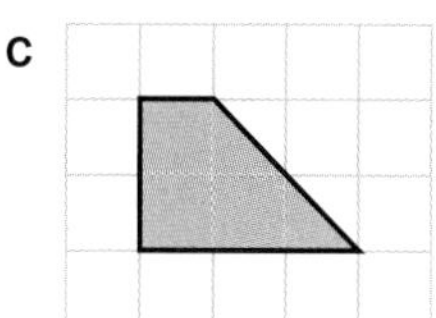

Q6 hint

For scale factor 3, multiply each side length by 3.
For scale factor 5, multiply each side length by 5.

5b

7 Real In a school play, to make the actors look very small, all the props need to be 15 times their real size.

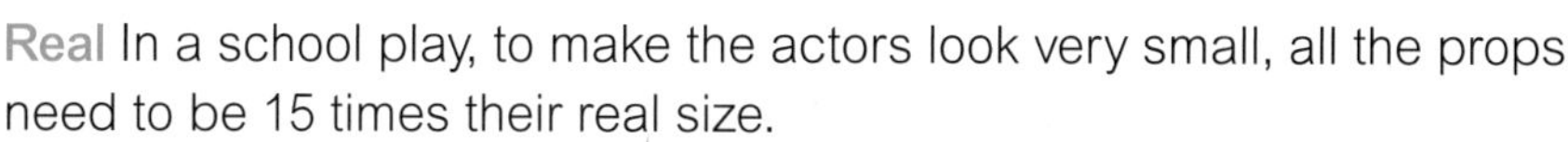

a A real DVD case is 15 mm thick. How thick is a DVD case in the play? Give your answer in centimetres.

b A real calculator is 14 cm long. How long is a calculator in the play? Give your answer in metres.

5a

5a

8 For each of these enlargements:

- **i** Write the ratio of the length of a side of the **object** to the corresponding length in the **image**. Give the ratio in its simplest form.
- **ii** Write the scale factor of the enlargement.

a

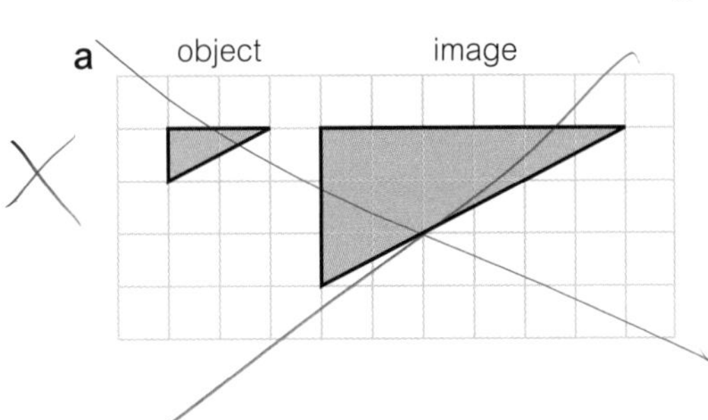

b

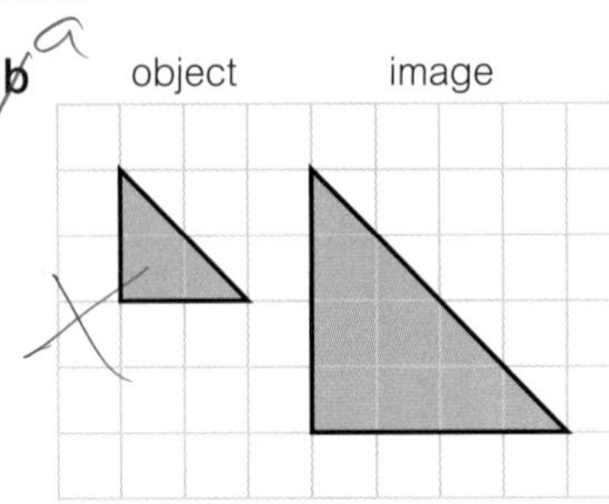

c

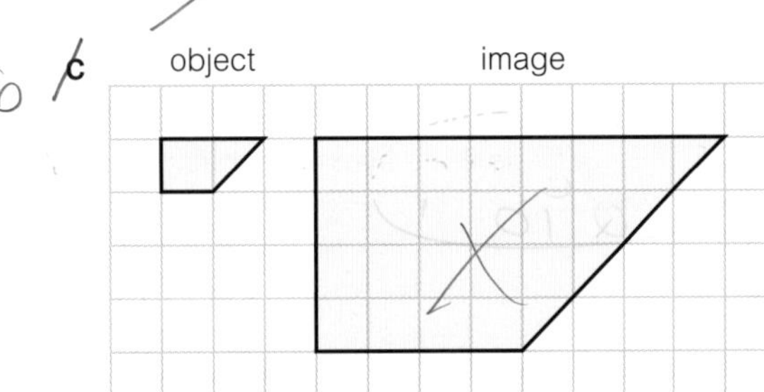

> **Key point**
> The original shape is called the **object**. The enlarged shape is called the **image**.

> **Q8a hint**
> **i** Length of object = 2 squares, length of image = 6 squares, so ratio is 2 : 6, which simplifies to 1 : □.
> **ii** All side lengths of image are 3 times longer than side lengths of object, so scale factor is □.

5a

9 Real / Reasoning A photo printing service offers the following size prints.

5″ × 5″, 7″ × 5″, 8″ × 6″, 8″ × 8″, 16″ × 12″

Sam wants two prints, one to be an enlargement of the other.

- **a** Would a 16″ × 12″ print be an enlargement of an 8″ × 6″ print? Explain your answer.
- **b** Would an 8″ × 6″ print be an enlargement of a 7″ × 5″ print? Explain your answer.
- **c** Would an 8″ × 8″ print be an enlargement of a 5″ × 5″ print? Explain your answer.

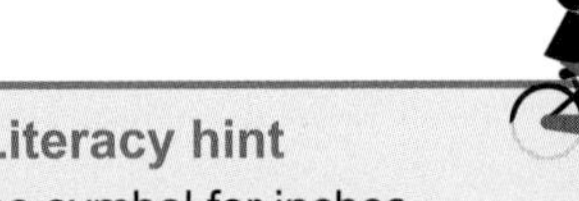

> **Q9 Literacy hint**
> ″ is the symbol for inches.

> **Q9 Strategy hint**
> You might want to draw a sketch to help you.

5a

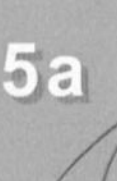

10 Reasoning Amanda says, 'If I enlarge a shape by scale factor 3, the perimeter of the image will be 3 times the perimeter of the object.'
Is she correct? Explain your answer.

Explore

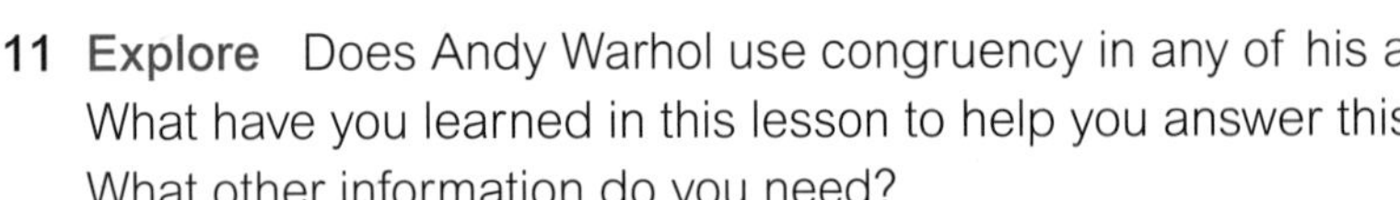

11 **Explore** Does Andy Warhol use congruency in any of his art works?
What have you learned in this lesson to help you answer this question?
What other information do you need?

Reflect

12 **Reflect** Look back at this lesson.
List all the new mathematical words you learned. Be careful to spell them correctly.
Write a short definition for each of them. Where possible, use your own words.
Draw your own shape or shapes with each definition, to show what you mean.

10.2 Symmetry

You will learn to:
- Recognise line and rotational symmetry in 2D shapes
- Identify all the symmetries of 2D shapes
- Identify reflection symmetry in 3D shapes.

CONFIDENCE

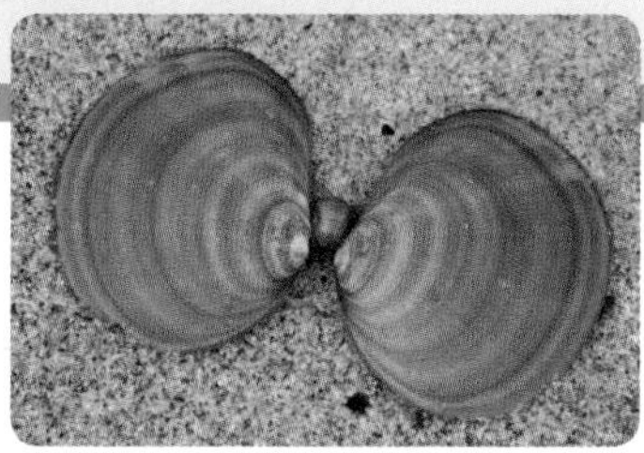

Why learn this? Understanding reflection helps us to appreciate the patterns found in nature. This is useful in science as well as drawing, painting and design.

Fluency
Which of these shapes can be folded exactly onto themselves?

Explore
Is there symmetry in snowflakes?

Exercise 10.2

Warm up

1 Read this without a mirror.

gnitirw rorrim si sihT

2 Write down the names of these 3D shapes.

a 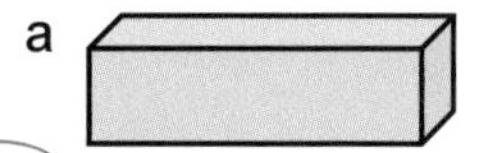 b 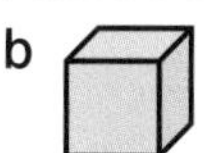 c 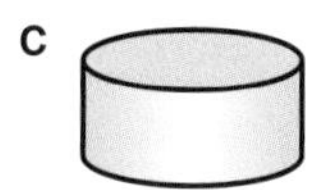 d 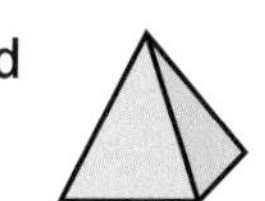

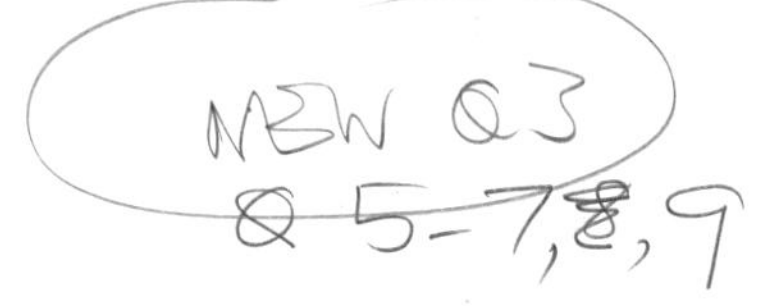

4a

3 Copy these shapes. Draw all the **lines of symmetry** (mirror lines) on the shapes.
The first one is done for you.

a 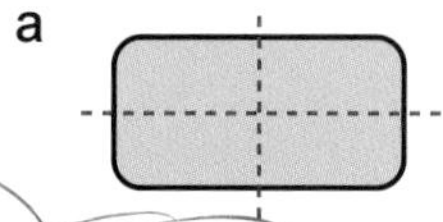 b  c  d 

Key point
If you fold a shape along a **line of symmetry**, both halves fit onto each other perfectly.

Discussion Which has more lines of symmetry, a square or a circle?

Investigation — **Problem-solving / Reasoning**

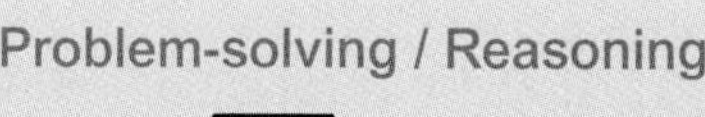

Here is a regular hexagon made from right-angled triangles.
How many ways can you shade two triangles so that the hexagon is symmetrical?
Now try with four triangles.
Can you make the hexagon symmetrical by shading three triangles? Explain your answer.

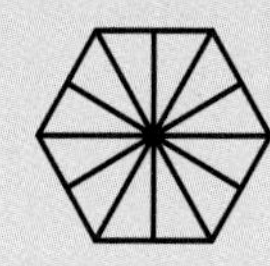

5c

4 Write down the **order of rotational symmetry** of each of these shapes.

a 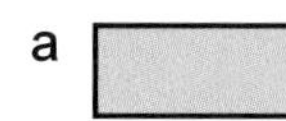  b  c   d 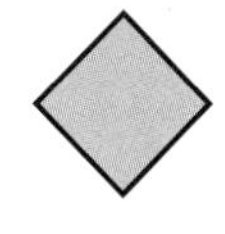

e 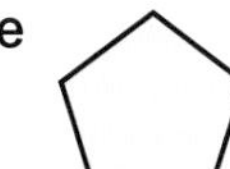 f  g  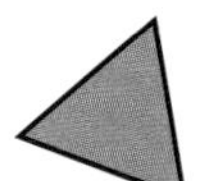 h  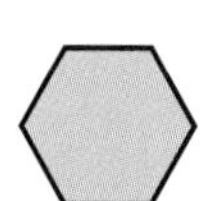

Key point
When a shape is rotated through 360°, the **order of rotational symmetry** is the number of times it looks exactly the same as it did at the start.

Discussion What is the order of rotational symmetry of these shapes?

5a

5 Copy and complete this table.

Shape	Number of lines of symmetry	Order of rotational symmetry
parallelogram	0	2
rectangle		
square		
kite		
rhombus		
isosceles triangle		
equilateral triangle		

Q5 hint

Draw each shape first.
A parallelogram has no lines of symmetry and order of rotational symmetry 2.

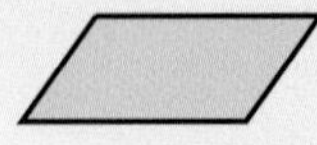

6c

6 This cuboid has reflection symmetry. The three **planes of symmetry** are shaded red in the diagrams.

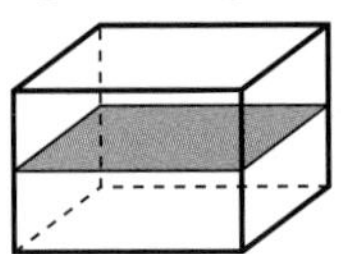 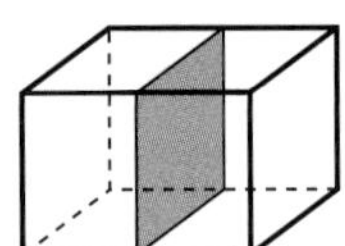 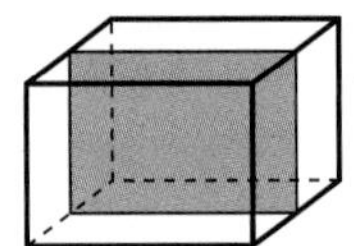

Which of these 3D shapes have reflection symmetry?

A 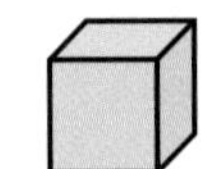 B 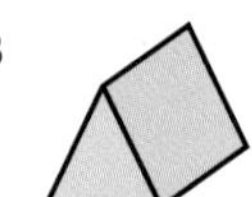 C  D  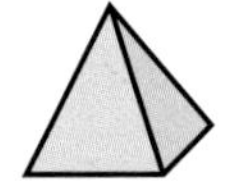

Key point

If a 3D shape has reflection symmetry, the mirror line is called a **plane of symmetry**.

Discussion Does a cylinder have reflection symmetry? What about a dice?

6c

7 STEM Scientists look for symmetry in molecules because it can help predict chemical properties.

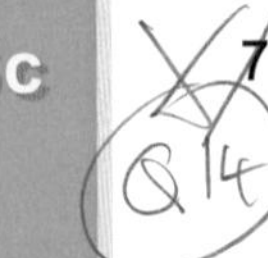

water

a How many planes of symmetry does this 3D model of a water molecule have?

b How many planes of symmetry does this 3D model of an ammonia molecule have?

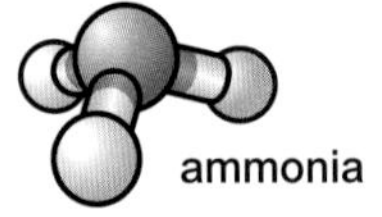
ammonia

Q7 Literacy hint

The formula for water is H_2O – two hydrogen atoms and one oxygen atom.
Ammonia (NH_3) is used in cleaning products and to make fertiliser.

Explore

8 Explore Is there symmetry in snowflakes?
What have you learned in this lesson to help you answer this question?
What other information do you need?

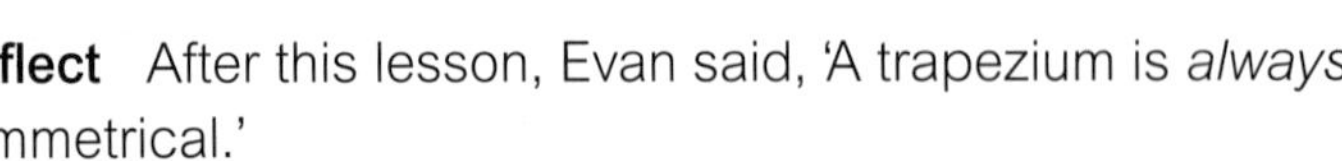

Reflect

9 Reflect After this lesson, Evan said, 'A trapezium is *always* symmetrical.'
Robyn said, 'A trapezium is *never* symmetrical.'
Claire said, 'A trapezium is *sometimes* symmetrical.'
Who is correct, Evan, Robyn or Claire?
Use what you have learned in this lesson, and what you know about trapeziums, to explain.

Q9 hint

You could draw diagrams to help you.

Subject links: Science (Q7)

10.3 Reflection

You will learn to:

- Recognise and carry out reflections in a mirror line
- Reflect a shape on a coordinate grid
- Describe a reflection on a coordinate grid.

CONFIDENCE

Why learn this?
Symmetry and reflections are used a lot in science. Scientists use the reflection of light to measure distances, such as the distance between the Earth and the Moon.

Fluency
Here is a coordinate grid.

- Which is the x-axis and which is the y-axis?
- What are the coordinates of the point A?

Explore
What symmetries are there in nature?

Exercise 10.3

Warm up

1 Here is a coordinate grid.
Make a copy of the grid, then plot and label these points.
A (3, 2) B (−2, 3) C (2, −1) D (−1, −2)

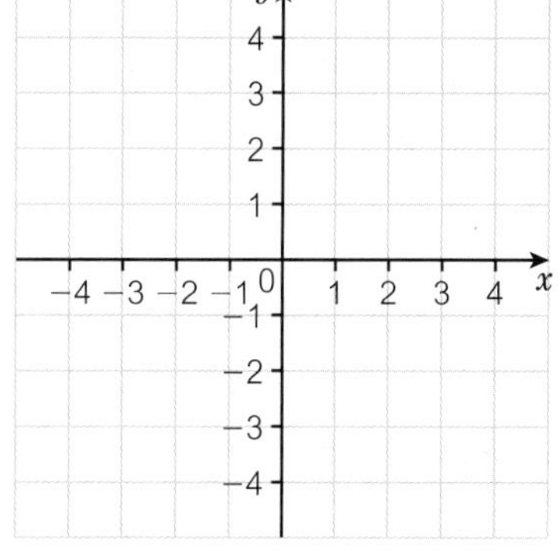

2 The diagram shows some straight lines on a coordinate grid.
Match each line with the correct equation.
$x = -2$ $y = 1$ $x = 3$ $y = -2$ $y = x$

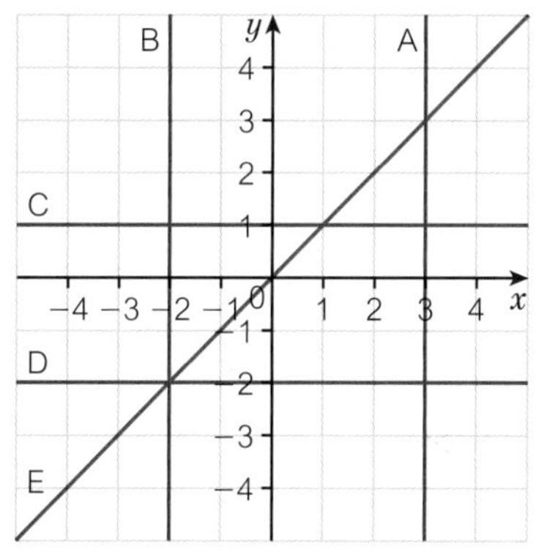

Worked example

Is the green shape a correct reflection of the yellow shape in the mirror line? Give a reason for your answer.

No. The green shape should be one square from the mirror line, not on the mirror line.

This is a correct reflection.

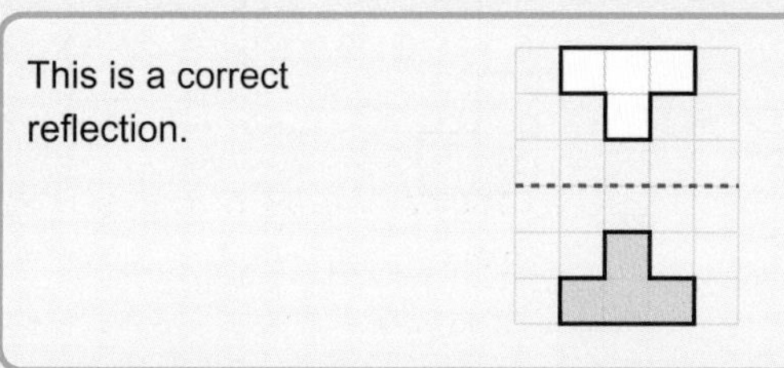

Key point
A **reflection** is a type of **transformation**. You reflect shapes in a **mirror line**.
All points on the object are the same distance from the mirror line as the points on the image, but on the opposite side.

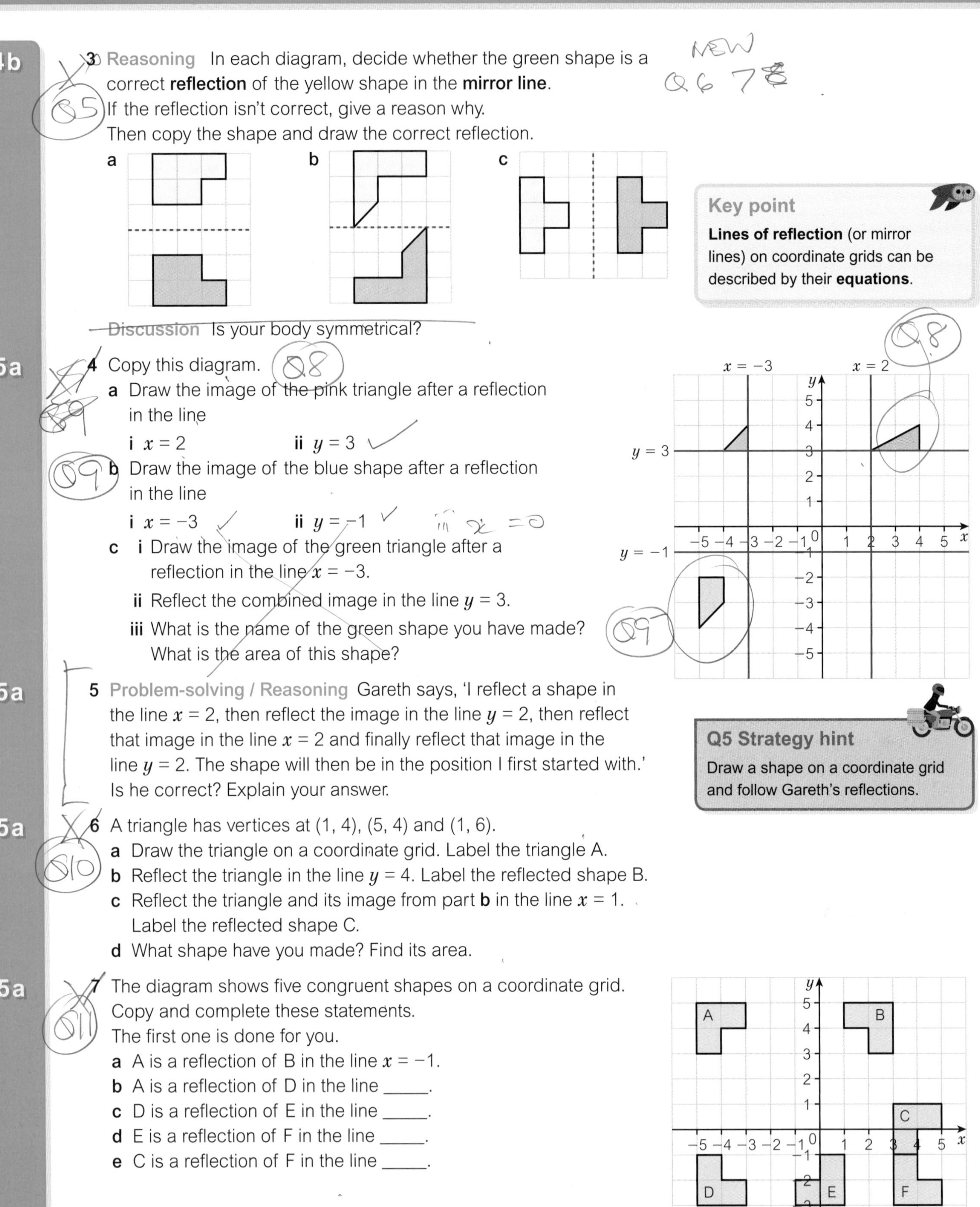

4b **3 Reasoning** In each diagram, decide whether the green shape is a correct **reflection** of the yellow shape in the **mirror line**.
If the reflection isn't correct, give a reason why.
Then copy the shape and draw the correct reflection.

a b c

Key point

Lines of reflection (or mirror lines) on coordinate grids can be described by their **equations**.

Discussion Is your body symmetrical?

5a **4** Copy this diagram.

a Draw the image of the pink triangle after a reflection in the line
 i $x = 2$ ii $y = 3$

b Draw the image of the blue shape after a reflection in the line
 i $x = -3$ ii $y = -1$

c i Draw the image of the green triangle after a reflection in the line $x = -3$.
 ii Reflect the combined image in the line $y = 3$.
 iii What is the name of the green shape you have made? What is the area of this shape?

5a **5 Problem-solving / Reasoning** Gareth says, 'I reflect a shape in the line $x = 2$, then reflect the image in the line $y = 2$, then reflect that image in the line $x = 2$ and finally reflect that image in the line $y = 2$. The shape will then be in the position I first started with.'
Is he correct? Explain your answer.

Q5 Strategy hint

Draw a shape on a coordinate grid and follow Gareth's reflections.

5a **6** A triangle has vertices at (1, 4), (5, 4) and (1, 6).

a Draw the triangle on a coordinate grid. Label the triangle A.

b Reflect the triangle in the line $y = 4$. Label the reflected shape B.

c Reflect the triangle and its image from part **b** in the line $x = 1$. Label the reflected shape C.

d What shape have you made? Find its area.

5a **7** The diagram shows five congruent shapes on a coordinate grid.
Copy and complete these statements.
The first one is done for you.

a A is a reflection of B in the line $x = -1$.

b A is a reflection of D in the line _____.

c D is a reflection of E in the line _____.

d E is a reflection of F in the line _____.

e C is a reflection of F in the line _____.

Topic links: Coordinates, Equations of lines, Area

Subject links: Science (Explore)

8 Copy this diagram.
Draw the images of these shapes after reflection in the lines given.
The first one is done for you.

a Shape A in the line $y = x$.
b Shape B in the line $y = -x$.
c Shape C in the line $y = x$.
d Shape D in the line $y = -x$.

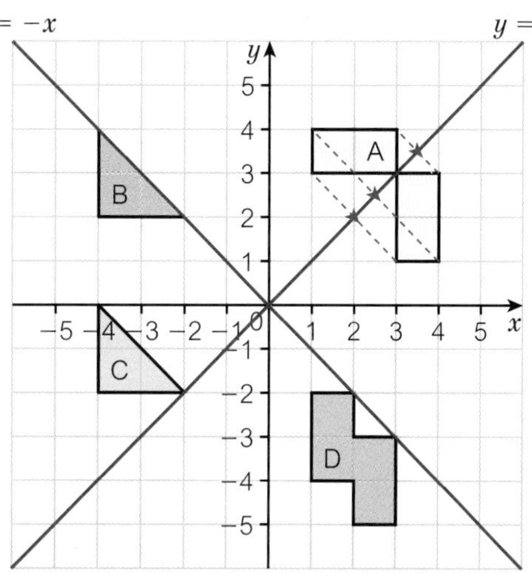

Key point

When you reflect a shape in the line $y = x$ or $y = -x$, count the distance from each vertex of the shape to the line, then count the same again the other side of the line.

Investigation **Reasoning**

In the diagram, triangle ABC has been reflected in the line $y = x$ to become triangle DEF.

1 Write down the coordinates of the vertices of the triangles ABC and DEF. Put your answers in a table like this.

	Coordinates of vertices					
Object ABC	A	(1, 4)	B		C	
Image DEF	D		E		F	

a What do you notice about the coordinates of the object and its image?
b Draw other shapes on a coordinate grid and reflect them in the line $y = x$.
c What can you say about the coordinates of each object and its image?

2 On a new grid, label the vertices of the green triangle and reflect it in the line $y = -x$.
a What do you notice about the coordinates of the object and its image?
b Draw other shapes on the grid to check this is always true.

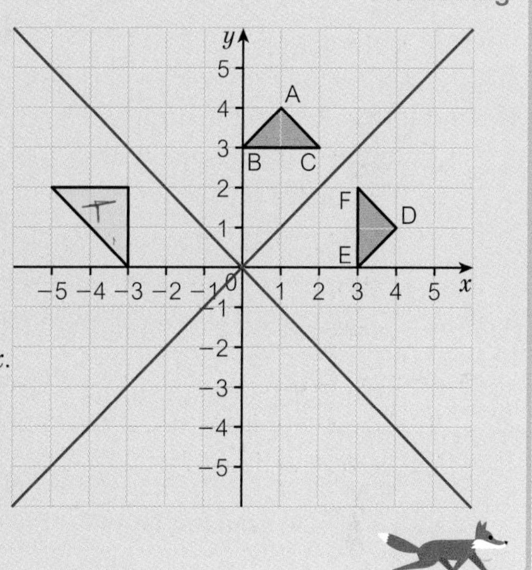

9 **Explore** What symmetries are there in nature?
Look back at the maths you have learned in this lesson.
How can you use it to answer this question?

10 **Reflect**

a Look back at Q3.
Write down the steps you took to draw the reflected images.
You might begin with:
Step 1: I found the mirror line.

b Look back at Q8.
Write down the steps you took to draw the reflected images.

c Which steps were the same or different for Q3 and Q8?

10.4 Rotation

You will learn to:

- Describe and carry out rotations on a coordinate grid.

CONFIDENCE

Why learn this? For fairground rides and moving machinery you need to be able to trace the path of an object as it rotates around a fixed point to check that it won't collide with anything.

Fluency
Name these regular polygons.

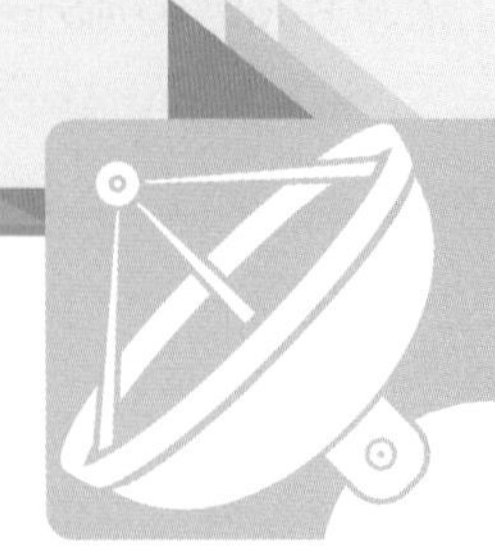

Explore
What does it mean when scientists say, 'The Earth rotates about its axis'?

Exercise 10.4

Warm up

1 Here is a coordinate grid. Write down the coordinates of the points A to G.

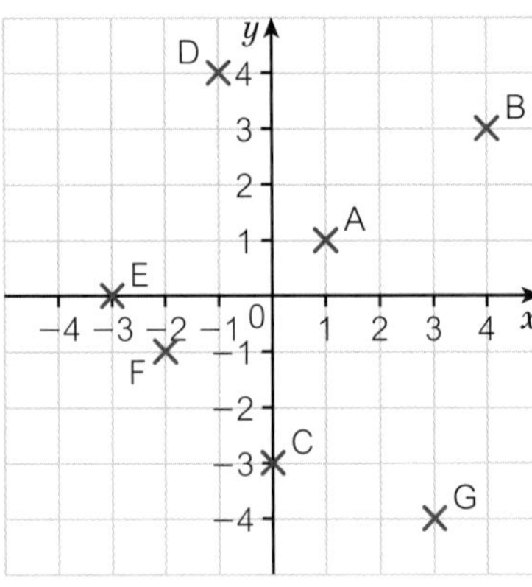

2 How many degrees are there in a
 a full circle
 b half circle
 c quarter circle?

3 Which of these arrows is **clockwise** and which is **anticlockwise**?

A

B

Q3 hint
Think of the numbers on a clock face. As you move clockwise the numbers increase.

4a

4 The grid shows four flags.

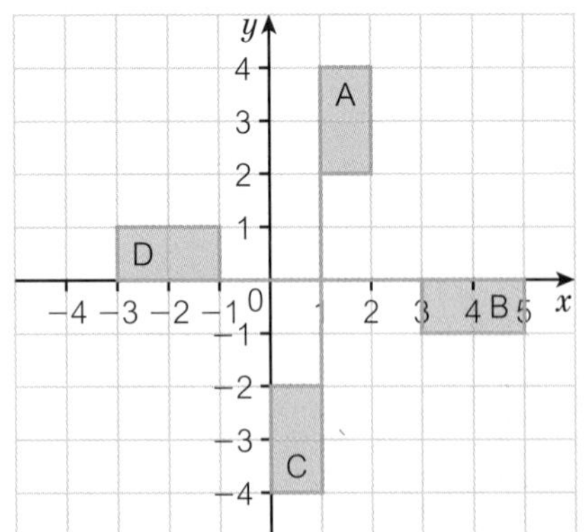

Describe these **rotations**. The first one is done for you.
 a A onto B
 90° rotation clockwise about (1, 0)
 b B onto A c D onto B d C onto D
 e A onto C f C onto A

Key point
A **rotation** is a type of transformation. You rotate a shape by turning it around a point, called the **centre of rotation**. To describe a rotation you also need to give the **angle** and direction (**clockwise** or **anticlockwise**).

 Topic links: Area **Subject links:** Science (Explore)

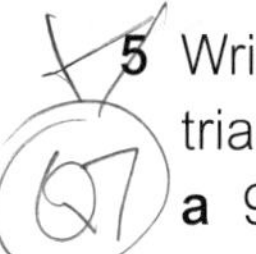

5 Write down the coordinates of the triangle after a rotation of

a 90° **clockwise** about (0, 1)

b 90° **anticlockwise** about (0, 0)

c 180° about (0, 0).

Discussion Why do you not need to state clockwise or anticlockwise with a 180° rotation?

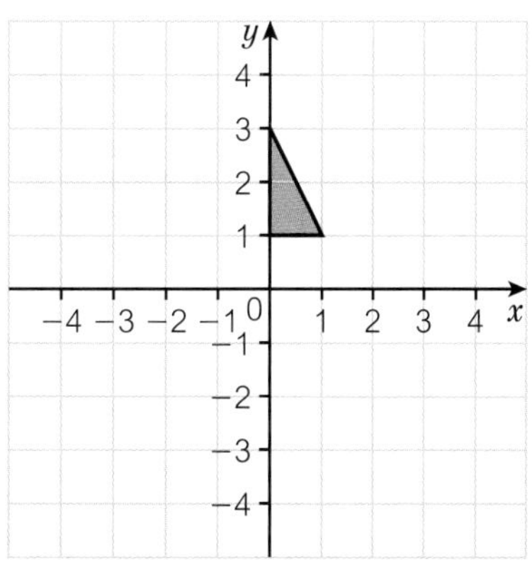

5c

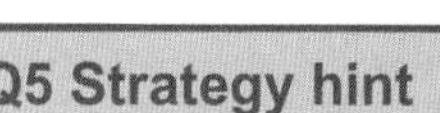

Q5 Strategy hint

Copy the grid and use tracing paper to draw the rotations to help you.

6 a Plot and join the points (0, 0), (2, 2), (4, 0) and (2, −2) on a coordinate grid. Label the shape A.

b Name the shape you have drawn and work out its area.

c Rotate your shape by 90°, 180° and 270° clockwise about (0, 0), showing all of these on the same diagram.

d Describe the shape you now have ~~and work out its area.~~

5c

Q6 hint

Use tracing paper to help you.

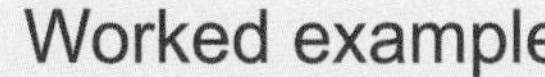

Worked example

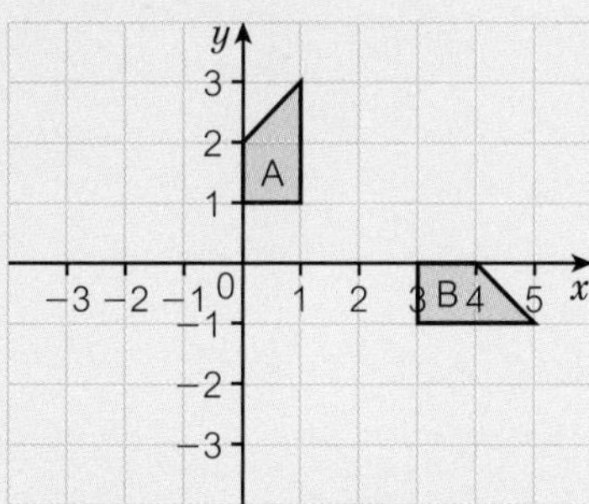

Describe the rotation that takes A to B

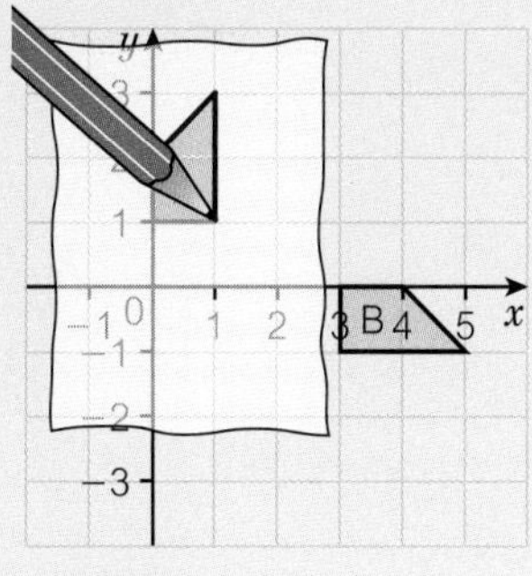

Trace the object shape

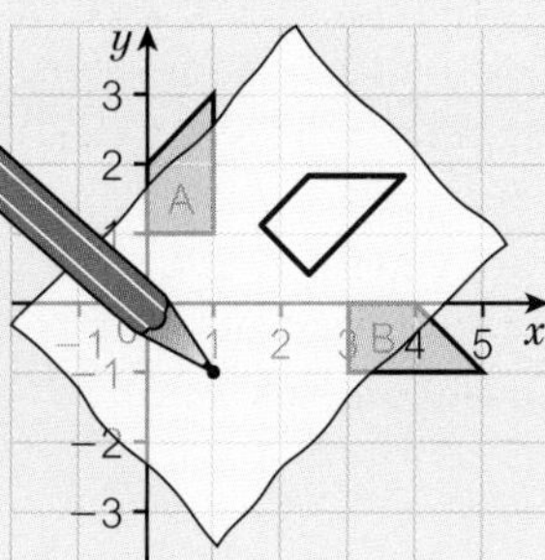

Rotate the tracing holding a point fixed with your pencil. Repeat for different points until your tracing ends up on the image

Give the direction, angle and centre of rotation.

Rotation clockwise through 90° about (1, −1).

7 Describe the rotation that takes

a A onto B

b A onto C

c B onto D

d B onto E

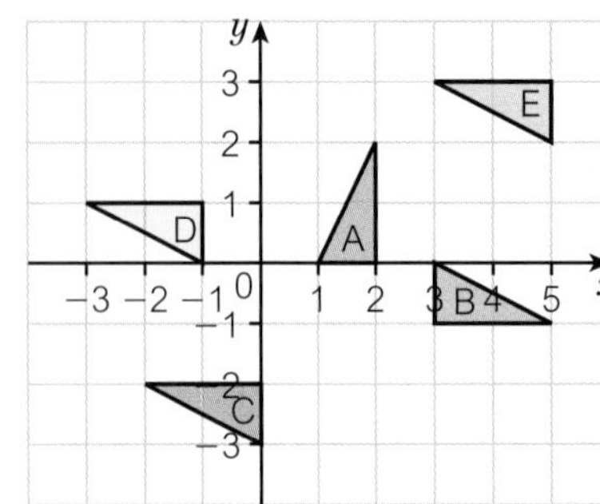

Q7 hint

Use tracing paper to help you.

Investigation — Real / Reasoning / Problem-solving

Work with a partner to solve this puzzle.

In the game of Tetris you have these seven different shape tiles that you need to rotate and move to fit in the grid without leaving any gaps.

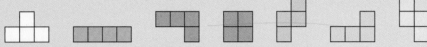

1 What is the order of rotation of each of the different shape tiles?

2 Is the purple shape a rotation of the green shape? Explain your answer.

In this particular game you use the tiles one at a time in the order shown above.

So far one tile of each has been used and fitted into the grid.

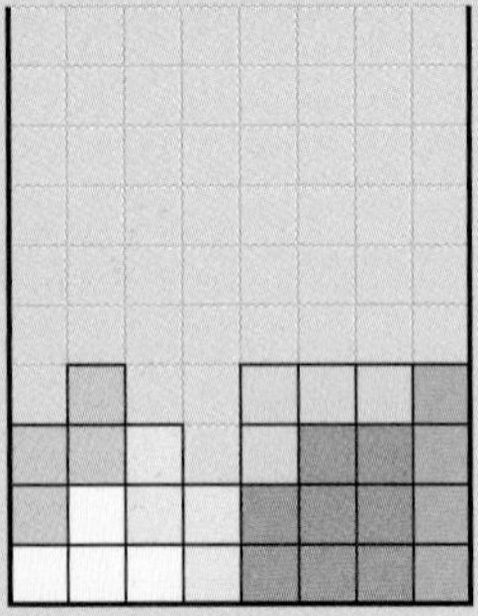

3 Carry on fitting one tile at a time into the grid.

4 Is it possible to complete the grid without leaving gaps?

5 Would it be easier if the tiles came in a different order?

6 Start with an empty grid and choose the order of the tiles and see if you can complete the grid without leaving any gaps.

Explore

8 **Explore** What does it mean when scientists say, 'The Earth rotates about its axis'?
What have you learned in this lesson to help you answer this question?
What other information do you need?

Reflect

9 **Reflect** In the last lesson you learned about reflection. In this lesson you learned about rotation. Look carefully at some of the shapes you reflected and rotated in these lessons. Can a reflection of a shape and a rotation of a shape give the same result?

10.5 Translations and combined transformations

You will learn to:
- Translate 2D shapes
- Transform 2D shapes by combinations of rotations, reflections and translations.

CONFIDENCE

Why learn this? With 3D modelling software, designers can use transformations to move objects around their screen.

Fluency
Which arrow points left and which points right?

A 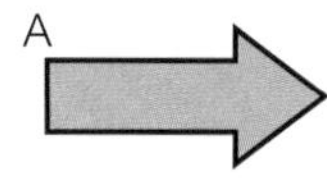 B 

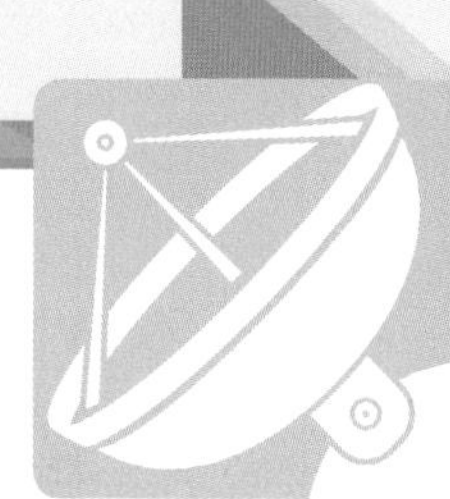

Explore
How many squares of a chessboard can the knight land on?

Exercise 10.5

Warm up

1 The diagram shows a green triangle on a coordinate grid.
Copy the diagram.
  a Draw the image of the triangle after a reflection in
    i $y = 1$ ii $x = -1$
  b Draw the image of the triangle after a rotation of
    i 90° clockwise about (0, 2) ii 180 about (2, 2).

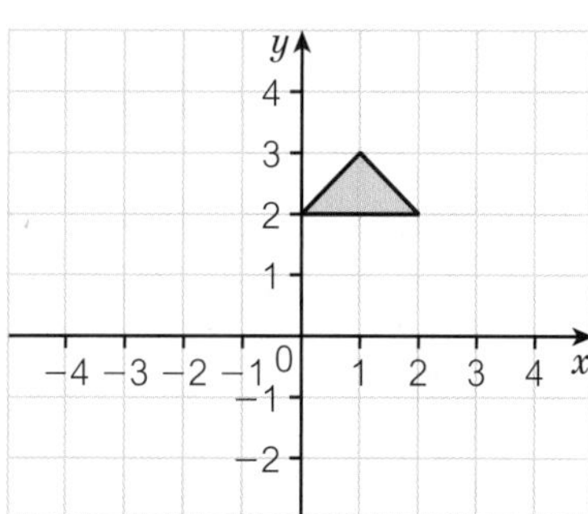

4a

2 Copy the orange shape on squared paper. Draw the image of the shape after these **translations**. Part **a** is done for you.

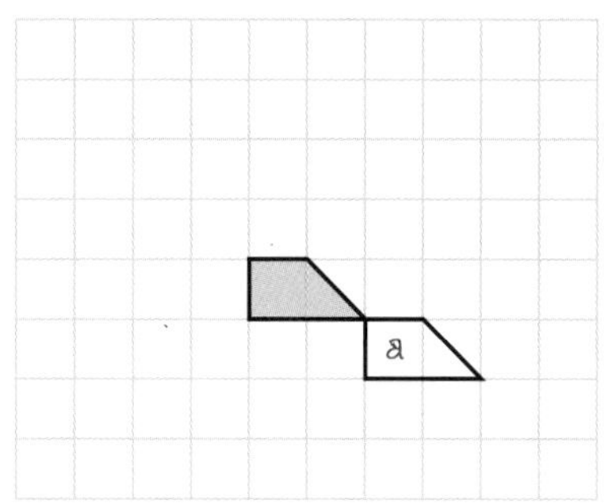

  a 2 squares right, 1 square down b 3 squares right, 2 squares up
  c 1 square left, 3 squares up d 2 squares left, 2 squares down
  e 4 squares left

Key point
A **translation** of a 2D shape is a slide across a flat surface. To describe a translation you need to give the movement left or right, followed by the movement up or down.

Q2b Strategy hint
Choose a vertex (corner) of the object. Count 3 squares right and 2 squares up and mark that point. Draw the shape in its new position.

4a

3 **Reasoning** Charlie translates shape A 4 squares left and 2 squares down to make shape B, then translates shape B 3 squares right and 4 squares up to make shape C.
Charlie says, 'If I translate shape A 1 square left and 2 squares up, I'll end up with shape C.'
Is he correct? Explain your answer.

Q3 Strategy hint
Draw a shape on a grid, label it A, then follow Charlie's instructions.

4a **4** Real In the game of chess, in one turn, a knight can move either 2 squares left or right followed by 1 square up or down, or 1 square left or right followed by 2 squares up or down. Copy this grid and show the different positions where the knight could move to in one turn.

5c **5** The diagram shows four triangles on a coordinate grid.

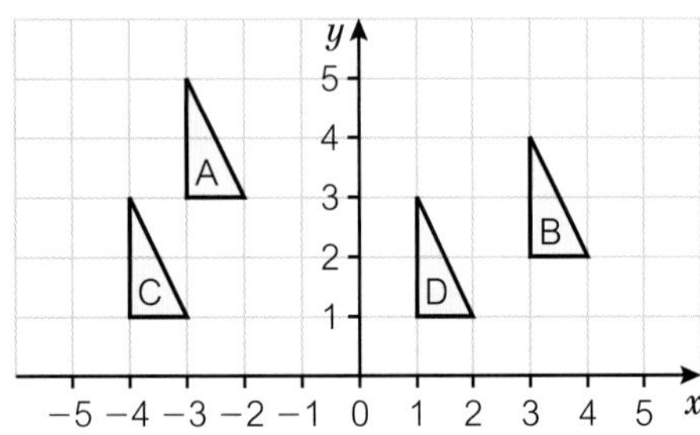

A
B
C
D

Triangle A to triangle B is a translation 6 squares right and 1 square down.
Describe each of these translations.

a triangle A to triangle D

b triangle A to triangle C

c triangle D to triangle B

Q5 hint

When describing a translation, always give the along movement first, then the up or down movement.

Worked example

Transform the red shape using this two-step transformation: translation 3 squares left and 1 square up, followed by a reflection in the line $x = -2$.

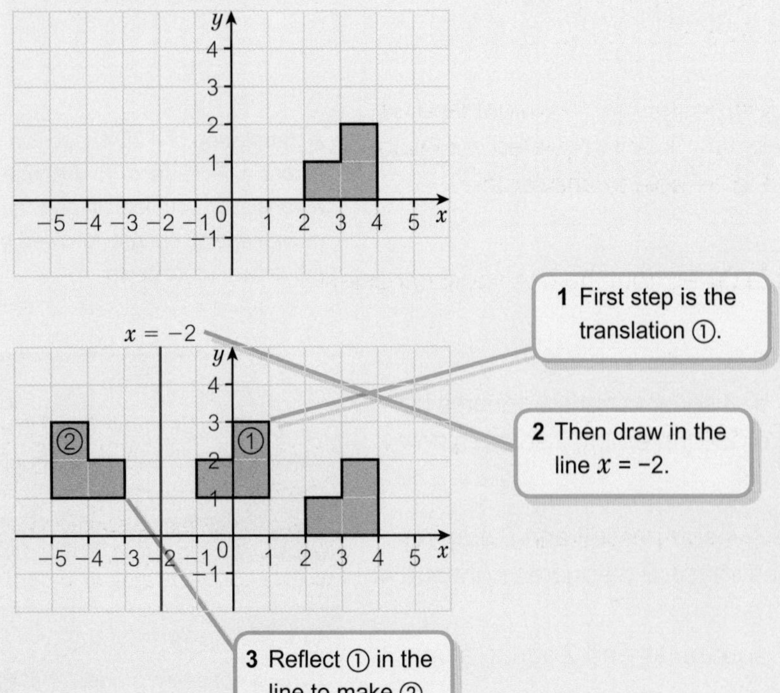

$x = -2$
①
②
3 Reflect ① in the line to make ②.

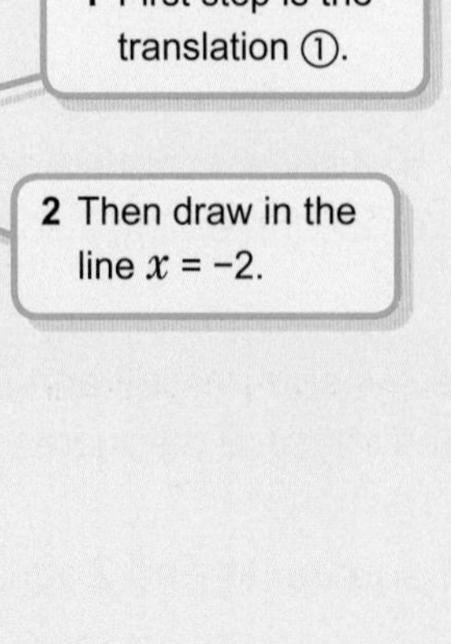

1 First step is the translation ①.
2 Then draw in the line $x = -2$.

Topic links: Equations of lines, Coordinates

6 Copy this diagram four times.
On separate copies, transform the triangle using these two-step transformations.

a Translation 4 squares right followed by a reflection in the line $y = 1$.

b Rotation 180° about (−1, 2) followed by a reflection in the line $x = 2$.

c Rotation 90° anticlockwise about (−1, 4) followed by a translation 2 squares right and 4 squares down.

d Reflection in the line $x = -1$ followed by a rotation 90° clockwise about (−1, 1).

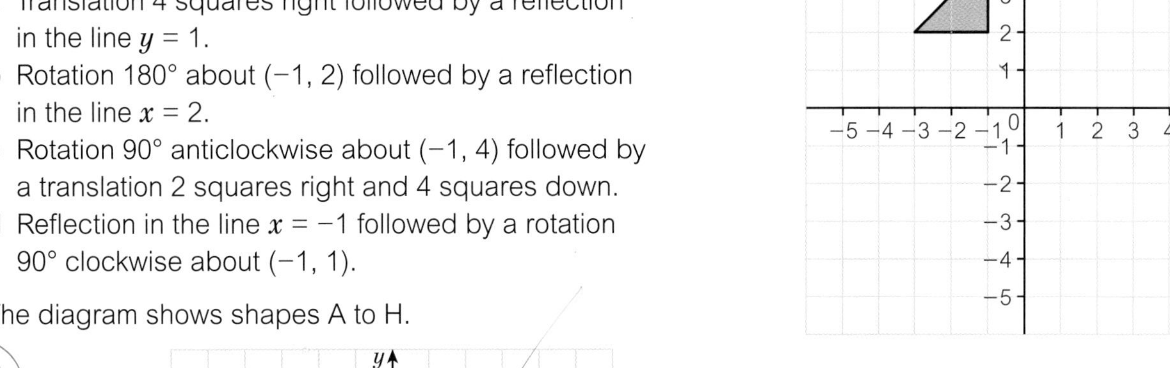

7 The diagram shows shapes A to H.

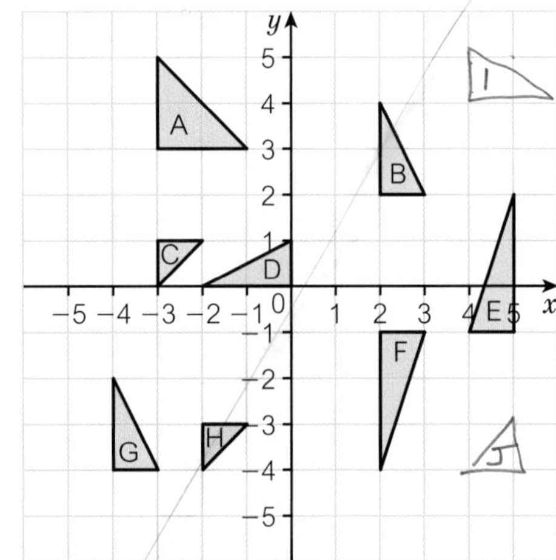

Write true (T) or false (F) for each of these statements.
If your answer is false, explain why.

a G is a translation of B.

b F is a reflection of B.

c E is a rotation of F.

d H is a translation of C.

e G is a rotation of D.

f C is a reflection of A.

g A is a translation of B.

h B is a rotation of D.

Key point

When a shape is transformed by a translation, rotation or reflection, the image has exactly the same side lengths and angles as the object.

8 Explore How many squares of a chessboard can the knight land on?
Is it easier to explore this question now you have completed the lesson?
What further information do you need to be able to answer this?

9 Reflect Write these transformations in order, from the one you find easiest to the one you find hardest:

A Reflection in horizontal line

B Reflection in vertical line

C Rotation of 90° (either clockwise or anticlockwise)

D Rotation of 180°

E Translation

Write a hint, in your own words, for the transformation you found the hardest.

Q9 Strategy hint

Look back at some of the transformation questions in this lesson to help you.

10 Check up

Shapes and symmetry

1 Write down the number of lines of symmetry for each of these shapes.

a 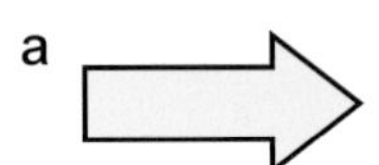 **b** 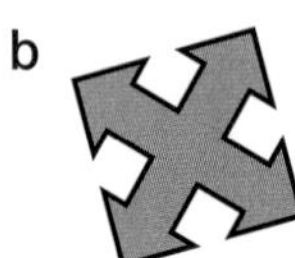 **c** 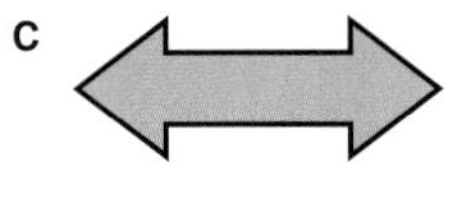 **d** 

2 Aaron says, 'A rectangle has these four lines of symmetry.'
Is Aaron correct? Explain your answer.

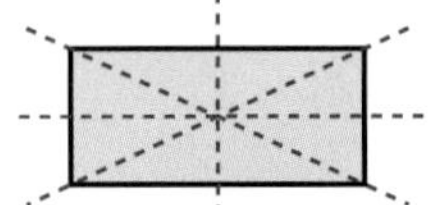

3 Which pairs of arrows are congruent?

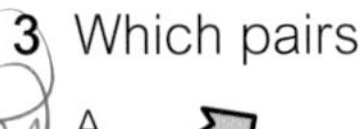

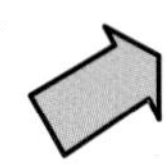

4 Write down the order of rotational symmetry of each of these shapes.

a 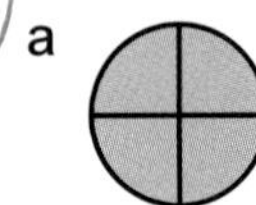 **b** 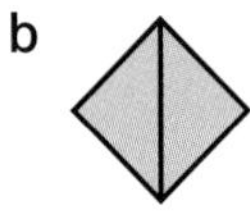 **c** 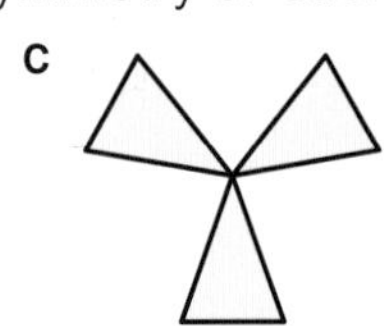

5 Copy and complete this table.

Shape	Number of lines of symmetry	Order of rotational symmetry
Square		
Equilateral triangle		
Parallelogram		
Kite		

Translations, reflections and enlargements

6 Copy this shape on to squared paper.
Draw the image of the shape after these translations.

a 3 squares right, 2 squares down. Label this shape A.

b 4 squares left, 1 square up. Label this shape B.

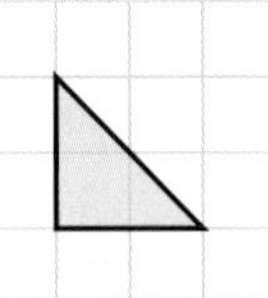

7 Describe each translation.

a shape A to shape B

b shape B to shape C

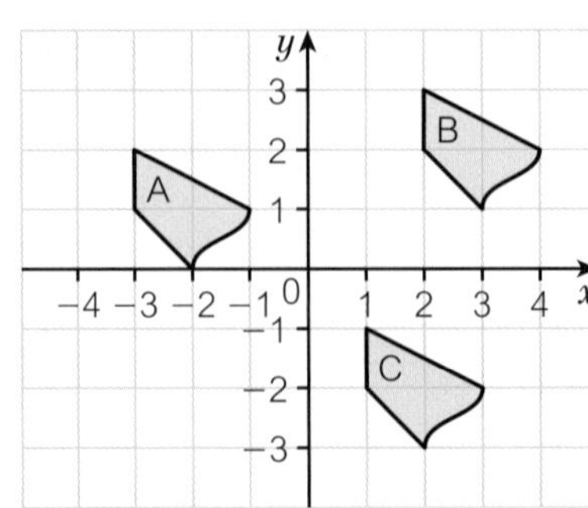

8 **a** Draw the original shape from Q6 enlarged by scale factor 2.

b Write down the ratio of the length of the sides of the original shape to the enlarged shape.

9 Copy this diagram.
Draw the image of the shape after a reflection in the line:
a $y = 1$. Label your reflected shape A.
b $x = -1$. Label your reflected shape B.

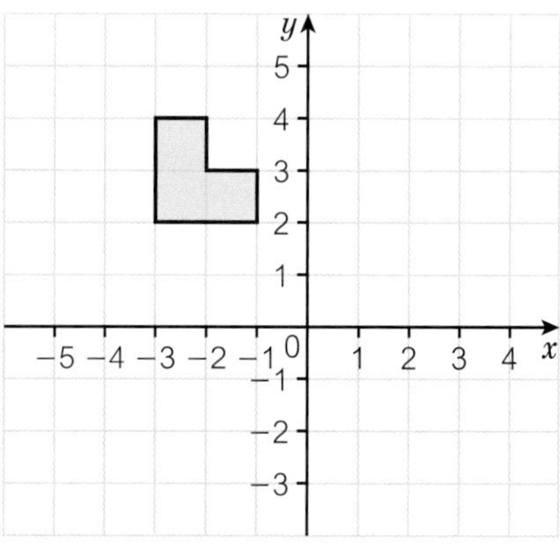

Rotations and combined transformations

10 Use your diagram from Q9.
Draw the image of the shape after these rotations.
a 90° clockwise about (–2, 1). Label this rotated shape A.
b 180° about (–3, 1). Label this rotated shape B.

11 The diagram shows two shapes A and B.
Shape A has been rotated to give shape B.
Arthur describes the rotation as
rotation, 90°, about (2, 1)
What is missing from Arthur's description?

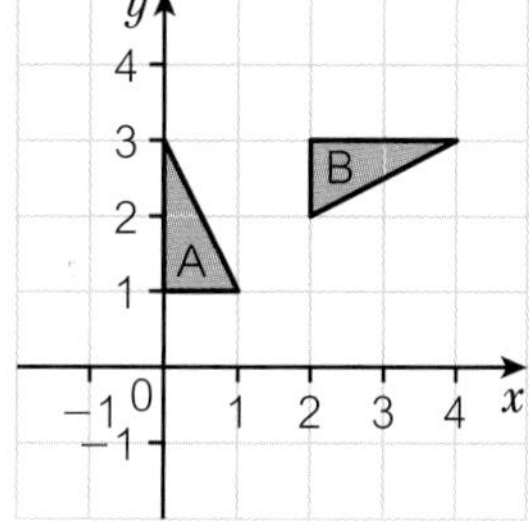

12 Copy this diagram and carry out these transformations on the shape.
a A translation 2 squares left and 1 square down followed by a reflection in the line $x = -1$.
b A rotation 90° anticlockwise about (2, 2) followed by a translation 2 squares right and 1 square up.

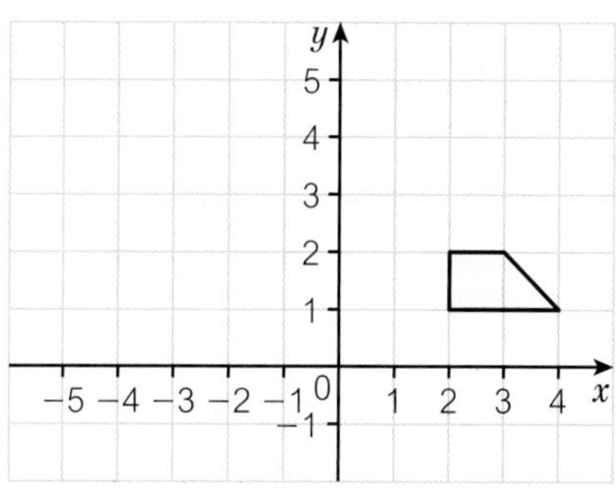

13 How sure are you of your answers? Were you mostly
Just guessing Feeling doubtful Confident
What next? Use your results to decide whether to strengthen or extend your learning.

Challenge

14 a Nigel says, 'Every shape that has 2 lines of symmetry also has order of rotational symmetry 2.'
Is Nigel correct? Explain your answer.
b Paul says, 'Every shape that has order of rotational symmetry 2 also has 2 lines of symmetry.'
Is Paul correct? Explain your answer.

10 Strengthen

You will:

- Strengthen your understanding with practice.

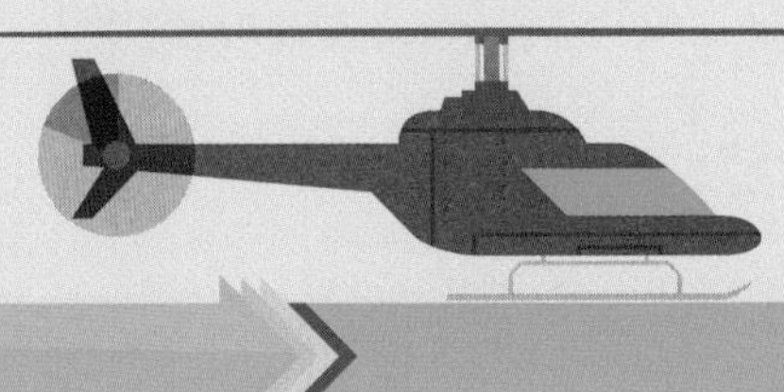

Shapes and symmetry

4a **1** Copy each shape and draw on the lines of symmetry.

a 1 line of symmetry

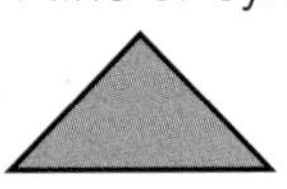

b 1 line of symmetry

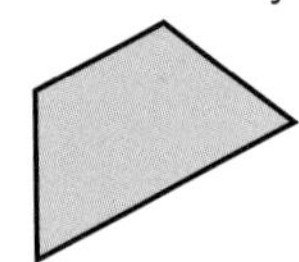

c 2 lines of symmetry

d 2 lines of symmetry

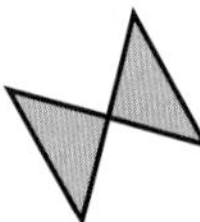

5c **2** How many lines of symmetry do each of these shapes have?

a 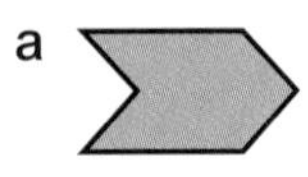 **b** 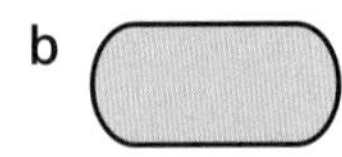 **c** 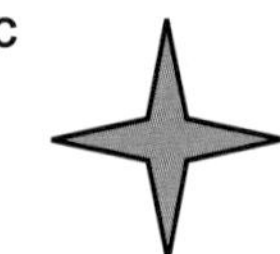 **d** 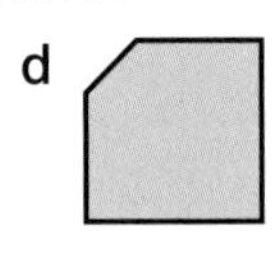

5c **3** Which of these shapes are congruent to shape A?

5c **4** Copy each shape and shade in the congruent parts of each shape in the same colour.

a 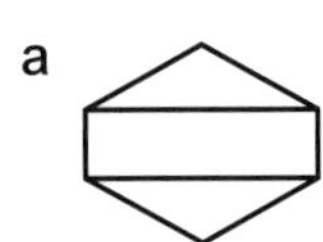 **b**  **c** 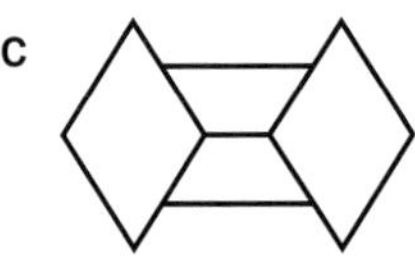

5c **5** Match the correct order of rotational symmetry card to each of these shapes.

A 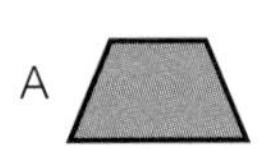 Order 4 B 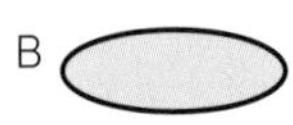 Order 3

Order 5 D 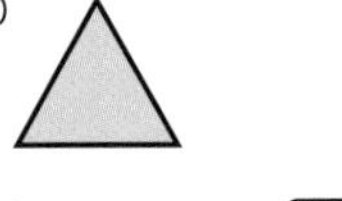 Order 1 C 

E  Order 2 

Q1a hint

Check using tracing paper.

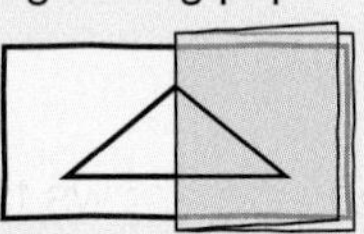

Q1c hint

The diagonal in a rectangle is *not* a line of symmetry.
You can use a mirror to check your line of symmetry by placing the mirror on the line.

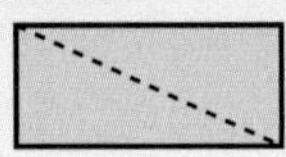

Q3 hint

You are looking for shapes that are the same size and shape as A.
Use tracing paper to trace shape A.
Which of the other shapes will your tracing fit onto exactly?

Q4a hint

In this shape only the triangles are congruent, so leave the rectangle blank.

Q5 hint

Trace each shape.
Turn the tracing paper through 360° and count how many times your tracing fits exactly over the shape.

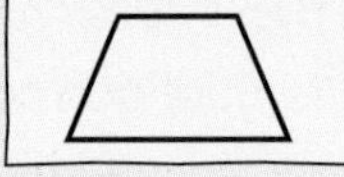

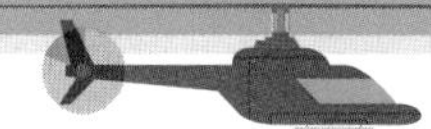

5c

6 Barney thinks this shape has order of rotational symmetry 1. Hannah thinks this shape has order of rotational symmetry 0. Who is correct? Explain your answer.

Q6 hint

Is it possible for a shape to fit onto itself 0 times?

5a

7 Copy and complete this table.

Shape	Number of lines of symmetry	Order of rotational symmetry
Rectangle		
Isosceles triangle		
Square		
Parallelogram		

Q7 Strategy hint

Draw each of the shapes.

Translations, reflections and enlargements

4a

1 The grid shows triangles A to E.
Describe the translation that takes

a A to B b B to C
c C to D d D to E
e E to A f E to C

Q1 hint

Choose one vertex (corner) of the shape. Give the number of squares right or left followed by the number of squares up or down.

4a

2 Copy this shape on to squared paper.
Draw the image of the shape after these translations.

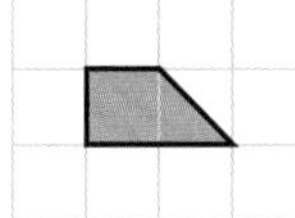

a 2 squares left, 1 square down. Label your translated shape A.
b 4 squares left, 3 squares up. Label your translated shape B.
c 1 square right, 4 squares down. Label your translated shape C.
d 3 squares right, 2 squares up. Label your translated shape D.

Q2a hint

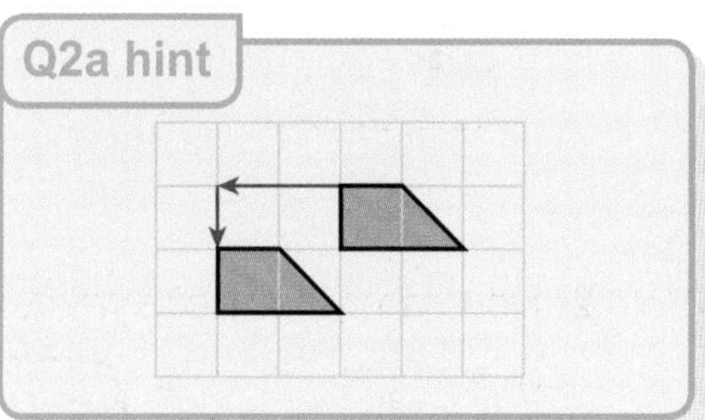

5a

3 Copy this diagram.
Draw the reflection of the triangle in the line

a $y = 1$. Label the image A. .
b $x = 2$. Label the image B.
c $y = 3$. Label the image C.
d $x = 0$. Label the image D.

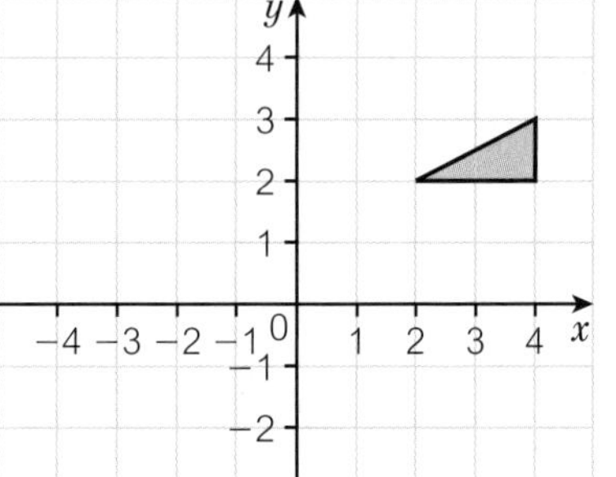

Q3a hint

Draw $y = 1$.
Check: put your finger at different points along the line $y = 1$. Do they all have a y-coordinate of 1?
Check your original shape and your reflection are the same distance from your line $y = 1$.

5a

4 Copy this shape on to squared paper.

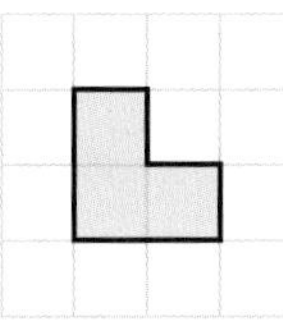

a i Enlarge the shape by a scale factor of 2.
ii Write down the ratio of the length of the sides of the original shape to the enlarged shape.

b i Enlarge the shape by a scale factor of 3.
ii Write down the ratio of the length of the sides of the original shape to the enlarged shape.

c i Enlarge the shape by a scale factor of 4.
ii Write down the ratio of the length of the sides of the original shape to the enlarged shape.

Q4a hint

Every 1 square on the original shape (object) is worth 2 squares on the enlarged shape (image).
object : image
1 : 2

Rotations and combined transformations

5c

1 Copy the diagram and draw the image of the triangle after these rotations.

a 90° anticlockwise about (0, 0). Label your rotated shape A.

b 90° clockwise about (2, 0). Label your rotated shape B.

c 180° about (0, 0). Label your rotated shape C.

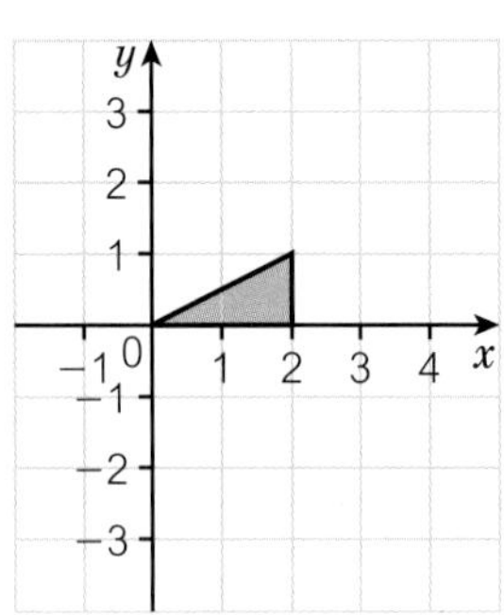

Q1a hint

Trace the triangle on tracing paper. Put your pencil on the point (0, 0) and turn your tracing paper 90° (quarter turn) anticlockwise.

Q1c hint

180° is half a turn.

5c

2 Copy this diagram.

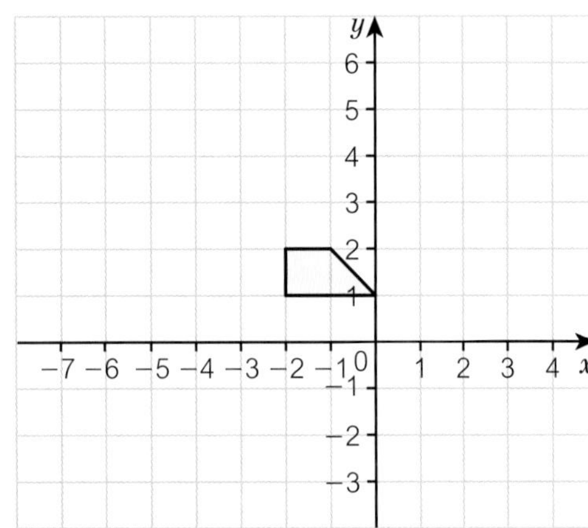

Do you have enough information to carry out these rotations?
If the answer is no, explain what extra information you need.
If the answer is yes, draw the image of the shape.

a Rotation 90° about (0, 1).

b Rotation 90° clockwise about (1, 1).

c Rotation 90° anticlockwise.

d Rotation clockwise about (0, 1).

e Rotation 180° about (1, 0).

f Rotation 90° anticlockwise about (−4, 2).

Q2 hint

For a rotation about a point, you must know

- angle of rotation
- direction of rotation (clockwise or anticlockwise)
- centre of rotation.

Q2e hint

Do you need clockwise or anticlockwise for a 180° rotation?

5a

3 Copy this diagram. Transform the shape using these transformations.

The first one is done for you.

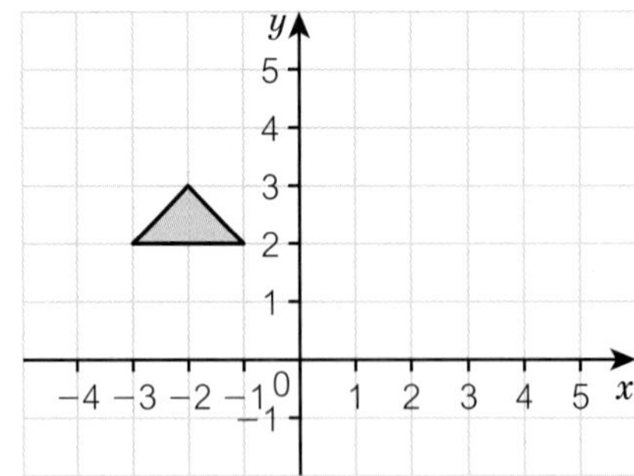

a A translation 3 squares right and 1 square up followed by a reflection in the line $y = 2$.

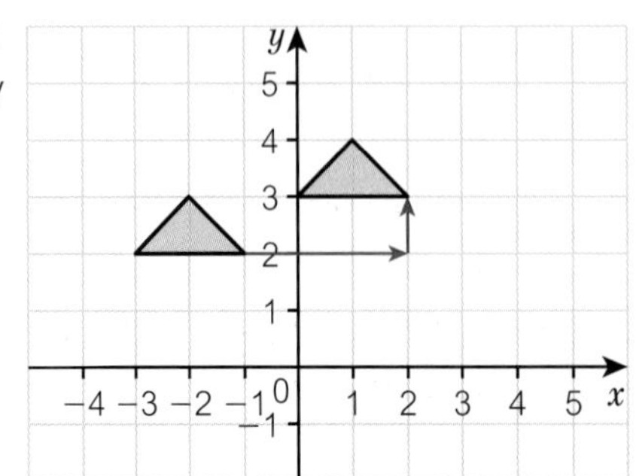

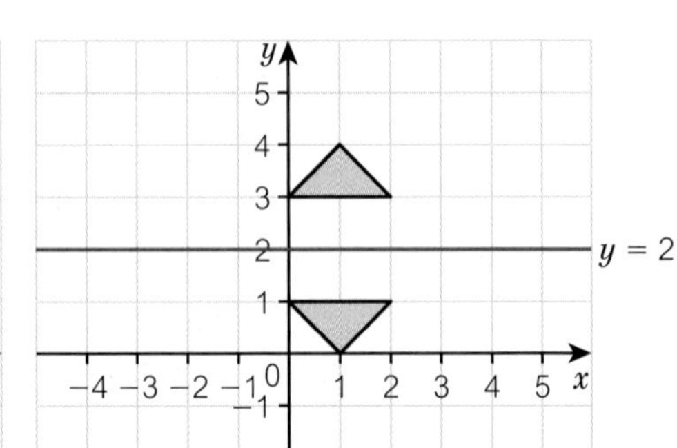

b A rotation 90° clockwise about (−1, 2) followed by a translation 2 squares right and 3 squares down.

c A reflection in the y-axis followed by a translation 2 squares left and 2 squares up.

d A reflection in the line $y = 1$ followed by a rotation 180° about (0, 0).

Enrichment

1 a Copy this rectangle on a square grid. Draw the image of the rectangle after a rotation of 90° clockwise about the red dot.
Repeat the rotation of the image, 90° clockwise about the red dot.
Finally repeat the rotation of the new image, 90° clockwise about the red dot.

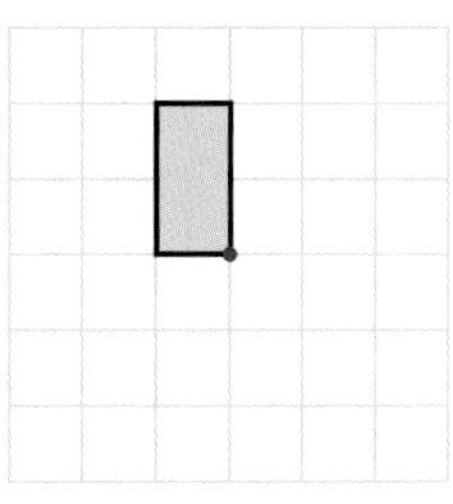

b What is the order of rotational symmetry of your combined final shape?

c Does your new shape have any lines of symmetry? Explain your answer.

2 Ellen makes candles. This is the smallest candle she makes.
These are the dimensions of the other candles she makes.

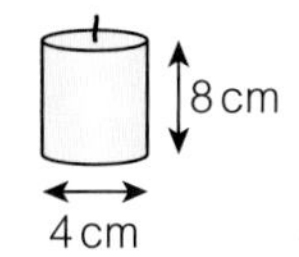

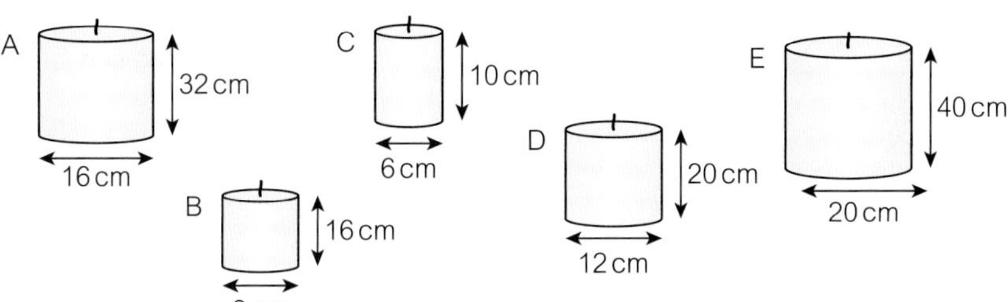

Which of these candles are not enlargements of the smallest candle? Explain your answers.

Q2 Literacy hint

A dimension is a measurement of length. Height and width are dimensions.

3 a Problem-solving Copy and shade the parts of this shape that are congruent. Use different colours for each type of shape.
You will need two different colours.

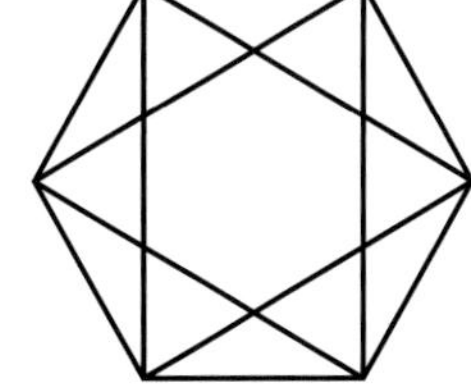

b Use the parts to make two regular hexagons that are congruent to the hexagon in the middle.

Q3b hint

All the parts of the same colour make one hexagon. All the parts of the other colour make the other hexagon.

4 **Reflect** In these lessons you have answered questions about

reflection rotation translation

Write a definition for each of them, using one of these descriptions:

flips over changes position turns around

For each definition, draw a sketch to show what the definition means.
How did your definition help you choose the shapes?

10 Extend

You will:

- Extend your understanding with problem-solving.

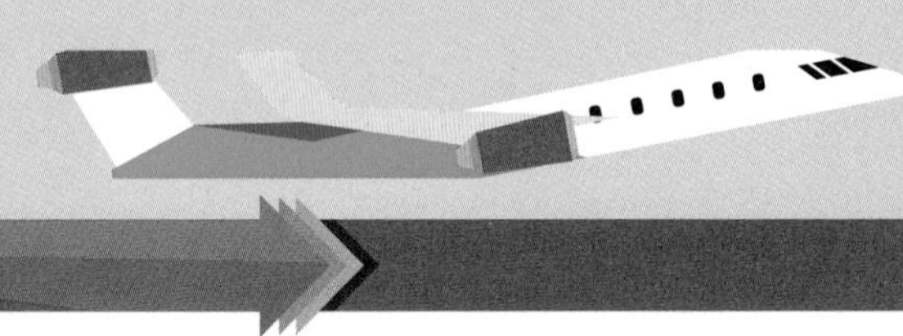

5b

1 The diagram shows four triangles. Triangle A has been rotated 180° about the point (−1.5, 3) to get triangle B. Describe the rotation that takes

a B onto C

b C onto D

c D onto A

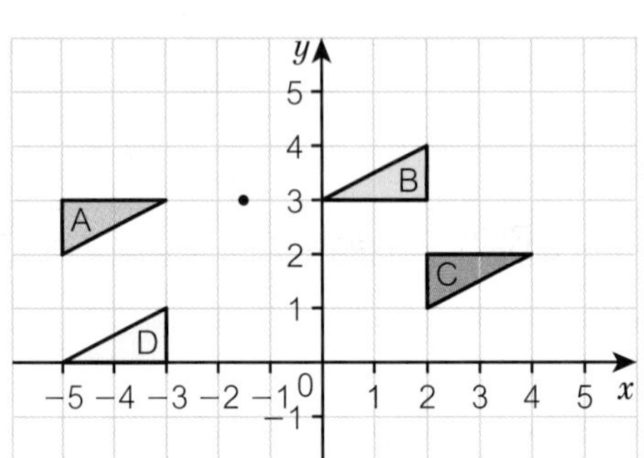

Q1 hint

Use tracing paper to find the centres of rotation.

5b

2 The diagram shows four triangles. Describe the rotation that takes

a A onto B

b B onto C

c B onto D

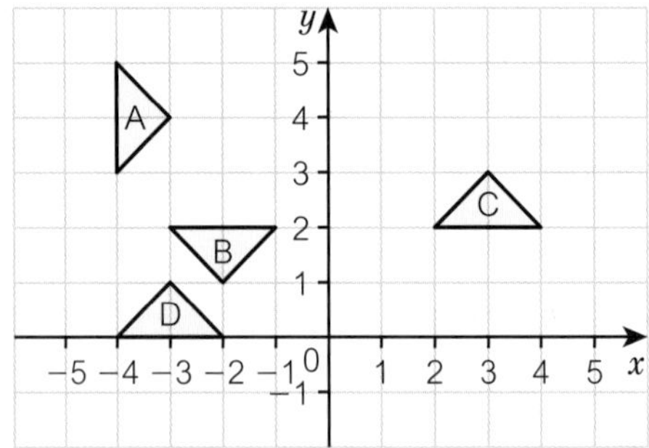

5b

3 Describe the rotation that takes

a A onto B

b C onto D

c B onto C

d E onto F

e F onto G

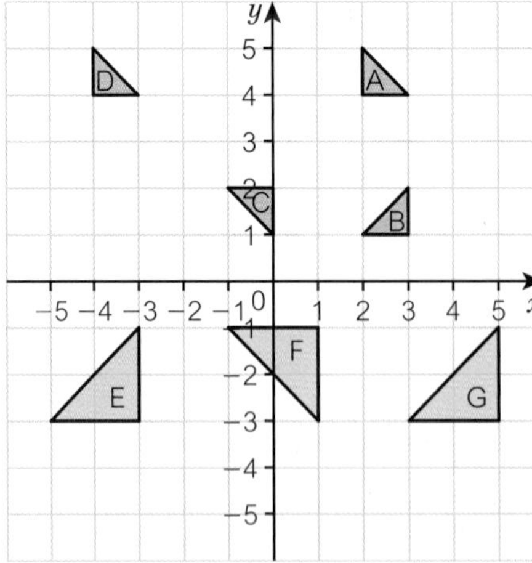

5a

4 This is the logo for a new brand of clothing. Copy the logo on to a square grid. Enlarge the logo using a scale factor of 3.

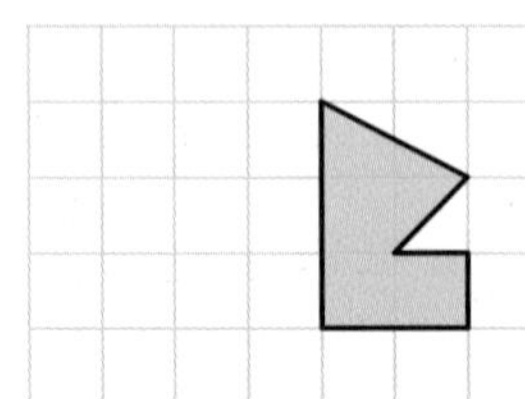

Topic links: Perimeter, Area

Subject links: Science (Q14)

5 **Reasoning** The diagram shows three rectangles A, B and C on a centimetre square grid.
B and C are both enlargements of A.

a What is the scale factor of enlargement of A to B?

b What is the scale factor of enlargement of A to C?

c What is the scale factor of enlargement of B to C?

d Copy and complete this table.

Rectangle	Perimeter (cm)	Area (cm^2)
A	6	2
B		
C		

e Copy and complete this table. Write each ratio in its simplest form.

Rectangles	Ratio of lengths	Ratio of perimeters	Ratio of areas
A : B	1 : 2		
A : C			

f What do you notice about the ratios you found in part **e**?
Explain what these ratios tell you.

6 **Problem-solving** Ingrid drew this shape on a centimetre square grid.
She enlarged the shape using a scale factor of 5.
Without drawing the enlargement, work out

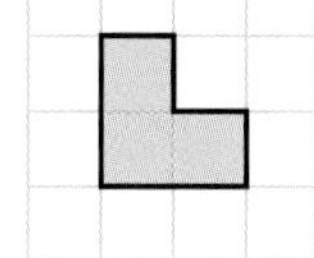

a the perimeter of the enlargement

b the area of the enlargement.

Draw the enlargement to check your answers to part **a** are correct.

Q6 hint

Use your answers to Q5 part **f** to help.

7 The diagram shows a blue parallelogram and a green parallelogram.
Describe the reflection that takes the blue parallelogram on to the green parallelogram.

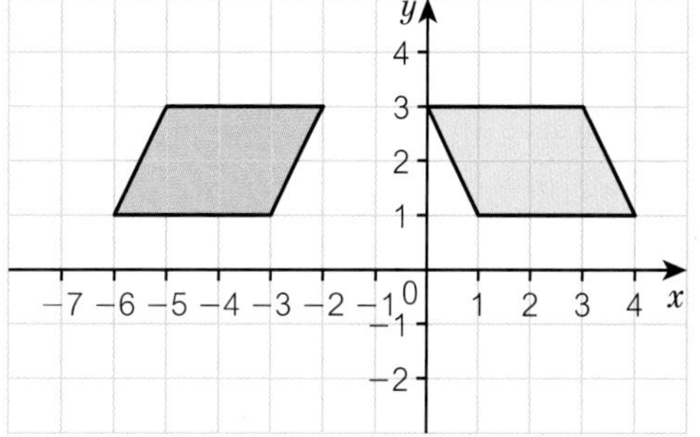

8 The diagram shows triangles ABC and DEF.
Triangle ABC has been reflected to make triangle DEF.

a Write down the equation of the mirror line.

Triangle DEF is reflected in the line $x = 6$ to become triangle GHI.

b Copy and complete this table showing the coordinates of the vertices of the triangles.

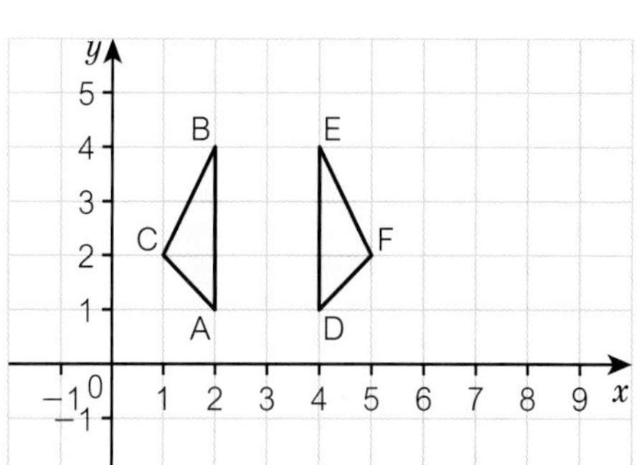

Triangle ABC	A (2, 1)	B (2, 4)	C (1, 2)
Triangle DEF	D (□, □)	E (□, □)	F (□, □)
Triangle GHI	G (□, □)	H (□, □)	I (□, □)

Triangle GHI is reflected in the line $x = 9$ to become triangle JKL.

c Without drawing triangle JKL, work out the coordinates of the vertices of triangle JKL.
Explain how you worked out your answer.

5a

9 Make two copies of this diagram.

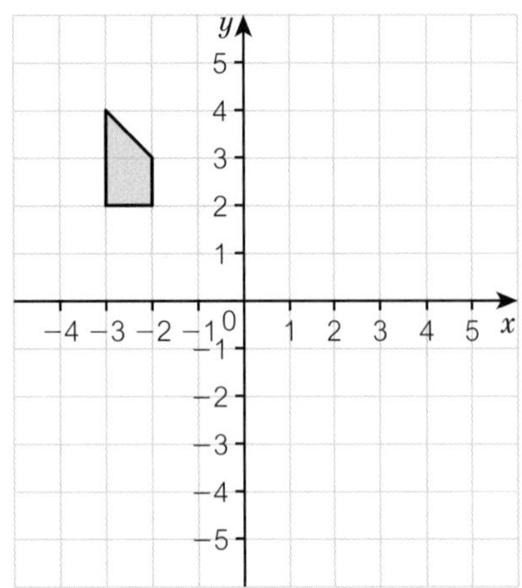

a i On the first copy, transform the object by carrying out a translation 6 right and 2 down, followed by a rotation 180° about (2, −1).

ii Describe fully the single transformation that will take the image back to the object.

b i On the second copy, transform the object by carrying out a rotation 90° clockwise about (−3, −1), followed by a rotation 90° anticlockwise about (2, −1).

ii Describe fully the single transformation that will take the image back to the object.

Q9ai hint

Draw the shape after each transformation.

Q9aii hint

Is it a translation, reflection or rotation? Remember to give all the information.

5a

10 **Problem-solving**

a Rohan translates a shape 2 squares right and 3 squares up. He then translates the image 5 squares left and 1 square down. What single translation has the same effect as these two translations combined?

b Janet translates a shape 3 squares left and 2 squares down. What translation must she now do to the image so that the combined effect of both translations is a single translation of 7 squares left and 4 squares up?

c Explain how you can answer parts **a** and **b** without drawing and translating shapes.

Q10 Strategy hint

Draw a shape on squared paper, then carry out the translations.

6b

11 Copy this diagram.

a Reflect the shape in the line $y = x$.

b Reflect the combined shape in the x-axis, then reflect the newly combined shape in the y-axis.

c How many lines of symmetry does your final shape have?

d What is the order of rotational symmetry of your final shape?

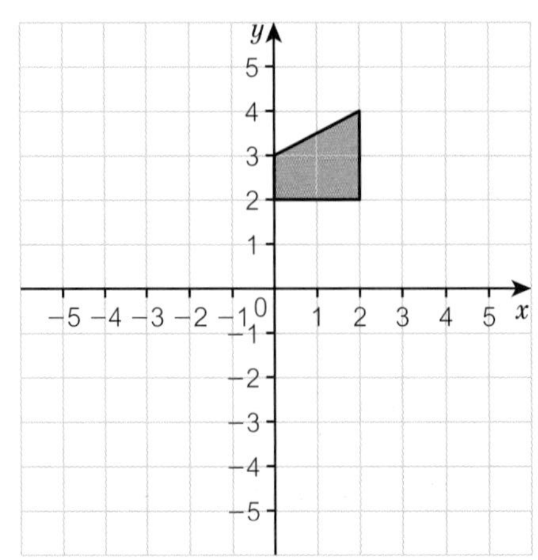

Q11a hint

Each vertex on the image needs to be the same distance from the mirror line as the corresponding vertex on the image.

6b

12 **Reasoning** Copy this diagram.

a i Transform the object by carrying out a reflection in the line $y = -x$, followed by a translation 2 squares left and 6 squares down.

ii Describe fully the single transformation that will take the image back to the object.

b i Transform the object by carrying out a reflection in the line $x = -2$, followed by a reflection in the line $y = x$, followed by a rotation 90° anticlockwise about (1, −2).

ii Describe fully the single transformation that will take the image back to the object.

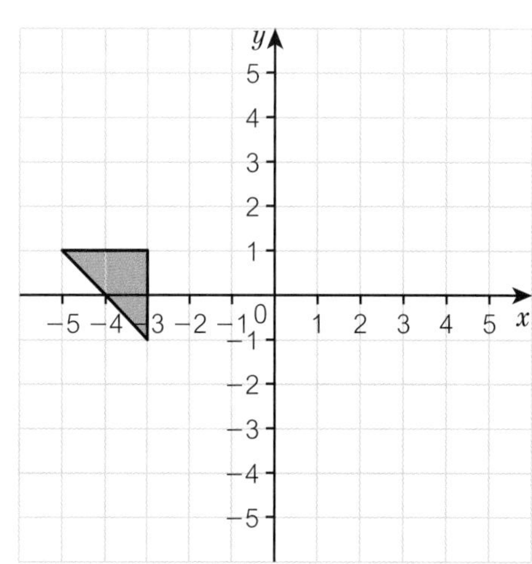

6c

13 **STEM** Greenhouse gases slow down or prevent the loss of heat from earth to space. These diagrams show the representations of molecules of three different greenhouse gases.
How many planes of symmetry does each molecule have?

a Methane (CH_4)

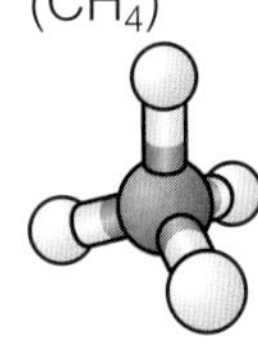

b Carbon dioxide (CO_2)

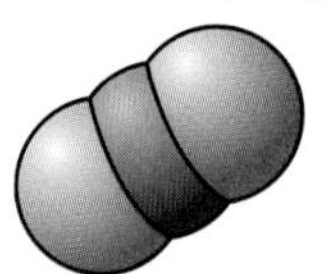

c Chlorofluorocarbon (CFC)

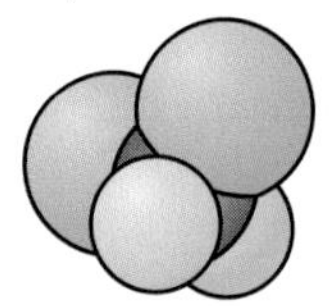

Q13a hint

Imagine a mirror cutting through the shape. Will the shape look the same?

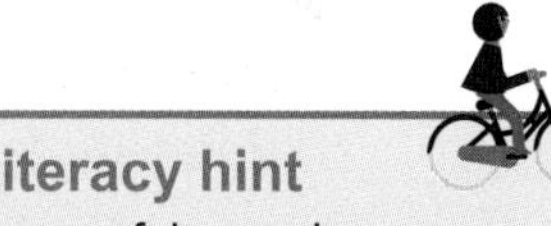

Q13c Literacy hint

CFC is a powerful greenhouse gas, thousands of times worse than CO_2.

Investigation — Problem-solving / Reasoning

The diagram shows kite 1.
Kite 1 is reflected in the x-axis to form kite 2.
Kite 2 is reflected in the y-axis to form kite 3.
Kite 3 is reflected in the x-axis to form kite 4.

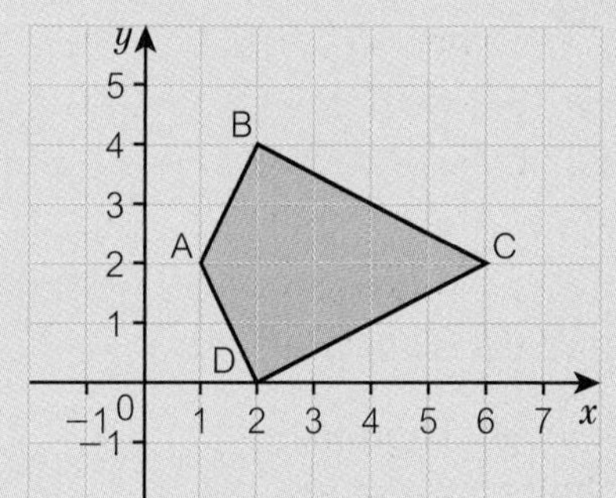

1 Fill in the coordinates in the table.

	A	B	C	D
Kite 1				
Kite 2				
Kite 3				
Kite 4				

2 What reflection would take kite 1 on to kite 4

3 Experiment with reflecting a different shape in the line $y = x$ and then in the line $y = -x$. What do you notice?

Reflect

14 **Reflect** Look back at the questions you answered in these Extend lessons. They were all about transformations.
List all the other mathematics topics you used to answer these questions.
Beside each one, write the type of transformation you used it for.

10 Unit test

4a **1** How many lines of symmetry does each shape have?

a 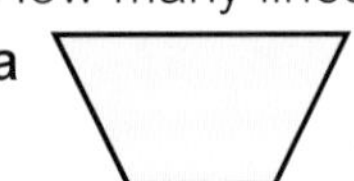

b

c 

d 

4a **2** Katie says, 'This triangle has these 3 lines of symmetry.'
Is she correct? Explain your answer.

4a **3** Copy this shape on to squared paper.
Draw the image of the shape after the translation 2 squares right, 4 squares down.

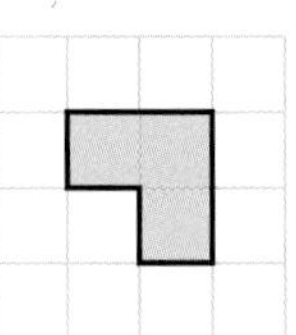

5c **4** Write the letters representing the congruent parts of each shape.

a

A B C

b 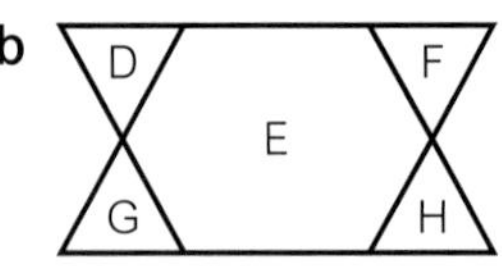

c 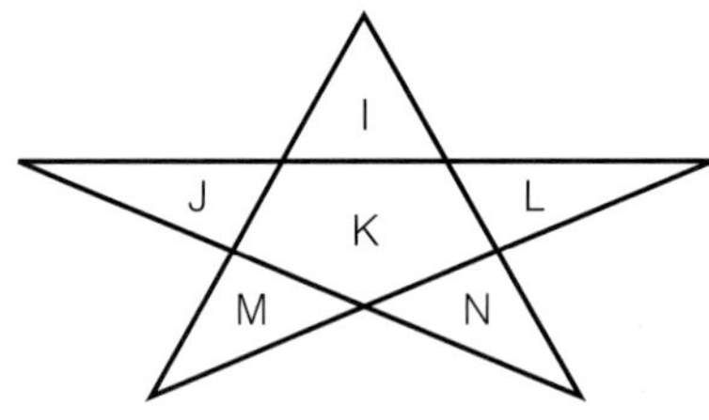

5c **5** In the diagram shape A has been rotated to give shape B.
Dianne describes the rotation as
rotation, 90°, anticlockwise.
What is missing from Dianne's description?

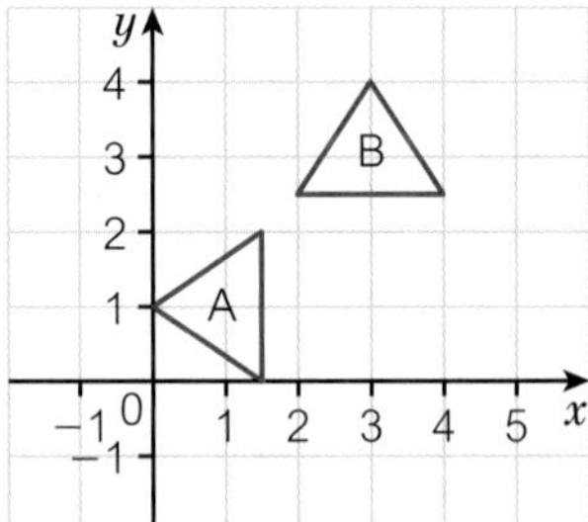

5a **6** Copy the diagram and draw the image of the triangle after these transformations.

a Reflection in $x = 1$. Label this shape A.

b Reflection in $y = 1$. Label this shape B.

c Rotation 90° clockwise about (3, −1). Label this shape C.

d Rotation 180° about (1, 0). Label this shape D.

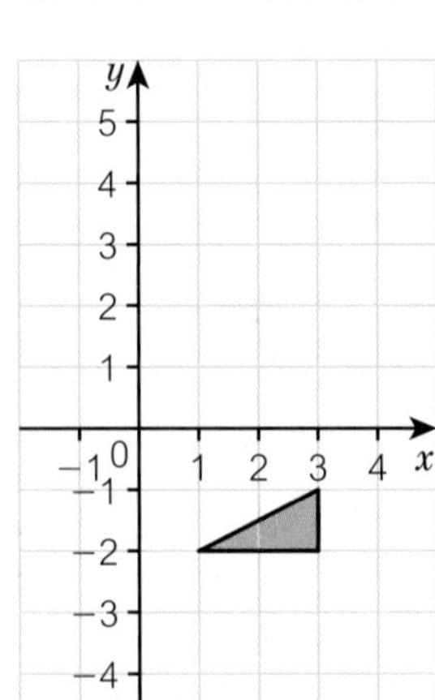

5a **7** For each shape write

a the number of lines of symmetry

b the order of rotational symmetry.

A 

B 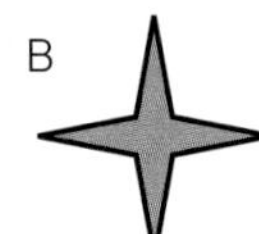

C 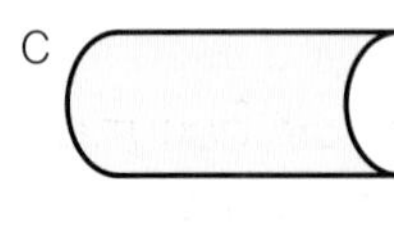

8 On this grid, Brian reflects the red shape in the line $y = 2$ and gets the blue shape. 5a
Explain the mistake that Brian has made.

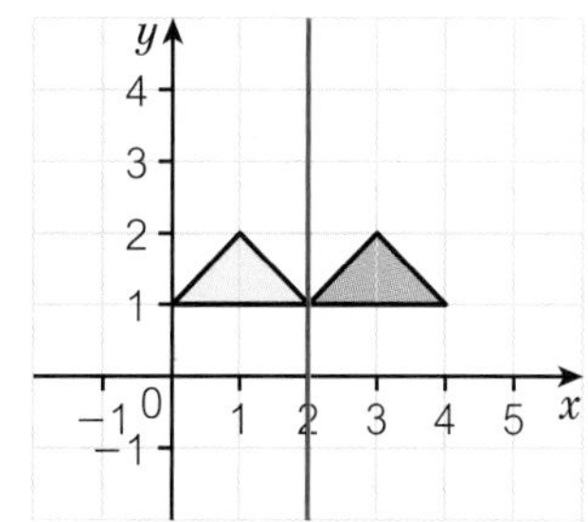

9 Copy the diagram in Q6. 5a

a Transform the shape using a rotation 90° anticlockwise about (1, −1) followed by a translation 3 squares right and 1 square down.

b Transform the shape using a translation 2 squares left and 1 square down, followed by a reflection in the x-axis.

10 a Draw the shape from Q3 enlarged by scale factor 3. 5a

b Write the ratio of the length of the sides of the original shape to the enlarged shape.

11 The diagram shows two shapes, A and B. 5a
Describe a two-step transformation that will transform shape A to shape B.

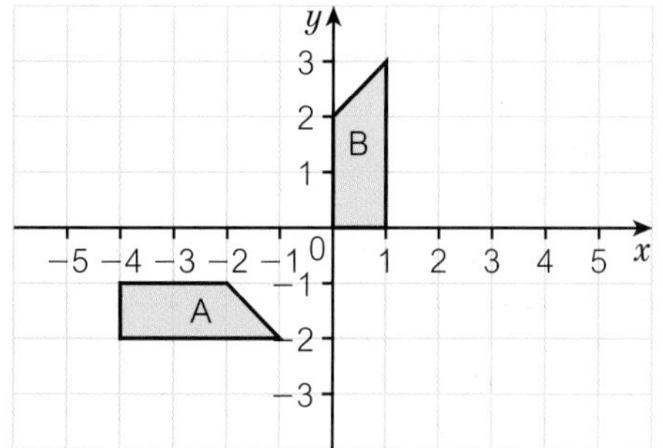

12 How many planes of symmetry do these 3D shapes have? 6c

a

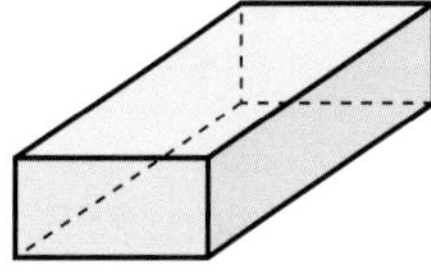

b

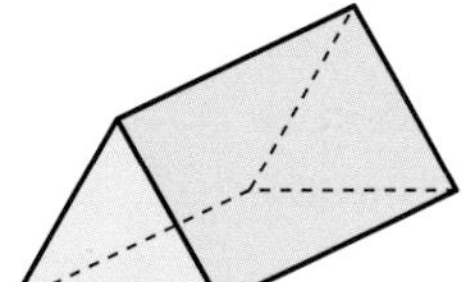

c

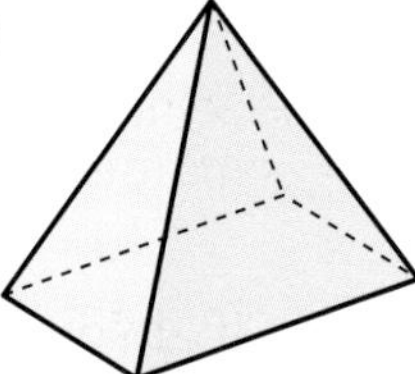

Challenge

13 Split each diagram into four congruent shapes. Each shape must contain a triangle, a square, a hexagon and a circle.

a

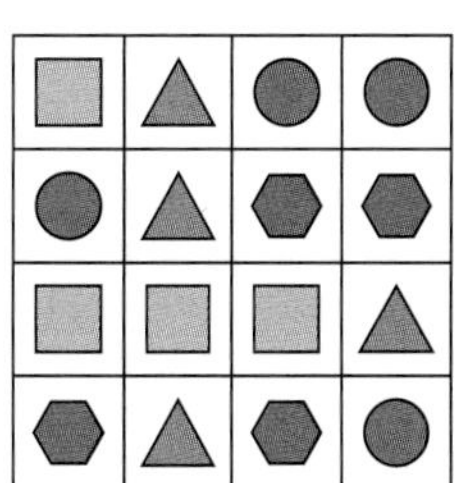

b

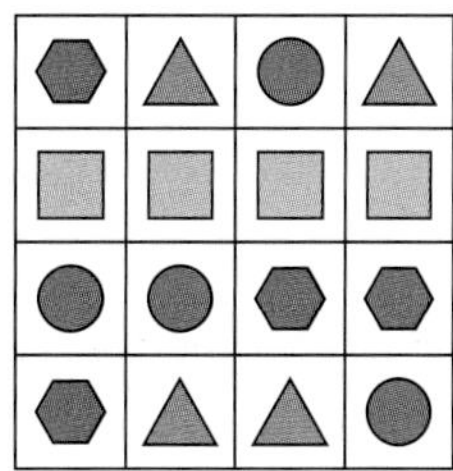

Q13 hint

The triangle, square, hexagon and circle can be in a different order within the congruent shapes, i.e. the outline shapes are congruent, but not the patterns within them.

14 Reflect List the four transformations you have learned about in this unit. Reflect
Draw a sketch for each of them to remind you what each transformation does.
Now read this sentence carefully.

After ______________ the shape and its image are congruent.

Complete this sentence with one or more transformations.
Explain your choice of word(s).